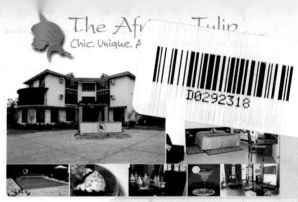

The African Tulip
Chic. Unique. A...

D0292318

Each Room Features

- Wireless Internet access
- Air Conditioners
- Satellite and local Tv
- Direct Dial telephone
- Mini Safe
- Hair Dryers
- Large Bathrooms
- Mini Bar

Other amenities

- Laundry Service
- Spacious Lounge
- Fully stocked bars
- Business centre
- Conference room
- Swimming pool
- Gift Shops

Contacts
44/1 Serengeti Road
P. O. Box 15171, Arusha, Tanzania   Tel: +255-27-2543004/2543005
Email: info@theafricantulip.com   www.theafricantulip.com

Visit Tanzania with
ROY SAFARIS LIMITED
ARUSHA TANZANIA

"We go thru' every measure
to give you Wild pleasure"

Roysafaris@intafrica.com   www.roysafaris.com

Footprint story

It was 1921

Ireland had just been partitioned, the British miners were striking for more pay and the federation of British industry had an idea. Exports were booming in South America – how about a handbook for businessmen trading in that far away continent? The Anglo-South American Handbook was born that year, written by W Koebel, the most prolific writer on Latin America of his day.

1924

Two editions later the book was 'privatized' and in 1924, in the hands of Royal Mail, the steamship company for South America, it became The South American Handbook, subtitled 'South America in a nutshell'. This annual publication became the 'bible' for generations of travellers to South America and remains so to this day. In the early days travel was by sea and the Handbook gave all the details needed for the long voyage from Europe. What to wear for dinner; how to arrange a cricket match with the Cable & Wireless staff on the Cape Verde Islands and a full account of the journey from Liverpool up the Amazon to Manaus: 5898 miles without changing cabin!

1939

As the continent opened up, the South American Handbook reported the new Pan Am flying boat services, and the fortnightly airship service from Rio to Europe on the Graf Zeppelin. For reasons still unclear but with extraordinary determination, the annual editions continued through the Second World War.

1970s

Many more people discovered South America and the backpacking trail started to develop. All the while the Handbook was gathering fans, including literary vagabonds such as Paul Theroux and Graham Greene (who once sent some updates addressed to "The publishers of the best travel guide in the world, Bath, England").

1990s

During the 1990s the company set about developing a new travel guide series using this legendary title as the flagship. By 1997 there were over a dozen guides in the series and the Footprint imprint was launched.

2000s

The series grew quickly and there were soon Footprint travel guides covering more than 150 countries. In 2004, Footprint launched its first thematic guide: Surfing Europe, packed with colour photographs, maps and charts. This was followed by further thematic guides such as Diving the World, Snowboarding the World, Body and Soul escapes, Travel with Kids and European City Breaks.

2012

Today we continue the traditions of the last 90 years that have served legions of travellers so well. We believe that these help to make Footprint guides different. Our policy is to use authors who are genuine experts who write for independent travellers; people possessing a spirit of adventure, looking to get off the beaten track.

Tanzania Handbook

Lizzie Williams

With its multitude of uncrowded locations that are home to a staggering variety of animals, Tanzania offers what most people hope to see on a visit to the African continent: the drama of the wildebeest migration unfolding along an infinite savannah; the gleaming snows of Mount Kilimanjaro; the proud Masai warriors stalking the plains; or the exotic palm-fringed beaches on the spice islands of Zanzibar.

Tanzania is serious about protecting its natural heritage and almost a quarter (23%) of its landscape has been allocated to game reserves and national parks. The town of Arusha is the safari capital of East Africa and the starting point for trips to the vast plains of the Serengeti, the birthplace of man at the Olduvai Gorge, the natural beauty of Lake Manyara and the Ngorongoro Crater.

In contrast to the flat plains, Tanzania is home to the tallest mountain in Africa; every year thousands of people fulfil their lifetime ambition of climbing to the top of Kilimanjaro. The country has a long coastline steeped in a Swahili culture that has been alive since the first dhows arrived on the trade winds from Asia.

A walk through the narrow, twisting passageways of Zanzibar's capital, Stone Town, reveals beautiful Arabian architecture, while the Indian Ocean offers excellent opportunities for diving, snorkelling, fishing, sailing and even swimming with dolphins. Here, on some of the best beaches in the world, it is impossible not to relax in the dazzling sun and warm azure waters.

THIS PAGE Path to Mount Kilimanjaro and the 'roof of Africa'
PREVIOUS PAGE A fine bull elephant dwarfed by the wall of the Ngorongoro Crater

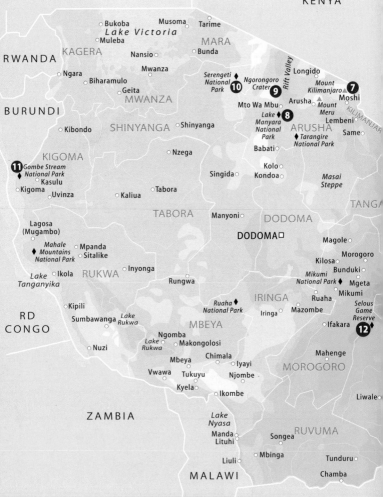

UGANDA

KENYA

Bukoba
Musoma
Tarime

Lake Victoria

Muleba

MARA

KAGERA

Nansio

Bunda

RWANDA

Ngara

Mwanza

Biharamulo

Serengeti
National
Park

Geita

Ngorongoro
Crater

10

9

Rift Valley

Longido

Mount
Kilimanjaro

Arusha

7

Moshi

Mount
Meru

KILIMANJARO

MWANZA

Mto Wa Mbu

8

BURUNDI

Lake
Manyara
National
Park

Lembeni

Kibondo

Shinyanga

ARUSHA

Same

SHINYANGA

Babati

Tarangire
National
Park

Nzega

KIGOMA

Kolo

Masai
Steppe

TANG

11 Gombe Stream
National Park

Singida

Kondoa

Kasulu

Nzega

Kigoma

Uvinza

Kaliua

Tabora

TABORA

Manyoni

DODOMA

DODOMA

Magole

Lagosa
(Mugambo)

Morogoro

Kilosa

Bunduki

Mahale
Mountains
National Park

Mpanda

Sitalike

Inyonga

Rungwa

Mikumi
National Park

Mgeta

Mikumi

*Lake
Tanganyika*

Ikola

RUKWA

Ruaha
National Park

IRINGA

Ruaha

Selous
Game
Reserve

Kipili

Mazombe

Iringa

Sumbawanga

*Lake
Rukwa*

Ifakara

12

RD
CONGO

Nuzi

Mbeya

Ngomba

*Lake
Rukwa*

Makongolosi

MBEYA

Mahenge

MOROGORO

Mbeya
Chimala

Iyayi

Vwawa
Tukuyu
Njombe

Kyela

Ikombe

Liwale

ZAMBIA

*Lake
Nyasa*

Manda
Lituhi

Songea

RUVUMA

Mbinga

Tunduru

Liuli

Chamba

MALAWI

MOZAMBIQUE

The alleyways of Stone Town, where little has changed for hundreds of years

Don't miss...
See colour maps at end of book

Pemba
Island
Tanga   6
Muheza   Chake Chake
2 Pangani
Stone   Zanzibar Island
Town   5
4   5
Bagamoyo
Dar es Salaam
Kisarawe   1
Kisiju
PWANI
Mafia
Island
Mohoro   Indian
Ocean
Kilwa Kivinje
Kilwa Masoko
3
LINDI
Lindi
Mingoyo
Nachingwea   Mtwara
Masasi MTWARA
Newala

Game-viewing from above: floating over the Serengeti

Itineraries for Tanzania

Vast areas of Tanzania are dedicated to game parks and reserves, and most visitors go on safari (which means 'journey' in Kiswahili). The principal draw card is the Big Five: lion, leopard, elephant, rhino and buffalo, but there are other fascinating species too. The most popular regions are the Northern Circuit parks: the vast plains of the Serengeti where the annual wildebeest migration is staged, the natural beauty of Lake Manyara and the animal-stuffed Ngorongoro Crater, to name but a few. In the south, less visited but equally impressive, are the Selous Game Reserve and Ruaha National Park, which are wild, remote and virtually untouched. Tanzania's other main attraction is a mountain that needs no introduction – snow-capped Kilimanjaro – and, for many people, watching the sun rise over Uhuru Peak at the top is one of Africa's most satisfying achievements. Tanzania's coastal attractions include palm-fringed, pearly white-sand beaches, and the coral reefs surrounding the offshore islands teem with life and colour. Zanzibar evokes romantic images of narrow winding streets in Stone Town, fragrant spices and the azure Indian Ocean; the resorts here offer the classic sun, sea and sand type of holiday. In the west of Tanzania are the great lakes: Lake Victoria is Africa's largest freshwater lake and Lake Tanganyika is its deepest; here the highlight is visiting chimpanzees at Gombe or Mahale.

ITINERARY ONE: (1-2 weeks)
The northern circuit & the Big Five

Tanzania's Northern Circuit attracts the majority of tourists; it is an extremely popular route as it includes the best known of the national parks. All the safari operators offer combinations of a few or all of the following parks, and how long you go for depends on how many parks you want to visit and how many nights you want to stay in each. Popular routes take in Lake Manyara National Park, Ngorongoro Conservation Area and the Serengeti National Park. Less visited, the Tarangire National Park, a dry-season retreat for many animals, is also splendid for game-viewing. To see the Ngorongoro Crater and Lake Manyara you will need three days and two nights. To see these two plus the Serengeti you will need four days and three nights, and if you

Contents

AROUND LAKE VICTORIA
NORTHERN CIRCUIT GAME PARKS
NORTH TO KILIMANJARO
ARUSHA
CENTRAL REGION
ZANZIBAR & PEMBA
DAR ES SALAAM
SOUTHERN TANZANIA
COASTAL TANZANIA

Contents

Essentials

Planning your trip

Best time to visit Tanzania

Thanks to its location near the equator, Tanzania has a moderate climate and long sunny days for most of the year, though there are variations depending on topography and elevation. Daytime temperatures average between 25 and 30°C. The hottest season is January to February and the coolest month is August. Humidity varies, being high along the coastal strip and on Zanzibar but much lower in the interior highlands. There are long rains, *masika*, from March to May and short rains, *mvuli*, fall from October to December. Even in these months, however, there is an average of four to six hours of sunshine each day. On the coast, high temperatures are cooled by ocean breezes, so it is rarely overpoweringly hot, although humidity levels peak just before the rains arrive and it can become uncomfortable. On peaks above 1500 m the climate is cooler, with permanent snow on the highest peaks, such as Kilimanjaro where night-time temperatures drop well below zero.

In terms of avoiding the rains, the best time to visit is between May and October, but Tanzania has much to offer all year round. The wildebeest migration in the Serengeti occurs from November to June. If you are planning a trekking holiday, the best months are May to September. Travelling by road, especially in the more remote areas or through the parks and reserves, is easier during the dry months, as road conditions deteriorate significantly in the rainy seasons making travel on unsealed roads difficult. As a result, many of the safari lodges drop their rates significantly, sometimes by as much as 50%, during the rainy low season from the beginning of April to the end of June. High season on Zanzibar is from September to January as this is the time Europeans visit looking for some winter sun; it gets especially busy around the Christmas and New Year period. Finally, bear in mind that malaria peaks during the rainy seasons, when mosquitoes are prolific.

What to do in Tanzania

Ballooning

The Serengeti National Park is the top spot for a gentle float over the animals in a balloon and, for many, this excursion is the highlight (albeit expensive) of a visit to the park. Most of the lodges and camps in the Seronera and Western Corridor can organize this activity. Tourists are picked up around 0500 and driven to the site where the lift-off will take place. Watching the balloon inflate is part of the experience. Once the balloon rises, passengers can watch the sunrise high above the plains when the grasslands turn from blue to gold. This is quite a spectacular experience, especially during the months of the wildebeest migration. Flights last 60-90 mins and cost US$500 per person and the price includes a bush breakfast with champagne. For more information, see www.balloonsafaris.com.

Birdwatching

Apart from all the mammals, Tanzania also boasts a vast selection of birds with 1108 recorded species, of which 23 are endemic. Birdwatching is a popular pastime and can easily be combined with wildlife watching. Apart from the national parks, good spots for birdwatching include the Usambara Mountains and the foothills of Kilimanjaro.

The #**1** Essential Travel Download*

Get TripAdvisor Mobile - **FREE**

- Browse millions of traveller reviews, photos & maps
- Find hotels, restaurants & things to do
- See what's nearby
- Apps available for iPhone, Android, Nokia, Palm Pre, & Windows Mobile

* From "iPhone Travel Apps: 10 Essential Downloads" on Frommers.com

Packing for Tanzania

Before you leave home, send yourself an email to a web-based account with details of traveller's cheques, passport, driving licence, credit cards and travel insurance numbers. Be sure that someone at home also has access to this information.

A good rule of thumb when packing is to take half the clothes you think you'll need and double the money. Laundry services are generally cheap and speedy in Tanzania and you shouldn't need to bring too many clothes. A backpack or travelpack (a hybrid backpack/suitcase) rather than a rigid suitcase covers most eventualities and survives the rigours of a variety of modes of travel. A lock for your luggage is strongly advised – there are cases of pilfering by airport baggage handlers the world over. Light cotton clothing is best, with a fleece or woollen clothing for evenings. Also pack something to change into at dusk – long

sleeves and trousers (particularly light coloured) help ward off mosquitoes, which are at their most active in the evening. During the day you will need a hat, sunglasses and high-factor suncream. Modest dress is advisable for women, particularly on the coast, where men too should avoid revealing their shoulders. Tanzania is a great place to buy sarongs, known in East Africa as *kikois*, which in Africa are worn by both men and women and are ideal to cover up when, say, leaving the beach. Footwear should be airy because of the heat: sandals or canvas trainers are ideal. Trekkers will need comfortable walking boots and ones that have been worn in if you are climbing Kilimanjaro. Those going on camping safaris will need a sleeping bag, towel and torch, and budget travellers may want to bring a sleeping sheet in case the sheets don't look too clean in a budget hotel.

Most tour operators will be able to arrange safaris particularly aimed at birdwatchers. The following websites have comprehensive bird checklists for Tanzania: www.tanzania birding.com or www.tanzaniabirds.net.

Climbing and hiking

Although Kilimanjaro tops the list as Africa's most famous – and highest (5895 m) – mountain to climb, with organized treks that take 5-6 days, Tanzania also has many other mountain ranges and attractive peaks. They vary from the dramatic crater of Mount Meru and the active volcano of Ol Doinyo Lengai to tamer options, such as the Usambara Mountains and the comparatively gentle slopes of the Crater Highlands. Tour operators and trekking companies will put together an itinerary that suits your preferences. Bear in mind, there are no mountaineering or outdoor outfitters in

Tanzania, so when preparing for a trek in the country, you'll need to bring most of your own gear. There are many small reserves and forests around the country that have nature trails and are ideal for birdwatching, and many safari lodges offer guided game walks. Details of local operators are listed in the relevant chapters.

Diving and snorkelling

Undoubtedly one of East Africa's greatest tourism assets is the vast areas of coral reefs that stretch south from the equator. There is an abundance of tropical reef fish as well as large pelagic fish, and if lucky, you will encounter barracuda, manta rays, whale and reef sharks, hawksbill and green turtles, and schools of dolphins are often seen. The main diving areas of Tanzania are found off the islands of Pemba, where there are dramatic drop-offs, and Zanzibar and

Mafia, where there are fringing reefs and coral gardens. On the mainland, you can dive at the offshore islands around Dar es Salaam. The best time to dive in Tanzania is between Oct and Apr before the long rains, when the average water temperature is 27°C and visibility ranges from 10-30 m, increasing to 20 to 40 m around Pemba and Mafia islands. Conditions are ideal for first-timers, and there are many PADI dive schools. Non-divers can enjoy the reefs by snorkelling from the beach or a boat, which can be arranged at all the coastal resorts. Details of local operators are listed in the relevant chapters.

Fishing

Fishing is not a particularly popular pastime for visitors to Tanzania's rivers and lakes, and there are virtually no facilities. However, deep-sea fishing is very popular with tourists on the coast, especially in the deep Pemba Channel. This reaches depths of 823 m and is home to three varieties of marlin – black, blue and striped – as well as sailfish, spearfish, swordfish, yellowfin tuna, tiger shark, mako shark and virtually every game fish popular with anglers. A gentle north current runs through the channel, acting much like a scaled-down version of the Gulf Stream, which is forced up by the lip in the north of the channel, also referred to locally as the Sea Mountain, which creates rips and eddies that bring nutrients to the surface and concentrates the fish in a very tight area. The fishing season is usually from Aug to the end of Mar. A number of operators offer excursions in customized boats, some with high-tech tackle and equipment. Details of local operators are listed in the relevant chapters.

Kiteboarding

Kiteboarding is the latest craze on Zanzibar, and with cross-shore winds, wide flat sandy beaches, shallow waves and virtually no

obstructions, the best beaches are at Paje on the east coast and Ras Nungwi on the north coast. The wind is best from Apr to Nov when it picks up to 12-20 knots in the afternoon. The centres can organize lessons for beginners and also rent out equipment to experienced boarders. For further information, contact **Kite Centre Zanzibar**, www.kitecentrezanzibar.com; **Kiteboarding Zanzibar**, www.kiteboardingzanzibar.com; and **Paje by Kite**, www.pajebykite.net.

Riding

There are a few opportunities to go horse or camel riding, especially around Arusha and Moshi. These include fun short camel rides from the Meserani Snake Park (page 241) and longer 7-day horse safaris for experienced riders in the foothills of Kilimanjaro arranged with **Equestrian Safaris**, www.safaririding. com. On horseback it's possible to get very close to wildlife, as animals do not have an inherent fear of horses.

Spectator sports

The most popular spectator sport is football (**Tanzania Football Federation**, www.tff. or.tz) and at the weekends there are fixtures for the Premier League at large stadiums in Dar es Salaam, Arusha, Mwanza, Morogoro, Dodoma and Tanga. Cricket (**Tanzania Cricket Association**, www.tanzaniacricket. com) is popular with the Asian communities and there are matches over the weekends at grounds in Dar es Salaam. Occasional sailing regattas are held at the yacht clubs in Dar es Salaam and Tanga. The **Kilimanjaro Marathon** (Kilimanjaro Marathon, www. kilimanjaromarathon.com) is an annual event in Feb which starts and ends in Moshi and attracts a number of Tanzanian and Kenyan professional runners, as well as international participants (see box, page 218). Check the daily press for information on sports fixtures.

Park entry fees

Prices as of 1 January 2012. Children's fees are for ages 5-16; under 5s go free. Entry is per 24 hours or part thereof.

In an initiative to avoid large cash payments at the entry gates of the parks administered by **Tanzania National Parks Authority (TANAPA)**, there is now an electronic ticketing system of paying park fees by a pre-paid TANAPA TemboCard (also referred to as a Smart Card after the successful similar project in neighbouring Kenya) or by credit card (Visa and MasterCard) at 'point of sale' machines at the gates. This system is currently in place at the Serengeti, Mount Kilimanjaro, Arusha, Tarangire, Lake Manyara, Mikiumi, Ruaha and the Udzungwa Mountains national parks, and is expected to be extended to cover most of TANAPA's 16 parks.

If you are on an organized safari, your tour operator will organize these for you, but if you are visiting the parks independently, you need to work out how many parks you are going to visit and for how long to calculate what your park entry fees, vehicle costs and camping fees are going to be. You then purchase a pre-paid TANAPA TemboCard with US dollars cash, Tanzanian shillings, credit card or traveller's cheques at branches of **CRDB Bank** (www.crdbbank.com) in Dar es Salaam, Arusha, Iringa, Kilombero, Moshi, Morogoro, Musoma or Usa River. Alternatively, you can pay at the CRDB Bank's credit card machines at the park gates. Anyone over the age of 16 must have their own card; under 16s can be paid for with a parent's card (remember under 5s are free). Money on the cards is not refundable, but you can always pay any additional fees at the gates by using the credit card machines. Note: Entry fees to the Ngorongoro Conservation Area are still paid on arrival in US dollars cash.

For further details contact **Tanzania National Parks Authority (TANAPA)**, Arusha, T027-250 3471, www.tanzaniaparks.com.

Arusha, Tarangire and Lake Manyara

Adult	US$35
Child	US$10

Gombe Stream

Adult	US$100
Child	US$20

Katavi, Kitulo, Mikumi, Mkomazi, Ruaha, Rubondo, Saadani and Udzungwa

Adult	US$20
Child	US$5

Kilimanjaro

Adult	US$60
Child	US$10

Mahale

Adult	US$80
Child	US$30

Serengeti and Ngorongoro Conservation area

Adult	US$50
Child	US$10

Vehicle entry to parks

Up to 2000 kg	US$40 (foreign)
	TSh 10,000 (Tanzanian)
2000-3000 kg	US$150 (foreign)
	TSh 25,000 (Tanzanian)

Note Only Tanzanian registered vehicles are allowed down into the crater itself, for which the additional Crater Service Fee is US$200 per vehicle.

Tanzania's UNESCO World Heritage Sites

Ruins of Kilwa Kisiwani (page 113) and **Ruins of Songo Mnara** (page 115)
Designated World Heritage Sites in 1981, the ruins of these two ancient settlements lie on tiny islands off the remote south coast. From 2004, they have also been on the UNESCO's List of World Heritage in Danger, in a bid to call for more attention to safe-guarding and preserving them. From the 13th to 17th century they were wealthy East African ports dealing with the trade that crossed the Indian Ocean, and helped create the rich Swahili civilization still evident on the coast today.

Stone Town, Zanzibar (page 142)
Awarded World Heritage status in 2000, Stone Town was inscribed for its rich cultural heritage of trading activity between Africa and Asia, illustrated today by the fine architecture and structure of the town that is still functioning today after more than a millennium. Its other criteria for inscription is the importance it played in the suppression of the slave trade. Once a slave port, it was also the base for anti-slavery opponents such as David Livingstone.

Kilimanjaro National Park (page 221)
Kilimanjaro National Park encompasses 756 sq km and was declared a national park in 1993 and UNESCO site in 1987. At 5895 m, Mount Kilimanjaro is the highest point in Africa and one of the tallest free-standing dormant volcanoes in the world.

Ngorongoro Conservation Area (page 281)
Located 180 km west of Arusha and covering an area of 8288 sq km, this is dominated by the spectacular collapsed caldera of the Ngorongoro Crater. The rich pasture and permanent water on the crater floor provides sustenance to large populations of animals. It was designated in 1979 not only for its ecological value, but also for its geological value, and includes the Olduvai Gorge site where the remains of many early hominoids and early pre-historic creatures have been unearthed.

Serengeti National Park (page 292)
Covering 14,763 sq km as Tanzania's first national park, this is one of the world's greatest refuges for wildlife and was designated a national park in 1952 and a World Heritage Site in 1981. The wildebeest migration between the Serengeti and the Masai Mara in neighbouring Kenya is perhaps one of the most impressive natural events on the globe.

Kondoa Rock Art Sites (page 334)
Tanzania's newest World Heritage Site, which was inscribed in 2006, the Kondoa cave system lies in the remote interior about 280 km south of Arusha bordering the Rift Valley. Here there are over 150 rocky walled shelters with hundreds of cave paintings of elongated figures, hunting scenes and animals. They are a testament to the early hunter-gatherers and the beliefs associated with different societies living in this region over a 2000-year period.

Selous Game Reserve (page 360)
The vast 54,600 sq km Selous became a World Heritage Site in 1982 for its undisturbed wilderness and diversity of wildlife, which has seen hardly any impact by humankind. It is believed that before the migration of early man and, much later, before the urbanization by relatively modern man, this is largely what the whole of East Africa looked like. It also gained protection for its exceptionally large populations of big game, including herds of elephants hundreds strong.

Watersports

As well as diving and snorkelling, many hotels and resorts on the coast organize windsurfing, jet skiing, parasailing and sea-kayaking, and many types of boat are available from an inflatable banana boat or a glass-bottom boat, to catamaran sailing and a sunset cruise on a traditional white-sailed dhow. Swimming with dolphins is a popular excursion on the southwest of Zanzibar. Details of local operators are given in the relevant chapters.

Going on safari → *See also How to organize a safari, page 259.*

No visit to Tanzania is complete without going on safari. There are a number of game parks and reserves run by the **Tanzania National Parks Authority** (**TANAPA**) (www.tanzaniaparks.com), and some in the private sector, such as ranches or game areas, run by the local communities. These offer visitors the chance of seeing splendid African landscapes and wildlife including the Big Five: elephant, buffalo, rhinoceros, lion and leopard, along with countless other animals and innumerable bird species. Along with wildlife, some of the parks have been gazetted to preserve the vegetation, such as Udzungwa, or unique locations, such as Mount Kilimanjaro, and marine life is protected in the marine parks off the coast and islands. Some of the parks and reserves are world famous, such as the Serengeti and Ngorongoro Crater, and have excellent facilities and receive many visitors, while others rarely see tourists and have few amenities.

The best time of day to spot animals is early in the morning and late in the afternoon, as many animals sleep through the intense midday heat. Animals can most easily be seen during the dry season, when the lack of surface water forces them to congregate around rivers and waterholes. However, the rainy seasons, from October to November and March to June, are when the animals are in the best condition after feeding on the new shoots, and there are chances of seeing breeding displays and young animals. The disadvantage of the wet season is that the thicker vegetation and the wider availability of water mean that the wildlife is more spread out and more difficult to spot; also, driving conditions are far harder in deep mud as none of the park roads are paved. However, prices for lodges can be up to 50% lower during the rainy seasons. Driving around endlessly searching for animals is not usually the best way to view animals, and drives can be broken up by stops at waterholes, picnic sites and hides. Time spent around a waterhole with your engine switched off gives you an opportunity to listen to the sounds of the bush and experience the rhythms of nature as game moves to and from the water. Tanzania's game parks and reserves are well organized; following the few park rules will ensure an enjoyable stay.

Organizing a safari

Most people visit the parks and reserves on an organized safari, which involves staying at a safari lodge or tented camp, or at the cheaper end of the scale at a campsite, and going out on game drives in a specially adapted vehicle with a guide, although it's still a good idea to take along some wildlife and bird identification books. You can pre-book a safari from your home country, or there are a huge number of safari companies in Tanzania, which are listed in the relevant chapters. Ensure that the company is properly licensed and is a member of the **Tanzania Association of Tour Operators** (**TATO**) (www.tatotz.org), which represents over 240 of Tanzania's tour operators and is a good place to start when looking for a safari. Avoid companies offering cheap deals on the street – they will almost always turn out to be a disaster and may appear cheap because they do not include national park entrance fees or use accommodation outside of the park boundaries. Generally speaking, because of their geographical location and accessibility, Tanzania's parks are grouped into three circuits: the northern circuit, the southern circuit and the western circuit. Safaris to the northern circuit (the Ngorongoro Conservation Area, Serengeti, Lake Manyara, Tarangire and Arusha national parks) are best arranged from Arusha (see page 258). For safaris to the southern circuit (Mikumi, Udzungwa and Ruaha national parks and Selous Game Reserve) and the western circuit (Kitavi, Gombe Stream and Mahale national parks) arrangements are best made in Dar es Salaam (see page 72).

Costs vary enormously depending on duration, season, where you stay and how many are in a group. At the very top end of the scale, staying in the most exclusive tented camps and flying between destinations, expect to pay in excess of US$500 per person per day; for larger mid-range lodges with buffet meals, around US$280-350 per person per day (more if you opt for air transfers); and for camping safaris using the basic national park campsites and the services of a safari cook, about US$180-250 per person per day. At first glance these prices may appear to be high, but remember a considerable portion of safari costs are park entry fees. Safaris do not run on every day of the week, and in the low season you may also find that they will be combined, meaning if you are on a six-day safari you could expect to be joined by another party say on a four-day safari. See page 24 for safari accommodation options and page 259 for 'How to organize a safari'.

Transport

It is worth emphasizing that most parks are some way from departure points. If you go on a three-day safari by road, you will often find that at least one day is taken up with travelling to and from the park, often on bad bumpy and dusty roads – leaving you with less time on safari in the park itself. The easiest option, which is of course the most expensive, is to fly; most parks and reserves have a good network of airstrips, and there are daily flights. If you are confident about driving on the poorly maintained tracks within the parks and are prepared to camp, you can also self-drive. In some parks there is the option to hire a guide from the park HQ to accompany you in your own vehicle. On your own safari remember that you will need to budget for vehicle, camping and park entry fees (see box, page 8).

Getting to Tanzania

Air → *See also Transport in Dar es Salaam, page 73.*

The majority of travellers arrive in Tanzania through Dar es Salaam's **Julius Nyerere International Airport** (JNIA), which is 13 km southwest of the city centre along Nyerere Road (see page 46). There are also direct international flights to **Kilimanjaro International Airport (KIA)**, halfway between Arusha and Moshi, about 40 km from each (see page 236), and to **Zanzibar International Airport (ZAN)**, 4 km southeast of Stone Town (see page 132). There is a departure tax of US$50 (US$25 from Zanzibar) on all international flights leaving Tanzanian airports but this is included in the price of the ticket. Airport information can be obtained from the **Tanzania Airports Authority** (www.taa.go.tz). The national carrier, **Air Tanzania**, went bankrupt a few years ago. Presently, **Precision Air** is Tanzania's principal airline, with a far-reaching domestic and regional network, and while it is currently extending its international network, it also partners with

Kenya's national carrier, **Kenya Airways**, on code-share routes. It is not generally cheaper to arrange a return to Nairobi and a connecting return flight to Dar es Salaam, but for travellers who are only visiting the northern circuit parks, it is easier to fly to Nairobi, given that Arusha is only 273 km to the south of Nairobi, and enter Tanzania through the Namanga land border from Kenya. There are regular shuttle buses between Nairobi and Arusha and Moshi (see box, page 15). You can also fly from Nairobi to Kilimanjaro. Nairobi is served by more airlines than Dar es Salaam, so air fares are more competitively priced. When flying to Tanzania from the north, getting a window seat is definitely a good option as, cloud permitting, you may be lucky enough to glimpse the gleaming top of Mount Kilimanjaro.

From Europe
British Airways flies between London and Dar es Salaam and flying time is nine hours 40 minutes. **KLM** has direct flights between Amsterdam and Dar es Salaam, and **Lufthansa**, between Frankfurt and Dar es Salaam. Non-direct flights from Europe may work out economical: **Egypt Air** offers flights via Cairo; **Emirates**, via Dubai; **Ethiopian Airlines** via Addis Ababa, and **Turkish Airlines**, via Istanbul. To Kilimanjaro (Arusha/Moshi), there are flights with **Ethiopian Airlines** and **KLM**, which touch down on the way to Dar es Salaam. To Zanzibar, **Ethiopian Airlines** has flights via Dar es Salaam, and **Kenya Airways** has flights via Nairobi. Italy, Spain and Switzerland have charter flights directly to Zanzibar. Airlines with daily direct flights from Europe to Nairobi include **Kenya Airways**, which flies from London, Amsterdam, Paris and Rome, and then has connecting flights to Dar es Salaam, Kilimanjaro and Zanzibar; try also **British Airways**, **KLM** and **Virgin Atlantic**.

Jet lag is not an issue if flying from Europe to Tanzania as there is only a minimal time difference.

From North America
There are no direct flights from the USA to Tanzania. Americans have to change planes in Europe or the Middle East depending on which carrier they choose. It is usual to fly via London, Amsterdam or Dubai if travelling from the USA. Alternatively, **Delta Airlines** has a code-share agreement with **South African Airways** who run daily direct flights from Atlanta and New York to Johannesburg, from where there are connections to Dar es Salaam.

From Australia, New Zealand, and Asia
There are no direct flights from Australia, New Zealand and Asia to Tanzania, but a number of indirect routes via Kenya, the Middle East (see below) or South Africa. Between them **Qantas** and **South African Airways**, on a code-share agreement, fly between Perth and Johannesburg, and on some flights, the same plane continues to and from Sydney. **Singapore Airlines**, which code shares with **Air New Zealand**, runs flights which link Wellington with Johannesburg via Sydney and Singapore. **Air Malaysia** has flights from Perth, Melbourne, Sydney and Darwin in Australia, and Auckland in New Zealand to Kuala Lumpur, connecting with a flight to Johannesburg. **Cathay Pacific** flies from Hong Kong to Johannesburg. From Johannesburg there are connections to Dar es Salaam on **South African Airways** and **Precision Air** or via Nairobi on **Kenya Airways**. To and from Nairobi, **Kenya Airways** flies between Mauritius and Nairobi, where it connects with the **Air Mauritius** flight to/from Perth. From Asia, **Kenya Airways** also has direct flights between Bangkok, Hong Kong, Guangzhou and Nairobi, from where you can again connect to Tanzania.

From Africa and the Middle East

South African Airways and **Precision Air** have direct flights between Johannesburg and Dar es Salaam. From Cape Town, you'll have to change in Johannesburg. South African no-frills airline **1 Time** has a good-value twice-weekly direct flight from Johannesburg to Zanzibar. Nairobi is served by just about all the African airlines, so you can connect to Dar es Salaam, Kilimanjaro or Zanzibar from there with **Kenya Airways**, **Precision Air** and **Fly 540**. From the Middle East, **Emirates** has direct flights from Dubai to Dar es Salaam; **Qatar Airways**, from Doha, and **Gulf Air**, from Bahrain, which also touch down in Zanzibar. **Kenya Airways** has direct flights between Dubai and Muscat and Nairobi, from where again you can connect to Tanzania.

Airlines

1 Time, www.1time.aero.
Air Malaysia, www.malaysia-airlines.com.
Air Mauritius, www.airmauritius.com.
Air New Zealand, www.airnewzealand.com.
Cathy Pacific, www.cathaypacific.com.
British Airways, www.britishairways.com.
Delta, www.delta.com.
Egypt Air, www.egyptair.com.
Emirates, www.emirates.com.
Ethiopian Airlines,
www.ethiopianairlines.com.

Gulf Air, www.gulfair.com.
Kenya Airways, www.kenya-airways.com.
KLM, www.klm.com.
Lufthansa, www.lufthansa.com.
Precision Air, www.precisionairtz.com.
Qantas, www.qantas.com.au.
Qatar Airways, www.qatarairways.com.
Singapore Airlines, www.singaporeair.com.
South African Airways, www.flysaa.com.
Turkish Airlines, www.turkishairlines.com.
Virgin Atlantic, www.virgin-atlantic.com.

Rail

There are two railway lines operating passenger services in Tanzania. The first is the **Tanzania Railway Corporation's Central Line**, which runs between Dar es Salaam and both Kigoma and Mwanza. If arriving into Tanzania by ferry from Zambia you are most likely to connect with the train at Kigoma. The second is the **TAZARA (Tanzania and Zambia Railway Authority)** line, which runs from Kapiri Mposhi in Zambia through the south of Tanzania via Mbeya, Iringa and Morogoro to Dar es Salaam. For details of both services, see box, page 18.

Road

Note: when departing from Tanzania across any land border, you will be asked to show your yellow fever vaccination certificate as Tanzania is considered an endemic country.

From Kenya The main road crossing is at Namanga, about halfway along the road between Arusha and Nairobi. As this border receives thousands of tourists on safari each week en route between the Kenyan and Tanzanian parks, it is reasonably quick and efficient. There are regular shuttle buses (see box, page 15) connecting Nairobi with Arusha (5½ hours) and Moshi (seven hours), on a good road. A cheaper alternative is to do the journey in stages by taking a minibus from Ronald Ngala Road in Nairobi to Namanga, crossing the border on foot, and then catching another minibus to Arusha. This will take a little longer than the shuttle, but will cost half the price. There are also international long-distance

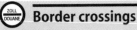

Border crossings

Tanzania–Kenya
Lunga Lunga, see page 99.
Taveta, see page 212.
Namanga, see page 237.
Isebania, see page 305.

Tanzania–Malawi
Songwe, see page 388.

Tanzania–Mozambique
Mtambaswala–Negomano, see page 126.
Kilambo–Namoto, see page 126.

Tanzania–Rwanda
Rusumo, see page 317.

Tanzania–Uganda
Mutukulu, see page 322.

Tanzania–Zambia
Tunduma-Nakonde, see page 383.

bus services between Nairobi and **Dar es Salaam**, about 14 hours, which also go via the Namanga border and stop in **Arusha** and **Moshi**. Other routes are Nairobi to **Musoma** and **Mwanza** on Lake Victoria in northwestern Tanzania, around 13½ hours, which go via the border at Isebania; and Mombasa to **Tanga**, around four hours, which connect with buses to and from **Dar es Salaam**, and cross the border at Lunga Lunga on the coast. Local buses and minibuses (*dala-dalas*) frequent the quieter border crossing at Taveta, between Voi and Moshi. Visas for both Tanzania and Kenya are available at all the borders.

From Malawi Travellers entering Tanzania from Malawi will pass through the Songwe border, 115 km southeast of Mbeya and 50 km north of Karonga in Malawi. There are buses between Lilongwe and Mzuzu, and Mzuzu and Karonga in Malawi to the border, and then buses run from Kyela, 5 km north of the Tanzanian side of the border, to Mbeya. Some (including **Scandinavia Express**, below) have direct services between Kyela and Dar es Salaam (13 hours). Most nationalities do not require a visa for Malawi. For more information, see page 388.

From Mozambique Getting to Tanzania from Mozambique is fairly difficult, and presently the best option is the car ferry, or without a vehicle, *mokoro* ride, across the Ruvuma River at the Kilambo-Namoto border approximately 40 km southeast Mtwara. There is public transport of sorts on this route in the form of *dala-dalas*, which in Mozambique are called *chapas*. There is a new bridge crossing the Ruvuma River some 275 km inland, which connects southern Tanzania at Masuguru Village, 240 km from Lindi, with northern Mozambique at Negonane Village in the Cabo Delgado Province, 275 km from Mocimboa da Praia on the coast. While the road between Lindi and the bridge is reasonable, the roads on the Mozambique side are very difficult and become impassable during and after heavy rain. Nevertheless, there is now a border control at the bridge, but no public transport on this route. For more information, see page 126. It is essential to have a visa for Mozambique which can be arranged at the embassy in Dar es Salaam.

From Rwanda The border with Rwanda is at Rusumo, although those in private vehicles must be aware that there have been incidents of banditry on the roads to the southwest of Lake Victoria. This is roughly 160 km on a fairly good road from Rwanda's capital of Kigali

Kenya–Tanzania shuttle services

Shuttle buses run daily between Kenya and Tanzania: Nairobi (city centre)–Nairobi Jomo Kenyatta International Airport–Arusha (via the Namanga border post)–Kilimanjaro International Airport–Moshi. The operators utilize 20- to 30-seat buses with comfortable individual seating, and drivers assist passengers during the border crossings. There is an early morning and an early afternoon departure. Expect to pay about US$30 for Nairobi to Arusha, US$40 for Nairobi to Moshi, and US$20 from Kilimanjaro International Airport to Arusha or Moshi. The journey time from Nairobi to Arusha is 5½ hours and it's another 1½ hours to Moshi via the airport. The company websites have booking facilities, timetables, prices and information about where to meet the buses, and they can also be booked at the company town offices, or through hotels or local tour operators.

AA Shuttles, www.aashuttles.com.
Impala Shuttles, www.impalashuttle.com.
Regional Luxury Shuttle, www.regionalluxuryshuttle.com.
Riverside Shuttles, www.riverside-shuttle.com.

and is served by regular minibuses, but on the Tanzanian side there is only sporadic public transport to Mwanza (usually one bus a day) or *dala-dalas* link the regional towns. For more information, see page 317.

From Uganda There is a crossing at Mutukulu, 82 km northwest of Bukoba, and as this road has recently been tarred, there are through buses between Bukoba and Masaka (89 km) and Kampala (218 km). For more information, see page 322. However, unless you are in the extreme northwest of Tanzania anyway, the easiest way to get from Tanzania to Uganda is via Nairobi (Kenya). **Scandinavia Express** (below) has buses from Dar via Arusha and Moshi to Nairobi and on to Kampala.

From Zambia The Tunduma–Nakonde border is 115 km southwest of Mbeya and roughly 1000 km northeast of Lusaka. There are buses to the border from Mbeya, but little public transport on the Zambian side. However, there are through buses between Dar es Salaam and Lusaka with **Scandinavia Express** (below). For more information, see page 383.

Bus

Although there are several companies that ply the cross-border routes, **Scandinavia Express**, www.scandinaviagroup.com, are the most reliable for travellers on the most popular routes. Buses are speed-limited, luggage is securely locked up either under the bus or in overhead compartments, complimentary DVDs, drinks, sweets and biscuits are offered, and the buses stop at roadside restaurants for lunch. They operate on the following routes: between **Dar es Salaam** and **Nairobi**, with stops in **Moshi** and **Arusha**; between Nairobi and **Musoma** and **Mwanza** – the route from Dar es Salaam to northwest Tanzania is quicker via Kenya than across country because of the appalling roads; between **Mombasa** and **Tanga**, which connects with buses to and from **Dar es Salaam**; and between **Dar es Salaam** and **Lusaka** in Zambia. Additionally, from **Nairobi**, they also have services to **Kampala** in Uganda, so die-hard fans of African bus travel can travel all the way from Kampala in Uganda to Lusaka in Zambia with **Scandinavia Express**. See Dar es Salaam Transport (page 73) or the relevant chapters for more details.

Car

If you are driving, border crossings between Tanzania and its neighbours can be laborious or simple, depending on your preparation and the state of your vehicle's paperwork. If in a private car, you must have a registration document, a driving licence printed in English with a photograph, and for a foreign-registered vehicle, a Carnet de Passage issued by a body in your own country (such as the Automobile Association). You will also be required to take out third-party insurance for Tanzania from one of the insurance companies who have kiosks at the border posts. Most car hire companies will not allow you to take a rented vehicle out of the country, but some may consider it if you only want to go to Kenya. If crossing the border into Kenya in a car registered in Tanzania (or vice versa), you'll be issued with a temporary import permit. See page 20 for information about hiring a car in Tanzania.

Overland trucks

Overland truck safaris are a popular way of exploring East Africa by road. They demand a little more fortitude and adventurous spirit from the traveller, but the compensation is usually the camaraderie and life-long friendships that result from what is invariably a real adventure, going to places the more luxurious travellers will never visit. The standard overland route most commercial trucks take through East Africa (in either direction) is from Nairobi a two-week circuit into Uganda to see the mountain gorillas via some of the Kenya national parks, then crossing into Tanzania to Arusha for the Ngorongoro Crater and Serengeti, before heading south to Dar es Salaam, for Zanzibar. If you have more time, you can complete the full circuit that goes from Tanzania through Malawi and Zambia to Livingstone to see the Victoria Falls, and then another three weeks from there to Cape Town in South Africa via Botswana and Namibia. There are several overland companies with departures almost weekly from Nairobi, Dar es Salaam, Livingstone and Cape Town.

Overland truck safari operators

Africa Travel Co, www.africatravelco.com.
Acacia Africa, www.acacia-africa.com.
Dragoman, www.dragoman.com.
Exodus Travels, www.exodus.co.uk.

Explore, www.explore.co.uk.
Kumuka Worldwide, www.kumuka.com.
Oasis Overland, www.oasisoverland.co.uk.

Sea and lake

A US$5 port tax is applied to all ferry tickets departing from Tanzanian ports, but is included in fares. From Burundi there is, in theory, a Lake Tanganyika ferry to Kigoma from Bujumbura every Monday. However, at the time of writing this was currently suspended, though the service may resume at any time. From Mpulungu (Zambia) there is a weekly ferry on Friday that arrives in Kigoma on Sunday (see page 355 for further details). From Nkhata Bay (Malawi) on Lake Nyasa (also known as Lake Malawi) there is a ferry to Mbamba Bay, though this is a very erratic service and should not be counted on.

Transport in Tanzania

Air → *See also Transport in Dar es Salaam, page 73.*

There are a number of airlines that offer extensive air coverage of the country and there are 62 airports and airstrips managed by the **Tanzania Airports Authority** (www.taa. go.tz). Regular daily flights connect the major towns and cities and some of the safari destinations, all of which can be reached within a couple of hours' flying time from each other. There's a fair amount of competition, so flights are very affordable. Many of these airlines run services in circuits, and flights may involve intermediate stops as the plane drops passengers at different airstrips on each circuit and may often return on the same route. For example, a flight to the Serengeti may actually 'drop down' at several safari lodges. The smaller airlines will only fly with the required minimum of passengers, though sometimes this is only two people. Note that on the smaller aircraft, the baggage allowance is 15 kg so you may have to leave luggage at hotels in Dar or Arusha, which most will allow for a small fee. All tickets can be booked online or can be bought directly from the airline desks at the airports. Specific schedules are detailed under each relevant chapter.

Airlines

Air Excel, Arusha, T027-254 8429, www.air excelonline.com, has flights to/from Dar es Salaam, Arusha, Kilimanjaro, Lake Manyara, the Serengeti and Zanzibar.
Auric Air, Dar, T022-212 6043, www.auric air.com, has flights to/from Dar es Salaam, Arusha, Bukoba, Iringa, Lake Manyara, Mbeya, Mwanza and the Serengeti.
Coastal Air, Dar, T022-284 2700, www. coastal.cc, has flights to/from Dar es Salaam, Arusha, Dodoma, Kilwa, Tarangire, Mafia Island, Lake Manyara, Mwanza, Pemba, Ruaha, Selous, Serengeti, Tanga and Zanzibar, and in Rwanda, Kigali.
Precision Air, Dar, T022-286 0701, www. precisionairtz.com, has flights to/from Dar es Salaam, Kigoma, Kilimanjaro, Musoma, Mwanza, Bukoba, Mtwara, Shinyanga and Zanzibar. Regionally they fly to Nairobi and Mombasa in Kenya, Entebbe in Uganda, and Johannesburg in South Africa.
Regional Air, Arusha, T027-250 2541, www.regionaltanzania.com, has flights to/from Dar es Salaam, Arusha, Kilimanjaro, Lake Manyara, Ngorongoro Crater, Pangani, Saadani, the Serengeti and Zanzibar.
ZanAir, Zanzibar, T024-223 3670, www.zanair.com, has flights to/from Dar es Salaam, Arusha, Pemba, Selous and Zanzibar, and in Kenya, Mombasa.

Air charter

Several companies offer small planes for charter, especially between the parks and islands, and have flights most days of the week, which can work out economical for groups of 4-6 people.
    Flightlink, Dar, T0782-354 448, www. flightlinkaircharters.com; **Indigo Aviation**, Dar, T022-226 4528, www.indigoair.co.tz; **Kilimanjaro Air Safaris**, T027-275 0523, www.kiliair.com; **Renair**, Mwanza, T028-256 2069, www.renair.com; **Zantas Air**, Dar, T022-213 0476, www.zantasair.com.

Train services in Tanzania

There are two services on the TAZARA line. The first train departs from Dar es Salaam at 1550 on Tuesday, gets to Mbeya at 1315 on Wednesday, the Zambia border at Tunduma at 1700 on Wednesday, and Kapiri Mposhi at 0925 on Thursday. In the other direction it departs from Kapiri Mposhi at 1600 on Tuesday, gets to Tunduma at 1015 on Wednesday, Mbeya 1415 on Wednesday, and arrives in Dar es Salaam at 1235 on Thursday. The second service is a slower and more basic train (you don't get meals in your compartment for example) and leaves Dar es Salaam at 1350 on Friday, gets to Mbeya at 1410 on Saturday, the border at Tunduma at 1840 on Saturday, and Kapiri Mposhi at 1340 on Sunday. In the other direction it leaves Kapiri Mposhi at 1400 on Friday, gets to Tunduma at 1030/Saturday, Mbeya 1430/Saturday, and arrives in Dar es Salaam at 1545 on Sunday. Approximate fares between Dar es Salaam and Kapiri Mposhi: 1st class US$45, 2nd class US$35, 3rd class US$25; between Dar es Salaam and Mbeya: 1st class US$25, 2nd class US$18, 3rd class US$9. If you are crossing the border, immigration officers board the train, and visas for both Zambia and Tanzania can be bought with US$ cash; money changers also get on the train as only cash of each respective country is accepted in the dining cars.

The Kigoma/Mwanza train departs from Dar es Salaam on the Central Line at 1700 on Tuesday and Friday, and gets to Tabora at 1825 on Wednesday/Saturday. In Tabora, the train is 'split' and carriages are attached to the respective locomotives going to either Kigoma or Mwanza. This process, in theory and according to the timetable, takes a couple of hours (but in reality can take several hours), while the carriages are shunted around and passengers may have to swap carriages depending on which direction they are going in. The trains then depart from Tabora again at 2130 and arrive in Kigoma and Mwanza respectively at 1725 Thursday/Sunday. In the other direction, the trains depart from Kigoma/Mwanza at 1700 on Thursday and Sunday, get to Tabora at 0400 on Friday/Monday where they 'split', and the Dar-bound train departs from Tabora at 0725, and arrives in Dar at 0850 on Saturday/Tuesday. Approximate fares between Dar es Salaam and Kigoma or Mwanza: 1st class US$40, 2nd class US$30, 3rd class US$15.

Rail

Trains in Tanzania are very slow and can be very late (you are likely to forget what day you actually departed), and you may well arrive at your destination hot, filthy and exhausted. But they cover vast distances in the interior of Tanzania, transport many thousands of Tanzanian people across the country and are undoubtedly a memorable and adventurous way to travel. If you have the time, it's a marvellous way to get off the beaten track and experience everyday African life as the trains trundle slowly across the sparse landscape. There are three classes of travel: first class in a compartment sleeping two or four; second class in a compartment sleeping six, and third class sitting. First class is the best bet, as some of the other rickety carriages are very old and lights and washbasins may not always function. Third class gets very uncomfortable and crowded; you'll be sitting among piles of boxes and live chickens for possibly up to 50 hours. All compartments on Tanzanian trains are sexually segregated unless you book the whole compartment (a single traveller could pay for a two-berth). While the trains themselves are a little grubby and more than a little infested by cockroaches, the bedding is very clean. Security can be an issue; it is essential to guard your possessions fiercely and keep cabin doors locked at all times. In fact you'll be given a piece of wood to wedge into the window to prevent anyone from opening it from the outside at night when the trains pull into stations. The trains have dining cars, which turn into rowdy bars late at night, and each first- and second-class carriage has a steward who can deliver a plate of adequate chicken and rice or *ugali* and beef or similar, which you can eat in your compartment. In the morning the steward comes round again with tea and coffee and the trains stop for a while at a trackside village for breakfast, when the enterprising villagers set up a row of stalls of street food next to the train.

Railway companies

There are two railway companies in Tanzania. Tickets for both can be bought at the stations, preferably in advance. **Central Line**, T022-211 7833, www.trctz. com. Trains run by the Tanzania Railway Corporation, between Dar es Salam and Kigoma with a branch line to Mwanza.

TAZARA, T022-226 2191, www.tazarasite. com. This is the name of the Tanzania-Zambia Railway Authority and the trains run from Dar es Salaam, southwest via Morogoro, Iringa and Mbeya to Kapiri Mposhi in Zambia.

Road

Bus → *See also Transport in Dar es Salaam, page 73.*
There is an efficient network of privately run buses across the country. On good sealed roads, buses cover 50-80 km per hour, but on unsealed or poorly maintained roads they may average only 20 km per hour. Larger buses give a considerably more comfortable ride than minibuses and have more space for luggage, and are to be recommended on safety grounds as well. If you are taking a shorter journey (Dar–Morogoro or Mwanza–Musoma, say), the bus will leave when full. You can join an almost full bus and leave promptly for an uncomfortable journey, either standing or on a makeshift gangway seat. Or you can secure a comfortable seat and wait until the bus fills, which can take one or two hours on a less busy route. On the main routes it is possible to book ahead at a kiosk at the bus stand, and this is wise rather than turning up at the departure time on the off-chance. On the larger and more travelled routes (Dar–Arusha, Dar–Mbeya, Dar–Mombasa in Kenya) there is a choice of 'luxury', 'semi-luxury' and 'ordinary' buses, and fares vary by a few dollars. The difference between them is that the 'luxury' and 'semi-luxury' buses often have air conditioning and only take the number of people the buses are designed to seat. On the 'ordinary' services, the buses are usually older, carry additional standing passengers and stop more frequently en route, making the journey considerably slower. Fares on all buses are very reasonable, for example on a 'luxury' bus the fare from Arusha to Dar es Salaam (a journey of 650 km or eight hours) is around US$18, on a semi-luxury bus it's US$12, and on an ordinary bus US$9. Consistently recommended is **Scandinavia Express**, which has its own terminal in Dar es Salaam, T022-218 4833, www. scandinaviagroup.com. They are very popular so book ahead when possible.

Car
Driving is on the left side of the road. The key roads are in good condition, and there has been considerable road-building going on in Tanzania in recent years. The best roads are

the tarmac ones from Dar es Salaam to Zambia and Malawi, Dar es Salaam to Arusha, Arusha to the Ngorongoro Crater and the road from Arusha to the Kenyan border at Namanga. Away from the main highways, however, the majority of roads are bad and hazardous. Most of the minor roads are unmade gravel with potholes; there are many rough stretches and they deteriorate further in the rainy season. Road conditions in Tanzania's parks and reserves are extremely rough and, during the rainy season, many are passable only with high-clearance 4WD vehicles. Fuel is available along the main highways and towns, but if you're going way off the beaten track, consider taking a couple of jerry cans of extra fuel. Also ensure the vehicle has a jack and possibly take a shovel to dig it out of mud or sand. If you break down, it is common practice in Tanzania to place a bundle of leaves 50 m or so before and behind the vehicle to warn oncoming motorists.

Car hire Most people visit the national parks on an organized safari, but if you're confident driving in Tanzania, there is also the option to hire a car. Car hire is not as well organized in Tanzania as it is in Kenya. There are fewer companies (although this is changing) and they are more expensive. Also, many of the vehicles are poorly maintained and you may find it difficult to hire a car without a driver. In saying that, however, by contrast to the rest of the country, hiring a Suzuki jeep on Zanzibar is a popular way to explore the island. To hire a car you generally need to be over 23, have an international driving licence, or pay a small fee to have your own country licence endorsed in Tanzania, and a credit card. Always take out the collision damage waiver premium, as even the smallest accident can be very expensive. Costs vary between the different car hire companies and are from around US$60-80 per day for a normal saloon car or a jeep on Zanzibar, rising to US$100-150 for a 4WD. Deals can be made for more than seven days' car hire. Finally, Tanzania's rather hefty 20% VAT is added to all costs. It is essential to shop around and ask questions of the companies about what is and what is not included in the rates and what the provisions are in the event of a breakdown. On safari you will have to pay the park entrance fees for the car and the driver, if you have one, although Tanzania residents pay a lot less than international visitors for park entry fees. Most of the tour operators listed in the book will be able to arrange vehicle hire.

Dala-dala
Called *dala-dala*, it is said, because they charged a dollar, although this seems a high sum, these are local private buses and passenger vehicles using Toyota (or other) minibuses. On Zanzibar they may also be small trucks. They are by far the most prevalent mode of urban and rural transport and are cheap, US$0.30 for a short journey, rising to US$0.50 for a longer one. However, they get very crowded, and there is often a squeeze to get on. But fellow travellers will be very helpful in directing you to the correct *dala-dala* if you ask (most have a sign indicating their route and destination on the front), will advise on connections, fight on your behalf to try to get you a seat and tell you when to get off at your destination. Many *dala-dalas* have inspirational messages on the front and back windows like 'God is Great', 'Viva Manchester United', or (rather ominously) 'Still Alive'.

Hitchhiking
In the Western sense (standing beside the road and requesting a free ride) hitchhiking is not an option. However, truck drivers and many private motorists will often carry you if you pay and, if you are stuck where there is no public transport, on that basis you can approach likely vehicles. Nevertheless, it is not generally recommended and women alone should be especially wary of hitchhiking.

Taxis

Hotels and town centre locations are well served by taxis, some good and some very run-down but serviceable. Hotel staff, even at the smallest locations, will rustle up a taxi even when there is not one waiting outside. If you visit an out-of-town centre location, it is wise to ask the taxi to wait – it will normally be happy to do so for benefit of the return fare. There is a bargaining element: none of the cabs have meters, so you should establish the fare (*bei gani?* – how much?) before you set off. Prices are generally fair, as drivers simply won't take you if you offer a fare that's too low. A common practice is for a driver to set off and *then* go and get petrol using part of your fare to pay for it, so often the first part of a journey is spent sitting in a petrol station. Also be aware that taxi drivers never seem to have change, so try and accumulate some small notes for taxi rides.

Tuk-tuks

These motorized three-wheel buggies are starting to feature in many African cities and are cheap and convenient. The driver sits in the front, whilst two or three passengers can sit comfortably on the back seat. They offer a service that is at least half the price of regular taxis. They do not, however, go very fast, so for longer journeys stick to taxis. In Tanzania they are known as *Bajajis*, after the Bajaj Auto Company that manufactures many of them.

Sea and lake

Ferries

Between Dar es Salaam and Zanzibar there are several sailings each day on modern hydrofoils and an older ferry (see page 75 for details). These are reliable and pleasant and, on the newer ones, movies are shown and refreshments are available. On Lake Victoria, the main sailings are between Mwanza and Bukoba, though small islands and some other lakeside towns are served. On Lake Tanganyika boats go from Kigoma to various small ports south. Fares for non-residents greatly exceed those for residents, though they are not overly expensive. On Lake Nyasa (also known as Lake Malawi) there is a boat going from the northern port of Itungi to Mbamba Bay, the last Tanzanian port on the east shore (see page 386).

Maps

The best map and travel guide shop in the UK is **Stanfords**, 12-14 Long Acre, Covent Garden, London WC2 9LP, T020-7836 1321, www.stanfords.co.uk, with branches in Manchester and Bristol. The *Michelin Map of Africa: Central and South*, www.michelintravel. com, covers Tanzania in detail. In South Africa, **Map Studio**, T+27 (0)21-460 5400, www. mapstudio.co.za, produces a wide range of maps covering much of Africa, which are available to buy online or there are shops in Johannesburg and Cape Town. In Tanzania you can pick up locally produced maps of the most popular parks, such as the Serengeti, in book and gift shops and some of the lodges stock them.

Where to stay in Tanzania

There is a wide range of accommodation on offer, from top-of-the-range lodges and tented camps that charge US$300-1000 per couple per day, to mid-range safari lodges and beach resorts with double rooms with air conditioning and bathroom for around US$150-250, standard small town hotels used by local business people for around US$50-100 per room, and basic board and lodgings used by local travellers at under US$20 a day. At the top end of the market, Tanzania now boasts some accommodation options that would rival the luxurious camps in southern Africa – intimate safari camps with unrivalled degrees of comfort and service in stunning settings. The beach resorts too have improved considerably in recent years, and there are some highly luxurious and romantic options that are in commanding positions next to the Indian Ocean.

Generally, accommodation booked through a European agent will be more expensive than if you contact the hotel or lodge directly, and most of Tanzania's hoteliers have websites. Hotels in the towns and cities usually keep the same rates year-round, but safari lodges and beach resorts have seasonal rates depending on weather, periods of popularity with overseas (especially European) visitors, and events like the wildebeest migration in the Serengeti, for example. Low season in East Africa is generally around the long rainy season from the beginning of April to the end of June, when most room rates drop considerably and it may be possible to negotiate rates, especially if you plan to stay a few days. Some establishments even close during this period, though the resorts on Zanzibar remain open throughout the year. For more expensive hotels, airlines, game park entrance and camping fees, tourists are charged approximately double the rate locals are charged – resident and non-resident rates. Most upmarket hotels will publish non-resident rates in US dollars, but these can be paid in Tanzania shillings as well as foreign currency. This really makes no difference but check the rates for Tanzania shillings against US dollars, and make a fuss if it's not a fair exchange rate. Credit cards are widely accepted at the larger places, but may attract a surcharge of around 5%. VAT at 20% is added to all service charges, though this is usually included in the bill.

Hotels

A few international hotel chains, such as **Hyatt** and **Holiday Inn** among others, have hotels in Dar es Salaam. Quality of local town and city hotels varies widely, and some tend to be bland with poor service and dated decor, while others are newly built with good amenities, and, increasingly, much nicer options are opening outside the major towns. For instance, many guesthouses have opened up on coffee farms around Arusha. In some areas, Stone Town on Zanzibar being the prime example, there is the opportunity to sleep in some historical and atmospheric hotels. Here, even the cheaper establishments are beautiful old houses decorated with fine antiques and Persian carpets, with traditional Zanzibar four-poster beds swathed in mosquito nets. Some of the beach hotels on the mainland and islands are resorts, which are in the most part appealing and sensitively built to blend in with the coastal forest in low-lying timber and thatched structures. These offer a range of watersports and activities where guests stay for their entire holiday, and while they will appeal to those who enjoy the all-inclusive package holiday experience, they may not appeal to more independent travellers. However, also on the coast is some small, simple beach cottage-type accommodation, which is mostly in good locations and is excellent value. At the budget end, there's a fairly wide choice of cheap accommodation.

Price codes

Where to stay

$$$$	over US$300	$$$	US$100-300
$$	US$50-100	$	under US$50

Unless otherwise stated, prices refer to the cost of a double room including tax, not including service charge or meals.

Restaurants

$$$	over US$30	$$	US$15-30	$	under US$15

Prices refer to the cost of a main course with either a soft drink, a glass of wine or a beer.

A room often comprises a simple bed, basic bathroom, mosquito net and fan, but may have an irregular water or electricity supply; it is always a good idea to look at a room first to ensure it's clean and everything works. It is also imperative to ensure that your luggage will be locked away securely for protection against petty theft, especially in shared accommodation. At the very bottom of the budget scale are numerous basic board and lodgings in all the towns that cost under US$10. For this you get a bare room with a bed and a door that may or may not lock. Unless these are exceptionally secure or good value, they are generally not recommended and are often simply rooms attached to a bar that, more often than not, are rented by the hour. The word hotel (or in Kiswahili, *hoteli*) means food and drink, rather than lodging. It is better to use the word guesthouse (in Kiswahili, *guesti*.

Camping

Away from the campsites in the national parks and game reserves, camping in Tanzania is fairly limited to the road that runs from Kenya all the way to Malawi in the south. This is part of the great African overland route and independent overlanders and commercial trucks on camping safaris travel in either direction. Campsites have sprung up along this route to accommodate the vehicles and campers and some are very good; indeed better than what is on offer in the national parks. The better ones have bars and restaurants, simple sleeping huts for those that don't want to camp, guards for tents and vehicles, and clean ablution blocks with plenty of hot water. However, you should always have your own tent and basic equipment, as these cannot be hired, and have adequate supplies of fresh water and food. In Dar es Salaam there are a few campsites that, for a small fee, will allow you to park your vehicle safely for a few days whilst you go to Zanzibar. Note camping on Zanzibar is illegal and sleeping on the beach is not permitted. If you are going off the beaten track and planning to bush or free camp outside official or designated campsites, seek local advice in advance. The land on which you are planning to camp may be privately owned or be traditional lands under the control of a nearby village. In some instances, advance permission and/or payment is required. Do not rely on local water supplies or rivers and streams for potable water. Any water taken from a stream should be filtered or boiled for several minutes before drinking. Never bush camp on the side of a busy road or near a town; it's an invitation to be robbed in the middle of the night.

Safari options

All safari companies offer basically the same safari but at different prices, depending on what accommodation is booked. For example, you can choose a three-day safari of the Ngorongoro Crater and Serengeti, and the options would be camping (the companies provide the equipment) or a lodge safari, making it considerably more expensive. For those who want to spend more, there is the option of adding flights between destinations or staying at one of the luxury private tented camps. Either way, you are likely to have the same sort of game-viewing experiences, but the level of comfort you enjoy on safari depends on where you stay and how much you spend.

Safari lodges vary and may be either typical hotels with rooms and facilities in one building, or individual *bandas* or *rondavels* (small huts) with a central dining area. Standards vary from the rustic to the modern, from the simply appointed to the last word in luxury. Some of the larger lodges in the parks of the northern circuit are enormous impersonal affairs with little atmosphere that were built some decades ago, though comfort and service is good. But at the newer ones, efforts have usually been made to design lodges that blend into their environment, with an emphasis on natural local building materials and use of traditional art and decoration. Most lodges serve meals and have lounges and bars, sometimes swimming pools, and they often have excellent views or overlook waterholes or salt licks that attract game.

There are **campsites** in most national parks. They are extensively used by camping safari companies. Vehicles, guides, tents and equipment, as well as food and a cook, are all provided, but you'll need to take your own sleeping bag and possibly a sleeping mat. Facilities are very basic – the Serengeti campsites, for example, have nothing more than a long drop loo – but sleeping here at night is really exciting: the campsites are unfenced and are often visited by hyena and lion. Many of the camps advertise hot running water for showers. This is accurate when the sun is out, otherwise the water may be cold. Do not leave food scraps or containers where they may attract and harm animals, and be careful about leaving items outside your tent. Many campsites have troupes of baboons nearby that can be a nuisance, and a hyena can chew through something as solid as a saucepan. If you are camping on your own, you will almost always need to be totally self-sufficient, with all your own equipment. The campsites usually provide running water and firewood. Camping should always have minimal impact on the environment. All rubbish and waste matter should be buried, burnt, or taken away.

A **luxury tented camp** is really the best of both worlds: the comfort of extremely high facilities and service, combined with sleeping closer to the animals. They are usually built with a central dining and bar area, are in stunning well-designed locations, and each tent will have a thatched roof to keep it cool inside, proper beds, a veranda and a small bathroom at the back with solar-heated hot water. The added benefit is that camps are usually fairly small, with just a few tents, so the safari experience is intimate and professional.

Food and drink in Tanzania

Food

Cuisine on mainland Tanzania is not one of the country's main attractions. There is a legacy of uninspired British catering (soups, steaks, grilled chicken, chips, boiled vegetables, puddings, instant coffee). Tanzanians are largely big meat eaters, and a standard meal is *nyama choma*, roasted beef or goat meat, usually served with a spicy relish, although some like it with a mixture of raw peppers, onions and tomato known as *kachumbari*. The main staple or starch in Tanzania is *ugali*, a mealie porridge eaten, all over Africa. Small town hotels and restaurants tend to serve a limited amount of bland processed food, omelette or chicken and chips, and perhaps a meat stew but not much else. Asian eating places can be better, but are seldom of a high standard. There is a much greater variety in the cities and the tourist spots; both Dar es Salaam and Zanzibar, in particular (with its exquisite coastal seafood), do a fine line in eateries. The Swahili style of cooking features aromatic curries using coconut milk, fragrant steamed rice, grilled fish and calamari, and delicious bisques made from lobster and crab. A speciality is *halau*, a sweet dessert made from almonds.

Some of the larger beach resorts and safari lodges offer breakfast, lunch and dinner buffets for their all-inclusive guests, some of which can be excellent while others can be of a poor standard and there's no real way of knowing what you'll get. The most important thing is to avoid food sitting around for a long time on a buffet table, so ensure it's freshly prepared and served. Vegetarians are catered for, and fruit and vegetables are used frequently, though there is a limited choice of dishes specifically made for vegetarians on menus and you may have to make special requests.

Restaurant prices are low; it is quite possible to get a plate of hot food in a basic restaurant for US$3, and even the most expensive places will often not be more than US$30 per person with drinks. The quality, standard and variety of food depends on where you are and what you intend to pay. The service in Tanzanian restaurants can be somewhat slower than you are used to and it can take hours for something to materialize from a kitchen. Rather than complain, just enjoy the laid-back pace and order another beer.

Various items can be bought at temporary roadside shelters from street vendors who prepare and cook over charcoal, which adds considerably to the flavour. It's pretty safe, despite hygiene being fairly basic, because most of the items are cooked or peeled. Snacks include barbecued beef on skewers (*mishkaki*), roast maize (corn), samosas, hard-boiled eggs, roast cassava (looks like white, peeled turnips) and *mandazi* (a kind of sweet or savoury doughnut). Fruits include oranges (peeled and halved), pineapples, bananas, mangoes (slices scored and turned inside-out), paw-paw (*papaya*) and watermelon. These items are very cheap and are all worth trying and, when travelling, are indispensable.

Most food is bought in open-air markets. In the larger towns and cities these are held daily and, as well as fresh fruit and vegetables, sell eggs, bread and meat. In the smaller villages, markets are usually held on one day of the week. Markets are very colourful places to visit and, as Tanzania is very fertile, just about any fruit or vegetable is available. Other locally produced food items are sold in supermarkets, often run by Asian traders, whilst imported products are sold in the few upmarket supermarkets in the larger cities, such as **Shoprite**.

Drink

Sodas (soft drinks) are available everywhere and are very cheap, and are bought in refundable 300 ml bottles. On the coast, especially Zanzibar, freshly squeezed fruit juices are delicious. Bottled water is fairly expensive, but is available in all but the smallest villages. Tap water is reputedly safe in many parts of the country, but is only really recommended if you have a fairly hardy traveller's stomach. **Coffee**, when freshly ground, is the local Arabica variety, with a distinctive, acidic flavour. In the evenings, particularly, but all day at markets, bus and railway stations there are traditional Swahili coffee vendors with large portable conical brass coffee pots with charcoal braziers underneath. The coffee is sold black in small porcelain cups and is excellent. On the coast chai (**tea**) is drunk in small glasses, black with lots of sugar, and is surprisingly refreshing. **Local beers** (lager) are decent and cheap and are sold in 700 ml refundable bottles. Brands include Kilimanjaro and Safari lager, tasty Tusker imported from Kenya or Castle from South Africa. Imported **wines** are on the expensive side, but there's a good choice of European or South African labels. Surreptitiously, **palm wine** is drunk at the coast.

Imported **spirits** are widely available, and local alternatives that are sold in both bottles and sachets of one tot include some rough vodkas and whiskies and the much more pleasant *Konyagi*, a type of scented gin distilled from sugarcane.

Shopping in Tanzania

Tanzania has several interesting craft items for sale, including Makonde and ebony wood carvings, soapstone carvings, musical instruments, basketware and textiles. Masai crafts, such as beaded jewellery, decorated gourds and spears, are available to buy in northern Tanzania as well as the red checked Masai blankets. *Mkeka* are plain, straw-coloured mats woven from sisal by craftsmen in Karatu, near the Ngorongoro Crater. The women of Mafia Island make more colourful *mkeka* from dried and twisted palm fronds. In Zanzibar, you can find old tiles, antique bowls and the famous carved wooden Zanzibar chests. Brightly coloured sarongs called *kangas* are worn by women all over Tanzania. They're sold in pairs and emblazoned with a traditional proverb. Woven with vertical stripes, *kikois* are similar but are traditionally worn by the men on the Swahili Coast as wrap-around sarongs. These are made into other items including clothes, cushion covers and bags. You can pick up bags of Zanzibar spices direct from the market. Tanzania is the world's only source of tanzanite, a semi-precious stone found in the open mines around Arusha. The deep blue of tanzanite is magnificent, ranging from ultramarine to a light purplish blue. Fakes abound, so if you're going to invest in one of Tanzania's largest exports, be sure to do it right. Don't buy from dealers on the street; most licensed curios shops and jewellers stock different grades, cuts, and colours. Also look out for Tingatinga paintings, which have a unique Tanzanian style (see box, page 56).

Most tourist areas have numerous places to buy these items; Dar es Salaam, Arusha and Stone Town on Zanzibar are dotted with curio shops, the roads on safari routes to and from the parks and reserves have plenty of roadside stalls where safari minibuses can conveniently pull in, and stalls line the roads behind the beach resorts. Prices in tourist shops are largely fixed, though in the depths of the quiet low season, can be negotiable. Prices at roadside stalls or markets are always negotiable. See page 30 for tips on bargaining.

Festivals in Tanzania

There are a number of festivals held on Zanzibar each year including the Festival of the Dhow Countries and the Sauti za Busara Swahili Music and Cultural Festival. For information on these see page 160.

February

Kilimanjaro Marathon, Moshi, www.kilimanjaromarathon.com (see box, page 218). Run on a 42-km route in the foothills of Kilimanjaro at an altitude of 800-1100 m, this is open to professionals and amateurs and is growing in popularity with international visitors to Tanzania. The Kili(man)jaro Adventure Challenge is a 6-day climb of Kilimanjaro, a 2-day mountain bike race around the mountain, followed by the marathon.

May

Goat Races, Dar es Salaam, www.goatraces.com. If you're in Dar in May, don't miss the unusual and hilarious Goat Races. Goats are released from their traps and then the owners, by any means possible without actually touching them, cajole their goats on to the finishing line. Betting is an integral part of the event, proper racing programmes are drawn up, and the goats are paraded around the ring before each race. Winners are picked up by their owners and cheered by the crowds, while the losers bleat despondently.

September

Bagamoyo Festival of Arts and Culture, Bagamoyo, www.tasuba.ac.tz. The Bagamoyo College of Arts (see page 85) organizes the annual 6-day festival, which features traditional performances of music and dance, acrobatics, exhibitions of art and sculpture, local hip hop and reggae bands and much more.

Tanzacat, Dar es Salaam, www.tanzacat.com. From the Yacht Club on the Msasani Peninsula, this is one of Africa's largest sailing regattas, which is run over 10 days on Olympic standard courses and ends when the 50 or so participating catamarans race to Zanzibar.

October

Diwali, Dar es Salaam. This is the Hindu and Sikh Festival of Light, which is celebrated by the large Asian population in Dar es Salaam with a street parade in the city centre and fireworks displays.

Responsible travel

The tourism industry in Tanzania is very important for the country's economy and creates thousands of jobs. Many national parks and game reserves, valuable archaeological sites and museums are funded by visitor entry fees, which in turn promote their protection. Additionally, some of the tour operators, private reserves and lodges fund conservation and community projects. By earning from tourism, the poorer people who rely on the land for their livelihoods are more likely to protect their environments for the benefit of tourism and these projects are well worth supporting.

10 ways to be a responsible traveller
There are some aspects of travel that you have to accept are going to have an impact, but try to balance the negatives with positives by following these guidelines to responsible travel.

• **Cut your emissions** Plan an itinerary that minimizes carbon emissions whenever possible. This might involve travelling by train, hiring a bike or booking a walking or canoeing tour rather than one that relies on vehicle transport. See opposite page for details of carbon offset programmes. Visit www.seat61.com for worldwide train travel.

• **Check the small print** Choose travel operators that abide by a responsible travel policy (if they have one it will usually be posted on their website). Visit www.responsibletravel.com.

• **Keep it local** If travelling independently, try to use public transport, stay in locally owned accommodation, eat in local restaurants, buy local produce and hire local guides.

• **Cut out waste** Take biodegradable soap and shampoo and leave excess packaging, particularly plastics, at home. The countries you are visiting may not have the waste collection or recycling facilities to deal with it.

• **Get in touch** Find out if there are any local schools, charities or voluntary conservation organizations that you could include in your itinerary. If appropriate, take along some useful gifts or supplies; www.stuffyourrucksack.com has a list of projects that could benefit from your support.

• **Learn the lingo** Practise some local words, even if it's just to say 'hello', 'thank you' and 'goodbye'. Respect local customs and dress codes and always ask permission before photographing people – including your wildlife tour guide. Once you get home, remember to honour any promises you've made to send photographs.

• **Avoid the crowds** Consider travelling out of season to relieve pressure on popular destinations, or visit a lesser-known alternative.

• **Take only photos** Resist the temptation to buy souvenirs made from animals or plants. Not only is it illegal to import or export many wildlife souvenirs, but their uncontrolled collection supports poaching and can have a devastating impact on local populations, upsetting the natural balance of entire ecosystems.
CITES, the Convention on International Trade in Endangered Species (www.cites.org) bans international trade in around 900 animal and plant species, and controls trade in a further 33,000 species.

Several organizations, including WWF, TRAFFIC and the Smithsonian Institution have formed the Coalition Against Wildlife Trafficking (www.cawtglobal.org).

• **Use water wisely** Water is a precious commodity in many countries. Treating your own water avoids the need to buy bottled water which can contribute to the build-up of litter.

• **Don't interfere** Avoid disturbing wildlife, damaging habitats or interfering with natural behaviour by feeding wild animals, getting too close or being too noisy. Leave plants and shells where you find them.

Code green for hikers
• Take biodegradable soap, shampoo and toilet paper, long-lasting lithium batteries and plastic bags for packing out all rubbish.
• Use a water filter instead of buying bottled water, and save fuel at remote lodges by ordering the same food at the same time. Only take a hot shower if the water has been heated by solar power.
• If no toilet facilities are available, make sure you are at least 30 m from any water source.
• Keep to trails to avoid erosion and trampling vegetation. Don't take short cuts, especially at high altitude where plants may take years to recover.

Code green for divers and snorkellers
• Help conserve underwater environments by joining local clean-ups or collecting data for Project AWARE (www.projectaware.org).
• Choose resorts that properly treat sewage and wastewater and support marine protected areas.
• Choose operators that use mooring buoys or drift diving techniques, rather than anchors that can damage fragile marine habitats such as coral reefs.
• Never touch coral. Practise buoyancy control skills in a pool or sandy area before diving around coral reefs, and tuck away trailing equipment.
• Avoid handling, feeding or riding on marine life.
• Never purchase marine souvenirs.
• Don't order seafood caught using destructive or unsustainable practices such as dynamite fishing.

How should I offset my carbon emissions?
Carbon-offsetting schemes allow you to offset greenhouse gas emissions by donating to various projects, from tree planting to renewable energy schemes. Although some conservation groups are concerned that carbon offsetting is being used as a smoke-screen to delay the urgent action needed to cut emissions and develop alternative energy solutions, it remains an important way of counterbalancing your carbon footprint.

For every tonne of CO_2 you generate through a fossil fuel-burning activity such as flying, you pay for an equivalent tonne to be removed elsewhere through a 'green' initiative. There are numerous online carbon footprint calculators (such as www.carbonfootprint.com). Alternatively, book with a travel operator that supports a carbon offset provider like TICOS (www.ticos.co.uk) or Reduce my Footprint (www.reducemyfootprint.travel).

It's not all about tree-planting schemes. Support now goes to a far wider range of climate-friendly technology projects, ranging from the provision of energy-efficient light bulbs and cookers in the developing world to large-scale renewable energy schemes such as wind farms.

Essentials A-Z

Accident and emergency

Police, fire and ambulance T111.

Bargaining

Whilst most prices in shops are set, the exception are curio shops where a little good-natured bargaining is possible, especially if it's quiet or you are buying a number of things. Bargaining is very much expected in the street markets, whether you are buying an apple or a Masai blanket. Generally traders will attempt to overcharge tourists who are unaware of local prices. Start lower than you would expect to pay, be polite and good humoured and, if the final price doesn't suit – walk away. You may be called back for more negotiation if your final price was too high, or the trader may let you go, in which case your price was too low. Ask about the prices of taxis, excursions, souvenirs and so on at your hotel.

Children

Tanzania has great appeal for families: animals and safaris are very exciting for children (and their parents), especially when they catch their first glimpse of an elephant or lion. However, small kids may get bored driving around a hot game park or national park all day if there is no animal activity. It's a good idea to get children enthused by providing them with checklists for animals and birds and perhaps giving them their own binoculars and cameras. In the parks, there are considerable reductions to entry fees for children under 16, and under 5s go free. At some safari lodges children are not permitted at all, whereas others are completely child-friendly. There are also considerable discounts on accommodation at the beach for children, especially in

the family-orientated resorts of Zanzibar, which have either specific family rooms or adjoining rooms suitable for families, and often extra amenities for children.

Disposable nappies, formula milk powders and puréed foods are only available in major cities and they are expensive, so you may want consider bringing enough of these with you. It is important to remember that children have an increased risk of gastro-enteritis, malaria and sunburn and are more likely to develop complications, so care must be taken to minimize risks. See Health, page 31, for more details.

Customs and duty free

The official customs allowance for visitors over 18 years includes 200 cigarettes, 50 cigars, 250 g of tobacco, 2 litres of wine, 1 litre of spirits, 50 ml of perfume and 250 ml of eau de toilette. There is no duty on any equipment for your own use (such as a laptops or cameras).

Disabled travellers

The towns have very uneven pavements, which are invariably blocked by parked cars, and wheelchairs are impossible to accommodate on public road transport, so you will probably need to come to Tanzania on an organized tour or in a rented vehicle. With the exception of the most upmarket hotels, there are few designated facilities for disabled travellers. A few of the game park lodges have ground-floor bedrooms, in contrast to most hotels where the bedrooms are upstairs and there are no lifts. Safaris should not pose too much of a problem given that most of the time is spent in the vehicle, and wheelchair-bound travellers may want to consider a camping or tented safari which provides easy access to a tent at ground level. Most tour operators are accommodating and should be able to make special arrangements for disabled travellers.

Based in Kenya, **Go Africa Safaris & Travel**, Nairobi, T+ 254 (0)20-235 3883, www.go-africa-safaris.com, organizes tailor-made safaris in East Africa in vehicles adapted for wheelchairs, uses selected accommodation with disabled facilities and has some specialist equipment such as hoists, plus it can cater for visually and hearing-impaired clients.

Also based in Kenya, **Victoria Safaris**, Nairobi, T+254 (0)20-225 2015, www.victoria safaris.com, again organizes tailor-made safaris for wheelchair-users and the visually and hearing impaired, and with a little planning, can arrange a Mt Kilimanjaro trek on the Marangu Route for those in wheelchairs, which involves utilizing extra porters.

Dress

Travellers are encouraged to show respect by adhering to a modest dress code in public places, especially in the predominantly Muslim areas on the coast and islands. In the evening at social functions there is no particular dress code, although hosts will feel insulted if you arrive for dinner in shorts, sandals or bare feet, and you will be expected to dress up a little in the more upmarket lodges and hotels. On safari, clothes in muted brown and khaki colours are the best. This is certainly true of the more remote parks where seeing unexpected bright colours may startle the animals. But in the Serengeti or Ngorongoro Crater, where the animals are so used to seeing hordes of tourists each day, it is not so important.

Drugs

The use of *bhangi* (cannabis) is relatively widespread, but is illegal. Penalties for possession of any drugs are extremely harsh. In some rural areas, locally distilled alcohol is available, but it can be dangerous to the uninitiated and should be avoided.

Embassies and consulates

For embassies and consulates of Tanzania, see http://embassy.goabroad.com.

Gay and lesbian travellers

Homosexuality is illegal in Tanzania and is considered a criminal offence, so extreme discretion is advised. There are no specific gay clubs or bars. Nevertheless, while Tanzanians generally consider being gay to be 'un-African', they do accept that non-Africans may be gay.

Health

See your GP or travel clinic at least 6 weeks before your departure for general advice on travel risks and vaccinations. Make sure you have travel insurance, get a dental check, know your own blood group and, if you suffer from a long-term condition such as diabetes or epilepsy, make sure someone knows or that you have a Medic Alert bracelet/necklace (www.medicalert.co.uk). If you wear glasses, take a copy of your prescription. Specialist advice should be taken on the best anti-malarials to use.

Vaccinations

Basic vaccinations recommended include polio, tetanus, diphtheria, typhoid, and hepatitis A. Note: Travellers from non-endemic countries travelling to Tanzania do not require a yellow fever vaccination certificate. However, travellers from non-endemic countries that travel through Tanzania will be asked to show the certificate after departing Tanzania and arriving at other destinations, which include all land borders in Tanzania and very possibly your home country – so it's essential that you get a certificate for any visit to Tanzania.

Health risks
Altitude sickness
Altitude sickness can strike from above 3000 m and is a response to the lack of

oxygen in the air. The best way of preventing altitude sickness is a relatively slow ascent when trekking to high altitude and spending some time walking at medium altitude, to acclimatize to the rarefied air. There are no specific factors such as age, sex or physical condition that contribute to the condition – some people get it and some people don't, though it's a good idea not to ascend to high altitude if you are suffering from a bad cold or chest infection and certainly not within 24 hrs of scuba-diving. Symptoms include headache, lassitude, dizziness, loss of appetite, nausea and vomiting. If the symptoms are mild, the treatment is rest, painkillers (preferably not aspirin-based) for the headaches and anti-sickness pills for vomiting. Should the symptoms be severe, it is best to descend to a lower altitude immediately – the symptoms disappear very quickly with even a few 100 m of descent.

Cholera

There are occasional outbreaks of cholera in the more impoverished rural areas of the country. The main symptoms of cholera are profuse watery diarrhoea and vomiting, which may lead to severe dehydration. However, most travellers are at extremely low risk of infection, and the disease rarely shows symptoms in healthy well-nourished people. The cholera vaccine, Dukoral, is only recommended for certain high-risk individuals such as health professionals or volunteers.

Diarrhoea

Diarrhoea can refer either to loose stools or an increased frequency of bowel movement, both of which can be a nuisance, but symptoms should be relatively short lived. Adults can use an antidiarrhoeal medication to control the symptoms but only for up to 24 hrs. In addition, keep well hydrated by drinking plenty of fluids and eat bland foods. Oral rehydration sachets taken after each loose stool are a useful way to keep well hydrated. These should always be used when treating children and the elderly.

Bacterial traveller's diarrhoea is the most common form; if there are no signs of improvement, the diarrhoea is likely to be viral and not bacterial and antibiotics may be required. Also seek medical help if there is blood in the stools and/or fever.

The standard advice to prevent problems is to be careful with water and ice for drinking. If you have any doubts then boil the water or filter and treat it. Food can also transmit disease. Be wary of salads (what were they washed in, who handled them), re-heated foods or food that has been left out in the sun having been cooked earlier in the day. There is a simple adage that says wash it, peel it, boil it or forget it. Also be wary of unpasteurized dairy products as these can transmit a range of diseases.

Hepatitis

Hepatitis means inflammation of the liver. Viral causes of the disease can be acquired anywhere in the world. The most obvious symptom is a yellowing of your skin or the whites of your eyes. However, prior to this all that you may notice is itching and tiredness. Pre-travel hepatitis A vaccine is the best bet. Hepatitis B (for which there is a vaccine) is spread through blood and unprotected sexual intercourse: both of these can be avoided.

HIV/AIDS

Africa has the highest rates of HIV and AIDS in the world. Efforts to stem the rate of infection have had limited success, as many of the factors that need addressing such as social change, poverty and gender inequalities are long-term processes. Visitors should be aware of the dangers of infection from unprotected sex and always use a condom. If you have to have medical treatment, ensure any equipment used is taken from a sealed pack or is freshly sterilized. If you have to have a blood transfusion, ask for screened blood.

Malaria

Malaria is present in almost all of Tanzania and prophylactics should be taken (take expert advice before you leave home). It can start as something just resembling an attack of flu. You may feel tired, lethargic, headachy, feverish, or, more seriously, develop fits, followed by coma and then death. Have a low index of suspicion because it is very easy to write off vague symptoms, which may actually be malaria. If you have a temperature, go to a doctor as soon as you can and ask for a malaria test. On your return home, if you suffer any of these symptoms, get tested as soon as possible.

To prevent mosquito bites wear clothes that cover arms and legs and use effective insect repellents. Repellents containing 30-50% DEET (Di-ethyltoluamide) are recommended; lemon eucalyptus (Mosiguard) is a reasonable alternative. Rooms with a/c or fans also help ward off mosquitoes at night. If your doctor or travel clinic advises you to take anti-malarials, ensure you finish the recommended course.

Rabies
Avoid dogs and monkeys that are behaving strangely. If you are bitten by a domestic or wild animal, do not leave things to chance: scrub the wound with soap and water and/ or disinfectant, try to at least determine the animal's ownership, and seek medical assistance at once. The course of treatment depends on whether you have already been satisfactorily vaccinated against rabies.

Schistosomiasis (bilharzia)
Bilharzia is a disease carried by parasitic snails living in fresh water; it occurs in most of the freshwater lakes of Tanzania, including Lake Victoria and Lake Tanganyika, and can be contracted from a single swim. Symptoms can appear within a few weeks and for many months afterwards. These include fever, diarrhoea, abdominal pain and spleen or liver enlargement. A single drug cures this disease, so get yourself checked out as soon as possible if you have any of these symptoms, or alternatively avoid swimming in any freshwater lakes or rivers – chlorinated swimming pools are safe.

Sun
Protect yourself adequately against the sun. Apply a high-factor sunscreen (greater than SPF15) and also make sure it screens against UVB. Prevent heat exhaustion and heatstroke by drinking enough fluids throughout the day (your urine will be pale if you are drinking enough). Symptoms of heat exhaustion and heatstroke include dizziness, tiredness and headache. Use rehydration salts mixed with water to replenish fluids and salts and find somewhere cool and shady to recover. If you suspect heatstroke rather than heat exhaustion, you need to cool the body down quickly (cold showers are particularly effective).

Ticks and fly larvae
Ticks usually attach themselves to the lower parts of the body often after walking in areas where cattle have grazed, and swell up as they suck blood. The important thing is to remove them gently, so that they do not leave their head in your skin because this can cause a nasty allergic reaction. Do not use petrol, Vaseline, lighted cigarettes, etc to remove the tick but, with a pair of tweezers, remove the beast gently by gripping it at the attached (head) end and rock it out in the same way that a tooth is extracted. Some tropical flies that lay their eggs under the skin of sheep and cattle also do the same thing to humans with the result that a maggot grows under the skin and pops up as a boil. The best way to remove these is to cover the boil with oil, Vaseline or nail varnish to stop the maggot breathing, then to squeeze it out gently the next day.

Water
There are a number of ways of purifying water. Dirty water should first be strained through a filter and then boiled or treated. Bringing water to a rolling boil at sea level is sufficient to make the water safe for drinking, but at higher altitudes you have to boil the water for a few minutes longer to ensure all microbes are killed. There

are sterilizing methods that can be used and there are proprietary preparations containing chlorine or iodine compounds. Chlorine compounds generally do not kill protozoa (eg giardia). There are a number of water filters now on the market. Make sure you take the spare parts or spare chemicals with you and do not believe everything the manufacturers say.

Other diseases and risks

If you are unlucky (or careless) enough to be bitten by a venomous snake, spider, scorpion or sea creature, try to identify the culprit, without putting yourself in further danger. Victims should be taken to a hospital or a doctor without delay. Tsetse fly is present in most game areas in Tanzania and can transmit sleeping sickness (African trypanosomiasis). However this disease is extremely rare in humans (though domestic animals can get it), but tsetse flies do administer a wicked bite.

If you get sick

There are private hospitals in Dar es Salaam, Arusha and Stone Town, which have 24-hr emergency departments and pharmacies, and have a high standard of healthcare. However, for extreme emergencies or surgery, visitors with adequate health insurance will be transferred to a private hospital in Nairobi, Kenya, which has the best medical facilities in East Africa. In other areas of Tanzania, facilities range from government hospitals to rural clinics, but these can be poorly equipped and under staffed. It is essential to have travel insurance, as hospital bills need to be paid at the time of admittance, so keep all paperwork to make a claim.

If you are planning to travel in more isolated areas, consider the **Flying Doctors' Society of Africa**, based at Wilson Airport in Nairobi, Kenya, T+254 (0)20-699 3000, www.amref.org. For an annual tourist fee of US$50, it offers free evacuation by air to a medical centre or hospital, and the service covers Tanzania. This may be worth considering if you are visiting remote regions, but not if visiting the more popular parks as adequate provision is made in the case of an emergency. The income goes back into the service and the **African Medical Research Foundation** (AMREF) behind it.

Useful websites

www.btha.org British Travel Health Association.
www.cdc.gov US government site that gives excellent advice on travel health and details of disease outbreaks.
www.fco.gov.uk British Foreign and Commonwealth Office travel site has useful information on each country, people, climate and a list of UK embassies/consulates.
www.fitfortravel.scot.nhs.uk A-Z of vaccine/health advice for each country.
www.travelhealth.co.uk Independent travel health site with advice on vaccination, travel insurance and health risks.

Holidays

All along the coast and on the islands the **Islamic calendar** is followed and festivals are celebrated. These include **Id-ul-Fitr** (end of Ramadan, variable); **Id-ul-Haji** (Festival of Sacrifice, variable); **Islamic New Year** (Jun) and **Prophet's birthday** (Aug). **Note** During Ramadan and other Muslim holidays, it's considered very offensive to eat and drink in public.

1 Jan New Year's Day
12 Jan Zanzibar Revolution Day (Zanzibar)
Mar/Apr Good Friday; Easter Monday
7 Apr Shiekh Abeid Amani Karume Day
26 Apr Union Day
1 May Mayday Workers' Day
7 Jul Industrial Day
9 Dec Independence Day
25 Dec Christmas Day
26 Dec Boxing Day

Insurance

Before departure, it is vital to take out comprehensive travel insurance. There are a wide variety of policies to choose from, so shop around. At the very least, the policy should cover medical expenses, including repatriation to your home country in the event of a medical emergency. If you are going to be active in Tanzania, ensure the policy covers whatever activity you will be doing (for example, trekking or diving). If you do have something stolen whilst in Tanzania, report the incident to the nearest police station and ensure you get a police report and case number. You will need these to make any claim from your insurance company.

Internet

Internet cafés are plentiful in the major towns and range from sophisticated cybercafés with fast connections to small shops and business centres that may just have a single computer. Costs are little more than US$1 per hr, but in more out-of-the-way places where a satellite connection is relied upon, the price is higher. Wi-Fi is available at Dar es Salaam's **Julius Nyerere International Airport**, in some of the more upmarket hotels in Dar es Salaam and Arusha, and the beach resorts on Zanzibar. Most safari lodges don't have internet.

Language → *See also page 424.*

Tanzania is a welcoming country and the first word that you will hear and come to know is the Kiswahili greeting '*Jambo*' – 'hello', often followed by '*Hakuna matata*' – 'no problem'! Lengthy greetings are important in Tanzania, and respect is accorded to elderly people, usually by the greeting '*Shikamoo, mzee*' to a man and '*Shikamoo, mama*' to a woman.

There are a number of local languages, but most people in Tanzania, as in all East Africa, speak Kiswahili and some English.

Kiswahili is the official language of Tanzania and is taught in primary schools. English is generally used in business and is taught in secondary schools. Only in the remote rural regions will you find people that only speak in their local tongues. A little Kiswahili goes a long way, and most Tanzanians will be thrilled to hear visitors attempt to use it. Since the language was originally written down by the British colonists, words are pronounced just as they are spelt.

Media

Newspapers and magazines
Tanzania has several English-language newspapers. The best are the *Daily News* (www.dailynews.co.tz) and the *Guardian* (www.ippmedia.com), which both cover eastern and southern African news and syndicated international news and are available online. There are also a number of newspapers published in Kiswahili. An excellent regional paper, *The East African* (www.theeastafrican.co.ke), published in Nairobi, comes out weekly and has good Tanzanian coverage and provides the most objective reporting on East African issues. On a local level, the weekly *Arusha Times* (www.arushatimes.co.tz) has good local news and sports. Copies of international newspapers from Europe and the US usually filter to the street vendors in Dar and Arusha a few days after publication, along with well-thumbed magazines, such as *Time* and *Newsweek*.

Radio
Radio Tanzania broadcasts in Kiswahili, and news bulletins tend to contain a lot of local coverage. There are several popular FM stations that can be picked up in the cities, such as Radio Free Africa, Clouds FM and Radio One FM, which mostly broadcast imported pop, rap and hip-hop music. *BBC World Service* is broadcast to Tanzania; check the website for frequencies (www.bbc.co.uk/worldservice).

Television

Television Tanzania began to transmit in 1994, and it's widely believed that Tanzania was the last country in the world to get TV. Prior to that, Julius Nyerere believed (in accordance with his socialist principles) that TV would increase the divide between rich and poor. There are now numerous national and local stations (Dar es Salaam broadcasts no fewer than 15), which have a mixture of English and Kiswahili home-grown programmes and foreign imports. Most hotels have DSTV (Digital Satellite Television), South African satellite TV, with scores of channels including news and movies. The most popular with Tanzanians are the sports channels for coverage of European football.

Money

→ *US$1=TSh 1590, £1=TSh 2520, €1=TSh 2100 (Mar 2012)*

Currency

The Tanzanian currency is the Tanzanian Shilling (TSh), not to be confused with the Kenyan and Uganda Shilling which are different currencies. Notes currently in circulation are TSh 200, 500, 1000, 5000 and 10,000. Coins are TSh 50, 10 and 20 but these are hardly worth anything and are rarely used. As it is not a hard currency, it cannot be brought into or taken out of the country, however there are no restrictions on the amount of foreign currency that can be brought into Tanzania. The easiest currencies to exchange are US dollars, UK pounds and euros. If you are bringing US dollars in cash, try and bring newer notes – because of the prevalence of forgery, many banks and bureaux de change do not accept US dollar bills printed before 2005. Sometimes lower denomination bills attract a lower exchange rate than higher denominations. Banks (and ATMs) generally only dish out notes in increments of 10,000 TSh, which are often too large for people to have change – break bigger notes at larger establishments and save small change for

taxis, snacks and drinks, small souvenirs and the like.

Changing money

There are plenty of banks with ATMs and bureaux de change (known as forex bureaux) in the cities and at both Julius Nyerere International and Zanzibar International airports, and most small towns have at least one bank. All banks have a foreign exchange service, and bank hours are Mon-Fri 0830-1500, Sat 0830-1330. Forex bureaux are open longer hours and some open on Sun. Many large hotels and the airlines publish prices in US$, but they can be paid in TSh – just ensure that you are getting a reasonable exchange rate from US$ to TSh. Some national park entrance fees are paid in US$ cash, but Tanzania National Parks Authority (TANAPA) now have a system in place for electronic ticketing of either pre-paying for an 'e-ticket' or 'smart card' at banks or paying at 'point of sale' machines at gates to the most popular parks, which accept Visa and Mastercard (see Park fees, page 8 for information). Visitors should not change money on the black market as it is illegal. However, there is an exception to this rule – at land borders where there are no banks, there are informal moneychangers and it is deemed acceptable to make use of these to change a small amount of local or US$ cash to last until you reach the next bank. Be very careful during these transactions as scams and short-changing is common, and always have the required amount to change ready – you do not want to be dipping into your money belt in such a public place as a border crossing.

Credit cards

Visa, Mastercard, Plus and Cirrus cards are accepted; acceptance of Diners Club and American Express is, however, limited. Credit cards are accepted by large hotels, upmarket shops and restaurants, airlines and major tour operators, but of course will not be taken by smaller hotels and restaurants, curio markets and so on. There may be a surcharge of up to 5% so check first if paying a sizeable bill. Banks in Tanzania can advance cash on credit cards, and almost all now have ATMs, even in the smallest towns. In Dar es Salaam, many shopping malls and petrol stations also have ATMs. However, on the islands, a little bit of planning ahead is required. On Zanzibar, the only banks and ATMs are in Stone Town, so ensure you get enough cash before heading to the north or east coasts unless you intend to use only a credit card at the resorts. On Pemba, the only bank with an ATM is the People's Bank of Zanzibar in Chake Chake, but don't rely on this – rather bring cash from Zanzibar or the mainland.

Traveller's cheques
The major advantage of traveller's cheques (TCs) is that if they are lost or stolen there is a relatively efficient system for replacement. The drawback is that increasingly fewer places in Tanzania are willing to change them (try Barclay's Bank), and those that do, ask to see the purchase agreement (the slip issued at the point of sale that in theory you are supposed to keep separately from your TCs). Another disadvantage is the time it takes to cash them and the commission charged, which ranges from 2% to 5%.

Opening hours

Banks Mon-Fri, 0830-1530, Sat 0830-1330. **Post offices** Mon-Fri 0800-1630, Sat 0900-1200. **Shops** Generally Mon-Sat 0800-1700 or 1800. Small shops and kiosks and markets in the bigger towns are open daily. In Muslim areas, shops may close early on Fri.

Post

The Tanzania Post Office (www.posta.co.tz), has branches across the country, even in the smallest of towns. The postal system is fairly reliable, and letters to Europe take about 5-7 days and to the US about 10 days. If sending parcels, they must be no longer than 105 cm and have to be wrapped in brown paper and string. There is no point doing this before getting to the post office as you will be asked to undo it so that the parcel can be checked for export duty. Items have been known to go missing, so post anything of personal value through the fast post service known as EMS, a registered postal service available at all post offices, or with a courier company such as DHL (www.dhl.co.tz), which has offices in the major towns.

Safety

The majority of the people you will meet are honest and ready to help you, so there is no need to get paranoid about your safety. However, theft from tourists in Tanzania does occur and it will be assumed that foreigners in the country have relative wealth. Visitors on tours or who are staying in upmarket hotels are generally very safe. Otherwise, it is sensible to take reasonable precautions by not walking around at night and by avoiding places of known risk during the day. Petty theft and snatch robberies can be a problem, particularly in the urban areas. Don't wear jewellery or carry cameras in busy public places. Bum-bags are also very vulnerable as the belt can be cut easily. Day packs have also been known to be slashed, their entire contents drifting out on to the street without the wearer knowing. Carry money and any valuables in a slim belt under clothing.

Always lock room doors at night, as noisy fans and a/c can provide cover for sneak thieves. Be wary of a driver being distracted in a parked vehicle, whilst an accomplice gets in on the other side – always keep car doors locked and windows wound up. You also need to be vigilant of thieves on public transport; guard your possessions fiercely and be wary of pickpockets in busy places like the bus and train stations. Never accept food and drink from a stranger on public transport as it might be doped so they can rob you. Crime and hazardous road conditions make travel by night dangerous.

It's not only crime that may affect your personal safety; you must also take safety precautions when visiting the game reserves and national parks. If camping, it is not advisable to leave your tent or banda during the night. Wild animals wander around the camps freely in the hours of darkness, and a protruding leg may seem like a tasty take-away to a hungry hyena. This is especially true at organized campsites, where the local animals have got so used to humans that they have lost much of their inherent fear of man. Exercise care during daylight hours too – remember wild animals can be dangerous.

Telephone → IDD 000. Country code 255.

You can make calls from public coin or card phones in boxes on the street or at post offices; the latter are found in even the smallest towns where you can buy phonecards. In the larger towns there are also **Tanzania Telecommunications Company Ltd (TTCL)** offices (www.ttcl.co.tz), which are usually within the post office or nearby. Connections are quick and about a third of the price of a call through hotels, which are expensive for phone calls and faxes. In larger towns, private shops also offer international phone services, usually with additional internet. Telephone calls from Tanzania to Kenya and Uganda are charged at long-distance tariffs rather than international.

If you have a mobile phone with roaming, then you can make use of Tanzania's cellular networks, which cover most larger towns, the urban sections of the coast, Zanzibar and the tourist areas but not some of the parks and reserves or the southwest of Tanzania away from the towns and the main road. SIM and top-up cards for the pay-as-you-go mobile providers are available just about everywhere; in the towns and cities these often have their own shops, but you can buy cards from roadside vendors anywhere, even in the smallest of settlements. Indeed, mobile phones are now such a part of everyday life in Tanzania that many establishments have abandoned the less reliable local landline services and use the mobile network instead. You will see from listings for hotels and restaurants in this book that mobile numbers are sometimes offered instead of landline numbers: they start T07. Indeed, if you find a taxi driver or tour guide you like, get their mobile number as this is the best way to reach them. Quite remarkably, fishermen now use mobile phones to check the market prices of fish in the fish markets on Zanzibar and in Dar es Salaam before deciding where they are going to sell their catch.

Time

GMT +3. Malawi, Rwanda and Zambia are GMT +2, so when crossing from Tanzania, clocks go back 1 hr.

Tipping

It is customary to tip around 10% for good service, and this is greatly appreciated by hotel and restaurant staff, most of whom receive very low pay. You can make individual tips, or most large hotels and beach resorts have tip boxes in reception for you to make a contribution at the end of your stay which is shared amongst all staff. Taxi drivers don't need tipping since the price of a fare is usually negotiated first. How much to tip the guide/driver (on a camping trip the cook too) on safari is tricky. Remember that wages are low and there can be long lay-offs during the low season. Despite this, there is also the problem of excessive tipping, which can cause problems for future clients being asked to give more than they should. It is best to enquire from the company at the time of booking what the going rate is. As a very rough guide you should allow US$8-20 per guide/driver per day. Always try to come to an agreement with other members of the group and put the tip into a common kitty. For example, if you are in a group of four that would like to tip US$20 per day, each would contribute US$5 per day to the tip kitty, and the member of staff's total tip at the end of a seven day safari would be US$140. It is also expected (and important) that you tip guides and porters if climbing Kilimanjaro (see page 223).

Tour operators

If you plan to book an organized tour from your own country, the best bet is to locate a travel agent with links to tour companies in Tanzania. Within Tanzania there is a bewildering array of tour operators offering safaris in Tanzania and East Africa, with most having offices in Dar es Salaam (see page 72) or Arusha (see page 258). There is no reason why you cannot deal with them directly and they may often be cheaper and better informed than travel agents in your home country. Many companies offer tailor-made guided trips for small groups to the more remote parts of the country, which can be economical for families or groups travelling together. See page 10 for parks and safaris,

page 24 for safari accommodation options, and page 259 for 'How to organize a safari'.

UK and Ireland
Abercrombie & Kent, T0845-070 0600, www.abercrombiekent.co.uk.
Acacia Africa, T020-7706 4700, www.acacia-africa.com.
Africa Explorer, T020-8987 8742, www.africa-explorer.co.uk.
Africa Travel Centre, T0845-450 1520, www.africatravel.co.uk.
Africa Travel Resource, T01306-880 770, www.africatravelresource.com.
Aim 4 Africa, T0114-255 2533, www.aim4africa.com.
Expert Africa, T020-8232 9777, www.expertafrica.com.
Explore, T0870-333 4001, www.explore.co.uk.
Global Village, T0844-844 2541, www.globalvillage-travel.com.
Odyssey World, T0845-370 7733, www.odyssey-world.co.uk.

Okavango Tours and Safaris, T020-8347 4030, www.okavango.com.
Rainbow Tours, T020-7226 1004, www.rainbowtours.co.uk.
Safari Consultants Ltd, T01787-888590, www.safari-consultants.co.uk.
Safari Drive, T01488-71140, www.safaridrive.com.
Somak, T020-8423 3000, www.somak.co.uk.
Steppes Africa, T01285-880980, www.steppestravel.co.uk.
Tanzania Odyssey, T020-7471 8780, www.tanzaniaodyssey.com.
Tim Best Travel, T020-7591 0300, www.timbesttravel.com.
Wildlife Worldwide, T0845-130 6982, www.wildlifeworldwide.com.

Australia
African Wildlife Safaris, T+61 (0)3-9249 3777, www.africanwildlifesafaris.com.au.

Classic Safari Company, T+61 1 300-130218, www.classicsafaricompany.com.au.
Peregrine Travel, T+61 (0)3-8601 4444, www.peregrine.net.au.

North America
Adventure Centre, T+1 800-228 8747, T151-0654 1879, www.adventure-centre.com.
Africa Adventure Company, T+1 954-491 8877, www.africa-adventure.com.
Bushtracks, T+1 707-433 4492, www.bushtracks.com.
Tanzania Odyssey, T+1 186-6356 4691, www.tanzaniaodyssey.com.

South Africa
Go2Africa, T+27(0)21-481 4900, www.go2africa.com.
Pulse Africa, T+27 (0)11-325 2290, www.pulseafrica.com.
Wild Frontiers, T+27 (0)72-927 7529, www.wildfrontiers.com.

Tourist information

The Tanzania Tourist Board has its offices in the IPS Building, 3rd Floor, Samora Av/Azikiwe St, Dar es Salaam, T022-211 1244, www.tanzaniatouristboard.com. Contact them in advance and they will send you a brochure. The Tourist Information Office for drop-in visitors is at the Matasalamat Mansion, Samora Av, Dar, T022-213 1555, Mon-Fri 0800-1630, Sat 0830-1230. Tanzania National Parks Authority (TANAPA) has its HQ in Arusha, T027-250 3471, www.tanzaniaparks.com (see page 237).

Useful websites

www.marineparks.go.tz Website for Tanzania's Marine Parks and Reserves Authority who manage the Mafia Island Marine Park and smaller reserves off Dar es Salaam.
www.tanzania.go.tz Website for the Tanzanian government.
www.tanzaniaculturaltourism.com Website for the Tanzania Cultural Tourism Programme, which has information about the various initiatives around the country.
www.tanzaniaparks.com Tanzania National Parks Authority (TANAPA).
www.tanzaniatouristboard.com Official website of the Tanzania Tourist Board.
www.tfcg.org The website for the Tanzania Forest Conservation Group, with more information on the mountains and forests in the region.

www.zanzibar.net Good general information about Zanzibar including history and culture.
www.zanzibartourism.net Official site for the Zanzibar Commission for Tourism.

Visas and immigration

Almost all visitors require a visa, with the exception of some African countries. A transit visa valid for 14 days costs US$30 per person; a single-entry visa valid for 3 months costs US$50 (the exception are US and Irish citizens for whom a single entry is US$100); a multi-entry visa valid for 12 months costs US$100. Single-entry and transit visas can be obtained on arrival at the port of entry into Tanzania. Passport photos are not required. However, multiple-entry visas cannot be issued at the point of entry and must be obtained in advance through Tanzania's embassies. Your passport must be valid for a minimum of 6 months after your planned departure date from Tanzania, whether you need a visa or not. For more information visit Tanzania's Ministry of Home Affairs website, www.moha.go.tz.

It is straightforward to get a visa at the point of entry (ie border crossing or airport) and many visitors find this more convenient than going to an embassy. Visas are issued at all the road borders, at Julius Nyerere International Airport, Kilimanjaro International Airport, Zanzibar International Airport, at the ports in Zanzibar and Kigoma and on the

TAZARA train from Zambia. Visas are paid for in US$ cash, but the airports and the land borders frequented by tourists, such as Namanga (between Nairobi and Arusha) will also accept euros or UK pounds.

It is worth remembering that there is an agreement between Tanzania, Kenya and Uganda that allows holders of single-entry visas to move freely between all 3 countries without the need for re-entry permits. Also remember that, although part of Tanzania, Zanzibar has its own immigration procedures and you are required to show your passport on entry and exit to the islands. You'll be stamped in and out but ensure your 3-month Tanzania visa doesn't expire when on Zanzibar.

Visas can be extended at the **Immigration Headquarters**, Ohio/Ghana Av, Dar es Salaam, T022-211 8637, www.moha.go.tz, Mon-Fri, 0730-1530. There are also immigration offices in Arusha and Mwanza (see pages 264 and 316), or on Zanzibar, go to the port. You will be asked to show proof of funds (a credit card should be sufficient) and your return or onward airline ticket or tour voucher. Occasionally, independent travellers not on a tour may be asked for these at point of entry; those travelling through Tanzania on the way to somewhere else on a 14-day transit visa will most certainly be asked for these.

Voltage

230 volts AC at 50 Hz. Square 3-pin British-type sockets. Travellers with round-pin plugs will require adaptors. Hotels usually have 2-pin round sockets for razors, phones etc. Some hotels and businesses have back-up generators in case of power cuts, which are more common at the end of the dry seasons, and some more remote places off the national grid only use generators.

Weights and measures

Metric.

Women travellers

Tanzania does not have a high record of sexual crime, and tourists are unlikely to be targeted. It is a relatively safe country for women to travel in, but always keep vigilant, especially for petty theft, and follow the usual common sense about avoiding travelling alone after dark and avoiding quiet places. Women may experience unwanted attention from men, but this can usually be dealt with if you are assertive. Tanzanian women will generally be very supportive if they see you are being harassed and may well intervene if they think you need help. Older Tanzanian women are very much respected, so a few sharp words from them will diffuse any manner of situations. Women should be aware that the coast, and particularly Zanzibar, is largely Islamic. It's fine to lie on the beaches in Zanzibar, as these are at tourist resorts (although see guidelines on page 141), but in local villages and in Stone Town, remember to cover up in loose-fitting and non-revealing clothing so you don't cause offence. Many women travellers ignore this advice and seem to think because they're on an all-inclusive beach holiday, it entitles them to wear what they want. It doesn't. Non-Islamic women generally are not welcome around mosques.

Working in Tanzania

Whilst there is a fairly large expatriate community in Dar es Salaam working in construction, telecommunications and the import/export industry, there are few opportunities for travellers to obtain casual paid employment in Tanzania and it is illegal for a foreigner to work there without an official work permit. A number of NGOs and voluntary organizations can arrange placements for volunteers, especially in the teaching or medical professions, see www.volunteerafrica.org, or www.tanzaniavolunteers.com.

Contents

Footprint features

Dar es Salaam

At a glance

◉ **Getting around** Taxis are available on every street corner and there are plenty of *dala-dalas* and local buses. But traffic can be chaotic and the city is compact enough to walk around the main sites.

◔ **Time required** 1-2 days, an extra day if you want to explore the coastal suburbs.

◑ **Weather** Uncomfortably sticky and humid in Mar before the rains, with high temperatures. Pleasantly warm for the rest of the year and wet towards end Mar-May.

✕ **When not to go** A good year-round destination.

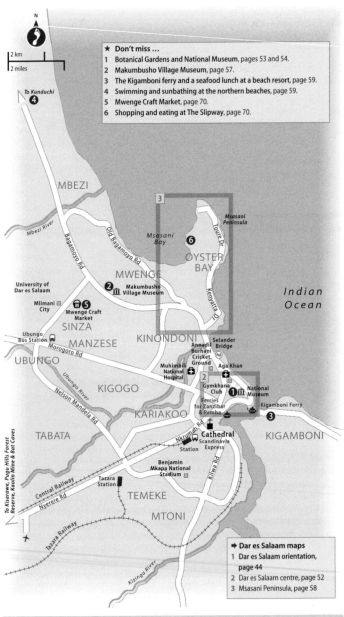

★ **Don't miss ...**
1 Botanical Gardens and National Museum, pages 53 and 54.
2 Makumbusho Village Museum, page 57.
3 The Kigamboni ferry and a seafood lunch at a beach resort, page 59.
4 Swimming and sunbathing at the northern beaches, page 59.
5 Mwenge Craft Market, page 70.
6 Shopping and eating at The Slipway, page 70.

➜ **Dar es Salaam maps**
1 Dar es Salaam orientation, page 44
2 Dar es Salaam centre, page 52
3 Msasani Peninsula, page 58

Dar es Salaam, meaning 'haven of peace' in Arabic, is far from peaceful these days but, by African standards at least, it is a relatively relaxed, unassuming yet atmospheric city. It's hardly a hive of activity for tourists – there are a handful of local museums, art galleries and craft markets to visit, and some interesting architecture of the 'faded colonial grandeur' category, alongside mosques, an attractive Lutheran church and a Roman Catholic cathedral that dominates the harbour front. But, with a rapidly increasing population estimated at 3.5 million, it is a thriving port, business centre and administrative base for the country (even though its status as capital city was removed in 1973), and you could do far worse than spend a couple of days here simply watching urban Tanzanian life go by. People are relaxed and friendly, the main sights of the city centre are easily walkable, and it's home to some excellent international-standard hotels and restaurants.

The city dates from 1857 and was successively under the control of Zanzibar, Germany and Britain before achieving self-determination in 1961, with all these influences leaving their mark on its character. During German occupation in the early 20th century, it was the centre of the colonial administration and the main contact point between the agricultural mainland and the world of trade and commerce in the Indian Ocean and along the Swahili Coast. Today, the ocean provides a sparkling backdrop to the city, with everything from small fishing boats to cruise liners and tankers visiting the port. And, should the urban bustle prove too much, nearby beaches to the north and south of town provide an easy escape. Further afield, Dar is the main springboard for ferries or flights to the islands of Zanzibar, Pemba and Mafia and to game parks across the country.

Arriving in Dar es Salaam → *Colour map 1, B6. 6°50'S 39°12'E. Phone code: 022. Population estimated at 3,200,700. Altitude: sea level.*

Getting there

Air International and domestic flights arrive and depart from **Julius Nyerere International Airport (JNIA)** ① *13 km southwest of the city centre along Nyerere Rd, T022-284 2402, www.taa.go.tz.* The airlines have desks at the airport and there are a range of facilities including a cafeteria and bar, 24-hour bureaux de change and ATMs and, airside, duty free and souvenir shops. For those international visitors requiring a visa for Tanzania (see page 41), the visa desk is just before immigration at international arrivals. To get from the airport to the city, there is a taxi stand in the main hall; organize your taxi here and not with the touts. A large board here has a list of hotels/destinations with fares: to the city centre and ferry terminal, US$25; Ubungo bus station, US$30; the Msasani Peninsula, US$35; Kunduchi, US$50; Kigamboni, US$50; and Bagomoyo, US$120. Taxi drivers prefer TSh rather than US$, and fares work out cheaper if you pay in shillings. Most hotels and tour operators also provide transport inclusive of a holiday package or, at the very least, can arrange a shuttle bus. The drive from the airport to the city centre takes around 30-50 minutes, but during 'rush hour' in Dar, 0800-1000 in the morning and 1600-1900 in the evening, traffic is very congested, so allow plenty of time. From the public bus stop on Nyerere Road, which is a five-minute walk from the terminal building, there are also regular *dala-dalas* and minibuses which cost no more than US$2. However, these are very crowded, there can be a problem with luggage which will normally have to be accommodated on your knees, and there is the possibility of petty theft. (From the city centre to the airport, these depart from the New Post Office stand on Azikiwe Street.) If you arrive after dark, the only sensible option is to take a taxi. ▸▸ *For airlines see Transport, page 73.*

Bus The main bus station for up-country travel is on Morogoro Road in the Ubungo area, 6 km to the west of the centre. It is well organized and modern, with cafés and shops, and is reasonably secure as only ticket holders and registered taxi drivers are allowed inside; nevertheless watch out for pickpocketing. For a few shillings you can hire a porter with a trolley for luggage. However, the ticket offices are on Morogoro Road outside, which means that if a taxi drops you here, then you are very likely to be pounced upon by a crowd of touts who want to take you to their preferred bus company. Hang on to your luggage tightly and ignore them. A taxi from Ubungo into the city centre should cost around US$5-8. Outside on Morogoro Road, you can also catch a local bus or *dala-dala* to the centre, though again these are crowded and there is a problem if you are carrying a large amount of luggage. The best bus company recommended for foreigners, **Scandinavia Express** (see page 15), has an office at the Ubungo Bus Station where all their buses stop, though it also has a downtown terminal on the corner of Nyerere and Msimbazi roads where all their services start and finish. ▸▸ *For details, see page 73.*

Ferry Ferries to and from Zanzibar and Pemba go from the jetty on Sokoine Drive, opposite St Joseph's Cathedral. Each company has a ticket office on or around the wharf. After disembarking from the ferry, taxis are readily available on the main road outside. ▸▸ *For details, see page 75.*

Train Trains to the central regions of Tanzania (the Dar–Tabora–Kigoma/Mwanza line), run from the **Central Railway Station** ① *Sokoine Dr, T022-211 7833, www.trctz.com.* The

Stesheni *dala-dala* terminal is in front of the station and it's only a short walk to the ferry terminal. Trains for the southwest (the Dar–Mbeya–Zambia line) leave from **TAZARA Station** ① *T022-286 5187, www.tazarasite.com*, some 5 km from the centre. There are plenty of *dala-dalas* and a taxi costs about US$5.►► *For details, see page 76.*

Getting around
Dala-dalas These are cheap at around US$0.40 for any journey (see page 20). The front of the vehicle usually has two destinations painted on the bonnet or a sign stating its destination, and sometimes another stating the fare. The main terminals (stands) in the city centre are at the Central Railway Station (Stesheni) and the New Post Office (Posta) on Azikiwe Street. From both, if there are not enough passengers, the *dala-dala* will make a detour to the Old Post Office on Sokoine Drive to pick up more people.

Taxis Taxis are readily available in the city centre and are parked on just about every street corner. They cost around US$2-3 per kilometre. Any car can serve as a taxi, they are not painted in a specific colour but many have a thin green strip along the side. If you are visiting a non-central location and there is no taxi stand at the destination, you can always ask the driver to wait or come back and pick you up at an allotted time. Most of Dar's taxi drivers have cell phones, so it is easy enough to get the number and call the driver when you want to be picked up. Taxis do not have meters so always negotiate fares before setting off on your journey. Although they start with a higher price, they don't usually intentionally try to rip you off, and if you offer a price that's too low they simply won't accept the fare. A short journey within the city centre should cost no more than US$3-4, and a longer journey to the Msasani Peninsula around US$8-10.

Tuk-tuks (bajajis) These have increased in number over the past few years and are at least half the price of regular taxis. They don't go very fast, though, and are quite uncomfortable, so for longer journeys stick to taxis. For more information on them, see page 21.

Tourist offices
If you contact the **Tanzania Tourist Board** ① *IPS Building, 3rd floor, Samora Av/Azikiwe St, T022-211 1244, www.tanzaniatouristboard.com*, in advance they will post out brochures. The **Tourist Information Office** ① *Matasalamat Mansion, Samora Av, T022-213 1555, Mon-Fri 0800-1600, Sat 0830-1230*, for drop-in visitors has a limited range of glossy leaflets about the national parks and other places of interest, and the staff are reasonably helpful.

There are two free monthly publications available from some hotels and travel agencies: the *Dar es Salaam Guide*, which has transport timetables and good articles about destinations and sights in the city, and *What's Happening in Dar es Salaam*. The latter is better for information about upcoming events.

When to visit
The hottest months are December to the end of March, when the Indian Ocean is warm enough to swim in at night. The long rains are from March to May and the short rains November to December. The best season to visit is June to October, although there is sun all the year round, even during the rains, which are short and heavy and bring on intense humidity.

Background

Zanzibar period 1862-1886

The name Dar es Salaam means 'haven of peace' and was chosen by the founder of the city, Seyyid Majid, Sultan of Zanzibar. The harbour is sheltered, with a narrow inlet channel protecting the water from the Indian Ocean. An early British visitor in 1873, Frederic Elton, remarked that "it's healthy, the air clear – the site a beautiful one and the surrounding country green and well-wooded."

Despite the natural advantages it was not chosen as a harbour earlier, because of the difficulties of approaching through the narrow inlet during the monsoon season and there were other sites, protected by the coral reef, along the Indian Ocean coast that were used instead. However, Majid decided to construct the city in 1862 because he wanted to have a port and settlement on the mainland, which would act as a focus for trade and caravans operating to the south. Bagamoyo (see page 80) was already well established, but local interests there were inclined to oppose direction from Zanzibar, and the new city was a way of ensuring control from the outset.

Construction began in 1865 and the name was chosen in 1866. Streets were laid out, based around what is now Sokoine Drive, running along the shoreline to the north of the inner harbour. Water was secured by the sinking of stone wells, and the largest building was the Sultan's Palace. An engraving from 1869 shows the palace to have been a substantial two-storey stone building, the upper storey having sloping walls and a crenellated parapet, sited close to the shore on the present-day site of Malindi Wharf. In appearance it was similar in style to the fort that survives in Zanzibar (see page 132). To the southwest, along the shore, was a mosque and to the northwest a group of buildings, most of which were used in conjunction with trading activities. One building that survives is the double-storeyed structure now known as the Old Boma, on the corner of Morogoro Road and Sokoine Drive. The Sultan used it as an official residence for guests and, in 1867, a western-style banquet was given for the British, French, German and American consuls to launch the new city. Craftsmen and slaves were brought from Zanzibar for construction work. Coral for the masonry was cut from the reef and nearby islands. A steam tug was ordered from Germany to assist with the tricky harbour entrance and to speed up movements in the wind-sheltered inner waters. Economic life centred on agricultural cultivation (particularly coconut plantations), and traders dealt with the local Zaramo people as well as with the long-distance caravan traffic.

Dar es Salaam suffered its first stroke of ill-luck when Majid died suddenly in 1870, after a fall in his new palace, and was succeeded as Sultan by his half-brother, Seyyid Barghash. Barghash did not share Majid's enthusiasm for the new settlement and, indeed Majid's death was taken to indicate that carrying on with the project would bring ill-fortune. The court remained in Zanzibar. Bagamoyo and Kilwa predominated as mainland trading centres. The palace and other buildings were abandoned, and the fabric of Dar rapidly fell into decay. Nevertheless, the foundation of a Zaramo settlement and Indian commercial involvement had already been established.

Despite the neglect, Barghash maintained control over Dar es Salaam through an agent (*akida*) and later a governor (*wali*) and Arab and Baluchi troops. An Indian customs officer collected duties for use of the harbour, and the Sultan's coconut plantations were maintained. Some commercial momentum had been established, and the Zaramo traded gum copal (a residue used in making varnishes), rubber, coconuts, rice and fish for cloth, ironware and beads. The population expanded to around 5000 by 1887, and comprised a cosmopolitan mixture of the Sultan's officials, soldiers, planters, traders and shipowners, as well as Arabs, Swahilis and Zaramos, Indian Muslims, Hindus and a handful of Europeans.

German period 1887-1916

In 1887 the German East African Company under Hauptmann Leue took up residence in Dar es Salaam. They occupied the residence of the Sultan's governor, whom they succeeded in getting recalled to Zanzibar, took over the collection of customs dues and, in return for a payment to the Zaramo, obtained a concession on the land. The Zaramo, Swahili and Arabs opposed this European takeover, culminating in the Arab revolt of 1888-1889, which involved most of the coastal region as well as Dar es Salaam. The city came under sporadic attack, and the buildings of the Berlin Mission, a Lutheran denomination located on a site close to the present Kivokoni ferry, were destroyed. When the revolt was crushed, and the German government took over responsibility from the German East Africa Company in 1891, Dar es Salaam was selected as the main centre for administration and commercial activities.

The Germans laid out a grid street system, built the railway to Morogoro, connected the town to South Africa by overland telegraph and laid underwater electricity cables to Zanzibar. Development in Dar es Salaam involved the construction of many substantial buildings, and most of these survive today. In the quarter of a century to 1916, several fine buildings were laid out on Wilhelms Ufer (now Kivukoni Front), and these included administrative offices as well as a club and a casino. Landing steps to warehouses and a hospital were constructed on the site of the present Malindi Wharf and, behind them, the railway station. Just to the south of Kurasini Creek was the dockyard where the present deep-water docks are situated. A second hospital was built at the eastern end of Unter den Akazien and Becker Strasse, now Samora Avenue. The post office is on what is now Sokoine Drive at the junction with Mkwepu Street. A governor's residence provided the basis for the current State House. The principal hotels were the Kaiserhof, which was demolished to build the New Africa Hotel, and the Burger Hotel, razed to make way for the present Telecoms building. The area behind the north harbour shore was laid out with fine acacia-lined streets and residential two-storey buildings with pitched corrugated-iron roofs and first-floor verandas, and most of these survive. Behind the east waterfront were shops and office buildings, many of which are still standing.

British period 1916-1961

In the 45 years that the British administered Tanganyika, public construction was kept to a minimum on economic grounds, and business was carried on in the old German buildings. The governor's residence was damaged by naval gunfire in 1915 and was remodelled to form the present State House. In the 1920s, the Gymkhana Club was laid out on its present site behind Ocean Road, and Mnazi Moja ('Coconut Grove') was established as a park. The Selander Bridge causeway was constructed, which opened up the Oyster Bay area to residential construction for the European community. The Yacht Club was built on the harbour shore (it is now the customs post) and, behind it, the Dar es Salaam Club (now the Hotel and Tourism Training Centre), both close to the Kilimanjaro Hotel Kempinski.

As was to be expected, road names were changed, as well as those of the most prominent buildings. Thus, Wilhelms Ufer became Azania Front, Unter den Akazien became Acacia Avenue, Kaiser Strasse became City Drive. Other streets were named after explorers Speke and Burton, and there was a Windsor Street. One departure from the relentless Anglicization of the city was the change of Bismarck Strasse to Versailles Street – it was the Treaty of Versailles in 1918 that allocated the former German East Africa to the British.

The settling by the various groups living in the city into distinctive areas was consolidated during the British period. Europeans lived in Oyster Bay, to the north of the city centre, in large Mediterranean-style houses with arches, verandas and gardens surrounded by solid security walls and fences. The Asians lived either in tenement-style blocks in the city centre or in the Upanga area between the city and Oyster Bay, where they built houses and bungalows with small gardens. African families built Swahili-style houses, initially in the Kariakoo area to the west of the city. Others were accommodated in government bachelor quarters provided for railway, post office and other government employees. As the population increased, settlement spread out to Mikocheni and along Morogoro Road and to Mteni to the south.

Independence 1961-present

During the early years of Independence Dar es Salaam managed to sustain its enviable reputation of being a gloriously located city with a fine harbour, generous parklands, tree-lined avenues (particularly in the Botanical Gardens and Gymkhana area), and a tidy central area of shops and services. New developments saw the construction of high-rise government buildings, most notably the Telecoms building on the present Samora Avenue, the New Africa Hotel, the massive cream and brown Standard Bank Building (now National Bank of Commerce) on the corner of Sokoine Drive and Maktaba Street, and the Kilimanjaro Hotel on a site next to the Dar es Salaam Club on Kivukoni Front.

But with the Arusha Declaration of 1967 (see page 403), many buildings were nationalized and somewhat haphazardly occupied. The new tenants of the houses, shops and commercial buildings were thus inclined to undertake minimal repairs and maintenance. In many cases it was unclear who actually owned the buildings. The city went into steady decline, and it is a testament to the sturdy construction of the buildings from the German period that so many of them survive. Roads fell into disrepair, and the harbour became littered with rusting hulks.

The new government changed the names of streets and buildings, to reflect a change away from the colonial period. Thus, Acacia became Independence Avenue, the Prince of Wales Hotel became the Splendid. Later, names were chosen to pay tribute to African leaders – Independence Avenue changed to Samora, and Pugu Road became Nkrumah Street. President Nyerere decided that no streets or public buildings could be named after living Tanzanians, and so it was only after his death that City Drive was named after Prime Minister Edward Sokoine.

Old Dar es Salaam was saved by two factors. First, the economic decline that began in the 1970s (see page 403) meant that there were limited resources for building new modern blocks for which some of the old colonial buildings would have had to make way. Second, the government decided in 1973 to move the capital to Dodoma. This didn't stop new government construction entirely, but it undoubtedly saved many historic buildings.

In the early 1980s, Dar es Salaam reached a low point, not dissimilar from the one reached almost exactly a century earlier with the death of Sultan Majid. In 1992 things began to improve. Japanese aid allowed a comprehensive restoration of the road system, colonial buildings were classified as of historical interest and were preserved, most notably the Old Boma on Sokoine Drive, the Ministry of Health building on Luthuli Road and the British Council headquarters on Samora Avenue. The Askari Monument was cleaned up, the Cenotaph Plaza relaid, and the Botanical Gardens restored.

Places in Dar es Salaam

Today, there's a great sense of civic pride in the city; the original German and Swahili buildings sit alongside gleaming new tower blocks, and the smooth streets, while still retaining their colourful African atmosphere with informal markets and frenetic transport, are neat and orderly. Very usefully, signposts now clearly show not only the street names but places of interest, hotels and major institutions such as banks or embassies. The main road into Dar es Salaam – the 109-km branch road off the Arusha–Mbeya road that neatly dissects the middle of the country – was for years a ribbon of potholed and broken tar. But this too is now a super-smooth highway. ➤➤ *For listings, see pages 61-76.*

Walking tour of the old town

A walking tour (about half a day) of the historic parts of old Dar es Salaam might start at the **Askari Monument** at the junction of Samora Avenue and Azikwe Street. The bronze statue, in memory of all those who died in the First World War, but principally dedicated to the African troops and porters, was unveiled in 1927. It was cast by Morris Bronze Founders of Westminster, London, and the sculptor was James Alexander Stevenson (1881-1937), who signed himself 'Myrander'. There are two bronze bas-reliefs on the sides of the plinth by the same sculptor, and the inscription, in English and Swahili, is from Rudyard Kipling.

Proceeding towards the harbour, on the left is the **New Africa Hotel**, on the site where the old **Kaiserhof Hotel** stood. This was once the finest building in Dar es Salaam, the venue for the expat community to meet for sundowners. The terrace outside overlooked the Lutheran church and the harbour, while a band played in the inner courtyard. Across Sokoine Drive, on the left is the **Lutheran church**, with its distinctive red-tiled spire and tiled canopies over the windows to provide shade. Construction began in 1898. Opposite is the **Cenotaph**, again commemorating the 1914-1918 war, which was unveiled in 1927 and restored in 1992.

Turning left along Kivukoni Front, there is a fine view through the palm trees across the harbour. Just past Ohio Street, on the shore side, is the **Old Yacht Club**. Prior to the removal of the club to its present site on the west side of Msasani Peninsula in 1967, small boats bobbing at anchor in the bay were a feature of the harbour. The Old Yacht Club buildings now house the harbour police headquarters. Further along Kivukoni Front is the first of an impressive series of German government buildings. The first two, one now the High Court and the other the present Magistrates' Court on the corner of Luthuli Road, were for senior officials. In between is the old **Secretariat**, which housed the governor's offices. On the other corner of Luthuli Road is the German Officers' Mess, where some gambling evidently took place as it became known as the **Casino**.

The eastern part of the city resembles an eagle's head (it is said the Msasani Peninsula is one of the eagle's wings). At the tip of the eagle's beak is a pier and the ramp for the ferry that goes over to Kigamboni and, just a little further round the promontory, the fish market (see page 56), constructed in the British period for the use of the governor. Past Magogoni Street is the **Swimming Club**, constructed in the British period and now mostly used by the Asian community.

Following Ocean Road, on the left is the present **State House**, with a drive coming down to gates. This was the original German governor's residence. It had tall, Islamic-style arches on the ground floor, rather similar to those in the building today, but the upper storey was a veranda with a parapet, and the roof was supported on cast-iron columns. The building was bombarded by British warships in 1914 and extensively damaged. In

1922 it was rebuilt and the present scalloped upper-storey arches added, as well as the tower with the crenellated parapet.

The **German Hospital** is further along Ocean Road, with its distinctive domed towers topped by a clusters of iron spikes. It is an uneasy mixture of the grand (the towers) and the utilitarian (the corrugated-iron roofing). It was completed in 1897 and was added to during the British period with single-storey, bungalow-style wards to the rear.

Turning left past the baobab tree down Chimera Road and taking the left fork, Luthuli Road leads to the junction with Samora Avenue. The area either side of this boulevard, one of the glories of Dar es Salaam in the German era, was laid out as an extensive park. The flamboyant trees and *oreodoxa* (Royal Palms) still border it.

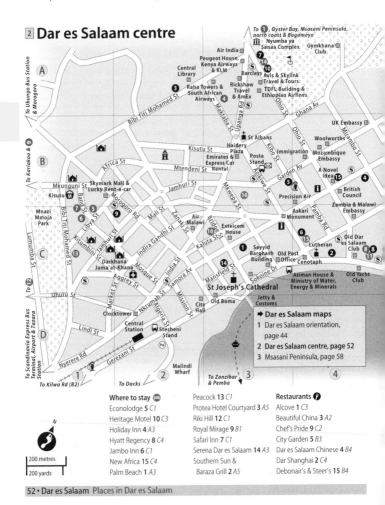

2 Dar es Salaam centre

Where to stay 🛌
Econolodge 5 *C1*
Heritage Motel 10 *C3*
Holiday Inn 4 *A3*
Hyatt Regency 8 *C4*
Jambo Inn 6 *C1*
New Africa 15 *C4*
Palm Beach 1 *A3*
Peacock 13 *C1*
Protea Hotel Courtyard 3 *A5*
Riki Hill 12 *C1*
Royal Mirage 9 *B1*
Safari Inn 7 *C1*
Serena Dar es Salaam 14 *A3*
Southern Sun &
  Baraza Grill 2 *A5*

Restaurants 🍴
Alcove 1 *C3*
Beautiful China 3 *A2*
Chef's Pride 9 *C2*
City Garden 5 *B3*
Dar es Salaam Chinese 4 *B4*
Dar Shanghai 2 *C4*
Debonair's & Steer's 15 *B4*

➡ **Dar es Salaam maps**
1 Dar es Salaam orientation, page 44
2 Dar es Salaam centre, page 52
3 Msasani Peninsula, page 58

200 metres
200 yards

The first Director of Agriculture, Professor Stuhlmann, began laying out the **Botanical Gardens** in 1893. The building that houses the Agriculture Department, as well as the Meteorological Station and the Government Geographer, lies just to the southwest and was completed in 1903, by which time the gardens were well established, Stuhlmann using his position as Chief Secretary from 1900-1903 to channel resources to their development. The gardens became the home of the Dar es Salaam Horticultural Society, which still has a building on the site and has undergone some rehabilitation with most of the exhibits labelled. Today it's a welcome escape from the city, and the peacocks give it an exotic air. It is one of the few places in the world to see the coco-de-mer palm tree, apart from the Seychelles.

To the left of the gardens is **Karimjee Hall**, built by the British, which served as the home of the Legislative Council prior to Independence. It then became the home of the National Assembly, the Bunge. In the same area is the original **National Museum** (see page 54), a single-storey stone building with a red-tiled roof and arched windows constructed as the King George V Memorial Museum in 1940, changing its name in 1963. A larger, modern building was constructed later to house exhibits, and the old building was used as offices.

Walking west down Sokoine Drive you return to the **New Africa Hotel**.

Proceed west along Sokoine Drive past the National Bank of Commerce building on the right. On the corner with Mkwepa Street is the German **Post Office** completed in 1893. Although the façade has been remodelled to give it a more modern appearance, the structure is basically unchanged. Just inside the entrance is a plaque to the memory of members of the Signals Corps who lost their lives in the First World War in East Africa. There are some 200 names listed with particularly heavy representation from South Africa and India, whose loyalty to the British Empire drew them into the conflict.

On the opposite corner to the post office is the site of the old customs headquarters, the **Seyyid Barghash Building**, constructed around 1869. The building on the corner with Bridge Street is the modern multi-storey **Wizaraya Maji, Nishati na Madim** (Ministry of Water, Energy and Minerals), which is on the site of the old Customs House. Next door, sandwiched between the ministry building and Forodhani Secondary School, is the **White Fathers' House** – called **Atiman House**. It is named after a

To 3, Aga Khan Hospital, Oyster Bay, Msasani Peninsula, north coast & Bagamoyo

Chimera Rd
German Hospital
2
Botanical Gardens
Samora Av
Karimjee Hall (Parliament)
National Museum & House of Culture
Shaaban Robert St
Ocean Rd
Luthuli Rd
Banda Beach
Madaraka St
Old Secretariat & 'Casino'
State House
Luthuli Rd
Kivukoni Front
High Court & Magistrates Court
Magogoni St
Swimming Club
Fish Market
Site of Berlin Mission
5
6
To Kigamboni & southern beaches ▼

heroic and dedicated doctor, Adrian Atiman, who was redeemed from slavery in Niger by White Father missionaries, educated in North Africa and Europe, and who worked for decades as a doctor in Tanzania until his death, circa 1924. Atiman House was constructed in the 1860s in the Zanzibar period and is the oldest surviving house in the city, excluding administrative buildings. It was built as a residence for the Sultan of Zanzibar's Dar es Salaam wives and sold by the Sultan to the White Fathers in 1922.

Continuing along Sokoine Drive to the west, the next building is **St Joseph's Roman Catholic Cathedral**. Construction began in 1897 and took five years to complete. St Joseph's remains one of the most striking buildings in Dar es Salaam, dominating the harbour front. It has an impressive vaulted interior, shingle spire and a fine arrangement of arches and gables.

On the corner of Morogoro Road is Dar's oldest surviving building, the **Old Boma** dating from 1867. It was built to accommodate the visitors of Sultan Majid and features a fine Zanzibar door and coral-rag walls. On the opposite corner is the **City Hall**, a very handsome building with an impressive façade and elaborate decoration.

On the corner of Uhuru Street is the **Railway Station**, a double-storey building with arches and a pitched-tile roof, the construction of which began in 1897. Between the station and the shore was the site of the palace of Sultan Majid and of the hospital for Africans constructed in 1895 by Sewa Haji, but which was demolished in 1959.

Turning right in front of the railway station leads to the **clock tower**, a post-war concrete construction erected to celebrate the elevation of Dar es Salaam to city status in 1961. A right turn at the clock tower leads along Samora Avenue and back to the Askari Monument.

Religious buildings
There are other notable buildings in the city. On Mosque Street is the ornate **Darkhana Jama'at-Khana** of the Ismaili community, three storeys high with a six-storey tower on the corner topped by a clock, a pitched roof and a weathervane.

There are several other mosques, two (**Ibaddhi Mosque** and **Memon Mosque**) on Mosque Street itself (clearly signposted and stringed with coloured lights used for religious occasions), one on Kitumbini Street, one block to the southwest of Mosque Street (a **Sunni Mosque** with an impressive dome), and there are two mosques on Bibi Titi Mohamed Street, the **Ahmadiyya Mosque** near the junction with Pugu Road and the other close by. On Kitsu Street, there are two Hindu temples, and on Upanga Road is a grand Ismaili building, decorated with coloured lights during festivals.

St Alban's Church on the corner of Upanga Road and Maktaba Street was constructed in the interwar period. St Alban's is a grand building modelled on the Anglican church in Zanzibar. This is the Anglican Church of the Province of Tanzania and was the Governor's church in colonial times. The **Greek Orthodox Church**, further along Upanga Street, was constructed in the 1940s. **St Peter's Catholic Church**, off the Bagamoyo Road, was constructed in 1962 and is in modern style with delicate concrete columns and arches.

National Museum and House of Culture
① *Shaaban Robert St next to the Botanical Gardens, between Sokoine Dr and Samora Av, T022-211 7508, www.houseofculture.or.tz, 0930-1800, US$3, children (5-16) US$2.*
The museum opened in 1940 in the former King George V Memorial Museum building next to the Botanical Gardens. King George V's car can still be seen in the newer wing, which was built in front of the old museum in 1963. The museum is in a garden where a few peacocks stroll and where there is a sculpture in memory of victims of the 1998 American Embassy bombing.

Casuarina cones

A particularly fine set of casuarina trees can be found along Ocean Road in Dar es Salaam. Strangely, they are also found in Australia. Quite unlike most other trees in East Africa, the theory is that the seed-bearing cones were carried by the cold tidal currents from the west coast of Australia into the equatorial waters flowing west across the Indian Ocean to the shore of Tanzania and then north along the East African coast in the Somalia current, eventually germinating after a journey of about 10,000 km.

Created in 2004 by US artist Elyn Zimmerman, it comprises a group of six related geometric forms that surround a granite-rimmed pool. Their flatness and thinness, as well as their striking silhouettes and outlines, were inspired by shapes used in traditional African art, shields and other objects including Tanzanian stools, which Zimmerman said greatly influenced her work. Very interestingly, the very same artist designed the World Trade Centre Memorial in 1993, after a bomb set by terrorists exploded on the site of the World Trade Centre in New York. That sculpture was a cenotaph to an attack that predated both the 7 August 1998 bombings in Dar es Salaam and Nairobi, and the 11 September 2001 attacks in New York. Zimmerman's 1993 sculpture was destroyed in the 2001 attack at the World Trade Centre.

The museum has excellent ethnographic, historical and archaeological collections. The old photographs are particularly interesting. Traditional craft items, headdresses, ornaments, musical instruments and witchcraft accoutrements are on display. Artefacts representing Tanzanian history date from the slave trade to the post-colonial period. Fossils from Olduvai Gorge include those of Zinjanthropus – sometimes referred to as Zinj or 'nutcracker man' – the first of a new group of hominid remains collectively known as *Australopithecus boisei*, discovered by Mary Leakey. The coastal history is represented by glazed Chinese porcelain pottery and a range of copper coins from Kilwa.

West towards Kariakoo

The area to the northwest of India Street, on either side of Morogoro Road, was an Asian section of the city in the colonial period and, to a large extent, still is. Buildings are typically several storeys high, the ground floor being given over to business with the upper storeys being used for residential accommodation. The façades are often ornate, with the name of the proprietor and the date of construction prominently displayed. Two superb examples on Morogoro Road, near Africa Street, are the premises of M Jessa. One was a cigarette and tobacco factory and the other, a rice mill.

Further to the west is the open Mnazi Mmoja (coconut grove) with the **Uhuru Monument** dedicated to the freedom that came with Independence; celebrations take place here every year on 9 December to commemorate Independence Day. The original Uhuru monument is a white obelisk with a flame – the Freedom Torch. A second concrete monument, designed by R Ashdown, was erected to commemorate 10 years of Independence. This was enlivened with panels by a local artist. On the far side of the space is **Kariakoo**, laid out in a grid pattern and predominantly an African area. It became known as Kariakoo during the latter part of the First World War, when African porters (the carrier corps, from which the current name is derived) were billeted here after the British took over the city in 1916. The houses are Swahili style. The colourful **market** in the centre and the shark market on the junction of Msimbazi and Tandamuti streets are well worth a visit but watch out for pickpockets.

Tingatinga art

It is easy enough to recognize Tingatinga paintings for their powerful images and vivid colours. Canvasses are crowded with exaggerated figures of birds, fish and all manner of African creatures, with giant heads and eyes, that roam rainbow landscapes and brilliant seas. Details of traditional village life or hospital and markets scenes take on an almost cartoon-like appearance. It's a style of pop art and is considered to be the only indigenous painted art of East Africa. The custom of painting on walls using natural pigments had been in existence in Africa for centuries, but it wasn't until the arrival of the Europeans that African painters were encouraged to produce canvasses.

Tingatinga art was created in the dusty back streets of Dar es Salaam by Edward Tingatinga in the late 1960s. Born in 1937 in the Tanga region of southern Tanzania, he went to Dar in 1959 in search of work. After attempting several jobs, he worked on building sites and began painting murals on the walls. He then progressed to boards and canvasses and used an enamel bicycle paint that is especially glossy. He sold his paintings underneath a baobab tree at the Morogoro Stores in Oyster Bay which attracted the rich Europeans. He took on several young apprentices and taught them his unique style. Tragically, in 1972, only four years into his discovery of art, he was shot dead by police who accidentally mistook his car for the getaway car in a local robbery. But his students continued to use the Tingatinga style and took on more apprentices, and the Tingatinga Art Cooperative Society was established six years after his death. In 1997, a Swedish customer introduced the art to a gallery in Stockholm and exhibitions appeared in other European cities. This instigated a TSh 60 million donation to build the gallery and workshop at Oyster Bay. After 25 years underneath a baobab tree, Tingatinga got its own home; Edward Tingatinga would no doubt have been impressed by the success of his legacy.

Further information

The Tingatinga Arts Cooperative is at the Morogoro Stores in Oyster Bay, off Haile Selassie Road, near Q Bar Guest House, T022-266 8075, www.tingatinga.org. There is a gallery of paintings for sale and more stalls outside on the street. Open daily 0900-1800.

Fish market and Banda Beach

At the point of the eagle's beak, where the ferry leaves for Kigamboni, is the **Kivukoni Fish Market**. A fish market has been on this site since time immemorial. It was formerly part of an old fishing village called Mzizima, which was located between what is now State House and Ocean Road Hospital. The village met its demise when Seyyid Majid founded Dar es Salaam in 1862, although the fish market survived. In 2002, the Japanese government funded a substantial expansion programme, and a new fish market was built. There are now zones for fish cleaning, fish frying, one for shellfish and vegetables, another for firewood and charcoal, an auction hall for wholesale vendors and buyers, and a maintenance area for the repair of boats, fishing nets and other tools of the trade. The complex is one of a kind and provides employment for 100 fishermen catering to thousands of daily shoppers. As you can imagine, this is an extremely smelly place. Fresh fish can be bought here, and there is an astonishingly wide variety of seafood from blue fish, lobster and red snapper to calamari and prawns. Be warned though, the vendors are quite aggressive and you'll need to haggle hard. You can also buy ice here to pack the fish.

Just north of the market is a stretch of sand known as **Banda Beach**, a well-known place for sittin' on the dock of the bay. Fishing boats, mostly lateen-sailed *ngalawas*, are beached on the shore.

Gymkhana Club
Further along Ocean Road, past State House and the hospital, are the grounds of the Gymkhana Club, which extend down to the shore. Amongst other sports practised here (see page 71) is golf; there is an 18-hole course featuring what are called 'browns' as opposed to 'greens'. There were various cemeteries on the shore side of the golf course, a European cemetery between the hospital and Ghana Avenue, and a Hindu crematorium beyond.

Nyumba ya Sanaa Complex
ⓘ *Junction of Ohio St, Ali Mwinyi Rd and Bibi Titi Mohammed St, northwest of the Serena Dar es Salaam Hotel, T022-213 1727, Mon-Fri 0800-2000, Sat-Sun 0800-1600.*
This art gallery has displays of paintings in various styles, including oil, watercolour and chalk, as well as carvings and batiks. You can see the artists at work, and there is also a café on site. The centre was started by a nun, and the present building was constructed with help from a Norwegian donation in the early 1980s. Traditional dances are held here on Friday evenings at 1930.

Oyster Bay
At the intersection of Ocean Road and Ufukoni Road, on the shore side, is a rocky promontory which was the site of European residential dwellings constructed in the interwar period by the British. These are either side of Labon Drive (previously Seaview Road). Continuing along Ocean Road is Selander Bridge, a causeway over the Msimbazi Creek, a small river edged by marsh that circles back to the south behind the main part of the city. Beyond Selander Bridge, on the ocean side, is Oyster Bay, which became the main European residential area in the colonial era (Rita Hayworth had a house here) and, today, is the location of many diplomatic missions. There are many spacious dwellings, particularly along Kenyatta Drive, which looks across the bay. The area in front of the **Oyster Bay Hotel** is a favourite place for parking and socializing in the evenings and at weekends, particularly by the Asian community, and there are ice cream sellers and barbecue kiosks.

Around Dar

Makumbusho Village Museum
ⓘ *Bagamoyo Rd, about 9 km from the city centre, on the right-hand side of the road just before the Millennium Towers complex, T022-270 0193, www.villagemuseum.homestead. com, 0930-1900, US$3, Tanzanians and children US$1, photos US$3, video cameras US$20. Taxis cost about US$10 from the city centre, or take a* dala-dala *from the New Post Office (Posta) heading towards Mwenge, which pass the entrance. Ask for Makumbusho bus stop or get off when you see the tall Millennium Towers and walk back a few metres.*
The museum gives a compact view of the main traditional dwelling styles of Tanzania, with examples of artists and craftsmen at work. There are constructions of tribal homesteads from 18 ethnic groups, with examples of furnished dwelling huts, cattle pens, meeting huts and, in one case, an iron-smelting kiln. Traditional dances are performed daily from 1400 to 1800, with performers recruited from all over Tanzania. It's worthwhile having a guide to explain the origin of the dances, which end with a display of tumbling and acrobatics. There is a café and

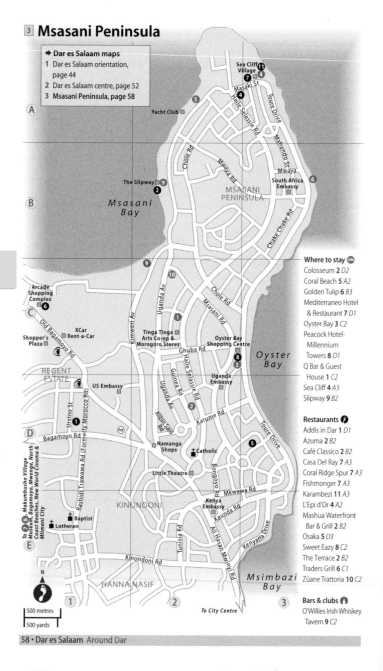

3 Msasani Peninsula

→ Dar es Salaam maps
1 Dar es Salaam orientation, page 44
2 Dar es Salaam centre, page 52
3 Msasani Peninsula, page 58

Sea Cliff Village

Yacht Club

Masaki St

Halle Selassie Rd

Toure Drive

Matanda St

Mwaya Rd

Chole Rd

Mwaya
South Africa Embassy

The Slipway

Msasani Bay

MSASANI PENINSULA

Chake Chake Rd

Where to stay
Colosseum 2 D2
Coral Beach 5 A2
Golden Tulip 6 B3
Mediterraneo Hotel & Restaurant 7 D1
Oyster Bay 3 C2
Peacock Hotel-Millennium Towers 8 D1
Q Bar & Guest House 1 C2
Sea Cliff 4 A3
Slipway 9 B2

Arcade Shopping Complex 6

Old Bagamoyo Rd

XCar Rent-a-Car

Shopper's Plaza

REGENT ESTATE

Uganda Av

Chole Rd

Msasani Rd

Kimwert Av

Tinga Tinga Arts Co-op & Morogoro Stores

Oyster Bay Shopping Centre

Oyster Bay

US Embassy

Ghuba Rd

Halle Selassie Rd

Guinea Rd

Uganda Av

Uganda Embassy

Ursino St

Bagamoyo Rd

Rashidi Trawawa Rd (Formerly Morocco Rd)

Albii Sara Rd

Karume Rd

Namanga Shops

Catholic

Little Theatre

Toure Drive

KINONDONI

Bongoyo Rd

Mkwawa Rd

Kenya Embassy

Kaunda Rd

Baptist

Lutheran

Tunisia Rd

Ali Hasan Mwinyi Rd

Kinondoni Rd

Kenyatta Drive

HANNA NASIF

Msimbazi Bay

Restaurants
Addis in Dar 1 D1
Azuma 2 B2
Café Classico 2 B2
Casa Del Ray 7 A3
Coral Ridge Spur 7 A3
Fishmonger 7 A3
Karambezi 11 A3
L'Epi d'Or 4 A2
Mashua Waterfront Bar & Grill 2 B2
Osaka 5 D3
Sweet Eazy 8 C2
The Terrace 2 B2
Traders Grill 6 C1
Zûane Trattoria 10 C2

Bars & clubs
O'Willies Irish Whiskey Tavern 9 C2

To Mikumbusho Village Museum, Bagamoyo, Mwenge, North Coast Beaches, New World Cinema & Mlimani City

To City Centre

N

500 metres
500 yards

an unusual compound, the Makumbusho Social Club, where the public is welcome. The small, corrugated-iron, partly open-sided huts are each named after one of Tanzania's game parks.

Kigamboni and the southern beaches

The beaches on Kigamboni are the best of those close to the city and, like the beaches to the north, have resorts (see Where to stay, page 63) that are popular with day visitors, especially at the weekends. The Kigamboni ferry (which takes cars) leaves from the harbour mouth close to the fish market, just before Kivukoni Front becomes Ocean Road, at regular intervals and takes less than 10 minutes. The ferry runs 0400-0100 and costs US$1 per vehicle and US$0.20 per person. Foot passengers can walk directly on to the ferry from the city side and catch taxis and *dala-dalas* at Kigamboni that follow the beach road for several kilometres to most of the more accessible resorts. Hotels such as **Ras Kutani** and the **Amani Beach Hotel** are further down this road, around 30 km from the ferry, and you will need to contact these lodges to arrange transport if you are not driving yourself.

The small town of Kigamboni spreads up from where the ferry docks and is the site of Kivukoni College, which provided training for CCM party members (see page 404), but has now been turned into a school and a social science academy. Just before the college, which faces across the harbour to Kivukoni Front, is the Anglican church and a free-standing bell. The Anglican church was formerly a Lutheran church. The new Lutheran church, a fine modern building, lies 500 m into Kigamboni.

Northern beaches

ⓘ *To get to either beach, a taxi from the city will cost in the region of US$15. To get to Kunduchi by public transport take a dala-dala from the New Post Office (Posta) in the city to Mwenge about 10 km along the Bagomoyo Rd, then change to one heading to Kunduchi (clearly signposted on the bonnet of the vehicle). Both rides will cost US$0.30. To get to Mbezi, take the same Kunduchi dala-dala from Mwenge, and at the sign for the White Sands Hotel on Bagamoyo Rd a couple of kilometres before the Kunduchi turn off, ask to get off (look out for the Kobil service station). At this junction you can catch a bicycle taxi for US$0.70 or a tuk-tuk for US$2 for the couple of kilometres to the hotels. Do not walk along this road, as there have been muggings.*

The shore close to Dar es Salaam is not particularly good for swimming. The best beaches are at **Kunduchi**, some 25 km north of the city, and **Mbezi Beach**, 20 km north of the city. These beaches are separated by a lagoon but both are easily accessed off the Bagamoyo Road on good tarmac side roads. Most of the hotels and resorts along this coast (see page 64) welcome day visitors who want to enjoy the facilities and beaches, including **Kunduchi Beach Hotel**, **Bahari Beach Hotel**, **Jangwani Sea Breeze Resort** and the **White Sands Hotel**. Some charge a fee of US$5-10 for the day, and it's worth paying to use the hotels' private (and guarded) beaches – the stretches of beach between the hotels should not be visited unaccompanied, people have been mugged here. Some also charge an extra fee if you bring your own food and drink. This is because many Indian families bring full-on picnics for a day at the beach and the hotel benefits little from selling food and drink. Most have restaurants and bars with bands playing at weekends and public holidays, and some offer a variety of excursions to nearby islands and also windsurfing. Snorkelling is a bit hit and miss because the water is not always very clear, especially during the rainy seasons.

There is a good beach on the uninhabited **Bongoyo Island**, 2 km north of Msasani Peninsula. The island is a marine reserve popular for diving and snorkelling and has a few short walking trails. Simple seafood meals are available from beach kiosks. It's a popular destination for a day trip from Dar es Salaam; boats take 30 minutes, cost US$12 return and leave from **The Slipway** on Msasani Peninsula (see Shopping, page 70) at 0930, 1130, 1330 and 1530, and return at 1030, 1230, 1430 and 1700. A similarly good beach can be found on **Mbudya Island**, 4 km north of Bongoyo Island, but there are no facilities here. Boat rides are available from **White Sands Hotel, Jangwani Sea Breeze Resort** and **Bahari Beach Hotel**.

Kisarawe and Pugu Hills Forest Reserve

ⓘ *25 km southwest of the city centre, T0754-565 498, www.puguhills.com, US$3 per person. To get there, follow Nyerere Rd to the south of the city and 200 m after the airport turn-off, turn right for 11 km to the village of Kisarawe. Once there, turn left at the Agip petrol station and the track into the reserve is a little further along on the right; its 3 km to the forest station. This short road may require a 4WD after heavy rains, but there is a longer alternative track to the forest station – ask in the village for directions. Dala-dala to Kisarawe leave from Narungumbe St next to the Tanzania Postal Bank on Msimbazi St in Kariakoo.*

In the peaceful rural hill town of Kisarawe it is hard to believe that you are just 32 km southwest of the hustle and bustle of Dar es Salaam. During the colonial period Kisarawe was used by European residents of the capital as a kind of hill station to escape from the coastal heat. It receives a higher rainfall than Dar because of its slightly increased elevation. There is little to see in the town itself (although Julius Nyerere worked as a teacher here before he entered full-time politics) but the surrounding countryside is very attractive, in particular the nearby rainforest at Pugu Hills Forest Reserve. It constitutes one of the few remaining parts of a coastal forest, which 10 million years ago extended from Mozambique to northern Kenya. It was gazetted as a reserve in 1954, at which time it stretched all the way to Dar's international airport and was home to many big game animals, including lions, hippos and elephants. Since then, the growth of the metropolis, as well as the urban demand for charcoal (coupled with the lack of alternative sources of income), has seen a large reduction in the forested area. In the past few years a concerted effort has been made to counter this process, and a nature trail has been established in order to encourage people to visit the area. Although Pugu contains flora and fauna which are unique to the forests of this district, you are unlikely to come across many animals in the forest. Having said that, quite astonishingly, a lion was spotted here in 2010 (as the crow flies, or the lion walks, it's not that far from the very northern reaches of the Selous Game Reserve). You might also spot Sykes' or vervet monkeys, bush squirrel or banded mongoose. The forest is a very beautiful spot and the perfect tonic for those in need of a break from Dar es Salaam. Most visitors spend the night in the lodge here (**Pugu Hills**), though you can visit just for for lunch (about US$10) and a short walk through the forest; you will still need to make a reservation for this with the lodge (see page 65).

Pugu Kaolin Mine and the Bat Caves

A further three to four kilometres on from the Pugu Hills Reserve is Pugu Kaolin mine, which was established by the Germans in the early 1900s. Kaolin is a type of fine white clay that is used in the manufacture of porcelain, paper and textiles. The deposits here at Pugu are reputed to be the second largest in the world, and should the market for it pick up, the mining of kaolin will clearly constitute a further threat to the survival of the remaining rainforest. If you continue through the mine compound you come to a disused railway tunnel, 100 m long and German built (the railway was re-routed after the discovery of kaolin). On the other side of this are a series of man-made caves housing a huge colony of bats. In the early evening at around 1800 or 1900 (depending on the time of year) the bats begin to fly out of the caves for feeding. It is a remarkable experience to stand in the mouth of the caves surrounded by the patter of wings, as huge numbers of bats come streaming past you.

⦿ Dar es Salaam listings

For sleeping and eating price codes and other relevant information, see pages 22-26.

⦿ Where to stay

As far as top-grade accommodation is concerned, hotels in Dar es Salaam have improved in recent years and there is excellent international standard accommodation in the city centre, on Msasani Peninsula and on the beaches to the north and south of the city. The lower end of the market is reasonable value, although it is always sensible to check the room and the bathroom facilities and enquire what is provided for breakfast. Also check on the security of any parked vehicle. If you're pre-booking, ask about transfers from the airport, even at the budget end.

City centre *p51, map p52*

$$$$ Hyatt Regency, Kivukoni Front, T022-212 0777, www.daressalaam.kilimanjaro.hyatt.com. Occupying a commanding position in the centre of the city overlooking the harbour, this new 8-storey hotel enclosed in blue glass offers 5-star luxury with contemporary decor, 180 rooms and excellent restaurants (see page 66). There's also a spa, a beautiful swimming pool on the 1st floor, a gym, shopping arcade and casino. The **Level 8** bar has stunning views over the city (see Bars and clubs, page 68). Rates start from US$315.

$$$$-$$$ Southern Sun Hotel, Garden Av, T022-213 7575, www.southernsun.com. An excellent upmarket offering from the quality South African chain, with friendly and helpful staff, nice location next to the Botanical Gardens (the peacocks regularly fly into the hotel's gardens) and close to the National Museum. 152 well-equipped rooms with Wi-Fi, gym, swimming pool and a popular restaurant and bar (see Restaurants, page 65).

$$$ Holiday Inn, north of the junction of India and Azikwe streets, T022-213 9250,

www.holidayinn.co.tz. An impressive newly built glass tower, with 124 contemporary a/c rooms with satellite TV, Wi-Fi and coffee maker, plus gym, travel desk and 2 restaurants. The **Al Dar Sheesha Bar** is on the 11th floor. Doubles from US$160.

$$$ New Africa Hotel & Casino, corner Azikiwe St and Sokoine Dr, T022-211 7050, www.newafricahotel.com. Central and within walking distance of the ferry terminal, great harbour views from the higher floors. 126 rooms with satellite TV, Wi-Fi and comfortable made-for-hotel furnishings. Not badly priced given its location (a double starts from US$160). Facilities include 2 restaurants (the **Sawasdee**, see page 66, is well-known for its Thai food), bar, casino and a lovely indoor heated swimming pool, and massages are available.

$$$ Palm Beach, 305 Ali Hassan Mwinyi Rd, opposite the junction with Ocean Rd, T022-213 0985, www.pbhtz.com. Stylish art deco hotel completely refurbished and painted in a striking petrol-blue colour, a little away from the centre of town but not on the beach, as the name suggests. 32 rooms with cool and modern decor, TV and Wi-Fi, airy bar and restaurant, popular beer garden with barbecue.

$$$ Peacock Hotel, Bibi Titi Mohamed St, T022-212 0334, www.peacock-hotel.co.tz. Well-run and centrally located modern hotel. 93 rooms with a/c and satellite TV in a tower block, good value, a double starts from US$135. Great views of downtown Dar from the restaurant on the top floor, which serves good buffet meals with occasional theme nights. The unmistakable building has been 'cocooned' in blue glass to make it cooler inside.

$$$ Protea Hotel Courtyard, Ocean Rd, next to the Aga Khan Hospital, T022-213 0130, www.proteahotels.com. A quality hotel with good facilities, a bit more character than some of the larger hotels and with excellent food and service. The 52 rooms, with a/c, TV and Wi-Fi, overlook a central lush garden and swimming pool, there's a bar, restaurant and 24-hr coffee shop.

$$$ Serena Dar es Salaam Hotel, Ohio St, T022-211 2416, www.serenahotels.com. This was a Mövenpick Hotel that, at the time of writing, had just been taken over by Serena so a refurbishment is expected. It's a landmark building on the city's skyline. The 230 spacious rooms have all mod cons including a/c and Wi-Fi, the best are at the rear overlooking the lovely gardens and very large swimming pool surrounded by palms. There's a full range of facilities, including a shopping arcade, gym, restaurants (see page 66), a popular bar, coffee shop and a bakery.

$$ Heritage Motel, corner Kaluta and Bridge Sts, T022-211 7471, www.heritage motel.co.tz. Easy to locate in the city centre, this new hotel in a tall, yellow building is conveniently located for the ferry terminal. It has 50 simply furnished but comfortable and spotless single, double and triple rooms with a/c and TV, though some are a little cramped. There's a restaurant and bar and parking in a secure complex across the road. Excellent value for money.

$$-$ Riki Hill Hotel, Kleist Sykes St, west of Mnazi Mmoja Park, T022-218 1820, www.rikihotel.com. This budget hotel in a smart white block several storeys high has 40 bare but comfortable a/c rooms with spotless bathrooms. There's a restaurant with very good à la carte food, bar, shop and bureau de change. It's slightly to the west of the city centre but not far from the Scandinavia Express bus terminal.

$ Econolodge, corner of Libya St and Band St, T022-211 6048, www.econohotel.8m. com. A plain but functional place with sparsely furnished, clean, self-contained single, double and triple rooms, the cheapest double is US$20; pay US$10 more on all rooms for a/c. There's a small TV lounge and rates include basic breakfast. There is no alcohol in this Indian area on and around Libya St but you could walk around the corner to the Peacock Hotel (see above).

$ Jambo Inn, Libya St, T022-211 4293, www.jamboinnhotel.com. Centrally located budget option that has been popular with backpackers since the 1980s. It has 28 en suite single, double and triple rooms with reliable hot water and working fans. Rates are as low as US$20 for a double and for a little more you can get a/c. There's an affordable restaurant (see page 66), internet café and small shop downstairs. The staff are friendly and helpful and well used to international visitors.

$ Royal Mirage, corner Amani and Livingstone streets, T022-218 1462, www.royalmiragetz.com. A fairly new 7-storey pink block with 60 well-maintained budget rooms that have a little bit more decor (mirrors and pictures) and are larger than most, all with a/c and fan, TV, and some have fridges, though hot water can be unreliable. The restaurant is reasonable, and there's an internet café, beauty salon and parking. Doubles start from US$65.

$ Safari Inn, Band St, T022-213 8101, www. darsafariinn.com. Another simple budget option in the same central area and similar to the Jambo Inn (see above), with 40 rooms, only 3 with a/c, in a square concrete block down an alleyway (security guards are at the entrance), continental breakfast is included but there's no restaurant, and it has an internet café on the ground floor. Doubles are US$21 and a single is US$16.

Msasani Peninsula *map p58*
$$$$ Oyster Bay Hotel, Toure Dr, T022-260 0530, www.theoysterbayhotel.com. This beautifully chic boutique hotel has recently opened, with 8 stylish and massive (70 sq m) suites in a whitewashed villa facing the Indian Ocean. Its British owners also own Beho Beho in Selous and place the same emphasis on luxury and relaxation here. There's a quiet lawned garden, with swimming pool and outdoor eating terrace, and the interior is furnished with a mix of contemporary and antique African crafts. Rates are from US$400 per person full board.

$$$$-$$$ Hotel Sea Cliff, Toure Dr, T022-260 03807, www.hotelseacliff.com. Stylish whitewashed hotel with thatched *makuti* roof set on a low cliff in manicured grounds on the northern tip of the peninsula. 94 spacious and modern a/c rooms with ocean view, and 20 cheaper units in garden cottages, all with satellite TV. Try the **Coral Cliff** and **Ngalawa** bars, **Alcove Restaurant** and the beautifully positioned **Karambezi** café bar overlooking the bay (see Restaurants, page 67). There's also a swimming pool, gym, casino and extensive shopping mall (see Shopping, page 70).

$$$ Colosseum, Haille Selassie Rd, T022-266 6655, www.colosseumtz.com. Located in the middle of the peninsula and not near the ocean with odd but attractive mock-Roman architecture. The 42 a/c rooms have satellite TV and some have kitchenettes. There's a bar, pizzeria and continental restaurant. It's well known for its fitness facilities (used by Oyster Bay residents), which include a 20-m pool, a gym on 2 floors, 2 squash courts and the Cleopatra Spa.

$$$ Coral Beach, Coral La, T022-260 1928, www.coralbeach-tz.com. Mid-range option in good location overlooking Msasani Bay. 62 smart rooms with satellite TV and Wi-Fi, some with balconies and ocean views, bright and breezy lobby area, restaurant and bar overlooking the swimming pool and a tiny man-made beach, gym, sauna and jacuzzi.

$$$ Golden Tulip, Toure Dr, T022-260 0288, www.goldentulipdaressalaam.com. Reasonably good value in this area, from US$110 for a double for 91 fairly simple a/c rooms with satellite TV, balconies or terraces, most with ocean views. There's a restaurant, bar and café, but it's let down by poor service and mediocre food. The highlight, though, is the huge infinity pool set in lovely gardens facing the sea, which non-residents can use for US$7.

$$$ Peacock Hotel – Millennium Towers, 10 km north of the city on Ali Hassan Mwinyi Rd (New Bagomoyo Rd), part of the Millennium Towers shopping centre, T022-

277 3431, www.peacockmillennium.com. In a glass tower block with ultra modern decor and facilities, all 60 rooms have a/c, satellite TV and internet access. The executive suites are twice the size of the standard rooms, and the junior suites have an extra spare bedroom, both for only US$20 more. There's a swimming pool, gym, 2 restaurants and bars. A smart business hotel near the **Makumbusho Village Museum** and **Mwenge Craft Market**.

$$-$ Hotel Slipway, at The Slipway, see Shopping, page 70, T022-260 0893, www.hotelslipway.com. Part of the Slipway, with 39 smallish but modern a/c rooms with satellite TV, Wi-Fi, some with kitchenettes, arranged around an inner courtyard in the shopping/leisure development. There's no pool but great location next to shops and restaurants (some rooms can be noisy); also used as 'day rooms' which they let out during the day for people who have returned to Dar from safari and are not flying out until the evening.

$ Q Bar and Guest House, off Haile Selassie Rd, behind the Morogoro Stores, T0754-282474, www.qbardar.com. Smart 4-storey block next to the popular bar (see Bars and clubs, page 69), with 12 comfortable and spacious, good-value but quite often noisy rooms with a/c, fridge, cool tiled floors and Tingatinga paintings on the walls, a couple have 4 beds and are ideal for backpackers in a party mood. Separate dining room for guests on the 2nd floor, breakfast included.

Southern beaches p59

The simpler resorts within a few kilometres of the Kigamboni ferry accept day visitors for a fee of around US$3-7 and they are fine places for a seafood lunch on the beach.

$$$$ Ras Kutani, 28 km south of Kigamboni ferry (or can organize charter flights), reservations through the **Selous Safari Company**, T022-212 8485, www.selous.com. Small and intimate resort with only 9 luxurious cottages, 4 suites and a family house with their own plunge pools, all beautifully decorated and in a superb location on a hill overlooking the ocean and the wide arch of white sandy isolated beach and freshwater lagoon. There's a swimming pool, and snorkelling and kayaking are available, but no diving is permitted in this area. All rates are full board and are about US$250 per person.

$$$ Amani Beach Hotel, 30 km south of the Kigamboni ferry, next to **Ras Kutani**, T0754-410 033, www.amanibeach.com. Closed in rainy season Apr-Jun. Rustic and peaceful beach resort set in 30 ha of tropical woodland around a wide bay, 10 individual whitewashed a/c double cottages, extra beds can be arranged for children, with Swahili furnishings and 4-poster beds, garden terraces and hammocks, swimming pool, tennis court, snorkelling equipment, restaurant and bar. Rates per cottage start at US$185.

$$-$ South Beach Resort, 8 km south of the Kigamboni ferry, Mjimwema, T022-282 0666, www.southbeachresort-tz.com. A rather brash concretey resort with 36 a/c rooms and balconies in a characterless block, with a large swimming pool set in a huge paved area, outdoor disco, pool tables, restaurant, shisha lounge and the **Whisky Shack** bar. But it's a good beach and fine if you're in a holiday mood. You can also camp or sleep in partially open red huts, although the campsite is a long walk from the facilities.

$ Kipepeo, 7 km south of the Kigamboni ferry, Mjimwema, T0732-920 211, www.kipepeovillage.com. One of the more relaxed and friendly beach resorts in this area, with 20 rustic en suite huts built on stilts in a grove of coconut palms, plus cheaper beach bandas for US$25 for 2, sharing good ablutions and hot showers with campers. Overlanders can leave vehicles for a small daily fee while they go to Zanzibar. Very good food and drinks are served on the beach or at the rustic thatched beach bar.

$ Mikadi Beach, 2 km from the Kigamboni ferry, T0754-370 269, www.mikadibeach.

com. Popular campsite in a grove of coconut palms right on the beach. You can hire a tent or there are 12 simple reed and thatch double bandas with mattresses and mosquito nets, 2 with en suite bathrooms. Also clean ablutions, a swimming pool and a very good bar that gets busy at the weekends and offers simple home-cooked meals. For a small fee you can park vehicles here whilst you visit Zanzibar.

$ Sunrise Beach Resort, 7 km south of Kigamboni ferry, Mjimwema, T022-550 7038, www.sunrisebeachresort.co.tz. Simple thatched resort with 32 characterless bandas with balconies, some have a/c, restaurant and bar, sun loungers on the beach, watersports including jet skiing and snorkelling. A far better option for camping than the neighbouring **South Beach Resort**, with decent ablutions and an open camp kitchen and there are also 15 simply furnished permanent tents under thatch for US$15.

Northern beaches *p59*

Most beach resorts accept day visitors for a fee of around US$4-10. Note: It is unsafe to walk along the beach between the northern hotels. The hotels' private beaches are watched by security guards and at the end of the beaches are signs warning guests of the danger of mugging – take heed.

$$$$-$$$ Bahari Beach, Kunduchi, T022-265 0708, www.laicohotels.com. Newly opened upmarket resort with 96 smart rooms in double-storey thatched rondavaals set in gardens along the beach, with balconies, ocean views, a/c and satellite TV. There's a swimming pool with bar, tennis courts, buffet meals, live band and traditional dancing with dinner, gift shop, tour desk and watersports centre.

$$$ Beachcomber Hotel, Mbezi Beach, T022-264 7772/4, www.beachcomber.co.tz. A rather old-fashioned concrete development, with 36 a/c rooms, satellite TV and Swahili decor. There's a health club with sauna, steam bath and massage, watersports facilities, large swimming pool with bar, and simple but adequate food in the restaurant. It's affordable though, and a double is little more than US$100.

$$$ Kunduchi Beach Hotel & Resort, Kunduchi, T022-265 0050, www.kunduchi. com. Elegant resort with a mixture of African and Islamic-style architecture and decor, 138 sea-facing a/c rooms with satellite TV, Wi-Fi and minibar. The excellent restaurants serve continental cuisine and seafood, and there's a swimming pool, tennis and squash courts, gym, beach with palms and flowers, live music at weekends, watersports and trips to offshore islands. The **Wet 'n' Wild Water Park** (see What to do, page 72) is just next door.

$$$ Mediterraneo Hotel & Restaurant, Kawe Beach off Old Bagomoyo Rd, midway between the city (10 km) and the northern beaches, T022-261 8359, www.mediterraneo tanzania.com. Relaxing set up in pretty gardens, with 21 simple and brightly painted bungalow-style rooms with cool tiled floors and shady verandas. Good value from US$125 for a double and extra beds available for adults and children, fantastic restaurant (see page 68), swimming pool, chilled lounge/bar with cushions and upturned wooden dugout canoes in the sand. Boat trips to the islands are available.

$$$ White Sands, Mbezi Beach, T022-264 7620/6, www.hotelwhitesands.com. Smart offering with 88 sea-facing rooms in thatched villas, with balconies, satellite TV, a/c and minibar, and 28 1- or 2-bed garden apartments with kitchenettes. There's a swimming pool, gym, spa, watersports, including a PADI dive centre, and boat trips are available. It has several restaurants and bars and is well known for its Sat night seafood buffet. **Water World Waterpark** is adjacent to the hotel (see page 72).

$ Jangwani Sea Breeze Resort, Mbezi Beach, T022-264 7215, www.jangwanisea breezeresort.com. A little old fashioned but excellent value from only US$70 for a double, very friendly and right on the beach. 34

simple a/c rooms with TV set in bungalows surrounded by flowering shrubs. There are 2 swimming pools, boat trips to the islands, watersports, gym, 3 restaurants, lively bar, barbecues and live music at the weekends.

Kisarawe and Pugu Hills Forest Reserve *p60*

$$-$ Pugu Hills, Pugu Hills Forest Reserve, 35 km south of Dar, T0754-56 5498, www. puguhills.com. Quiet retreat with 4 smart bamboo huts erected above the forest floor on poles, with hardwood floors and Swahili furnishings. There's a swimming pool, fabulously rustic restaurant offering snacks and 4 dishes a day, including 1 vegetarian dish, and lovely nature trails through the forest. The resort can arrange visits to a local cattle market. Camping available, US$10 per person.

⊘ Restaurants

Most of the hotels, including those on the beach out of town, have restaurants and bars. While the city centre has a fair number of good places to eat, many of these are only open during the day, cater for office workers and do not serve alcohol. The best places for dinner and evening drinks are out of the centre on the Msasani Peninsula.

City centre *p51, map p52*

The best and more formal restaurants can be found in the hotels. For cheap food there are numerous daytime canteen-style places offering filling Tanzanian and Indian dishes clustered around Jamhuri and Libya streets, and on the corner of Morogoro Rd and Jamhuri St stalls serve *chips mayai* (omelettes with chips in) for breakfast.

$$$ Baraza Bar & Grill, Southern Sun Hotel, Garden Av, see Where to stay, page 61. Open 1000-2200. A deservedly popular restaurant with upmarket African decor serving a mix of Swahili and continental food, including pastas, curries, grills, seafood and vegetarian dishes, the weekend brunch goes on until 1300. There's an outdoor terrace onto the pool area and a relaxed bar, and at night the Botanical Gardens next door are partially floodlit around the hotel.

$$$ L'Oliveto, Serena Dar es Salaam Hotel, Ohio St, see Where to stay, page 62. Open 1200-1500, 1900-2300. Upmarket Italian restaurant with bright contemporary decor and good service, well-known for its home-made pasta and steaks with rich sauces. The hotel's other restaurant, the **Serengeti** (0730-2300) has themed nights every day of the week such as Mediterranean, Oriental, seafood, Tex-Mex or Indian, plus good-value buffet breakfasts and lunches.

$$$ Oriental, Hyatt Regency, Kivukoni St, city centre, see Where to stay, page 61. Open 1830-2300. Very smart 1st-floor restaurant serving a pricey but superb and varied Southeast Asian menu – try the dim sum or beautifully presented sushi – with an excellent wine list, including a comprehensive South African selection, and impeccable service. Bookings advised.

$$$ Sawasdee, New Africa Hotel, corner Azikiwe St and Sokine Dr, see Where to stay, page 61. Open 1900-2300. Exceptionally good and very authentic Thai food cooked by chefs from Bangkok, elegant decor, attentive service and fantastic setting on the hotel's 9th floor, with wonderful harbour views.

$$ Alcove, Samora Av, T022-213 7444, www.alcovetz.com. Mon-Sat 1200-1500, daily 1900-2230. Long-established and smart Indian and Chinese restaurant, more upmarket than most in the city centre, offering tasty Indian kebabs, tandoori and masala dishes; the long Chinese menu is equally as good. There's a fully stocked bar and efficient professional service. They have another branch in the **Hotel Sea Cliff** (see Where to stay, page 63).

$$ Beautiful China, Bibi Titi Mohamed St, T022-215 0548. Mon-Sat 1200-1500, 1800-2300. Excellent and authentic Chinese restaurant with typical red-lantern type decor and fluorescent lights. Véry long menu of seafood, duck, lamb and pork dishes,

plenty of vegetarian options and attentive chefs who will cook to order.

$ Chef's Pride, virtually opposite **Jambo Inn Hotel**, on road between Libya St and Jamhuri St. 0800-2300. A split-level restaurant with tasty food, fast service and always packed so you may have to wait for a seat and share a table, offering Chinese, Indian and Tanzanian dishes; try *matoke* (savoury bananas) with beef stew or fresh fish in coconut.

$ City Garden Restaurant, corner of Garden Av and Pamba St, T022-213 6347. Open 0800-2200. African, Indian and Western meals, including full English breakfasts, sandwiches, salads, steaks with sauces and fresh fish, excellent juices, milkshakes and coffees, tables are set in a shady garden, good service and consistently popular, especially at lunchtime when there are buffets.

$ Dar es Salaam Chinese Restaurant, basement of NIC Investments House, Samora Av. Mon-Sat 1200-2000. Cafeteria with good, inexpensive Chinese cuisine – soups and vegetable stir-fries cost little more than US$2 – also African and some continental dishes. Has been going some 30 years.

$ Dar Shanghai, Luther House, Sokoine Dr, T022-213 4397. Open 1200-2300. Chinese and Tanzanian menus, canteen-style atmosphere, the food's not brilliant (the noodles may actually be spaghetti) but it's quick, cheap and filling. No booze but soft drinks.

$ Debonair's and **Steer's**, corner of Ohio St and Samora Av, T022-212 2855. Quality South African chains. **Debonair's** serves pizza and salads, while **Steer's** offers burgers, ribs and chips. Also in the Steer's Complex is **Hurry Curry**, an Indian takeaway, **Chop Chop**, Chinese, and a coffee shop. Eat at plastic tables in a/c surroundings or takeaway.

$ Jambo Inn, Libya St, T022-211 0711, see Where to stay, page 62. Open 1100-2330. Bright spotlessly clean canteen with plastic tables, some outside next to the street, excellent cheap Indian menu, huge inflated chapattis like air-cushions, also Chinese and European dishes, good choice for vegetarians.

There's no booze in this Indian area, but they serve delicious fresh juice and ice cream.

Cafés
Sno-cream, Mansfield St. 0900-1200. Established in Dar in the 1960s, an old-fashioned ice cream parlour within a short walk of the ferry terminal serving excellent ice cream, including incredibly elaborate sundaes with all the trimmings.

Msasani Peninsula *map p58*
$$$ Addis in Dar, 35 Ursino St, off Old Bagamoyo Rd, Oyster Bay, T0713-266 299. Open Mon-Sat 1200-1430, 1800-2300. Small and charming Ethiopian restaurant with an outside terrace, great place to try spicy beef, lamb and chicken stews, and plenty of choice for vegetarians. Everything is served on woven platters and scooped up with *injera*, a sponge-like bread used as your eating utensil. Ethiopian honey wine before your meal and coffee afterwards completes the experience. They also sell beautiful Ethiopian silver jewellery.

$$$ Azuma, The Slipway, T022-260 0893. Tue-Sun 1800-2300. Japanese and Indonesian restaurant, authentic cuisine with elegant decor and good views over the bay. Very good sushi. If you book ahead, the chef will come out from the kitchen and prepare food at your table.

$$$ Karambezi, Hotel Sea Cliff, see Where to stay, page 63. Mon-Fri 0630-1030, 1200-2200, Sat and Sun 0630-2200. Beautiful setting on wooden decking on a low cliff overlooking the ocean. The menu is varied, with pizzas, pastas, seafood and grills and a good selection of wines. It's a fine place for weekend brunch, to share a seafood platter, or a cocktail at sunset.

$$$ The Terrace, at The Slipway, T022-260 0893. Mon-Sat 1800-2230. Upstairs from the **Mashua Waterfront Bar & Grill** (see below) with the same outstanding ocean views, fine Italian cuisine and extensive menu of barbecued grills and seafood, impeccable service and romantic ambience and decor,

with Moorish painted arches and intimate tables on the terrace.

$$$-$$ Fishmonger, at Sea Cliff Village, T0754-304 733. Mon-Thu 1700-2300, Fri-Sun 1200-2300. Good fish and seafood US$12-20, though the non-fishy options are limited. Pleasant modern seaside decor and outdoor terrace upstairs in the shopping centre.

$$$-$$ Osaka, Chaza Lane off Toure Dr, look for the sign as it's down a dirt road, T0755-268 228. Tue-Sun 1230-1430, 1830-2230. Quality sushi and teppanyaki restaurant decorated with Japanese lanterns and wall hangings, and with a lovely outdoor patio. Authentic food and you can watch the chefs. Set menu lunch specials.

$$$-$$ Sweet Eazy, Oyster Bay Shopping Centre, Toure Dr, T0745-754 074, www. sweeteazy.com. 1100-2400. Stylish cocktail bar and restaurant with lovely outdoor terrace with water features and Swahili arches, African and Thai cuisine, fish dishes include red snapper and parrot fish, plus lobster and seafood platters. There's a stage with great dinner/dance-type bands on Thu, Sat and Sun, happy hour 1700-1900.

$$ Casa Del Ray, at Sea Cliff Village, T0773-438 834. Tue-Thu 1100-2130, Fri-Sun 1100-2300. Mexican restaurant (possibly the only one in Tanzania) with a full range of nachos, tacos, burritos and quesadillas, plus good combo steak/seafood dishes, fun atmosphere with Mexican-themed decor, plenty of cocktails and, of course, tequila.

$$ Mashua Waterfront Bar & Grill, at The Slipway, T022-260 0893. Open 1200-2400. Great location on the waterfront offering sunset views over the ocean and a broad terrace with sea breezes. Grills, burgers, salads, pizza, a varied selection of seafood and a popular bar.

$$ Zûane Trattoria, Mzinga Way, off Haile Selassie Rd, near the Morogoro Shops, T022-260 2272. Open 1200-1400, 1900-2230. Simple, homely and genuine Italian, great thin-based pizza, home-made pasta; the steaks, calamari and tuna are worth trying too, gooey desserts, often busy with loyal customers so the service is not great, but well worth finding in its tricky location down a side road.

$$-$ L'Epi d'Or, Haile Selassie Rd, at the junction of Chole Rd, T022-260 1663. Tue-Sun 0700-2230. Bistro-style café and French bakery with outside terrace tables, serving very good sandwiches, with imaginative fillings, pastries, croissants, cappuccino and fresh juice, and it's a Wi-Fi hotspot. There are some beautiful cream cakes in the chilled cabinet here, and it's a popular spot for Sun brunch. The dinner menu includes wood-fired pizzas and Lebanese mezzes.

$$-$ Traders Grill, The Arcade, Old Bagomoyo Rd, T0784-706 188. Open 1830-2300. Mock English-style pub with draught beer, informal atmosphere, predominantly a steakhouse with generous sized T-bones and rumps, but also does seafood, the grilled prawns are good, especially on Wed, Fri and Sun, when you can eat as many as you want for US$7.

$ Coral Ridge Spur, at Sea Cliff Village, T022-260 0380. Open 1100-2300. Quality South African steak and ribs chain, geared up for families with a play area, Wild West decor, big portions and help-yourself salad bar.

Northern beaches *p59*

$$ Mediterraneo, Kawe Beach, off Old Bagomoyo Rd, midway between the city and the northern beaches, see Where to stay, page 65. Open 1200-2300. Lovely setting right on the beach, the bar/lounge area has low tables and cushions set in the sand and offers Wi-Fi, a varied and inventive menu of Italian home-made pasta, wood-fired pizza, seafood and Swahili-style buffets, and a divine tiramisu, plus a good choice of Italian and South African wines.

Cafés

Café Classico, at The Slipway. 0700-2200. Good location with tables on the main square overlooking the harbour and a modern a/c interior, speciality coffees and teas, English and continental breakfasts, sandwiches, salads and light meals.

Bars and clubs

Dar es Salaam *p46, maps p52 and p58*
There are few nightclubs as such in Dar, though many of the hotels and restaurants mentioned above crank it up late in the evening with live music or a DJ, especially at weekends when tables are cleared away for dancing. Hotels that have regular discos and/or live music in attractive outdoor settings include the **Jangwani Sea Breeze Resort** and **White Sands Hotel** on the northern beaches (see page 64); and **South Beach Resort** on the southern beaches (page 63).

Al Dar Sheesha Bar, Holiday Inn (see page 61). Open 1100-2400. Has stunning city and ocean views from the 11th floor and serves snacks and a good choice of cocktails.

Bottleneck Bar, New Africa Hotel, corner Azikiwe St and Sokine Dr, city centre, see Where to stay, page 61. Open 1000-2400. Popular for after-work drinks with rattan furniture and palms, long cocktail list, happy hour 1730-1930.

Club Bilicanas, Mkwepu St, city centre, T022-202 1604, www.bilicanasgroup.com. Open 2000-0400. Far and away the most sophisticated and popular club in Dar, it has been imaginatively designed with a VIP lounge, 7 bars and glass decor, and has all the effects you'd expect from a world-class club. Cover charge is US$4-12 depending on the event.

Kibo Bar, Serena Dar es Salaam Hotel, Ohio St, city centre, see Where to stay, page 62. Open 1000-2400. Upmarket hotel bar with a good range of imported drinks, bar meals, pleasant patio tables overlooking the palm-filled gardens. It has an occasional live band and shows sport on TV.

Level 8, Hyatt Regency, Kivukoni St, city centre, see Where to stay, page 61. Open 1700-0100. A luxurious bar on the 8th floor of the Hyatt, with rooftop terrace and mesmerizing views of the port and downtown Dar at night (go here for sunset). Subtle lounge music and occasional live jazz, 90 cocktails plus champagne and cigars.

O'Willies Irish Whiskey Tavern, Chui Bay Rd, off Kimweri Av, Msasani Peninsula, T022-260 1273, www.owillies.com. 1100-late. Lively (sometimes raucous) themed pub, with events on each night like pub quiz on Mon, karaoke on Wed and a Celtic band on Sat, popular with expats, great ocean views from the rooftop terrace, Guinness on tap and, as the name suggests, lots of whiskey, large portions of food, such as burgers, fish and chips and Irish stew.

Q Bar, off Haile Selassie Rd, behind the Morogoro Shops, Oyster Bay, T0754-304 733. Open 1700-0200. A friendly and popular expat venue, with good bar meals, cocktails and shooters, pool tables, lots of TVs – gets packed when European football is showing – live music on Wed and Fri, and Sat is 1970s soul night. There are also budget rooms here (see Where to stay, page 63).

⊕ Entertainment

Dar es Salaam *p46, maps p52 and p58*
Casinos
There are several places advertising themselves as casinos dotted around the city centre, but many of these are just seedy slot-machine joints. The nicest proper casinos, with gaming tables, waiter service and bars, are at the **New Africa Hotel**, the **Hyatt Regency** and the **Hotel Sea Cliff**. These generally open about 1200 for the slot-machines and from 1700 for the gaming tables and stay open until 0400 or 0500.

Cinema
Programmes are in the newspapers. Tickets are about US$6.
Century Cinemax, in the **Mlimani City Shopping Mall**, San Nujoma Rd, Mikocheni, near the university, T022-277 3053. Modern 4-screen complex showing Hollywood movies 1200-2200.
New World Cinemas, New Bagamoyo Rd, Mwenge, T022-277 1409. Shows mostly Indian/Bollywood movies on 2 screens 1400-2200.

Live music
The **British Council** and the **Alliance Française** (see Cultural centres, page 76) often host concerts by touring artists. African and Indian bands and artists play regularly at the hotels and restaurants especially at weekends.

Theatre
Little Theatre, corner Haile Selassie Rd and Ali Hassan Mwinyi Rd, Oyster Bay, T0784-277 388. The home of the amateur dramatic Dar es Salaam Players presents drama, comedy or musical productions on an occasional basis. The Christmas pantomime is particularly popular.

⊙ Shopping

Dar es Salaam *p46, maps p52 and p58*
There are shops along Samora Av (electrical goods, clothing, footwear) and on Libya St (clothing and footwear). Supermarkets, with a wide variety of imported foods and wines, are on Samora Av between Pamba Av and Azikawe St; on the corner of Kaluta St and Bridge St; opposite Woolworth's on Garden Av; and in **Shopper's Plaza** on the Msasani Peninsula. The **Mlimani City Shopping Mall**, Sam Nujoma Rd, Ubungo, near Dar University is also home to a huge **Shoprite** supermarket, and there is another branch on Nyerere Rd on the way to the airport. A popular location for buying fruit and vegetables is the market on Kinondoni Rd, just north of Msimbuzi Creek.

The **Namanga Shops**, are at the corner of Old Bagamoyo and Ali Hassan Mwinyi roads on the way to the Msasani Peninsula, and are basically stalls selling household supplies and food; there's a good butcher's towards the back. **Manzese Mitumba Stalls**, Morogoro Rd, Manzese, has great bargains for second-hand clothing, and Uhuru St has several *kanga* shops (the traditional wrap-arounds worn by women). **Ilala Market**, on Uhuru St, sells vegetables, fresh and dried fish and second-hand clothing.

Fresh fish and seafood can be bought at the **Fish Market** on Ocean Rd, just past the Kigamboni ferry, which is an interesting place to visit (see page 56).

Bookshops
Second-hand books can be found at the stalls on Samora Av, on Pamba St (off Samora), on Maktaba St and outside Tancot House, opposite Luther House. Most of these also sell international news magazines, such as *Time*, *Newsweek*, *New African*, etc.
A Novel Idea, corner of Ohio St and Samora Av, T022-260 1088, and in the shopping malls (see below), www.anovelideatanzania. com. The best bookshop in Dar by far, and perhaps one of the most comprehensive bookshops in East Africa, with a full range of new novels, coffee table books, maps and guide books.

Curios and crafts
In the city centre, traditional crafts, particularly wooden carvings, are sold in various shops along Samora Av to the south of the Askari Monument, and from stalls along Ali Hassan Mwinyi Rd near the intersection with Haile Selassie Rd. But the place to go for curios in Dar is the **Mwenge Craft Market**, along Sam Njoma Rd, close to the intersection with New Bagamoyo Rd, 10 km or about 30 mins from the city centre towards the northern beaches. Open 0800-1800. This is easily reached by *dala-dala* from the New Post Office (Posta) stand, and is just around the corner from the Mwenge *dala-dala* stand. Well known for its Makonde carvings, there is a vast number of shops and stalls here offering goods at very reasonable prices (all are negotiable) and you can watch the carvers at work.

Jewellery
For tanzanite, the beautiful blue-violet gemstone only mined in Tanzania, try **Lithos Africa**, in the **Hyatt Regency Hotel** (see Where to stay, page 61), T0753-603 666, www.lithosafrica.com,

or **Jewelex**, in the **Oyster Bay Shopping Centre** (below), T022-260 0787.

Shopping malls
Mlimani City Shopping Mall, San Nujoma Rd, Mikocheni, near the university. Mon-Sat 1000-2000, Sun 1000-1800. Dar's most modern shopping mall with a cinema complex, one of the biggest **Shoprite** supermarkets in Tanzania, and a plethora of smaller shops covering everything from clothes to electronics.
Oyster Bay Shopping Centre, see also Where to stay, page 62, Msasani Peninsula. Small group of shops next to the hotel with supermarket, internet café, gift and art shops and restaurants.
Sea Cliff Village, Hotel Sea Cliff, see Where to stay, page 63, Msasani Peninsula. Mon-Sat 0930-1800, Sun 1000-1500, restaurants stay open later. A very attractive modern piazza-style mall attached to the hotel with a branch of the excellent bookshop **A Novel Idea** (see above), a French bakery, upmarket jewellery and clothes boutiques, forex bureaux, a food court and restaurants. There's also a vastly overpriced supermarket catering for expats, but it has a good selection of imported items.
Shoppers' Plaza, Old Bagamoyo Rd, Msasani Peninsula, T022-270 1545, www.shoppers. co.tz. Mon-Sat 0830-1730, Sun 1000-1500. Has a useful variety of small shops, including a large supermarket that is open Mon-Sat until 2030 and Sun until 1800, a branch of **A Novel Idea** (see above), and a **Standard Bank** with an ATM.
The Slipway, Msasani Peninsula, facing Msasani Bay, T022-260 0893, www.slipway. net. Mon-Sat 1000-1800, Sun 1000-1500, restaurants later. Pleasant waterfront development in a converted boatyard, expensive, high-quality goods can be found here at a number of boutiques and specialist shops, plus there's a branch of **A Novel Idea** (see above), an internet café, several restaurants, an ice cream parlour and a **Barclay's Bank** with an ATM. There's

also a craft market selling tablecloths, cushions and beadwork, and a Tingatinga workshop (see box, page 56 for more information about Tingatinga art) and hotel rooms (see Hotel Slipway, page 63). **Woolworth's**, in the New PPF Towers building on Ohio St, T022-212 6909, www.w-stores.co.tz. Mon-Fri 0900-1730, Sat 0900-1300. This is a quality South African clothing and home store very similar to the UK's Marks & Spencer.

⚙ What to do

Dar es Salaam *p46, maps p52 and p58*
Cricket
Almost entirely a pursuit of the Asian community. There are regular games at weekends at: **Annadil Burhani Cricket Ground**, off Aly Khan Rd; **Gymkhana Club**, off Ghana Av; **Jangwani Playing Fields**, off Morogoro Rd, in the valley of Msimbazi Creek; and **Leaders Club**, Dahomey Rd, off Ali Hassan Mwinyi Rd. For information about fixtures, visit the website of the **Tanzania Cricket Association**, www.tanzaniacricket.com.

Diving
Diving takes place in the **Dar es Salaam Marine Reserve** off the north coast, which includes the 4 uninhabited islands of Mbudya, Pangavini, Fungu Yasin and Bongoyo. All dive sites are accessible from the shore within 25 mins by boat. The best time to dive is Oct-Feb when visibility is excellent and dives average 20-25 m. Although the variety of fish is good, it's not exceptional as it is in Zanzibar and Pemba, and the marine life has suffered from the consequences of illegal dynamite fishing off the coast here. Nevertheless, moray eels, blue-spotted stingrays, lion scorpion and crocodile fish may be spotted on the reefs. Of particular note is Ferns Wall, on the seaward side of Fungu Yasin Reef, where you'll find large barrel sponges, gorgonian fans and 2-m-long whip corals. Reef sharks are often spotted here. Another favourite is

Mwamba, a unique reef comprising large fields of pristine brain, rose and plate corals. **Sea Breeze Marine Ltd**, White Sands Hotel (see page 65), T0754-783 241, www.sea breezemarine.org. A PADI centre, single dives start from US$50 and also offers Open Water courses.

Fishing
Deep-sea fishing can be arranged through many of the hotels on the beaches, see Where to stay, pages 63-64.

Football
Benjamin Mkapa National Stadium, Taifa Rd, off Nelson Mandela Rd to the south of the city. Dar es Salaam has 2 clubs, **Simba** and **Young Africans**, and there is intense rivalry between them and a local derby at the 60,000-seater stadium is hugely popular. The national team, **Taifa Stars**, also play regularly here, mostly against other African teams.

Golf
Gymkhana Club, Ghana Av, T022-212 0519, www.gymkhana.co.tz. Established in 1916 as a horse-riding club, this now has a full range of sporting facilities, including an 18-hole golf course, tennis and squash courts, and cricket, football and rugby pitches. Visitors can obtain temporary membership to play golf and the pro-shop rents out clubs. Here, because of a shortage of water, you will be playing on browns not greens.

Sailing
Yacht Club, Chole Rd, Msasani Peninsula, T022-260 0132, www.daryachtclub.com. Visitors can obtain temporary membership here and there's a restaurant, bar and swimming pool. The club organizes East Africa's premier sailing event, the Dar to Tanga (and back) Yacht Race every Dec.

Swimming
The beaches around the city centre are not suitable for swimming, but many of the larger hotels on the northern beaches allow

non-guests to use the facilities for a small fee (see page 59).

Water World, White Sands Hotel, see Where to stay, page 65, Mbezi Beach, Tue-Sun 1000-1800, US$5, children (under 12) US$4. One of the swimming pools here has several different water slides and games for children.

Wet 'n' Wild, next to Kunduchi Beach Hotel, Kunduchi Beach, T022-265 0326, Tue-Sun, 0900-1800, US$5, children (under 8) US$4. A large complex largely, though not exclusively, for children, with 7 swimming pools, 24 water slides – 2 are very high and 1 twists and turns for 250 m – a jungle gym for small children, fast-food outlets and a main restaurant.

Tour operators

A variety of companies offer tours to the game parks, the islands (Zanzibar, Pemba, Mafia) and to places of historical interest (Kilwa, Bagamoyo). It is well worth shopping around as prices (and degrees of luxury) vary. It is important to find an operator that you like, offers good service and does not pressure you into booking something. This is just a small selection. You can find more on the Tanzania Association of Tour Operators website: www.tatotz.org.

Authentic Tanzania, Kuanda Rd, Oyster Bay, T0786-019 965, www.authentictanzania.com.

Bon Voyage Travel, Barclay's Bank Building, Ohio St, also has a desk at the airport, T022-211 8023, www.bonvoyagetz.com.

Cordial Tours, corner Jumhuri and India streets, T027-213 6259, www.cordialtours.com.

Easy Travel & Tours, Raha Towers, Bibi Titi Mohamed St, T022-212 1747, www.easytravel.co.tz.

Ebony Tours & Safaris, Chole Rd, Oyster Bay, T022-260 1459, www.ebony-safaris.com.

Emslies Travel, TDFL Building, Ohio St, T022-211 4065, www.emsliestravel.com.

Fortune Travels & Tours, Jamhuri St, T022-213 8288, www.fortunetz.com.

Hima Tours & Safaris, PPF House, Morogoro Rd, T022-211 1083, www.himatoursnsafaris.com.

Hippo Tours & Safaris, Nyumba ya Sanaa Building, Ohio St, T022-212 8662, www.hippotours.com.

Hit Holidays, Bibi Titi Mohamed St, T022-211 9024, www.hitholidays.com.

Kearsley Travel & Tours, Kearsley House, Makunganya St, T022-211 5026, and Sea Cliff Village, T022-260 0461, www.kearsleys.com.

Planet Safaris, Nyumba ya Sanaa Building, Ohio St, T022-213 7456, www.planetsafaris.com.

Reza Travel & Tours, Jamhuri St, T022-213 4814, www.rezatravel.com.

Rickshaw Travel (American Express Agents), Serena Dar es Salaam Hotel, Ohio St, T022-213 7275, www.rickshawtravels.com.

Skylink Travel & Tours, Amani Place, Ohio St, opposite Serena Dar es Salaam Hotel, T022-211 5381; airport, T022-284 2738; Mayfair Plaza, Old Bagamoyo Rd, T022-277 3983, www.skylinktanzania.com.

Takims Holidays Tours & Safaris, Mtendeni St, T022-211 0346/8, www.takimsholidays.com.

Walji's Travel, Zanaki St/Indira Ghandi St corner, T022-211 0321, www.waljistravel.com. **Wild Things Safaris**, Mbezi Beach, off Bagomoyo Rd, T022-261 7166, www.wildthingsafaris.com.

⊘ Transport

Dar es Salaam *p46, maps p52 and p58*
Air

For details of international airlines serving Tanzania, see Essentials, page 11. The following airlines offer daily scheduled flights from Dar es Salaam, but these can change regularly and it's always best to check with the airlines before making plans. It's also necessary to reconfirm your bookings a day or so before flying since timings often change. The airlines generally run services in circuits, so flights may involve many intermediate stops as the plane drops passengers at different airstrips on each circuit. Many flights using small planes have a baggage limit of 15 kg per person.

Air Excel has daily scheduled circuits between Dar, **Zanzibar** and **Arusha**, from where they connect with a circuit of the lodges in the **Serengeti**. They also touchdown at **Kilimanjaro** to meet **Air Kenya** flights from Wilson Airport in Nairobi.

Coastal Air has daily scheduled circuits from Dar to **Zanzibar**, **Arusha**, **Serengeti** and **Mwanza**; to **Zanzibar**, **Pemba** and **Tanga**; to **Mafia Island** and **Kilwa**; and to **Selous** and **Ruaha** on a circuit that's come from **Zanzibar**. It also has a direct daily flight between Dar and **Dodoma**.

Fly 540 has direct flights between Dar and **Kilimanjaro**, **Mwanza**, **Mtwara** and **Nairobi** in Kenya.

Precision Air has numerous flights between Dar and **Zanzibar**, some of which are on a circuit that also includes **Kilimanjaro**. There are also flights on a circuit between Dar and **Shinyanga**, **Kigoma**, **Mwanza** and **Bukoba**; and flights between Dar and **Mtwara**. It also has international flights between Dar and Zanzibar and either

Nairobi or **Mombasa** in Kenya on the same circuits, and direct flights between Dar and **Johannesburg** in South Africa.

ZanAir has several daily flights from Dar to **Zanzibar**, some of which continue on to **Pemba**, and to **Arusha** and the **Serengeti**, and a flight to the **Selous**, which has come from **Zanzibar**.

Airline offices Air Excel, Arusha, T027-254 8429, www.airexcelonline.com. **Air Malawi**, corner India and Zanaki streets, T022-212 7746, www.airmalawi.com. **British Airways**, at the Serena Dar es Salaam Hotel, Ohio St, T022-2113 8202, www.british airways.com. **Coastal Air**, airport, T022-284 2700, www.coastal.cc. **Emirates**, Haidery Plaza, Kisutu St, T022-211 6100, www.emirates.com. **Ethiopian Airlines**, TDFL Building, Ohio St, T022-211 7063, www.flyethiopian.com. **Fly 540**, airport, T0752-540 540, www.fly540.com. **Kenya Airways**, Peugeot House, Bibi Titi Mohammed/Ali Hassan Mwinyi Rd, T022-211 9377, www.kenya-airways.com. **KLM**, Peugeot House, as above, T022-211 3336, www.klm.com. **Precision Air**, airport, T022-286 0701, corner of Samora Av and Pamba Rd, T022-213 0800, www.precisionairtz.com. **South Africa Airways**, Raha Tower, Bibi Titi Mohammed St, T022-211 7044, www.flysaa.com. **ZanAir**, Zanzibar airport, T024-223 3670, www.zanair.com,

Bus

The main bus station is Ubungo Bus Station on Morogoro Rd, 6 km from the city centre, which can be reached by bus, *dala-dala* or taxi. Outside on the road is a long line of booking offices. Recommended for safety and reliability is Scandinavia Express, which while all its buses stop at Ubungo, also has its own terminal on Nyerere Rd at the corner of Msimbazi St (taxi from the city centre approximately US$3), T022-218 4833, www.scandinaviagroup.com. There is a small airport-style arrival and departure lounge at this terminal with its own restaurant. Buses are speed-limited, luggage is securely locked

The dala-dalas of Dar es Salaam

Ownership of one or more minibuses, or *dala-dalas*, remains a favourite *mradi* (income-generating project) for Dar es Salaam's middle class and, judging by the numbers squeezed into their interiors and the speed at which they travel between destinations, those returns are handsome. Realizing that they can't monitor the number of passengers using their buses, the *dala-dala* owners stipulate how much they expect to receive at the end of the day from the 'crew' they hire to operate the vehicle; anything left over constitutes the crew's wages. It is a system that appears to work to everyone's advantage other than that of the passenger, who suffers the consequent overcrowding and the suicidal driving as *dala-dala* competes with *dala-dala* to arrive first and leave fullest.

The basic crew of each *dala-dala* is made up of two people: the driver (clearly picked for the ability to drive fast rather than well) and the conductor, or in Dar slang *Mgiga debe* – literally 'he who beats on a tin can', and so named because he slaps the vehicle to indicate to the driver that they are ready to depart. It is his job to collect money and issue tickets, harangue passengers who fail to make room for one more, as well as to entertain the remainder of the bus with hair-raising acrobatic stunts hanging from the door of the bus. Supplementing this basic crew at either end of the journey is a tout, who bawls out the intended destination

and route, attempting to attract or, if necessary, intimidate people (at times this stretches to actual manhandling of passengers) into entering his *dala-dala*.

The *dala-dala* network radiates from three main terminals (also known as 'stands') in the city centre, **Posta** on Azikiwe Street opposite the New Post Office, and if there are not enough passengers, they will also make a detour to the Old Post Office on the Kivukoni Front to pick up more people; **Stesheni**, close to the Central Railway Station; and **Kariakoo**, around the Uhuru/Msimbazi Street roundabout for destinations south and at the central market for those in the north. From each of these you can catch *dala-dalas* to destinations throughout Dar es Salaam, although the four main routes are along Ali Hassan Mwinyi to Mwenge (for the Makumbusho Village Museum, Mwenge Craft Market and the university); along the Kilwa Road to Temeke, Mtoni and Mbagala; to Vingunguti via Kariakoo and Ilala (for the TAZARA Railway Station); and along the Morogoro Road to Magomeni, Manzese and Ubungo (for the long-distance bus station). Most *dala-dalas* have the start and ending point of their route clearly painted on the front or side of the vehicle, and it's also fine to ask someone where to find the *dala-dala* you're looking for (newspaper/phonecard sellers are the most helpful). For a *dala-dala* going to the airport ask for '*Uwanja wa Ndege at Minazi Miretu*'.

up either under the bus or in overhead compartments, and complimentary DVD, drinks, sweets and biscuits are offered. There are 2 different kinds of buses; the Deluxe service has a/c and an onboard toilet, while the Semi-luxury service doesn't. Buses depart daily for **Arusha** (9 hrs), Deluxe at 0830, US$15, and Semi-luxury at 0915,

US$10; **Mbeya** (12 hrs), Semi-luxury at 0645 and 0745, US$11; **Tanga** (6 hrs) Deluxe at 0800, US$6.50, and Semi-luxury at 1530, US$4.50; **Dodoma** (4 hrs) Deluxe at 0915, US$6.50, and Semi-luxury at 1100, US$5. International destinations are **Mombasa** and **Nairobi** in Kenya, **Kampala** in Uganda and **Lusaka** in Zambia.

There are numerous other bus companies at Ubungo, including: **Al Saedy**, T0715-380838; **Dar Express**, T0754-373415; **KLM Express**, T022-255 6327; **Royal Coaches**, T022-212 4073, and **Tashreef**, T022-238 5247.

Car hire
Car hire can be arranged through most of the tour operators. Alternatively try:
Avis, Amani Place, opposite the Serena Dar es Salaam Hotel, Ohio St, T022-211 5381, www.avis.com; **Green Car Rentals**, Nukrumah St, along Nyerere Rd, T022-218 3718, www.greencarstz.com; **Lucky Rent-A-Car**, Skymark Mall, corner of Morogoro Rd and Libya St, T022-213 5843, www.luckyrentacar-tz.com; **XCar Rent-A-Car**, Old Bagamoyo Rd, near Shopper's Plaza, T022-277 1126, www.xcarrentals.com, or **Xpress Car Rental**, Haidery Plaza, Kisutu St, T022-212 8356, at the Holiday Inn, see Where to stay, page 61, T022-213 9250, www.xpresstours.org.

Ferry
All ticket offices of the ferry companies with services to **Zanzibar** and **Pemba** are on Sokoine Dr adjacent to the jetty and are generally open 0600-2000. Ignore the touts who may follow you to the offices to claim credit and take commission. The companies themselves advise travellers to completely ignore them and it is easy enough to book a ticket on your own. Payment for tickets is in US$ cash only, though £ and € cash may be accepted at a push. Most ferries are fast and comfortable hydrofoils or catamarans that take on average 90 mins to reach Zanzibar. Fares for non-residents greatly exceed those for residents, though they are not overly expensive and are inclusive of port tax. The trip is generally reliable and pleasant, and on the newer boats movies are shown and refreshments are available. Some services continue on to Pemba.

Ferry companies Azam Marine, T022-212 3324, www.azammarine.com. Runs 5 catamarans with daily departures at 0700,

0930, 1230 and 1530. From Zanzibar to Dar, ferries depart at the same times. On Mon, Thu and Fri they also operate a service from Dar to **Pemba** via Zanzibar at 0700 which arrives in Zanzibar at 0840, departs again at 0930 and arrives in Pemba at 1135. The return boat on Mon, Thu and Fri departs Pemba at 1230, arrives in Zanzibar at 1435, departs again at 1600 and arrives in Dar at 1740. Fares: from Dar to Zanzibar, economy class US$35, children (under 12) US$25, 1st class US$40 per person; from Dar to Pemba, economy class US$60, children (under 12) US$30, first class US$65 per person.
Fast Ferries, T022-213 7049, www.fastferries tz.com, operate *Sea Express I and II*, with a daily departure from Dar at 0715 that arrives in Zanzibar at 0915, and departs Zanzibar for the return at 1600. On Mon and Wed, the ferry continues from Zanzibar (departing at 1000) to **Pemba** where it arrives at 1200, leaving Pemba at 1300 to return. Fares: Dar and Zanzibar, economy class US$35, children (under 12) US$20, 1st class US$40, children (under 12) US$25; from Dar to Pemba, economy class US$60, children (under 12) US$30, 1st class US$65 per person.
Flying Horse (Africa Shipping Corporation), T022-212 4507. The outward journey to Zanzibar departs at 1230 and takes 2-3 hrs, the overnight return from Zanzibar departs at 2200, but passengers are not let off at Dar until 0600 when Customs open. However, tourists are accommodated in a comfortable lounge with a/c and provided with mattresses to sleep on until 0600. A good option for budget travellers as the fare is only US$20 each way and you save on accommodation for 1 night.
Mega Speed Liners, T0713-282 365, www.megaspeedliners-zanzibar.com. Runs the *Sepideh*, which leaves Dar daily except Wed and Sun at 0715, and returns from Zanzibar at 1600. It continues on to **Pemba** on Mon, Tue and Sat at 0930, where it arrives at 1130, leaving Pemba at 1230 to return. Fares are similar to the other fast ferries above.

Sea Star, T0777-411 505. Departs Dar at 1030, the return leaves Zanzibar at 0700, again for similar fares.

Train
The **Central Railway Station** is off Sokoine Dr at the wharf end of the city at the corner of Railway St and Gerezani St, T022-211 7833, www.trctz.com. This station serves the Central Line that runs through to **Kigoma** on Lake Tanganyika and **Mwanza** on Lake Victoria.

TAZARA Railway Station is at the junction of Mandela Rd and Nyerere Rd, about 5 km from the city centre, T022-226 2191, www.tazarasite.com. It is well served by *dala-dala*, and a taxi from the centre costs about US$5. This line runs southwest to **Iringa** and **Mbeya** and on to **Tunduma** at the Zambia border and terminates at **Kapiri Mposhi** in Zambia. For details of services on both lines, see Train travel in Tanzania, page 18.

⊙ Directory

Dar es Salaam *p46, maps p52 and p58*
Cultural centres
Regular films, concerts and talks are on offer, as well as libraries and language courses. **Alliance Française**, at the French Embassy, Ali Hassan Mwinyi Rd, Upanga, T022-213 1406, www.ambafrance-tz.org. **British Council**, corner of Ohio St and Samora Av, T022-216 5300, www.britishcouncil.org.

Embassies and consulates
For a full list of foreign representatives in Dar es Salaam, visit the government's website, www.tanzania.go.tz or go to http://embassy.goabroad.com.

Immigration
Corner of Ohio St and Garden Av, T022-211 8637, Mon-Fri 0730-1530.

Medical services
Hospitals Muhimbili National Hospital, off United Nations Rd, northwest of the centre towards Msimbazi Creek, T022-215 1298, www.mnh.or.tz. **Aga Khan Hospital**, Ocean Rd at the junction with Ufukoni Rd, T022-211 5151, www.agakhanhospitals.org. Both these hospitals are well equipped and staffed. See also **Flying Doctors Society of Africa**, page 34.

Pharmacies In all shopping centres; small dispensaries are also found in the main residential areas.

Police
The **main police station** is on Gerazani St near the Central Line railway station, T022-211 5507. There are other police stations including on Upanga Rd on the city side of Selander Bridge, T022-212 0818, and on Ali Hassan Mwinyi Rd at the junction with Old Bagamoyo Rd (Oyster Bay), T022-266 7322. Other police stations can be found on the website, www.policeforce.go.tz. Always inform the police of any incidents – you will need a police statement for any insurance claims. **Emergencies** For police, ambulance and fire brigade, T112.

Contents

Footprint features

Border crossings

Coastal Tanzania

At a glance

⊖ **Getting around** Self-drive
or public buses are really the
only options.
◷ **Time required** 1 week to
explore the north coast and spend
a day or 2 on the beaches around
Pangani; 4-5 days to get down to
Kilwa; 1-2 nights on Mafia Island.
☼ **Weather** Tropical and balmy
most of the year.
✕ **When not to go** There are heavy
showers in the afternoons Mar-May.

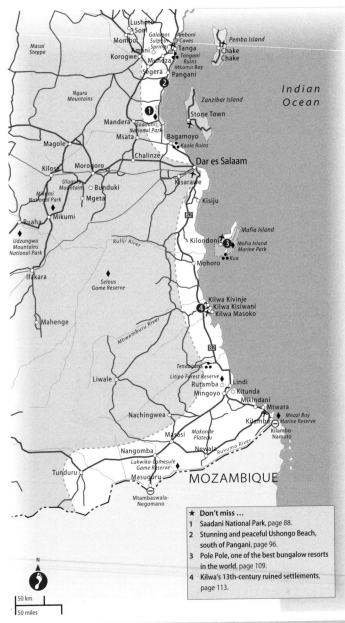

Lushoto
Soni
Mombo
Galanos
Sulphur
Springs
Amboni
Caves
Pemba Island
Chake
Chake
Amani
Korogwe
Muheza
Tanga
Tongoni
Ruins
Mkoma Bay
Segera
Pangani **2**
Masai
Steppe
Nguru
Mountains
Zanzibar Island

*Indian
Ocean*

Stone Town

Mandera
1
Saadani
National Park
Msata
Bagamoyo
Kaole Ruins
Magole
Morogoro
Chalinze
Kilosa
Uluguru
Mountains
Bunduki
Dar es Salaam
Mgeta
Kisarawe
Mikumi
National Park
Mikumi
Kisiju
B2
Ruaha
Mafia Island
Udzungwa
Mountains
National Park
Rufiji River
Kilondoni
3
Mafia Island
Marine Park
Ifakara
Selous
Game Reserve
Mohoro
Kua
Mahenge

Kilwa Kivinje
Kilwa Kisiwani
4
Kilwa Masoko
Liwale
Mbwemburu River

B2

Tendaguru
Litipo Forest Reserve
Rutamba
Lindi
Mingoyo
Kitunda
Mikindani
Nachingwea
Mtwara
Mnazi Bay
Marine Reserve
Masasi
Makonde
Plateau
Kilambo
Kilambo-
Namoto
Nangomba
Newala
Ruvuma River
Lukwika-Lumesule
Game Reserve
Tunduru
Masuguru
MOZAMBIQUE
Mtambaswala-
Negomano

★ **Don't miss …**

1 Saadani National Park, page 88.
2 Stunning and peaceful Ushongo Beach,
south of Pangani, page 96.
3 Pole Pole, one of the best bungalow resorts
in the world, page 109.
4 Kilwa's 13th-century ruined settlements,
page 113.

N

50 km
50 miles

The 800 km of the Tanzanian mainland coast has blindingly white beaches, coconut groves and mangrove swamps with nearby coral reefs and natural lagoons, but much of it is virtually undiscovered by modern tourism. Generally overlooked in favour of Zanzibar, the coast (away from Dar es Salaam) is rarely visited and has little development of any kind (tourist or otherwise), with just a few farming and fishing villages dotted along its shoreline. Yet there are vivid reminders of the Swahili past to be found as well as evidence of the coast's bloody and fascinating history. Palatial remnants of Persian and Omani kingdoms still remain, and ancient mosques, dating from the 12th century, testify to the far-reaching roots of Islam.

Bagamoyo was the last point reached by slave caravans before shipment; its fortified houses still stand, as does the tree under which the slaves were gathered to be sold. There is also the fading grandeur of Tanga in the north, and the relatively undiscovered island of Mafia, location of the Mafia Island Marine Park, which is home to large populations of whale sharks and is a wonderful place for scuba-diving. Towards the Mozambique border is the historic ruined city of Kilwa.

Things are beginning to change, however; there is now a clutch of upmarket beach resorts, and the newly tarred road from Dar es Salaam to Bagamoyo has improved transport and accessibility. Also, the beaches around Pangani have flourished with tourist development in recent years and now offer some excellent rustic beach resorts, which you should enjoy while tourism there is still in its infancy. In the future, this part of Tanzania could attract many more visitors.

Roads south are improving too, and – slowly but surely – the 21st century is arriving here, with oil and bio fuel developments creeping in. They've not changed the beauty of these areas yet, but if you want to visit them in their most pristine state, don't leave it too late.

Arriving in Coastal Tanzania

Getting there

North coast Although there is a new tar road from Dar es Salaam to Bagamoyo, north of here the road deteriorates into a sandy track; there is no access along the coast to Saadani and the coastal towns of Tanga and Pangani further north, as there is presently no crossing over the Wami River. Instead, these are reached from the inland road. From Dar this stretches the 109 km to the junction at Chalinze before heading north towards Moshi and Arusha, off which are roads that go east, back towards the coast. Beyond Tanga the road continues on to the border with Kenya; there is good access along this route from Dar to Mombasa (Kenya) and the journey can easily be made in a day by bus.

South coast Off the coast is the island of Mafia, which is now partially protected as the Mafia Island Marine Park. It's an idyllic setting and a paradise for scuba-divers and snorkellers and, with its stunning lodges, was for a long time a haven for those only at the luxury end of the market; however, a clutch of cheaper options have opened recently too. Flights connect Dar es Salaam and Mafia Island, as well as Kilwa and Mafia Island and Dar es Salaam and Mtwara. The main coastal road south from Dar es Salaam to Lindi and then on to the border with Mozambique has recently been tarred (see box, page 126). It passes the town of Kilwa, with the small island of Kilwa Kisiwani just off the mainland. This is the location of the intriguing Kilwa ruins and, although very remote, is worth the trouble to get to. Buses make the journey from Dar es Salaam to Kilwa, Lindi and on to Mtwara, but these are long journeys and, outside the towns, there are few facilities along this road.

Bagamoyo

Bagamoyo, whose name means 'lay down my heart' in Kiswahili, has a host of historical associations and, as the oldest town in Tanzania, is currently being considered as Tanzania's eighth World Heritage Site (for a list of the others, see page 9). The town has seen Arab and Indian traders, German colonial government and Christian missionaries, and although Bagamoyo is no longer the busy port city that it once was, it does have dozens of ruins. Unfortunately, however, most are fairly dilapidated as the town hasn't seen the attention to restoration afforded to the likes of Zanzibar's Stone Town. With luck, this will change if it's awarded World Heritage status. In recent years, many of the buildings have lost their intricate carved doors and window frames, as they have either been stolen or sold. About a decade ago, a clutch of large holiday resorts were built on the beach to the north of town but, with a couple of exceptions, they haven't proved popular and today they are mostly empty or cater for local conferences. These days, the resorts to the north of Dar or lovely Ushongo Beach south of Pangani appear to be far more popular with foreign visitors.

Bagamoyo makes a very interesting day trip from Dar es Salaam and the journey only takes about 90 minutes. Be aware, though, that the public beaches are not that great and there's a fair amount of debris along them. You should not wander around public places in swimwear or shorts (this will offend the local Muslim community) and you should also be aware of the possibility of petty theft and muggings on the beaches. If you do want to swim and sunbathe, go to one of the resorts. ▸▸ *For listings, see pages 88-90.*

Arriving in Bagamoyo → *Phone code: 023. Altitude: sea level. Population: 82,500. Colour map 1, B5. 6°20'S 38°30'E.*

Getting there Bagamayo is about 70 km north of Dar es Salaam by road; there are several *dala-dalas* a day between Dar es Salaam and Bagamoyo, and some of the Bagomoyo hotels offer a shuttle service to their guests. From Dar, get a *dala-dala* to the bus stand at Mwenge and swap to another to Bagamoyo. The journey shouldn't cost more than US$2.

Getting around There are a number of taxis at the bus stand but all destinations in Bagamoyo are within walking distance. It is a good idea to hire a guide; being with a local person provides security to get to places on isolated roads. Any of the hotels can organize guides if you're staying overnight, or you can pick up a guide at either the Holy Ghost Mission or Livingstone's Church, or go to the **tourist office** ① *Boma St, T023-244 0155, 0800-2000.* Expect to pay around US$10-15 for a three- to four-hour walking tour. Alternatively, you may be able to negotiate with local people to hire a bike for an hour or two.

Background

The coastal area opposite Zanzibar was first settled by fishermen and cultivators. Towards the end of the 18th century, 12 or so Muslim diwans arrived to settle, build dwellings and establish their families and retinues of slaves. These diwans were all related to Shomvi la Magimba from Oman. They prospered through levying taxes whenever a cow was slaughtered, or a shark or other large fish caught, as well as on all salt produced at Nunge, about 3 km north of Bagamoyo.

Bagamoyo's location as a mainland port close to Zanzibar led to its development as a centre for caravans, and an expansion of commerce in slaves and ivory soon followed. Although the slave trade officially ended in 1873, slaves continued to be sold and traded in Bagamoyo until the end of the 19th century. During this time, it was not uncommon to see hundreds of slaves walking through the streets of Bagamoyo chained together by the neck. There was also a growing trade in sun-dried fish, gum copal and the salt from Nunge. Copra (from coconuts) was also important and was used to make soap. A boat-building centre was established, which supplied craft to other coastal settlements.

In 1880 the population of the town was around 5000, but this was augmented by a substantial transient population, in residence after completing a caravan or undertaking preparations prior to departure. The numbers of those temporarily in town could be considerable. In 1889, after the slave trade had been suppressed, significantly reducing the numbers passing through, it was still recorded that 1305 caravans, involving 41,144 people, left from Bagamayo for the interior.

The social composition of the town was varied. There were the initial Muslim Shomvi and the local Zaramo and Doe. Among the earliest arrivals were Hindus from India, involving themselves in administration, coconut plantations and boat-building. Muslim Baluchis, a people based in Mombasa and Zanzibar, and, for the most part, mercenary soldiers, also settled and were involved in trade, financing caravans and land-owning. Other Muslim sects were represented, among them the Ismailis who settled in 1840 and by 1870 numbered 137. A handful of Sunni Muslims from Zanzibar established shops in Bagamoyo, some Parsees set up as merchants, and a small group of Catholic Goans was engaged in tailoring and retailing.

In 1888 the German East Africa Company signed a treaty with the Sultan of Zanzibar, Seyyid Khalifa, which allowed the company to collect customs duties along the coast. The Germans rapidly made their presence felt by ordering the Sultan's representative (the

Mangroves

Up and down the coast of East Africa you come across stretches of mangrove forest. Ecologically, these can be described as evergreen saline swamp forests, and their main constituents are the mangroves Rhizophora, Ceriops and Bruguiera. These are all described as viviparous, which means the seeds germinate or sprout when the fruits are still attached to the parent plant. Mangrove forests support a wide range of other plants and animals, including a huge range of birds, insects and fish.

Economically, mangrove forests are an important source of building poles, known on the coast as *boriti*, which were once exported in large quantities to the Arabian Gulf. Their main property is that they are resistant to termite attack. Mangrove bark is also used as a tanning material, and charcoal can be obtained from mangrove wood. As with so many natural resources in East Africa, care needs to be taken in the use of mangrove forests. Their over-exploitation could lead to the delicate balance that is found in the forests being upset, with serious consequences for these coastal regions.

Liwali) to lower the Sultan's flag; on being refused, they axed down the flag-pole. Later in the year a dispute between a member of the company and a townsman culminated in the latter being shot. The Usagara trading house of the company was besieged by irate townspeople, 200 troops landed from the *SS Moewe*, and over 100 local people were killed.

Further resentment was incurred when the Germans set about registering land and property, demanding proof of ownership. As this was impossible for most residents, there was widespread fear that property would be confiscated.

One of the diwans, Bomboma, organized local support and enlisted the help of Bushiri bin Salim al-Harthi, who had earlier led Arabs against the Germans in Tabora. Bushiri had initial success. Sections of Bagamoyo were burned and Bushiri mustered his troops in Nzole, about 6 km southwest of the town, ready for an assault. The German government now felt compelled to help the company; Hermann von Wissmann was appointed to lead an infantry force comprising Sudanese and Zulu troops. Admiral Denhardt, commanding the German naval forces, played for time by initiating negotiations with Bushiri, whose demands included being made governor of the region from Dar es Salaam up to Pangani, payment of 4000 rupees a month (about US$10,000 in present-day values), and the right to keep troops.

By May 1889 Wissmann had consolidated his forces and built a series of fortified block houses. He attacked Nzole, and Bushiri fled. The alliance of the diwans and Bushiri weakened, and, in June, the Germans retook Saadani, followed in July, by Pangani. Bushiri was captured and executed at Pangani in December. Bomboma, and another of the diwans leading the resistance, Marera, were also both executed, and other diwans were deposed and replaced by collaborators who had assisted the Germans.

It was now clear that the German government intended to extend their presence and, in October 1890, rights to the coast were formally purchased from the Sultan of Zanzibar for four million German marks.

In early 1891 German East Africa became a formal colony, but in April it was decided to establish Dar es Salaam as the capital. Commercial activity in Bagamoyo revived and, in the last decade of the century, rebuilding began, with the construction of new stone buildings including a customs house and the boma, which served as an administrative centre.

The caravan trade resumed, and there was a further influx of Indians, together with the arrival of Greeks who established a European hotel. William O'Swald, the Hamburg trading company, arrived, and the company Hansing established vanilla plantations at Kitopeni and Hurgira. An important Koran school was established in the town. Yet, despite these developments, Bagamoyo was destined for steady decline: its harbour was unsuitable for deep draught steamships and no branch of the railway was built to serve the port. The ending of German rule further reduced commercial presence in the town, and the last century saw Bagamoyo decline further, lacking even a sealed road to link it to Dar es Salaam. These days, thanks to the new tar road from Dar es Salaam, trade has improved considerably, and it's now easily reachable by tourists.

Bagamoyo

Where to stay 🛏
Badeco Beach **2**
Bagamoyo Beach Resort **3**
Kasiki Marine Camp **5**
Lazy Lagoon Island **6**

Livingstone Club **4**
Millennium Old Post
Office **8**
Millennium Sea Breeze
Resort **7**

Travellers' Lodge **1**

Old Bagamoyo

On the south approach to the town, on the road from Kaole, is the fully restored **Old Fort** (sometimes referred to as the Old Prison). It is the oldest surviving building in Bagamoyo having been started by Abdallah Marhabi around 1860, and extended and strengthened by Sultan Baghash after 1870, and then by the German colonialists. It was used as a police post until 1992. Initially, one of its functions was to hold slaves until they could be shipped to Zanzibar. It is said there is an underground passage through which the slaves were herded to dhows on the shore, although this passage is not apparent today. Since its restoration in 1992, it's a particularly handsome building: whitewashed, three storeys high, and with buttresses and battlements and an enclosed courtyard. For a small fee and if anyone's there, you should be able to go inside.

Off to the right on the path to Badeco Beach Hotel is the **German cemetery**, with some 20 graves dating from 1889/1890; most are Germans killed during the uprising led by Bushiri in those years (see page 82). There are also graves of two females: one a German nurse and one a German child who died six days after birth. A German deed of freedom for a slave is reproduced on a tree. The cemetery is well tended, surrounded by a coral wall. In the grounds of the **Badeco Beach Hotel** (see Where to stay, page 89) is the site of the tree reputedly used by the German administration for executions; it is marked by a plaque.

Continuing along India Street, on the left is an old two-storey building, **Liku House**, with an awning supported by slender iron columns and a central double door. This served as the first administrative headquarters for the Germans from 1888 until the boma was completed in 1897. German explorer Emin Pasha stayed there in 1889 and fell drunk from the balcony, which resulted in a fractured skull and six weeks in hospital. He was a member of Henry Morton Stanley's party. Today it's used as the District Commissioner's office.

The **German Boma** is a two-storey building topped by crenellations, constructed in a U-shape. There are pointed arches on the first floor and rounded arches on the ground floor. This was the German administrative centre and governor's residence from 1897. Unfortunately it's now no more than a ruin and needs urgent restoration. Until 1997 it served as the local District Commissioner's office but, after heavy rain during El Niño and after a long period of poor maintenance, the office had to be relocated as the balcony caved in under the weight of heavy water. Since then the roof has been stripped off by vandals.

On the shore side is a semi-circular levelled area on which was a monument with brass commemorative plaques erected by the Germans. With the fall of Bagamoyo to the British, the monument was razed and replaced with the present construction which commemorates the departure of Burton and Speke to Lake Tanganyika from nearby Kaole in 1857. The old German plaques have been reset in the walls which support the levelled area, on the shore side. To the left is an Arabic two-storey building fronted by six columns, a fretted veranda and curved arch windows, said to be the **Old Bagamoyo Tea House**. It is thought to be one of the oldest buildings in the town, constructed by Abdallah Marhabi in 1860 as a tea house, general store and hotel. Later, under the British, it was used as both a school and a bank. In front of the boma is the **Uhuru Monument**, celebrating Tanzania's Independence in 1961, and a derelict bandstand.

Continuing north along India Street there is a particularly fine residential house on the right, with columns and arched windows, just before Customs Road. This leads down to the **Customs House**, built in 1895 by Sewa Haji and rented to the Germans. It is a double-storey lime-washed building, with an open veranda on the first floor, buttresses and arched

Bagamoyo College of Arts

After Independence in 1961, the new Ministry of Culture founded the National Theatre Company and the National Dance Company. In 1980 the government broke up both groups in favour of the government-funded Bagamoyo College of Arts, also known as Taasisi ya Sanaa na Utamaduni Bagamoyo (TASUBA), which in Kiswahili means 'institute of art and culture'. It is a school for the arts where music, drama, dance and painting are taught, and is one of very few training institutions in Africa offering practical training in the arts. Most of the 40 or so students are Tanzanian, and only Africans are permitted to apply. Most of the training focuses on East African and Swahili culture, but several artists from Europe, America and the Far East attend seminars and events throughout the year. Students learn traditional drumming, dance, acting, sculpture, carving and painting, as well as instrument manufacture and stage management.

There's not much to see for most of the year, but you may see the students practising around the buildings and, on Friday and Saturday nights, there are occasional concerts or film evenings. The main thatched theatre unfortunately burnt down in 2003, but in 2008 the new theatre, financed by Sweden, Norway and the Tanzania government, opened; with 1800 seats, it is the largest theatre in East Africa. The annual six-day Bagamoyo Festival of Arts and Culture is held in the last week of September and focuses mainly on Tanzanian and East African music, dance and theatre. Music includes ngoma, afro jazz, bongo flava, reggae, African fusion and taarab.

For more information, contact Bagamoyo College of Arts, along the road to Kaole to the south of Bagamoyo, T023-244 0032, www.tasuba.ac.tz.

windows. It looks on to a walled courtyard and the beach, but many of the stone pillars on the beach side have collapsed. Opposite the Customs House are the ruins of the **Usagara Company Store**, built in 1888 with the arrival of the German commercial presence. The unusual construction had stone plinths on which were mounted cast-iron supports for the timber floor, raised to keep the stores dry. The cast-iron supports have cups surrounding them in which kerosene was poured to prevent rats climbing up to eat the stored grain.

Halfway down Customs Road is the covered **Fish Market**, with stone tables for gutting fish. When not used for this purpose, they are marked out with chalk so informal games like checkers can be played with bottle-tops. At the top of Customs Road, just before the intersection with India Street is the former **post office**, with a fine carved door and a blue-painted upstairs veranda; it is now the **Millennium Old Post Office Hotel** (see Where to stay, page 89). Further north along India Street is a series of Arabic buildings in various states of repair.

Continuing north, on the right, is the **Jama'at Khana**, the Ismaili mosque, which dates from 1880, double-storeyed with a veranda and carved doors. Behind the mosque on the beach side are some 150 tombs in the Ismaili Cemetery. On the right, beyond the mosque, is the **Bagamoyo District Hospital**, now part of Muhimbili Teaching Hospital in Dar es Salaam, which is based on the original Sewa Haji Hospital, constructed in 1895. On the death of Sewa Haji in 1896, the hospital was run by the Holy Ghost Mission and then, from 1912, by the Germans. The present hospital, where goats loll about in the covered walkways between the wards, has some handsome old buildings and some more modern blocks. In 2006 the roof of the original building was renovated.

At the northern end of the town on the right is a substantial **mosque** and Muslim school with curved steps up to the carved door, over which is a delicate fretted grill.

Close to the intersection of Sunda Road and Mongesani Street, at the western approach to the town, is the white **Block House**, constructed in 1889 by Hermann Wissman during the Bushiri uprising (see page 82). There is a mangrove pole and coral stone roof and an outside ladder, which enabled troops to man the roof behind the battlements. The walls have loopholes through which troops could fire, standing on low internal walls, which doubled as seating, to give them the height to fire down on their adversaries. Behind the Block House is a disused well.

The **slave track** to the interior departed from this point, a 1500-km trail that terminated at Ujiji on Lake Tanganyika. Off Caravan Street is the **Caravanserai**, a courtyard with single-storey buildings at the front and a square, two-storey building with a veranda at the centre (the corner of which is collapsing). This latter building was used for storing ivory and other precious commodities. It was here that preparations were made to fit out caravans to the interior, and it was believed to be surrounded by a large fenced area to hold livestock and temporary shelters for porters. The great explorers – Burton, Speke, Grant, Livingstone, etc – passed through here at various times in the latter half of the 1800s. Today it is the headquarters for the Bagamoyo Department of Antiquities.

North of the centre
Livingstone's Church This is a simple construction with a tin roof, curved arch windows and wooden benches. Its formal name is the Anglican Church of the Holy Cross. Above the entrance is the sign 'Through this door Dr David Livingstone passed', referring to the fact that his body was kept in the church prior to it being returned to England and buried in Westminster Abbey.

Cross by the Sea There's a monument in green marble surmounted by a cross on the path leading to the sea from Livingstone's Church. It marks the spot where, in 1868, Father Antoine Horner of the French Holy Ghost Fathers crossed from Zanzibar (where they had operated a mission since 1860) and stepped ashore to establish the first Christian church on the mainland.

Holy Ghost Mission Opposite the path to the Cross by the Sea is **Mango Tree Drive**, which was established in 1871 as the approach to the Mission. A statue of the Sacred Heart, erected in 1887, stands in front of the **Fathers' House**, which was begun in 1873 – the third storey finally added in 1903. In 1969 the building was taken over by MANTEP as a training centre for educational management.

Behind the Fathers' House is the **First Church**, construction of which started in 1872. It comprises a stone tower topped with arches with a cross at the centre and crosses on the pediments at each corner. The main building is a simple rectangular structure with a tin roof, unusually behind and to the side of the tower, so that the tower sits at one corner.

It was here on 24 February 1874 that the body of David Livingstone was brought by the missionary's African followers, Sisi and Chuma, who had carried their master 1500 km from Ujiji. Speke, Burton, Grant, Stanley, Peters, Emin Pasha and Wissmann all visited the church at one time or another.

Following the path to the right of the First Church is a cemetery where the early missionaries are buried. Further down this path is a small shrine built by freed slaves in 1876 with the sign 'Salamnus Maria' picked out in flowers. A great baobab tree, planted in

1868, stands to the side of the First Church. At the base can be seen the links of the chain where Mme de Chevalier, a mission nurse, tethered her donkey.

The **New Church**, constructed of coral blocks, begun in 1910 and completed in 1914, stands in front of the First Church. A small iron cross commemorates the centenary, in 1968, of the Holy Ghost Mission in Bagamoyo.

The **Mission Museum** is housed in the **Sisters' Building**. The displays present a history of Bagamoyo and there are relics and photographs from the slave period. One intriguing exhibit is the uniform, presented by HA Schmit in 1965, that he wore during the East African Campaign under von Lettow (see page 400). Adjacent to the museum is a **craft workshop**, with *Ufundi* ('craftsmen') picked out in flowers.

One of the main activities of the Holy Ghost Mission was to purchase slaves and present them with their freedom. A certificate of freedom was provided by the German authorities. These freed slaves had originally been captured hundreds of kilometres away in the hinterland, and the Mission undertook to rehabilitate them in **Freedom Village** just to the north of the main Mission buildings.

Kaole Ruins → Colour map 1, B5.

ⓘ 0800-1600. It is possible to walk around the ruins, but it's a good idea to take a guide for security, which should cost around US$3.

The Kaole Ruins are 5 km south of Bagamoyo, along the road past Taasisi ya Sanaa na Utamaduni Bagamoyo (TASUBA; Bagamoyo College of Arts; see box, page 85), on the coastal side of the present-day village of Kaole. The site consists of the ruins of two mosques and a series of about 30 tombs, set among palm trees. Some of the tombs have stone pillars up to 5 m high. The older of the two mosques ('A' on the site plan) dates from some time between the 13th and 15th century. The remains of a vaulted roof constructed from coral with lime mortar can be seen, which formed the *mbirika* at the entrance. Here ceremonial ablutions took place, taking water from the nearby well. There is some buttressing with steps that allowed the muezzin access to the roof to call the faithful to prayer. The recess (*kibula*) on the east side, nearest to Mecca, has faint traces of an inscription on the vaulting.

The stone pillars that mark some of the tombs were each surmounted by a stone 'turban', and the remains of some of these can be seen on the ground. Delicate porcelain bowls with light green glaze were set in the side of the pillars, and the indentations can be seen. The bowls, identified as celadon made in China in the 14th century and the main indication of the likely age of the structure, have been removed for safekeeping to the National Museum in Dar es Salaam. Some of the tombs have frames of dressed coral and weathered obituary inscriptions. Bodies would have been laid on the right side, with their faces towards Mecca.

Mosque 'B' is of later construction and has been partially restored. It is similar to the triple-domed mosque at Kilwa Kisiwani (see page 114) in style, and it is thought that the builder may well have been the same person.

The community that gave rise to these ruins would have been founded during the Muslim period, AD 622-1400. The first Muslim colonies were established from AD 740 by sea-borne migrations from the Persian Gulf down the East African coast as far as Sofala, the area round the Zambezi River. The settlement at Koale would have traded mangrove poles (see box, page 82), sandalwood, ebony and ivory. It is suggested that Koale might have had several hundred inhabitants. The dwellings would have used timber in their construction and would therefore have been less durable than the all-stone mosques and tombs. As they were on more fertile soil inland, they rapidly became overgrown when the dwellings collapsed. The settlement went into gradual decline as the shore became more densely packed with mangroves, making its use by dhows difficult, and commercial activity shifted to Bagamoyo.

Saadani National Park → *For listings, see pages 88-90. Colour map 1, B5.*

ⓘ *www.tanzaniaparks.com, 0630-1830, US$20, children (5-16) US$5, vehicle US$40.*
About 60 km north of Bagamoyo, Saadani was gazetted as a National Park in 2005 and is the only national park in East Africa with ocean frontage. Some of the animals come down to the beach, especially in the early morning, and you may be lucky enough to see vervet monkeys or elephants frolicking in the sand (on a handful of occasions both have been seen venturing into the crashing surf). This makes Saadani one of the more special parks to visit in Tanzania. Its boundaries have been expanded to include land north of the Mligaji River, which contains the only permanent elephant population in the area, as well as sable antelope. It also incorporates the Zaraninge forest, noted for its variety of indigenous vegetation and animal and birdlife, and land south of the Wami river. The total protected area now covers over 1100 sq km, with the park headquarters based at Mkwaja Ranch. It has plentiful game, including giraffe, hartebeest, waterbuck, wildebeest, eland, buffalo, hippo, crocodile, reedbuck, black and white colobus monkey and warthog. Also present, but harder to see, are lion, leopard, elephant, sable antelope, greater kudu and the Beisa oryx. To the north of the reserve is a green turtle-breeding beach and here, **A Tent With a View Safari Lodge** (see page 90) has started its own turtle hatchery to help conserve this endangered species. A particular highlight is the thousands of flamingos found in the salt marshes in the Wami River estuary. There is also an extensive range of bush, river and sea birds.

Arriving in Saadani National Park
Generally, the park is accessible all year round, but the access roads are sometimes impassable during April and May. The best game viewing is in January and February and from June to August. **Coastal Air** will stop here on request between Zanzibar and Dar es Salaam, and charter flights can also be arranged. Although its only 60 km north of Bagamoyo, you can't get directly to the park from there by road, as there is no crossing over the Wami River. Instead, you have to drive on the inland road from Dar via Chalinze and Msata and turn right at Mandera, which is 60 km from the village of Saadani. This is roughly a 200-km drive from Dar and takes about 4½ hours. From the north, Saadani is 35 km south of the ferry at Pangani but a 4WD is needed for the sandy track. The lodges operate shuttles from Dar for about US$75 each way.

⊚ Bagamoyo listings

For sleeping and eating price codes and other relevant information, see pages 22-26.

⊛ Where to stay

Bagamoyo *p80, map p83*
Bagamoyo has a splendid, curved, palm-fringed beach, though often the sea is too rough for swimming. There are a few beach resorts around town but some are becoming rather faded and thus overpriced. It seems a lot was expected of Bagamoyo's tourism when these huge resorts were built a few years ago but they rarely have more than a handful of guests and, as a result, with a couple of exceptions, service and standards have slipped considerably. Some offer full-board package rates.
$$$$-$$$ Lazy Lagoon Island, private luxury island 2 km off the coast, a 20-min

boat ride across the water from a jetty close to Mbegani Fisheries (a private airstrip is nearby), 8 km east of Bagamoyo, reservations **Foxes Safari Camps**, Dar, T0784-237 422, www.tanzaniasafaris.info. A beautiful thatch-and-wood construction on a perfect swathe of beach, 12 bandas with en suite bathrooms, swimming pool, spacious lounge and restaurant area, linked to the rooms by a nature trail through the indigenous forest. Price includes all meals, seafood is a speciality, and dining is outside with an exceptional view of the lights of Bagamoyo in the distance. Snorkelling, kayaking, windsurfing and sailing, fishing and boat trips cost extra.

\$\$\$ Millennium Old Post Office Hotel, corner of India St and Customs Rd, T023-244 0201/3, www.millennium.co.tz. Owned by the same company as the **Sea Breeze**, below, and with the same contact details, this is a neat option in the converted Bagamoyo 19th-century post office. It has 5 upstairs rooms with cool tiled floors, Zanzibari beds, satellite TV, a/c and fridge, but, while it is a beautiful building, the interior sadly hasn't been refurbished in the style of the historic building. Furthermore, it's not on the beach and can be noisy. The downstairs post office hall is now the bar, restaurant and reception. Doubles from US\$120.

\$\$\$ Millennium Sea Breeze Resort, adjacent to the **Bagamoyo College of Arts**, T023-244 0201/3, www.millennium.co.tz. Accommodation in attractive double-storey thatched rondavaals, with wrought-iron staircases, satellite TV and minibar, but decor is starting to look rather faded. Set in pleasant grounds, though, with a swimming pool, extensive buffets for lunch and dinner, and 2 bars. Dhow trips available. Full- and half-board rates available.

\$\$\$-\$\$ Kasiki Marine Camp, approximately 7 km east of Bagamoyo along the road to Dar es Salaam, T0744-278 590, www.bagamoyo.org/kasiki.htm. Quiet resort with 6 simple bungalows, the price includes breakfast (US\$56), or there's full-board

accommodation at twice the cost (US\$108). The restaurant specializes in Italian cuisine and you can buy items such as home-made pesto from the Italian chef. Can organize boat trips, and there are massages on offer.

\$\$\$-\$\$ Livingstone Club, 2 km to the north of town, T023-244 0059, www.livingstone.ws. Fairly new complex, with 40 a/c rooms with fridge and minibar in 10 brick cottages with thatched roofs in lovely gardens. The restaurant has an international menu. Facilities include a swimming pool, tennis courts, watersports, and it is possible to arrange local excursions. Rates for a double with breakfast start at US\$95, or there are half- of full-board rates.

\$\$-\$ Bagamoyo Beach Resort, at the north end of town, continue along India St, T023-244 0083, www.bagamoyo.org/bagbeach.htm. Another good option with French management, 18 a/c and traditional-style rooms, with thatched roofs, a/c and hot water, set in pretty gardens facing the ocean. Given the French influence, the food is exceptional, plus there's a pleasant open-air bar with thatched roof overlooking the beach. Sports facilities include wind-surfing, snorkelling, mini-golf and volleyball, and there's a pool. Doubles from US\$65, or you can camp for US\$8 per person.

\$\$-\$ Travellers' Lodge, at north end of town on India St, T023-244 0077, www.travellers-lodge.com. The best mid-range option, with friendly German management and good-value, traditional thatched self-contained bungalows with a/c or fans, all built out of local materials. Excellent bar, restaurant serving plenty of seafood and watersports. Doubles from US\$75, and camping is available in the grounds (US\$10 per person).

\$ Badeco Beach Hotel, off India street near the German Cemetery, T023-244 0018, www.badecobeachhotel.com. A simple German-run resort that has been around for many years, good location and handy for the sights but on the rather scruffy and busy town beach. The rooms are in faded thatched cottages, with restaurant and bar, cheap from US$25 for a double. The shady campsite has reasonable ablutions and a basic kitchen shelter; camping at U$12 per tent includes a basic cold breakfast.

Saadani National Park p88
$$$$ Saadani Safari Lodge, 1 km north of Saadani Village, reservations, Dar T022-277 3294, www.saadanilodge.com. Nestled among palms and spread across the beach, the 9 attractive cottages here have makuti thatch roofs, wooden floors and sailcloth walls, and the spacious bathrooms have solar-heated hot water. Behind is a hide overlooking a waterhole where you can be served tea and cake, and a fire is lit on the beach for drinks before dinner. Activities include game drives, fishing and boat rides on the Wami River, and snorkelling in the ocean.
$$$$ A Tent with a View, about 30 km north of Saadani Village, reservations Dar, T022-211 0507, www.saadani.com. This has 8 tented bandas with en suite bathrooms, elegantly perched on stilts individually spaced out along the beach, and large balconies with hammocks, decorated in bright colours. There are another 2 units at beach level. Activities include walking safaris through the bush and on the beach, birdwatching by canoe on the Mafue River, and game drives and a boat safari on the Wami River. A cultural tour offers an opportunity to meet the local fishing community in Saadani Village. There are 2 rates: US$195 per person per night sharing full board, with the option of paying for activities separately depending on what you want to do, or US$295 per person per night sharing, including all safari activities and park entry fees.
$$$ Kisampa, just on the edge of the southeastern boundary of the park on the banks of the Wami River, access is by road transfer to the river and then a canoe crossing, or by charter flight, reservations,

Dar T0769-204 159, www.afrikaafrikasafaris. com. A small eco-friendly camp with compost toilets and bush 'bladder' showers hanging from trees, with 6 spacious cottages with furnishings made from natural materials and verandas with hammocks, extra tents can be put up for children. Good set meals – they make their own bread and produce their own honey. Activities include game drives into Saadani, bush walks, village visits, fishing and canoeing on the river.

❼ Restaurants

Bagamoyo p80, map p83
For restaurants and bars, the hotels are your best bet, but there are some snack bars near the covered market on Caravan St.

❾ Shopping

Bagamoyo p80, map p83
There are some small general and pharmacy stores on School St. The covered market on Caravan St is excellent for fruit, vegetables, meat and dried fish. Fresh fish can be found at the fish market on Customs Rd. Some of the larger resorts have (tacky) curio shops.

❿ Transport

Bagamoyo p80, map p83
Dala-dala
Several *dala-dalas* a day leave from the bus stand opposite the covered market on Caravan St. A journey to **Dar** costs US$2 and takes 1-2 hrs, swap vehicles in Mwenge.

⓭ Directory

Bagamoyo p80, map p83
Medical services Bagamoyo District Hospital, India St, T023-244 0008.
Police Intersection of Caravan St and Boma St at south end of town, T023-244 0026.

Tanga and around

Tanga, Tanzania's second biggest seaport, is an attractive place with a sleepy ambience and many fine German and Asian buildings in its centre. It has a natural deep-water harbour and was briefly the German colonial capital, following the treaty between the Sultan of Zanzibar and the German East Africa Company. Much of its wealth came from the sisal plantations in the hinterland but, with the advent of alternative rope-making fibres, this industry has fallen into decline, adversely affecting the region. Nearby places of interest include the enormous Amboni limestone caves, the Shirazi ruins at Tongoni, dating from the 10th century, and offshore coral gardens, consisting of three reefs: Mwamba Wamba, Mwamba Shundo and Fungu Nyama. The Usambara Mountains are worth a detour; Lushoto and Amani can be visited either on the way to Tanga, or when travelling to Kilimanjaro and Arusha, and Pangani, on the coast south of Tanga, makes for a decent beach-holiday destination. ▸▸ For listings, see pages 99-104.

Tanga → *For listings, see pages 99-104. Colour map 1, B5. Phone code: 027. Altitude: sea level. Population: 24,400. 5°5'S 39°2'E.*

The centre of Tanga (meaning 'sail' in Kiswahili) is a congested grid of roads centred around the bustling market. The buildings along Market Street are old and traffic-stained, but the street is a hive of activity of small traders, food kiosks and women carrying bunches of vegetables. There are a number of interesting colonial buildings around Market Street and Independence Avenue. Most are in a poor state of repair, but it's a relaxing and easy walk around the tree-lined streets, and it's easy to imagine that Tanga was very grand in its heyday. It's a very friendly place, where men on bicycles bumping in and out of the potholes will take the time to say *'jambo'*. Further out of town on Hospital Road towards the Yacht Club, are the quieter and sedate leafy suburbs of the more upmarket residential area, where the large houses look out into the bay from a hill. There are good views to uninhabited Toten Island out in the bay, especially when the tide is low and the yellow sandstone cliffs of the island are exposed.

Arriving in Tanga

Getting there There are scheduled air services between Tanga and Dar es Salaam, Pemba and Zanzibar. Bus services take four to six hours to cover the 460 km from Dar es Salaam via Chalinze and Segera (the junction on the Dar–Moshi road), where the branch road to Tanga veers off to the right. There are also services from Moshi to Tanga, 360 km. *Dala-dalas* take one to three hours between Tanga and the Kenyan border and there is also the option of getting the **Scandinavia Express** bus from Mombasa to Tanga, which then goes on to Dar. There is presently not the option of driving between Dar and Tanga on the coast road, as there is no crossing on the Wami River, but in a 4WD it is possible to drive from Saadini National Park up to Tanga via Pangani, having got to Saadini from Dar via Mandera first (see page 88). In the past there have been ferry services between Tanga and Zanzibar and Pemba. However, tragically, the *MV Spice Islander* that used to serve this popular route capsized in 2011 in the Pemba Channel, and more than 200 lives were lost. It is, however, possible to organize motorboat transfers from the beach resorts in Pangani south of Tanga (see page 96) to Zanzibar. ▸▸ *For further details, see Transport, page 103.*

Getting around Taxis, buses and *dala-dalas* can be found in Uhuru Park. However, most of Tanga is within walking distance. Taxis are advisable after dark. Bikes can be hired at several places; try around the bus stand or wherever there is a row of bikes lined up on the side of the street. You can organize tours through the **Tanga Youth Development Association (TAYODEA)**, an organization that is well worth supporting as it employs disadvantaged young local people as guides and 30% of fees taken from tourists go into community projects. For more information on the tours they offer, see What to do, page 103.

Background

Carl Peters and the German East Africa Company arrived in 1885 and, in 1888, leased a 16-km-wide strip from the Sultan of Zanzibar along the entire coast of what is now Tanzania, between the Ruvuma and the Umba rivers. The Germans appointed agents (calling them *akidas*), though they were often not of the same tribe as the people they administered, to collect taxes and enforce law and order.

With the advent of European settlement and trade, Somalis arrived, trading in cattle but seldom intermarrying. Islanders from the Comoros also settled around Tanga.

Agriculture in the Usambara area (see page 203) expanded and, with the construction of the railway to Moshi, Tanga became a flourishing port. Tanga was the site of a substantial reversal for the British during the First World War. Allied troops, including 8000 Indian soldiers, found it difficult to disembark through the mangrove swamps and were repulsed by the well-organized German defence and some hostile swarms of bees that spread panic among the attackers. Over 800 were killed and 500 wounded, and the British abandoned substantial quantities of arms and supplies on their withdrawal.

After the eventual German withdrawal from Tanga, the German population was steadily replaced by Greek plantation owners. Tanga's prosperity declined with the collapse in sisal prices in the late 1950s, and the large estates were nationalized in 1967. Some have now been privatized, and sisal has made a modest recovery.

The African groups in the Tanga area, excluding those in the coastal belt, number six. The **Pare**, who now live in the Pare Hills, came originally from the Taveta area of Kenya in the 18th century. The **Zigua** inhabited the area south of Tanga and have a reputation for aggression: Bwana Heri attacked and defeated the force of the Sultan of Zanzibar in 1882. The **Nguu** clan to the west occupy the Nguu Hills, and the **Ruvu** clan inhabit the Pangani islands. The **Shambaa** are around the Lushoto area and are closely allied with the **Bondei**, who occupy the area between Tanga and Pangani.

Places in Tanga

The open space in the centre of town is **Uhuru Park**, originally named Selous Square after the celebrated naturalist and hunter (see box, page 361). At the junction of the square with Eukenforde Street are the German buildings of **Tanga School**, the first educational establishment for Africans in Tanzania.

On Market Street to the east of Uhuru Park is **Planters Hotel**. This once grand wooden building is now virtually derelict, but reputed to have seen wild times, when Greek sisal plantation owners came into town for marathon gambling sessions at which whole estates sometimes changed hands. It was an ornate building, with arches, columns and plinths. The ground floor had a bar, with a huge antique corner cabinet full of miniatures.

Proceeding north across Independence Avenue brings you to the **Tanga Library**, originally the King George VI Library. The west wing was opened in 1956 and the east wing in 1958 by the then governor, Sir Edward Twining. There is a courtyard behind with cloisters and Moorish arches. To the west is the **Old Boma**, a substantial structure in typical style. Opposite the boma is a building from the German period with keyhole-style balustrades. Further to the west down Mombasa Road leading down to the shore is **St Anthony's Cathedral**, a modern 1960s octagonal building with a free-standing bell tower, a school and various mission buildings. On Boma Road is a small, white **Greek Orthodox church**.

Following Independence Avenue back east you reach the **clock tower** and the **post office**. To the west of the clock tower is the German Monument in marble, decorated with an eagle and oak leaves, dedicated to the 18 who died in 1889 during the Arab Revolt led by Bushiri (see page 82) and listing the five German naval vessels, under the command of Admiral Denhart, that supported Major Hermann Wissmann on the ground.

Just to the east of the clock tower are some ruins thought to be part of the fortifications built during the First World War. On the corner of Independence Avenue and Usambara Street is the **Old Court House**, dating from the German period. Today it has been fully restored and serves as the Tanga Medical Hospital. It is a fine, double-fronted building with a Mangalore-tiled roof, offices on the mezzanine level, a fluted façade and fretwork over the windows.

The **German Cemetery** is on Swahili Street and contains the graves of 16 Germans and 48 Askaris killed in the action of 4-5 November 1914. One of the Askaris is listed as *sakarini* ('crazy drunk'). Also buried here is Mathilde Margarethe Scheel (1902-1987), known as 'Mama Askari', who looked after the welfare interests of the African soldiers of the *Schutztruppe* (see box, page 401) after Tanganyika became a British protectorate. Crossing over the railway line along Hospital Road to Ocean Drive is the old Tanga Club of the British period. Further east of the centre, the **Bombo Hospital** is a handsome German building, with a three-storey central block, a first-floor veranda overlooking the ocean, a Mangalore-tiled roof and a gatehouse.

Tanga

200 metres
200 yards

Where to stay 🛏
Inn by the Sea 6
Kola Prieto 3
Mkonge 2

Ocean Breeze 5
Panori 1
Raskazone 8
Tanga Beach Resort 4

Restaurants 🍴
Food Palace 3
Patwas 1
Yacht Club 2

Around Tanga

Toten Island

You can arrange a boat trip out to Toten Island, which faces the town in the bay about 1 km offshore. It's very overgrown, though, and surrounded by mangroves, so it's best to go at low tide when access to the beach is easier. Though they are difficult to find, there are ruins of two 15th-century mosques and some German graves here; hence its name – Toten means 'the dead' in German. **TAYODEA** (see page 103) can organize a small motorboat to get you there and back for about US$30 per group, and the full guided tour lasts about four hours.

Amboni Caves → *Colour map 1, B5.*

ⓘ *0900-1600, US$3. The caves are 8 km to the north of Tanga on the road to Horo Horo at the Kenyan border. They are badly signposted. The best way to get there is to cycle. It's a good way to meet the local people, the birds are numerous and you might spot a dikdik. Bikes can be hired in town for about US$1 per hr. Tours can be arranged through TAYODEA (see page 103), whose guides will cycle with you to the caves for US$25 per person including bikes, entry fees, lunch and sodas. Before entering the mouth of the cave you are required to write your name in the official record book, which is kept in the tour guide's office. All visitors entering the caves are recorded in case someone becomes lost. Take a powerful torch and go in pairs with a guide. There have been fatalities when people have explored the caves alone.*

Formed during the Jurassic Age some 150 million years ago, when reptiles were dominant on land, these natural limestone caves extend over a wide area, lying mostly underground and accessed through openings in the gorges of the Mkilumizi River and the Sisi River. They form the most extensive cave system in East Africa (estimated at over 230 sq km). There are chambers up to 13 m high, with stalactites and stalagmites. A German-Turkish survey in 1994 found that there are 10 separate cave systems, and the longest cave is 900 m. Only one of the caves is used for guided tours.

The location is of great religious significance to local people, and offerings to ensure fertility are made in one of the shrines. There are many legends associated with the caves, including beliefs that they form a 400-km underground passage to the foothills of Mount Kilimanjaro. The main cave, known as *Mabavu*, is said to be the home of the Snake God. The Digo people were reputed to dispose of unwanted albino babies in a section of the caves known as the Lake of No Return. The caves were also used by the Mau Mau as a refuge during the troubles in Kenya. A guide will escort you round the caves, illuminating the chamber with a burning torch. The caves are home to many thousands of bats (called *popo* in Kiswahili) – watching the 'popo flight', when the bats fly out of the cave entrance at sunset, is popular.

On the way back to Tanga you can stop at the **Galamos Sulphur Springs**, 3 km from the caves off the Tanga–Mombasa road. Discovered by a local Greek sisal planter, Christos Galamos, the springs are hot and sulphurous and are said to relieve arthritis and cure skin ailments. A small spa was erected, but it has now fallen into disrepair. It is still possible to bathe in the springs, however but they are very smelly and muddy underfoot. From Amboni Village, the guide will take you to the Ziggi River. Here, children will look after your bicycles and you can pay a small fee to cross the river by canoe. The springs are on the other side.

Tongoni Ruins → *Colour map 1, B5.*

ⓘ *18 km south of Tanga on the road to Pangani, about 1 km off the road. 0900-1600, US$2 if the caretaker is there to collect the fee. Buses or dala-dala from Tanga cost about US$1 and will take up to 1 hr. A return taxi will cost about US$10-12; ask the driver to wait for you.*

The legend of the Shirazi migration

Ali ben Sultan Hasan of Shiraz in Persia (now Iran) had a dream in AD 975 in which a rat with jaws of iron devoured the foundations of his house. He took this as a sign that his community was to be destroyed. The court in Shiraz ridiculed the notion but his immediate family and some other followers resolved to migrate. They set out in seven dhows from the nearby port of Bushehr and sailed through the mouth of the Persian Gulf, into the Indian Ocean. There they were caught in a great storm and separated, making landfalls at seven different points on the East African coast where they settled. Among these were Tongoni, Kilwa, and the islands of Zanzibar, Pemba, and Tumbatu in present-day Tanzania.

The Tongoni Ruins date from the Shirazi period (see box, above), and the settlement was started at the end of the 10th century. The community would have been similar to that at Kaole (see page 87), but it was almost certainly larger. There are 40 tombs, some with pillars, and the remains of a substantial mosque. The mosque is of the type found along the north part of the East African coast. There is a central *musalla* (prayer room) with arches leading to aisles (*ribati*) at each side. The mosque is constructed of particularly finely dressed, close-grained coral, especially on the lintel of the *kibula*, the side of the building that faces towards Mecca. The roofs were coral on mangrove rafters. There are depressions in the pillars where there were porcelain bowls, all apparently removed during the German period. It is said that Tongoni was founded by Ali ben Sultan Hasan at much the same time as he established the settlement at Kilwa (see page 112). There are Persian inscriptions at Tongoni that would seem to establish a link with Shiraz. Vasco de Gamma visited the settlement in 1498. Again **TAYODEA** (see page 103) runs four-hour guided tours out here by car for US$30 per person.

Amani Nature Reserve → *For listings, see pages 99–104.*

The Amani Nature Reserve, part of the Eastern Usambara Mountains, is 25 km from Muheza on a dirt road that most of the year requires a 4WD vehicle, as it is steep and winding in places.

Arriving in the reserve
To get there, you will need to make a connection at Muheza on the road linking Tanga to the Dar es Salaam to Moshi highway. There is a bus that leaves Muheza at around 1400 daily for the 25-km trip to Amani, which takes about an hour and costs US$1. In the mornings the bus leaves Amani when full, usually around 0800. The reserve charges a one-off fee of US$30 per adult, US$5 children (under 16), and a US$10 fee for photography.

A sprawling, bustling town, 35 km west of Tanga along a good road, Muheza provides a link between the coastal beaches and the lush, cool Usambara Mountains. Access to the Amani Nature Reserve is from here (see below) and, although it's part of the Usambara Mountains, which are dealt with in the North to Kilimanjaro chapter (see page 203), Amani is in the eastern mountains and accessed from the Tanga side. **Scandinavia Express** buses stop here en route between Dar and Tanga and Mombasa, but accommodation is very primitive and there are better options in either Tanga, Korogwe to the west, or Amani.

Background

In 1898, the Germans established an agricultural research institute here that was the envy of Africa. With the twin benefits of the north railway from Tanga to Moshi and the Amani Institute, the Usambara area flourished under settler farming. By 1914, 40,000 ha were under sisal, 80,000 ha under rubber and 14,000 ha under cotton; there were also extensive areas of tobacco, sugar, wheat and maize. One of the great lessons of farming in Africa is that crops have to be carefully adapted to local conditions. Amani Institute tested soils, experimented with insecticides and developed new varieties. After 1914, Amani turned its hand to the war effort, developing a local quinine for use against malaria from cinchona bark and manufacturing chocolate, tooth-powder, soap and castor oil.

In 1997 the Nature Reserve was established to protect the biodiversity of the flora and fauna of the sub-montane rainforests of the East Usambara Mountains. This joint venture of the Tanzanian and Finnish governments seeks to protect an area whose biological significance in terms of plant and animal diversity has been compared to the Galapagos Islands. There are, for instance, three endemic bird species: the Usambara alethe, Naduk eagle owl and the Usambara weaver. The rainforests also provide the water supply for 220,000 people in Tanga.

Visiting the reserve

The total area of the Amani Nature Reserve is 8380 ha, which includes 1065 ha of forests owned by private tea companies under the management of the **East Usambara Tea Company**. It also includes the **Amani Botanical Garden**, established in 1902, which has over 460 plant species and is one of the largest botanical gardens in Africa. Amani also has a medical research centre run by the Tanzanian government. Birdlife and small animals such as monkeys abound. It is excellent hiking country.

The reserve's **information centre** is housed in the recently rehabilitated old German Station Master's house (there was a short railway line here, built in 1911 but abandoned in 1924) in the small settlement of **Sigi**, which is also the entrance gate to the reserve. A small resthouse has also been constructed nearby. The **East Usambara Catchment Forest Project** has made efforts to strengthen the villagers' rights to manage their own forests, and pilot farm forestry activities have been set up in a number of villages in an effort to improve local land husbandry. A dozen forest trails have been established, including three driving routes. The **East Usambara Conservation Area Management Programme** created and maintains the nature trails, as well as training guides in an effort to encourage village collaboration and conservation efforts. Short or long walks can be arranged, and the guides are very knowledgeable about local species, bird and insect life and the uses of traditional plants.

Pangani → For listings, see pages 99-104. Colour map 1, B5. Phone code: 027. 5° 25' S, 38° 58' E.

Pangani Village, 52 km south of Tanga, is located at the point where the Pangani River empties itself into the Indian Ocean. The river passes through the north side of the village, separating the old buildings and the present-day market from the farms and small houses on the south side. The river itself has a car and passenger ferry that runs from early morning to 1800. There are some handsome old Arab houses in town, though these are in poor repair. Around Pangani there are some excellent beaches. There has recently been a mushrooming of resorts, similar to those on the north coast of Zanzibar, with thatched cottages, laid-back rustic bars and restaurants serving fragrant Swahili seafood, and, increasingly, a good choice of watersports. None of them are in the super luxury category

Tanzania's 'White Gold'

Sisal (*Agave sisalana*) is a stiff, spiky plant that looks a bit like a yucca and is used to make rope, twine and sacks (and an exceptionally little known fact – dartboards). It's strong enough to make ropes big enough to moor large ships. It is grown in many places in Tanzania and is an important export crop. It was introduced in 1882 on estates around Pangani by Dr Richard Hindroph, who imported 1000 plants from Florida. Only 62 survived the voyage via Hamburg but from such a small nucleus, the plant flourished in Tanzania's favourable climate. By 1913, Tanzania was the biggest producer of sisal in the world,

and it became known as the 'white gold' of Tanzania. Much of it went to the German Navy during the First World War, as heavy duty rope to secure battleships. The industry flourished until the 1960s, when nationalization of the economy and the replacement of natural fibres by synthetic fibres sent the industry into decline. Nevertheless, it's recovered significantly since the 1990s, as the worldwide use of natural fibres is becoming popular again, and investment has meant that there has been some exploration into new uses for sisal, including making cloth, paper, bricks and roof tiles from it.

but instead are friendly and informal retreats for mid-range and budget travellers. When choosing where to stay, bear in mind that while the resorts to the north of town are more than adequate, most are on cliff tops from where it is a short walk to the beach, and much of the surrounding landscape is made up of sisal plantations.

Ushongo Beach, to the south of town, is glorious – a long swathe of white sand backed by towering coconut palms. It's possible to swim even in low tide in water that averages around 25°C and, when the tide does go out, it's possible to cycle along the smooth sand on the edge of the surf. In the afternoons you will be greeted by the delightful sight of school children walking home along the beach. This is one of Tanzania's best kept secrets and makes a fine and more peaceful alternative to Zanzibar or the Kenyan coast for a beach holiday away from mass tourism. Another great advantage of visiting Pangani is the unbelievably friendly and helpful **Pangani Cultural Tourism Programme**, which can organize a vast range of tours and activities in the region, most of which involve interaction with the local community.

Arriving in Pangani

The approach to Pangani is along the unpaved road from Tanga. The road is fine in the dry season but becomes slippery in the wet. Much of it passes through a vast sisal plantation. There are regular buses from Tanga until about 1400, which take about two hours (depending on the season) and cost US$1.50. It is only 52 km but the road is very bumpy. The bus will drop off outside the beach resorts between Tanga and Pangani. None of them are more than 1 km off the road. Once in Pangani, an option for budget travellers is to stay in cheap accommodation in town and hire a bike from places at the bus stand, take the ferry across the river and cycle to one of the beach resorts south of town for lunch and to enjoy the beach. If you get back too late for the ferry, which stops at 1800, you can try and negotiate with a local boatman to take you across. Bring cash with you from Tanga; although there is a bank in Pangani, it doesn't change money and has no ATM. This has caused problems for travellers before, who have had to return to Tanga and then go back to Pangani to pay for hotels. Be aware, as in other places in Tanzania, it's fine to wear bikinis and shorts on the beach, but in town it's important to cover up so as not to offend the Muslim community.

Background

Swahili for 'distribute' or 'arrange', it comes as no surprise that Pangani was one of the earliest ports established by the Arab settlers. A prosperous port during the 19th century, the community was ruled by an Arab Liwali, five Shirazi Jumbes and a network of *akidas*. Indian traders financed parties under *akidas* to collect ivory and rhinoceros horn in the interior, and there was some trading in slaves. The town prospered as the trade in ivory and slaves flourished. It was at Pangani that Bushiri, leader of the Arab revolt of 1888-1889, was finally captured and executed (see page 82).

The mouth of the Pangani River is crossed by a sand bar. This provided shelter for dhows, and prevented them from being pursued by steam vessels when the slave trade was being suppressed after 1873. However, it also meant that vessels of deeper draught could not use the port. Traffic drifted steadily to the newer facilities at Tanga, subsequently accelerated by the railway linking Tanga to Dar es Salaam and Moshi.

In 1930 the population was around 1500 but the substantial houses on the north side of the river, built largely by slave labour, have since fallen into disrepair. In the early 20th century, the economy of the town shifted to reliance on the sisal plantations, but the price of sisal fell drastically with the advent of synthetic fibres in the mid-1960s (see box, page 97). There are still many coco-palms and some fishing.

Places in Pangani

The old **Customs House**, originally built in 1916 as the post office, and the old **CCM Building** are both fine structures, unfortunately in poor repair. Next to the Customs House is the old slave depot, built around 1850 and still largely intact, with some characteristic carved doors and the remnants of whipping posts. It is also thought that there are underground tunnels and pits that lead to the river, along which weak slaves were taken to be washed out to sea. Just by the ferry is a plaque recording the capture of Pangani by the British on 23 July 1916, and the **Uhuru** or **Jamhuri Monument**, celebrating Independence. The **Boma** is also a handsome building. Built in 1810, it is said that slaves were buried alive to strengthen the foundations. The distinctive roof was added in the German period. It is now the District Commissioner's Office but some of the original carved doors remain.

Across the river by ferry (US$0.30, US$2.50 cars) is the village of **Bweni**. From the hill behind the village are fine views of Pangani and of the Indian Ocean. It is possible to hire a boat, through the **Pangani Cultural Tourism Programme** (see What to do, page 103), to travel up the river for around two hours (around US$25-35 for a boat taking up to eight people). There are many birds, best seen at dusk, and crocodiles further upstream. You will also see local fishermen in dugout canoes and vast coconut plantations beside the river. Men climb the trees to collect coconuts or the sap from cut branches – used to make *mnazi*, an alcoholic drink.

Mkoma Bay

This is a tranquil area about 3 km north of Pangani on the road to Tanga. There are several places to stay, all set in attractive, well-kept gardens with good sea views at the edge of a small cliff. Steps lead down to the beach, which is quiet but a little rocky in places and does not have the brilliant white sands found elsewhere. Along the coral shoreline, in the area known as Mkomo and Mwanaunguja, the fossilized remains of dinosaurs have been found, estimated to be 200-300 million years old.

Border crossing: Tanzania–Kenya

Lunga Lunga

The Lunga Lunga border is on the A14, 61 km north of Tanga and 106 km south of Mombasa, and is open 24 hours. While unpaved in places, the road is reasonable. Formalities at the border are fairly efficient, and visas for Tanzania and Kenya can be purchased. Remember you can go into Kenya and return to Tanzania on the same visa, if it's still valid, without paying for a new one. You'll also need to produce a yellow fever vaccination certificate to enter Kenya from Tanzania. The nearest banks (with ATMs) are at Ukunda (the turn-off to Diani Beach, 92 km north of the border) in Kenya, and Tanga in Tanzania. There are through buses from Tanga to Mombasa with Scandinavia Express that leave daily at 1315, take four hours and cost US$7. In the opposite direction, buses leave Mombasa at 0800 and arrive in Tanga at 1200. Very usefully, these drop off at Ukunda at the turn-off to Diani Beach, where there are taxis and tuk-tuks to take you on to the beach resorts.

Diani Beach is the most popular tourist beach in Kenya with about 20 km of dazzling white sand, coconut trees, clear sea and a coral reef that is exposed at low tide. It has a whole string of hotels – from large all-inclusive resorts to simple beach cottages – linked by a coast road with restaurants, dive schools, shopping centres and a golf course. See *Footprint Kenya Handbook*.

Maziwe Marine Park

About 8 km off the coast of Pangani, Maziwe Island is incorporated in the Maziwe Marine Park. It used to harbour mangrove forests and causarina trees, but it was partly submerged in 1978-1979 due to erosion resulting mainly from clearance of the island's vegetation cover. It also used to be a nesting site for green turtles (which are still commonly seen at the surrounding reef) but, because the island is now sometimes completely covered in water at high tide, there is a danger of them being washed away. Any turtle eggs found on the island are removed to a site on Ushongo Beach. Today, the highlight is snorkelling off the offshore reefs, although the quality can be disappointing in the rainy seasons when the water is not clear. Over 200 species of fish, 35 genera of coral (soft and hard) and a number of sea-grasses, algae and sponges are found in and around the reserve. Boats can be arranged through the resorts.

⊙ Tanga and around listings

For sleeping and eating price codes and other relevant information, see pages 22-26.

⊖ Where to stay

Tanga *p91, map p93*
$$$ Tanga Beach Resort, Karume Rd, about 2 km east of town on the seafront, T027-264 5424, www.tangabeachresort.com. Opened in 2009, this is the best and most modern hotel in Tanga, with 46 well-furnished a/c rooms, Wi-Fi, satellite TV and smart bathrooms, some have balconies and sea views. There are 2 restaurants, 2 bars, a very large swimming pool, spacious lawned gardens and large car park. Day trips to the Amboni Caves and boat rides to Toten Island can be organized, as well as pick up from the airport. Doubles from US$130.
$$ Mkonge Hotel is about 1 km east from the centre along Hospital Rd, which leads into Ocean Dr, T027-264 3440, www.mkongehotel.com. Set in grounds by the sea, in what was originally the HQ of a sisal company built

in 1951, this has excellent service. There are lovely views over the bay and vervet monkeys play in the gardens. The 48 rooms have a/c and satellite TV and start from a very reasonable US$80, and there's a good bar and restaurant and a swimming pool. It's worth coming here just to eat in the lovely surroundings (see Restaurants, page 102).

$$-$ Panori Hotel, east of the centre, south of Hospital Rd, in a quiet area beyond the Yacht Club and the other hotels, T027-264 6044, panori@africaonline.co.tz. Colonial-style building with new wing added in 1997 (though there is nothing new any of the furnishings), with 22 rooms, some have a/c and TV. Indian and international food in an attractive open banda restaurant, and bar built around a mango tree. Well run and comfortable with secure parking.

$ Raskazone Hotel, Fertilizer Rd, east of centre off Hospital Rd, T027-264 3897. Rooms with a/c and minibar are on offer, or slightly cheaper rooms without a/c. It also has a restaurant and a garden bar, and the old colonial building is covered in established creepers. Breakfast is included. You can camp here for US$5 per person.

$ Inn by the Sea, close to the Mkonge Hotel on Ocean Dr, T027-264 4614. The 24 rooms have a/c or fans, and mosquito nets. Price includes breakfast but there is no restaurant or bar (Muslim owned). A good location on cliffs overlooking the harbour. Rather neglected in recent years but clean and at US$12 a room, cheap, and has secure parking.

$ Hotel Kola Prieto, India St, T0784-489 526, kolaprieto@hotmail.com. A modest block and centrally located with friendly Indian owners, the basic self-contained rooms are well looked after and clean, with a/c, hot water and TV, some have 3 beds, a cold buffet breakfast is included, great city views from the higher floors and cheap Indian dishes in the downstairs restaurant.

$ Ocean Breeze, just off Independence Av, T027-264 4545. Superb value, this is easily the best budget option in town. Neat and fairly modern block, with 55 rooms but fills up quickly and is deservedly popular. Self-contained rooms with a/c, mosquito nets and cool tiled floors cost only US$8. The restaurant serves curries, grilled chicken and fish.

Amani *p95*

$ Emau Hill Forest Camp, to get here, go through Amani Nature Reserve and out the other side, follow the road for 6 km, turn right at the sign for Emau Hill (4WD only), email ahead to get directions, T0782-656 526, emauhill@gmail.com. This is a mission post and school that offers some accommodation in rooms or in 3 tented bandas for US$45 per person full board, or you can pitch a tent for US$7.50 per person. There's a dining banda and bar, and the menu makes good use of local produce. It's a lovely forested spot: along the border of the plot is a winding creek, with lots of bushbabies and birds in the trees. They can provide bird lists and printed guides for local walks.

$ Sigi Resthouse, near to the Amani Forest Information Centre, T027-264 6907, usambara@twiga.com. Very comfortable triple rooms with mosquito nets and en suite showers, and toilets in a new smart white wooden block. Serves fresh produce and can make arrangements for guided forest walks. Also camping for US$5.

Pangani *p96*

The better accommodation options are on the beaches to the north and south of town. There are, however, a couple of budget places in town itself – useful if arriving late. You are likely to notice the former Mashado Beach Resort, on the cliff top on the hill south of the river ferry (and nowhere near the beach), which was built as a luxury hotel in the mid-1990s. However, under different owners, it's gone bankrupt a few times since then and is again presently closed. It remains somewhat of a folly in Pangani.

$ Seaside Community Hostel, right by the beach about 1 km to the east of town, T027-263 0318. Offers 10 simple but good-quality rooms with nets and fans from US$20, set in a large and well-tended garden where you can camp (US$5 per person), with a simple restaurant and bar under thatch selling beer, soft drinks, local dishes and some seafood.

$ Safari Lodge, Tanga Rd, straight up the road from the ferry, T027-263 0013. Probably the better of the rough board-and-lodging places in town, the 9 rooms are US$7-10 depending on size, breakfast of eggs and bread is available but not included in the rate. Tatty but clean. Simple local meals and cold beers are available on the thatched terrace outside, friendly service and a good place to meet the locals. There are another 10 rooms in the annex building.

Beaches south of Pangani

To get to the resorts on beautiful Ushongo Beach south of Pangani you will need to take the ferry. All the lodges seem to use the same taxi guy, so expect to pay about US$40 for a transfer. As you drive south from the ferry and follow the signs to the beach hotels there is a fork in the road. Turn left to **The Tides Lodge**, **Ushongo Beach Cottages** and **Beach Crab Resort** (reached in that order). Turn right to **Tulia Beach Lodge** and **Emayani Beach Resort**.

$$$$ The Tides Lodge, 16 km south of Pangani, T0784-225 812, www.thetides lodge.com. Intimate lodge with 13 spacious and stylish thatched and brightly painted cottages, with verandas, romantic bar and restaurant lit by lamps, and a swimming pool. Seafood is a speciality. Arranges snorkelling trips to the marine park, deep-sea fishing, kayaking in nearby mangrove swamps, which is ideal for birdwatching, and sunset cruises on the Pangani River. This is the most upmarket lodge on Ushongo Beach and gets consistently good reports. Doubles from US$300 full board and can organize charter flights from Dar or Zanzibar.

$$$ Emayani Beach Resort, 17 km south of Pangani, T0782-457 668, reservations, Arusha T027-264 0755, www.emayanilodge. com. Thatched resort on the beach, the 12 bungalows have verandas with ocean views surrounded by coconut trees. Rates are half board, considerable discounts for children, friendly cocktail bar, swimming pool, watersports, lots of boats for fishing and snorkelling, and it has its own airstrip.

$$$-$$ Tulia Beach Lodge, 10 km south of Pangani, T027-264 0680, www.tuliabeach lodge.com. Neat set-up with 7 makuti-thatched cottages with white stone walls, facing the ocean, plus a pleasant bar and restaurant with good set meals for dinner. Activities include sundowner trips on a dhow and fishing rods can be hired. Doubles from US$95 with a buffet breakfast, and half- and full-board rates are available.

$$$-$$ Ushongo Beach Cottages 16 km south of Pangani, T0784-214 412, www. ushongobeach.com. A bit different from the other resorts in that the 1- or 2-bedroom cottages have kitchenettes for self-catering. Fruit and veg are available locally and you can buy fresh seafood directly from the fishermen. Alternatively, there's a higher full-board rate, which includes food and your own cook, or you can eat out at the other lodges along the beach. All drinks are available and there's a good range of watersports.

$$$-$ The Beach Crab Resort, 17 km south of Pangani, T0784-543 700, www.thebeach crab.com. Highly rated by travellers, this is run by friendly Sonja and Alex who were part of a German TV series that followed their progress in setting it up; hence its popularity with Germans. Accommodation is in en suite thatch-and-reed bungalows (from US$120 for a double) or cheaper permanent tents with camp beds, again under thatch (from US$30 for a double), or you can camp for US$4. There's a sociable bar with pool table, good food in the restaurant, including beach seafood BBQs, and they rent out bikes, snorkelling gear and windsurfing boards.

Beaches north of Pangini

All the resorts to the north of Pangani are off the Tanga road.

$$$ Mkoma Bay Tented Lodge, 4 km north of Pangani at Mkoma Bay, T027-263 0000, www.mkomabay.com. Set on a low cliff overlooking the beach, with whitewashed buildings decorated with antiques, beautifully furnished tents or cheaper bandas, all have en suite bathrooms with hot water and flush toilets and mosquito nets, and a self-catering family house. There's a swimming pool, well-stocked bar, restaurant offering excellent food. Boat trips on the Pangani River and walking tours of Pangani can be arranged, and they rent out mountain bikes.

$$$-$$ Tinga-Tinga, perched on the cliff 2 km north of Pangani, T027-263 0022, www.tingatingalodge.com. Set in a grove of coconut palms, 10 neat makuti-thatch cottages, with fans, minibar, satellite TV and tea and coffee stations, stone showers and locally made furniture. The partially open restaurant and bar specializes in seafood and Cajun dishes and has good ocean views. Rates are very good value, from US$80 for a double, and service is of a high standard – think welcome drink and damp face towel on arrival. Activities include snorkelling, Pangani walking tours and dhow cruises.

$$$-$ Peponi Beach Resort, further north from Mkoma Bay, 15 km north of Pangani at Kigombe Village, T0748-202 962, www.peponiresort.com. Thatched bandas with 2-5 beds and en suite bathrooms; for a group of 4 or more, accommodation can work out about US$40 per person, which includes continental breakfast and dinner, and there's camping for US$5 per person. Good restaurant and pleasant bar that can get especially lively if there is a crowd. Game fishing in the Pemba Channel on the resort's own dhow, snorkelling trips can also be arranged, and there's a swimming pool and a good stretch of sheltered beach.

● Restaurants

Tanga *p91, map p93*
$$ Mkonge Hotel, on Ocean Dr, see Where to stay, page 99. Open 0700-2200. Fantastic setting overlooking the town and bay and set in lovely gardens. Dine inside

in a dark wood dining room or outside on the terrace. Serves up very good grills and salads, or try the excellent prawn curry; there's a full bar and some wines.

$$ Yacht Club, Ocean Dr, T027-264 4246, www.tangayachtclub.com. 1100-1500, 1800-2300. Day membership US$2, for which you can use the bar and restaurant. You need to buy a book of tickets to pay for meals and drinks. Very large menu, good seafood, well-stocked bar. A real expat hangout, but entertaining nonetheless, and the service is excellent. Dining tables are spread out on lovely stone terraces overlooking the bay – a perfect place for sundowners.

$ Food Palace, Market St, look for the red corrugated roof, T027-264 2816. Open 0800-2200, closed Mon evening and during Ramadan. Serves grills, curries, ice cream and fruit juices. The Indian food is cheap and superb for around US$5 a plate, plus extra for rice and naan bread. It's cooked from scratch, so expect to wait about 30-45 mins. Takeaway also available. There's no alcohol but you can take your own.

$ Ocean Breeze Hotel, just off Independence Av, see Where to stay, page 100. Open 1100-2300. Terrace restaurant serves excellent curries, grilled chicken and fish, and cold beer. Popular and busy and the outside area is lively for a few drinks in the evening.

$ Patwas Restaurant, Mkwakwani St, off Market St just south of market. Mon-Sat 0800-2000. Well run, with snacks of egg-chop (Scotch egg), meat chop, kebabs, burgers, curries and samosas. Excellent ice-cold drinks: lemon, mango, pineapple, papaya, lassi and milkshakes. Recommended for cheap eats.

Pangani *p96*
There are many small food stalls along the river front, where you can get items such as chapatti, omelette and rice very cheaply. Otherwise, look to the hotels which have excellent restaurants, mostly under thatch on the beach and serve superb Swahili seafood.

☺ What to do

Tanga *p91, map p93*
**Tanga Youth Development Association
(TAYODEA)**, Independence Av, T027-264
4350, www.tayodea.org. An organization
that is well worth supporting, as it employs
disadvantaged young local people as
guides, and 30% of fees taken from tourists
go into community projects. They can take
you on a walking tour around town to see
the historical buildings; to Amboni Caves;
Tongani Ruins; arrange a boat ride to Toten
Island; or a visit to a working sisal plantation.
Costs are in the region of US$20 per person
for a walking tour and other prices are in the
listings. Guides will rightly expect a tip, and
bike/boat hire is extra.

Pangani *p96*
Pangani Cultural Tourism Programme,
Jamhuri St (or Harbour Rd), next to the
post office, T0732-976 460. Mon-Sat 0800-
1600. This is one of the excellent **Tanzania
Cultural Tourism Programmes** and part
of the fees goes towards local community
development projects; it is an excellent
initiative to support. All the guides carry
ID and, along with the staff in the office,
speak excellent English and are a mine of
local information. Depending on transport,
an average day trip costs US$15-20 per
person. On offer are walks through the town;
excursions to local farms, coconut and sisal
plantations; visits to homes for a traditional
meal and, perhaps, to have your hair plaited
or hands and feet decorated with henna;
river cruises to the mangrove swamps;
and fishing with local fishermen. Can also
arrange bicycle hire, snorkelling and other
excursions. Further details and bookings
of the programmes can be obtained from
the **Tanzania Cultural Tourism Programme**
office at the Museum/Old Boma or the
Tanzanian Tourist Board tourist information
centre in Arusha (see page 236), www.
tanzaniaculturaltourism.com.

⊖ Transport

Tanga *p91, map p93*
Air
Tanga Airport is 3 km west of town on the
A14 towards Dar es Salaam. **Coastal Air**,
Tanga Airport, T0773-733 446, Dar, T022-
284 2700, www.coastal.cc, has 2 daily
flights on a circuit between Tanga,
Pemba, **Zanzibar**, and **Dar**.

Bus and dala-dala
Buses and *dala-dalas* leave from the bus
station south of the town on the other
side of the railway track. Buses for **Dar** run
0800-1600 about every 30 mins, 5-6 hrs, a
regular bus costs US$9 and a semi-luxury
one US$11. To **Moshi**, 4-6 hrs, US$11; to
Pangani, regularly until about 1400, 1-2 hrs,
US$1.50. Although it is only 52 km, the road
is very bumpy and buses may take over
2 hrs depending on the season. The bus will
drop off outside the beach resorts between
Tanga and Pangani. None of them are more
than 1 km off the road. There are also several
departures a day to **Lushoto**, 3-4 hrs, US$3.

The **Scandinavia Express** office is on
Mkwakwani St, south of the stadium, T027-
264 4337, www.scandinaviagroup.com. Daily
buses to **Dar**, 0730 and 1300, 5 hrs, US$9.
The 1300 service has come from **Mombasa**
in Kenya; heading towards Mombasa
(5-6 hrs, US$9) it stops in Tanga at 1245.

Pangani *p96*
Bus
The bus stand in Pangani is on Jamhuri St
opposite the ferry. There are no buses to
Bweni on the other side of the river. The only
regular service is to **Tanga** (1-2 hrs, US$1.50).
All the resorts can arrange transfers from
Tanga, and seem to use the same taxi driver,
Mohammed, T0713-808 534, and his fleet.

Motorboat
To the south of Pangani the string of lodges
around Ushongo Beach can organize
motorboat transfers to **Kendwa** on the

north coast of Zanzibar (see page 170), which take about 3 hrs, and cost around US$50 per person, depending on how many people are in the boat; the minimum charge for a boat is US$130-150. As weather and wave conditions are normally mild in the first few hours after dawn, boats usually leave Ushongo Beach at around 0700 and return from Zanzibar around 1000. This is a very useful service; the best place to enquire is at the **Beach Crab Resort**, where you may be able to tag along with another group. However, remember, as these boats originate from Ushongo Beach, you'll have to arrange for a boat to come and pick you up again after a few days on the island.

Note There was concern that people arriving at Kendwa (where there is no immigration) and then leaving Zanzibar through the port at Stone Town might get into trouble as they wouldn't have an entry stamp for Zanzibar. However, travellers have reported that the immigration people in Stone Town are fully aware that people arrive and depart in Kendwa from Ushongo Beach and have reported no problems. Remember, it is illegal for foreigners to go from the mainland to the islands by dhow.

● Directory

Tanga *p91, map p93*
Medical services Bombo Regional Hospital, on Ocean Dr to east of town centre, T027-264 4390. **Police** off Independence Av, near Tanga library.

Mafia Island

Mafia, the southernmost of the Tanzanian islands, is a wonderful little island at the centre of the largest marine park in East Africa. At around 20 km long and 8 km wide, it's a real sleepy backwater, a remnant of the old Swahili coast and a place to visit now if you want to see how Zanzibar was 30 years ago. Unlike Zanzibar and Pemba which, along with a number of smaller islands, form the semi-autonomous state of Zanzibar, Mafia is politically an integral part of mainland Tanzania. The inhabitants are mainly fishermen, but other industries involve the coconut palms and cashew nut tree plantations. Geographically, as well as politically, the island, with its central areas covered with bush, light woodland and plantations, is much more like the mainland in character than the other islands. The coast is generally lined with palm trees, but there are no sweeping sandy beaches like those on Zanzibar. Here the shoreline is narrow and mangrove forests are widespread, so it's not primarily a beach destination. It is, however, an excellent diving destination. The recent gazetting of Mafia Island Marine Park – the largest protected area in the Indian Ocean – which includes surrounding villages in its conservation efforts, means that the millions of fish and coral species that thrive in the warm waters around Mafia are fully protected. ▸▸ *For listings, see pages 109-111.*

Arriving on Mafia Island → *Phone code: 023. Colour map 1, B6. 7°45'S 39°50'E.*
Getting there **Mafia Airport** is just to the north of the main town of Kilindoni, on the western side of the island, and about 15 km from the lodges at the southeastern tip of the island around Chole Bay. All the places to stay on the island will collect you in their vehicles. Flights from Dar es Salaam take 30-40 minutes. **Coastal Air**, T022-284 2700, T023-240 2426 (Mafia), www.coastal.cc, have 2 flights a day on a circuit between Mafia, Zanzibar and Dar, and will also stop at Kilwa (page 112) on request. ▸▸ *For further details, see Transport, page 111.*

Getting around There are few taxis on the island; indeed there are very few vehicles of any sort, and Mafia has no public transport system. The upmarket lodges and hotels ferry their guests around the island, and budget travellers have the option of walking, hitchhiking – which can involve lengthy waits – or hiring a bicycle. Enquire at **New Lizu Hotel** in Kilindoni (see Where to stay, page 111).

Background

There is evidence of foreign, probably Shirazi, settlers on Mafia from as early as the eighth or ninth century. From the 12th to the 14th century it was an important settlement, and the remains of a 13th-century mosque have been found at Ras Kismani, at the southwestern point of the island. By the 16th century, when the Portuguese arrived, it had lost much of its importance and was part of the territory ruled by the king of Kilwa. There is little left on the site of the settlement from the 12th to 14th century, although old coins and pieces of pottery are still found occasionally, particularly to the south of Kilindoni where the sea is eating away at the ruins. On the nearby island of Juani, however, are extensive ruins of the town of Kua. The town dates back to the 18th century, and its five mosques go back even further to the 14th century. In 1829 the town was sacked by Sakalava cannibals from Madagascar, who invaded, destroyed the town and dined on the inhabitants.

Mafia Island

N

2 km
2 miles

Where to stay 🛏
Big Blue 5
Blue House 7
Butima Beach 9
Chole Foxes Lodge 12
Chole Mjini Lodge 1
Harbour View 8
Kinasi Lodge 6
Lua Cheia Beach Camp 13
Mafia Island Lodge 2
New Luzi 4
Pole Pole 3
Ras Mbisi Lodge 11
Shamba Kilole
Eco-Lodge 14
Whale Shark Lodge 10

From the beginning of the 19th century, traders from all over the world were plying these coastal waters. '*Americani*' cloth proved itself to be the most popular of all the traded goods among the resident population. The trading of goods and of slaves was soon to be followed by the interest of European politics but, it was not until the end of the century, that this affected territorial rights. Under the treaty of 1890, Mafia, along with Zanzibar and Pemba, were initially allotted to the British sphere. However, it was later agreed that Mafia should go to Germany in exchange for some territory on the southern border, which was allocated to the British Territory of Nyasaland (now Malawi). The island was therefore included in the purchase of the coastal strip from Sultan Seyyid Ali, and the German flag was raised in 1890.

The Germans established a headquarters at Chole and, in 1892, a resident officer was posted here together with a detachment of Sudanese troops. A large two-storey boma was constructed, with various other buildings such as a gaol. The site seemed ideal, with good anchorage for dhows but, with the opening of a regular coastal steamship service a deeper harbour was needed and the headquarters were moved to Kilindoni in 1913.

During the First World War, it became clear that Mafia represented an extremely useful base from which attacks could be launched. In particular, the British needed a base from which to attack the SS *Königsberg*, which was wreaking havoc up and down the East African coast. In January 1915 a British expeditionary force under Colonel Ward landed on the island at Kisimani, and the islands were captured with little resistance. A garrison of about 200 troops remained on the island. The *Königsberg* had been damaged and gone into the mouth of the River Rufiji for repairs. The delta, with its many creeks and maze of streams, provided the perfect hiding place. It was important that the British should find and destroy the ship before any further damage could be done. In 1915, a British warplane was assembled on Mafia, took off from there, spotted the ship and boats, then went into the delta to destroy it. This was the first use of aerial reconnaissance in warfare. The wrecked remains of the crippled boat could be seen until 1979, when it finally sank out of sight into the mud.

For a short period, the islands were under military rule and were later administered by Zanzibar. In 1922 the islands were handed over by the government of Zanzibar to become part of the Tanganyika Territory under the United Nations Mandate.

These days, the coconut industry is particularly important and Mafia has the largest coconut factory in East Africa at Ngombeni Plantation. It produces copra (dried kernels), oil, coir yarn and cattle cake. More recently, geological surveys have shown that the Mafia Deep Offshore Basin, an area of 75,000 sq km, contains deposits of oil and gas. Exploration has already started and, given the extreme poverty of many of the people on the island, the onset of employment opportunities has given a renewed sense of optimism to Mafia's inhabitants – ecological concerns notwithstanding.

Around Mafia Island

Kilondoni → *Colour map 1, B6.*
Kilondoni is the main town and a refreshingly simple place. The only road is flanked on either side for a kilometre or so by classic Swahili buildings with carved doors and, in the centre of town, there is a small market. Whilst dhows remain commonplace to this day all along the East Coast of Africa, the huge ocean-going *jahasi* are increasingly rare. Here, on the beach at Kilondoni, there are usually three or four of these giant boats, which are still in service providing an essential means of trade with the mainland. This working beachfront at Kilondoni is one of the highlights of a visit to Mafia. On the shore you can watch the construction of boats 20-25 m in length and weighing up to 100 tonnes. Timbers are prepared by hand and the frame of the boat is made from naturally V-shaped forked branches of trees.

Ruins at Kua
① *Local fishermen will take you to Kua for US$3-4.*
The largely 18th-century ruins of the town of Kua are on Juani Island to the south of Mafia Island. The remains are tucked away inconspicuously on the western side of the island, covering a large area of about 14 ha. In 1955, when the site was cleared of bush, one observer stated that he believed that these ruins were 'potentially the Pompeii of East Africa'. However, the remains still require a lot of work on them to bring them up to anything like that standard. There are several houses, one of which was clearly double-storeyed. Beneath the stairs leading to the upper level is a small room in which slaves could be confined for punishment. Under the building is the *haman* (bathroom), with a vaulted ceiling of curved coral blocks. A soil pipe runs from the remains of an upper room

Swimming with whale sharks

Measuring up to 12 m in length and weighing around 13 tonnes, the whale shark is the largest fish in the world. Known as 'Papa Shillingi' along the Swahili coast, from the story that its spots derived from God throwing shillings at it, this solitary beast swims off the coast of Mafia and its lagoons during feeding times from October to March. Its mouth alone can measure up to 1.5 m, which can be filled with as many as 350 rows of teeth. And yet, it's perfectly safe to swim with ...

Whale sharks are the gentle giants of the Indian Ocean and eat only plankton, so there's no danger of a repeat of a grisly scene from *Jaws*. No special skills are required if you want to try swimming with them – as long as you can snorkel, you can have a go. However, because the whale shark can cover huge distances,

as with any wild animal, there's no guarantee you'll find one.

The main hotels on the island all offer snorkelling trips, especially to see whale sharks during the season, and it's an unforgettable experience – even seasoned divers have been silenced by the awkward beauty of these enormous beasts gliding beneath them. As with any wildlife encounter, always respect their space and you may just be rewarded: there have been several reports of whale sharks playing with swimmers, even allowing them to tickle their tummies and scratch away their parasites.

Whale sharks are vulnerable and relatively little is known about their behaviour and biology. To find out more, and to share your experiences, go to www.whalesharkproject.org, and contribute towards their survival.

to a pit below. Two mosques and a series of tombs, some with pillars, are nearby. The evidence suggests that the town did not have a protective wall and that the inhabitants were mainly involved in agricultural pursuits on the island rather than in sea-trading.

There is also a cave on the island, formed by the action of the sea. The water streaming out of the cave as the tide turns is reputed to cure *baridi yabis* ('cold stiffness' – rheumatism) and other ailments. The cure is not effective, however, unless the hereditary custodian of the cave is paid a fee, and the spirits of the cave appeased by an offering of honey, dates or sugar.

Nororo Island

Nororo is a small island 12 km off the north coast of Mafia, with a fishing community of about 50 local boats. There are two small *hotelis* selling rice, *ugali* and fish, and it's possible to camp on the beach in a thatched shelter.

Baracuni Island

This is a beautiful small island with fine beaches about 12 km off the northwest coast of Mafia and an hour's sailing from Nororo. It's used as a base for fishing dhows. You need to have your own food, water and tent if you want to stay there.

Mafia Island Marine Park → *Colour map 1, B6.*

ⓘ *Park fee of US$20 per day, children (5-16) US$10, payable whether or not you go diving. All the lodges (see Where to stay, below) have dive schools and rent out equipment. Note that during Apr-Sep the monsoon winds blow too hard, making it impossible to dive outside the lagoon and leading to a deterioration in visibility.*

The legend of Ras Kismani

The town of Ras Kismani was originally settled by the Sakalava from Madagascar. The townspeople built a large ship, and when it was completed they invited the local people of Kua to a feast. During the celebrations, the Sakalava seized several children and laid them on the sand in the path of the ship as it was launched.

The Kua people planned revenge at their leisure. Seven or eight years later they invited the Sakalava of Ras Kismani to attend a wedding at Kua. The celebrations were in a special room beneath a house. Gradually the hosts left, one by one, until only an old man was left to entertain the guests. As he did so, the door was quietly bricked up, and the bodies remain to this day. A message was sent to the headman at Ras Kismani that the account was now squared. Within a month, Ras Kismani was engulfed by the sea.

To protect an internationally significant ecosystem, the Mafia Island Marine Park (the first in Tanzania) was opened in July 1995. The project is backed by the World Wildlife Fund, which contributes human and financial resources for its development and maintenance. Here you can experience some of the best deep-sea diving in Tanzania. There is something here for everyone, from the most experienced diver to those who want to snorkel in the shallower pools. The coral gardens off Mafia are marvellous: wonderfully vivid fish, shells, sponges, sea cucumber and spectacular coral reefs. Two of the most beautiful reefs are the Okuto and Tutia reefs around Juani and Jibondo Islands, a short distance from Chole Bay. About 1 km off Mafia's coastline there is a 200-m deep contour along the seabed of the Indian Ocean. The depth contributes to the wide variety of sea life. Due to its position alongside the barrier, the island is the meeting place of large oceanic fish and the vast variety of fish common to the Indian Ocean coral reefs. There are over 400 species of fish in the park. Mafia Island and some of the uninhabited islands around are also traditional breeding sites for the green turtle. Sadly, you would be very lucky to see these, as the local population is now close to being wiped out; they are killed both as adults for their meat and as eggs. Another threatened species is the dugong, which lives in sea grass such as that found between Mafia and the Rufiji delta. Because of their strange shape, early sailors thought they had breasts (giving rise to the legend of the mermaid). This strange beast is protected by law, but hunting continues. It's also possible to swim and snorkel with whale sharks at certain times of the year, particularly between October and March, and most local hotels offer this through their diving schools (for more information, see box, page 107).

Diving The diving around Mafia can be described as a 'shallow Pemba with more fish'; there are beautiful reefs and beautiful fish life. Jino Pass and Dindini Wall are two sites to the northeast of Chole Bay. Both reefs have flat tops at 8 m, dropping vertically in a spectacular wall to 25 m with a sandy bottom. Whip corals 2-3 m long grow out from the walls. There are a couple of interesting (if tight) swim-throughs and a long tunnel cave at 20 m on Dindini Wall. Impressive sightings include huge malabar, potato and honeycomb groupers, giant reef rays, green turtles, great barracuda, kingfish, bonito, shoals of bluefin trevalley and snappers in their thousands.

On the eastern entrance to Chole Bay lies Kinasi Pass. There is a recommended drift dive in the Pass but it must be dived on an incoming tide and is for experienced divers only if diving on a spring tide. The Pinnacle in the centre of the mouth of the Pass is a good opportunity to see large rays, groupers, eagle rays and jacks. It's best dived on a slack or gentle incoming tide, and you will need an experienced guide to find the site.

◉ Mafia Island listings

For sleeping and eating price codes and other relevant information, see pages 22-26.

🛏 Where to stay

Mafia Island *p104, map p105*
There are few places to stay on the island, and most of the top-end lodges close during rainy season from the beginning of Apr to the end of May. Most of the lodges on the eastern side of the island lie within the Mafia Island Marine Park, so there is the additional park fee of US$20 (children 5-16 US$10) per day. However, the beach on that side of the island is better and has less seaweed than the beaches around Kilondoni. All of the places offer diving, as well as boat and snorkelling trips to see whale sharks.

$$$$ Chole Mjini Lodge, on the 1 sq km Chole Island, T0784-520 799, www.chole mjini.com. Best described as rustic luxury in a stunning setting on its own island, this lodge is truly eco-sensitive, built by local people using local materials, and revenues have helped to establish a school and medical centre on the island. The 7 rooms are actually treehouses, built partially on stilts, with private bathrooms with long-drop toilets, solar-heated water for the showers and kerosene lamps for lighting. There is a restaurant and bar area, the meals being primarily seafood, and snorkelling and diving are on offer. Rates vary seasonally from US$300 for a double full board.

$$$$ Kinasi Lodge, 100 m up the beach from **Mafia Island Lodge**, T0777-424 588, www.kinasilodge.com. Set up on a hillside above the bay, on the site of an old cashew plantation, the lodge has a dozen rooms arranged in thatched cottages around a stylish central dining and lounge area. Its beach is not quite as nice as its rivals' but

it has a beautiful main complex with old coastal traditional decor, and a small library, bar with billiards table, lounge with satellite TV and Wi-Fi, patio and dining room. The swimming pool overlooks the beach, there's a spa, and diving and other watersports can be arranged.

$$$$ Lua Cheia Beach Camp, Ras Bweni in the extreme northwest of the island, T0777-424 588, www.luacheiabeach.com. The most remote and newest of the lodges, some 55 km from the airport and under the same ownership as **Kinasi Lodge**, **Lua Cheia** has 6 tents under thatch with decks in the sand on a secluded 2-km beach facing northwest for the sunset. It's built adhering to eco-friendly principles using local materials and solar power. There's a bar and restaurant with lounge areas and leather sofas and furniture made from dhows. Activities include snorkelling, kayaking, game fishing, windsurfing, and there's a swimming pool and massages available.

$$$$ Pole Pole, between **Kinasi Lodge** and **Mafia Island Lodge**, Chole Bay, reservations Dar, T022-260 1530, www.polepole.com. 7 spacious bungalows on stilts with wide verandas facing the Mafia Island Marine Park and the islands of Chole, Juani and Jibondo. Built using natural materials, the decor is stunning, with hard wood floors and mahogany furniture, and linen imported from Italy. This is a beautiful, peaceful spot, and the emphasis is on relaxation, with a massage parlour that overlooks the sea, and an unusual swimming pool shaped in a series of circles. The lodge shares a dive school with the nearby **Mafia Island Lodge**.

$$$$ Ras Mbisi Lodge, on the west coast, about 15 km north of the airport, T0754-663 739, www.mafiaislandtz.com. A fairly new lodge with 9 tented bandas, all en suite and with private balconies, set in lovely grounds by the beach and made from sustainable coco-wood. At the time of writing, there were no other lodges in the area, so it currently has an air of seclusion about it. They grow their own vegetables here and, as much as possible, source food from nearby villages for their restaurant overlooking the beach. They can arrange visits around the island to local villages and to Chole Bay and the marine park.

$$$ Butiama Beach, to the southwest of Kilindoni, T0787-474 084, www.butiama beach.com. Another Italian-owned spot, with 8 spacious thatched bungalows set well apart among palms, with large terraces and hammocks; a couple are for families. Nice playful decor of kikoy fabric and old dhow sails, good food, pleasant beach bar and relaxing semi-open lounge; by the time you read this they may have a swimming pool. Dhow trips, village excursions and massages on offer.

$$$ Mafia Island Lodge, Chole Bay, reservations Dar, T022-211 6609, www.mafialodge.com. Well managed by Gabriel, an Italian-American, this larger lodge is in a lovely setting overlooking Chole Bay, with friendly and efficient staff. There are 35 comfortable and colourful a/c rooms, 2 of which are for families. The relaxing thatched bar and restaurant are the main hub of the lodge and the food is excellent. The lodge has its own beach, where there's a dive centre, and has windsurfing boards and hobicats for rent. Doubles from US$190 half board.

$$$ Shamba Kilole Eco-Lodge, T0786-903 752, www.shambakilolelodge.com. A pretty spot with just 6 en suite stone chalets under elevated thatched roofs, with home-made furniture and patio; each has a sofa that can be used as a third bed. There's a restaurant and bar. As the name suggests, it runs on eco-friendly principles, such as compost toilets and recycling. The swimming pool is especially deep (for dive courses), and it has its own PADI dive school and can also organize snorkelling, boat trips and village visits. One of the less expensive options with doubles from US$130.

$$ Big Blu Diving College, just down the beach from **Mafia Island Lodge**, T0787-474 108, www.bigblumafia.com. This Italian-run place is a dive centre but has 3 simple but comfortable thatched bandas on the beach, with private bathrooms, from US$45 per person including breakfast. There's also a lovely bar/restaurant here, with low stone seats and giant colourful cushions, serving lunch for US$16 and dinner for US$20. It's organized by a local cooperative as part of the Mafia Island Self Sustaining Programme. Single dives US$40, double dives US$70 and snorkelling US$15. Internet access available.

$$-$ Chole Foxes Lodge, on Chole Island, T0787-877 393, www.cholefoxeslodge.webs. com. A friendly, locally run place, with simple reed huts with flush loos and cold showers. There's a small beach from where you can swim at high tide (note that on Chole Island there are no wide sandy beaches as they are under the mangrove trees). Basic meals include lots of fish, doubles from US$50 with breakfast or US$70 half board, and you can camp for US$10 per person. Guided walks around Chole Island to see the flying foxes at dusk, dhow trips, snorkelling and other watersports can be arranged.

$ Blue House, Utende Village by Chole Bay, signposted on the left if driving towards the bay, T0755-828 825, www.bluehousemafia. com. This guesthouse, run by the enterprising and friendly Mohammed, is the only budget accommodation in Chole Bay, and has 5 basic sea-facing and self-contained reed huts from US$30 for a double with breakfast and US$50 half board. The rustic and relaxing restaurant and bar right on the sand serves seafood, grilled over an open fire. Activities include diving and snorkelling, dhow trips, and guided village walks and bike rides.

$ Harbour View, on the harbour in Kilindoni, T0755-560 314. The location is fun – there's a lot of local life here, with food stalls and boat building. But the lodge itself is fairly gloomy. Rooms have mosquito nets, fans and their own bathrooms. Price includes breakfast, but lunch and dinner need to be pre-ordered. The bar is in an enormous thatched building towards the harbour.

$ New Lizu Hotel, in the centre of Kilondoni, T023-240 2683. A basic guesthouse in a good location, offering simple rooms with nets and fans for about US$7-8, not including breakfast. It is aimed at the resident market, so don't expect anywhere near a Western level of comfort or facilities, but the place is friendly and there is a restaurant here serving fish, rice, etc, but you need to pre-order dinner.

$ Whale Shark Lodge, about 2 km from the airport in the opposite direction from Kilidoni, T0755-696 067. There are 4 bungalows here, quite basic with squat toilet, shower and fan. The price includes a basic breakfast, and dinner might be fish or calamari with chapatti or rice. The restaurant and bar are set on a low cliff that overlooks the bay, where whale sharks come to bathe at sunset, and there's access to the beach. Doubles from US$20 or you can camp for US$6 per tent.

○ What to do

Mafia Island *p104, map p105*
Diving
For more information on diving on Mafia Island, see page 108.

Almost all the lodges have dive schools or can arrange diving trips or courses.

Fishing
Fishing is at its best Sep-Mar, when the currents and the northeast monsoon (*kaskazi*) give rise to an enormous variety of fish. When the south monsoon (*kusi*) blows during the rest of the year, fishing can be rather sparse. Big game fish that can be caught in the area include marlin, shark, kingfish, barracuda and red snapper.

Game fishing, diving and other boat excursions can be arranged at **Chole Mjini Lodge, Pole Pole** and **Kinasi Lodge**. Guests are taken out by an experienced skipper. **Kinasi Lodge** is a member of the International Game Fishing Association and has weighing facilities. It also holds a fishing competition every Feb.

○ Transport

Mafia Island *p104, map p105*
Air
Mafia Island's airport is at Kilindoni. **Coastal Air**, Dar T022-284 2700, T023-240 2426 (Mafia), www.coastal.cc, has 2 daily flights between Mafia Island and **Dar** (30 mins, US$110). They will also run a daily service between Mafia and **Kilwa**, if there are enough takers, leaving Mafia at 1110 (30 mins, US$110) and Kilwa at 1150 on the return to Mafia.

Kilwa

Of exceptional historical interest, Kilwa is a group of three settlements magnificently situated on a mangrove-fringed bay, dotted with numerous small islands. It grew up as a gold trade terminus and, when its fortunes faded, some magnificent ruins were left behind. These are said to be some of the most spectacular on the East African coast but are today succumbing slowly to the encroaching jungle and the relentless cycles of the tide. Once an important centre of Swahili culture and civilization, the baked limestone, coral blocks, fig tree roots growing through the windows and a few shattered tiles give witness to many years' habitation here. If Kilwa was in Kenya, it would be full of tourists – it is an extraordinarily rewarding place to visit. As it is, it gets just a handful of visitors each week. The town itself is pleasant and quiet, with a few local bars and restaurants and a busy market. The area is, however, beginning to see changes, due to potential industrial developments involving oil and biofuels: there's talk of extending the harbour for freight ships; the road to Dar has improved, there are better bus facilities and even a couple of new internet cafés in town (although the electricity supply is still fairly erratic). In the future, as the infrastructure improves, it is unlikely that Kilwa will remain as unspoilt and inaccessible as it is at present. ⟫ *For listings, see page 116.*

Arriving in Kilwa → *Colour map 1, C6. 9°0'S 39°0'E.*
Getting there The B2 road from Dar es Salaam to Kilwa is part tar, part dirt but there is a 60-km stretch about 180 km north of Kilwa, that is very rough and takes three hours. There

is now a new bridge over the Rufiji River, so there is no more hassle catching ferries or buses waiting overnight at the crossing. The whole journey takes about eight to 10 hours, depending on the weather. There are a couple of direct buses a day to Kilwa from the **Ubungo Bus Station** in Dar or, alternatively, you could take one of the numerous buses heading for destinations south of Kilwa, such as Mtwara, Lindi or Nachingwea. Seats closer to the front are recommended as the going is rough. The bus will drop you off at **Nangurukuru**, a village on the B2, 12 km west of the coast and Kilwa Masoko, where you have to transfer to a minibus or pickup *dala-dala* to complete the journey (US$1).

Coastal Air flies to Kilwa from Dar on its circuit between Zanzibar, Pemba and Mafia, if there are enough passengers needing the service. It's always best to check with Coastal before making firm plans. A charter is a possibility, particularly for groups. ⟫ *For further details, see Transport, page 116.*

Kilwa area

To Dar es Salaam

Kilwa Kivinje

Nangurukuru

Indian Ocean

Kilwa Masoko

Kilwa Kisiwani

To Lindi & Mtwara

Sanje ya Kati Island

Songo Mnara Island

Nisas Haven

N

10 km
10 miles

Getting around The town is split between **Kilwa Kisiwani** (Kilwa on the Island), 2 km offshore; **Kilwa Kivinje** (Kilwa of the Casuarina Trees) on the mainland, and **Kilwa Masoko** (Kilwa of the Market), which was built as an administrative centre on a peninsula and is the site of the main present-day town. There is a superb beach a stone's throw from Kilwa Masoko centre and another, even better one, a few miles north of the town (ask for *Masoko pwani*). There are frequent *dala-dalas* between Kilwa Kivinje and Kilwa Masoko.

Background

Kilwa Kisiwani contains the ruins of a 13th-century city of the Shirazi civilization, which is well preserved and documented. The town was founded at the end of the 10th century by Shirazis (see box, page 95) and flourished with the core of commercial activity based on the trade of gold from Sofala (in present-day Mozambique). It grew to be the largest town on the south coast and prospered to the extent that Kilwa could maintain an independent status, with its own sultan and coinage.

The large stone town that grew up thrived, and the architecture was striking. The largest pre-European building in equatorial Africa was located here, the **Husuni Kubwa**. However, Kilwa's fortunes were reversed in the 14th century. Vasco da Gama was said to have been impressed by the buildings of Kilwa and, in 1505, a large Portuguese fleet arrived and took the town by force. Their aim was to take control of the Sofala gold trade, and they did this by erecting a garrison and establishing a trading post in the town from where they set up a gold trade link with the interior. Without the gold trade, the Shirazi merchants were left with little to maintain their wealth and the town quickly went into decline. Having taken over the gold trade, and thus triggering the decline of the town, the Portuguese decided there was little point in staying in Kilwa, now an out-post that was expensive to maintain. So they withdrew and continued the gold trade from further afield.

Deprived of the main source of income, the town continued to decline. In 1589 disaster struck, when a nearby tribe, the Zimba, attacked the town, killing and eating many of the inhabitants. In the 17th century, with the arrival of the Oman Arabs, Kilwa began to revive, and many of the buildings were taken over by the sultans as palaces. The slave trade (see page 397) made a significant impact on this area and Kilwa Kivinje on the mainland flourished, thanks to the caravan route from the interior, which terminated at the port.

Places in Kilwa

Kilwa Kisiwani

Getting there Small dhows in the harbour at Kilwa Masoko will take you across the 2-km channel for US$8 (with a motor), or it's possible to get there in a passenger boat for US$0.30; these usually depart when full and take about 20 minutes, but can take up to an hour if there is little wind. However, it is first necessary to get a permit to visit the site (approximately US$2) from the Department of Antiquities at the district commissioner's offices (Monday-Friday 0800-1500), which are on the road leading to the harbour. Alternatively, **Kilwa Seaview Resort** (see Where to stay, page 116) and the other resorts are able to arrange the whole trip, including boat, permit and guide for around US$30 per person, plus an additional US$10 per person if using a vehicle to get to the harbour. Jamilla, who works at Kilwa Seaview, is an extremely knowledgeable guide and will take you through the ruins, giving some background information on the buildings and their former inhabitants. Allow at least half a day for your visit and note that the ruins are spread around the island so some walking is unavoidable. You'll need to bring water and sun protection.

Gereza Fort The original Gereza was built in the 14th century. The one standing today was built by the Omani Arabs in the 19th century on the site of the original on the orders of the Imam of Muscat. It is a large square building built of coral set in lime. The walls, with circular towers at the northeast and southwest corners, are very thick, and it has an impressive entrance of fine wood carving.

Great Mosque (Friday Mosque) This mosque is said to have been built in the 12th century and is probably the largest of this period on the east coast. It was excavated between 1958 and 1960, and parts of it have been reconstructed. The oldest parts that remain are outer sections of the side walls and the north wall. The façade of the *mihrab* (the niche that points towards Mecca) is dated from around 1300. The domed chamber was supposed to have been the sultan's prayer room. The water tanks and the slabs of stone were for rubbing clean the soles of the feet before entering the mosque.

Great House The large single-storey building is said to have been the residence of the sultan, and the remains of one of the sultans are said to reside in one of the four graves found within its walls. The building is an illustration of the highly developed state of building and architectural skills in this period, with examples of courtyards, reception rooms, an amphitheatre that is unique to this part of the world, latrines, kitchens and cylindrical clay ovens.

Small Domed Mosque About 150 m southwest of the Great House, this is without doubt the best preserved of all the buildings in Kilwa. It is an ornamental building with beautiful domes. The long narrow room on its east side is thought once to have been a Koran school.

House of Portico Little remains of this once large building. There are portico steps on three of its sides, from which it gets its name, and its doorway has a decorated stone frame.

Makutini Palace (Palace of Great Walls) This large, fortified building is believed to date from the 15th century. It is to the west of the Small Domed Mosque and is roughly triangular in shape. Its longest wall, which ran along the coast, is in ruins. Within the complex is the grave of one of the sultans.

Jangwani Mosque The ruins of this stone building are concealed under a series of mounds to the southeast of the Makutini Palace. This mosque was unique for having ablution water jars set into the walls, just inside the main entrance.

Kilwa Masoko

To **5**, Airstrip & Masoko Pwani

Mapinduzi St

Football Ground

School

Jimbiza Beach

District Office

Harbour

N

200 metres
200 yards

Where to stay
Hilton Guest House
  & Restaurant **1**
Kilwa Dreams **5**
Kilwa Ruins Lodge **4**
Kilwa Seaview Resort **6**
Kimbilio Lodge **8**
New Mjaka Guest Houses **3**

Malindi Mosque This mosque to the east of the Gereza Fort was said to have been built and used by immigrants from Malindi on the Kenya coast.

Husuni Kubwa This building is thought to be the largest pre-European building in equatorial Africa. It is about 1-2 km to the east of the main collection of ruins on top of a steep cliff. It is certainly an exceptional construction, with over 100 rooms and a large conical dome that reaches about 30 m above the ground. The mosque has 18 domes on octagonal piers, separated by high barrel vaults. The piers are decorated with bowls of white porcelain set in the plaster.

Husuni Ndogo This is a smaller version of Husuni Kubwa, separated from it by a small gully. It is said to have been built in the 15th century, with walls 1 m thick and towers in the corners.

Kilwa Kivinje → *Colour map 1, C6.*

About 29 km north of Kilwa Masoko, Kilwa Kivinje is an attractive historical trading centre, whose heyday was during the slave trading times of the 18th and 19th centuries, but which remained the district headquarters up until 1949. It retains many interesting old buildings dating back to the 19th century as well as the colonial period, and is somewhat reminiscent of Bagamoyo. A handsome old boma on the shore dates from the German period, as does the covered market. Several fine though rather dilapidated houses stand along the main street. There is an old mosque in the centre and, to the east of the town, is a cemetery with tombs and pillars. The town can be reached by *dala-dala* from Kilwa Masoko, heading for Manguruturu, costing about US$1. There are half a dozen or so each day.

Songo Mnara and offshore islands

Songo Songo is an island about 25 km northeast of Kilwa Kivinje, protected by a reef, lying close to the site of a large natural gas field in a Lower Cretaceous sandstone reservoir. The Songo Songo gas field contains unusually dry petrogenic gas, which is 97% methane. From 2003 the Songas Project has been operational, and the gas is being extracted from the gas field and piped to Dar es Salaam to fuel a power station that was until recently fuelled by more expensive oil. Songo Songo, **Jewe Island** and the surrounding smaller islands are an important marine bird breeding site. Access is by dhow, and there is usually at least one service each day transporting the gas employees, which takes around three hours each way, arranged in Kilwa Kivinje.

About 10 km south of Kilwa Kiswani there is another group of islands. To get there you can hire a motorized dhow from **Kilwa Seaview** (US$100 for up to five people), or it's possible to catch a local boat from Kilwa Masoko through the district headquarters office. The ruined buildings at **Songo Mnara** are exceptional. The settlement is surrounded by the remains of a wall and the main mosque is distinguished by herringbone stonework and a double row of unusually high arches at one end. The Sultan's Palace, with its high walls, is extensive and was evidently at least two storeys high. The doorways, faced with slender stonework, are particularly fine. The building to the east of the palace has a room with a vaulted roof and porcelain bowls set into the stonework. There are three other smaller mosques, two of which abut the surrounding wall. Fragments of porcelain and earthenware abound, and some relics have been identified as Egyptian, dating from the 14th and 15th centuries. About 3 km southwest of Songo Mnara is an area known as **Sanje Majoma**, which also contains the ruins of a number of once-beautiful houses, complete with courtyards and stone arches.

Sanje ya Kati is a nearby uninhabited island, which was once settled by the Shanga people who are now extinct. In the 13th century they were considered a force to be reckoned with and strongly resisted foreign control. There are ruins of oblong-shaped houses, estimated to date from the 14th to 15th century.

◉ Kilwa listings

For sleeping and eating price codes and other relevant information, see pages 22-26.

● Where to stay

Kilwa *p112, map p114*
Kilwa Masoko
$$$ Kilwa Ruins Lodge, Jimbiza Beach, T023-201 3226, www.kilwaruinslodge.com. 14 rooms of varying standards, some large and spacious overlooking the beach and others, much smaller, in wooden bungalows up on the hill, which are not particularly good value, all have a/c, en suites, fans and mosquito nets. This is a popular game-fishing lodge, and all the rooms are named after different fish. There's a pleasant bar area off the beach and a restaurant with a pool table, darts board and TV lounge. There's a small swimming pool in the well-kept grounds. Prices vary depending on the room, but are around US$70-110 per person half board.
$$$ Kimbilio Lodge, Jimbiza Beach, next to the **Kilwa Ruins**, T0785-991 681, www.kimbiliolodges.com. This Italian-run lodge is predominantly a PADI diving resort, with 6 en suite bandas near the beach with verandas; the foot wash to stop sand coming in is a nice touch. The popular restaurant (with Italian chef) is well known for its pasta and pizza and for its daily fresh fish. Good guides for day tours. Doubles from US$130.
$$$-$$ Kilwa Seaview Resort, set on a cliff overlooking Jimbiza Beach, T023-201 3064, www.kilwa.net. Spotless rooms with bathrooms are in stone bandas and many have views over Kilwa Kisiwani. There's access to Jimbiza Beach, as well as a swimming pool. The atmospheric restaurant and bar has a palm-thatched roof, built around an old baobab tree, and serves tasty 3-course dinners and good seafood dishes. Activities include day trips to Kilwa Kivinje, fishing and dhow trips. Doubles from US$100, and some bandas sleep up to 4 from US$130, so good value per person.
$$ Kilwa Dreams, in a very pretty location on Pwani Beach, 3 km out of town, T0784-585 330, www.kilwadreams.com. This small, pleasant but isolated lodge has 7 thatched en suite bungalows with mosquito nets and terraces, a bar, restaurant and gift shop. Popular with anglers, it has 3 fully equipped fishing boats and can organize day trips. Doubles from US$60 including breakfast. Danish-run and involved in supporting a local medical clinic.
$ Hilton Guest House, Mapinduzi St, T0777-547 588. Simple rooms with fan, with or without bathroom, a bit run down and dingy but all less than US$5. There is a restaurant adjoining the guesthouse, offering local dishes and breakfast, the fish here is good.
$ New Mjaka Guest House/Majaka Enterprises, there are 2 of these, both with the same name, T023-201 3071. One is on the main road to the harbour in the centre of town near *NMB*; the other is 500 m down the road near the harbour. They're both similar, serve local food and offer clean rooms with en suite, mosquito net and fan. The choice depends mainly on how close you want to be to town.

● Transport

Kilwa *p112, maps p112 and p114*
Air
Coastal Air, Dar T022-284 2700, T023-201 3004 (Kilwa), www.coastal.cc, flies between Kilwa and **Dar** (2 hrs) via **Mafia** (30 mins). On the Kilwa part of the circuit the flight leaves Mafia at 1110, arrives in Kilwa at 1140, departs

again at 1150 and arrives back in Mafia at 1220. **Note** The plane will only call at Kilwa if there are enough passengers needing the service, so it's always best to check with **Coastal Air** before making firm plans. A charter is a possibility, particularly for groups.

Bus

Buses go direct between **Kilwa** and the Ubungo bus station in **Dar**, and from both places they depart at 0500-0600 (8-10 hrs, US$15). Confirm exact departure time and book a ticket the day before you travel. There are some direct buses south to **Lindi**, **Mtwara** and **Masasi**, although they're few and far between, and you may have to catch buses coming from Dar at **Nangurukuru**. They start arriving from about 1400 onwards but you cannot guarantee a seat.

Lindi and around

Despite the fact that Lindi translates from Ki Mwera (a local language) as 'a pit latrine', the place still has a great deal of charm, albeit faded. It was an important port for early traders and travellers, and the Arab influence is visible. The centre has many attractive colonial buildings, but poor communications, and the collapse of the Groundnut Scheme (see box, page 399), one site for which was at nearby Nachingwea, has hampered development. Since the opening of the deep-water harbour at Mtwara in 1954, Lindi's harbour, too shallow for modern ships, is only used by local fishing boats, and the quay is slowly crumbling away. Around Lindi Bay there are several attractive beaches fringed with palm trees. ▶▶ *For listings, see pages 120-121.*

Arriving in Lindi → *Phone code: 023. Population: 40,000. Colour map 1, C6. 9°58'S 39°38'E.*
Getting there The airstrip is at Kikwetu about 25 km north of town but at present there are no commercial flights. The only way to get there is by road, perhaps breaking your journey at Kilwa, as the daily bus journey from Dar takes eight hours; more if it's the rainy season. The road both south and north of Kilwa has seen extensive improvements over recent years but repairs are ongoing and there are still stretches which can be impassable in heavy rains. The 175-km drive between Kilwa and Lindi can take up to five hours depending on road conditions, but would normally take about three. Seek advice on road conditions before travelling. ▶▶ *For further details, see Transport, page 121.*

Getting around Lindi itself is a very compact town and most of the places of interest are within walking distance. *Dala-dalas* can be caught at the market, the bus stand or along the main streets (Kawawa, Market and Mchinga roads).

Places in Lindi

Initial settlement was by Shirazi migrants (see box, page 95). Being the main seaport for Lake Nyasa (now Lake Malawi), it was a destination for slave caravans from the interior in the 19th century. The only remnant of this Omani Arab period is the massive **round tower** on the beach side of the stadium.

The colonial German powers chose Lindi as the administrative headquarters of the Southern Province, a huge administrative area that encompassed the whole of the south of Tanganyika right across to Lake Nyasa, at the end of the 19th century. A **Custom House** and store for the German East African Company were constructed close to the remains of the fort. These, and other buildings of the colonial period, are now very dilapidated. One

German building, the **police station**, is still in use; it's easily identifiable by its solid build and ornamental finishes. The German **Boma** is disappearing behind the trees growing out of it.

Lindi has a long history as a trading port for ivory, beeswax and mangrove poles. Rock salt is extensively mined nearby. Its advantages were the comparatively easy approach along the Lukuledi River valley and the relative proximity of Mozambique, source of much of the produce.

There are fine examples of Asian-inspired architecture along **Market** and **Kawawa roads**, dating from when the town used to support an Asian community trading in grain, sisal and cashew nuts.

There are ornamental decorative finishes on some of the buildings, especially the mosques, such as those on Makongoro Street facing the stadium. The modest **mosque** next to the bus station possesses a wonderful elaborately carved and colourful door.

Lindi is now essentially a Muslim town, and the Muslim brotherhoods or *tariqa* are quite active. You are likely to hear, if not see, noisy celebrations at night on feasts such as *maulid*, the commemoration of the Prophet's birth. It involves Koran school teachers and their students singing in turn, drumming, lots of incense and, possibly, deep-breathing exercises known to Muslim mystics as *dhikr*. If you want to see a *maulid*, dress modestly and exercise discretion. Other rather high-pitched drums heard at night are for girls' initiation ceremonies or spirit possession dances – no contradiction for the local brand of Islam.

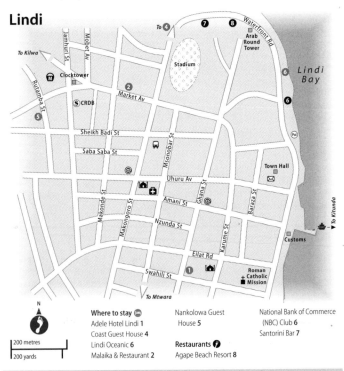

Lindi

Where to stay
Adele Hotel Lindi **1**
Coast Guest House **4**
Lindi Oceanic **6**
Malaika & Restaurant **2**

Nankolowa Guest
House **5**

Restaurants
Agape Beach Resort **8**

National Bank of Commerce
(NBC) Club **6**
Santorini Bar **7**

200 metres
200 yards

Cashew nuts

Cashew nuts are the main export product in the Lindi, Mtwara and Kilwa regions of Tanzania. They grow on massive trees, rarely more than 10 m tall, but with sprawling, shady crowns, which line many of the streets in these districts. They supply elephant repellent, poison, furniture varnish and, of course, nuts. Two properties combine to make them so versatile. First, cashew nuts come attached to cashew apples, a tasty, brightly coloured fruit that is easily fermented. Second, between the shell and the kernel, cashew nuts contain a noxious oil strong enough to cause serious wounds. Hence the use of cashew nuts to drive off elephants: the animals detest the smell of the burning oil.

The oil makes the shelling difficult and the shelled nuts expensive. The trick is to burn the shells and the oil of the nuts, but not the kernels, by roasting them quickly and then, as quickly, extinguishing the fire. If people do this in their back yards in old gasoline drums, the kernels end up spotty, half raw, half charred. Nuts like these are sold cheaply in the countryside and sometimes in Dar. Better quality ones, shelled in factories, are much more expensive, and a handful might cost more than a meal.

Cashew trees are not indigenous to Africa. They entered Tanzania from Mozambique, where they had arrived from Brazil, a fringe benefit of Portuguese colonialism. For a long time, Mozambique was the only African cashew nut exporter, the nuts being sent to Goa, Portugal's colonial possession in India, for processing. In Tanzania, efforts to build up production only started in the late 1940s; British reluctance to support cashew production was partly due to colonial officials' fear of drunkenness among Africans, since cashew apples make a good raw material for distilling a high-voltage liquor.

The present centre of town around the bus stand dates from the British period. The historic centre of the town between Kawawa Road and the beach is now a poor area, with a reputation for rampant witchcraft. Here the last descendant of the once-dominant Jamalidini family, of Mombasa origins, lives in a mud hut on a waterlogged compound. Several of the newer houses resemble pillboxes made of cement or breeze-blocks or, occasionally, mud and wattle.

The beach doubles as a boulevard and football pitch in the evenings, and you sometimes see fishermen unloading their catch, including octopus, kingfish and sharks (caught outside the bay). The catch of the day is for sale after dark at the bus stand, freshly cooked. The beach by the town is good for swimming, but you are likely to be observed by the locals.

Mitema

There are several excellent beaches around Lindi Bay, the best probably at Mitema, 4 km north of the town, just a 10-minute drive from the centre. This is where Lindi's few expatriates go swimming. The long beach, often deserted, is sheltered by palms and closed off at each end by rocks and enormous baobab trees. Occasionally you may meet a herd boy with his goats or a couple of Lindi's Asian traders in their 4WD vehicles. The ground is a bit rocky at low tide and the waves are high in the evening but it makes an enjoyable excursion – if you don't have your own transport make arrangements with *dala-dala* operators at the bus stand.

Kitunda and 'ngambo'

Many of Lindi's residents come from 'ngambo', which means 'the other shore' and, in Lindi, it refers to the peninsula across the bay, Kitunda being the beachside village. For a negligible fare, and at approximately half-hour intervals from Lindi harbour until 1800, you can take a wooden motorboat ferry to Kitunda. Here the water is clearer than at Lindi, though mangroves make swimming difficult at low tide. You can hire a dug-out very cheaply from a local fisherman to paddle along the shore or across the bay. Take the owner along for safety. Locals can show you around the hill behind the village. You will be shown many edible plants and odd animals, such as *ndandanda*, a small wedge-shaped fish with large eyes at the top of its head that uses its fins for crawling and jumping in shallow water. The sisal and coconut estates here are in terminal decline and there are the remains of a railway and jetty jutting out over the water, a good vantage point for swims at high tide. Across the hill to the south lie the villages of **Mwitingi**, once the home of Arab plantation owners, and **Shuka**, where locals catch sharks.

Kikwetu

Kikwetu is a breezy promontory 25 km north of Lindi, the location of the town's **airfield** and also of the last sisal estate to close in the area. It closed in 1999 after 100 years of production because sisal, used as coarse fibre for sackcloth and ropes, was no longer profitable (see box, page 97). Hidden among the large fields is the manager's mansion, from where there are excellent views. There is regular transport to the airport; to see the mansion, a 20-minute walk away from the roadside village, ask for '*kambi*' and the locals will show you.

Kisiwa cha popo

This small island in Lindi Bay is famed for its large bat population. Chiroptera fanciers can take a boat trip to the island where the trees are heavy with sleeping bats hanging from the branches during the day. You may also see crocodiles if you take a boat ride south across the Lukuledi River estuary, to the other side of Lindi Bay.

⊙ Lindi listings

For sleeping and eating price codes and other relevant information, see pages 22-26.

⬤ Where to stay

Lindi *p117, map p118*

There is 1 decent hotel in Lindi, but beyond this, there's little choice. Most options are cheap guesthouses with very basic amenities, and little English is spoken.

\$\$ Lindi Oceanic Hotel, Waterfront Rd towards the ferry, T0713-261 336, info@ lindioceanichotel.com. Built in 2008, this is the top hotel in town with a swimming pool, 2 restaurants (1 indoor and 1 outdoor), serving either buffet food or an à la carte menu, a bar and access to the beach. The

smart rooms all have a/c, en suite facilities, mosquito nets, fans, minibars, TVs, safes and balconies. Doubles from a very reasonable US\$60 and there's a secure car park.

\$ Adele Hotel Lindi, Ghana St, T023-220 2310, T0784-703 332. This guesthouse has been open for some years, but has recently added 7 spacious, en suite rooms in a new block, all with a/c, TV, mosquito net and fridge. In the old block there are 15 cheaper self-contained rooms with mosquito nets and TVs. There is an outside restaurant but dinners need to be ordered in advance. Unusually for a guesthouse in Lindi, there's a bar that sells beer. Good value and well run. The owner also runs 2 other guesthouses in town: the **Adele Guest House (\$)**, Ghana St, T023-220

2571, not far from the hotel; and the **Veronica Adela ($)**, Swahili St, T023-220 2570. Both are low budget with en suite or shared facilities.

$ Coast Guest House, about 500 m north of the ferry, T0754-628 105. This simple place has 17 rooms with nets and fans, most have bathrooms which have been newly tiled, and there are some singles with shared bathrooms. It's in a good location amongst palm trees on the beach, about a 20-min walk from the bus stand. Expect to pay around US$8, including a basic breakfast.

$ Malaika Hotel, Market Av, T0713-263 335. This has 8 rather grubby self-contained rooms, with TVs, fans and mosquito nets. Also has a restaurant with limited, if any, choice – despite what's on the menu. US$10 for a double room and breakfast. If you want to stay near the bus station, this is a good option.

$ Nankolowa Guest House, Rutamba St, signposted from the clock tower, T023-220 2727. Good value, self-contained double rooms; single rooms have shared toilet. Price includes large breakfast, and they serve other good meals on request, after a long wait.

🍴 Restaurants

Lindi *p117, map p118*
All hotels have restaurants, although many expect food to be pre-ordered, and there are snack bars around the bus station that serve sweet, milky tea, as well as *maandazi*, chapattis and other snacks. Fresh fruit and simple fare can be purchased at the market on Jamhuri St. The fishermen's catch of the day is for sale, freshly cooked, at the bus stand after dark.

A couple of bars on Waterfront Rd serve food. **Santorini Bar** is a friendly place which does good chicken and chips, and **Agape Beach Resort**, next door, has a few thatched gazebos around the rather tired gardens. Both serve beer, as do some of the small bars on Makongoro St down towards the stadium, which also serve local food. The **National Bank of Commerce (NBC) Club**, also called the **Lindi Club**, on the beach, further down from Market Av, is a bit dilapidated, but the sea view makes it one of the most pleasant locations for a drink. With plenty of notice they can cook something basic.

⊖ Transport

Lindi *p117, map p118*
Bus
The bus to **Dar** leaves at 0500 from the bus stand on Makongoro Rd (12-20 hrs, US$20), it stops at **Kilwa** along the way (US$10). There are also a few direct buses to Kilwa leaving at 0900 and 1300 for the same price. To **Mtwara**, buses run fairly frequently (about 4 hrs, US$3). To **Nachingwea** and **Newela**, there are daily buses (5-6 hrs, both about US$5); the road rising up to the Makonde plateau is pretty grim.

① Directory

Lindi *p117, map p118*
Medical services Sokoine Hospital, T023-220 2027/8. There is a **medical clinic** at the corner of Amani St and Msonobar St. **Police** Police station, housed in an old German building beside the waterfront, towards the NBC Club, T023-220 2505.

Mikindani and Mtwara

Mikindani is, for now at least, a sleepy fishing village with an interesting history, reflected in crumbling old Arab-style buildings with carved doors and elaborate balconies. However, changes are likely in the near future as oil and gas companies move in, following successful discoveries by prospectors. At the time of our visit, some areas of pristine palm forest beyond the village were already being cleared to make space for workers' camps, and the village's peaceful way of life will inevitably be altered. This really is a 'go now, before it's too late' destination. The two best places to stay in the region are here, the Old Boma and 10° South, which both offer good value accommodation, excellent food and trips to the region's local attractions including the Mnazi Bay Marine Reserve.

Mtwara, 10 km to the south, is more modern and is the administrative centre of the south coast region. There is little to see here, though it offers facilities, such as a bank and post office, and the immigration office is here if you are planning to cross the border into Mozambique.
▶ *For listings, see pages 125-128.*

Mikindani → *For listings, see pages 125-128. Phone code: 023. Colour map 1, C6.*

The small town of Mikindani is 11 km northwest of Mtwara on the Mtwara to Lindi road. Unlike most towns in this region, Mikindani has managed to retain much of its traditional Arab charm. It is a very Muslim town, so you should dress and act appropriately. It is located beside a sheltered circular lagoon that is itself an inlet from the larger Mikindani Bay, fringed with palm forests and mangroves. The lagoon has made an excellent harbour for the dug-out canoes and dhows of local fishermen for centuries, and there has been a settlement here for almost 1000 years. When the Arabs arrived, Mikindani grew in prosperity, its importance as a trading centre being greatest in the 15th century. Later, with the arrival of the first Europeans, notably the explorer Dr Livingstone, and with the subsequent ban on the slave trade, Mikindani began to decline. There was a revival when the German colonial government briefly made the town the district headquarters in 1890. However, by the 1950s, production of groundnuts and oil seed demanded larger ships, for which the port was unsuitable, and Mikindani declined once more.

Arriving in Mikindani
Getting there There are plenty of *dala-dalas* that cover the 11 km between Mtwara and Mikindani and through buses between Lindi and Mtwara stop here. If you fly in to Mtwara, you'll need to get a *dala-dala* or a taxi to Mikindani. **The Old Boma** (see Where to stay, page 125) can arrange a pickup, if you're staying there. ▶ *For details, see Transport, page 128.*

Places in Mikindani
Much of the town's traditional character remains. There is an interesting mix of thatched mud houses and Arab-style buildings, including several fine two-storey townhouses with elaborate fretwork balconies. Arabs, Portuguese, Germans and British have all occupied the town at different times. The 500-year-old Portuguese fort was used as a slave prison and later bombarded by the British in the First World War. There is an old slave market, now a collection of small art shops, and a fort, dating from the German period and built in 1895, which has been renovated to become a hotel. Most of the other old colonial buildings are in a poor state of repair. Mikindani was the port from which Livingstone departed on his

Trade Aid UK, Livingstone House and the Old Boma

Since 1996, a British charity called Trade Aid UK has been working in Mikindani helping local people build and develop sustainable ecotourism businesses, and thus alleviate poverty. They started by rehabilitating and converting the old German Boma and turning it into the best hotel in the area, in the process training local people in all kinds of skills, from masonry and gardening to hotel management. Profits from the hotel are ploughed back into the local community and are used to fund projects involving education, conservation and sustainable employment. The **Old Boma** is the base for the charity, which actively encourages small businesses within the village by providing micro-credit loans and business advice. So far, some 150 loans have been given, involving around 450 local people who act as business partners, in enterprises as diverse as beekeeping, fishing, furniture making, hair-dressing, shop keeping and catering.

Aside from encouraging local employment, Trade Aid are also keen to preserve the village of Mikindani, where many of the buildings, all with stories to tell, are slowly crumbling. **Livingstone House**, for example, claims to have been the great explorer's base while he was in the area, and may have even greater historical significance, since Trade Aid recently discovered ornately carved Zanzibari doors, 200 years' old or more, inside. Other than a few add-ons by Indian traders in the late 19th century, the structure has remained relatively untouched compared to other examples of Arab buildings of this time. Working closely with Tanzania's Department of Antiquities and the Ministry of Natural Resources, Trade Aid is now involved in restoring the building to its former glory, as they did so successfully with the Boma.

Trade Aid takes on volunteers; to find out more, or to offer financial or practical help, contact Trade Aid in either the UK or in Mikindani: www.tradeaiduk.org.

final journey to the interior in 1867 (see page 340) and a house with a fine carved door bears a plaque to mark the site where the explorer is said to have camped.

A walk up the hill behind the Old Boma will bring you to a very large hole. A witchdoctor saw his lucky chicken scratching in this spot several years ago and, ever since, has been digging for the German gold that he firmly believes is buried there.

Mtwara → *For listings, see pages 125-128. Phone code: 023. Population: 80,000. Colour map 1, C6. 10°20'S 40°20'E.*

Mtwara is a sizeable town that came to prominence during the British period. It has been a centre for agricultural processing and has a factory for shelling and canning the cashew nuts that are grown extensively in the southeast (see box, page 119). Although the town itself is set a little way from the shore, Mtwara boasts a magnificent sheltered harbour. However, the port, built in 1948-1954, has never been used to capacity, as there is relatively little traffic generated in this economically depressed region. The second deepest port in Africa, it was built as part of the ill-fated scheme to grow and export groundnuts from southern Tanzania, a project that included the construction of a railway from Mtwara to Nachingwea – now dismantled. The scheme was implemented after the Second World War, when the British had taken control of what was then Tanganyika from the Germans, and the groundnuts were expected to make up for post-war food shortages in the United Kingdom and to provide exports to the rest of Europe. There are current plans to dredge and widen the port's entrance channel to facilitate the handling of larger modern vessels.

Arriving in Mtwara

Getting there The airport is 4 km to the south of town. The only airline that presently flies between Mtwara and Dar is **Fly 540**, although **Precision Air** has previously served the route and may do so again in the future. Buses leave from Dar early in the morning and take roughly 12 hours. It's about 640 km along a mostly tarred but occasionally

Mtwara

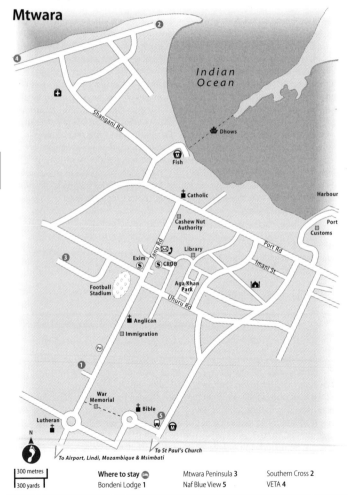

300 metres
300 yards

Where to stay 🛏
Bondeni Lodge **1**

Mtwara Peninsula **3**
Naf Blue View **5**

Southern Cross **2**
VETA **4**

rough, unsurfaced road, and you are advised to break the journey in either Lindi or Kilwa.
▸ *For further details, see Transport, page 128.*

Places in Mtwara

The town has one site of particular interest, **St Paul's Church**, which houses some remarkable murals of Biblical scenes painted by German priests. There are some **beaches** about 2 km from the town centre good for swimming and diving.

Mnazi Bay Marine Reserve

ⓘ *The reserve is 30 km south of Mtwara, 22 km along a dirt track off the main road, which is in a good state of repair and accessible to all vehicles because of a gas drilling operation on the peninsula. The road is, however, frequented by fairly heavy traffic and is liable to flooding during the wet season. The charge for entering the reserve is US$20, children (5-16) US$10 for a 24-hr period. 10° South and its dive centre Eco2 Diving offer tailor-made diving safaris to the reserve, with night beach camps and dives in the afternoon and morning; prices depend on the duration of the safari and the number of people involved. The Old Boma in Mikindani can also arrange excursions here.*

Mnazi Bay Marine Reserve was gazetted in 1999 and is similar in status to the Mafia Island Marine Park further up to the coast to the north. It offers superb snorkelling and scuba-diving and, as the reef along the coast is not tidal, it is good for swimming at all times of the day. Within the reserve, **Msimbati Beach** is a pristine, white sandy beach that shelves steeply. There is a fabulous coral reef lying offshore and turtles are common.

The self-proclaimed 'Sultan of Msimbati', a British eccentric named Leslie Latham Moore, came to these parts after the First World War. He attempted to declare Independence from Tanganyika – a situation that was briefly tolerated before he was arrested. The remains of his dilapidated house can still be seen.

Geological surveys on **Msimbati Island** in the Ruvuma Basin have shown several oil seeps, some with characteristics of true degraded crude oil. There is also a gas seep on the island, believed to be of biogenic origin. This basin lies at the southern end of the large East African Karoo Rift System that extends from Somalia. Exploration licences have been granted to the oil companies, and there is a new gas installation offshore.

⦿ Mikindani and Mtwara listings

For sleeping and eating price codes and other relevant information, see pages 22-26.

⦿ Where to stay

Mikindani *p122*

There are 2 excellent places to stay and eat in Mkindani, catering for all budgets.
$$$ The Old Boma, off the main Mikindani Bay Rd, overlooking the bay, T0784-360 110, www.mikindani.com. A characterful 100-year-old converted fort run by the British charity, Trade Aid UK. It has 9 standard and superior rooms, the latter with balconies overlooking

the coast. All have fans, en suite bathrooms, tremendous views and are individually furnished with beautiful local-style beds and handicrafts. Rates are US$140-175 for a double, depending on the room, and include breakfast. Even if you're not staying, come and eat here, as the food is superb, made using their own organically grown vegetables. They also stock a good range of wines. There is a swimming pool for use by guests or diners, and email for guests only. The hotel can arrange excursions to local attractions such as Mnazi Marine Reserve for US$75 and town tours for US$15. Free Swahili language and

Border crossing: Tanzania–Mozambique

Namoto

The Kilambo–Namoto border with Mozambique (0600-1800) over the Ruvuma River is approximately 40 km southeast of Mtwara, but it's a difficult border crossing, with or without a vehicle, as there is no bridge over the river.

If you're in a vehicle, there is a sporadic car ferry – water level permitting; it does run most days but cannot navigate the river in very low or neap tides. Be prepared to camp here for a day or two if it's necessary to wait for the ferry. You'll need to avoid the crossing altogether during heavy rains, as the road on the Mozambique side can be washed away. The ferry costs in the region of a (negotiable) US$25 per vehicle but, if there is only one vehicle, it could cost nearer US$100. Both border posts are no more than a collection of huts, but you should be able to change a few Tanzanian shillings into Mozambique metical (or vice versa) and buy a soda and basic snack. From Namoto, it's roughly 125 km to **Moçimboa da Praia**, the first main town on the 247 road south of the border, which has a petrol station (though supplies are erratic and there's sometimes only diesel), a bank with an ATM, district hospital and cell phone coverage. This road is tough – expect anything from pot-holed gravel to deep sand – and is encroached on either side by dense bush, making it single track in places; during heavy rains it is virtually impassable. From Moçimboa da Praia, it's another 360 km south to **Pemba** on a reasonable tarred road, though there are some stretches of deep pot holes. **Note** You cannot buy third-party insurance on the Mozambique side of the border until you reach Pemba. South of the border, you must tell the police (there is a checkpoint at Moçimboa da Praia) this is what you intend to do; anywhere south of Pemba, the police will fine you if you don't have it.

If you don't have a vehicle, Kilambo is an hour's *dala-dala* ride south of Mtwara, and then you need to walk, get a bicycle taxi or hitch the further 4 km to the river itself. You can cross the Ruvuma on the car ferry, if it's running, or by *mokoro*, which should cost in the region of US$8. If water levels are low, you may have to wade to get to and from the boat on the Tanzanian side. On the Mozambique side, it's a 3-km walk to the

cookery lessons. It is run as a training centre for local people, so profits are ploughed back into the community (see box, page 123). Highly recommended.

$$-$ 10° South (Ten Degrees), just off of the bay road, T0784-855 833, www.ten degreessouth.com. 4 en suite rooms in a block in the garden with terraces and sea views for US$60, plus 5 cheaper, simple but very clean guesthouse rooms in the main house with shared bathrooms for US$20. The thatched bar and restaurant is popular with local expats and has a wooden deck, which is ideal for sundowners, and serves excellent food, including local fish, calamari and a variety of good Western dishes. There's

usually a BBQ on Sat evenings. Eco2 Diving, is attached to the guesthouse, see What to do, below.

Mtwara *p123, map p124*
$$ Naf Blue View Hotel, Sinani St, in the town centre, T023-233 4465, T0776-467 066, nafblueviewhotel@gmail.com. Don't be put off by the name, it's the best accommodation option in Mtwara town. (N, A and F are the initials of the owner's 3 children.) The 9 a/c en suite rooms have nets, satellite TV and fridge, and there's a small, spotless restaurant that serves Chinese, Indian and local food. Doubles from US$65, including breakfast.

Mozambique border post at Namoto, from where there are daily landcruiser pickup *chapas* (taxis) to Moçimboa da Praia, or, if there are other vehicles, you can hitch. If the road is washed away, the only option is to walk the 15 km from Namoto to **Quionga**, the next village, and get transport from there. Be prepared for a long bumpy ride and make sure you have lots of water. There is very simple accommodation in Moçimboa da Praia – the best of which is the Pensao Leeta, which has basic rooms in a three-storey building opposite the petrol station, with a restaurant next door, and Chez Natalie, 2 km from town, which has comfortable chalets overlooking a lagoon and you can order meals. From Moçimboa da Praia, it is reasonably easy to find transport further south to Pemba.

Visas Visas for Tanzania are available at Kilambo. It is essentials to have a visa for Mozambique. These can be obtained from the embassy in Dar es Salaam. (If Namoto gets electricity any time soon – to power computers – then they may be available at the border.) Another awkward aspect of this border, is it's very quiet and rarely used – you may have to ask around to gather the various immigration and customs officials.

Mtambaswala–Negomano

There is a new bridge crossing the Ruvuma River some 275 km inland: the 720-m Unity Bridge, which opened in 2010 and was built by the Chinese. It connects southern Tanzania at Mtambaswala village, 240 km from Lindi, with northern Mozambique at Negonane village in the Cabo Delgado Province, 275 km from Moçimboa da Praia on the coast. While the road between Lindi and the bridge is reasonable, the roads on the Mozambique side are very difficult and become impassable during and after heavy rain. Nevertheless, there are now border posts on both sides of the bridge, and the nearest town to the bridge (170 km) on the Mozambique side, Mueda, has facilities including petrol stations, basic accommodation, restaurants, shops and a bank with an ATM. Traffic on this route is expected to increase rapidly as the roads are improved, but you'll still need to get up-to-date local information on conditions before attempting this route.

$ Bondeni Lodge, Tanu Rd, south of police station, T023-233 3769. Plain but spacious rooms with fans, nets and en suite bathrooms with squat toilets. The garden bar and restaurant has satellite TV and is a popular place for a few beers, though you may have to wait a long time for a hot plate of food.

$ Mtwara Peninsula Hotel, west of town near the football station, T023-233 3638. Run-down but adequate board and lodgings, some rooms have TV and fridge, all have a/c and en suite bathrooms. Good restaurant, with an extensive menu of seafood, curries and some vegetarian dishes.

$ Southern Cross Hotel, also known as Msemo Hotel, about 2 km north of town

on the Shangani Peninsula, T023-233 3206. The 9 rooms in terraced bungalows have great views over the bay and are clean and spacious with bathroom, a/c, TV and fridge. The food is OK, but service is notoriously slow, with seafood and curry dishes from US$6. Dhow trips around the bay are available. Doubles from US$35 and you may be able to negotiate to camp here.

$ VETA, about 2 km north of town on the Shangani Peninsula, T023-233 4094, www.veta.go.tz. A local conference and training centre, this new and rather characterless place offers 20 clean en suite rooms that are bland, typical conference bedrooms with fans, TV and hot water. However, it overlooks the ocean, staff are friendly and efficient, and there's a large canteen-type restaurant serving local food.

🍴 Restaurants

Mikindani *p122*
Most definitely head to **The Old Boma** or **10° South** to eat. The other hotels offer a limited selection of inexpensive simple meals, with little variety – usually rice with chicken or fish. The best cheap street food is at the fish market, beside the beach, where fresh fish and cassava chips are sold.

Mtwara *p123, map p124*
Restaurants are pretty much limited to the hotels; the **Naf Blue View** and **Southern Cross** have the greatest choice.

⏾ What to do

Mikindani *p122*
Diving
Eco2 Diving, at **10° South**, see Where to stay, above, T0784-855 833, www.eco2tz.com. Offers PADI dive courses up to divemaster level. A PADI open water course costs in the region of US$400, and recreational dives cost from US$75, with discounts if you book diving and accommodation packages at either **The Old Boma**, or **10° South**. Dives go to 12 local reefs, and also to the Mnazi Bay Marine Reserve as either day trips or over-nighters.

🚍 Transport

Mikindani *p122*
Bus and dala-dala
All buses stop at Mikindani en route to **Mtwara**. *Dala-dala* to **Mtwara** (US$0.40).

Mtwara *p123, map p124*
Air
Fly 540, Dar, T0752-540 540, www.fly540.com, has a daily flight which leaves Dar at 1630, arrives in Mtwara at 1730, departs again at 1800 and arrives back in Dar at 1900; US$160 1-way.

Bus and dala-dala
There are several buses a day between Mtwara and **Dar**; they leave from both destinations at 0500-0600 and take around 12 hrs (US$18), but if it's dry all the way through and the road has been graded, they may take around 10 hrs. The bus stand is on Market St. Book a ticket the day before and confirm departure time. There are also regular direct buses and *dala-dala* to **Lindi** (US$2) and **Mikindani** (US$0.40), and all buses stop at both places en route to/from **Dar**.

ℹ Directory

Mtwara *p123, map p124*
Immigration The immigration office is to the south of the NBC Club, Tanu Rd. **Police** The police station is across the road from the immigration office.

Contents

Footprint features

Zanzibar & Pemba

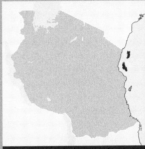

At a glance

⊖ **Getting around** Buses, *dala-dala* and taxis go almost everywhere on Zanzibar, but transport on Pemba is much more limited. Cars, motorbikes and bikes can be hired, and local boatmen will take you in their dhows.

✪ **Time required** 3 days for a beach break after a safari or trek, 1-2 weeks to explore the islands and still have time to chill. At least 1 day in Stone Town.

☀ **Weather** Hot and sticky Nov-Dec and Apr-May. Jun-Oct has a cooler, balmier climate and is the best time to visit.

✖ **When not to go** Many places close in the rainy season (Apr-Jun). During Ramadan local cafés and bars will be shut, although tourist restaurants and hotels stay open.

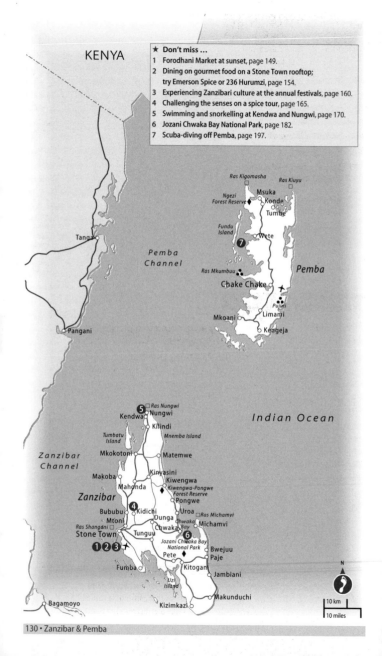

KENYA

★ Don't miss ...
1 Forodhani Market at sunset, page 149.
2 Dining on gourmet food on a Stone Town rooftop;
  try Emerson Spice or 236 Hurumzi, page 154.
3 Experiencing Zanzibari culture at the annual festivals, page 160.
4 Challenging the senses on a spice tour, page 165.
5 Swimming and snorkelling at Kendwa and Nungwi, page 170.
6 Jozani Chwaka Bay National Park, page 182.
7 Scuba-diving off Pemba, page 197.

Ras Kigomasha   Ras Kiuyu

Ngezi   Msuka
Forest Reserve   Konde
                    Tumbe

Tanga   Fundu
           Island   Wete

Pemba
Channel   Pemba

           Ras Mkumbuu

           Chake Chake

Pangani

                    Pujini
           Mkoani   Limami
                    Kengeja

                              Indian Ocean

           Ras Nungwi
      Kendwa Nungwi

           Kilindi
Tumbatu   Mnemba Island
Island   Mkokotoni   Matemwe

Zanzibar   Kinyasini
Channel   Makoba   Kiwengwa
           Mahonda   Kiwengwa-Pongwe
Zanzibar   Forest Reserve
                        Pongwe
      Bububu Kidichi
      Mtoni   Uroa Ras Michamvi
Ras Shangani Dunga Chwaka
Stone Town   Tunguu Chwaka Michamvi
❶❷❸   Bay
                Jozani Chwaka Bay
                National Park   Bwejuu
           Pete   Paje
Fumba
           Kitogan   Jambiani
      Uzi
      Island

Bagamoyo   Makunduchi
           Kizimkazi

N

10 km
10 miles

The very name Zanzibar conjures up exotic and romantic images. The main town on Zanzibar Island, Stone Town, with its intriguing, winding alleyways, old Arabian townhouses and heaving port, is steeped in history, full of atmosphere and immensely attractive. Zanzibar's coastlines offer some of the best beaches in the world, but sand and surf vary depending on which side of the island you're on. On the east coast, waves break over coral reefs and sand bars offshore, and low tide reveals small pools of starfish. Up north, ocean swimming is much less susceptible to the tides, and smooth beaches of white sand make for dazzling days in the sun. Roads to the southeast coast take visitors through the Jozani Chawka Bay National Park, the only national park on the islands, which is home to Zanzibar's rare red colobus monkeys and a number of other primate and small antelope species.

Zanzibar attracts hundreds of thousands of visitors a year and, to some extent, the island has suffered from the consequences of mass tourism. In recent years, its popularity as a European charter destination has seen the growth of all-inclusive resorts housing tourists on sun, sea and sand holidays, from which they experience little of the island outside the compound of their resort.

Quite by contrast, Pemba is hardly visited at all and is infinitely more difficult to get around. The sea around Pemba is dotted with desert islands and is the location of some of the best scuba-diving in the Indian Ocean. The Pemba Channel drops off steeply just off the west coast and the diverse species of marine life and coral are exceptional. Unlike Zanzibar, tourism is still in its early stages here and a visit is truly a Robinson Crusoe experience.

Arriving on Zanzibar → *Colour map 1, B6. 6°12'S 39°12'E.*

Getting there → *Phone code: 024.*

Immigration The islands that make up the Zanzibar Archipelago – Unguja (commonly known as Zanzibar Island), Pemba and numerous smaller islands – lie roughly 30-50 km off the coast of mainland Tanzania. Visa requirements are the same as they are for Tanzania but, whilst still part of Tanzania, the islands are administered autonomously and have their own immigration procedures. Therefore, you will be asked to show your passport to an immigration official on entry and exit and have it stamped in and out. Likewise, your passport will be stamped on arrival once back on mainland Tanzania. If you fly directly into **Zanzibar International Airport** from outside Tanzania, visas are available on arrival. Note that the agreement between Tanzania, Kenya and Uganda that allows holders of single-entry visas to move freely between all three countries without the need for re-entry permits, also covers travel to Zanzibar.

Air International and domestic flights arrive and depart from **Zanzibar International Airport** ① *T024-223 3979, www.zanzibar-airport.com*, 6 km to the southeast of Stone Town along Nyerere Road. There are numerous daily flights between Dar es Salaam and Zanzibar which take 20 minutes and cost from around US$75 one-way. Zanzibar International Airport also serves flights from other destinations on the mainland, including Nairobi and the rest of East Africa, as well as European charter flights. Visitors arriving on Zanzibar from outside Tanzania can obtain a visa on entry. The airport has a snack bar, souvenir shops, bureaux de change and ATMs. You can organize a taxi at the taxi stand outside arrivals, or else at the desk for the Zanzibar Commission for Tourism (see below). Ignore the touts who will endeavour to pull your bags out of your hands in an effort to get you into their taxi. Fares vary depending on your destination, but expect to pay in the region of US$60-70 to the north or east coasts for up to four or six people depending on the size of the vehicle. To get from the airport to Stone Town, a taxi costs around US$10. Transport from the airport to destinations across the island is included in holiday packages and most hotels and tour operators will provide transport to take you directly to your coastal resort, or at the very least can organize an airport transfer. The small airport at Pemba is near Chake Chake and the smaller airlines link Pemba with Dar es Salaam and Zanzibar. Taxis meet the flights and, again, the resorts organize transfers. There is an international airport departure tax of US$50 and a domestic departure tax of US$5, although these are usually included in the price of your ticket; check with your airline. ➤ *For airlines, see Transport, page 166.*

Ferry Ferries to Zanzibar and Pemba leave from the jetty on Sokoine Drive opposite St Joseph's Cathedral in Dar es Salaam, and each company has a ticket office on or around the wharf. There are frequent ferries between Dar and Stone Town on Zanzibar, from big, old slow overnight boats to 90-minute hydrofoils. How much you pay depends on the level of comfort and how quickly you want to get there, but fast ferry fares start from US$35 each way (see Dar es Salaam, page 75, for further information). There are less frequent ferry services between Dar and Mkoani on Pemba from US$60 each way, all of which stop at Zanzibar en route. ➤ *For further details, see Transport, page 166.*

Getting around

Public transport on Zanzibar in the way of buses and *dala-dalas* is cheap, the longest journey is no more than US$2, with regular services, and the main roads around the island are all good tar. *Dala-dalas* on the islands are usually converted pickup trucks with bench-like seating. However, they are crowded, uncomfortable and can be very tiresome. A 60-km journey across the island can take up to three hours, since stops are frequent. On Pemba, *dala-dalas* and the odd bus run up and down the main roads from early morning to early afternoon and their regularity rather depends on how many people want to use them. An alternative on Zanzibar, and by far the quickest and best way to reach the beaches, is to either go directly from the airport (see above) or book a seat on one of the daily tourist minibuses. These will usually take you right to your hotel door for about US$15 per person. They can be booked through Stone Town's tour operators and most budget hotels, and leave Stone Town at around 0800, returning mid-morning from their various destinations.

If you want to drive yourself, cars, jeeps and motorbikes can be hired and, for a group of four people, hiring a car can sometimes work out cheaper than paying for individual transfers. Hiring a car is not especially difficult. Drivers must be over 25 and have an international driver's licence. A licence from your own country is permissible but you need to get this endorsed locally by the police for a fee of about US$10, and you'll get a temporary 15-day driver's permit. Without this permit you may get harassed at the police road blocks on the island, of which there are several. The tour operator that you hire the car from will take care of all of this during a 20-minute drive around to the respective offices whose stamps and signatures are needed. Car hire costs around US$40-60 per day for something like a small Suzuki jeep including insurance, but do read the small print to ensure that the cover is adequate. Motorbikes and scooters cost around US$35 per day with helmet and insurance. Most tour operators (see page 165) can organize car hire.

If you can handle the heat, then cycling can be an excellent way to explore; in fact, it will soon become apparent that most Zanzibaris own bikes. Many beach hotels rent out bikes for around US$10-15 per day and some offer them free to guests. Watch out for motorists, though, as they generally have little respect for cyclists and expect them to get out of the way or leave the road when they want to pass.

Best time to visit

Due to their proximity to the equator, the climate on the islands is generally tropical, but the heat is tempered by a sea breeze throughout the year. The average temperature fluctuates between 25 and 30°C. There are long rains from March to mid-June and short rains in November and December. The hottest time is after the short rains from December to February, with temperatures up to 34°C at midday. The most comfortable time of year is June to October, with lower temperatures, little rain and plenty of sun, made bearable by the cooling winds from the southeast, known as the *Kusi* or the southeast monsoons. From October to March the winds change, blowing from the northeast, and they are known as the *Kaskazi* or the northeast monsoons. Bear in mind when booking flights and accommodation, there are high and low seasons. The Muslim month of Ramadan is one festival most tourists aim to avoid (especially those travelling to Stone Town), as many restaurants close during the day, and eating and drinking in public before nightfall can be very awkward. However, Eid-al-Ftir (end of Ramadan) is an excellent day to be in Stone Town as feasting and partying take over and all are welcome.

Tourist information and maps

The **Zanzibar Commission for Tourism (ZCT)** ① *T024-223 3485, www.zanzibartourism.net*, is the official government tourist body. There are two very helpful offices and both are open 0800-1800; one is at the airport just after baggage reclaim and the other is at the port, just on the left as you disembark from the ferry. Both can immediately organize taxis to town

Zanzibar Island

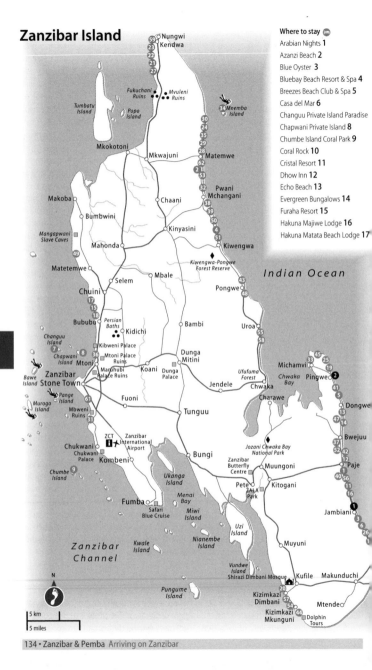

Where to stay
Arabian Nights **1**
Azanzi Beach **2**
Blue Oyster **3**
Bluebay Beach Resort & Spa **4**
Breezes Beach Club & Spa **5**
Casa del Mar **6**
Changuu Private Island Paradise
Chapwani Private Island **8**
Chumbe Island Coral Park **9**
Coral Rock **10**
Cristal Resort **11**
Dhow Inn **12**
Echo Beach **13**
Evergreen Bungalows **14**
Furaha Resort **15**
Hakuna Majiwe Lodge **16**
Hakuna Matata Beach Lodge **17**

and transport to the coast with their official drivers. They have a list of hotels and can call ahead on your behalf. In the case of the port, they can then organize someone from the hotel to come to the port and walk you to the closer hotels with your luggage. Their website is a good source of information. The tour operators (see page 165), which have offices all over Stone Town, also provide comprehensive information for visitors to the islands and can book hotels, transfers and car hire, and arrange excursions.

The best maps available are produced by **The Zanzibar Gallery** ⓘ *Gizenga St*, in Stone Town; *Illustrated Zanzibar Map* and *Illustrated Pemba Map*, both have extra information about weather, distances and very usefully, *dala-dala* routes. Each costs around US$0.50 and is available from The Gallery and various other outlets in Stone Town and Dar es Salaam. Try the bookshops in Dar such as **A Novel Idea**, see page 70, or in Stone Town, see page 161.

Note that the only banks and ATMs on Zanzibar are in Stone Town, so make sure you have enough cash before you head off to other parts of the island. Avoid changing money on the street in Stone Town.

Safety

Zanzibar is a reasonably safe place to travel in and, by using the usual common-sense precautions like leaving valuables in a hotel safe and not flashing your wealth, you shouldn't have any trouble. There have been a few isolated incidents of violent robberies of tourists in Stone Town and its environs. Be careful walking after dark, especially in poorly lit areas, particularly in Stone Town by the Big Tree on Mizingani Road and the Malindi area near the port. Always take a taxi late at night or, if this is not possible in the confined streets of Stone Town, ask your restaurant or hotel to ask someone to accompany you on the walk home. Exert caution on quiet beaches and stay within shouting distance of other people.

If you've hired a vehicle, you may encounter one of the numerous police road blocks around the islands. Standard fines (for offences such as speeding) are issued on the spot and you will be given a receipt. If the police are not willing to give a receipt, or they claim that your papers are not in order, they may be looking for a small bribe. Insist that you want to go to the police station to deal with it.

The use of recreational drugs is highly illegal and, though you may be offered marijuana on Zanzibar, you will get into all sorts of serious trouble if caught negotiating with a dealer.

One of the biggest annoyances are the *papasi* (unlicensed and often intrusive touts) or 'beach boys'. These are usually young men who hound visitors trying to earn commission by taking them to hotels or tour operators, or who sell anything from curios to snorkelling trips. See box, page 143.

Background

The origin of the name Zanzibar is disputed. The Omani Arabs believe it came from *Zayn Zal Barr*, which means 'Fair is the Island'. The alternative origin is in two parts – the early inhabitants of the island were from the mainland and were given the name *Zenj*, a Persian word that is a corruption of *Zangh* meaning negro. The word *bar* meaning 'coast' was added to this to give 'Negro Coast'.

The earliest visitors were Arab traders who brought with them Islam, which has remained the dominant religion on the island. They are believed to have arrived in the eighth century. The earliest remaining building is the mosque at Kizimkazi, which dates from about 1100. For centuries the Arabs had sailed with the monsoons down from Muscat and Oman in the Gulf to trade in ivory, slaves, spices, hides and wrought-iron. The two main islands, both of roughly similar size, Unguja (known as Zanzibar Island) and Pemba, provided an ideal base, being relatively small islands and thus easy to defend. From here it was possible to control 1500 km of the mainland coast from present day Mozambique up to Somalia. A consequence of their being the first arrivals was that the Arabs became the main landowners.

In 1832 Sultan Seyyid Said, of the Al Busaid dynasty that had emerged in Oman in 1744, moved his palace from Muscat to Zanzibar. Said and his descendants were to rule there for 134 years. In 1822, the Omanis signed the Moresby Treaty, which made it illegal for them to sell slaves to Christian powers in their dominions. To monitor this agreement, the United States in 1836 and the British in 1840 established diplomatic relations with Zanzibar and sent resident consuls to the islands. The slaving restrictions were not effective and the trade continued to flourish. Caravans set out from Bagamoyo on the mainland coast, travelling up to 1500 km on foot as far as Lake Tanganyika, purchasing slaves from local rulers on the way, or, more cheaply, simply capturing them. The slaves, chained together, carried ivory back to Bagamoyo. The name Bagamoyo means 'lay down your heart' for it was here that the slaves would abandon hope of ever seeing their homeland again. They were shipped to the slave market in Zanzibar's Stone Town, bought by intermediary traders, who in turn sold them on without any restrictions.

All the main racial groups were involved in the slave trade. Europeans used slaves in the plantations in the Indian Ocean islands, Arabs were the main capturers and traders, and African rulers sold the prisoners taken in battle to the traders. Nevertheless, it is the perception of the African population than the Arabs were mainly responsible.

Cloves had been introduced from Southeast Asia, probably Indonesia, prior to the advent of Sultan Seyyid Said. They flourished in the tropical climate on the fertile and well-watered soils on the western areas of both Zanzibar and Pemba. Slaves did the cultivation and harvesting, and the Sultan owned the plots: by his death in 1856 he had 45 plantations. Other plantations were acquired by his many children, as well as by numerous concubines and eunuchs from the royal harem. In due course, cinnamon, nutmeg, black pepper, cumin, ginger and cardamom were all established, their fragrance was everywhere and Zanzibar became known as the 'Spice Islands'. Slaves, spices and ivory provided the basis of considerable prosperity, mostly in the hands of the Arab community, who were the main landowners and who kept themselves to themselves and did not intermarry with the Africans.

This was not true of a second group that came from the Middle East to settle on the East African coast, the Shirazis (see box, page 95). Intermarriage between Shirazis and Africans gave rise to a coastal community with distinctive features and a language derived in part from Arabic. This became known as Swahili. In Zanzibar the descendants of this group were known as the Afro-Shirazis. They were not greatly involved in the lucrative slave, spice and ivory trades. They cultivated coconuts, fished and became agricultural labourers. Those Shirazis who did not intermarry retained their identity as a separate group.

Two smaller communities were also established. Indian traders arrived in connection with the spice and ivory trade and, as elsewhere, settled as shopkeepers, traders, skilled artisans, money-lenders, lawyers, doctors and accountants. The British became involved in missionary and trading activities in East Africa while attempting to suppress the slave trade. And, when Germans began trading on the mainland opposite Zanzibar, things needed to be sorted out with the Sultan of Zanzibar, who controlled the 10-mile coastal strip that ran for 1500 km from Mozambique to Somalia. The Germans bought their strip of the coast from the Sultan for £200,000. The British East African Company had been paying the Sultan £11,000 a year for operating in the Kenyan portion. In 1890, Germany allowed Britain to establish a protectorate over Zanzibar in return for Heligoland, a tiny barren island occupied by the British, but strategically placed opposite the mouth of the River Elbe, 50 km from the German coast. In 1895 Britain took over responsibility for its section of the mainland from the British East African Company and agreed to continue to pay the £11,000 a year to the Sultan. The British mainland territory (later Kenya), was administered by a Governor, to whom the British representative in Zanzibar, the Resident, was accountable.

The distinctive feature of Zanzibar as a protectorate (Kenya had become a colony in 1920) was recognized in 1926 when the British Resident was made directly responsible to the Colonial Secretary in London. Germany had by this stage lost control of its section of the mainland when, as a result of its defeat in the First World War, the territory was transferred to British control and became Tanganyika.

The colonial period

Further legislation in 1873 had made the slave trade illegal, the slave market in Zanzibar was closed and the Protestant cathedral erected on the site. But slavery lingered on. The trade was illegal, but the institution of slavery existed openly until Britain took over the mainland from the Germans in 1918, and covertly, it is argued, for many years thereafter. Many former slaves found that their conditions had changed little. They were now employed as labourers at low wage rates in the clove plantations. Zanzibar continued to prosper with the expansion of trade in cloves and other spices. The fine buildings that make Zanzibar Stone Town such a glorious place were constructed by wealthy Arab slavers and clove traders, British administrators and prosperous Indian businessmen and professionals. These structures were so soundly built that they have survived for the most part without repairs, maintenance and redecoration to the present day.

The wealth of the successive Sultans was considerable. They built palaces in Stone Town and around Zanzibar. Islamic law allowed them to have up to four wives, and their wealth

Princess Salme of Zanzibar

Princess Sayyida Salme was born at Mtoni Palace on Zanzibar in 1844 and was the daughter of Sultan Seyyid Said who ruled from 1804 to 1856. Her mother was one of his concubines and a former Circassian slave from southern Russia, who was tall and strong with startling blue eyes, pale ivory-coloured skin and black hair that came down to her knees (Circassian women were thought to be highly beautiful and spirited which made them desirable as concubines at the time). Salme inherited her mother's great beauty and intelligence and was unusually skilled for a young woman in the royal family; she could swim, ride a horse, shoot, was fluent in both Kiswahili and Arabic and could write. The princess was very keen on learning about Western cultures and she convinced her father to permit her to take English lessons so she could communicate with the wives of Western dignitaries, whose husbands came to greet the Sultan. When her father died in 1856, she was declared of age at 12 years old and received her paternal heritage of a plantation, residence and £5500. Her brother Sayyid Thuwaini bin Said al-Said became Sultan of Muscat and Oman, while her other brother Majid bin

Said became the Sultan of Zanzibar. (She was also the half-sister of Barghash bin Said who took the throne after Majid.)

The princess fell in love with a young German businessman from Hamburg, Rudolph Heinrich Ruete, whom she met across the balconies on the rooftops of Stone Town. (It is reputed that the courtship took place on the second-floor balcony of today's People's Bank of Zanzibar on Cathedral Street behind the Old Fort.) But because of her strict Islamic upbringing, Salme was restricted from coming into contact with men, let alone Western men. Nevertheless, they had a secret love affair and she became pregnant. As it was impossible for the princess to conceal her pregnancy from her family, she eloped to Germany with Ruete in 1866. En route to Hamburg she converted to Christianity and was baptized in a small English church in Aden in Yemen. (She also gave birth to their son while they were in Yemen.) Once in Germany, she married Ruete in 1867 and adopted the name Frau Emily Ruete. She learned to speak and write German, she dressed beautifully in the cumbersome Western dress, ran a household herself and had three more children. Sadly, her marriage

enabled them to exercise this privilege and raise numerous children. Until 1911 it was the practice of the Sultan to maintain a harem of around 100 concubines, with attendant eunuchs. The routine was established whereby the Sultan slept with five concubines a night, in strict rotation. The concubines had children, and these were supported by the Sultan.

Social practices changed with the succession of Khalifa bin Harab, at the age of 32, as Sultan in 1911. He was to reign until his death, in 1960, at the age of 81. The harem and concubines were discontinued – apart from anything else, this proved a sensible economy measure. Gradual political reforms were introduced and the practice of Islam was tolerant and relaxed. Social pressures on non-Muslims were minimal. But the office of the Sultan was held in considerable awe. As the Sultan drove each day to spend the afternoon a few kilometres away at his palace on the shore, his subjects would prostrate themselves as he passed. In 1959, when it was suggested that there should be elected members of the Legislative Councils and Ministers appointed to deal with day-to-day matters of state, the Sultan received numerous delegations saying change was unnecessary and the Sultan should retain absolute power.

was not to last long, as her husband was tragically killed in a tram accident in 1870.

His death left Salme in difficult financial circumstances and she tried to get some support from her estranged family in Zanzibar. However, Majid had died two months after her husband, and her half-brother Barghash, who was now on the throne, refused to have anything to do with her. After all, she had eloped with a foreigner and broken Islamic law and, having converted to Christianity, had given up the faith of her birth. Nevertheless, Salme tried repeatedly to get some kind of settlement of her claims and to become reunited with her family and childhood friends in Zanzibar, but her brothers, first Barghash then Khalifa, refused to meet with her and, in October 1888, bitterly disappointed, Emily Ruete left Zanzibar for the last time.

During this period, and partly to alleviate her economic problems, she wrote *Memoirs of an Arabian Princess from Zanzibar*, which was first published in the German Empire in 1886, later in the United States and Britain. It was the first known autobiography of an Arab woman. The book presents an extraordinary and intimate picture of life in Zanzibar between 1850 and 1865. It covers Salme's life in Mtoni Palace and describes both her privileged and inferior position as a woman in the royal family. She writes about the dress, jewellery and customs of the concubines at the palace, and also provides a fascinating inside portrait of her powerful father, whom she speaks of with great affection, as well as her brothers Majid and Barghash.

After 25 years living in Beirut in Lebanon, Emily moved back to Germany in 1917. By this time the generation which had known her in Zanzibar had died and, with them, the animosity towards her; so, in 1922 Sultan Seyyid Khalifa bin Harub finally bestowed a pension upon her. Emily Ruete, née Princess Salme of Zanzibar, died in Germany in 1924 at the age of 79. Ironically, she was the longest survivor of all Said's children and perhaps today her name is better known than those of Said, Majid and Barghash themselves. She was laid to rest in the grave of her husband at a cemetery in Hamburg. With her ashes was buried a small bag of sand from a Zanzibar beach which was found in her possessions, and which she had carried with her since her last visit to the island in 1888.

However, there were significant tensions. Several small Arab Associations combined to form the Zanzibar National Party (ZNP) in 1955 and their main objective was to press for Independence from the British without delay, while two African associations, active with small landless farmers and agricultural labourers, formed the Afro-Shirazi Party (ASP) in 1957.

Although the ZNP tried to embrace all races, the fact was that they were seen as an Arab party, while the ASP represented African interests. Arabs comprised 20% of the population, Africans over 75%. Elections to the Legislative Council in 1955 were organized on the basis of communal rolls – that is, so many seats were allocated to Arabs, so many to Africans, and so on. This infuriated the ZNP who wanted a common electoral roll so that they could contest all seats. They boycotted the Legislative Council, but the next elections, in 1957, were held on the basis of a common roll, and the ZNP did not win a single one of the six seats that were contested. ASP took five and the Muslim League one. But in the next four years, the ZNP greatly increased its efforts, and wealthy Arab landowners and employers flexed their economic muscles to encourage support for ZNP among Africans. ZNP was greatly assisted in 1959 by a split in the ASP. Sheikh Muhammed Shamte, a Shirazi with a large clove plantation in Pemba, formed the Zanzibar and Pemba People's Party (ZPPP). In the run-up to Independence, the ZNP, ASP and ZPPP contested the next three elections, which were on the most part deadlocked between the ZNP and ASP which formed a coalition.

In 1962 a Constitutional Conference was held at Lancaster House in London, attended by the main figures of the three political parties. A framework was duly thrashed out and agreed, with the Sultan as the constitutional Head of State. The number of seats was increased from 23 to 31 and women were given the vote. Elections in 1963 saw ASP gain 13 seats, ZNP 12 and ZPPP six. A ZNP/ZPPP coalition government was formed under the leadership of Shamte of ZPPP. Once again ASP had the majority of the popular vote with 54%. Independence was set for later that year, on 10 December.

The old Sultan had died in 1960 and was succeeded by his son Abdullah bin Khalifa, who was to reign for less than three years, dying of cancer in July 1963. His son, Jamshid Bin Abdullah, became Sultan at the age of 34.

The revolution

It has been described as 'the most unnecessary revolution in history'. At 0300 on the night of 12 January 1964, a motley group of Africans, armed with clubs, pangas (similar to machetes), car springs and bows and arrows, converged on the Police Headquarters at Ziwani on the edge of Stone Town. John Okello, a labourer and leader of the attacking force, had campaigned for the ASP in the three elections in the run-up to Independence. Highly religious, Okello was convinced he had been given orders in his dreams by god to break the powerful position of the Arabs and to found the revolutionary state on Zanzibar and Pemba, and to do this he had built up a small army of determined African nationalists. The attackers stormed the building and, in a matter of moments, the police had fled and the mob had broken into the armoury. Thus armed, they moved on to support other attacks that had been planned to take place simultaneously at other key installations – the radio station, the army barracks and the gaol. By midday, most of the town was in the hands of Okello's forces.

As the skirmishes raged through the narrow cobbled streets of historic Stone Town, the Sultan, his family and entourage (about 50 in all) were advised to flee by the Prime Minister and his Cabinet. Two government boats were at anchor offshore. The Sultan's party was ferried to one of these, and it set off to the northwest to Mombasa, in nearby Kenya. The government there, having gained Independence itself only a month earlier, had no desire to get involved. The Sultan was refused permission to land, and the boat returned southwards down the coast to Dar es Salaam in Tanganyika. From there the party was flown to Manchester and exile in Britain.

Okello began the business of government by proclaiming himself Field-Marshal and Leader of the Revolutionary Government, and members of the ASP were allocated ministries, with Abeid Karume as Prime Minister. But as a semblance of order was restored, it was clear that Okello was an embarrassment to the ASP government and, by 11 March, he was expelled from Zanzibar, resuming his former career of wandering the mainland, taking casual employment and languishing for spells in prison. Meanwhile there was considerable mayhem throughout the islands, as old scores were settled and the African and Arab communities took revenge upon one another. Initial figures suggest that 12,000 Arabs and 1000 Africans were killed before the violence ran its course.

The union

Instability on the islands, army mutinies in Kenya, Tanganyika and Uganda earlier in the year, the presence of British troops in the region and some ominous remarks by the US

Sensitivity to Zanzibar culture

Zanzibar has a relaxed and sympathetic attitude to visitors. However, the islands are predominantly Muslim and, as such, Zanzibaris feel uncomfortable with some Western dress styles. In the towns and villages, it is courteous for women to dress modestly, covering the upper arms and body, with dress or skirt hemlines below the knee. Wearing bikinis, cropped tops, vests that reveal bra straps, or shorts causes offence. For men there is no restriction beyond what is considered decent in the West, but walking around the towns bare-chested or with no shoes is considered offensive. Zanzibaris are either very vocal in expressing their offence or, by contrast, are too polite to say anything. It is because of the latter behaviour that many tourists continue not to heed this advice. When on the beach it is acceptable to wear swimwear but, if

a fisherman or harvester wanders by, it is polite to cover up. Some tourists sunbathe topless on the beaches – this is hugely insensitive and completely inappropriate. It is worthwhile remembering that whilst you may see other tourists wandering around in inappropriate dress, this doesn't mean that you should do the same. Behave like a responsible tourist and cover up. Other sensitivities to consider are during the holy month of Ramadan when most Muslims fast during daylight hours. It is considered the height of bad manners to eat, drink or smoke in the street or public places at this time. Although alcohol is freely available, drunken behaviour is not regarded with tolerance and is considered offensive by most non-drinking Muslims. Finally, public displays of affection are also considered to be inappropriate.

Ambassador in Nairobi about Communist threats to the mainland from Zanzibar, all served to make Karume anxious. He felt vulnerable with no army he could count on and what he saw as hostile developments all around. He needed some support to secure his position.

On 23 April 1964, Karume and Julius Nyerere signed an Act of Union between Zanzibar and Tanganyika to form Tanzania. Zanzibar became semi-autonomous and retained its own president and House of Representatives, with a full set of ministries and the control of its own foreign exchange earnings. In 1977, the mainland party and ASP merged to form Chama Cha Mapinduzi (CCM), which remains in power on both the mainland and the islands today. Nevertheless, the legitimacy of the Act of Union has been called into question, as it was a deal between two leaders (one of whom had come to power unconstitutionally) without any of the democratic consultation such a radical step might reasonably require. Separatist movements have emerged, most notably the Civic United Front (CUF), which was a party formed in 1992 when Tanzania's constitution was changed to allow for a multi-party system. At the time, the CUF called for greater autonomy, and some members wanted complete Independence. But under the ruling pro-union CCM, Zanzibar remained, and still is, part of Tanzania.

In recent years, internal political conflicts have been more pointed in Zanzibar than on the mainland, with the CCM and the equally popular CUF clashing in closely run elections – particularly in 2001 and 2005 when there were outbreaks of violence between their supporters after tense and closely contested elections. However, talks brokered in 2009 have been hailed as a breakthrough, and elections in 2010 were peaceful following the approval of a power-sharing agreement between the CCM and CUF. Since then, Zanzibar has been administered by a unity government.

Stone Town

It may not have a particularly romantic name, but Stone Town is the old city and cultural heart of Zanzibar, where little has changed for hundreds of years. It's a delightfully romantic place of narrow alleys, more than 50 crumbling mosques, two imposing cathedrals and 1700 grand Arab houses with giant brass-studded wooden doors. Most of the buildings were built by the Omani sultans in the 19th century when Zanzibar was one of the most important trading centres in the Indian Ocean. European influences, such as balconies and verandas, were added some years later. Despite its name, the walls of the houses are not, in fact, made of stone but from coralline rock, which is a good building material, but erodes easily. Since Stone Town was deservedly declared a World Heritage Site by UNESCO in 2000, the Stone Town Conservation Authority has been working towards restoring the ancient town before these buildings are lost forever, and many of Stone Town's historical houses have now been beautifully renovated. Most hotel accommodation is in the restored old houses and rooms are decorated with antiques, Persian rugs and the delightful four-poster Zanzibarian beds. At least two nights is warranted in Stone Town to soak up the atmosphere, to take one or more of the interesting half- or full-day tours on offer and to learn a little about its fascinating history. ▶ *For listings, see pages 153-167.*

Arriving in Stone Town → *See also Arriving on Zanzibar, page 132.*

Getting there If arriving at the airport (see page 132), which is 6 km southeast of town, you will be badgered by the many taxi drivers. Expect to pay in the region of US$10 to hotels in town. Not all hotels in Stone Town are easily accessible by car right to the front door, but for an extra tip the taxi drivers usually help visitors with their luggage into the hotels. You can also get a *dala-dala* from the airport to Benjamin Mkapi (Creek) Road in Stone Town, which will cost less than US$1. However, these are generally full of people, there'll be little space for luggage and you will have to walk the final leg to your hotel. Some of the more upmarket hotels and resorts offer free airport pickups.

The ferry terminal is in the Malindi area of Stone Town. You can take a taxi directly from the port for little more than US$4 to anywhere in town. Alternatively, you can go to the **Zanzibar Commission for Tourism** (**ZCT**) desk at the port (see page 133) and they will phone the hotels to arrange someone to meet you, walk you to your hotel and help with luggage. The booking offices for the ferries are clustered around the jetty where you will need to reconfirm the date of your return ticket to Dar if you have not already done so when booking the ticket. The dhow harbour is next to the port, but remember it is illegal for foreigners to travel between the mainland and the islands by dhow. ▶ *For further details, see Transport, page 166.*

Getting around Stone Town is compact enough to walk around and, in any case, most of the streets are too narrow for vehicles. However, taxis are available and a short taxi ride around town shouldn't cost more than US$5. The main bus and *dala-dala* terminal is on Benjamin Mkapi (Creek) Road opposite the **Central Darajani Market**. Routes around Stone Town and across the island run throughout the day and all *dala-dalas* have their destination marked on them.

If you have not pre-booked accommodation in Stone Town, you need to walk around and find a hotel that suits.

Papasi

In Stone Town you will undoubtedly come into contact with street touts – young men who will tout for business, offering hotels, transfers, spice or other tours in the hope of earning commission. You may well be pounced upon after you get off the ferry; other hotspots include the streets in Shangani around the post office. Some can be very persistent, and most are certainly irritating; in Kiswahili the word means 'tick' (as in the parasite).

One of the most common ploys *papasi* use is to tell visitors that your hotel of choice no longer exists, is full, or not safe or clean etc. Take this with a pinch of salt, as it could well be that they just want to take you somewhere where they know they'll get better commission. You also have a better chance of getting a discount on your hotel room if you arrive alone, since the hotel can then give you the discount instead of paying commission. Most *papasi* are also hoping that your stay on the island will mean ongoing work for them as your guide, so if you do use one to help you find a hotel, they'll invariably be outside waiting for you later. When arranging tours and transport to the coastal resorts, never make payments on the street; deal directly with a hotel or one of the many tour operators and organize everything in the confines of their office and get a receipt.

A polite 'no thank you' is usually enough to rid yourself of the services of *papasi*, but other strategies include saying that you have already booked hotel accommodation, carrying your own bags to a restaurant first, having a drink and then looking for accommodation later. Or saying you have been on all the tours and that you are leaving tomorrow and have already bought the ferry ticket. Taxi drivers look for hotel commissions too, but most are legitimate and once you are 'spoken for' by a taxi driver, the hassles from touts usually diminish.

Overall, *papasi* are not well tolerated by most licensed companies and locals get annoyed when tourists become distressed by the unwanted attention. In short, some travellers complain bitterly about them, while others actually make firm friends and enjoy their additional helpful local knowledge and services (*dhow* trips for example). It's just a case of your personal preference whether you ignore them or not.

Places in Stone Town

The area west of Benjamin Mkapi (Creek) Road is the original Stone Town and a tour of it will take at least a day. But it is such a fascinating place that you could easily spend a week wandering the narrow streets and still find charming and interesting new places.

Central Darajani Market
ⓘ *Daily 0800-1800.*

A good place to start a walking tour is from the Central Darajani Market on Benjamin Mkapi (Creek) Road opposite the *dala-dala* terminal. This was opened in 1904 and remains a bustling, colourful and aromatic place. Here you will see Zanzibarian life carrying on as it has done for so many years – lively, busy and noisy. Outside are long, neat rows of bicycles carefully locked and guarded by their minder while people are buying and selling inside the market. Fruit, vegetables, meat and fish are all for sale here, as well as household implements, many of them locally made, clothing and footwear. On Wednesday and

Stone Town

Where to stay 🛏
236 Hurumzi **10** *C4*
Abuso Inn **2** *D2*
Africa House **1** *D2*
Beyt al Chai **21** *D1*
Chavda **6** *D3*
Clove **7** *C4*
Dhow Palace **9** *D2*
Emerson Spice **3** *C4*
Flamingo Guest
 House **11** *E4*
House of Spices **4** *C5*
Karibu Inn **17** *D2*
Karibu Zanzibar **29** *D2*
Kholle House **17** *D2*
Kiponda **18** *C4*
Kisiwa House **5** *D2*
Malindi Guest House **20** *A6*
Mashariki Palace **8** *C3*
Mazzon's **23** *D2*
Mbweni Ruins **12** *E4*

Princess Salme Inn **13** *A6*
Pyramid Guesthouse **26** *B5*
Shangani **30** *D2*
St Monica's Hostel **27** *D5*
Swahili House **14** *C5*
Tembo House **31** *D2*
Zanzibar **33** *D3*
Zanzibar Coffee
 House **15** *D4*
Zanzibar Grand
 Palace **16** *B5*
Zanzibar Ocean View **19** *E4*
Zanzibar Palace **37** *C4*
Zanzibar Serena Inn **36** *D1*
Zenji **38** *A5*

Restaurants 🍴
Archipelago **9** *C2*
Dolphin **7** *D2*
Green Garden **2** *D4*
La Fenice **5** *D2*

La Taverna **6** *C5*
Lazuli **10** *D2*
Livingstone's **4** *C2*
Luckmaan's **12** *D5*
Luis Yoghurt Parlour **11** *D3*
Mercury's **1** *B4*
Monsoon **3** *C2*
Old Fort **18** *C3*
Pagoda **13** *D2*
Silk Route **14** *C3*
Stone Town Café **15** *D2*
Terrace **16** *D1*
Tower Top **22** *C4*
Tradewinds **17** *D2*
Zenji Café &
 Boutique **19** *A5*

Bars & clubs 🍸
Dharma Lounge **8** *E4*
Sunset Bar **20** *D2*
Tatu **21** *D2*

Saturday there is also a flea market selling antiques and bric-a-brac. Note that the chicken, fish and meat areas are not for the squeamish – the smell and flies can be somewhat overwhelming.

Anglican Cathedral
ⓘ 0800-1800, US$5.

Returning to Benjamin Mkapi (Creek) Road, after a further 200 m south there is a large crossroads. To the right is Sultan Ahmed Mugheiri Rd and, after about 50 m, another right leads into the cathedral courtyard. The building to the left of the entrance to the courtyard is the **Anglican Missionary Hospital**, which is constructed on top of the old slave chambers. The Anglican Cathedral was built in 1887 on the site of the old slave market to commemorate the end of the slave trade. You can pick up guides here who will, for a small fee, give you a short tour of the slave chambers and cathedral. The altar is on the actual site of the slave market's whipping post. The marble columns at the west end were put in upside down, while the bishop was on leave in the UK. Other points of interest are the stained-glass window dedicated to David Livingstone who was instrumental in the abolition of the slave trade, and the small wooden crucifix said to have been made from the wood of the tree under which Livingstone died in Chitambo in Zambia. If you can, try to go up the staircase of the cathedral to the top of the tower from where you will get an excellent view of the town. There are services in Swahili every Sunday, and in English on the first Sunday of the month.

Beit El-Amani
ⓘ Mon-Sat 0900-1800, US$3.

Meaning 'House of Peace' and located about 400 m south of the cathedral at the end of Benjamin Mkapi (Creek) Rd, this was built by the British in 1925 as a memorial to the end of the First World War. Its architecture and domed shape were based on the Aya Sophia Mosque in Istanbul. Although fairly run down and shabby, it has some interesting exhibits relating to Zanzibar's history, including items from the sultans, the slave traders and European explorers and missionaries. Livingstone's medicine chest is here, and the story of the German battleship the *Königsberg,* sunk during the First World War in the Rufiji Delta (see page 105), is documented. There are also displays of local arts and crafts. If you are out of season for the Spice Tour (see box, page 165), it has an interesting exhibition on clove production.

Stone Town's western tip

The People's Gardens on Kaunda Road, also known as the Victoria Gardens, were originally laid out by Sultan Barghash for the use of his extensive harem. The grand pavilion was renovated in 1996 by German aid agencies. Many of the plants in the garden were added in the 1880s by naturalist and British Resident Sir John Kirk. Opposite the gardens and behind a white wall is the **State House**. Originally built as the British Residency, it was designed to complement the earlier Arabic buildings such as the People's Palace. Since Independence the building has housed the President's Office. Note that photography is not permitted around the State House.

The **Africa House Hotel** (see Where to stay, page 153) is on Suicide Alley and was once the **English Club**, opened in 1888 (the oldest such club in East Africa), see box, page 147. One of the great events at the English Club used to be the New Year's Eve fancy dress ball, when great crowds of dumfounded Zanzibaris would gather to stare at the crazy *wazungu* (whites) in their costumes. It has been beautifully restored to its former glory, and the upstairs terrace bar is one of the best places in Zanzibar for a drink at sunset (see also Bars and clubs, page 160). A little further down Suicide Alley is **Tippu Tip's House**, named after the wealthy 19th-century slave-trader. Although his real name was Hamed bin Mohammed el Marjebi, everybody called him by his nickname Tippu Tip, which referred to a nervous twitch affecting his eyes. Owner of several plantations on Zanzibar and more than 10,000 slaves by 1895, he was the most notorious of all slavers, making him Livingstone's arch-enemy during his quest for the abolition of the slave trade. The house is not open to the public but it has a splendid carved wooden door and black-and-white marble steps.

Also at the western tip of the town off Shangani Street is the building now known as **Mambo Msiige**, which was built in 1847 and was once owned by a slave-trader. Its name, meaning 'do not imitate', is a reference to its various architectural styles. It is said that the owner used to bury slaves alive within the walls of the building and added many thousands of eggs to the mortar to enhance the colour. Since then, the building has been used as the headquarters of the Universities Mission to Central Africa and, later, as the British Consulate.

Old Fort and around

The Old Fort (also known as the Arab Fort or *Ngome Kongwe*) is in the west of the town next to the House of Wonders (see below). This huge structure was built in 1700 on the site of a Portuguese church, the remains of which can be seen incorporated into the fabric of the internal walls. Its tall walls are topped by castellated battlements. The fort was built by Omani Arabs to defend against attacks from the Portuguese, who had occupied Zanzibar for almost two centuries. During the 19th century the fort was used as a prison and, in the early 20th century, it was used as a depot for the railway that ran from Stone Town to Bububu. It is possible to reach the top of the battlements on the west side and look at the towers. The central area is now used as an open-air theatre, with a traditional music and dance show on Tuesdays, Thursdays and Saturdays at 1900 (see Restaurants, page 157), and is a venue during Zanzibar's festivals (see page 160). The fort also houses an art

Zanzibar under the British – the English Club

The British in Zanzibar (as everywhere) were profoundly insular and, in general, reluctant to establish social relations with other communities. This was expressed in the formation of the English Club, which subsequently provoked every other significant community to establish its own club, thereby underscoring the religious and racial divisions in the society.

Although the English Club was formed some time before the turn of the 20th century, it was only in 1907 that it began to look seriously for substantial premises. A suitable building, now the Africa House Hotel, was located in Shangani just back from the shore, and, backed by a government loan, the club opened in 1908 on its new site, with a restaurant, a committee room that doubled as a library, a bar and a billiards room.

In 1911 the club proposed taking over two rooms in an adjoining building to provide accommodation for out-of-town members. The government was approached to provide the capital to buy a lease and to refit the rooms. It agreed on condition that the rooms would be made available to the government for officials and their wives and other visitors needing accommodation in Stone Town.

The Secretary, EWP Thurston, reported that the constitution of the club did not allow Americans or Europeans, and that it was a 'Man's Club', and there were the "strongest social and sanitary reasons against ladies occupying rooms." The government reacted vigorously to the proposed exclusions.

Women were allowed in to use the library in the mornings and between 1800 and 2000 in the evenings. They were also admitted to take lunch and dinner in the restaurant. As for the Committee's 'sanitary' objections to women using the accommodation, these were dismissed by the government as the "merest bogies of their perfervid imaginations." In April 1912 the club gave way, and the two rooms were added. Later, some garages were built on the shore side of the building, and more rooms for women were added above them.

In 1916 the club had plans to demolish a warehouse on the shore and build a swimming pool and squash courts. But the war interfered with these plans and they never went ahead. The space was cleared, however, and became known as 'German Forodhani' (Forodhani means 'customs house' – the German Consulate was nearby) or 'Shagani Steps'. Coloured lights were strung from cast-iron telegraph poles (two can still be seen on the site) and, on Tuesday evenings the Sultan's band played a selection of classical and popular music for the benefit of locals who sat around on the grass and those taking sundowners in the club's veranda bar.

gallery, several small shops selling crafts and spices, and a café with tables in the shade of a couple of large trees.

On the south side of the fort you can take a walk down Gizenga Street with its busy bazaars. This will lead you to **St Joseph's Catholic Cathedral**, designed by Henri Espérandieu, who designed the Basilica in Marseille and loosely based this work on it. The twin-spire cathedral is well used and holds regular Mass (Monday to Friday 0700, 0900 and 1630, Sunday 0600), which incorporates local elements, including Swahili drumming (be warned, though, it lasts about two hours). When not in use, the doors may be closed, in which case entrance can be gained by the back door, through the adjoining convent. On the opposite side of the road is the **Bohora Mosque**. To the east of the cathedral, in the centre of Stone Town on Hammani Street, are the **Hammani Persian Baths**, which were built by Sultan Barghash in 1888 for use as public baths and maintained their function until 1920. Today they are a protected monument. The building of the baths was overseen by a specialist team from Persia. If you want to look inside, ask for the caretaker who will show you around for a small fee (US$2). There is no water anymore, so you have to imagine how it would have been in its heyday.

Beit-el-Ajaib (House of Wonders)
① *0900-1800, US$4, children (under 6) US$1.*
Close to the fort and opposite the Forodhani Park, Zanzibar's tallest building, houses the **Museum of History and Culture**. It has four storeys surrounded by verandas and was built in 1883 by a British marine engineer for Sultan Barghash to serve as his palace. The name 'House of Wonders' came about because it was the first building on the island to have electricity and even a lift. It has fine examples of door carving. At the entrance are two Portuguese cannons, which date from the 16th century. In 1896, in an attempt to persuade the Sultan to abdicate, the palace was subjected to a bombardment by the British navy. Inside, the floors are of marble and there are various decorations that were imported from Europe. Although a little unkempt and dusty, there are several well-labelled permanent exhibitions on the history of the Swahili Coast and the struggle for Independence (the building once served as the local headquarters of Tanzania's political party CCM). Some of the more interesting displays are on traditional dress and religion, and, in the Swahili maritime section, there's a life-size dhow on show. The third floor is empty, but you can walk out onto the wrap-around veranda to get marvellous views over Stone Town

Forodhani Park
In front of the House of Wonders and the Old Fort are the former Jamituri (or Forodhani) Gardens. This park was completely overhauled in 2009 to the tune of more than US$2 million by a grant from the Aga Khan Trust for Culture. It was once the location for the port's customs sheds, before the port was moved in 1936 to the deepwater anchorage. In the middle is a domed bandstand with Arabic arches where the Sultan's band once played to the public. Nearer the sea is a white concrete arabesque arch, which was built in 1956 for the visit of Princess Margaret, although this was never officially used, as the princess arrived at the dhow harbour instead. She did, however, visit the gardens and planted a tree. Today, the well-kept gardens are a pleasant place to stroll and watch the young boys diving quite spectacularly off the sea wall. During the day, there are a couple of simple garden cafés selling drinks and snacks, and by night the park is transformed into the wonderful **Forodhani Market** (see box, page 149).

Adjacent to the park is Zanzibar's **Orphanage**, which has previously been an English Club and an Indian School. The road here passes through a tunnel and, if you follow it, the second building on the right has a plaque on the wall that reads: "This building was the British Consulate from 1841 to 1874. Here at different times lived Burton, Speke, Grant and Kirk. David Livingstone lived here and in this house his body rested on its long journey home." If the tide is low enough it is possible to pass down the side of the British Consulate and onto the beach, from where the magnificent houses can be viewed to their best advantage. Today, this building houses **Livingstone's Bar and Restaurant**, another good sundowner location with tables on the beach (see page 158).

Forodhani Market

In Forodhani Park between the Old Fort and the sea, this charming nightly food market, which opens at dusk, is a lively, atmospheric place to eat and shouldn't be missed on a visit to Stone Town. There are dozens of stalls selling an extraordinary variety of snacks and seafood cooked on charcoal burners under paraffin lamps, and it's fun to wander around even if you don't feel hungry. It has the best and the cheapest seafood anywhere; you can get prawn and lobster kebabs, giant crab claws, grilled calamari, octopus tentacles and mussels, and fish including kingfish, tuna, barracuda, red snapper and blue marlin. Non-seafood snacks include corn on the cob, cassava, curries, chicken and beef kebabs, falafels and samosas, and keep your eyes peeled for delicious local specialities like *mantabali* (African pizza), *mishkaki* (skewer-grilled marinated meat), *chipsi mayai* (chip omelette) and *urojo* (a mango and ginger-based soup). You eat your feast on paper plates with small toothpicks and, if you're thirsty, try some fresh coconut milk or freshly squeezed sugar cane juice. You may need to haggle over some of the prices, but you will still come away very full and with change from US$10. Just inspect it carefully in the dim light to ensure everything is cooked well; if it's not, ask the vendor to throw it back on the coals for a little longer.

Palace Museum and around

ⓘ *Mizingani Rd, north of the House of Wonders, 0830-1800, US$3, children (under 18) US$1.*
The Beit al-Sahel (People's Palace), built in the 1890s, is where the sultans, their families and harems lived until their rule was finally overturned by the revolution of 1964. Following the revolution, it was renamed the People's Palace and was used by various political factions until it was turned into a museum in 1994. There are three floors of exhibits, which are reasonably distracting, and good views over town from the top floor. A variety of furniture on show includes the Sultan's huge bed. Look out for the formica wardrobe with handles missing – obviously very fashionable at the time. One room shows memorabilia of Princess Salme, whose father was the first Sultan of Zanzibar and whose mother was a slave (see box, page 138). Another exhibition concentrates on the period between 1870 and 1896 and the changes in Stone Town following the introduction of water pipes and electricity. At the top of the stairs on the first floor are some fine larger-than-life portraits of Sultan Seyyid Said and his two sons Majid and Barghash.

Heading north from the Palace Museum is the **Old Customs House**, which was built in 1865 and now houses the **Dhow Countries Music Academy**. Look for the signboard outside advertising *taarab* music concerts (about US$7) performed regularly by the students on the top floor. It was originally a house of one of the Sultan's daughters, Zam Zam Humud bin Ahmed, and from 1928 served as the customs house for the port until it fell into disrepair in 1987. The house was fully restored in 2002 and features many beautifully carved wooden doors, decorated with fish, lotus and anchor chain motifs, and there's a fine balcony with four iron pillars supporting the two verandas. Just north of here is the **Big Tree**, a giant fig that was planted in 1911 by Sultan Khalifa. Traditionally it sheltered local dhow builders; today it does the same for taxi drivers and is also a good place to organize trips to the islands on boats that leave from the little beach in front.

Zanzibar doors

At last count, there were 560 original carved doors in Zanzibar. When a house was built, the door was traditionally the first part to be erected, with the rest of the house built around it. The tradition originates from the countries around the Persian Gulf and spread through Afghanistan to Punjab in India where such doors were reported in the first half of the 12th century. They started to feature in Zanzibar houses in the 15th century, but most of those surviving today were built in the 18th to 19th centuries. The greater the wealth and social position of the owner of the house, the larger and more elaborately carved his front door. The door was the badge of rank and a matter of great honour amongst merchant society. British explorer Richard Burton remarked in 1872: "the higher the tenement, the bigger the gateway, the heavier the padlock and the huger the iron studs which nail the door of heavy timber, the greater the owner's dignity." Set in a square frame, the door is a double door opening inwards that can be bolted from the inside and locked from the outside by a chain and padlock. Popular motifs in the carvings on the doors include the frankincense tree, which denotes wealth, and the date palm denoting abundance. Some of them feature brass knockers, and many are studded with brass spikes. This may be a modification of the Indian practice of studding doors with sharp spikes of iron to prevent them being battered in by war elephants. In AD 915, an Arab traveller recorded that Zanzibar island abounded in elephants and, in 1295, Marco Polo wrote that it had 'elephants in plenty'. These days there are no elephants, and the studs are there merely for decoration. The doors are maintained by the Stone Town Conservation and Development Authority who keep a photographic record and a watchful eye that they are not removed and exported.

Na Sur Nurmohamed Dispensary

Often called the 'Old Dispensary', this very ornate building is on Mizingani Road, north of the Big Tree. It was built in 1887 by Thaira Thopen, Zanzibar's richest man at the time, to commemorate Queen Victoria's Silver Jubilee. It's one of the most imposing of Stone Town's buildings, with four grand storeys and wrap-around decorative balconies. It served as a dispensary in colonial times and was one of the first buildings to be successfully restored to its former glory. Today it is the **Stone Town Conservation and Development Corporation**. Inside is a small tourist development known as the Zanzibar Cultural Centre (0900-1800) with fixed priced curio shops and a small, very pleasant cheap restaurant with a shady courtyard.

Port and dhow harbour

Further up Mizingani Road is the main port and the dhow harbour, which is a lively and bustling part of the Malindi quarter. The deepwater harbour has wharfs piled high with containers, and the landing is most frequently used by boats and hydrofoils from Dar es Salaam and Pemba. Built in 1925, the port remains essentially the 'industrial' end of town, with docks, cargo sheds and a clove distillery. The dhow harbour is at its busiest in the morning when the dhows arrive and unload their catches, and buyers bargain and haggle over the prices. These days very few dhows cross the Indian Ocean, unlike times gone by when fleets would arrive carrying goods from Arabia and the Orient, returning loaded with slaves, ivory and the produce of the islands' plantations. The best time to see one of these large ocean-going dhows is between December and March, before they return on the southwesterly monsoon. There is still plenty of smaller dhow traffic all year round between Zanzibar and the mainland, most bringing building materials and flour to Zanzibar.

Livingstone House

On Malawi Road, Livingstone's House was built around 1860 for Sultan Majid. It was also used by many missionaries and explorers as a starting point for expeditions into deepest, darkest Africa. Most notably, David Livingstone lived here before beginning his last journey to the mainland in 1866. Since then, it's been a laboratory (among other things) for research into clove production.

Around Stone Town → *For listings, see pages 153-167.*

Mbweni Ruins

ⓘ *At the Mbweni Ruins Hotel (see Where to stay, page 157) 6 km south of Stone Town off Nyerere Rd to the airport, T024-223 5478/9, www.mbweni.com, free, but for US$15 you can book a day tour through the hotel, which includes transport, lunch, a visit to the ruins and the gardens, and use of the beach and swimming pool.*

In 1857 Livingstone gave a powerful lecture at Cambridge University about the horrors of slavery. As a result, Anglican members of four universities (Cambridge, Oxford, Durham and Dublin) formed a committee which came to be named the Universities' Mission to Central Africa (UMCA). The aim was to attempt to stop slavery and promote Christianity in Central Africa. The Mbweni Ruins were originally the St Mary's School for Girls, built in 1871 by the UMCA for freed slave girls on 30 acres of land called Mbweni Point Shamba. The girls were trained as teachers so that they could be sent to the mainland to help run mission stations there. Originally there was an old Arab house on the property that was made into the entrance building. Then dormitories and school rooms were added, making the building into a huge square built around an open courtyard, where today two royal palm trees flourish. The construction was overseen by Edward Steere, who also built the Anglican Cathedral on the site of the old slave market in Stone Town (see page 145). In 1882 St John's Church was built nearby for the use of the freed slaves; it is still in use today and has a fine carved door and a tower (you can stop at the church just before the turn-off to the ruins). A village of slaves freed by the British was set up around the school, and each family had a plot of land big enough to build a house with a small vegetable garden. The school was moved to smaller premises in 1920 and finally closed in 1939, and St Mary's slowly fell into a tate of ruin – wild fig trees took root in the walls and bats and birds occupied the former rafters. Today the site can be visited from the **Mbweni Ruins Hotel**, and there is a nature walk through the hotel's lovely botanical gardens that meanders around the ruins. The gardens have more than 650 plant species of which 150 are palms. Day visitors are welcome at the hotel's restaurant, or they run shuttles between town and the hotel during the day so you can book a day tour (see above).

Changuu Island

ⓘ *Tour operators run half-day tours for about US$30, but it is just as easy – and cheaper – to find a boat yourself. Many boats will take you across to the island (about 20 mins), and come back at a prearranged time to pick you up for about US$10 per person. Ask around on the beaches in front of the Big Tree or Tembo Hotel. Pay when you have been safely deposited back on the mainland. There is also a US$4 landing fee on the island.*

Also known as **Prison Island**, Changuu Island is almost 5 km northwest of Stone Town and is roughly 800 m long and 230 m wide at its broadest point. It lies on a coral reef approximately 6 m above the high-tide mark, and much of the reef is exposed at low tide. All over the island there are disused pits where coral was quarried over the centuries for building in Stone Town. There are some sweet-scented citrus and frangipani trees here interspersed among the indigenous trees. The island was once owned by an Arab who used it for 'rebellious' slaves. Some years later, in 1893, it was sold to General Mathews, a Briton who converted it into a prison. However, it was never actually used as such and was later converted to serve as a quarantine station for yellow fever in colonial times. Sailors were taken off the ships and were monitored here for one or two weeks before being permitted to continue on with their journey. The prison is still relatively intact and a few remains of the hospital can be seen, including the rusting boilers of the laundry. There is good snorkelling, windsurfing and sailing from the beautiful little beach, though jellyfish can sometimes be a problem. The island is also home to giant tortoises, which were brought over from Aldabra (an atoll off the Seychelles) in 1919 as a gift from the then British governor of the Seychelles. From just four individuals, the population now numbers around 100. They stand up to a rather staggering 1 m high and the older ones have their ages painted on their shells (some are 150 years old). You can buy leaves to feed them but under no circumstances sit on them. There is a simple café serving cold beers and basic meals, such as grilled fish and salad, and the old quarantine buildings on the southwest of the island have now been turned into a smart lodge, the **Changuu Private Island Paradise**, see Where to stay, page 156.

Chapwani Island
① You can only visit this island if you are staying at the lodge.
Also known as **Grave Island**, Chapwani Island is a nearby private island with one exclusive lodge on it (see page 157). There is an interesting cemetery with headstones of British sailors and marines who lost their lives in the fight against slavery and in the First World War. The island itself is 1 km long and 100 m wide, with a perfect swathe of beach on the northern edge. The forested section is home to a number of birds, duikers and a population of colobus monkeys (how they got here is a bit of a mystery).

Chumbe Island
① The island is a private conservation project and has an all-inclusive resort of the same name (see page 157). A day trip can be booked directly with the park, T024-223 1040, www.chumbeisland.com, or through one of the tour operators, US$100 per person including transport, snorkelling equipment, nature trail guides and a buffet lunch. Note that they only take day visitors when they're not fully booked with overnight visitors – it's best to book 2 or 3 days in advance.
Approximately 4 km offshore, southwest from the Mbweni Ruins, lies the **Chumbe Island Coral Park**. This is an important marine park with a wonderful reef of coral gardens in a pristine state and is shallow (between 1-3 m according to tides). If you swim up to the reef ridge, it's possible to spot shoals of barracuda or dolphins.

There are nearly 400 species of fish here: groupers, angelfish, butterfly fish, triggerfish, boxfish, sweetlips, unicornfish, trumpetfish, lionfish, moorish idols, to name but a few. The snorkelling opportunities are excellent but scuba-diving is not permitted in the park. There are nature trails through the forest on the island, which is home to the rare roseate tern and the coconut crab, the largest land crab in the world, which can weigh up to 4 kg. It is now also a refuge for the shy Ader's duiker, introduced to the island with the assistance of the World Wide Fund for Nature. For great views across to Zanzibar and a bird's eye view of the reefs that surround the island, you can climb the 131 steps to the top of the lighthouse that was built by the British in 1904. The lighthouse keeper's cottage next to the lighthouse is now the visitor centre and next to it is an old mosque.

◉ Stone Town listings

For sleeping and eating price codes and other relevant information, see pages 22-26.

◉ Where to stay

Don't rush off to the beach, there are some simply stunning places to stay in Stone Town that cater for all budgets, and sleeping in an atmospheric historic townhouse is a magical experience.

Stone Town *p142, map p144*
$$$$ Zanzibar Palace Hotel, Kiponda, T024-223 2230, www.zanzibarpalacehotel. com. This lovely boutique hotel has 9 a/c rooms individually furnished in stunning Arabian styles. Extras include satellite TV, DVD players and Wi-Fi. Tea and coffee is served in the bedrooms before breakfast, and some of the rooms have huge stone baths as their centrepiece. It's worth checking the website to choose a room before booking because all are so different. Bar/lounge, spa and gourmet 5-course dinners in the restaurant.
$$$$ Zanzibar Serena Inn, Shangani St, Shangani Sq, T024-223 3567, www.serena hotels.com. One of the best hotels in East Africa and a member of Small Luxury Hotels of the World. Stunning restoration of 2 historic buildings in Stone Town right on the seafront, with 51 luxury rooms and 10 suites and a swimming pool. Beautifully decorated with antique clocks, Persian rugs, carved staircases, chandeliers and brass-studded doors. The several restaurants have excellent but pricey menus and **The Terrace** is on the rooftop (see Restaurants, page 158). Wonderful location with first-class service.
$$$ Africa House Hotel, Suicide Alley, T0774-432 340, www.africahousehotel.com.

This used to be the English Club in the pre-Independence days and is now restored to its former glory with many archways, studded wooden doors and cool stone floors. The 15 rooms have a/c, satellite TV and Wi-Fi, and are tastefully furnished with antiques, original photographs and paintings by local artists. The library houses a rare collection of many 1st editions and antiquarian books, there's a restaurant (see page 158) and the famous **Sunset Bar** (see page 160).
$$$ Beyt al Chai, Kelele Sq, opposite **Serena Inn**, T0774-444 111, www.bluebayzanzibar. com/beyt-al-chai. This boutique hotel takes its name from its previous occupation as a tea house. It has just 5 individually decorated rooms with 4-poster Zanzibari beds, silks and organza fabrics in an opulent Arabian style, some have corner stone baths. The lovely first-floor lounge looks out over the square, and the restaurant is highly recommended (see Restaurants, page 158).
$$$ Chavda, Baghani St, T024-223 2115, www.chavdahotel.co.tz. A good mid-range establishment in a large restored Arab mansion, with 38 large a/c rooms with satellite TV – comfortable and well decorated, if slightly inauthentic. Reasonable restaurant serving international, Chinese and Indian food and a breezy rooftop bar with excellent views. Doubles from US$130.
$$$ Dhow Palace, just off Kenyatta Rd, T024-223 0304, www.dhowpalace-hotel. com. A good family option with old and new wings, 30 a/c rooms with Wi-Fi, satellite TV, good modern bathrooms and traditional furnishings. There's a lovely interior courtyard with a very attractive swimming pool and a restaurant. Like its sister hotel, the **Tembo House**, it's 'dry', so no alcohol. Doubles from US$110.

$$$ Emerson Spice, Tharia St, T0775-046 395, www.emersonspice.com. From the owner of the former **Emerson & Green Hotel**, which was Stone Town's original 'boutique' hotel in the 1990s, this is New Yorker Emerson Skeens' new venture, which he painstakingly restored from a near-ruin and took over 2 years to decorate. It opened to great acclaim in early 2011. With an impressive pale blue interior, with wrap-around carved wooden balconies, the 12 beautiful rooms feature exotic Zanzibari, art deco and Indian touches and exquisite stained-glass windows. Breakfast is served in bed or on your tranquil balcony, and the ground floor tea room offers spiced coffee or delicious iced ginger tea. The gourmet food in the rooftop restaurant is simply outstanding (see Restaurants, page 157) and reservations for dinner are required when you book a room. Doubles from US$175.

$$$ 236 Hurumzi, Hurumzi St, T024-223 2784, www.236hurumzi.com. A charming and quirkily restored 19th-century Omani merchant's house that is literally riddled with staircases to get to the 24 individually themed rooms (the Ballroom has soaring ceilings) with old (some would say shabby) Zanzibari furniture and fittings, original stucco decor, ornate carved doors and stone baths, lower rooms have a/c. The highlight here is the spectacular open-sided rooftop restaurant, **Tower Top** (see Restaurants, page 158). This is the 2nd tallest building in Stone Town so the views over the rooftops are quite spectacular.

$$$ Kholle House, south of Malindi Rd, not far from the **Precision Air** office, T0799-898 200, www.khollehouse.com. Built in 1860 by Princess Kholle, the daughter of the first Sultan of Zanzibar, and newly opened after 3 years of immaculate restoration. 10 a/c rooms, all different so choose when booking, the larger ones have balconies and gold-painted stone bathtubs, while the small ones are comfortable and start from just US$110 for a double, delightful rooftop tea house/bar (but no restaurant) and a swimming pool in a well-tended garden.

$$$ Kisiwa House, Baghani St, off Kenyatta Rd, T024-223 5654, www.kisiwahouse.com. Smart offering, with 11 a/c rooms in an Omani merchant's house (1840) and still owned by the family's descendants, with traditional antiques and Persian rugs but very modern bathrooms, satellite TV and Wi-Fi. Rooftop restaurant/bar and peaceful courtyard tea salon with palms and fountain. Special touches include perfumed incense.

$$$ Mashariki Palace, off Hurumzi St, behind the **House of Wonders**, T024-223 7232, www.masharikipalacehotel.com. A new and exceptionally stylish Italian-run boutique hotel set in a wing of a former palace where the sultan's religious advisor was housed. 18 rooms with balconies or mezzanine floors, thick stone whitewashed walls, lofty ceilings and carved doors, but refreshing contemporary decor and luxurious fixtures and fittings, satellite TV, a/c and Wi-Fi. Lovely rooftop sun terrace, massages available, no restaurant but bar, and breakfast and afternoon tea and cakes are included.

$$$ The Swahili House, Kiponda St, T0777-510 209, www.theswahilihouse.com. Again a fairly new restoration of a 5-storey 19th-century mansion. 22 elegant a/c rooms built around a courtyard, with Swahili furnishings. The larger rooms are higher up, though the staircases are very steep. There's a downstairs café, attractive rooftop terrace with bar, restaurant and sunbathing area with jacuzzi and, given its height, excellent views over Stone Town, so it's worth dropping in even if you're not staying. Doubles from US$130.

$$$ Tembo House Hotel, Forodhani St, T024-223 3005, www.tembohotel.com. This is a beautifully restored historic building that was the American Consulate in the 19th century. The 37 rooms are decorated with antique furniture and have a/c, satellite TV and balconies overlooking either the ocean or swimming pool courtyard. Great location, and the terrace is good for watching the comings and goings on the public beach. There's an excellent restaurant (no alcohol), and the staff are very friendly. Doubles from US$120.

\$\$\$ Zanzibar Grand Palace, Malindi Rd, Malindi, T024-223 5638, www.zanzibar grandpalace.com. Newly opened in 2011, a mid-range hotel near the port but on a peaceful grassy square. The building is new so doesn't have the old character or atmosphere of other places, but it's built in typical Stone Town style and has 34 well-equipped and smartly decorated rooms with satellite TV and Wi-Fi. Rooftop restaurant with views of the harbour, café and spa. Doubles from US\$130.

\$\$\$ Zanzibar Hotel, at the back of the **Dhow Palace Hotel**, off Kenyatta Rd, T0774-333 222, www.zanzibarhotel.co.tz. An elegant hotel with beamed ceilings, Persian rugs, velvet curtains and chandeliers in a 19th-century house. 12 rooms centred around a surprisingly large and peaceful lawned garden full of palms, which is home to some vervet monkeys and a dik-dik (rescued by the owner). It's the sister hotel of **Africa House**, which is a 3-min walk away and where breakfast is served. Doubles from US\$115.

\$\$\$-\$\$ Zanzibar Coffee House, Market St, T024-223 9379, www.riftvalley-zanzibar. com. Restored 1885 house with 8 individually decorated a/c rooms, each named after a type of coffee, with floors and walls painted in cool pastel colours, Zanzibari beds, antique lamps and Wi-Fi, some on are en suite, others have private bathrooms in the corridors. Breakfast is served on the rooftop and it adjoins the pleasant café of the same name (see Restaurants, page 160). Doubles from US\$90.

\$\$ Abuso Inn, Shangani St, opposite **Tembo House Hotel**, Shangani, T024-223 5886, www.abuso-inn-zanzibar-town-hotel. com. Exceptionally friendly hotel run by the Abubakar family, who have lived in Stone Town since the 1870s. The building was rebuilt in 2005, but all effort has been taken to preserve the architecture and decor. One of the nicest features is the elaborate woodwork on the arches in the lounge leading to the 24 a/c rooms, which are spacious and spotless; most have sea views. Doubles from US\$80

\$\$ Clove, Hurumzi St, behind the **House of Wonders**, T0777-484 567, www.zanzibar hotel.nl. A simple Dutch-run option in a nice quiet square with 8 rooms, 2 for families, fans and hot water. The building itself is quite modern by Stone Town standards, but the interiors include Zanzibari-style elements and traditional beds. Bookings for a minimum of 2 nights. There's a pleasant rooftop terrace with sea views and free Wi-Fi.

\$\$ House of Spices, Kiponda St, T024-223 1264, www.houseofspiceszanzibar.com. Best known for its excellent restaurant (see page 158), but also has 4 lovely small rooms, carefully decorated with rich textiles and antiques, windowless but cool with whirring fans, and a separate entrance on to the street. A double goes from US\$80, or all the rooms can be rented as an apartment for 7 people for US\$250, and there's a delightful antique Zanzibari baby's cot.

\$\$ Karibu Zanzibar Hotel, Shangani, to the east of **Beyt al Chai** and Kelele Sq, not to be confused with **Karibu Inn** below, T024-223 0932, www.karibuzanzibarhotel.co.tz. This is a straightforward friendly guesthouse, with 9 spotless rooms (2 of which have 5 beds and are available individually as dorm beds), each with its own bathroom, Zanzibari beds, nets, a/c and TV. Doubles from US\$60.

\$\$ Mazson's Hotel, Kenyatta Rd, Shangani, T024-223 3062, www.mazsonshotel.net. A whitewashed 1830s merchant's house with wrap-around balconies. The 28 rooms are very plain compared to most, though they do have a/c, fridge and TV, but at US\$90 for a double, it is overpriced for what you get. Nevertheless it's in a great central location with a basic rooftop restaurant.

\$\$ Shangani, Kenyatta Rd, across from the Old Post Office, T024-223 3688, www. shanganihotel.com. Clean and straightforward, with 28 en suite rooms, a/c, TV, fridge, fans and balconies overlooking the old town. There are nicer places to stay in this price range – with more polite managers – but the location is central and convenient, and they have an internet café next door. Doubles from US\$75.

$$-$ Zenji Hotel, Malawi Rd, Malindi, T0774-276 468, www.zenjihotel.com. A consistently well-regarded small hotel near the port, owned by a friendly and helpful Zanzibari/Dutch couple, very community focused, with all locally made furniture and decor and locally sourced food. The 9 individually decorated rooms are reasonably priced from US$50, including a generous buffet breakfast served on the roof. The delightful **Zenji Café & Boutique**, is downstairs (see Restaurants, page 160).

$ Flamingo Guest House, off Mkunazini St, just north of junction with Sokomuhogo St, not far from Vuga Rd, T024-223 2850, www.flamingoguesthouse.com. Simple option with management well-used to backpackers. 18 rooms, most with shared showers, a small book exchange and satellite TV in the lobby, and breakfast is served on an upstairs terrace with views over town. Very good value at around US$10-15 per person.

$ Hotel Kiponda, Nyumba ya Moto St, behind the **Palace Museum**, T024-223 3052, www.kiponda.com. Another nicely restored building, with simple clean double/twins, triples and 1 shared room with 5 beds, mosquito nets, fans, some rooms are en suite, others have spotless shared bathrooms. Breakfast is served on the breezy open roof with sea views (their fresh avocado and passion fruit juices are renowned), which also has Wi-Fi. Rates are from US$20 per person.

$ Karibu Inn, Forodhani St, Shangani, T024-223 3058, karibuinnhotel@yahoo.com. Very popular budget no-frills option and deservedly so, with good management and one of the best locations in Stone Town, tucked away behind the Old Fort. 25 rooms all with bathrooms and fans, doubles from US$40, a/c is US$10 extra, dorms for US$15 per person, a simple breakfast is included and it's a 50-m walk to coffee shops, etc.

$ Malindi Guest House, Funguni Bazaar, Malindi St, T024-223 0165, www.malindi guesthouse.com. Popular with budget travellers since 1976 and near the port. The 14 clean rooms sleep 2-4 and are around a central courtyard with plants, some are en suite while others have shared facilities. Breakfast is at the rooftop coffee-shop and bar, with views of the fishermen landing their catch every morning. The only down side is that Malindi is not the safest part of Stone Town after dark – exercise caution if coming home late at night. From US$25 per person.

$ Pyramid Guesthouse, Kokoni St, behind the Ijumaa Mosque near the seafront, T024-223 3000, pyramidhotel@yahoo.com. Charming staff, modest accommodation in 11 rooms, a mixture of self-contained en suite doubles/twins/triples and dorms for as little as US$15 per person. They vary in size (so ask to see a few) and are reached by very steep staircases. A fruit, bread and egg breakfast is served on the roof.

$ St Monica's Hostel, Sultan Ahmed Mugheiri Rd, T024-223 6772, www.stmonicahostel zanzibar.s5.com. An old characterful building next to the Anglican Cathedral, which, in the 1890s, was nurses' accommodation, with 15 very clean and comfortable but simple rooms with or without bathrooms and either fans or a/c, some with balconies and views of the cathedral. The restaurant is next door for breakfast and traditional Swahili dishes. From US$15 per person.

$ Princess Salme Inn, Mizingani St, Malindi, T0777-435 303, www.princesssalmeinn.com. Named after the beautiful princess (see box, page 138), a basic but friendly and cheap place near the port (again be wary if walking back after dark). Doubles with fans from only US$35, some en suite, or there are shared bathrooms in the corridors. Good and filling breakfasts are taken in the rooftop lounge, which has sea views, Wi-Fi and comfortable couches, you can cook in the kitchen and beers are available.

Around Stone Town p151
$$$$ Changuu Private Island Paradise, T0773-333 241, reservations Arusha T027-254 4595, www.privateislands-zanzibar.com. On Changuu or 'Prison' Island (page 151), this smart lodge, a 20-min boat ride from

Stone Town, has 5 deluxe thatched cottages on the beach with ocean views, roomy bathtubs and outdoor showers, and 12 standard rooms in the restored quarantine buildings with views across to Stone Town. Good food, including 4-course seafood dinners, swimming pool and floodlit tennis court, great snorkelling and you can see the giant tortoises. Rates from US$380 for a double half board.

$$$$ Chapwani Private Island, T0777-433 102, www.chapwaniisland-zanzibar.com. Chapwani or 'Grave' Island (page 152), about 15 mins from Stone Town by boat, offers super-privacy in only 10 rooms in 5 bandas right on the beach, with 4-poster beds and colourful African fabrics. Seafood is the main feature on the restaurant menu. There's a swimming pool and a relaxing bar with day beds, cushions and lanterns, and fishing and snorkelling can be arranged. At night there are fantastic views of Stone Town. Rates from US$320 for a double half board.

$$$$ Chumbe Island Coral Park, T024-223 1040, www.chumbeisland.com. The utmost care has been taken to minimize the environmental impact of this resort; sustainably harvested local materials were used in the construction of the 7 luxury cottages and dining area, there is solar power and composting toilets, and rainwater is collected as the source of fresh water. Recognition of these efforts has been given through various awards and nominations over recent years. The emphasis is very much on the wildlife, coral reefs and ecology of the island, and a stay here makes for an interesting alternative to the other beach resorts. Excellent food. Rates from US$250 per person, including all meals and soft drinks, boat transfers, snorkelling trip and forest trail.

$$$ Mbweni Ruins Hotel, 6 km south of Stone Town off Nyerere Rd, T024-223 5478/9, www.mbweni.com. Built in the spacious grounds of the ruins of the first Anglican Christian missionary settlement in East Africa (see page 151), and on a private beach. 13 rooms with a/c and fans, 4-poster beds and balconies, some have extra beds for kids. Stunning tropical gardens full of butterflies, where bushbabies may be seen in the evening, open-air restaurant and bar under thatch, swimming pool, free shuttles to Stone Town 3 times a day, and also offers tranquil kayak trips through the mangroves. Doubles from US$180.

$$$-$$ Zanzibar Ocean View, Kilimani Rd, 2 km south of Stone Town off Nyerere Rd, T024-223 3882, www.zanzibaroceanview. com. On the beachfront at Kilimani and the closest beach resort to Stone Town, this is the sister property of the **Amaan Bungalows** in Nungwi (page 174). The 58 simple a/c rooms are comfortable with TV, balconies and sea or garden views. There's a restaurant and bar, but overall it's let down by indifferent service and lack of character.

Restaurants

Stone Town *p142, map p144*

A Stone Town 'must-do' is to eat at the Forodhani Market in the evening (see box, page 149). For breakfast, look out for stalls in the back streets selling *chai tangawizi* (ginger tea) and *mandazi* (fried dough balls), which in Zanzibar are often infused with cardamom. There are some excellent restaurants in Stone Town, most serving fresh seafood, and the hotels have good restaurants and bars, many of which are on rooftops and are open to non-guests. Remember that if you are looking for a venue to watch the sunset, sunset around the equator is always between 1815 and 1845. Since this is a Muslim society, not all of the restaurants serve alcohol, so check beforehand if a bottle of wine is an essential part of your dining pleasure. During Ramadan some restaurants do not open during the day (this doesn't apply to those in the tourist hotels).

$$$ Emerson Spice, Tharia St, see Where to stay, page 154. Dinner from 1900 (except Thu). This beautifully resorted and incredibly romantic teahouse with its delicately carved wooden trellises and hanging lanterns is on the rooftop of Emerson's new hotel. The 5-course degustation menu is now considered the best Zanzibari seafood on the island, and the experience is magical. A sample menu might be lemongrass calamari, squid-ink risotto, coconut kingfish baked in banana leaf, and palate-cleansing sorbets, such as custard apple with saffron or mango with cardamom. Reservations are essential (in fact book before you arrive on the island); cocktails are from 1730 and dinner is served at 1900.

$$$ The Terrace, at the **Serena Inn**, Kelele Sq, see Where to stay, page 153. Open for dinner only 1930-2200. An expensive but special and romantic place for a treat set on a quiet terrace with ocean views in one of the most beautiful of the restored buildings on Zanzibar – go up there after a drink in the hotel's bar. Famous for its top-class seafood – think sailfish tartare, lobster medallions, giant crab claws and, for dessert, heavenly dark chocolate and lemongrass mousse. Superb winelist.

$$$ Tower Top Restaurant, 236 Hurumzi, see Where to stay, page 154. Open 1130-1600, 1900-2200. Here you can eat in wonderful surroundings on the rooftop, 81 steps up from the street; if you are not staying here you need to book a day ahead. The semi-fixed dinner menus with an emphasis on seafood have one seating starting at 1900; arrive from 1730 for cocktails, then take all evening to enjoy the excellent food, while sitting on cushions with your shoes off. On Fri-Sun evenings, there's traditional *taarab* entertainment. The lunch menu has wraps, sandwiches and pizza.

$$$ Tradewinds, at the **Africa House Hotel**, see Where to stay, page 153. Open 1900-2200. As well as the terrace **Sunset Bar**, which is perfect for sundowners, the fairly formal restaurant here is on the 2nd floor with a menu of Swahili dishes and seafood. Nicely decorated with an old map of Africa painted on the ceiling and outside tables with ocean views, but service is notoriously slow and food overpriced.

$$$-$$ Beyt al Chai, Kelele Sq, see also Where to stay, page 153. Open 1200-1530, 1900-2200. Popular and romantic Zanzibari-themed restaurant with carved wooden ceiling beams and brightly coloured cushions, the sophisticated menu includes a delicate 'trio of tuna' dish, seafood casserole poached in lemongrass, mouth-watering crab and coconut soup or giant piri-piri prawns.

$$$-$$ House of Spices, Kiponda St, see Where to stay, page 155. Mon-Sat 1000-2200. Beautifully decorated restaurant and wine bar in a restored 18th-century spice merchant's house, tables are on terraces on the 2nd floor. Delicious food, a mix of seafood (whole lobster is the speciality) and Italian, with good home-made ravioli and thin-crust pizzas. Good choice of Italian and South African wine. The lovely scented shop here sells nicely packaged tea and spice gift boxes.

$$$-$$ Monsoon, in the tunnel building between Forodhani Park and the Old Fort, T0777-410 410, www.monsoon-zanzibar. com. 1000-2400. A touristy spot and worth a mention for the location and fun Zanzibari atmosphere, with cushions on the floor indoors, lovely garden terrace outside, fully stocked bar and *taarab* music in the evenings, but the menu over-sells the mediocre not-always-hot Swahili-themed cuisine and service is notoriously bad.

$$ La Fenice, Shangani St, see **Tatu** and **Africa House**, T0777-472 729. Open 1100-2200. Authentic Italian cuisine with a great choice of creamy risottos, home-made pasta with seafood sauces, meat grills and real gelato ice cream. Tastefully furnished with African masks and breezy veranda overlooking the ocean.

$$ Livingstone's, in the old British Consulate building, on the seafront just down from Kenyatta Rd, T0773-271 042. Open 1200-1630, 1830-2230, bar open later. In a great location on the beach, with a varied menu of continental and Swahili dishes, salads and pastas. Lively and popular, with occasional bands and artwork for sale on the walls. If you want a candlelit table on the sand in the evenings, it's best to book ahead. Wi-Fi available.

$$ Mercury's, Mizingani Rd, near The Big Tree, T024-223 3076. Open 1200-2400. Named after Freddie, with an atmospheric wooden outdoor terrace overlooking the harbour, serves pizzas, pasta, seafood and ice cream, but food is very average and overpriced and it's a better a late-night venue (see page 160).

$$ The Old Fort Restaurant, inside the fort, T0777-878 737. Tue, Thu and Sat 1900-2200. Dinner here is a rather tacky tourist affair and the restaurant itself is nothing special, with tables scattered haphazardly under trees, but the draw card is the live *taarab* band and traditional dancing in the fort's amphitheatre. The buffet features seafood, salads and fruit for US$18 or watch the show only for US$7.

$$ Silk Route, Shangani St, T024-223 2624. Tue-Sun 1130-1500, daily 1800-2300. Indian restaurant with chandeliers, brightly coloured decor and rooftop tables. The long menu includes tandoori chicken and lamb with spinach, Zanzibar fish, such as red snapper, and vegetarian options, such as paneer curry and chickpeas in tamarind sauce. Serves cocktails, some wine and lassis.

$$-$ Archipelago, Kenyatta Rd, opposite the National Bank of Commerce, T024-223 5668. Open 0800-2200. Healthy breakfasts, traditional Swahili dishes, salads, burgers and daily specials of grilled fish – look out for swordfish or marlin. Great coffee, the 'flat white' is arguably the best in town, and quite delicious desserts, such as sticky date pudding and frangipani tart. Outdoor terrace with modern furniture overlooking the ocean. No alcohol.

$$-$ La Taverna, Darajani St near the market, T0776-650 301. Open 1100-2300. Stone Town's most authentic Italian restaurant run by a family from Milan with a pretty street-side terrace decked with bougainvillea. Excellent crispy thin-based pizza, the seafood toppings are not surprisingly the favourite, plus meat dishes, home-made pasta and sandwiches during the day.

$ Dolphin Restaurant, Kenyatta Rd, T024-223 1987. Open 1100-2100. Long-standing, family-run place serving mainly seafood, popular with local people, and little English is spoken. Nothing special but well located near the post office and one of the cheapest places where you can sit down. A sandwich will cost you about US$2 and tasty grilled fish or beef curry little more than US$5.

$ Green Garden Restaurant, off Mkunazini St or Sultan Ahmed Mugheiri Rd, T0773-849 636, www.greengardenstonetown.com. 1200-2400. Set in a little square with palms and pot-plants, this restaurant, with its open-air kitchen, is quite hard to find but it is very popular with travellers and serves very good pizza and grilled fish with chips and salad and has Wi-Fi. No alcohol but inventive 'mocktails'.

$ Luis Yoghurt Parlour, Gizenga St, near the **Gallery Bookshop**, T0765-759 579. Mon-Sat 1000-1500, 1800-2100, closes for long periods in low season while the owner goes away. Very small place serving excellent lassi, yoghurt drinks, milk shakes, fresh fruit juices, spiced tea and fabulous Italian ice cream. Main meals include unusual Goan curries with fish or lentils for vegetarians.

$ Lukmaan's, Mkunazini House, Sultan Ahmed Mugheiri Rd, T0777-482 131. Open 0800-2100. Traditional Swahili canteen-style restaurant and probably the cheapest sit-down option in Stone Town, with filling dishes from US$2. Tricky to find, but ask, as everyone knows where it is. Try the fish in coconut sauce, spinach and beans, and fish or beef biyriani or pilau rice – cooked in big pots, they may run out of the most popular dishes by 1700. No alcohol.

$ Pagoda Chinese Restaurant, Suicide Alley, behind **Africa House**, Shangani, T024-223 4688. Open 1130-1400, 1830-2200. In the unlikely event that you are craving a Chinese while in Stone Town, this hotchpotch of upstairs brightly lit rooms has an authentic menu, including good hot and sour soups and duck (rare in this part of the world), generous portions and sells beer.

$ Stone Town Café, Kenyatta Rd just south of the post office, T0777-843 377. Open 0800-2200. The sister restaurant to the **Archipelago**, with modern a/c interior and outside tables that are good for people-watching on the street. Popular for breakfasts of fresh fruit, yoghurt and muesli or avocado on toast, lunch includes salads, quiche or falafels, and has more substantial mains for dinner, such as chicken kebabs or pizza. No alcohol.

Cafés

Lazuli, off Kenyatta Rd just south of the post office, Shangani, T0776-266 679. Mon-Sat 1100-2100. With a fresh all-white interior and colourful tablecloths, this living room-sized restaurant serves great pancakes with fruit, spiced iced coffee, sandwiches, wraps made from chapattis, salads, burgers and some seafood.

Zanzibar Coffee House, Market St, see Where to stay, page 155. Open 0900-1800. Great coffee, which is grown on the owner's estate in the Southern Highlands of Tanzania near Mbeya, plus breakfasts of home-made muesli and crêpes, biscuits, muffins and croissants, milkshakes and smoothies. The coffee is roasted in a little back room so the aromas are wonderful, and you can buy coffee beans.

Zenji Café & Boutique, at the **Zenji Hotel**, Malwai Rd, Malindi, T0774-276 468, www.zenjicafeboutique.com. 0800-2000. Lovely a/c café near the port, with outside terrace and a craft shop where you can watch women make jewellery from beautiful paper beads (you can also buy packets of them). Great coffee and herbal teas, breakfasts, sandwiches using delicious home-made brown bread, and excellent chocolate brownies.

☏ Bars and clubs

Stone Town *p142, map p144*
Dharma Lounge, Vuga Rd, T0772-641 058. Tue-Thu and Sun 2000-0300, Fri and Sat 2000-0500. A popular and modern hi-tech club/cocktail bar with, a/c, big cushions to sit on, well-stocked bar, large dance floor and good selection of music.

Livingstone's (see Restaurants, page 159). Open 1200-2300. Once the British Consulate building now a lively bar and restaurant. At the weekend live music draws a mix of tourists and locals to the dance floor, and you might struggle to find a cosy corner. Lengthy cocktail list and outside tables on the beach.

Mercury's (see Restaurants, page 159). Open 0830-2400. Living rather tenuously off its name, this Freddie Mercury memorabilia-filled bar and restaurant, with its broad wooden deck, is a great place to watch the sunset and the locals playing football on the beach – they have some very skilled players. There's a fully stocked bar with good cocktails, and the Coconut Band plays on weekend nights.

Sunset Bar, at **Africa House**, see Where to stay, page 153. Open 1000-2400. The most popular bar in the town is on a wide marble upstairs terrace that looks out across the ocean – watching the sun set while dhows glide by is a nightly highlight. The beers and cocktails are cold and plentiful, although rather expensive, bar snacks include burgers and calamari and chips, there's free Wi-Fi, and it's a good place to meet people. The adjoining **Majlis Lounge** is where you can try traditional fruit-flavoured shisha pipes.

Tatu, Shangani St, opposite **Tippu Tip's House**, T0778-672 772, www.tatuzanzibar. com. 1200-2200 for food, bars open until 0100. Set on 3 floors ('tatu' means 3 in Kiswahili) in a lovely old house, with lattice wooden balconies overlooking the ocean, a restaurant, lounge and bar, fabulous cocktails and over 85 single malt whiskies (they claim to have the largest collection in East Africa), and the menu features tapas and pub-style grub. Close to **Africa House**, and the rooftop is certainly a competitor for a sunset venue.

❀ Festivals

Stone Town *p142, map p144*
Feb Sauti za Busara Swahili Music and Cultural Festival, 2nd week Feb, T024-223

2423, www.busaramusic.org. This 4-day festival attracts talent from all over East Africa, with performances in music, theatre and dance. *Sauti za Busara* means 'songs of wisdom' in Kiswahili. There are concerts (mostly in the Old Fort) of traditional music, from Swahili *taarab* and *ngoma* to more contemporary genres that mix African, Arab and Asian music.

Jul Festival of the Dhow Countries, first 2 weeks of Jul, T0773-411 499, www.ziff. or.tz. Celebrates and promotes the unique culture that grew as a result of Indian Ocean trade and the wooden sailing dhow. All nations around the Indian Ocean known as the dhow countries are included in the celebration, but the Swahili culture is the best represented. Zanzibari *taarab* music and traditional dances are performed by a rich ensemble of cultural troupes, and there are exhibits of arts and crafts, street carnivals, small fairs and canoe races. The highlight is the **Zanzibar International Film Festival**; screenings take place around Stone Town.

Aug-Dec Eid al-Fitr (in Kiswahili also called 'Idi' or 'Sikuku,' which means 'celebration'). The Muslim holiday that signifies the end of the holy month of Ramadan is without doubt the central holiday of Islam, and a major event throughout Tanzania, but especially observed on the coast and Zanzibar. Throughout Ramadan, Muslim men and women fast from sunrise to sunset, only taking meagre food and drink after dark. The dates for Eid al-Fitr vary according to the sighting of the new moon but, as soon as it is observed, the fasting ends and 4 days of feasting and festivities begin. Stone Town is the best place to witness this celebration; the whole town takes to the streets as people go from house to house visiting friends and relatives, and there is live Swahili *taarab* music and much rejoicing.

O Shopping

Stone Town *p142, map p144*
Stone Town has many shops selling wood carvings, Zanzibari chests, spices, jewellery,

paintings, antiques, *kikois* and *kangas* (sarongs), and lovely handmade leather beaded sandals. For most of these it's best just to wander the streets, get the measure of prices and then bargain hard. Most shops are along Kenyatta Rd in Shangani, Gizenga St behind the Old Fort, and on Hurumzi St behind the House of Wonders. Tourists are advised not to buy any products related to protected species on the islands, such as sea shells and turtles. For alcohol, there is an unnamed bottle shop on Kenyatta Rd opposite Zanzibar Gallery. Shops in Stone Town are usually open 0900-1400 and 1600-1800 or 1900 but some are open all day.

A Novel Idea, on the ground floor of **236 Hurumzi Hotel** (see page 154), Hurumzi St, T024-223 1186, www.anovelideatanzania. com. A great bookshop and a branch of the Dar es Salaam chain, selling guidebooks, maps and a full range of African coffee table and souvenir books, as well as fiction, as the name suggests.

Abeid Curio Shop, Cathedral St, opposite St Joseph's Cathedral, T024-223 3832. Sells antique Zanzibari furniture, including teak canopied beds inlaid with painted glass panels, clocks, and copper and brass, such as Arabic coffee pots. They can arrange international shipping.

Capital Art Studio, Kenyatta Rd, T0777-431 271. Sells wonderful prints of black-and-white photographs of old Zanzibar, which make great souvenirs and look particularly good when framed in heavy wood. The shop was opened in 1930 by Ranchod Oza who was the royal photographer at the time and today is run by his son. The Zanzibar entrance door is particularly fine.

Central Darajani Market, Benjamin Mkapi (Creek) Rd. Sells mainly fresh fruit and vegetables and meat. However, the shops nearby sell *kikois* and *kangas* (sarongs), wooden chests and other souvenirs. In fact, you can buy anything here, from freshly caught octopus to mosquito nets, and the spices are sold to real shoppers as opposed to the ready-packaged ones designed for tourists.

Doreen Mashika, Hurumzi St, near 236 Hurumzi Hotel, T0786-369 777, www.doreen mashika.com. Swiss/Tanzanian designer with a range of top-quality fashionable bags, shoes, jewellery and clothing. She uses some beautiful local fabrics and Masai beads.

The Gallery Bookshop, Gizenga St, T024-223 2244. The best bookshop in Stone Town for fiction, plus guidebooks, maps, pictorial books and some quality souvenirs. There are also a couple of stalls on Gizenga St selling second-hand novels.

Kanga Kabisa, off Suicide Alley, near Africa House, T024-223 2100, www.kangakabisa. com. Sells colourful men's, women's and children's clothes and accessories made from *kangas* as well as *kitenga*, which is a heavier batik-patterned cloth.

Mago East Africa, Cathedral St, T0777-457 795, www.magoeastafrica.com. Well-respected Italian designer for quality women's clothes using local fabrics which are also sold in Europe. Profits go towards supporting a team of local tailors in starting their own businesses.

Memories of Zanzibar, Kenyatta Rd, opposite Shangani post office, T024-223 9376, www.memories-zanzibar.com. Upmarket shop on 2 storeys, with quality souvenirs, jewellery, handbags, cloth, cushions, CDs and books. Ideal for those not in the bargaining mood – there are fixed prices on all the souvenirs you could possibly want and you can shop in a/c comfort.

Moto/Dada, Hurumzi St, near the Clove Hotel, T0777-466 304. This is the shop for 2 Zanzibari women's co-operatives. Moto makes beautiful handwoven and lined bags and baskets. Dada makes lovely packaged natural beauty products like body oils, foot scrubs and soap – orange and green tea, lemongrass and ginger, eucalyptus and sea salt or aloe vera and cinnamon are just some of the more than 60 varieties.

Tamim Curio Shop next door to Abeid's, see above, T024-223 2404. This is one of the best places to buy carved teak or mahogany Zanzibar chests. These were used by the sultans to transport their belongings and are still used today, typically to hold family heirlooms and other valuables and are often used as decoration in hotels. The ones with brass inlays are less often seen, but this shop is run by a brass artisan whose family brought the skill from Yemen in 1904. Again, shipping can be arranged.

Upendo Means Love, just off Gizenga St, near Karibu Inn, T0784-300 812, www. upendomeanslove.com. Sells great clothes for women and children made from *kangas* and *kikois*. All the proceeds go to running a sewing school and workshop where women are trained and employed.

Zanzibar Curio Shop, Hurumzi St, near the Clove Hotel, T0777-411 501. Antiques including old Zanzibar doors (yes, you can ship these for a price), chests, nautical instruments, traditional lamps and a good selection of the usual curios.

The Zanzibar Gallery, Mercury House, Gizenga St, Shangani, T024-223 2721, www.zanzibargallery.net. Reputedly the former home of Freddie Mercury, this beautifully decorated shop boasts the most comprehensive range of books in Zanzibar: guidebooks, maps, wildlife guides, coffee table books and the best of contemporary and historical fiction from the whole of Africa. The CD collection focuses on Swahili music such as *taarab*. Authentic artworks, antiques, fabrics and textiles from Zanzibar and mainland Africa, plus clothes and spiced candles and soaps. It also sells excellent postcards of photos taken by the owner.

⚙ What to do

Stone Town *p142, map p144*
In order to maximize your time in Zanzibar, it is worth considering going on a tour. All the tour companies listed under Tour operators offer the following range of tours:

City tour
A 3-hr guided walking tour includes most of the major sites of Stone Town, such as

Zanzibar dive sites

Pange Reef The first sandbank west of Stone Town, with a maximum depth of 14 m. There is an enormous variety of coral and lots of tropical reef fish, such as clown fish, parrot fish, moorish idol and many others. Pange reef is ideal for Open Water Diver courses, as it offers calm and shallow waters. This is also a good spot for night dives, where you may see cuttle fish, squid, crab and other nocturnal life.

Bawe Island Bawe has a reef stretching around it, with a maximum depth of 18 m. Here you will find beautiful corals, such as acropora, staghorn, brain corals and a large variety of reef fish.

Wrecks At 12 m, *The Great Northern* (built 1870), a British steel cable-laying ship, which sank on New Year's Eve 1902, has become a magnificent artificial reef and is home to a number of leaf fish, lionfish and morays. Parts of the ship can still be identified and some relics may still be found (though not taken). *The Great Northern* is an ideal wreck for the beginner diver as she is only 12 m below the surface and is also great for snorkelling.

The 30 m wreck of the *Royal Navy Lighter* is home to large schools of rainbow runners, trevally, sweepers and, sometimes, reef sharks, best suited for experienced advanced divers.

At 40 m, a steam sand dredger, *The Penguin*, is only suitable for very experienced deep-water divers. Here you can find huge numbers of barracuda, big stingrays and morays.

Murogo Reef Maximum depth 24 m, 25 mins from Stone Town by boat. Sloping reef wall, with a huge variety of coral and fish. Turtle are often seen here, and this is usually the preferred dive site for the Open Water Diver course.

Nyange Reef The largest of all reefs on the west coast of Zanzibar and containing several dive sites, all of which are unique. A new species of coral has recently been identified here, and marine biologists believe it to be endemic to Nyange.

Boribu Reef One of the best dive sites off Zanzibar; huge barrel sponges, large moray eels, pelagic fish and large lobsters are all features of this dive. In season, whale sharks pass through. The maximum depth is 30 m.

Leven Banks On the north coast, this site is popular with advanced divers as it lies near the deep water of the Pemba Channel and is home to big shoals of jacks and trevally. Famous for remote 'holiday brochure style' beaches and colourful reefs, the east coast diving is the most talked about on Zanzibar.

Mnemba Island Reached from Nungwi or Matemwe, also on the north coast, it has a wide range of sites varying in depth with exciting marine life. Great for snorkelling too. Pungu Wall, East Mnemba, is a recommended dive for experienced divers looking for sharks, rays and groupers. This site can only be dived in calm conditions.

Thanks to **Zanzibar Dive Centre-One Ocean**, www.zanzibaroneocean.com.

---

the market, national museum, cathedral, Beit al-Sahel and House of Wonders. If you are interested in the architecture, this is a good opportunity to learn more about the buildings. Costs are about US$15 per person for 2, US$11 per person for 3+.

Cruises

The Original Dhow Safari, T024-223 2088, www.dhowsafaris.net. A 2-hr sunset cruise which departs from the beach at the **Serena Inn** – book in advance through any hotel and meet at the Serena's reception at 1630. The views of Stone Town from the water at sunset are gorgeous, and *taarab* musicians play as you are served soft drinks and snacks. US$50 per person for 2, US$35 for 3, US$30 per person for 4+.

Safari Blue, T0777-423 162, www.safariblue. net, or book through any hotel or tour operator. This daily cruise (0930-1700) uses a 10-m *jahazi* (ocean-going dhow) and departs from Fumba, a 20-min drive to the southwest of Stone Town; transfers can be arranged. A full day trip around sandbanks, small islands and coral reefs includes use of top-quality snorkelling equipment with guides and instructors, sodas, mineral water and beer, and a seafood lunch of grilled fish and lobster, fruit and coffee. Dolphins can be seen most of the time. US$80 per person; Safari Blue does not run on Fri.

Diving *See also box, page 163.*
Zanzibar is a great place to go diving. It is worth noting that the best time for diving in Zanzibar is Feb-Apr and Aug-Nov. Expect to pay in the region of US$500 for a 4-day PADI Open Water course, US$75 for a single dive, and US$35 for a snorkelling trip with lunch.
Bahari Divers, near the **National Bank of Commerce** on the corner of Shangani St and Kenyatta Rd, T0777-484 873, www. baharidivers.com. PADI dive school with another dive shop in Nungwi (see page 175).
One Ocean Diving, bottom of Kenyatta Rd, on the seafront, T024-223 8374, www. zanzibaroneocean.com. PADI dive school, also operates from many of the resorts on the east coast (see page 181).

Dolphin tour
Humpback and bottlenose dolphins swim in pods off **Kizimkazi Beach** on the southwest of the island. However, despite what the tour operators tell you, they are not always that easy to spot and 'swimming' with them is not an apt description of the excursion, nor should it be encouraged. If you do go on a trip, bear in mind that, as cute as they seem, they are still wild animals and they live in a fragile ecosystem. The boatmen can get fairly close to the pods of dolphins and you

can slip into the water with snorkelling gear. If you're lucky, they may approach within 2-4 m and are likely to play around the hull of the boat. A dolphin tour includes transport by minibus to a boat at Kizimkazi, a route that easily allows for a visit of **Jozani Chwaka Bay National Park** (see page 182). Many of the small boats do not run to a timetable but wait to fill up, usually accommodating 6-8 tourists. Book this excursion through a tour operator and not with the touts in Stone Town. A half-day trip costs around US$35-40, depending on how many people go, and includes transport, lunch and snorkelling gear. A full day, including the dolphins in the morning and Jozani Chwaka Bay National Park in the afternoon, is about US$60.

Swahili cooking
Some of the tour operators can arrange a Swahili cooking lesson, and the normal drill is to begin at the **Central Darajani Market** to buy ingredients, then go to a family home to help prepare and cook lunch or dinner (usually on an outdoor cast-iron stove) before sitting down for a meal in the traditional way. Costs are around US$45 per person for a minimum of 2, the cost goes down for a larger group. Try **KV Tours & Travel** or **Zenji Zanzibar** (see Tour operators, below).

Spas
There are many regular spas at resorts around Zanzibar. In Stone Town, both the following places offer a relaxing diversion and specialize in traditional natural treatments using Zanzibari flowers and spices. Drop into reception or phone ahead to make an appointment.
Cinnamon Spa, Shangani St, T0777-908 000, www.cinnamonspa.net. Open 0800-2200. As the name suggests, the rooms here are beautifully scented with cinnamon, and the shop in reception sells some luxurious home-made body creams and soaps. The signature treatment is the *Princess Salme*: a papaya and sugar body scrub, followed by a milk and honey body wrap and a massage.

Spice tour

The exotic spices and fruits that are grown in the plantations around Stone Town have attracted traders from across the Indian Ocean for centuries, and there's ample opportunity to dazzle the senses on a spice tour. It's also a good opportunity to see the rural areas in the interior of the island and connect with local people. Without a guide, you will never find nutmeg sitting on the forest floor, think to peel the bark off a cinnamon tree, or know how to open a jackfruit or custard apple, but these are some of the fun things to do on a spice tour. The guide will carve off a root, branch or bark and then ask you to smell or taste it to guess what it is. Along the way, local children will scamper up a palm to cut a fresh green coconut for you. Almost all the ingredients of the average kitchen spice rack can be found on this tour, and you can buy packaged spices including turmeric, tandoori, vanilla beans, masala, hot chillies, black pepper, cloves, nutmeg, cinnamon sticks or powder, ginger and others. Most tours are by *dala-dala*, and usually last four hours and can be organized with any of the tour operators or hotels. A half-day tour costs around US$25 including lunch; longer tours include additional visits to the slave caves and beach at Mangapwani. They leave Stone Town around 0900 and return 1300-1600 (depending on whether or not you go to the beach).

Other treatments use coconut, cloves, sea salt and seaweed, among many other locally harvested ingredients.

Mrembo Spa, Cathedral St, near St Joseph's Cathedral, T0777-430 117, www.mtoni.com/mrembo. Open 0930-1800. The *singo* body scrub with ylang-ylang and jasmine is traditionally used by a bride in preparation for her wedding, while the *vidonge* body scrub using clove stems and buds and rosewater is used by men in Pemba to relieve aching muscles. Also try a massage using bags of hot sand (similar to a hot-stone massage) or the *mbarika* massage using hot leaves of the castor seed plant. The cool and tranquil treatment rooms are decorated with *kangas*, scented with incense, and *taarab* music is played in the background. There's another branch at **Mtoni Marine**, 8 km north of Stone Town (see Where to stay, page 172).

Tour operators

All the following operators offer the tours listed above and others, including dhow trips to offshore islands such as Changuu (or Prison) Island (page 151) or the Jozani Chwaka Bay National Park (see page 182).

They also offer transport to the north and east coast beaches (see Getting around, page 132), which can be combined with tours. For example, you can be picked up in Stone Town and taken to the east coast via the Jozani Chwaka Bay National Park, or on the way to the north coast, you have the option of combining a morning spice tour with, perhaps, a visit to the Mangapwani slave caves and ending with a transfer to the hotels in Nungwi. Some are also able to arrange visits to Pemba, domestic flights, and car and motorbike hire. This is certainly not a comprehensive list; there are many tour operators to choose from; it's just a case of finding one you like. There are more listed on the **Zanzibar Association of Tour Operators (ZATO)** website: www.zato.or.tz. Alternatively, you can book all excursions through your hotel. For information about Stone Town's *papasi* (touts), see box, page 143.

Black Pearl, Shangani St, next to the Silk Route restaurant, T024-223 9283, www.blackpearlzanzibar.com.

Discover Zanzibar Tours & Safaris, Sokomuhogo St, T024-223 2022, www.discoverzanzibartours.com.

Eco & Culture Tours, Hurumzi St, near 236 Hurumzi Hotel, T024-223 3731, www.ecoculture-zanzibar.org.

Exotic Tours & Safaris, 1st floor, Bombay Bazaar Building, Mlandenge, T024-223 6392, www.exoticzanzibar.com.

Fisherman Tours & Travel, Vuga Rd, T024-223 8790, www.fishermantours.com.

Gallery Tours & Travel, close to Mbweni Ruins Hotel (page 157), T024-223 2088, www.gallerytours.net.

Jambo Tours, inside the Old Fort, T024-223 4205, www.jambo-zanzibar.com.

Kawa Tours, in the Old Dispensary, Mizingani Rd, T0777-430 431, www.zanzibarkawatours.com.

KV Tours & Travel, T0773-132 334, www.kvtours.net.

Links Tours & Travel, at the port, T024-223 1081, www.linkstours-zanzibar.com.

Marzouk Tours & Travel, Hurumzi St, opposite 236 Hurumzi Hotel, T024-223 8225, www.marzoukzanzibar.com.

Ocean Tours, Kelele Sq, opposite Serena Inn, T024-223 8280, www.oceantourszanzibar.com.

Sama Tours, Changa Bazaar St, T024-223 3543, www.samatours.com.

Sun Tours & Travel, Hurumzi St, near 236 Hurumzi Hotel, T024-223 9695, www.suntoursznz.com.

Tabasam Tours & Travel, in the Old Dispensary, Mizingani Rd, T024-223 0322, www.tabasamzanzibar.com.

Tropical Tours & Safaris, Kenyatta Rd, opposite Mazson's Hotel, Shangani, T0777-413 454, www.tropicaltours.villa69.org.

Zenji Zanzibar, at the Zenji Hotel (see Where to stay, page 156), Malindi, T0774-276 468, www.zenjizanzibar.com.

⊙ Transport

Stone Town *p142, map p144*
Air
Several airlines have scheduled services to and from the mainland and Zanzibar, and some also fly between Zanzibar and **Nairobi** and **Mombasa** in Kenya. Expect to pay in

the region of US$75 one-way from Dar es Salaam and the flight takes 20 mins. Some also operate services between Zanzibar and **Pemba**, which cost around US$100 one-way and take 30 mins. For details of direct international flights serving Zanzibar, see Essentials, page 11. For information about arriving at Zanzibar International Airport, see Getting there, page 132.

Air Excel has daily scheduled circuits between **Dar**, Zanzibar and **Arusha**, from where they connect with a circuit of the lodges in the **Serengeti**.

Coastal Air has daily flights on a circuit that goes between **Dar** and **Zanzibar**, **Arusha**, **Serengeti** and **Mwanza**. Another circuit goes between **Dar**, **Zanzibar**, **Pemba** and **Tanga**, and another between **Dar**, **Zanzibar**, **Pemba** and **Selous**.

Fly 540 has daily flights between Zanzibar and **Dar**, a Mon-Fri flight between Zanzibar and **Kilimanjaro** via Dar, and direct daily flights between Zanzibar and **Nairobi** and **Mombasa** in Kenya.

Kenya Airways has direct daily flights between Zanzibar and **Nairobi** and **Mombasa** in Kenya.

Precision Air has several daily flights between Zanzibar and **Dar**, some of which are on a circuit that also includes **Kilimanjaro**. It also has international flights between Zanzibar and Dar to either **Nairobi** or **Mombasa** in Kenya on the same circuits. The Zanzibar flights also connect with their 4 weekly flights between Dar and **Johannesburg** in South Africa.

ZanAir has daily flights between **Dar** and **Zanzibar**, some of which continue on to **Pemba** and to **Arusha** and the **Serengeti**, and one of the flights goes from **Zanzibar** to **Dar** and then on to **Selous**.

Airline offices 1-Time, airport, T024-223 6583, www.1time.aero. **Air Excel**, Arusha, T027-254 8429, www.airexcelonline.com. **Coastal Air**, Shangani St, T024-223 3112, www.coastal.cc. **Emirates**, Dr. Salim Amur Rd, Malindi, T024-223 3322, www.emirates.com.

Ethiopian Airlines, opposite the Friday Mosque, off Malawi Rd, Malindi, T024-223 1527, www.flyethiopian.com. Fly 540, airport T0762-540 540, in the Old Cine Afrique building, Malawi Rd, Malindi, T024-223 5110, www.fly540.com. Gulf Air, airport, T024-223 3772, www.gulfair.com. Kenya Airways, opposite the Friday Mosque, Malawi Rd, Malindi, T024-223 2042, www.kenya-airways.com. Precision Air, behind the Old Dispensary, Kiponda, T024-223 4521, www.precisionairtz.com. ZanAir, Migombani St, to the west of Malawi Rd, Malindi, T024-223 3670, www.zanair.com.

Bus and dala-dala
The main bus and *dala-dala* terminal is on Benjamin Mkapi (Creek) Rd opposite the Central Darajani Market. They generally run from 0600 or 0700 to 1600 or 1800, depending on the destination, and a journey across the island costs US$2-4. Vehicles with lettered codes serve routes in and around Stone Town. A to **Amani**, B to **Bububu** and U to the **airport**, amongst others. Numbered vehicles go further afield. No 9 goes to **Paje**, **Jambiani** (3 hrs) and **Bwejuu** (4½ hrs). Other routes include No 1, Benjamin Mkapi (Creek) Rd to **Pwani Mchangani** and **Matemwe**; No 2, **Mangapwani**; No 6, **Chakwa**, **Uroa** and **Pongwe**; No 7, **Fumba**; No 10, **Makunduchi** and **Kizimkazi**; No 14 and No 16, **Nungwi**; and No 17, **Kiwengwa**. An alternative to the buses and *dala-dalas* is to organize a seat on one of the daily tourist minibuses to the coastal resorts (see Getting around, page 132).

Car hire
Car and motorbike hire can be arranged through most of the tour operators (for more details see Getting around, page 132). Alternatively try: Zanzibar Car Hire Ltd, Kenyatta Rd, Shangani, T024-223 5485, www.zanzibarcarhire.com; Zanzibar Express Car Hire, Nyerere Rd on the way to the airport, T0777-410 186, www.zanzibar expresscarhire.com, or Zanzibar Rent-A-Car, Nyerere Rd on the way to the airport, T024-223 1990, www.zanzibarrentacar.com.

Ferry
The booking offices of the ferry companies are on the approach road to the port at the end of Malawi Rd and are generally open 0600-2000. If at all possible, buy your ticket in advance, as it is easier to then go straight to the departure gate later with your luggage. As in Dar, the companies advise travellers to ignore the touts, and it is easy enough to book a ticket on your own. For details of ferry services between Dar, Zanzibar and Pemba, see Transport in Dar, page 75.
Azam Marine, T024-223 1655, www.azam marine.com. Fast Ferries, T024-223 4690, www.fastferriestz.com. Flying Horse, T0784-472 497. Mega Speed Liners, T0713-282 365, www.megaspeedliners-zanzibar.com. Sea Star, T0777-411 505.

❶ Directory

Stone Town *p142, map p144*
Immigration T024-223 9148. If you lose your passport whilst on Zanzibar, go to the immigration office at the port who will arrange for an emergency travel document to get you back to Dar, where the international embassies and high consulates are located.
Medical services The main public hospital is Mnazi Mmoja Hospital, Kuanda Rd near the State House, T024-223 0707 A better bet are the private hospitals: Zanzibar Medical & Diagnostic Centre, near Majestic Cinema, off Vuga Rd, T024-223 3113; Zanzibar Medical Group, off Kenyatta Rd, T024-223 3134, 24-hr emergency number T0777-410 954.
Police Malindi Police Station, Malawi Rd, near the corner of Benjamin Mkapi (Creek) Rd, T024-223 0772. Always inform the police of any incidents – you will need a police statement for any insurance claims.

North to Nungwi

The stretch of coastline immediately to the north of Stone Town was once an area of villas, recreational beaches and Sultans' out-of-town palaces. This is also the route that was once followed by the Bububu light railway (so named after the noise the train made) and an iron pipeline that carried domestic water supplies to the town during the reign of Sultan Barghash. Today, many of the ruined palaces can be visited, though little of their previous opulence remains and they are fairly overgrown. Nevertheless, they offer an interesting excursion off the road to Nungwi. At the northern end of the island are the villages of Nungwi and Kendwa. Until recently these were sleepy fishing villages hosting a couple of backpackers' lodges, but today the two settlements are almost joined together by a ribbon of hotel development, and this is one of the most popular spots on the island for a beach holiday. The party atmosphere along the Nungwi Strip may not appeal to everyone, but there is no denying that this is a wonderful stretch of palm lined beach. Days are warm and sunny, the Indian Ocean is a brilliant blue and the snorkelling and diving are excellent. ▸▸ *For listings, see pages 172-176.*

Maruhubi Palace ruins

The Maruhubi Palace ruins are about 3 km to the north of Stone Town. They were built in 1882 by Sultan Barghash for his harem of what is said to be one of the most impressive residences on the island. Built in the Arabic style, the main house had balustrade balconies, the great supporting columns for which can still be seen. From here you can imagine him looking out over his beautiful walled gardens, which are believed to have been inspired by the Sultan's 1875 visit to Richmond Park in London. An overhead aqueduct and lily-covered cisterns (or 'pleasure ponds') can also be seen on the site and are evidence of the extensive Persian Baths. On the beach are the remains of a fortified *seble* or reception area, where visiting dignitaries would have been welcomed. The palace was almost completely destroyed by a fire in 1899; the site is now very overgrown, and marble from the baths has long since been stolen.

Mtoni Palace ruins

About 2 km after the Marahubi Palace, just before the small BP oil terminus and next to **Mtoni Marine** (see Where to stay, page 172), are the ruins of the earlier Mtoni Palace. In 1828 and shortly before he relocated his court from Muscat to Zanzibar, Sultan Seyyid constructed the Royal Palace at Mtoni as his primary residence, and it is the oldest palace on the island. One of the most famous inhabitants was his daughter, Princess Sayyida Salme who was born here (see box, page 138, for her story). She described in her book, *Memoirs of an Arabian Princess from Zanzibar*, that Mtoni "had a large courtyard where gazelles, peacocks, ostriches and flamingos wandered around, a large bath-house at one end and the sultan's quarters at the other where he lived with his principal wife". The palace was abandoned by 1885, in favour of more modern residences built by Sultan Barghash (see Maruhubi Palace, above) and quickly fell into disrepair. Use as a storage depot in World War I caused further damage, and now only the walls and part of the roof remain.

Kibweni Palace

Around 3 km North of Mtoni, to the left-hand side of the road is Kibweni Palace. This fine whitewashed building is the only Sultan's Palace on the island to remain in public use, accommodating both the President and state visitors. Constructed in 1915 it was used as a country or 'rest house' for the royal family and was originally named Beit el-Kassrusaada ('Palace of Happiness') but that name fell into disuse and it's now commonly referred to by the name of the nearby village.

Persian Baths at Kidichi

ⓘ *1 km north of Kibwenii at Bububu, take a right-hand turn opposite a small filling station, along a rough dirt road. Follow the track for 4 km out through the clove and coconut plantations.*
Built on the highest point of Zanzibar Island by Sultan Seyyid Said in 1850, these baths were for his wife, who was the grand-daughter of the Shah of Persia, Fatah Ali, and are decorated in ornamental Persian stucco work. The remarkably preserved domed bathhouses have deep stone baths and massive seats. This is quite a contrast to the plain baths nearby at **Kizimbani**, which were built within Said's clove tree and coconut plantation. Persian poetry inscribed inside the baths at Kidichi has been translated (approximately) as "Pleasant is a flower-shaped wine/With mutton chops from game/Given from the hands of a flower-faced server/At the bank of a flowering stream of water". The beaches to the west of **Bububu** are good and are the location of several resorts (see Where to stay, page 172).

Mangapwani slave caves

ⓘ *Near the village of Mangapwani, about 20 km north of Stone Town. Many of the tour operators stop here on a spice tour. The caves can be reached independently by taking bus No 2 from Benjamin Mkapi (Creek) Rd. It's best to take a torch.*
These were used to hide slaves in the times when the slave trade was illegal but still carried on unofficially. The **Coral Cave** is a natural cavern in the coralline rock with a tapered entrance and a pool of fresh water at its deepest point. The cave itself is said to have been discovered when a young slave boy lost a goat that he was looking after. He followed its bleats, which led to the cave containing the freshwater stream (a blessing for the confined slaves). With care, you can reach the steps that lead down onto the chamber floor. **Mangapwani Slave Chamber** is a couple of kilometres up the coast from the Coral Cave. Although sometimes called the Slave Cave, it is a rectangular cell that has been cut out of the coralline rock, with a roof on top. It was built specifically for storing slaves, and its construction is attributed to one Mohammed bin Nassor Al-Alwi, an important slave trader. Boats from the mainland would unload their human cargo on the nearby beach, and the slaves would be kept here before being taken to Stone Town for resale, or directly to the nearby plantations. After 1873, when Sultan Barghash signed the Anglo–Zanzibari treaty which officially abolished the slave trade, both the caves continued to be used as a place to hide slaves, as an illicit trade continued for many years.

Tumbatu Island

Northwest of Zanzibar, the island of Tumbatu is the third largest island in the archipelago and, despite being only 8 km long by 3 km wide, it has a very individual history. The island contains **Shirazi ruins** of a large ancient town dating from the 12th century; about 40 of the stone houses remain. The **Mvuleni ruins** are in the north of the island and are the remnants of the Portuguese attempt to colonize Zanzibar. The island's people, the Watumbatu, are distinct from the people of Unguja. They speak their own dialect of Kiswahili and are fiercely independent, renowned for their aloofness and pride rather than their hospitality. They are strictly Muslim and generally do not welcome visitors to the island. They also have the reputation of being the best sailors on the East Coast of Africa.

Kendwa

South of Nungwi (see below), about 3 km by road or 30-40 minutes' walk along the beach (but only at low tide), is the small resort of Kendwa. It is reached by the same minibuses that transport visitors to Nungwi. The beach is especially known as a good place to swim (as is Nungwi) because the tide only retreats about 6 m at low tide, so swimming is possible at any time of day. A band of coral lies about 20 m offshore which offers interesting snorkelling, and trips can be organized by the hotels.

Nungwi

ⓘ *Tourist minibuses go from Stone Town throughout the day, take approximately 1 hr and cost about US$15 each way, ask from any hotel or tour operator. There are also local dala-dala and the No 14 and 16 buses from Benjamin Mkapi (Creek) Rd also goes to Nungwi. These take about 2 hrs and cost about US$1 each way.*

At the north tip of the island is Nungwi, about 56 km from Stone Town. It's a pleasant fishing village surrounded by banana palms, mangroves and coconut trees, with a local population of around 8000. However, tourism has rapidly expanded in this area and, today, it is the most popular beach resort on the island, with a string of large self-contained resorts and a firmly established reputation as the island's party destination. As well as resorts, there are a number of good budget beach-side bungalows, a short line of lively outdoor bars and restaurants, known as the 'Nungwi Strip', and a few dive schools. The accommodation is of a good standard and most of Nungwi's cottages are built in a traditional African style with makuti thatched roofs to blend in with the natural surroundings. The bars are fantastically rustic and you'll find beautifully carved Zanzibari furniture sitting on the beach.

Down on the beach, you'll often see local men working in groups to build dhows or dhow fleets heading out to fish in the mid-afternoon. Boat building here has been a traditional skill for generations, using historic tools; a 12-m boat takes approximately six months to build. Goats are slaughtered when certain milestones are reached (eg raising the mast), and verses and prayers are read from the Koran. Upon completion a big ceremony is organized and all the villagers are invited. Before the launch the boat builder hammers the boat three times in a naming ceremony.

The name of the village is derived from the Swahili word *mnara*, referring to the 70-ft lighthouse built here 1886 by Chance and Brothers. Currently it's in a restricted area, with access permitted only by special request and photography is prohibited.

Where to stay
Amaan Bungalows **1**
Baraka Annex **4**
Baraka Bungalows **2**
Double Tree Hilton Nungwi **8**
Essque Zalu Zanzibar **7**
Flame Tree Cottages **12**
Jambo Brothers Beach
  Bungalows **14**
Langi Langi **3**
Mnarani Beach
  Cottages **6**
Nungwi Inn **13**
Paradise Beach **9**
Ras Nungwi Beach **10**
Sazani Beach **11**
Smiles Beach **16**
Union Beach Bungalows **15**
Z **5**

Henna tattoos

The art of henna body-painting has been used for centuries as a woman's adornment in Asian and Middle East countries and it was imported to Zanzibar during the establishment of the Swahili culture. Known as *hina* in Kiswahili, the dye is obtained after pounding the dried leaves of the plant, then mixing them with water to form a paste. Lemon or lime juice is added to make the dye more reddish, and the colour can be further enhanced by adding cloves, tea, coffee or indigo. Sugar and oil are added to make it last longer. Today, henna occupies a special place in both rural and urban Zanzibar and Pemba in marriages and occasions such as births, naming and circumcision ceremonies and the Muslim holiday of Eid-al-Ftir (end of Ramadan). It is applied on the soles of the feet, ankles, palms and nails, and patterns represent good health, fertility, wisdom, protection and spiritual enlightenment; the more complex the design is, the more attractive the woman becomes. Rather delightfully, wives also paint themselves to gladden and welcome home their spouses who have been away for days, and men return the compliment by buying their wives new *kangas* (pieces of cloth worn by local women), shoes or jewellery.

Many visitors to Zanzibar (both male and female) get henna 'tattoos'. (For men a trailing vine or geometrical pattern around the upper arm that's popular for normal tattoos is the norm). Ladies or *wachoraji* (henna painters) offer this service at most of the beach resorts on the island, and you can also get tattoos done in the small art galleries in Stone Town, especially around Hurumzi Street behind the Old Fort, and they may be offered on a Spice Tour. Because henna is a natural dye (it's permanent on fabric or wood), and the skin reacts and absorbs the powder, it stains the skin and cannot be scrubbed off with soap and water. The tattoos usually last around two weeks (a consideration, perhaps, if you're going back to work after your holiday on Zanzibar), although they do fade during that time.

Green turtles frequently nest on Nungwi Beach; the locals bring the hatchlings to the two natural aquariums nearby, where they remain until they are big enough to be released into the sea. **Mnarani Aquarium** ① *0900-1800, US$5*, is a protected natural tidal rockpool, where you can see the turtles; the water is clearest about two hours before high tide. You can swim with the turtles here (they are very curious and nudge you in the water), and the resorts arrange trips and supply masks and snorkels for around US$20. The other natural aquarium is at the **Baraka Annex** ① *(see Where to stay, page 175) 0800-1830, US$5, swimming US$8*, where you can feed seaweed to the green turtles. Again, you can quietly slip into the water to swim with them (but you'll need your own snorkelling equipment if you want to put your head underwater, though there is little need as the water is crystal clear). The pool is also home to schools of red snapper and parrot fish.

⊙ North to Nungwi listings

For sleeping and eating price codes and other relevant information, see pages 22-26.

⊜ Where to stay

North to Nungwi *p168, map p134*
$$$$ Sea Cliff Resort & Spa, Mangapwani,
T0767-702 241-9, www.seacliffzanzibar.com.
A quality new resort on Mangapwani Beach
and sister property to the **Hotel Sea Cliff** in
Dar (page 63), built in mock-Arabic style
architecture with makuti thatched roofs.
There are 120 rooms, 2 very large rim-flow
swimming pools, tennis courts, spa, gym,
watersports centre, bike hire, walking trails
through a coconut plantation, a jetty into
the sea, a bar and restaurants. An excellent
all-round option with high standards.
$$$ Hakuna Matata Beach Lodge, Chuini,
10 km north of Stone Town, T0777-454 892,
www.hakuna-matata-beach-lodge.com. Built
around some ruins discovered here in 2004,
13 secluded a/c bungalows with terraces
and ocean views set in leafy gardens around
a small cove, some with sleeper couches for
children. An excellent restaurant serves the
usual seafood and, more unusually, game
meat like impala or ostrich. The bar is built
on stilts in the sea, and there's a spa.
$$$ Imani Beach Villa, Bububu Beach,
9 km north of Stone Town, T024-225 0050,
www.imani-zanzibar.com. Fairly secluded,
with only 7 clean, comfortable a/c rooms
and traditional-style furniture. The quality
and presentation of food is very high, with
fresh fish and organic vegetables from their
gardens, and you eat Swahili-style, seated on
cushions around low tables. The restaurant
is open to non-residents, and there's a
barbecue on Thu nights. US$110 double
B&B or US$700 for private use of the whole
house for up to 14 people half board.
$$$ Mtoni Marine, between the Maruhubi
and Mtoni ruins to the north, 8 km from Stone
Town, T024-225 0140, www.mtoni.com. Set
in an attractive palm tree garden with large

swimming pool, this good-value all-round
resort has 41 rooms with private verandas,
traditional furnishings and ocean views,
plus 4 apartments, with 1-3 bedrooms and
kitchenettes, which are ideal for families. The
open-air restaurant has barbecue buffets and
themed nights with live jazz or *taarab* music,
plus there's a beach cocktail bar, a sports
café and a sushi restaurant (the only one on
the island). There's also another Zanzibari
Mrembo Spa (see Stone Town, page 165).
$$-$ Furaha Resort, Bububu Beach, 9 km
north of Stone Town, T024-225 0010,
www.furahazanzibar.com. Fairly simple but
friendly option set on a quiet part of the
beach, with 13 large, comfortable a/c rooms
and Zanzibari beds; most of the rooms are
set around the swimming pool. There's a
terrace restaurant and bar with ocean views.
Doubles from US$60, singles are particularly
good value from US$35.

Kendwa *p170, map p134*
$$$$ Kilindi Zanzibar, reservations
Elewana Afrika, Arusha T027-250 0630,
www.elewana.com. Stunning new resort
with beautiful architecture and eco
principles, such as rainwater collection and
solar power. 15 very spacious and private
brilliant white villas with domed roofs to
keep them cool (makes a change from
makuti thatch), each with its own plunge
pool, some have 2 bedrooms and 3 have
rooftop gardens. There's an open restaurant,
bar with waterfall feature, beautiful spa with
its own walled garden, and unique T-shaped
infinity swimming pool next to the ocean.
All-inclusive rates are in excess of US$500
per person, but it's definitely competing as
one of Zanzibar's best luxury options.
$$ Kendwa Amaan Bungalows, T0777-417
127, www.kendwa.tanzania-adventure.com.
A mixture of 39 rooms in bungalows 50 m
from the beach or in the main building in
gardens set back on the hill. Rooms are simply
furnished and a little bare but with balconies

or verandas, mosquito nets and fans. The restaurant and bar under a giant thatched roof is on the beach with tables in the sand, and there are lots of hammocks to lounge around in. Offers free transfers to Nungwi.

$$ Kendwa Sunset Bungalows, T0777-413 818, www.sunsetkendwa.com. One of the better places to stay in Kendwa, perched on top of a small cliff above the beach, with a reasonably organized feel to it, friendly staff and a choice of accommodation ranging from new apartments to beach bandas – all are reasonably priced and most rooms have a/c. The good bar and restaurant does great fresh fish and pizzas, and the **Scuba-Do** dive centre is here (see page 176).

$$-$ Kendwa Rocks, T0774-415 475, www.kendwarocks.com. The original Kendwa backpackers' lodge but these days it gets consistently poor reports for its shabby accommodation, variable levels of service and surly staff. A much better venue for its restaurant, which serves pizza, seafood, veggie and Indian food, and the 24-hr **Mermaid Bar**, which is famous for its 'full moon' parties on the beach with DJs, acrobats and fire-eaters. **Zanzibar Watersports** has a centre here (see page 176). Basic thatched bandas on the beach from US$12 per person, or better quality bungalows for US$60 for a double.

$ White Sands Hotel, T0777-470 331, www.whitesandhotelznz.com. Basic set-up with en suite bandas or bungalows on the hillside near the beach with hot water; pay a little more for the larger rooms with ocean view. There's a thatched restaurant and bar with sunken cushioned area serving simple seafood but lacking ambience. Doubles from US$40.

Nungwi *p170, map p170*

The price of a hotel room in Nungwi varies from US$30-500, so the resort appeals to all budgets. In recent years, new hotels, including large, soulless package resorts, have been built here and they effectively join up Nungwi with Kendwa to the south. If you want to avoid the crowds, the northeast

of the peninsula is generally quieter and has some smaller, more intimate places to stay. The beach party crowds tend to hang out around the southern part of the village.

$$$$ Essque Zalu Zanzibar, T0778-683 960, www.essquehotels.com. Opened in 2011, this large resort, with its enormous thatched main building (the roof is more than 40 m high), now dominates a previously low-key part of east Nungwi. Italian-owned but so far popular with a mixture of international holidaymakers, it has 40 slick rooms and 9 super-luxury villas, a stylish restaurant and bar, expansive spa, stunning infinity swimming pool and pier into the ocean.

$$$$-$$$ Ras Nungwi Beach Hotel, T024-223 3767, www.rasnungwi.com. Quality and well-run resort which was one of the first in Nungwi with 32 rooms, some in the lodge, some beach chalets and 1 suite that is a huge detached house with a plunge pool and total privacy from the rest of the hotel. All are linked to the beach by pathways and have ocean views, 4-poster beds, carved doors, a/c and balconies. Restaurant, bar and lounge area are under thatched roofs, there's a large pool, spa, and **Zanzibar Watersports**, is here (see page 176). The hotel supports the local Nungwi Village community through the Labayka Development Fund, assisting with health and hygiene projects and schooling, and they offer an informative 3-hr village walk for US$25.

$$$$-$$$ The Z Hotel, T0732-266 266, www.theZhotel.com. An excellent boutique hotel with 35 elegant sea-view rooms boasting plasma TVs (unusually built within the mosquito nets over the beds), Wi-Fi and a classy mix of Zanzibari and contemporary decor. The 2 rooftop suites and 2 oceanside cottages are especially nice. The relaxing infinity pool overlooks the beach, and there's an open-air restaurant serving African-continental fusion food built up on stilts over the sea. The **Cinnamon Bar** is a perfect spot for sundowners, there's a spa, they have their own 'Z' dhow for sunsets cruises, and **East Africa Diving** has a base here.

$$$ Double Tree Hilton Nungwi, T024-224 0476, www.doubletree1.hilton.com. A modern resort, with 96 a/c rooms (1 suitable for wheelchairs) with satellite TV, Wi-Fi and balconies overlooking the ocean or pool in whitewashed blocks with thatched roofs, pool with swim-up bar, 2 restaurants with themed nights and live entertainment, gym and spa. A little impersonal but good standards and service from Hilton's mid-range brand. There are good views of the dhows moored off the village to the north of here.

$$$ Flame Tree Cottages, T024-224 0100, www.flametreecottages.com. Set in colourful gardens with coconut palms, frangipane and bougainvillea just off the beach, the 16 immaculate a/c cottages with terraces are all named after trees or plants that are common to Zanzibar. Some also have kitchenettes, and self-catering can be arranged for a small surcharge. Candle-lit restaurant specializing in seafood, swimming pool, and can organize yoga (www.yoga zanzibar.com). The whole place has an air of tranquillity about it. Doubles from US$120.

$$$ Langi Langi, T024-224 0470, www.langilangizanzibar.com. Pleasant thatched bungalows with 34 a/c rooms with verandas just across the track from the beach, some in 2-storey buildings next to the pool and cheaper units in garden cottages, plus a good-value 2-bedroom family house. Swimming pool in peaceful garden, internet café, very good restaurant on a pleasant deck over the beach with reasonably priced food, including mains of octopus and lobster. Doubles from US$120.

$$$ Mnarani Beach Cottages, T024-224 0494, www.mnarani-beach-cottages.com. A quiet and secluded spot near the lighthouse, and a 20-min walk from the main strip, with friendly management and a good atmosphere. 37 rooms ranging from simple cottages in the garden, to spacious family apartments with balconies and sea views in the main building, all with a/c and Zanzibari beds. Great seafront bar with hammocks, restaurant that focuses on seafood and international cuisine, library and internet facilities. Doubles from US$140.

$$$ Sazani Beach Hotel, near Ras Nungwi, T024-224 0014, www.sazanibeach.com. A quiet option about a 20-min walk from the 'strip', with 10 thatched bungalows with fans set in tropical gardens dotted with day-beds and hammocks and linked to the beach by sandy paths. Morning tea is brought to your veranda, the Pweza Juma bar and restaurant serves original dishes with local flavour, specializing in 3-course set dinners of seafood and barbecues. The secluded beach is good for kiteboarding and **Kiteboarding Zanzibar** is here (see page 176).

$$$-$$ Amaan Bungalows, T024-224 0026, www.amaanbungalows.com. This, the original Nungwi resort, was established more than 15 years ago and is really the centre of the whole Nungwi strip. Today it's a sprawling place with 58 rooms of varying standards but all very well maintained – the best are those with balconies right over the beach. The 2 restaurants and bars, the **Marina Grill** and **Infusion**, serve good quality food and are deservedly popular, plus there's an internet café and curio/coffee shop. Bicycles can be hired. Doubles with fan start from US$70, with a/c US$100.

$$ Nungwi Inn, T024-224 0091, www.nungwiinnhotel.co.tz. A neat and friendly set-up with 24 quieter-than-most bungalows in a pretty garden behind **Spanish Dancer Divers**, with spacious tiled bathrooms, terraces, a/c and Zanzibari beds. The beach restaurant and bar, with a relaxed atmosphere and chilled music, has a pizza oven, and it's worth making a detour for the chocolate, banana and honey pancakes. Doubles from US$65.

$$ Smiles Beach Hotel, T0714-444 105, www.smilesbeachhotel.com. A fairly simple family-owned place, with 16 a/c rooms, terraces or balconies in 2-storey pagoda-style houses with wide spiral staircases to the upper floors, but a bit exposed next to the beach track. The restaurant, just off the beach, serves traditional Swahili food; it's Muslim owned so no alcohol.

$$-$ Baraka Bungalows, T0777-422 901, http://barakabungalow.atspace.com. A simple local guesthouse with no direct sea frontage yet it is a beautiful little garden oasis with some of the best bungalows in this price range in Nungwi. The 12 rooms are simply furnished with terraces, fans and nets, good bathrooms, and 2 have a/c. US$50 for a double. The cheap restaurant serves generous portions; no alcohol but good juices such as avocado and cucumber. The sister guesthouse, **Baraka Annex**, T0776-465 017, is opposite Mnarani Beach Cottages on the northeastern side of the peninsula, about a 30-min walk from the main Nungwi drag. The 4 rooms here are more basic but cheaper at US$30 for a double with fans and nets, and breakfast is included. They also have a natural aquarium here to see turtles (see page 170).

$$-$ Paradise Beach Hotel, T0777-416 308. Again in the heart of things on the Nungwi strip, with 18 basic rooms with bathrooms and fans in a rather ugly, tired-looking block facing the sea, but cheap (from US$40 for a double), with a popular restaurant serving pizza and curries and a lively beach bar. Difficult to pre-book but you should be able to get a room. **Zanzibar Watersports** is on the beach here (see page 176).

$ Jambo Brothers Beach Bungalows, behind the **East Africa Diving** centre, T0777-492 355. A slightly simpler concern than some of its neighbours and set just back from the beach. The 15 rooms in large cottages with terraces have nets, fans and hot water, but it's a little scruffy and not as well maintained as some. Doubles from US$35 with breakfast, no restaurant but an easy stroll to the other places. Again, not easy to pre-book but it's easy to organize a room when you get off the minibuses in the centre of the village.

$ Union Beach Bungalows, T0777-454 706. Low budget with 10 bungalows on the beach but dotted around the main track

so very exposed, but clean with their own bathrooms, nets and fans. Doubles from US$35 including breakfast.

❼ Restaurants

Nungwi *p170, map p170*
All the hotels have restaurants and you can take your pick from the string along the Nungwi strip as you walk along the beachside track between the hotels. Most are open 0700-2300. The nicest, with wooden decks next to the beach, are the **Marina Grill** and **Infusion**, at Amman Bungalows, and the restaurant at **Langi Langi**. Menus are very similar and offer seafood, pizza and pasta; expect to pay in the region of US$8-10 for a main course rising to US$15 for lobster. The best of the more formal restaurants are at **Z Hotel** and **Double Tree** (see page 173).

❑ Shopping

Nungwi *p170, map p170*
You can buy basics at the small shops along the beachfront but it is much cheaper to go into the village where water, bread and other items are available. Remember to respect local custom if you go into the village. Women should cover their arms, shoulders and thighs. There's an unnamed bottle shop for alcohol on the track behind the beach near **Jambo Brothers**. There are several places for massages, manicures and pedicures, hair-braiding and henna tattoos (see box, page 171) at the resorts or along the beach track.

❻ What to do

North to Nungwi *p168, map p134*
The beaches around Kendwa and Nungwi are one of the few areas without a coral reef near to the shore, so you can swim at all tides here without walking out for miles to reach the sea, as is the case on the east coast. A number of places organize 'sunset cruises' on dhows for around US$15 per person.

Diving and snorkelling

There are more than 20 dive sites around the top of Zanzibar between Tumbatu Island in the west and Mnemba Island in the east. There is an abundance of tropical reef fish as well as large pelagic fish and, if lucky, you will encounter barracuda, manta rays, whale and reef sharks; hawksbill and green turtles, and schools of dolphins are often seen. The average water temperature is 27°C and visibility sometimes exceeds 40 m, with the average all year at 20 m. For more information on Zanzibar's dive sites, see box, page 163. Several dive schools operate on the north coast. Expect to pay in the region of US$55-75 for a single dive and US$400-500 for a 4-day PADI Open Water course. They can also organize snorkelling boat trips for around US$20-30. The most popular trip is to **Mnembe Island Marine Conservation Area**; a day trip includes 2 dives (or unlimited snorkelling) and lunch of barbecue fish on the beach. Snorkelling equipment for use from the beach can also be hired at the resorts or from some of the shops in Nungwi village.

East Africa Diving, in front of **Jambo Brothers Beach Bungalows**, Nungwi, and there's another centre at the **Z Hotel**, Nungwi, T0777-416 425, www.diving-zanzibar.com.
Scuba-Do, at **Kendwa Sunset Bungalows**, Kendwa, T0784-415 179, www.scuba-do-zanzibar.com.
Spanish Dancer Divers, in front of **Nungwi Inn**, Nungwi, T0777-417 717, www.spanishdancerdivers.com.
Zanzibar Watersports, at **Kendwa Rocks**, Kendwa, **Paradise Beach Hotel** and Ras Nungwi, both in Nungwi, T0773-235 030, www.zanzibarwatersports.com.

Fishing

Fishing trips go to the Pemba Channel just north of Nungwi. The yellowfish tuna

season is Aug-Nov and the billfish season for blue, black and striped marlin Nov-Mar. A 5-hr trip, including tackle and bait and refreshments, costs in the region of US$400-550 for 4-6 fishermen.
FishingZanzibar.com, at Ras Nungwi, T0773-875 231, www.fishingzanzibar.com.
Hooked on Fishing, at the **Z Hotel**, Nungwi, T0777-330 331, www.fishzanzibar.com.
Zanzibar Big Game Fishing, based at the Zanzibar Watersports centres (above), T0777-415 660, www.zanzibarfishing.com.

Kiteboarding

Kiteboarding Zanzibar, office near Jambo Brothers and at **Sazani Beach Hotel**, Nungwi, T0779-720 259, www.kiteboardingzanzibar.com. Offers lessons from 3 hrs (from US$80) to a 3-day course and rents out equipment to experienced boarders.

Parasailing and watersports

Zanzibar Parasailing, the office is on the beach just south of Jambo Brothers, T0779-073 078, www.zanzibarparasailing.com. A range of watersports can be arranged here and their pontoon with equipment is moored just off the beach. **Parasailing** takes around 1 hr for the boat ride with about 15 mins in the air and is best at sunset when you can see the other side of the peninsula; US$70, tandem US$110. **Waterskiing/wake-boarding**, US$45 for 10-15 mins or US$80 for a 30-min lesson. **Banana boat/rubber rings**, US$15 for 10-15 mins. Similar to the banana boat, the 'Fly-Fish' looks like a large inflatable mattress that can take 3 and it lifts some 5 m into the air as it's pulled along by boat, US$30 for 10-15 mins. Guided **jet-skiing** trips last 1 hr and go approximately 15-20 km from Nungwi to the tip of Tumbatu Island, Kendwa and back to Nungwi, US$180 for 1 rider or US$200 for 2.

To the northeast coast

The very northeast part of the island seems miles away from the party scene of the Nungwi area and has a more remote, 'get away from it all' feel. Villages like Matemwe stretch right up the coast, fringed with shady palms. The local people live a peaceful existence making a living from farming seaweed or octopus fishing. An extensive coral reef runs down the whole east coast of the island, protecting a long, idyllic white sandy beach that runs for miles and is one of Africa's most beautiful. The only problem here is that the ocean is tidal and, during some parts of the day, it's a very long walk over the tidal flats to reach the sea (look out for sea urchins when walking). Further south, particularly around Kiwengwa and Pongwe, there has been a mushrooming of fully inclusive resort properties along the coast, which are quite characterless and could quite frankly be anywhere in the world, many of them frequented by European package holidaymakers. For the most part, it is necessary to book these through a tour operator in Stone Town, Dar es Salaam or Europe (many are Italian- or Swiss-owned) – or take a chance on getting a room when you arrive, although several do not take 'walk-in' guests. This is particularly risky in high season from June to September and over the Christmas and New Year period. There is very little choice of budget accommodation along the stretch of coast around Pongwe or Kiwengwa, although Matemwe has more options. ▸▸ *For listings, see pages 179-181.*

Getting there

Minibus transfers can be arranged in Stone Town and cost around US$15. Bus No 6 goes from Benjamin Mkapi (Creek) Rd in Stone Town to Chwaka (1½ hours) and then continues north to Uroa and Pongwe, while the No 17 bus also goes along the better part of the beach road as far north as Kiwengwa. Both cost approximately US$1.50.

Dunga Palace

ⓘ *Dala-dalas to Chakwe pass the ruins but they are not well signposted off the main road.*

Just over 20 km down the road from Stone Town to Chwaka are the ruins of the Dunga Palace, which was built by Chief Mwinyi Mkuu Ahmed bin Mohamed Hassan. Legend has it that during the palace's construction slaves were killed in order that their blood could be mixed with the mortar to bring strength and good fortune to the building. During the 1920s a nearby well was found to be 'half full of human bones'. King Muhammed died in 1865 and was succeeded by his son Ahmed, who died without an heir in 1873, ending forever the line of the Mwinyi Mkuu. Unfortunately, there is little left of the palace today beside bits of wall and arches, and the area has been taken over by a plantation.

Chwaka Bay

At the end of this road, 32 km from Stone Town via Dunga you will reach Chwaka Bay. On the way you will pass the small **Ufufuma Forest**, a home for Zanzibar red colobus monkey, Ader's duiker, impala and many bird species, and also the site of several caves. The forest has been actively conserved since 1995 and, although it's not a very well-known attraction, tourists are welcome, with guided walks costing around US$5. Chwaka is a quiet fishing village overlooking a broad bay of shallow water and mangrove swamps. Its history is evident from a line of fine but decayed villas, standing above the shoreline on the coral ridge, and it was once popular as a holiday resort with slave traders and their families in the 19th century. There is a lively open-air fish market but little accommodation, and most visitors head north along the coast to the hotels.

North of Chwaka

The road from Chwaka heads north through the coastal fishing villages where there are several accommodation options and watersports centres on what is a fantastic beach. **Uroa** is a lovely fishing village 10 km north of Chwaka, and is close to an accessible reef, which offers suitable diving for novices. **Pongwe** is 5 km north of Uroa, and **Kiwengwa** another 10 km north of Pongwe, followed by **Pwani Mchangani**. From the main road between Kiwengwa and Pongwe, which is all tarmac now, there are sections where there seems to be one gated tourist package hotel after another (predominantly occupied by Italians). This is one of the most heavily developed stretches of coastline on Zanzibar and, in some respects, locals have taken badly to many of the largest and least considerate resorts at which many guests show flagrant disregard for Zanzibari culture (topless sunbathing is illegal on the island though in parts of Italian-Kiwengwa you would be forgiven for not believing so). Nevertheless, Kiwengwa is popular on account of its beautiful beach and the 'all-inclusive' appeal of a holiday here. The large barricaded resorts diminish as you head further up the coast road to **Matemwe**, a small village 45 km from Stone Town and 15 km north of Kiwengwa. Inland from Matemwe, is some of the most fertile land on the island, a centre for rice, sugar and cassava production. Matemwe beach itself makes few concessions to tourists in that it's a centre for gathering seaweed and fishing. Depending on the position of the tide, you'll either see scores of women wading fully dressed into the sea to collect their daily crop or fleets of dhows sailing away to fish. It's one of the most interesting stretches of coast on the island and beautiful in the sense that it's very much a place where the locals carry on their traditional way of life. About 4 km off the coast of Matemwe lies the small island of **Mnemba**. About 500 m in diameter and a stunning teardrop-shaped oasis of white sand, the island, surrounded by a circular coral reef, is renowned for its diving and game fishing. Quite remarkably, in the tiny forest in the middle of the island there is a population of suni antelope but, unlike the mainland, there are no mosquitoes, scorpions or snakes on the island. Green turtles nest on the beach between December and May. The island is privately leased and to visit it, it is necessary to stay in the exclusive lodge (see page 181).

Kiwengwa-Pongwe Forest Reserve

ⓘ *Behind the beach and about a 2-km walk from the village of Kiwengwa, or catch the No 117 dala-dala towards Kinyasini, 0730-1700, guided tours from the visitor centre US$10.*

This is a recently opened conservation area that covers about 3000 ha of scrubland, mixed thickets and coral rag forest where there is the option of 200-m, 400-m or 2-km nature trails. Wildlife is varied, and you might catch sight of the endangered red colobus monkey, Sykes and blue monkeys, although they are much shyer and less used to visitors here than at the Jozani Chwaka Bay National Park (page 182). The forest is also home to Aders duiker, several species of snake, clouds of butterflies and some 40 species of bird, including ones indigenous to Zanzibar, such as the Zanzibar sombre greenbul, crowned hornbill, collard sunbird and white-browed coucal. Many of the 100 or so plant species are used by local people for medicinal purposes. You can explore the interesting coral caves here, which have impressive stalactites formed by water dissolving from the calcium carbonate of the coral stone. Another curious feature are the roots that have forced their way through the ground and look like electric wires connecting the ceiling to the bottom of the caves. The cave system is divided into three parts: the north and south caves are over 200 m long, sometimes 200 m deep, are accessible by stairs and walkways (although they are a bit of a scramble) and have naturally formed holes in the ceilings to let sunlight in. The east cave is 50 m long, darker, has a lot of bats, and can only be entered by crawling. Although the caves were only re-discovered in 2002, it was thought that they were traditionally used by villagers to make sacrifices in order to gain assistance with earthly matters such as harvests and fertility. The caves were also used as hiding places in the First and Second World Wars, when young men hid to avoid being drafted, and their parents would sneak down in the dead of night to bring them food. When leopards were still present on the island (there were still some alive in the mid-1990s but they are now thought to be extinct), it is said that witchdoctors would sometimes keep them tethered in the caves, as they conferred status on the owners and induced terrible fear amongst the local people.

◉ To the northeast coast listings

For sleeping and eating price codes and other relevant information, see pages 22-26.

◉ Where to stay

North of Chwaka *p178, map p134*
Uroa
$$$ Uroa Bay Beach Lodge, T0778-672 806, www.uroabay.com. A fairly new resort and good value, with 61 rooms in low, thatched buildings surrounded by pretty flowerbeds, either sea- or garden-facing, some for families, with TV and a/c. Buffet meals are included but you have the option of paying more for the likes of lobster. There are 2 bars, 2 swimming pools, and at low tide a sandbar appears off the beach that you can swim to. From US$120 for a double.
$$ Tamarind Beach Hotel, T0777-411 191, www.tamarindhotelzanzibar.com. One of the older options on the east coast and fixtures and fittings could do with a spruce up, but it's affordable and has a relaxed and informal atmosphere. 18 simple bungalows near the beach with nets, ceiling fans and Wi-Fi, a pleasant restaurant, open-air bar, swimming pool, and they can arrange diving at Mnembe Island Marine Conservation Area, as well as snorkelling, game fishing, bike hire and massages. Doubles from US$70.

Pongwe
$$$ Pongwe Beach Hotel, T0784-336 181, www.pongwe.com. A deservedly popular small hotel that has retained its peacefulness, with 16 nice stone and thatch beach bungalows and Zanzibari beds set in lovely relaxing gardens with hammocks strung between the palms. Attractive swimming pool area with decking overlooking the beach. The food is excellent, including inventive 3-course set dinners, and there's a cocktail bar. They can arrange all the usual activities, such as snorkelling and game fishing, and also rent out jeeps. Doubles from US$180.
$$ Santa Maria Coral Park, T0777-432 655, www.santamaria-zanzibar.com. A relaxed budget spot on the beach near the village, with rustic thatched bungalows and double-storey reed huts with basic twin/doubles/triples with fans and nets, a generator provides electricity and hot water in the evenings, thatched restaurant and bar serving simple meals, such as fish, chicken, chips, rice and salad, can organize to rent a local boat for fishing and snorkelling. Doubles are US$60.

Kiwengwa
Bear in mind there's a string of back-to-back mostly Italian resorts along Kiwenga Beach. The ones below cater to visitors of mixed nationalities.
$$$$ Bluebay Beach Resort & Spa, T024-224 0240/4, www.bluebayzanzibar.com. One of the better all-round family resorts on the east coast set on 12 ha of palm-filled grounds and on a lovely stretch of beach, with 112 a/c rooms ranging from ultra-luxurious Sultan's Suites to pretty garden rooms with sea views, 4-poster beds, satellite TV and minibar. There are several restaurants and bars, disco, swimming pool, opulent spa, tennis court, children's club, watersports. **One Ocean Diving** have a base

here (see page 181). **Sultan Sands Island Resort** is the sister resort (same contact details) next door with 76 rooms and similar facilities (many of which are shared).

$$$$ Ocean Paradise Resort, T0774-440 990, www.oceanparadisezanzibar.com. Another good all-inclusive option with 100 a/c rooms in round thatched bungalows in 6 ha of pretty gardens sloping gently towards the beach, with satellite TV and terraces. A full range of facilities is on offer, including 3 restaurants, several bars, watersports and one of the largest swimming pools on the island.

$$$$-$$$ Shooting Star Lodge, T0777-414 166, www.shootingstarlodge.com. Still owned by the charismatic Elly, who opened this lodge 17 years ago as the first in Kiwengwa. It's a beautiful, intimate place to stay, with 16 rooms furnished in Zanzibari style, ranging from pretty garden rooms to top-class luxury suites with private pools and roof terraces. The open-air bar and restaurant on sand with *makuti* roof serves seafood, grills and traditional Zanzibari cuisine – some of the best food to be had on the east coast. There are bicycles for hire and a lovely infinity swimming pool 10 m above the beach.

Pwani Mchangani
$$$ Mchanga Beach Lodge, T0773-569 821, www.mchangabeachlodge.com. A small, low-key lodge, with 6 sea-view lodge rooms and 2 garden suites that can sleep up to 4 on the couches/day beds, with a/c and locally crafted Zanzibari furniture set in pretty gardens opening on to the beach – morning tea is brought to your terrace. Swimming pool right by the beach, open-air restaurant specializing in Swahili cuisine and seafood, internet available, snorkelling and diving can be arranged.

$$$ Next Paradise Boutique Resort, T0773-822 206, www.next-paradise.com. A boutique hotel with just 16 a/c rooms and suites, very spacious and stylish with decor of hand-carved dark wood furniture and bright organza fabrics. There's satellite

TV and terraces overlooking the beach or swimming pool. Day-beds are scattered around the flowering gardens, there's an open-air bar and good restaurant with well-presented Mediterranean and Swahili food. Intimate and peaceful and a popular spot for honeymooners.

Matemwe
$$$$ Matemwe Retreat, at the far north of the beach, www.asiliaafrica.com/Matemwe-Retreat. A luxury lodge with 4 stunning whitewashed stone and thatched private villas, each with rooftop terrace, private plunge pool, a fully stocked bar, Wi-Fi, bathtub with ocean views, stylish rustic-chic decor, a personal butler and guests can choose whether to have dinner in their private gardens or go to the restaurant at **Matemwe Lodge** (below). There's an infinity pool, spa treatments and all watersports can be arranged. Privacy comes at a price and rates are from US$390 per person.

$$$$ Matemwe Lodge, next to the Matemwe Retreat above and formerly the **Matemwe Bungalows**, www.asiliaafrica.com/Matemwe. Along with the Retreat, this is the most secluded spot on Matemwe beach and a fair distance from the closest resort to the south (and out of the 'beach-boy' zone). 12 upmarket thatched a/c bungalows, terraces with couches and hammocks, an open-air restaurant and bar serving good buffet lunches and set seafood dinners, swimming pool and, again, spa treatments and watersports can be arranged.

$$$$-$$$ Azanzi Beach Hotel, T0775-044 171, www.azanzibeachhotel.com. Classy hotel with 35 a/c rooms linked by wooden walkways through lush gardens, furnished in a contemporary style with lovely Zanzibari touches, such as carved wood furniture and doors, some have outdoor showers and free-standing baths. Swimming pool, spa, internet access and the **Mnemba View** bar and **Bridge** restaurant on the 1st floor of the main building have great views.

$$$ Matemwe Beach Village, T024-223 8374, www.matemwebeach.com. One of the nicest mid-range places to stay in Matemwe, with 20 pretty rooms, some of which sleep 4, and great wholesome food. The swimming pool cascades into another pool below, the thatched restaurant, bar and lounge is scattered with cushions and low tables, and its strongest point is its chilled atmosphere and friendly staff. It has its own dive school for trips to Mnembe Island Marine Conservation Area and is popular with divers on the 5-day PADI Open Water course. Doubles from US$160.

$$$ Sunshine Hotel, T0774-388 662, www.sunshinezanzibar.com. Recently opened and similar to **Matemwe Beach Village** next door. 15 comfortable and brightly decorated rooms with fans in 2-storey blocks with balcony. The well-designed central thatched area has a restaurant, bar and lounge on a mezzanine floor, all with lovely views over the 2 swimming pools or beach. There's a good menu that changes daily. Doubles from US$140.

$$$ Zanzibar Retreat, T0776-108 379, www.zanzibarretreat.com. Charming, small and hospitable hotel with just 10 rooms with a/c and Wi-Fi that can be made into triple or family rooms, elegant and sleek hardwood furniture and floorings, good-sized pool near the beach, relaxing bar, well above-average cuisine, arranges watersports, and staff can take you on village walkabouts. Doubles from US$140.

$$ Matemwe Baharini Villas, T0772-990 021, www.baharinivillasznz.com. Simple place with 15 stone bungalows sleeping 2-3 with makuti roofs. Don't be too put off by the untidy screens on the outside of the windows – inside the rooms are fine, with a/c, fans and nets. There's a decent-sized swimming pool overlooking the beach and a cavernous open-air restaurant. Doubles from US$80.

$$-$ Keys Bungalows, T0777-411 797, www.allykeys.com. A low-budget local guesthouse with plenty of character and chilled atmosphere. The 6 rustic bungalows are simply but nicely furnished, set back from the beach in lush gardens but only have cold water. There's a cool seating area outside with hammocks and loungers, and the bar right on the beach plays reggae music, serves fresh fish and uses old dhows for furniture. Rents out bikes and Vespa scooters. Doubles from US$60.

$ Mohammed's Restaurant & Bungalows, T0777-431 881. A decent low-budget family-run option in the middle of the village, with just 4 clean and basic bungalows right on the beach with nets and fans but cold showers. The small restaurant here serves surprisingly good meals, such as chicken and fresh fish, and the prawns in coconut are delicious. Can arrange snorkelling and fishing with the local boatmen. From US$15 per person.

Mnemba Island

$$$$ Mnemba Island Lodge, 15 mins by boat from Matemwe, central reservations, South Africa, T+27-11-809 4314, www.mnemba-island.com. This very stylish, very discreet and very expensive beautiful little private island has a reputation for being one of the world's finest beach retreats and is very romantic, with 10 stunning cottages well spaced along the beach and gourmet food. The US magazine, *Travel & Leisure* said of it: "It's the closest two people can get to being shipwrecked, with no need for rescue." If you can afford it, enjoy; fully inclusive rates are US$1500 per person in high season.

What to do

To the northeast coast *p177*
Diving
One Ocean Diving, T024-223 8374, www.zanzibaroneocean.com. On the east coast they have dive centres at **Azanzi Beach Hotel, Bluebay Beach Resort & Spa, Matemwe Lodge & Retreat, Ocean Paradise Resort** and **Sandies Neptune Pwani Beach**, and most of the other resorts can arrange diving with them at these. They offer daily dive excursions to the Mnembe Island Marine Conservation Area (see page 163).

Southeast Zanzibar

To get to the southeast of the island leave Stone Town's Benjamin Mkapi (Creek) Road at the junction that leads out through the Michenzani housing estate. Eventually the houses begin to peter out and are replaced by small fields of cassava, maize, banana and papaya. The road continues via Tunguu and Bungi to the Jozani Chwaka Bay National Park near Pete, before joining the coastal road linking the resorts of Jambiani, Paje and Bwejuu, about 50 km from Stone Town. There is a magnificent beach here that runs for nearly 20 km from Bwejuu to Jambiani, with white sand backed for its whole length by palm trees, laced with incredibly picturesque lagoons. You will see the fishermen go out in their dhows, while the women sit in the shade and plait coconut fibre, which they then make into everything from fishing nets to beds. ▶▶ *For listings, see pages 184-189.*

Getting there
The trip from Stone Town to Paje by minibus takes just over an hour and costs around US$15. Bus No 9 from Benjamin Mkapi (Creek) Road terminal in Stone Town serves Paje and continues to Jambiani and Bwejuu. Bus No 10 from Benjamin Mkapi (Creek) Road goes to Kizimkazi via Jambiani and Makunduchi.

Jozani Chwaka Bay National Park
ⓘ *35 km southeast of Stone Town, an easy stop-off en route to the southeast coast beaches, 0730-1700, US$10 which includes a guide for the 45-minute nature trail. Most people visit as part of a tour, usually combined with a dolphin tour, but you can get here independently by dala-dala and bus No 9 or 10 from Benjamin Mkapi (Creek) Road in Stone Town, which pass the entrance.*

Most of Zanzibar's indigenous forests have been lost to agriculture or construction, but the Jozani Forest in the centre of Zanzibar has been declared a protected national park (the only one on the islands). The park also incorporates the sea grass beds of Chwaka Bay to the north, the shores of which are fringed with mangrove forests. It covers 50 sq km, roughly 3% of the whole island. Because of human interference and the introduction of some alien plants and trees in the past, Jozani is not entirely an 'authentic' indigenous forest, but it is almost natural and most of the species seen here once existed throughout Zanzibar. (Kiwengwa-Pongwe Forest Reserve on the northeast of the island is considered to be the islands' last tract of completely virgin coral rag forest; see page 178). Jozani is home to roughly one third of the remaining endemic Zanzibar red colobus monkeys, one of Africa's rarest primates. The present population is believed to be about 2500. In Zanzibar the Kiswahili name for the red colobus monkey is *Kima Punju* – 'Poison Monkey'. It has associations with the kind of poisons used by evil doers. Local people believe that when the monkeys have fed in an area, the trees and crops die, and dogs will lose their hair if they eat the colobus. The monkeys appear oblivious to tourists, swinging above the trees in troups of about 40, babies to adults. They are endearing, naughty and totally absorbing.

The forest is completely managed by the local people, who operate tree nurseries and act as rangers and guides. Visitors can go on the guided forest walk which takes about 45 minutes. Stout shoes are recommended as there are some venomous snakes. Lizards, civets, mongooses and Ader's duiker are plentiful and easy to see, and there are also Sykes' monkey, bush babies, hyraxes and over 50 species of butterfly and 40 species of birds. From the visitor centre there's also a short walk that takes you through coral forest to an old tamarind tree, which marks the beginning of the **Pete-Jozani Mangrove Boardwalk**. The transition from coral forest to mangroves is abrupt, and the boardwalk, which is horseshoe-shaped, takes you through the mangrove swamp. Mangroves anchor the shifting mud and sands of the shore and help prevent coastal erosion. When the tide is out, the stilt-like roots are visible. Crabs and fish are plentiful and easily seen from the boardwalk.

Just beyond the village of Pete on the left before the entrance to the Jozani Chwaka Bay National Park, you can visit the **Zanzibar Butterfly Centre** ⓘ *T0773-999 897, www. zanzibarbutterflies.com, 0900-1700, entry US$5, the butterflies are most active 1030-1530.* This is a great new centre where the funds generated help local communities and conservation. They have a colourful collection of Tanzanian butterflies, often in their hundreds, farmed sustainably in the nearby villages, and provide tours lasting around half an hour to explain the project and the butterfly's life cycle.

ZALA Park

The road continues south to the village of Kitogani and, just south, is **ZALA Park** ⓘ *0900-1700, US$5,* which is primarily a small educational facility set up in conjunction with the University of Dar es Salaam for Zanzibari children to help them learn about and conserve the island's fauna. ZALA stands for Zanzibar Land Animals. Entry is free to local children if they are unable to pay, subsidized by the tourists' donations. The aim is to make it a self-funding enterprise in time. There is a small classroom where the children are taught. The adjacent **zoo** has a number of reptiles, including lizards, chameleons and indolent rock pythons weighing up to 40 kg, Eastern tree hyrax, as well as Suni antelopes, an endemic Zanzabari subspecies. Donations to support this worthwhile enterprise are appreciated.

Paje

Paje is the first village on this coast that you are likely to reach as it lies on the junction with the direct road from Stone Town. It has its share of guesthouses, and there is a convenient little supermarket, the **SupaDuka**, on the main road as you enter the village, which has a post office and a small café that does takeaway cooked food and can even provide car and bike hire. Once through the village, Paje offers a stunning strand of white sand and, with no rocks or sea urchins, this is one of the better places on the east coast to swim.

Bwejuu

Bwejuu is best known for its proximity to 'the lagoon' and the Chwaka Bay mangrove swamps. The mangrove swamp at Chwaka Bay can be reached by a small road leading inland from the back of Bwejuu Village. It is possible to find a guide locally, who can navigate the way through the maze of channels and rivers in the swamps. Here you can stroll through the shallow rivers looking at this uniquely adapted plant and its ecosystem; there is also a good chance of seeing a wide variety of crabs, which live in the mud-banks amongst the tangle of roots. The best snorkelling in the area is to be found at 'the lagoon', about 3 km to the north of Bwejuu, just past the pier at **Dongwe**. Bicycles and snorkels can usually be hired from any of the children on the beach.

Michamvi

Michamvi is a small village right at the tip of the eastern peninsula, another 5 km north of Dongwe and about 68 km from Stone Town. It lies between the sea and the picturesque Chwaka Bay, and the village appears at the bottom of the road and is split into Michamvi Pingwe (oceanic) and Michamvi (bay-side). Although there's a handful of hotels and lodges here, the area still has an 'off-the-beaten-track' feel to it. Local transport only goes as far as Bwejuu, from where you'll need to arrange a taxi.

Jambiani

The name Jambiani comes from an Arabic word for dagger, and legend has it that early settlers found a dagger here in the sand – evidence of previous visitors. These days the village, some 6 km south of Paje, spreads for several kilometres along the coast road and there are a number of resorts (see Where to stay, below).

Kizimkazi

Most people visit here as part of a tour to 'swim' with the large resident pods of humpbacked and bottlenose dolphins. The village is split into two parts: Kizimkazi Dimbani in the north, and Kizimkazi Mkunguni in the south. The coastline here is very different from the classic palm-backed lagoons of the east coast. Here a coral rag cliff elevates above the ocean and the beaches take the form of small coves rather than broad expanses of sand. Other than when the dolphin-trippers come in the mornings, it's a fairly quiet area, so if you're after a lively night scene, this wouldn't be your best option. The **Shirazi Dimbani Mosque** ruins are 3 km to the northeast of Kizimkazi and contain the oldest inscription found in East Africa – from AD 1107. The mosque has been given a tin roof and is still used. Its significance should not be underestimated for it may well mark the beginnings of the Muslim religion in East Africa. It was built by Sheikh Abu bin Mussa Lon Mohammed and archaeologists believe that it stands on the site of an even older mosque.

◉ Southeast Zanzibar listings

For sleeping and eating price codes and other relevant information, see pages 22-26.

◑ Where to stay

Paje *p183, map p134*
$$$ Hakuna Majiwe Lodge, on the borders of Paje and Jambiani, T0777-454 505, www.hakunamajiwe.net. Set on the beach with 20 individual and very attractively decorated rooms in stone and thatch, extra beds can be supplied for children, surrounded by palms and shrubs and sand (the name means 'place without stones'). The swimming pool is set back from the beach, and there's a huge open dining area with big sofas at the bar. Snorkelling and bike hire can be arranged.
$$$-$$ Arabian Nights, just south of the village, T0777-854 041, www.zanzibar arabiannights.com. The 11 rooms in stone cottages either facing the beach or around the garden or pool are well equipped, with

spacious bathrooms, private terraces, TVs and a/c. There's a bar, restaurant and a lounge area in an Arabian tent. There's also a nearby block with its own small pool and cheaper guesthouse rooms, which are good value at US$40-65 for a double. Buccaneer Diving has a base here (see page 189).
$$$-$$ Cristal Resort, at the end of the group of lodges on the beach, T0777-875 515, www.cristalresort.net. In a pretty location surrounded by palm trees and pines. 5 deluxe bungalows with a/c and spacious bathrooms, and 13 attractively rustic 'eco' bungalows, which are cheaper but nicer with fans, home-made furniture and terraces with sea views. Swimming pool and a chilled bar and restaurant on the beach with Wi-Fi.
$$$-$$ Dhow Inn, just to the north of the village, T0777-525 828, www.dhowinn.com. A small intimate place with just 5 a/c rooms in a very attractive double-storey thatched building, all tastefully decorated with large

Zanzibari beds, good value from US$110 for a double; 1 room has 3 bunks from US$30 per person. Good restaurant, comfortable lounge areas, swimming pool and Wi-Fi.

$$ Paje by Night, just south of the village centre, T0777-460 710, www.pajebynight. net. Very rustic verging on ethnic, with a vibey atmosphere, run by an Italian. 20 self-contained thatched bungalows, the 2-storey one sleeps 4, with ceiling fans and nets set about 50 m back from the beach around the swimming pool. Bar and restaurant with very good local and international food, including Swahili dishes, seafood and pizzas. An unashamed party place and the bar stays open all night (hence the name).

$$ Paradise Beach Bungalows, 1 km north of the village, T024-223 1387, www. zanzibar-paradise-bungalows.com. Run by a nice (but scatty) Japanese lady, Saori. 11 simple bungalows, with old furnishings and temperamental water pressure, a small restaurant and bar serving expensive Japanese meals that must be ordered in advance, but the sushi, sashimi and miso soup are superb. Bikes and snorkelling gear can be hired. Doubles from US$60.

$ Teddy's Place, just south of **Paje by Night**, T0776-110 850, www.teddys-place.com. A well-run and popular backpackers' spot right on the beach and built entirely on the sand. Basic thatched bandas with nets and fans, shared bathrooms, chilled bar and restaurant, with hammocks and furniture made from dhows, good music and a tasty choice of food, such as grilled fish and Swahili curries. Simple, friendly and cheap with dorms for US$15 and doubles from US$35.

Bwejuu *p183, map p134*

$$$$ Breezes Beach Club & Spa, 3.5 km north of the village, T024-224 0102, www.breezes-zanzibar.com. An established favourite on Zanzibar and a good mid-range all-inclusive choice with high standards, 70 smart rooms with either balconies or terraces, shopping arcade, spa, restaurants, bars, large swimming pool, gym, watersports

centre, tennis courts and disco. The **Rising Sun Dive Centre** is based here.

$$$$ The Palms, adjoining **Breezes**, towards Pingwe, T024-224 0294, www. palms-zanzibar.com. A stunning super-luxurious resort with just 6 very private villas, colonial decor, satellite TV, DVD player, private terrace with plunge pool, living room and bar. Facilities in sumptuous surroundings include tiered swimming pool, spa, gym, tennis court, elegant dining room, bars and lounge areas. Activities are organized at Breezes. Doubles from US$930.

$$$ Echo Beach, just south of **Breezes**, T0773-593 260, www.echobeachhotel. com. Owned by a British couple, one a French-trained chef and the other an interior designer, this place is very stylish with an excellent restaurant menu. The 9 rooms in local stone and makuti are individually designed with African antiques, silk fabrics and locally crafted wooden furniture, with spacious verandas, and the swimming pool and jacuzzi are near the beach.

$$ Evergreen Bungalows, 3 km north of the village, T024-224 0273, www.evergreen-bungalows.com. Reed-and-thatch bungalows set in a palm grove directly on the beach with 14 rooms, each with a different touch and decorated using local materials and a balcony. The double-storey ones are the nicest and have sea views; cheaper bandas are set further back and have no hot water but some sleep 4. Relaxing bar and restaurant with a good choice of Swahili dishes, and there's a dive school. Doubles from US$70.

$$ Sun & Seaview Bungalows, 2 km south of the village, about midway between Bwejuu and Paje, T0718-102 633, www.sun andseaviewbungalows.com. Set in pretty flowering gardens and owned by a friendly Italian, the 10 thatched bungalows have fans, nets and verandas, and face towards the sea, and the comfortable family house sleeps 4. Very good food includes local seafood and Italian dishes, and the bar/restaurant has comfy lounge areas and hammocks. Doubles from US$70.

$ Mustapha's Place in the village, the No 9 bus will drop you outside, T024-224 0069, www.mustaphasplace.com. A chilled, low-budget place run by Mustapha, a friendly Rastafarian. The 7 rooms are fun and bright, with paintings on the walls, and 1 called Treetops is on huge stilts. Prices range from US$35 for a double room with shared bathroom, to US$50 for a double room with bathroom, although some rooms can sleep up to 6 with floor space in the loft for US$15 per person. Very relaxing, with lovely gardens with hammocks, reggae music, bar where you can play drums, good seafood, and it's across the road from the beach, reached via a pretty pathway.

$ Robinson's Place, 2 km north of the village just past **Evergreen**, T0777-413 479, www.robinsonsplace.net. A very simple place in a similar vein to **Mustapha's**, but smaller (maximum of 12 guests) and run by the charming Rastafarian Edi and his wife Ann. All rooms have nets and some have bathrooms. There's no electricity here, just solar power and a generator, and they serve local Zanzibari dinners cooked over coals and eaten on cushions on the floor.

Michamvi p183

$$$$ Karafuu Hotel Beach Resort, north of Pingwe as the road turns inland to Michamvi, T0777-413 647/8, www.karafuuzanzibar.com. The name means 'cloves' in Swahili. A large but quiet and professionally run resort, with almost 100 a/c rooms with thatched roofs in spacious gardens. There are 3 restaurants, numerous bars, watersports, swimming pool, tennis courts, nightclub and diving. The beach is good, although watch out for the very sharp coral close offshore.

$$$$ Michamvi Sunset Bay, Michamvi Village, T0778-662 872, www.michamvi. com. A well-run, friendly and out-of-the-way South African-owned resort overlooking Chwaka Bay, with 20 attractive a/c rooms in 4 blocks facing the sea and the swimming pool, all with a balcony or terrace, contemporary decor and very spacious

modern bathrooms, some with double showers. The bar and restaurant serves quality international cuisine and, since the bay is calm, as well as the usual activities, kayaking and windsurfing are on offer.

$$$ Kichanga Lodge, off main road as it turns inland to Michamvi, then 1 km along a dirt road, T0773-175 124, www.kichanga. com. Sleepy place in a secluded cove with a half-moon beach. 23 pretty bungalows spread out in gardens, with fans, nets and private terraces; the spacious **Ocean Villas** are the best and have a mezzanine floor for extra beds. There's a bar and dining area in a breezy makuti-roofed building. Swimming pool, dive centre, bikes and canoes are for hire, and the gift shop makes up dresses to order out of traditional *kangas*.

$$$ Ras Michamvi Beach Resort, signposted with **Kichanga Lodge** off the road to Michamvi, then 1 km down a dirt road. T024-223 1081, www.rasmichamvi. com. This discreet and very pretty lodge right at the tip of the peninsula is built on low coral cliffs overlooking the beach. 15 a/c rooms in 4 stone bungalows with cool tiled flooring and big Zanzibari beds. There are 3 small beaches here, 1 of which – Coconut Beach – is backed by forest and has resident red colobus monkeys. The nice swimming pool and the restaurant are set above the beach with wide ocean views. Good value at US$180 for a double half board.

Jambiani p184, map p134

$$$$ Kikadini Villas, next door to **Hotel Casa del Mar**, T0777-707 888, www.kikadini. com. Smart resort with Arabian-style architecture and 5 beautifully decorated villas in understated Zanzibari style right on the beach that can be booked for exclusive use or as individual rooms. Villa Maroc is particularly suitable for loved-up couples, having a private roof terrace and bath to soak in under the stars. There's a candlelit restaurant or dinner can be cooked and served in your villa. They have a swimming pool and their own dhow for excursions.

\$\$\$ Coral Rock Hotel, 1 km south of the village on a coral rock above the sea, T024-224 0154, www.coralrockhotelzanzibar.com. Popular, friendly and recently refurbished with 14 smart a/c bungalows, nice Zanzibari beds and pleasant patios, some sleeping 3-4, plus 2 more upmarket beach villas with extra satellite TV. The food is exceptionally good with a nod at African fusion cooking and great seafood platters (worth coming to eat even if you're not staying). There's a pleasant swimming pool on the edge of the beach, and free 'toys' to use include windsurfing and snorkelling gear, kayaks and bikes. Doubles from US\$110.

\$\$ Blue Oyster Hotel, in the middle of the village, T024-224 0163, www.zanzibar.de. Deservedly popular and well run, the 13 rooms have beautiful carved beds and are arranged around a serene ornamental pool and garden or in 2-storey buildings with balconies and sea views. Good food is served in the rooftop restaurant, there's bike hire, and they have their own dhow for fishing and snorkelling. **Easy Blue Divers** is based here. Doubles from US\$80.

\$\$ Casa del Mar, next to the internet café in the village, T024-224 0400, www.casa-delmar-zanzibar.com. A rustic resort with 20 rooms arranged in 2 blocks with sea views, the ones on the 1st floor are bigger with a sleeping gallery for extra beds on the mezzanine. The swimming pool is set in tropical gardens, there's an excellent restaurant and bar and, although the service is sometimes slow, it's worth the wait for the generous portions and the fresh fruit cocktails (highly recommended). Doubles from US\$80.

\$\$ Red Monkey Beach Lodge, 2 km south of the village, T0777-713 366, www.red monkeylodge.com. At the southern end of the string of resorts in a lovely location on a gentle slope above the beach and popular with kiteboarders. It's named after the red colobus monkeys that can sometimes be spotted in the gardens. The 9 simple rooms with fans and nets are in whitewashed

stone cottages with makuti roofs. Evening meals change daily and there's a choice of 4 courses including seafood and sometimes barbecues. The relaxing bar can sometimes be in the party mood. Doubles from US\$90.

\$ Zanzest Beach Bungalows, just after **Red Monkey Beach Lodge**, T0777-430 992, www.zanzest.co.tz. Simple friendly budget resort and the last place at the southern end of the beach so very peaceful, with 15 thatched wooden bandas set in neatly tended gardens with bathrooms and fans, 2 with balconies on the 2nd floor with sea views. The restaurant/bar has a good choice of food (the wood-fired seafood pizza is delicious). US\$15 for a dorm and from US\$40 for a double.

Kizimkazi *p184, map p134*

\$\$\$\$ Unguja Lodge, in Kizimkazi Mikunguni, T0774-477 477, www.unguja lodge.com. A very atmospheric, discreet resort set in tropical gardens with huge baobab trees and palms. 11 stunningly designed a/c villas with makuti roofs, curved walls and private terraces; the 3 that don't have sea views have their own plunge pools as compensation. There's a large swimming pool, dive centre, comfortable bar and restaurant and a coral beach.

\$\$\$ Karamba, Kizimkazi Dimbani, T0773-166 406, www.karambaresort.com. This lovely, laid-back and alternative lodge has 19 pleasantly decorated rooms with fans and sea-facing terraces on a small cliff above the sea. It has its own yoga teacher and offers various yoga classes, Ayurvedic massage and even Vedic options on its extensive restaurant menu, which also includes sushi and sashimi, Indian, Italian and tapas. There's an infinity swimming pool, and at high tide steps go down the cliff straight into the sea.

\$\$\$ Swahili Beach Resort, Kizimkazi Mkunguni, T0777-844 442, www.swahili beachresort.com. On one of the better beaches in this area, with 19 a/c rooms in stone bungalows with veranda and satellite TV, most with sea views. There's a swimming pool, restaurant and pool bar, and **Adventure Fishing** (page 189) is based here. The hotel will cook your fish for dinner. There are more charismatic places to stay, perhaps, but it's good value from US$130 for a double half board.

$$-$ Promised Land Lodge, 1 km south of Kizimkazi Mkunguni, past **Swahili Beach Resort**, T0779-909 168, www.promised landlodge-zanzibar.com. A bit out of the way and a 20-min walk from the village, but a very chilled place, with 12 rooms in the main house or attractive whitewashed reed-and-thatch bungalows, each with bathrooms, fans and nets. There's a beach bar, restaurant serving good Swahili dishes, hammocks and day beds dotted around the sand for hanging out, a bonfire is lit on the beach in the evening, and bikes can be hired. Doubles from US$50.

🍴 Restaurants

As elsewhere on the island, restaurants are at the hotels and resorts and most are open to non-guests so you don't necessarily have to eat where you are staying. There are, however, a couple of exceptional places on the southeast coast.

Michamvi *p183, map p134*
$$$ The Rock Restaurant, at Pingwe, just south of where the road turns inland west to Michamvi, T0779-909 855, www.therock restaurantzanzibar.com. Open for lunch and dinner but only has 14 tables so reservations are essential. This really has to be seen to be believed. The thatched whitewashed restaurant with wrap-around balcony is remarkably built on a tiny coral islet about 50 m off the shore that actually becomes 'beached' at low tide when you can walk across (at other times you can wade or there is a boat). Naturally the menu focuses on seafood, most of it grilled on an open fire, but there are also inventive salads and pastas, and a good wine list including Moët & Chandon champagne. Expensive but very special, particularly if the moon rises above the ocean. Expect to pay in the region of US$100 for 2 for a 5-course meal with wine.

Jambiani *p184*
$$$-$ Alibi's Well, in the village about 200 m north of the **Blue Oyster Hotel**, T0786-231 988. Mon-Fri 1200-1800, dinner Fri only from 1830. This is run by the Jambiani Tourism Training Institute, a project sponsored by the **Hands Across Borders Society** (www.handsacrossborderssociety. org), which is a Canadian NGO working to empower and educate people in Jambiani, and well worth seeking out for its amazing food and beachside setting. Lunches are simple and include freshly made sandwiches, tacos and pizzas, juices, coffees and herbal teas, and amazing cakes – date, beetroot or carrot cake; the coconut and chocolate ganache one is sublime. Dinner is only served on Fri but is spectacular and should be booked in advance – each week showcases a different cooking style, and previous menus have included Indonesian, Lebanese, Austrian, sushi and tapas. A 3-course dinner costs in the region of US$20, which is excellent value for the very high standard. There's also a good choice of wines and cocktails.

🎉 Festivals

Southeast Zanzibar *p182*
Jul Mwaka Kogwa, held in the 3rd week of Jul. The traditional Shirazi New Year on Zanzibar and celebrated with traditional Swahili food, *taarab* music, drumming and dancing on the beach all night. Although the festival is celebrated around the island, the village of Makunduchi is the heart of the celebration. The men of the village have a play fight and beat each other with banana fronds to vent their aggressions from the past year. Then, the *mganga*, or traditional healer, sets fire to a ritual hut and reads which way the smoke is burning to determine the village's prosperity in the coming year.

☼ What to do

Diving

Expect to pay in the region of US$50 for a single dive and US$400 for a PADI Open Water Course.

Buccaneer Diving, at Arabian Nights Hotel, Paje, T0777-853 403, www.buccaneerdiving.com.

Easy Blue Divers, at Blue Oyster Hotel, Jambiani, T0777-422 488, www.easybluedivers.com.

Paje Dive Centre, despite its name this centre is now in Kizimkazi, on the main road in Kizimkazi Mkunguni, T0777-416 614, www.pajedivecentre.com.

Rising Sun Dive Centre, at Breezes Beach Club & Spa, Bwejju, T0774-440 885, www.risingsun-zanzibar.com.

Fishing

Adventure Fishing, at Swahili Beach Resort, Kizimkazi, T0777-416 614, www.zanzibaradventurefishing.com.

Kiteboarding

With its wide flat sand beach, shallow waves and virtually no obstructions, Paje is one of the best beaches for kiteboarding on the island. Conditions are good throughout the year, but the best months are Jun-Oct, when the Kusini winds blow, and Dec-Mar during the Kaskasi winds. These centres rent out equipment to experienced boarders for about US$20 per hr, and can arrange lessons from US$80.

Kite Centre Zanzibar, at Kinazi Upepo Hotel, next to the Cristal Resort, Paje, T0776-531 535, www.kitecentrezanzibar.com.

Paje by Kite, at Paji by Night Hotel, Paje, T0777-460 710, www.pajebykite.net.

Pemba Island

Pemba Island lies approximately 80 km northeast of Zanzibar Island (Unguja) and is about the same distance from the Tanzanian mainland, situated directly east of Tanga. Unlike Unguja, which is flat and sandy, Pemba's terrain is hilly, fertile and heavily vegetated. The early Arab sailors called it 'Al Huthera', meaning 'The Green Island'. Today more cloves are grown on Pemba than on Zanzibar Island. Pemba has a wealth of natural resources, ranging from beaches to mangrove ecosystems to natural forests. The coral reefs surrounding the island protect a multitude of marine species and offer some of the best scuba-diving in the world. Zanzibar Island is connected to the African continent by a shallow submerged shelf. Pemba, however, is separated from the mainland by depths of over 1000 m. During September and March the visibility around Pemba has been known to extend to a depth of 50 m, and there are great game fish, such as sharks, tuna, marlin and barracuda. While much of the coast is lined with mangroves, there are a few good stretches of shoreline and attractive offshore islands with pure, clean beaches and interesting birdlife. There are also some important ruins and charming Swahili villages. The tourism industry here is still in its infancy and the infrastructure is still quite basic, but is slowly beginning to develop, with new lodges opening up and a few more foreigners visiting than before, although nothing on the scale of visitors to Zanzibar.
▶▶ *For listings, see pages 194-198.*

Arriving on Pemba Island → *Colour map 1, B6. 5°0'S 39°45'E. Population: 300,000.*

Getting there

Pemba Airport is 7 km to the southeast of Chake Chake. There is just a simple semi-open waiting area with a snack bar. The island can be reached by air – the views of the uninhabited islands and reefs from a small low-flying plane are quite incredible – either from Zanzibar Island (30 minutes) or from Dar es Salaam (1¼ hours), with a touchdown in Zanzibar. **Coastal Air** also fly direct between Tanga and Pemba (25 minutes). You can take a *dala-dala* to Chake Chake or else taxis meet the flights; a more reliable option is to organize an airport pickup with your hotel.

Nearly all ferries coming into Pemba arrive at the town of Mkoani, on the southwestern end of Pemba Island. Very few ships or dhows actually use Chake Chake anymore, as the old harbour is silted up and only canoes can actually gain entrance. The journey between Zanzibar and Pemba takes about two to three hours, and prices are about US$40; from Dar es Salaam to Pemba via Zanzibar costs from US$60. For further details, see Getting there, page 132 and Transport, page 197.

Getting around

The island of Pemba is about 70 km long and 22 km wide. There is one tarred but bumpy main road in Pemba running from Msuka in the north to Mkoani in the south, which is served by public transport. There are buses or *dala-dala* along the main roads but these tend to operate in the mornings and early afternoons only, and there are very few vehicles after 1500. *Dala-dala* No 606 runs between Chake Chake and Wete, and the No 603 between Chake Chake and Mkoani. Each journey takes about one hour and costs US$1. Other less frequently run routes include the No 602 between Chake Chake and Konde, and the No 24 between Wete and Konde (for the Ngezi Forest). Besides this, it is very difficult to get around on public transport, and budget travellers will need to walk to get to the more out-of-the-way places.

It's possible to hire a car with a driver at around US$70-80 per day, which is effectively hiring a taxi for the day, but it is good value (especially if there are four in a car). Although not common, you may also be able to hire a self-drive car for about US$60 per day. You can rent out motorbikes for around US$40 and bicycles for around US$10. All the hotels organize these and remember that negotiation is necessary, as ever. Motorbikes are the most common form of transport on the island, more so than cars, as potholes are more readily avoided, and it's a little too hilly in most

Pemba Island

N

5 km
5 miles

Where to stay
Fundu Lagoon **2**
Jondeni Guest House **3**
Kervan Saray Beach **4**

Manta Resort **1**
Pemba Crown **5**
Pemba Lodge **6**
Pemba Misali Sunset Beach Resort **9**
Sharook Guest House **7**
Sharook 2 **8**
Verani Beach **10**
Zanzibar Ocean Panorama **11**

places for cycling. But they could also be considered dangerous due to erratic local driving practices; remember you won't have insurance if your motorbike is hired. The alternative is to jump on the back of a motorbike *boda boda* (taxi), which are plentiful.

Background

There is nothing on Pemba that holds as much historical or cultural significance as Stone Town on Zanzibar Island, but it is the site of many historical ruins that bear testament to its role in the spice trade and early commerce with the other Indian Ocean dynasties. The major income for islanders is from cloves, and the island actually produces about 75-80% of the archipelago's total crop. It is the mainstay of the island's economy. Also, unlike Zanzibar, production is largely by individual small-scale farmers who own anything from 10 to 50 trees each. Most of the trees have been in the family for generations, and clove production is very much a family affair, especially during the harvest when everyone joins in the picking. Harvest occurs about every five months and everything is worked around it – even the schools close. The cloves are then laid out in the sun to dry, and their distinctive fragrance fills the air.

The island is overwhelmingly Muslim, with more than 95% of the population following Islam. But the island is tolerant of other cultures, and alcohol is available at hotels, some guesthouses and in the police messes (where visitors are welcome). Local inhabitants do, however, like to observe modest dress and behaviour.

Around the island → *For listings, see pages 194-198.*

Mkoani → *Colour map 1, B6.*

Mkoani is Pemba's third largest town and the port of entry for ferries from Zanzibar and Dar es Salaam. The town is set on a hill overlooking a wide bay and comprises a mix of palm-thatch huts and rundown multi-storey apartment buildings. The landing stage is a modern jetty that projects out from the shallow beach on either side, where fishermen load their daily catch into ox-carts for the short trip to market. The main road runs directly from the port up the hill and most of this distance is rather surprisingly covered by a dual carriageway, complete with tall street lights on the central reservation. This, along with the ugly apartment blocks around town is evidence of the East German influence in Tanzania during the 1970s, which is also present at Chake Chake and Wete, and in the concrete estates on the edge of Stone Town on Zanzibar Island. Following the winding road up the hill from the port, the old colonial District Commissioners Office is on the right, where there is a bandstand in front of the compound. On the left is Ibazi Mosque, with a fine carved door. South of the dock there are steep steps down to the market by the shore.

Chake Chake → *Colour map 1, B6. 5°15'S 39°45'E. Phone code: 024.*

This, Pemba's main town, is about halfway up the west coast of the island and 28 km northeast of Mkoani. The town sits on a hill overlooking a creek and is fairly small, with a population of around 25,000. It is, however, the unofficial capital of Pemba, there are several government offices and it has the most shops on the island (although it has a dearth of accommodation). It's presently the only place on Pemba with an ATM (at the **People's Bank of Zanzibar** to the north of town). The bus stand is in the centre close to the mosque and next to the market, which is particularly pleasant to wander around with its spices, fresh fruit and fish on display, and some of the local stores stock some interesting *kikois* and *kangas* (sarongs) in patterns and colours not seen on Zanzibar Island. Chake

Clove production

It has been estimated that there are about 6 million clove trees on the islands of Zanzibar and Pemba and they cover about one-tenth of the land area. The plantations are found mainly in the west and northwest of the islands where the soil is deeper and the landscape hillier. To the east the soil is less deep and fertile and is known as 'coral landscape'.

Cloves were at one time only grown in the Far East and they were greatly prized. On his first trip back from the East, Vasco da Gama took a cargo back to Portugal and they were later introduced by the French to Mauritius and then to Zanzibar by Sayyid Said who was the first Arab Sultan. At this time all the work was done by slaves, who enabled the plantations to be established and clove production to become so important to the economy of the islands. When the slaves were released and labour was no longer free, some of the plantations found it impossible to

survive, although production did continue and Zanzibar remained at the head of the world's clove production.

Cloves are actually the unopened buds of the clove tree. They grow in clusters and must be picked when the buds are full but before they actually open. They are collected in sprays and the buds are then picked off before being spread on the ground to dry out. They are spread out on mats made from woven coconut palm fronds for about five days, turned over regularly so that they dry evenly – the quicker they dry the better the product.

There may be many clove trees on Zanzibar now – but there were even more in the past. In 1872 a great hurricane destroyed many of the trees and it was after this that Pemba took over from Zanzibar as the largest producer. Zanzibar, however, has retained the role of chief seller and exporter of cloves, so the Pemba cloves go to Zanzibar before being sold on.

Chake is also an excellent place to buy *halua*, a sticky sweet made of wheat gluten, sugar, nuts and spices that is wrapped in woven palm fronds.

The oldest surviving building in the town is the **Nanzim Fort**, which is thought to date back at least to the 18th century and possibly as far back as the Portuguese occupation (1499-1698). Records dating back to the early 19th century describe the fortress as being rectangular, with two square and two round towers at the corners, topped by thatched roofs. Round towers are typical of the Arab and Swahili architecture of the time, but the square towers are unusual and indicate possible Portuguese influence. Construction of the old hospital destroyed all but the eastern corner and tower, which now houses a municipal office. A battery, dating from the same period, overlooked the bay to the west, but only two cannons remain to mark the site. There are some handsome Moorish-style administrative buildings near the fort, with verandas, and a **clock tower**.

On the outskirts of town is a new hospital, built by the European Community overseas aid programme. A few kilometres north of town, towards Wete, there is a clove stem oil distillery at Wawi, which in addition to cloves, produces essential oils from lemongrass and eucalyptus. It is possible to visit the factory; ask around in town.

Ruins at Pujini

About 10 km southeast of Chake Chake, this settlement is thought to date back to the 15th century. There was a fortified enclosure and rampart surrounded by a moat, the only known early fortification on the East Africa coast. It is believed to have been built by a particularly unpleasant character, nicknamed Mkame Ndume, which means 'a milker of men', because he worked his subjects so hard. He was known to order his servants to carry the large stones used to build the fortress whilst shuffling along on their buttocks. The memory remains and local people believe that the ruins are haunted. The settlement and the palace of Mkame Ndume were destroyed by the Portuguese when they arrived on the island in about 1520. Today, the site is largely overgrown, and there is little left of the forticfications except for a crumbling staircase and some remains of 1 m thick walls. There are also the remnants of a two-chambered well that reputedly was used by the two wives of Ndume who lived in separate parts of the palace and never met. It is best to visit by hiring a bicycle (ask in Chake Chake).

Ruins at Ras Mkumbuu and Mesali Island

About 20 km west of Chake Chake, Ras Mkumbuu is probably Pemba's most important archaeological site, believed to date back about 1200 years, making it the oldest settlement south of Lamu Island in Kenya. It is the site of a settlement originating in the Shirazi period (see page 95). The ruins include stone houses and pillar tombs and the remains of a 14th-century mosque. Of interest are the tombs decorated with pieces of porcelain that suggest an early connection with the Chinese. Most people visit by boat on the way to **Mesali Island**, where the marine life on the reef make it excellent for diving and snorkelling and there is a fine beach. There are pleasant trails through the forest in the middle of the island, which is rich in birdlife and is also home to vervet monkeys and the Pemba flying fox (a large bat). Legend has it that the notorious 17th-century pirate, Captain Kidd, once had a hideout here and perhaps even buried some treasure during his stay. Dive schools regularly visit here, and most of the lodges and guesthouses can arrange boat trips here.

Wete

This town on the northwest coast of Pemba, about 30 km from Chake Chake, once served as a port for the clove trade; today the port has been surpassed by the more modern wharf at Mkoani, where the cloves are exported either on the ferries or special boats arranged by the government after harvest time. Wete is now a laid-back place on a hill overlooking the ocean, with houses and small shops lining the main road down to the dhow harbour. Clustered close to the dock area is a pleasant group of colonial buildings. The town has a post office and police station, and the market and *dala-dala* stand are about halfway up the hill.

The small island of **Mtabmwe Mkuu** opposite Wete, which means 'great arm of the sea', is linked to Pemba at low tide. It was once home to an 11th-century town, and a number of silver coins have been discovered at the site, though there is nothing to see today and a small fishing village stands on the spot.

Tumbe and Konde

Tumbe is at the north end of Pemba and is a busy fishing village with a market where people from all around buy their fish in the mornings. Local fishermen contract to provide catches for firms, which chill the fish and export it to the mainland. At the end of the cool season in October, there is a boat race here. Teams of men compete, paddling dug-out canoes, and the day is completed with a feast provided for contestants and onlookers. Konde is in the northeast of the island at the end of the tarmac road and is the furthestmost point of the *dala-dala* network. Access to Ngezi Forest is from here. There is no accommodation in Tumbe or Konde but both can be reached by *dala-dala* from Wete and Chake Chake.

Ngezi Forest Reserve

① *0730-1600, entry US$5 includes a guided walk along the sandy nature trail which is about 2 km long and takes about 1 hr.*

The reserve covers 1440 ha and compromises ancient coastal forest that once covered all of Pemba. The area was declared a reserve in the 1950s, after much of the island had been cleared for clove production. This is a thick blanket of forest, with vines and creepers and a dense undergrowth that supports a variety of plants and wildlife. It has its own plant species and subspecies that are unique to this area. Most of the 27 species of bird recorded on Pemba have been spotted in the forest, some endemic to Pemba including hadada, the African goshawk, the palm-nut vulture, Scops owl, the malachite kingfisher and the Pemba white eye. Much of the ground is ancient coral rag, often sharp-edged, containing pockets of soil. Mangrove forests grow on the tidal coastal creeks, and the incoming tide sees seawater running deep upstream, forming brackish swampy areas. The central area contains heather-dominated heathland where the soil is leached sand. The heather, *Philippia mafiensis*, is only found on Pemba and Mafia Islands.

Pemba's flying fox, a large fruit-eating bat, is found in Ngezi. Tree mammals include the Pemba vervet monkey and the Zanzibar red colobus monkey. Indolent-looking hyrax can also be seen climbing in the trees eating leaves. The Pemba blue duiker, an antelope about the size of a hare, is also here, though it is very shy and is rarely spotted. Feral pigs, introduced long ago by the Portuguese, can be found along with the Javan civet cat, which was probably brought to the island by southeast Asian traders for the production of musk for perfume. The only endemic carnivore in Ngezi is the marsh mongoose, which normally lives by ponds and streams. To the north of here is the secluded **Panga ya Watoro beach** on a peninsula that juts out from the island. At the end is the lighthouse at Ras Kigomasha, the far northwestern tip of the island (an easy walk from the Manta Resort). It's an odd-looking 38-m-high prefabricated iron structure that was built and shipped out to Pemba by the British in 1904. A concrete cover was added in the 1970s to prevent corrosion. It is still functioning today, using kerosene lamps that are lit every evening. For a tip of about US$2, the lighthouse keeper will allow you to climb to the top (not for the faint-hearted as the steps are on the outside), which is well worthwhile for the views over the ocean and south across the island.

◉ Pemba Island listings

For sleeping and eating price codes and other relevant information, see pages 22-26.

◐ Where to stay

Mkoani *p191, map p190*

$$$$ Fundu Lagoon, north of Mkoani across the bay near the village of Wambaa and reached on a 10-min speedboat ride organized by the resort, T0777-438 668, www.fundulagoon.com. This luxury British-owned development is the top place to stay on Pemba, with 18 very stylish tented rooms on stilts, overlooking a beautiful mangrove-fringed beach, and furnished with locally crafted hardwood furniture. 4 suites have private plunge pools and decks and are perfect for honeymooners. There's a restaurant, 3 bars, an infinity pool and spa, and all watersports are available, including diving, sailing and windsurfing. It supports local communities through its Village Fund and has built a school for 500 children and installed several water wells. Rates are between US$330 and US$670 per person, depending on the room and season.
$$$$ Pemba Lodge, Shamiani Island, T0777-415 551, www.pembalodge.com.

Opened in 2010, this remote eco-lodge on Shamiani is a 15-min boat ride from the southern tip of Pemba and is under the same ownership as **Mnarani Beach Cottages** in Nungwi (page 174). The 5 reed-and-makuti thatch bungalows are built on stilts 1 m above the ground and discreetly spaced at least 30 m apart along the beach. Each has showers using collected rainwater, solar power and furniture made from old dhows. Excellent food and views from the elevated bar and restaurant, activities include snorkelling and kayaking around the island and in the mangrove forests. Airport and ferry transfers are available. It's not luxury but a genuine Robison Crusoe experience. Rates from US$220 per person.

$$-$ Jondeni Guest House, Mkoani, T024-223 0879, www.jondeniguestlodge. com. A pleasant local guesthouse in a whitewashed bungalow at the top of a hill overlooking Mkoani, about a 15-min walk from the ferry. The 6 rooms are simple but spotless with fans, nets and Zanzibari beds, some are en suite, and there's a dorm room with 6 beds. The extremely friendly and helpful owner, Ali, serves good-value meals on the lovely porch, and arranges local excursions including snorkelling at Mesali Bay (US$40), sunset dhow cruises (US$15), bike, motorbike and car hire, and can arrange a pickup from the airport at Chake Chake (US$40 per car). The garden has views of the bay and hammocks and loungers. Doubles from US$50, dorm beds US$20, including breakfast.

$$-$ Zanzibar Ocean Panorama, Mkoani, T024-245 6166, T0773-545 418, www. zanzibaroceanpanorama.com. Again, up the hill in Mkoani with great ocean views and a 15-min walk from the ferry. A similar set up to Jondeni, next door, with 4 basic but clean rooms, 1 has dorm beds, with nets and fans, in a fairly new bungalow with broad thatched terrace. Good meals are served, especially the crab and grilled tuna, and they can organize the same activities and pickups from the airport. Rates are identical too (see

above). Both these places face west so the sunsets over the bay are spectacular.

Chake Chake p191, map p190
$$$ Pemba Misali Sunset Beach Resort, near Wesha, about 3 km west of Chake Chake and a 15-min drive from the airport, T0775-044 713, www.pembamisalibeach. com. Under the same ownership as **Amaan Bungalows** in Nungwi (page 174), this is a welcome new and well-run mid-range option on Pemba set on a beautiful beach on a little peninsula that is completely surrounded at high tide creating a little island. 39 neat a/c bungalows with either sea-facing or garden terraces, thatched restaurant and bar serving seafood and Swahili dishes. Activities include snorkelling, fishing on local dhows, kayaking and **Pemba Misali Divers** (see page 196) is based here. Doubles from US$120; packages with diving include 4 nights B&B accommodation and 6 dives from US$540 per person.

Wete p193, map p190
$ Pemba Crown Hotel, Wete Main Rd, T024-245 4191, T0777-493667, www. pembacrown.com. Handy location for the market and bus stand in an imposing and reasonably maintained white 4-storey block, with 15 en suite a/c clean rooms with nets, TV and fairly reliable hot water. There's no restaurant as such, but dinner can be pre-ordered. Doubles from US$35.

$ Sharook Guest House, near the market and bus stand, down the track that leads to the harbour, T024-245 4076, www.pemba living.com. Run by friendly Mr Sharook and his brother. 4 very simple but clean 2- or 3-bed rooms for US$20 per person regardless of how many in a room. There's a restaurant with the best food in town, though it has to be pre-ordered, and a lounge with satellite TV. They can arrange airport pickups, snorkelling trips to local islands and bicycle hire.

$ Sharook 2, on the road to the port, take the road opposite the **Pemba Crown Hotel**, and it's on the left about 10 m up a small track, same contacts as Sharook Guest House, above. Also known as the Annex and under the same ownership, this is slightly more comfortable, as it's in a fairly new purpose-built house. 8 en suite rooms sleeping 2-4 with gleaming black-and-white floor tiles, Zanzibari beds, fans and nets; again US$20 per bed. There's an internet café on the ground floor, good meals can be pre-ordered and a restaurant is planned on the roof (for now you can go up there for views of Fundu Island).

Ngezi Forest Reserve *p194, map p190*
$$$ Kervan Saray Beach, near Makangale Village, T0773-176 737, www.kervansaray beach.com. A very chilled lodge and the home of **Swahili Divers** (see What to do, opposite). It's primarily a diving centre with accommodation, although there's plenty here for non-divers too, such as kayaking, fishing and walks in the forest. Set in lovely gardens, with an open restaurant and bar/lounge area, the 11 clean and spacious rooms are in 6 bungalows and have traditional *barazza* beds, mosquito nets with fans inside and private bathrooms. US$160 per person full board, and there are some excellent packages such as 6 nights' full board with 10 dives for US$1250 per person.
$ Verani Beach Hotel, near Verani village, T0777-414 402, www.veranibeach.com. A rustic family-owned guesthouse on the beach a short walk to the Ngezi Forest, with a clutch of thatched huts. The rooms have concrete floors, Zanzibari beds and en suite bathrooms with warm (not hot) water, no electricity but kerosene lamps are lit in the evening. Good fresh seafood meals can be ordered in advance, and dinner is a barbecue on the beach. They can organize snorkelling and fishing on local dhows. Rates are US$45 per bungalow.

Panga ya Watoro Beach
$$$$ The Manta Resort (formerly Manta Reef Lodge), T0777-718 852, www.themanta

resort.com. Quiet and wonderfully remote location in the extreme northwest of the island on a cliff overlooking a private beach. There's a large central area with terrace, lounge, restaurant and spa, and 20 rooms in individual cottages, some with sea view, all attractively decorated. As well as a swimming pool and beach bar, snorkelling, kayaking and game fishing can be arranged, and there's a dive centre. Doubles from US$400.

○ What to do

Pemba Island *p189, map p190*
Diving
For more information on diving Pemba, see box, opposite.
    Fundu Lagoon and **The Manta Resort**, have their own dive centres, otherwise diving is arranged at the following:
Pemba Misali Divers, at Pemba Misali Sunset Beach Resort, T0763-586 712, www. pembamisalidivers.com. Single dive US$80, double dives US$120 and PADI Open Water course US$500. Has good-value diving packages if you're staying at the resort.
Swahili Divers, Kervan Saray Beach, T0773-176 737, www.swahilidivers.com. 5-star PADI Gold Palm Resort dive centre. Single dive US$70, double dives US$130 and PADI Open Water course US$450. Again, have very reasonable diving packages if you're staying at the lodge. Day guests can be picked up at Konde if they arrive by *dala-dala* by 0800.
Zanzibar Watersports, T0763-586 712, www.zanzibarwatersports.com. This company, which operates from the north coast of Zanzibar, has a yacht for a liveaboard diving option and trips begin and end at Mkoani. A 6-night trip with 18 dives and food costs in the region of US$2100-2400.

Tour operators
Most hotels and guesthouses can arrange excursions. Ali at **Jondeni Guesthouse** (see Where to stay, page 195) is keen to show travellers that Pemba has lots to offer, and is very helpful.

Dive Pemba

Pemba has some of the most spectacular diving in the world. The Pemba Channel separates Shimoni in Kenya from Pemba Island. The channel runs deep until it approaches the Pemba coastline and then begins a dramatic rise creating a sheer wall off the coast. Diving is characterized by crystal-clear blue-water drop-offs, along with pristine shallow reefs and hard and soft coral gardens. These offer glimpses of sharks and turtles, and encounters with eagle rays, manta rays, Napoleon wrasse, great barracuda, tuna and kingfish are the norm. Visibility can range from 6 m in a plankton bloom to 60 m, though 20 m is classed as a bad day and 40 m is average. The average sea temperature is a pleasant 26°C. Here are a few of the more famous dive sites with their descriptions, although there are many more spectacular sites around Pemba's smaller offshore islands.

Fundu Reef The visibility ranges from 20 to 40 m and there is a large sheer wall with overhangs and caverns. The coral is remarkable, especially the large rose coral and red and yellow sea fans. You can see many types of fish here including kingfish, triggerfish and wrasse. The reef is relatively shallow and therefore Fundu is a good spot for a first dive.

Kokota Reef Ideal for night diving, the waters are shallow and generally calmer, ranging from 8 to 20 m. Of all the creatures that come out after dark, the Spanish dancer is a particular attraction.

Manta Point Visibility averages from 20 to 40 m. Manta Point is one of the best sites in the world for close encounters with the giant manta rays that inhabit this area. The rays can be seen in groups of up to 15 and rise to depths as shallow as 9 m. The enormous variety of coral, fish and other marine life is so concentrated here that you should try and include at least two dives. This is truly one of the finest dive sites in the region.

Mesali Island Visibility averages between 40 and 50 m. This is a wall dotted with small caves and ridges. Large rivers of sand run off the top of the reef to form wide canyons that enter the wall at approximately 25 m. Gorgonian fans are in abundance below 20 m and, on a turning tide, the marine life is exceptional and the currents strong. Giant grouper drift lazily through the reef and hundreds of surgeonfish cruise below divers.

Njao Gap Njao Gap is well known for its amazing wall diving. Mantas can be seen here in season and the coral is spectacular, but what distinguishes this particular location is the profusion of titan trigger-fish. Visibility varies from day to day, but is usually good to 30 m.

☐ Transport

Pemba Island p189, map p190
Air

Coastal Air, T0785-627 825, Pemba Airport, T0777-418 343, www.coastal.cc, has 2 daily flights between Pemba and **Dar** (1 hr 15 mins) via **Zanzibar** (30 mins). Flights leave Dar at 1030 and 1400 and leave Zanzibar at 1100 and 1430. They return from Pemba to Dar via Zanzibar at 1200 and 1635. Dar US$130 one-way, Zanzibar US$95 one-way.

The afternoon flight continues from Pemba to **Tanga** (25 mins) at 1515, and returns from Tanga to Pemba at 1600; US$95.

Zanair, T024-223 3670, www.zanair.com, flies daily from **Zanzibar** to Pemba at 0945 and 1600, and from Pemba to Zanzibar at 1030 and 1500; US$100.

Ferry

The ticket offices of the ferry companies with services to **Zanzibar** and **Dar** are at the ferry terminal in Mkoani. Fares: from Dar to Pemba, economy class US$60, children (under 12) US$30, 1st class US$65 per person; from Zanzibar to Pemba, economy class US$40, children (under 12) US$30, 1st class US$45 per person. See also Dar es Salaam Transport, page 75.

Azam Marine, Dar T022-212 3324, Zanzibar T024-223 1655, www.azammarine.com. On Mon, Thu and Fri they operate a service from Dar to Pemba via Zanzibar at 0700 which arrives in Zanzibar at 0840, departs again at 0930 and arrives in Pemba at 1135. The return ferry departs Pemba at 1230, arrives in Zanzibar at 1435, departs again at 1600 and arrives in Dar at 1740.

Fast Ferries, Dar T022-213 7049, Zanzibar T024-223 4690, www.fastferriestz.com, operate a service on Mon and Wed that leaves Dar at 0715 to Zanzibar, from where it departs at 1000 to Pemba where it arrives at 1200; it leaves Pemba at 1300 to return to Zanzibar, where it departs again for Dar at 1600.

Mega Speed Liners, T0713-282 365, www.megaspeedliners-zanzibar.com, run the *Sepideh* which leaves Dar at 0715 and continues on to Pemba on Mon, Tue and Sat at 0930, where it arrives at 1130, leaving Pemba at 1230 to return.

ⓘ Directory

Pemba Island *p189, map p190*

Banks There are branches of the **People's Bank of Zanzibar**, in the 3 towns: Mkoani, Chake Chake and Wete, but only the bank in Chake Chake has an ATM and can change TCs. You need to bring cash from Zanzibar or Dar as only the couple of top-end lodges take credit cards, and these attract a surcharge of 6-9%. **Immigration** As in Zanzibar, if you lose your passport whilst on Pemba, go to the immigration office at the port in Mkoani, which will arrange for an emergency travel document to get you back to Dar, where the international embassies and high consulates are located.

Medical services The main public hospital is **Abdalla Mzee Hospital**, in Mkoani, but this is poorly equipped and in the event of an emergency you are strongly advised to get to Dar or at the very least Zanzibar. For diving medical emergencies, the nearest hyperbaric re-compression chamber is in Likoni in Kenya, which is reached by air; all divers are required to have adequate hyperbaric-medical insurance.

Contents

Footprint features

Border crossings

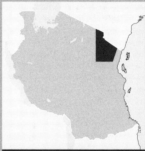

North to Kilimanjaro

At a glance

⊜ **Getting around** Buses regularly ply the Dar to Moshi road and there are connecting buses and *dala-dala* into the Usambara Mountains. Climbing operators include transfers to the ascent points of Kilimanjaro.
✪ **Time required** Dar to Moshi can be done in 8 hrs by bus or car, but allow an extra day if you want to go to the Usambara Mountains. A week is needed to climb Kili, which includes a night on either side in Moshi or Marangu.
☀ **Weather** Temperate all year around the bottom of the mountain; icy conditions at the top.
✕ **When not to go** Avoid climbing Kili in the long rainy season, late Mar to mid-May.

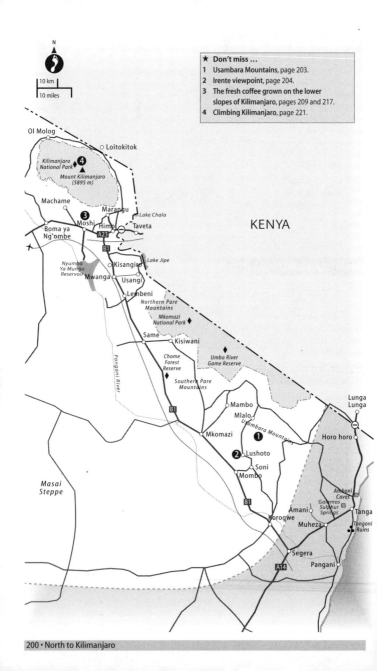

★ Don't miss ...
1 Usambara Mountains, page 203.
2 Irente viewpoint, page 204.
3 The fresh coffee grown on the lower slopes of Kilimanjaro, pages 209 and 217.
4 Climbing Kilimanjaro, page 221.

N

10 km
10 miles

Ol Molog
Loitokitok
Kilimanjaro National Park ◆ ❹
Mount Kilimanjaro (5895 m) ▲
Machame
Marangu
Lake Chala
Boma ya Ng'ombe
Moshi ❸ Himo
Taveta
A23
B1
KENYA
Nyumba Ya Mungu Reservoir
Kisangira
Lake Jipe
Mwanga
Usangi
Lembeni
Northern Pare Mountains
Mkomazi National Park ◆
Pangani River
Same
Kisiwani
Chome Forest Reserve ◆
Umba River Game Reserve ◆
Southern Pare Mountains
Masai Steppe
Lunga Lunga
Mambo
Mlalo
Usambara Mountains
B1
Mkomazi
❶
❷ Lushoto
Soni
Mombo
Horo horo
Amani Caves ▪
Galanos Sulphur Springs ▪
Amani
Korogwe
Muheza
Tanga
Tongoni Ruins
B1
Segera
Pangani
A14

The main road out of Dar es Salaam travels inland and joins the highway that runs the length of Tanzania and effectively links Kenya to the north with Malawi to the south. Travelling north from Dar to Arusha is a scenic drive of some 650 km through extensive farmland and sisal plantations, with the ever-present backdrop of the Pare and Usambara mountain ranges to the east. The main road is very busy, with a steady stream of buses linking Dar with Arusha, and the small regional towns offer petrol stations and services for bus passengers and drivers wishing to take a break from their journey. Away from the main road is the small mountain town of Lushoto, which is very attractive and a recommended spot for some good hiking in the hills. The forests and mountain scenery of the Usambara are not what is normally expected by visitors to Tanzania. Moshi is the town at the foot of Kilimanjaro, and climbs start just a few kilometres away at the entrance to the Kilimanjaro National Park. On the approach to Moshi you may well be rewarded with a glimpse of the snow-capped top of Kili when the mists lift off the summit in the late afternoon. Climbing Mount Kilimanjaro is an adventurous break from game viewing and reaching the 'Roof of Africa' is one of the continent's greatest challenges. It is the highest mountain in the world that can simply be walked up.

The road from Dar to Moshi

From Dar es Salaam, the main road (A7) goes 109 km to the west to Chalinzi and the junction with the main north–south road. North from Chalinzi it passes through regional centres, such as Karogwe, Mombo and Same, before reaching Moshi at the foothills of Kilimanjaro. This is where climbers begin their ascent of the mountain. The road will not hold your attention long: the small towns that you pass through are fairly nondescript, but they do provide facilities, such as petrol stations and shops, and access to the Usambara Mountains to the east. These are worth a detour for the good hiking opportunities, country lodges and the attractive town of Lushoto. Further north, closer to Moshi, are the Pare Mountains and Mkomazi National Park.
▸▸ *For listings, see pages 206-208.*

Getting there and around

The driving time between Dar and Moshi is roughly seven to eight hours, and there are scores of buses each day that ply this route. From Dar es Salaam, the A7 goes 109 km west to Chalinzi. This is possibly the most important road junction in Tanzania, despite Chalinzi not being much more than a straddling service centre for traffic. The A7, which is the main north–south road, goes southwest from Chalinzi to Morogoro (where there is the turn-off to Dodoma) and on to Iringa. It then continues until it eventually reach the Malawi and Zambia borders (see the Southern Tanzania and Central Region chapters). North from Chalinzi, the road becomes the A14. After 173 km, the A14 reaches Segera, another roadside service centre where many of the buses stop for a break. Here it splits: the A14 continues for another 74 km to Tanga (see page 91) on the coast, while the other branch of the road becomes the B1 and heads northwest towards Moshi. Near the village of Himo, 272 km northwest of Segera and 27 km before Moshi, the B1 joins the A23. To the east, the A23 goes about 15 km to the Taveta border with Kenya (see box, page 212) and, to the west, it goes another 27 km to Moshi via the foothills of Mount Kilimanjaro. From Moshi it is a further 80 km to Arusha on the A23. There are daily flights between Dar es Salaam and Zanzibar and **Kilimanjaro International Airport**, which lies roughly midway between Moshi and Arusha. ▸▸ *For further details, see Transport, page 219.*

Korogwe → *Colour map 1, B5. 5°0'S 38°20'E. Phone code: 022.*

Korogwe is a small town that you pass through on the way from Tanga or Dar es Salaam northwest to Moshi. It is 197 km north of Chalinzi and 24 km north of Segera. It lies at 52 m, on the north bank of Pangani/Ruvu Rivers, whose fertile valley, with its many settlements, stretches to the west. The local people are of the Zigua and Wasambaa ethnic groups but call themselves Waluvu. It is a local administrative centre, due to its position near the local sisal estates, the Dar es Salaam–Nairobi road and the Usambara and Pare Mountains. There are a few shops, a market, a hospital and a Christian mission. Most buses stop here at one of the many petrol stations in and around town, which also feature restaurants and shops catering for the bus passengers. There are a couple of reasonable places to stay and eat if you want to break the journey between Dar and Moshi but there's little reason to.

Mombo → *Colour map 1, B5.*

Mombo is another small town on the Dar es Salaam to Moshi highway, 38 km north of Korogwe. There's little of interest here; its main activity is the provision of services for travellers and, again, lots of buses stop here at either the oddly named **Liverpool Hill**

Breeze, 1.5 km north of Mombo, or the **Manchester Executive Inn** in town, which have petrol stations and serve fast food. It is worth a mention, however, as this is the junction with the road to Soni and Lushoto in the Usambara Mountains (see below). You can jump off the bus here and switch to one of the many *dala-dala* that climb the mountain road for 33 km from Mombo to Lushoto.

Usambara Mountains → *For listings, see pages 206-208. Colour map 1, A5.*

The Usambara Mountains are approximately 110 km long, range between 30 and 60 km in width and at their highest point at Mount Mgamba are 2440 m above sea level. They are accessible from Lushoto in the west and Amani (see page 95) in the east. The Usambaras are fairly unique in that they support tropical forests of the kind normally found only in West Africa and are home to euphorbias, acacias, giant ferns, palms, lobelias, camphors (Japanese and Usumbaru) eucalyptus and fig trees. Wildlife to be seen includes the elegant black and white colobus monkey, blue monkeys and a wide variety of birds. Several bird species are endemic, including the Usambara Eagle-owl and Usambara weaver. The views on the southern and western sides of the mountains are of spectacular vistas of the Masai plains below. Kilimanjaro can be seen on a clear day and, at the end of the day, the sun turns the land an unforgettable colour.

Lushoto is about 1½ hours or 33 km off the main Korogwe–Moshi road from the turn-off at Mombo. The road up to Lushoto via the small town of **Soni** is spectacular, as it twists and turns through the mountains, with glimpses of small waterfalls in Mlalo River. The tiny market town is reminiscent of an Indian hill station and the country lodges in the region have a charming colonial atmosphere. The climate changes quickly as you rise up into the mountains. Sunny days are warm, but cloudy and windy days get very cool, and it is comfortable to sit around a fire in the evening throughout the year. The big pull here is exploring the Usambara Mountains, dotted with streams and waterfalls and rural villages. There is plenty of opportunity for hiking or mountain biking through the deep forests and green hillsides; this part of Tanzania is a long way from the scorched plains of the game parks. From the hotels you can hire a guide for walks into the forest and up the peak of Kwa Mongo, a hike of three to four hours.

Lushoto → *Colour map 1, B5. 4°4'S 38°20'E. Phone code: 027. Altitude: 1500 m.*

Lushoto, at an elevation of around 1500 m, was the town chosen by early German settlers to escape from the heat and dust of the plains for the holidays. Back then it was called Wilhemstal (named after German Emperor Wilhem II) and the cool, fresh air and lush, green surroundings were greatly appealing. It was even once thought that it might develop into the capital of the colonial administration. It can get quite cold from June to September, so take warm clothes.

Many of the surrounding farms and government buildings are originally German. There is a very fine Dutch-style **Governor's House**, just out of town on the road going north. Other reminders of the colonial connection are the horse-riding arenas and the red tiles on some of the roofs of the buildings. There is a group of **German Alpine-style buildings** with flat red, rounded end tiles, chimney stacks and shutters on the east side of the main road near the Mission Hospital. The British changed the town very little. Their main contribution was to lay out a **cricket ground** just to the west of the town centre. Although football is played here now and not cricket, it is still possible to see the old weather-boarded cricket pavilion with a veranda, albeit in poor repair. East of the main road, near the Catholic church, is the **Parade Ground**. Horse riding was a favourite recreation of the Germans, and this was where the mounted officials were paraded in front of the timber review stand. The **Lutheran church**, just west of the centre, is an attractive building, with blue window frames, black-and-white walls, Mangalore tile roof, a front stone arch and a free-standing bell in a wooden tower.

The town also holds a fine **market** (close to the bus stand) that is very colourful and lively, with several small, inexpensive eating places, hair salons, tailors and a maize mill making *posho* (maize flour). Among the many products on sale is the locally produced pottery, with a variety of pots for cooking, storage or serving. One of the ancient beliefs of the Shambaa people is that Sheuta, their God or Supreme Being, made people from a handful of soil in the manner of a potter. In the Usambaras, potters are traditionally women, with the skills passed on from mother to daughter. Men are discouraged from participating in any stage of the potting process, as it is believed that to do so brings great misfortune including sterility. There is good fishing in the mountain streams, one of which runs through the centre of the town, but you'll need to be fully equipped.

This area is a place to enjoy the views and countryside. It is fertile and verdant, and there are plenty of tracks to walk along. One such walk takes about 45 minutes from Lushoto to reach **Irente viewpoint** 5 km away, from where the view of the hills and the Masai Plain 1000 m below really is breathtaking. Take the road out of town towards Irente and head for the children's home. Ask around and you'll be shown the track. On the way is the **Irente Biodiversity Reserve**, formerly and still referred to as **Irente Farm**, where fresh fruit, vegetables, preserves, bread and cheese are sold – the large garden is an excellent picnic spot and the **Mkuyu Lodge** is here (see Where to stay, page 207). There's also a hotel very near to the view point, aptly named **Irente View Cliff Lodge** (see page 207), with fantastic views from all the rooms.

Usambara Mountains Cultural Tourism Programme

ⓘ *Guides are available from the information centre, just off the road opposite the bus station, daily 0800-1800, which is run by the Friends of Usambara Society, T0787-094 725, www.usambaratravels.com. Here, there are details and photographs of each tour offered and you can discuss with the staff exactly what you would like to do. Further information is available from the* **Tanzania Cultural Tourism Programme** *office, or the Tanzanian Tourist Information Centre, both on Boma Rd in Arusha, see page 236, www.tanzaniaculturaltourism.com.*

Lushoto

To Governor's House, District Offices, Mlalo & ➍

Forestry Office

Old Cricket Ground

Pavilion

Catholic

Parade Ground

Council Offices

Lutheran

Mission Hospital

Friends of Usambara Society

NMB

Village Hall

Adventista

To Soni, Mombo & Dar es Salaam ➋➌➎

To ➐➑➒ & Irente Viewpoint

N

300 metres
300 yards

Where to stay
Eddies Lodge 3
Irente View Cliff Lodge 9
Karibuni Lodge 8
Lawns 2
Lushoto Sun 11
Mukyu Lodge 7
Muller's Mountain Lodge 4
St Eugene's Guesthouse 5
White House Annex 12

This has been one of the most successful of Tanzania's cultural tourism programmes and these days runs largely self-sufficiently. Local development projects benefiting from the scheme include maintaining traditional irrigation systems and soil erosion control for small farmers. It aims to involve and ultimately benefit the small local communities who organize tourist projects off the usual circuits. These include several one-day walking trips from Lushoto to the Irente Viewpoint overlooking Mazinde village 1000 m below (see above), a walking tour of Usambara farms and flora, the increasingly popular rock tour from Soni, and the Bangala River tour, which includes wading through the water. You can also visit and stay in **Carters Camp** at **Ndekia**. This is a hut precariously perched on a rocky outcrop, built by an American writer as his launch pad for hang-gliding. There are also longer three- to five-day excursions walking into the Western Usambara Mountains via the villages of **Lukozi**, **Manolo** and **Simga** to reach the former German settlement of **Mtae**, a small village perched high up on the western rim of the escarpment, and the tour to the **Masumbae Forest Reserve**. Another hike is to **Mlalo** and **Mount Seguruma** (2218 m), about 25 km north of Lushoto. One of the more ambitious tours offered is a seven-day bike ride from Lushoto to Moshi through the mountains. On overnight hikes and rides, you stay in local guesthouses and, in some cases, local homes, or the tourist office will supply tents and sleeping bags. The costs for all these trips varies greatly but expect to pay in the region of US$30-40 per person per day. There are additional costs for accommodation and food. Most of the guides are former students of the Shambalai secondary school in Lushoto, speak fair to good English, and can give you information on the history of, and daily life in, the Usambara Mountains.

Back on the road to Moshi → *For listings, see pages 206-208.*

Same → *Colour map 1, A5.*
A small town 126 km north of Korogwe and 103 km south of Moshi, Same is a base for a visit to Mkomazi National Park (see below). The market has covered and open sections, with a good selection of earthenware pots and bowls, baskets and mats. The bus station is particularly well organized, with bus shelters clearly displaying the destinations and routes of the various buses. A feature of the area is the hollowed-out honey-logs hanging from the trees. Every Friday there's a cattle market at Mgagau about 15 minutes drive away. Ask at the **Elephant Motel** (see page 208) for directions.

Mkomazi National Park → *Colour map 1, A5. 4° S, 38° E.*
ⓘ *www.tanzaniaparks.com, 0630-1830, US$20, children (5-16) US$5, vehicle US$40. Access to the park is through the Zange Gate, 7 km east of Same. There is very little tourist development in the park, it is well off the normal safari circuit and there is only one camp (see page 208). There are 3 small airstrips inside the reserve used by chartered planes.*
This national park of 3245 sq km lies about 100 km northwest of Tanga and is contiguous with Kenya's Tsavo National Park. In the rainy season herds of elephant, zebra and oryx migrate between the parks. The name means 'where the water comes from' in the local Pare language and refers to the Umba River on the southeastern border. Mkomazi Game Reserve was established in 1951 but, by 1988, heavy poaching had destroyed its rhino and elephant populations, and overgrazing by pastorals who brought their cattle into the reserve had taken its toll. In 1989 the government gave Tony Fitzjohn, a conservationist with the George Adamson Trust a mandate to rehabilitate the wilderness. He set about building an infrastructure of roads, airfields, water pumps and dams, and recruited anti-poaching rangers. These efforts have proved successful and now Mkomazi is so well

protected that the government upgraded it from a game reserve to a national park in 2005. In the 1980s, there were only 11 individual elephants; today there are over 1000.

The landscape is wide savannah dotted with baobab trees, which is an ideal environment for rhino. In the 1960s, it was thought Mkomazi was home to some 250 black rhino, but by the late 1980s there were none left. The **Mkomazi Rhino Sanctuary**, coordinated by the George Adamson Wildlife Preservation Trust (www.georgeadamson.org), has taken a lead role in relocating black rhino from South Africa to Mkomazi Reserve and Ngorongoro. The eight rhino that were released here in 2001 are kept in intensive protection zones and it is hoped that they will breed, after which they will be relocated within Tanzania to other traditional natural habitats. Another three rhino were transferred here in 2009 from a zoo in the Czech Republic. It is an expensive programme; the cost of transferring one rhino is put at over US$100,000.

African hunting dogs, the endangered wild dog and other big mammals, such as zebra, giraffes and gazelles, have also been reintroduced. The reserve is home to about 400 bird species including falcons, eagles, hawks, hornbills, barbets, starlings, weavers and shrikes.

◉ The road from Dar to Moshi listings

For sleeping and eating price codes and other relevant information, see pages 22-26.

● Where to stay

Korogwe *p202*
$ Motel White Parrot, from the bus stand turn left for 400 m, T022-264 1068. By far the best place to stay in Korogwe, this white double-storey building has 22 small but smart a/c rooms, with hot showers, satellite TV and phones. You can also camp at the back on grass for US$6 per person, and there's a toilet, a hot shower and a cooking shelter. There is also a separate thatched restaurant and bar.
$ Korogwe Transit Hotel, on the main road, T022-264 0640. Mosquito nets, private bath with hot water most of the time, some rooms have a/c, overpriced for what you get, front rooms have a balcony but are very noisy because of the traffic and many of the buses stop here. With the number of people around, security could be an issue.

Usambara Mountains *p203*
$$$-$ Mambo View Point Eco Lodge, 60 km or a 2-hr drive from Lushoto on a dirt road in the heart of the Usambaras near the village of Mambo; contact the lodge or

check the website for detailed directions, T0785-272 150, www.mamboviewpoint. org. Beautifully remote and worth the effort of getting here for the stunning and sweeping views from its cliff-top position at 1900 m across the Pare Mountains, Mkomazi National Park and, on a clear day, Mt Kilimanjaro. It has a variety of accommodation all perched right on the edge of the cliff, including thatched self-catering cottages, many with floor-to-ceiling windows in their own pretty gardens (US$90-110) and permanent furnished tents with en suite toilets and hot showers (US$60). There's also a campsite (US$8 per person) with ablutions and a cooking shelter. The restaurant serves good home-cooked meals, there are plenty of hikes, and visits to local villages and schools can be organized, as can pick up from Lushoto.
$$ Maweni Farm, 2 km from Soni up a good dirt road, at the foot of a large rockface, T0784-279 371, www.maweni.com. This guesthouse on an old colonial farm has 5 rooms in the main house and 8 in garden chalets, simply furnished but comfortable with reliable hot water. Lovely restaurant with veranda, organic locally grown food and home-made bread, bar serving local wine, lounge with fireplace, established

gardens, sauna and swimming pool, internet access. A very pretty setting next to a small lake, lots of nature trails through the forest, and they run 1- to 3-day guided hikes. Pickups can be arranged from the bus stand in Mombo.

$$-$ Muller's Mountain Lodge, 13 km from Lushoto on the road to Migambo, which is rough in places, signposted from Lushoto; start by heading north on the road that passes the post office, T0782-315 666, www.mullersmountainlodge.co.tz. Built in 1930 in the style of an English country home, it has brick gables, attractive gardens and orchards, and lovely views. 7 bedrooms, shared dining and living rooms with outsized fireplaces, large camping area on the hill above the house (US$4 per person), plus very good food and service; they offer guided walks and rent out mountain bikes. Pickups can be arranged from town.

Lushoto p203, map p204
There are a number of basic guesthouses around the market in Lushoto itself, but by far the best places to stay to enjoy the mountain scenery are the country lodges on the outskirts.

$$ Eddies Lodge, 1.5 km from town, T0784-360 624, www.eddieslodge.com. Comfortable self-contained rooms in single-storey brick buildings with satellite TV and 4-poster beds, some have self-catering kitchens and thatched roofs, set in manicured gardens where you can also camp (US$10 per tent). There's a restaurant and bar – meals are prepared from local farm produce – as well as a gym and sauna.

$$ Irente View Cliff Lodge, Irente Viewpoint, 5 km from Lushoto, T027-264 0026, www.irenteview.com. The newest and best-positioned mid-range lodge around Lushoto in a stunning cliff-top location with 16 comfortable rooms, balconies, satellite TV, tea and coffee trays, hot water, spacious grounds with amazing views, curio shop, restaurant and bar. Can organize guides for hikes. Doubles from US$65. There's an adjacent campsite (US$4 per person) with hot showers and its own bar serving cheap meals.

$$-$ Lawns Hotel, 1 km before town on Soni Rd, T027-264 0005, www.lawnshotel. com. Old colonial-style hotel, with wonderful views and fireplaces in the rooms, plus a veranda, restaurant and lively bar. Rates include a very good breakfast. Some rooms are self-contained, the cheaper ones have shared facilities. Given that the building is over 100 years old, the quality of the rooms varies, so look at a few. Run by a football-loving Cypriot who is quite a character and a good source of information about Tanzania. Camping is possible, US$7 per person, with fairly new ablutions block, hot water and a cooking shelter.

$$-$ Mukuyu Lodge, at Irente Biodiversity Reserve, formerly and still referred to as Irente Farm, 5 km southwest of town, 1.7 km before the Irente Viewpoint, go past the farm buildings and after 200 m turn right to the lodge and farm shop, T0788-503 002, www.irentebiodiversity reserve.org. Run by the Evangelical Lutheran Church of Tanzania, this property has a children's home, a school and church and a wonderful cheese factory. You can buy a picnic lunch for around US$5 from the farm shop (0800-1600) to take with you to climb to the viewpoint, including rich brown bread, several types of jam, fresh butter, cheese and fruit juice. Their produce is also for sale in shops in Moshi and Tanga. Accommodation on offer is in a simply furnished self-catering house, sleeping up to 6 (US$80), and 3 double/triple rooms in rondavels (from US$20), rates include a delicious farm breakfast, and dinner can be arranged on request. There's also a campsite with an ablution block and watchman (US$5 per person).

$$-$ St Eugene's Guesthouse, 2 km before Lushoto on the Soni Rd, T027-264 0055, www. steugeneshostel.com. Run by the Usambara sisters, 14 plain but comfortable self-contained rooms in a double-storey building decked with vines, hot water and phones.

Check out the white starched bed linen and hand-embroidered bed covers. Serves food, including delicious home-made ice cream, and in the farm shop you can buy home-made jam and marmalade made from various fruits, such as passion fruit and grapefruit, herbed cheeses and rather potent banana wine. This is a convent and a Montessori teacher training centre with modern buildings in gardens well tended by the sisters. Doubles from US$45 and all meals are available.

$ Karibuni Lodge, 1 km south of town on a hill to the left of the road, T0784-474 026. A stone house with a wide veranda, set in a lush tract of vegetation with a lounge and bar, self-catering kitchen or meals can be organized. Accommodation is in a 6-bed dorm, in rooms with or without bathrooms or you can pitch a tent in the garden. Can organize local guided walks.

$ Lushoto Sun Hotel, Boma Rd near the police station, T027-264 0082. Best of the simple board and lodgings, with 10 large, but a little gloomy, double rooms with nets and hot water for US$12, and safe parking. Good restaurant serving steaming plates of stew and *ugali* and chicken and chips.

$ White House Annex, in town near the market, T0784-427 471. A tidy 1-storey white house near the tourist office and bus stand, with 10 self-contained singles and doubles from US$10. There's a TV room, bar and small restaurant serving good local food in big portions. There is also an adjoining internet café.

Same *p205*

$$-$ Elephant Motel, T027-275 8193, www.elephantmotel.com. Simple but more than adequate, with 12 double rooms with mosquito nets reliable hot water, Wi-Fi and TV, and limited DSTV (BBC and CNN). 4 slightly more expensive rooms also have a/c and a fridge; doubles from US$35. Staff are helpful and there's a good restaurant and bar serving Western and Oriental dishes. Set in well-maintained gardens, you can also camp for US$5 per person, and there

are toilets and showers. You can organize a guide here to take you to some of the local farms or a cattle market.

Mkomazi National Park *p205*

$$$$ Babu's Camp, 11 km from the entrance gate of Zange, reservations Arusha, T027-254 5884, www.babuscamp.com. Not as luxurious as the usual tented camps, but simple and comfortable, and the only accommodation within the park. The 6 tents are spacious and have attached bathrooms with shower and toilet. Activities include day and night game drives, game walks, and they can ask permission to take guests to see the rhino in the enclosed area. Transport into the reserve is usually organized when you make a reservation.

❼ Restaurants

Lushoto *p203, map p204*

All guesthouses and lodges have restaurants and bars, and in town itself there are a number of cheap food stalls and local bars, again around the bus stand and market. It's worth dropping into the **Irente Biodiversity Reserve** and **St Eugene's Guesthouse** to buy their excellent fresh produce.

❽ Transport

Lushoto *p203, map p204*
Bus, dala-dala and 4WD

The road to Lushoto is good tar despite the 33-km gradual climb up from Mombo. Public transport is frequent and hitching is possible, as there are plenty of 4WDs who will give lifts in this area. Buses and *dala-dalas* from **Mombo** take about 1½ hrs and cost US$2. You can also get a direct bus from **Tanga**, but it is slow, 6 hrs, and there are also slow buses between Lushoto and **Arusha** (6 hrs) and **Moshi** (5½ hrs). Direct buses from **Dar** leave the stand on Mafia St in the Kariakoo area throughout the morning and take 7 hrs. The better option is to get a bus as far as **Mombo** and swap vehicles there.

Moshi and around

Moshi is the first staging post on the way to climbing Mount Kilimanjaro. It's a busy town of about 250,000 people and a pleasant place to spend a few days organizing your trip. Trekking expeditions depart from the town's tourist hotels into Kilimanjaro National Park early each morning. The two peaks of this shimmering snow-capped mountain can be seen from all over the town and it dominates the skyline except when the cloud descends and hides it from view. Moshi means 'smoke' – perhaps either a reference to the giant volcano that once smoked or the regular smoke-like cloud. Marangu is 27 km from Moshi and is the closest village to Kilimanjaro National Park, the entrance to which is 5 km away. Accommodation here is more expensive than in Moshi so, if you're on a tight budget, you should plan your assault on the mountain from Moshi. ▶▶ *For listings, see pages 213-220.*

Arriving in Moshi and Marangu

Moshi is 80 km east of Arusha on the A23, and 580 km northwest of Dar es Salaam. **Kilimanjaro International Airport** ⓘ *55 km west of Moshi, off the A23/Arusha road, T027-255 4252, www.kilimanjaroairport.co.tz,* is well served by domestic flights and some international flights. For details of these, see page 236. A taxi from the airport should cost around US$50 to Moshi, or you can arrange transfers with one of the hotels or tour operators. There are numerous buses in all directions from Moshi, and it is a pickup/drop-off terminus for the many daily buses between Dar and Arusha. It is also served by the daily Nairobi–Arusha–Moshi shuttle buses, which also call in at Kilimanjaro International Airport on their way past (see box, page 15). There is a steady stream of *dala-dalas* that cover the 27 km between Moshi and Marangu. ▶▶ *For further details, see Transport, page 219.*

Background

The area around Moshi is particularly fertile, due to the volcanic soils, and there are lots of melt-water streams fed by the snow. This is where Arabica coffee, the premium quality of the two coffee varieties, is grown by the Chagga people, helping them to become one of the wealthiest of the Tanzanian groups. All around the town and on the lower slopes of Kilimanjaro, vast plantations of coffee blanket the area. Notice that the low coffee bushes are grown with taller banana palms for shade. The first coffee grown in Tanzania was planted at the nearby Kilema Roman Catholic Mission in 1898. Growth was steady and, by 1925, 100 tonnes were being produced each year. The Chagga people are particularly enterprising and formed the Kilimanjaro Native Cooperative Union (KNCH) to collect and market the crop themselves.

Moshi is the centre of Tanzania's coffee industry; the Coffee Board is located here and coffee from all over Tanzania is sold at auction to international buyers. However, apart from the coffee produced in the immediate locality, the crop does not pass through Moshi, it is auctioned on the basis of certified type, quality and grade, and then shipped directly from the growing area to the buyer. Not all of the wealth generated by the sale of coffee makes its way back to the growing community. Local small farmers have been known to receive only half the Moshi export price. By the time the coffee is sold in London their purchase price amounts to only one-tenth of the London price. Interestingly, only 1-2% of the coffee grown in Tanzania is consumed in the country; simply because Tanzanians are traditionally chai (tea) drinkers. Moshi was the site of the signing of the Moshi Declaration after the war with Uganda in February 1979, which created the Uganda National Liberation Front (UNLF) government to replace Idi Amin.

Moshi → Colour map 1, A5.

Moshi is a pleasant town, with the former European and administrative areas clustered around the clock tower, and the main commercial area southwest of the market. Despite being an attractive town, there are few places worth visiting in Moshi itself, and many visitors stay here just long enough to arrange their trek up the mountain and to enjoy a hot shower when they get back. The limited sights include the (non-operating) **railway station** southeast of the clock tower, a two-storey structure from the German period, with pleasing low arches, a gabled roof with Mangalore tiles and arched windows on the first floor. On the corner of Station Road and Ghalla Road is a fine **Indian shop building** dating from the colonial period, with wide curved steps leading up to the veranda, tapering fluted stone columns and a cupola adorning the roof. To the north of town on the roundabout marking the junction with the Dar–Arusha road, the **Askari Monument** is a soldier with a rifle and commemorates African members of the British Carrier Corps who lost their lives in the two World Wars. **Shah Industries Ltd** ⓘ *T027-275 2414*, employ many disabled workers producing high-quality crafts, such as wood carvings, leatherwork, batiks and furniture. Their shop is on Karakana Street in the industrial area to the west of town.

Moshi

Where to stay	Parkview Inn 1
AMEG Lodge Kilimanjaro 11	Springlands 3
Bristol Cottages 7	YMCA 13
Buffalo Inn 10	
Honey Badger Lodge 6	**Restaurants**
Impala Kilimanjaro 12	Aroma Coffee House 3
Keys 14	Chrisburger 1
Kilemakyaro Mountain	Coffee Shop 7
Lodge 15	Deli Chez 6
Kilimanjaro Backpacker's 9	El Rancho 5
Kilimanjaro Crane 2	Indoitaliano 9
Kindoroko 8	Panda 4
Leopard 18	Salzburger 2
Mountain Inn 16	Tanzania Coffee Lounge 10
Mt Kilimanjaro View	
Lodge 4	
Newcastle 5	

Machame

Machame is 30 km northwest of Moshi; the road to the village turns off the Moshi–Arusha road (A23) 12 km west of Moshi. It is the start of the second most popular route up Kilimanjaro, the Machame Trail (see page 230), which is tougher than the Marangu Trail but is considered one of the most beautiful routes up. Machame itself lies in a fertile valley of farmland on the lower slopes of the mountain; the park gate is 4 km beyond the village. Accommodation is presently limited to the **Protea Hotel Aishi** (see page 215), but climb operators will transport you to the park gate from Moshi.

West Kilimanjaro

The road running in a northerly direction from Boma ya Ng'ombe, 27 km west of Moshi on the Moshi–Arusha road (A23), passes through Sanya Juu and Engare Nairobi to reach the village of Ol Molog, about 70 km north of the main road and on the northern side of the mountain very close to the border with Kenya. This was the main area for European farming in northern Tanzania prior to Independence. After Independence most estates were nationalized. These days while pockets of farmland still exist, most of the plains in this region are used by wildlife on a migratory route between **Arusha National Park** (see page 245)and Kenya's Amboseli National Park. In the dry season up to 600 elephant use this corridor, and it's an important calving area for zebra, wildebeest, and Grant's and Thompson's gazelles. In addition to its diverse habitats and wildlife communities, West Kilimanjaro is home to a number of Masai communities that depend on cattle grazing. There are a couple of lodges in this region (see Where to stay, page 216).

Marangu

Marangu is 11 km north of Himo, a village 27 km east of Moshi on the A23 road to the Kenya border (see box, page 212). It's a busy little village that most people visit only to attempt the climb on the Marangu Route to the summit of Kilimanjaro, and is 5 km south of the entrance gate to the Mount Kilimanjaro National Park. However, Marangu is also an excellent base for hiking, birdwatching and observing rural Africa in the foothills of the mountain, and the main tracks in the region radiate from the village and forest boundary through the cultivated belt of coffee and bananas. There are several waterfalls within a short walk of the village and, indeed, in the Chagga language, Marangu means 'a place with too many streams' in reference to the profusion of waterways running off the mountain. For full details of climbing Kilimanjaro, see page 226.

Foothill walks

ⓘ *Tanzania Cultural Tourism Programme office, or the Tanzanian Tourist Information Centre, both on Boma Rd in Arusha, see page 236, www.tanzaniaculturaltourism.com.*

The **Marangu/Mamba Cultural Tourism Programme** arranges guided walks through the attractive scenery of the valleys near Marangu and Mamba. **Mamba** is a small village 3 km from Marangu. From here you can also visit caves where women and children hid during ancient Masai-Chagga wars or see a blacksmith at work, using traditional methods to make Masai spears and tools. From Marangu there is an easy walk up Ngangu hill, a visit to a traditional Chagga home, or a visit to the home and memorial of the late Yohano Lawro, a local man who accompanied Dr Hans Meyer and Ludwig Purtscheller on the first recorded climb of Mount Kilimanjaro in 1889. He is reputed to have guided Kilimanjaro climbs until he was 70 and lived to the age of 115. Profits from the programme are used to improve local primary schools. Any of the Marangu hotels can organize guides from the programme.

Border crossing: Tanzania–Kenya

Taveta

Taveta is a small settlement in Kenya surrounded by sisal estates, 41 km east of Moshi, straddling the A23 road between Tanzania and Kenya. It is a thriving point of commerce for the Masai communities on both sides of the border and, for a small out-of-the-way place, it has an especially large twice-weekly market (Wednesday and Saturday). The border is open 24 hours, the crossing is efficient and quick, and visas for both Tanzania and Kenya are available (although if you only go in and out of Kenya you don't need to buy another visa to re-enter Tanzania as long as your original one is still valid. There are banks in Taveta with ATMs. The nearest banks on the Tanzania side are in Moshi.

Through buses between Moshi and Mombasa cross at Taveta, and there are also plenty of *dala-dalas* (in Kenya *matatus*) that go the 109 km from Taveta to Voi, the main town on the A109 between Nairobi and Mombasa. From Voi it is 156 km to Mombasa and 327 km to Nairobi. If you're not in a vehicle, the two border posts are 4 km apart but you can get a *boda-boda* (bicycle taxi) between them.

In Kenya, the A23 runs eastwards to Voi through the Taita Hills and, for a short distance, the road goes through **Tsavo West National Park** via Maktau and Mbuyuni gates (you don't have to pay the entrance fees if only transiting). The road is fairly well maintained murram for most of the way. Look out for the now-disused railway that follows the road: it served as a vital supply line to British forces during the First World War, when Tanzania was German East Africa. It was on these plains that one of the most eccentric campaigns of the war was fought. Here, the British, led by General Jan Smuts, pitted their wits against one of Germany's most charismatic generals, General Paul von Lettow, in a bizarre battle that featured fleets of Rolls Royces, blown-up railways lines, lack of men, lack of guns and a final surrender that came three months after the rest of the world had signed an armistice.

In town, the **Taveta Military Cemetery** is next to the District Commissioners Office and holds the graves of 127 soldiers who died in these battles (Taveta was invaded by Germany in August 1914). It is believed to be the only place where British and German soldiers were laid to rest side by side.

Taveta is actually on a piece of land that juts into Tanzania. The irregular shape of the border here was created in 1881 when Queen Victoria gave Mount Kilimanjaro to her grandson, then the Crown Prince of Prussia and later Kaiser Wilhelm II of Germany, as a wedding present. Consequently, the border was adjusted so that Kilimanjaro fell within the boundaries of the German colony of Tanganyika instead of the British protectorate of Kenya.

As you drive east from Taveta to Voi, the road crosses a number of 'elephant grids'; they serve the same purpose as cattle grids but are, naturally, much larger. From Voi, the road runs through the **Taru Desert** for another 156 km down to Mombasa. From Tanzania, it is not an unreasonable option to get a bus to Voi and go to one of the safari lodges around the main road there for a safari to Tsavo West and Tsavo East national parks (see *Footprint Kenya Handbook*).

Lake Chala

This undetermined deep-water crater lake straddles the border with Kenya and can be accessed from Himo on the A23 on the Tanzania side; the turn-off is 7 km after Himo towards Taveta, from where it's roughly another 15 km on a rough road to the lakeshore; it is 8 km north of Taveta on the Kenyan side. The picturesque lake is about 4 sq km and is totally clear, with 100-m-high steep and vegetated walls, and it is filled and drained by underground streams fed by the waters running off Kilimanjaro. It is a tranquil, beautiful place to explore on foot and, aside from plenty of fish, there are also monitor lizards, baboons, monkeys and common snakes. Unfortunately, you can't swim as there is still thought to be at least one crocodile in the lake (a British tourist was killed in 2002). A new campsite opened here in 2010, see Where to stay, page 216, which is expected to be a boon for tourism to this little-visited area.

◉ Moshi and around listings

For sleeping and eating price codes and other relevant information, see pages 22-26.

◎ Where to stay

Most of the hotels in Moshi and Marangu offer arrangements to climb Kili, or at the least will recommend a tour operator. They all offer a base from which to begin your climb, and there is an excellent choice of mid-range and budget places where you will enjoy the 'camaraderie' of other excited (or, afterwards, weary) trekkers. Ensure that the hotel will store your luggage safely whilst you are on the mountain. Facilities to consider include hot water and a comfortable bed, and of course cold beer and a good hot meal on your return from the climb. Some establishments also offer saunas and massages. The Marangu hotels are better located on the lower slopes of Kilimanjaro but are considerably more expensive. Almost all hotels can organize transfers from **Kilimanjaro International Airport** for about US$50-60.

Moshi *p210, map p210*
$$$ Impala Hotel Kilimanjaro, Lema Rd, Shantytown, T027-534 443, www.kilimanjaro. impalahotel.com. The smaller sister hotel to the **Impala** in Arusha, set in leafy and peaceful gardens about 2 km from the town centre. 11 rooms with satellite TV and Wi-Fi,

restaurant serving continental and Indian dishes, bar and 24-hr coffee shop, large swimming pool set on expansive lawns.
$$$ Kilemakyaro Mountain Lodge, 7 km from Moshi, take the Sokoine road out of town, T027-275 4925, www.kilimanjarosafari. com. Set in a 240-ha coffee plantation at an altitude of 1450 m above Moshi, a stay here will very much help climbers with acclimatization. The reception, bar and dining room are in the main house, a restored 1880s farmhouse, while the 20 rooms are in chalets dotted throughout the lovely palm-filled garden, which has a swimming pool. They can arrange climbs of Kilimanjaro and also Meru, day trips to Arusha National Park (see page 245), and picnics at local waterfalls.
$$ AMEG Lodge Kilimanjaro, off Lema Rd, near the Moshi International School, Shantytown, T0754-058 268, www.ameglodge.com. A modern if somewhat characterless lodge set in 1.5 ha of garden. 20 rooms with smart tiled en suite bathrooms and lovely bright contemporary furniture, satellite TV, phone and fan. The more expensive suites have a/c and internet access for laptops. Good value in this price range, with the cheapest double at only US$65. Swimming pool and pool bar, good restaurant serving both Western and Indian dishes, gym and business centre.

$$ Bristol Cottages, Rindi Lane, T027-275 0175, www.bristolcottages.com. Within walking distance of the bus stand, this is set in a pretty garden compound with parking and, although furnishings are a little old fashioned, it is spotlessly clean and adequate. The 8 cottages, including 3 family ones, are spacious and have a/c, satellite TV, reliable hot water and Wi-Fi, and there are another 9 more basic and cheaper rooms in the main building. The pleasant restaurant and bar serves continental and Indian food and can organize packed lunches. Rates include an English breakfast.

$$ Keys Hotel – Uru Road, Uru Rd, just north of the town centre, T027-275 2250, www.keys-hotel-tours.com. This hotel functions primarily as a base for budget climb operations. Accommodation is in 15 rooms in the main building, which have satellite TV and a/c, or 15 simpler round huts in the grounds, some with 3 beds. There is a restaurant, bar, internet access and swimming pool. The location itself is not particularly interesting and it's probably not as pleasant as some of the more rural locations; it is, nevertheless, a firm favourite with budget travellers. Doubles are from US$65 with breakfast, and camping is available in the grounds for US$5 per person. They also run **Keys Hotel – Mbokomu Road**, which is nearby and is usually referred to as the 'Keys Annex', with another 48 budget rooms, some with a/c, balcony and mountain views, and identical facilities including a swimming pool.

$$ Mt Kilimanjaro View Lodge, 16 km from Moshi, follow the unpaved road out of town north of the **YMCA** or arrange a pick up, bookings through the website, www.mtkilimanjaroviewlodge.com. A country retreat in the Kilimanjaro foothills, with great views and accommodation in colourful stone and thatch Chagga huts with bathrooms and home-made chunky wooden furniture. There's a restaurant and bar serving authentic African food, jacuzzi, lots of local walks to nearby waterfalls

and, in the evenings, traditional dancing and storytelling. An excellent opportunity to interact with the local Chagga people. Doubles from US$80, and they'll pick up 1-3 people from Moshi for US$30, and from **Kilimanjaro International Airport** for US$70.

$$ Mountain Inn, 6 km from Moshi on the road to Marangu, T027-275 2370, www.kilimanjaro-shah.com. 35 basic but comfortable rooms, some are triples, a dining room with a veranda, set meals and an à la carte menu, Indian food at the pool bar and restaurant (see page 217), lush gardens, swimming pool, sauna. This is the base for **Shah Tours**, see page 219, a quality operator for Kilimanjaro climbs.

$$ Parkview Inn, Aga Khan Rd, T027-275 0711, www.pvim.com. Local business hotel with little character but nevertheless spacious rooms with modern bathrooms, TV, a/c, internet, secure parking in a compound, spotless swimming pool and a restaurant serving continental and Indian food and can make up lunch boxes to takeaway.

$$ Springlands Hotel, Tembo Rd, Pasua area towards the industrial area, T027-275 3581, www.springlandshotel.com. Set in large, attractive gardens, this place offers all sorts of treats that are ideal to recover from a Kili climb. 37 rooms, restaurant, bar, swimming pool, TV room, massages, sauna, manicures and pedicures, bicycle hire, internet. Doubles are from US$70 with a generous breakfast. Base for **Zara Travel**, see page 219, a recommended operator for climbs.

$$-$ Kilimanjaro Crane, Kaunda St, T027-275 1114, www.kilimanjarocranehotels.com. 30 simple but neat rooms with mosquito nets and satellite TV. Facilities include swimming pool, sauna, gym, gardens, good views, pizza kitchen, several bars including one on the roof with fantastic views of the mountain. There is a very good bookshop in the lobby. A good mid-range option: single/double/triple US$40/50/60.

$ Kindoroko Hotel, Mawenzi Rd, close to market, T027-275 4054, www.kindoroko hotels.com. One of the best budget options in the middle of town, very organized and friendly and fantastically decorated. 46 rooms, which are on the small side but have satellite TV, some also have fridges, and bathrooms have plenty of hot water. Rates include a hot breakfast. Downstairs is a restaurant and bar, internet café and tour booking office, upstairs is the rooftop restaurant and bar with excellent views of Kili. A great place to meet other travellers even if you are not staying here. They operate their own Kili climbs on all routes, and rates include a night before and after the climb in the hotel. Single/double/triple US$20/35/45.

$ Leopard Hotel, Market St, T027-275 0884, www.leopardhotel.com. This centrally located hotel has 48 clean but cramped rooms in a 4-storey block, with balconies, a/c, satellite TV and tiled en suite bathrooms, half of which have a view of Kilimanjaro. Reasonable bar and restaurant downstairs, and a bar with nice views on the roof, but has fewer facilities or amenities than the other places.

$ Buffalo Inn, 2 blocks south and east of the bus station, T027-275 0270. Clean budget hotel with 35 rooms, very friendly, hot water with/without bathroom. Good restaurant and bar serving some Indian dishes. Will store your luggage if you are going on safari. Rates include breakfast.

$ Honey Badger Lodge, 6 km from town on the Dar road, T0767-551 190, www.honeybadgerlodge.com. A refreshing rural alternative to the town hotels, set in a grassy walled compound with 8 self-contained rooms with up to 5 beds, reliable solar-powered hot water, pleasant *makuti* thatch bar and swimming pool in the gardens where you also camp, there's a restaurant and you can self-cater in the kitchen. They can organize massages, drumming lessons and village walks.

$ Kilimanjaro Backpacker's Hotel, Mawenzi Rd, T027-275 5159, www. kilimanjarobackpackers.com. Here there are 10 rooms, which are small but comfortable with fans and shared bathrooms. There's a small restaurant and bar with TV showing sports, or guests can also use the facilities at the **Kindoroko** next door, which has the same owner. You can't argue with the price here; just US$7 for a dorm bed and from US$20 for a double.

$ Newcastle, close to the market on Mawenzi St, T027-275 0853. Offers 40 rooms on 5 floors, 36 with bathrooms, the rest with shared bathrooms, good views from the top, hot water, rooms are well kept though all the dark wood makes the place a little gloomy. Rooftop bar.

$ YMCA, Uhuru Highway, to the north of the clock tower, T027-275 1734. Facilities include gym, shop, several tour desks, bar, restaurant and Olympic-sized swimming pool (non-guests can use the pool for US$2.50). Mostly used by local people, this has 60 bare rooms with communal showers with hot water. Nevertheless, it's secure and clean with spotless sheets and mosquito nets and rates are from US$10 per person.

Camping

There is a good grassy campsite at the **Honey Badger Lodge**, 6 km from Moshi on the road to Dar. It is also possible to camp at the **Keys Hotel**.

Machame *p211*

$$$ Protea Hotel Aishi, 30 km from Moshi in Machame village, T027-275 6941, www. proteahotels.com. This is one of the nicest hotels in the region, run by South African chain Protea, and is an ideal base to conquer Kili on the Machame Trail (see page 230). The 30 rooms, with private facilities, have recently been completely refurbished to the highest standard. Set in well-kept gardens, there's also a restaurant, bar, swimming pool and gym. The hotel arranges mountain climbing, safaris and also nature trails in the area and rents out mountain bikes.

West Kilimanjaro *p211*

$$$$ Kambi ya Tembo, reservations Arusha, T0767-333 223, www.tanganyikawilderness camps.com. A traditional tented camp set on a 600-sq-km private concession, with 14 spacious tents and good views of either the mountain or across the Kenya border towards the Amboseli plains. There's a rustic semi-open-air restaurant and bar, picnics can be arranged and activities include game drives and walks with the Masai.

$$$$ Ndarakwai Ranch, reservations Arusha, T027-250 2713, www.ndarakwai.com. The 15 tents are spacious with en suite bathrooms and are fully and tastefully furnished, set under the spreading branches of an acacia tree. Views of Kilimanjaro are superb, and there is game in this region. Game drives, night drives, walks with the Masai, and there's a treehouse overlooking a waterhole. A conservancy fee of US$35 per day is charged and the minimum stay is 2 nights.

Marangu *p211*

$$$ Kilimanjaro Mountain Resort, about 2 km from Marangu Village and 3 km before the park gate, T027-275 8950, www.kilimountresort.com. Probably the smartest option in Marangu and still not unreasonably priced, with the 42 rooms with balconies, kettles and satellite TV going from US$110 for a double. They're set in picturesque gardens complete with duck pond, swimming pool and mountain views, good restaurant, bar with terrace in a mock-up of a Chagga hut, coffee shop serving freshly brewed Kilimanjaro Arabica coffee, gym and they can organize climbs.

$$$ Marangu Hotel, 5 km back from Marangu towards Moshi, T027-275 6594, www.maranguhotel.com. Long-established, family-owned and run country-style hotel, warm and friendly atmosphere, self-contained cottages with private baths and showers, hot water, set in 5 ha of gardens offering stunning views of Kilimanjaro, swimming pool, croquet lawn, one of the original operators of Kilimanjaro climbs with over 60 years' experience. Can arrange treks on all the routes. Also has a pretty campsite and will safely look after vehicles for overlanders doing the climb. Partnered with the Kilimanjaro Porters Assistance Project (see box, page 223).

$$ Ashanti Lodge, close to the Marangu Gate, T027-275 6443, www.ashantilodge. com. Old-style country hotel. Spacious but rather plain rooms with en suite bathrooms, in thatched bungalows in the garden. Bar, restaurant, can organize local cultural tours and safaris. There is ample parking, so if in your own vehicle and climbing Kili, you could negotiate to leave your car here.

$$ Babylon Lodge, 500 m from the post office on the Jarakea Rd, T027-275 6355, www.babylonlodge.com. Clean and comfortable, sited in well-kept gardens, built into the hillside, all 25 slightly small rooms have private facilities, and there's a bar and restaurant with a set 4-course meal each evening (US$10) and a swimming pool with sun deck.

$$ Nakara Hotel, about 3 km from Marangu village and 2 km before the park gate, T0784-605 728, www.nakarahotels.com. Old German building with 17 old-fashioned but adequate rooms, restaurant, cheery bar and fine gardens featuring banana trees and coffee bushes, but it lacks other facilities, such as a swimming pool. Climbs can be organized.

$ Coffee Tree Campsite, 2 km before the park gate and next to the **Nakara Hotel**, T027-275 6604. Grassy lawns for camping (US$8 per person), you can hire 2-man tents for US$8 and they sell beers, soft drinks, firewood and charcoal. Cook for yourself in the kitchen or eat at the restaurant at the **Nakara Hotel**. There's also a cabin that sleeps 5 for US$12 per bed with a toilet, and guests can use the camper's hot showers and wooden sauna – a godsend after the Kili climb.

Lake Chala *p213*

Camping

Lake Chala Safari Camp, accessed from Himo on the main road (A23), the turn-off is 7 km after Himo towards Taveta, from where it's roughly another 15 km on a rough road to the lakeshore, T0786-111 177, www.lakechalasafaricamp.com. Picturesque and remote campsite set under acacia trees, could be grassy if it has rained, thatch and stone newly built ablution block, with flush loos, and hot showers provided by a wood-burning stove, kitchen area with picnic tables, fireplace and grills, bar with views across the lake and simple local meals can be ordered with notice. US$10 per person, and you can hire a tent and bedding for US$20 per person.

❼ Restaurants

Moshi *p210, map p210*
The best restaurants are in the hotels. For Indian food and pizzas (an odd combination that seems to be very popular in Moshi), try the **Kilimanjaro Crane** and catch the sunset from the rooftop bar. Budget travellers should head for the restaurant at the **Kindoroko Hotel**. The menu's very good and includes authentic Indian dishes and 3-course set meals, and again there are Kili views from the rooftop. There are a few places around town where you can try the Arabica coffee grown on the lower slopes of Kili.

$$ El Rancho, off Lema Rd, Shantytown, T027-275 5115. Tue-Sun 1230-2300. Northern Indian food, good choice for vegetarians, very authentic and a full range of curries, each dish is prepared from scratch so it can take a while. However, there are plenty of diversions in the garden to keep you occupied, including table football, a crazy golf course and a pool table. There's a full bar with 16 brands of whisky.
$$-$ Indoitaliano, New St, T027-275 2195. Open 1200-2230. A wide selection of Indian and Italian food, with main dishes, such as pizza or mutton curry with naan bread, for around US$8. The outside veranda is popular and gets very busy from around 1900, when you may have to wait for a table. A good choice of imported wine is on offer and plenty of cold beer too.

$$-$ Mountain Inn, 6 km from Moshi on the road to Marangu, see Where to stay, page 214. Open 0700-2300. Probably the best of the restaurants in the out-of-town hotels, there's a formal dining room with veranda but the better option is the pool bar and restaurant; non-guests can swim. The long menu includes continental, Chinese and Indian dishes and snacks, such as sandwiches and salads, bar with satellite TV, and a nyama choma grill at the weekends.
$$-$ Panda, off Lema Rd, Shantytown, just south of the **Impala Hotel**, T0744-838 193. Open 1200-1500, 1800-2200. Good Chinese food served by ladies in Chinese clothes, tables set up in a house or dotted around the pretty garden, very good seafood, including king-size prawns and sizzling dishes.
$$-$ Salzburger, Kenyatta St, T027-275 0681. Open 1100-2200. A little bit difficult to spot down a dimly lit road a couple blocks west of the market, this has an unusual Austrian-themed menu and Bavarian pub-style decor (the Tanzanian owner used to live in Austria), and then, quite by contrast, the waiting staff have leopard-print uniforms. Good schnitzel, chicken and steak with excellent fries or, very unusually, mashed potato and fresh green veg.
$ Deli Chez, Hill St, T027-275 1144. Wed-Mon 1000-2200. Popular white-tiled restaurant with a/c and decorated with mirrors and plants. Comprehensive menu of good Indian and Chinese food, plus lighter meals, such as burgers and shakes, and ice cream desserts. No alcohol, though.

Cafés
Aroma Coffee House, Boma Rd, T027-275 134. Open 0800-1800. Pleasant café selling a good range of coffee from the region, including creamy cappuccinos and lattes and iced coffee, plus snacks and ice cream.
Chrisburger, Kibo Rd, close to the clock tower, T027-275 0419. Mon-Sat 0830-1530. Has a small veranda at the front and sells cold drinks and snacks, including burgers and

Kilimanjaro Marathon

The Kilimanjaro Marathon is held in Moshi at the end of February and runs on a 42.2-km route around the town and in the foothills of the mountain. The route is at an altitude of 800 to 1100 m and passes along a stretch of the Moshi–Dar road before crossing a landscape of banana plantations and smallholder farms, with Africa's highest mountain as a backdrop. It's open to professionals, many of whom are famed Tanzanian, Kenyan and Ethiopian long-distance runners, as well as amateurs. Established in 2002, it now attracts some 1500 runners for the full- and half-marathon and the 5-km fun run. Visit www.kilimanjaromarathon.com.

A new event, started in 2009, is the Kili(man)jaro Adventure Challenge, which is a six-day climb to the top of Kili (this part is not raced), a two-day/246-km mountain bike race around the mountain, followed by the marathon. Visit www.kilimanjaro-man.com.

---

very good fruit juice and sometimes home-made soup, closes mid-afternoon though. **Coffee Shop**, Hill St, near the bus station, T027-275 2707. Mon-Fri 0800-2000, Sat 0800-1630. Lovely food using fresh produce from Irente Farm in Lushoto – cakes, home-made jam, cheese and tea. Healthy breakfasts, and light meals include omelettes, carrot and lentil soup and quiche. Try the cheese platter with apple, pickle and brown bread. Garden to sit in at the back. Outlet of St Margaret's Anglican Church. It also sells Tanzanian coffee beans and has Wi-Fi.
Tanzania Coffee Lounge, Chagga St, opposite the fruit and vegetable market, T027-275 1006. Mon-Sat 0800-2000, Sun 0800-1800. A Western-style café serving good coffees, milkshakes, juices, muffins, bagels, waffles and cakes. Also has 8 terminals for high-speed internet and is consistently popular with travellers.

● What to do

Moshi *p210, map p210*
Tour operators
It is cheaper to book tours for Kilimanjaro from Moshi than it is from either Arusha or Marangu. Like booking an organized safari in Arusha for the game parks (see box, page 259), give yourself a day or 2 in Moshi to talk to a couple of the tour operators that

arrange Kilimanjaro climbs. Find one that you like, does not pressure you too much, and accepts the method of payment of your choice. Ignore the touts on the street. You may find, if it is quiet, that the tour companies will get together and put clients on the same tour to make up numbers. All tour operators below offer Kili climbs on most of the routes and most additionally offer climbs of Mt Meru, as well as multi-day safaris to the Northern Circuit parks, such as the Serengeti, Ngorogoro, Manyara, etc, which can be organized before or to follow on from your climb. This is a far from comprehensive list. A good place to start looking for a registered tour operator is on the **Tanzania Association of Tour Operators'** website (www.tatotz.org). Most of the hotels also organize climbs, and packages usually include a night's accommodation before and after the climb. The **Keys** (see page 214), **Marangu Hotel** (see page 216), **Mountain Inn** (see page 214) and **Springlands Hotel** (see page 214) have excellent long-established reputations. Also consider **Hoopoe Safaris** (see page 260), **Nature Discovery** (see page 261) and **Tropical Trails** (see page 262) in Arusha. For an idea of costs for an organized climb, see page 11.
Akaro Tours Co Ltd, ground floor of NSSF House on Old Moshi Rd, T027-275 2986, www.akarotours.com.

Kilimanjaro Crown Birds Tours & Safaris,
based in the Kindoroka Hotel, see page 214,
T027-275 1162, www.kilicrown.com.
Kilimanjaro Serengeti Tours & Travel Ltd,
Old CCM Building, Mawenzi Rd, T027-275
1287, www.kilimanjaroserengeti.com.
Kilimanjaro Travel Services Ltd,
THB Building, Boma Rd, T027-275 2124,
www.kilimanjarotravels-tz.com.
Mauly Tours & Safaris, Boma Rd,
opposite Exim Bank, T027-275 0730,
www.mauly-tours.com.
MJ Safaris International,
CCM Building, Taifa Rd, T027-275 2017,
www.mjsafarisafrica.com.
**Moshi Expedition & Mountaineering
(MEM)**, Kaunda St, T027-275 4234,
www.memtours.com.
Shah Tours and Travels Ltd, Sekou Toure
Way (with base at the Mountain Inn Hotel,
see Where to stay, page 214), T027-275
2998, www.kilimanjaro-shah.com.
Snow Cap, CCM Building, Taifa Rd,
T027-275 4826, www.snowcap.co.tz.
**Summit Expeditions & Nomadic
Experience**, based in Marangu, T027-275
3233, www.nomadicexperience.com.
Trans-Kibo Travels Ltd, YMCA Building,
T027-275 2207, www.transkibo.com.
Zara Tanzania Adventure, at Springlands
Hotel, see page 214, T027-275 0011,
www.zaratours.com, www.kilimanjaro.co.tz.

✈ Transport

Moshi *p210, map p210*
Air
Kilimanjaro International Airport is 55 km
west of Moshi, off the A23/Arusha road,
T027-255 4252, www.kilimanjaroairport.
co.tz. It is well served by domestic flights
and some international flights. For details of
these, see page 263. A taxi from the airport
should cost around US$50 to Moshi, or you
can arrange transfers with one of the hotels
or tour operators.

Bus and dala-dala
Moshi is 80 km east of Arusha on the A23,
580 km northwest of Dar es Salaam and
349 km southeast of Nairobi (Kenya). Local
buses and *dala-dala* to nearby destinations
such as **Marangu** and **Arusha** cost little
more than US$3 and go from the stand just
to the south of the main bus stand, which
are both on Market St. Those who organize
a Kili climb in Moshi will be transferred to
the park gates by their tour operator.

There are countless departures each day
to **Dar**, around US$15 'deluxe' and US$10
'semi-luxury', which take about 7 hrs and
stop for 20 mins at one of the roadside
restaurants in **Mombo** or **Korogwe** en
route. Both **Dar Express**, Boma Rd opposite
the **Aroma Coffee House**, T0744-286 847,

and **Royal Coaches**, Aga Khan Rd, T027-275 0940, offer a fast, reliable service. **Scandinavia Express**, Mawenzi Rd, south of the bus station, T027-275 1387, www.scandinaviagroup.com, are recommended for reliability and safety, and, as well as daily services to **Dar**, also have a daily service to/from **Moshi** and **Mwanza**, 22 hrs, US$22, via **Arusha** and **Nairobi** (you will have to buy a transit visa for Kenya; US$20).

From the main bus stand on Market St, there are also buses to/from **Tanga** which take 4-6 hrs and cost US$7. It is also possible to get a direct bus to **Mombasa**, cost approximately US$13, 7-8 hrs. These go through the Taveta border on to **Voi** in Kenya where they join the main road (A109) from Nairobi to Mombasa (see box, page 212).

Take lots of care at the bus stands in Moshi as pickpocketing is rife and you need to protect your belongings. On arrival, its best just to jump straight in a taxi as soon as you get off the bus. The hustlers, who try to get people on to their buses, can be particularly annoying too.

To Kenya There are several through shuttle services to **Nairobi** via Arusha and the Namanga border, see box page 237, which leave Moshi at around 0630 and 1100 daily, US$40, and can be booked through hotels or tour operators. These include **Impala Shuttle**, Kibo Rd, T027-275 1786, www.impalashuttle.com, and **Riverside Shuttle**, THB House, T027-275 0093, www.riverside-shuttle.com.

❶ Directory

Moshi *p210, map p210*
Medical services Kilimanjaro Christian Medical Centre (KCMC), 6 km out of town beyond Shantytown, T027-275 4383, www.kcmc.ac.tz. Mawenzi Moshi District Hospital, just north of Hill St T027-275 2321. **Police** Market St, T027-275 5055.

Kilimanjaro National Park

In The Snows of Kilimanjaro, *Ernest Hemingway described the mountain: "as wide as all the world, great, high, and unbelievably white in the sun, was the square top of Kilimanjaro." It is one of the most impressive sights in Africa, visible from as far away as Tsavo National Park in Kenya. Just 80 km east of the eastern branch of the Rift Valley, it is Africa's highest mountain, with snow-capped peaks rising from a relatively flat plain, the largest free-standing mountain worldwide, measuring 80 km by 40 km, and one of Earth's highest dormant volcanoes. At lower altitudes, the mountain is covered in lush rainforest, which gives way to scrub – there is no bamboo zone on Kilimanjaro – followed by alpine moorland until you get to the icefields. Try to see it in the early morning before the clouds mask it. Despite its altitude, even inexperienced climbers can climb it, provided they are reasonably fit and allow themselves sufficient time to acclimatize to the elevation.*

Arriving in Kilimanjaro National Park → *Colour map 1, A5.*

Getting there
Regular *dala-dalas* travel from the bus stand in Moshi the 30 km to the village of Machame (for the Machame Trail) and the 27 km to Marangu (for the Marangu Trail). They each take about 45 minutes and cost around US$3. Those who organize a Kili climb in Moshi will be transferred to the park gates by their tour operator. The hotels in Machame and Marangu will also be able to arrange an airport pickup from **Kilimanjaro International Airport**.

Climate
Kilimanjaro can be climbed throughout the year but it is worth avoiding the two rainy seasons (late Mar to mid-May and October to the beginning of December) when the routes become slippery. The best time to visit is January/February and September/October, when there is usually no cloud.

Park information
Anyone planning to climb Mount Kilimanjaro is advised to buy *Kilimanjaro: The Trekking Guide to Africa's Highest Mountain,* by Henry Steadman (Trailblazer Guides), which is full of practical information and covers preparing and equipping for the climb; much of the book's information is also available on Henry's website, www.climbmountkilimanjaro. com; *Kilimanjaro & East Africa: a Climbing and Trekking Guide,* by Cameron M Burns (Mountaineers Books), is also a useful guidebook. There are plenty of maps on the market, many of which now list GPS coordinates, and other locally produced maps and coffee-table books are available in both Moshi and Arusha. The tour operators that offer climbs have comprehensive information on their websites, as does the **Tanzania National Parks Authority (TANAPA)**, www.tanzaniaparks.com.

Altitude sickness
Altitude sickness is often a problem while climbing Kilimanjaro. If you know you are susceptible to it, you are advised not to attempt the climb. Symptoms include bad headache, nausea, vomiting and severe fatigue. It can be avoided by ascending slowly – if at all possible, spend an extra day halfway up to help your body acclimatize. Altitude sickness symptoms can often be alleviated by descending to a lower altitude. The drug Diamox

helps if taken before the ascent. Other more serious conditions include acute pulmonary oedema and/or cerebral oedema. In the former, the sufferer becomes breathless, turns blue in the face and coughs up froth. The latter is even more serious – symptoms are intense headache, hallucinations, confusion and disorientation and staggering gait. It is caused by the accumulation of fluid on the brain and can cause death or serious brain damage. If either of these conditions are suspected, the sufferer should immediately be taken down to a lower altitude to receive medical care. It is, however, normal to feel breathless and fatigued at high altitudes and these are not always precursors to the more serious conditions.

Guides

A guide is compulsory on all routes; it is essential to go with a tour operator that will supply not only guides but porters and relevant equipment (see Moshi tour operators, page 218). Marangu is the usual route for tourists, and only fit and experienced hikers or climbers should use the other routes.

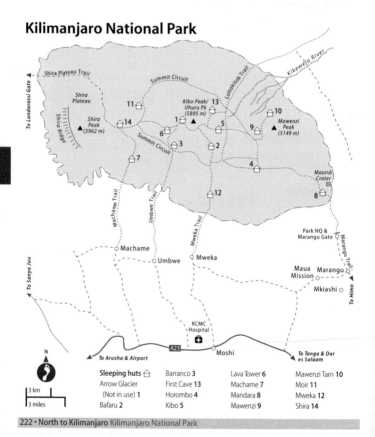

Kilimanjaro National Park

Sleeping huts
Arrow Glacier (Not in use) 1
Bafaru 2
Barranco 3
First Cave 13
Horombo 4
Kibo 5
Lava Tower 6
Machame 7
Mandara 8
Mawenzi 9
Mawenzi Tarn 10
Moir 11
Mweka 12
Shira 14

Tipping on Kilimanjaro

On the last day of the tour your guide will request a tip for himself and his cook and porters. Tipping is more or less mandatory, as a way of supplementing the low incomes of people who essentially have a remarkably physically demanding job. Porters, in particular, are very poorly paid (as little as US$10 a day) and cannot always afford the right equipment/clothes needed on the mountain. Remarkably, while you slog up, carrying just a day pack and a camera and wearing a warm waterproof jacket, it is these people that scuttle past you carrying luggage, gas bottles, chairs, full jerry cans of water and anything else needed for a comfortable hike. And they often go up and down Kili, time after time, in inadequate shoes and clothing fit only for the moderate climate at the base of the mountain where they live.

A good tour operator will have a fair tipping procedure in place or at least will be able to give advice. Many also introduce you to your team and provide an explanation of the jobs they do at the beginning of the climb – if they don't, request that they do and make a mental or written note of each individual person, so you know who to allocate tips to at the end of a climb. Generally, you should budget between 10-15% of your total climb cost for tips. However, if you feel your climb was particularly difficult or a certain person went out of his way to help you, or, on the flipside the staff were surly or weren't as helpful as they should have been, then this should be reflected in the tipping. Tip amounts listed are per group, not per trekker/client, so always try to come to an agreement with other members of the group and put the tip into a common kitty. If you are climbing in a small group, you should contribute more per person to the kitty. Very roughly allow US$15-30 per day for the head guide; US$10-20 per day for the assistant guide (those members of the team that accompany you along with the head guide on the final leg to Kibo/Uhuru Peak are considered assistant guides); US$8-12 per day for the cook; and US$4-10 per day per porter (some porters have extra jobs such as toilet cleaner, camp crew and waiter, so you may want to tip them a bit more). From the common kitty, the group should always hand out tips individually to the trekking team to ensure that the money goes to the person it's intended for (unscrupulous guides have been known to take 'commission' from the tips intended for porters, for example). You may want to have small denomination US$/TSh notes for this purpose.

For more information about the importance of tipping on Kilimanjaro, and for recommendations of responsible tour operators, visit the websites of the **Kilimanjaro Porters Assistance Project**, www.kiliporters.org, or the **African Ascent Project**, www.africanascentproject.com. (Both of these are committed to improving the working conditions of porters on Kili, including programmes to lend suitable equipment to porters). Something else to consider is that you won't need much 'stuff' on the mountain – you'll be wearing most of it anyway – and porters are limited to 20 kg of trekkers' packs and 5 kg of their own things. Kili is a hard slog for anyone – imagine what it's like climbing it over and over again with 25 kg on your back? Keep it light and leave the bulk of your luggage at a hotel. Finally, if you're never going to climb a big mountain again, think about making gifts of your specialist clothing and gear to your trekking team; it is after all these people who were responsible for your welfare on the mountain and (hopefully) got you to the top.

Equipment

Being well equipped will increase your chances of reaching the summit. In particular, be sure you have a warm sleeping bag, insulating mat, warm rainproof jacket, thermal underwear, gloves, wool hat, sunglasses or snow goggles, sun cream, large water bottle and first-aid kit. Some of these are available to buy or hire in Moshi from the tour operators. However, the quality is variable and it is best to come fully prepared. As regards clothing, it is important to wear layers as they provide better insulation than bulkier items, and sturdy, waterproof hiking boots should be well worn-in. Other essential items include a small daypack for things you'll need during the day – porters carry your main pack but tend to go on ahead by some distance – a head torch and spare batteries (essential for the final midnight ascent), toilet roll, and you may want to consider a light weight trekking pole. Energy snacks are also a good idea.

Costs

Climbing Mount Kilimanjaro is an expensive business, though everyone who makes it to the summit agrees that it is well worth it. The costs are much higher than those in the Alps or the Andes. Park fees alone, charged by **Tanzania National Parks**, are US$60 per person per 24 hours; add to this camping or hut fees of US$50 per person per day (whether you use the huts or not), a rescue fee insurance of US$20 per person, guides at US$20 per day, cooks US$15 per day and porters US$10 per day per 20 kg of luggage. These are the set fees that the tour operator must pay on your behalf to Tanzania National Parks and can amount to over US$900 for a six-day trip, though while everyone needs a porter, costs come down if a group are sharing a guide and cook. On top of this, other costs for the tour operators include the salaries of the guides and porters, the additional 20% VAT on the total invoice, 10% commission if booking through a third party travel agent, transport to the start of the trail, food and the costs of equipment. The absolute cheapest you will probably manage to do it for will be around US$1280 for the five-day Marangu Route. An extra day on this route (recommended) brings it up to about US$2010 per person. The other more technical or longer climbs are US$1575 or more.

Background

Formation

Kilimanjaro was formed about one million years ago by a series of volcanic movements along the Great Rift Valley. Until this point, the area was a flat plain at about 600-900 m above sea level. About 750,000 years ago volcanic activity forced three points above 4800 m – Shira, Kibo/Uhuru and Mawenzi. Some 250,000 years later Shira became inactive and collapsed into itself forming the crater. Kibo and Mawenzi continued their volcanic activity, and it was their lava flow that forms the 11-km saddle between the two peaks. When Mawenzi died out, its northeast wall collapsed in a huge explosion creating a massive gorge. The last major eruptions occurred about 200 years ago; Kibo now lies dormant but not extinct. Although Kibo appears to be a snow-clad dome, it contains a caldera 2.5 km across and 180 m deep at the deepest point in the south. Within the depression is an inner ash cone that rises to within 60 m of the summit height and is evidence of former volcanic activity. On the southern slopes the glaciers reach down to about 4200 m, while on the north slopes they only descend a little below the summit.

The meaning of Kilimanjaro

Since the earliest explorers visited East Africa, people have been intrigued by the name Kilimanjaro and its meaning. The Chagga people do not have a name for the whole mountain, just the two peaks: *Kibo* (or kipoo) means 'spotted' and refers to the rock that can be seen standing out against the snow on this peak; *Mawenzi* (or Kimawenze) means 'having a broken top' and again describes its appearance.

Most theories as to the origin of the name Kilimanjaro for the whole mountain break the word down into two elements: *kilima* and *njaro*. In Swahili the word for mountain is *mlima*, while *kilima* means hill – so it is possible that an early European visitor incorrectly used *kilima* because of its similarity to the two Chagga words Kibo and Kimawenzi.

The explorer Krapf said that the Swahili of the coast knew it as Kilimanjaro 'mountain of greatness', but he does not explain why. He also suggests it could mean 'mountain of caravans' (*kilima* = mountain, *jaro* = caravans), but while *kilima* is a Swahili word, *jaro* is a Chagga word. Other observers have suggested that *njaro* once meant 'whiteness' and therefore this was the 'mountain of whiteness'. Alternatively, *njaro* could be the name of an evil spirit, or a demon. The first-known European to climb Mount Kilimanjaro mentions 'Njaro, the guardian

spirit of the mountain', and there are many stories in Chagga folklore about spirits living here – though there is no evidence of a spirit called Njaro, either from the Chagga or from the coastal peoples.

Another explanation suggests that the mountain was known as 'mountain of water', because of the Masai word *njore* for springs or water and because all the rivers in the area rose from here. However, this theory does not explain the use of the Swahili word for 'hill' rather than 'mountain', and also assumes that a Swahili word and a Masai word have been put together.

The final explanation is from a Kichagga term *kilelema* meaning that 'which has become difficult or impossible' or 'which has defeated'. Njaro can be derived from the Kichagga words *njaare*, a bird, or else *jyaro*, a caravan. Thus the mountain became *kilemanjaare*, *kilemajyaro* or *kilelemanjaare*, meaning that which defeats or is impossible for the bird or the caravan. This theory has the advantage of being composed entirely of Chagga elements.

It seems possible either that this was the name given to the mountain by the Chagga themselves, or by people passing through the area, who heard the Chagga say *kilemanjaare* or *kilemajyaro*, meaning that the mountain was impossible to climb. Over time the name was standardized to Kilimanjaro.

Vegetation and wildlife

Kilimanjaro has well-defined altitudinal vegetation zones. From the base to the summit these are: plateau, semi-arid scrub; cultivated, well-watered southern slopes; dense cloud forest; open moorland; alpine desert; moss and lichen. The lower slopes are home to elephant, rhino, buffalo, leopard, monkey and eland. Birdlife includes the enormous lammergeyer, the scarlet-tufted malachite sunbird, as well as various species of starlings, sunbirds, the silvery-cheeked hornbill and the rufous-breasted sparrowhawk.

History

When, in 1848, the first reports by the German missionary Johannes Rebmann of a snow-capped mountain on the equator arrived in Europe, the idea was ridiculed by the

The snow sepulchre of King Solomon

Legend has it that the last military adventure of King Solomon was an expedition down the eastern side of Africa. Exhausted by his battles, the aged king was trekking home with his army when they passed the snow-covered Mount Kilimanjaro. Solomon decided this was to be his resting place. The next day he was carried by bearers until they reached the snows. As they steadily trudged up to the summit, they saw a cave glittering in the sunlight, frost sparkling in the interior, icicles hanging down to close off the entrance. As they watched, two icicles, warmed by the sun, crashed to the ground. They carried the old king inside and placed him on his throne, wrapped in his robes, facing out down the mountain. Solomon raised a frail hand to bid farewell. The bearers left with heavy hearts. The weather began to change and there was a gentle fall of snow. As they looked back they saw that icicles had reformed over the entrance.

Royal Geographical Society of Britain. In 1889 the report was confirmed by the German geographer Hans Meyer and the Austrian alpine mountaineer Ludwig Purtscheller, who climbed Kibo and managed to reach the snows on Kilimanjaro's summit. At the centenary of this climb in 1989, their Tanzanian guide was still alive and 115 years old. Mawenzi was first climbed by the German Fritz Klute in 1912.

The mountain was originally in a part of British East Africa (now Kenya). However, the mountain was 'given' by Queen Victoria as a gift to her cousin, and so the border was moved and the mountain included within German Tanganyika. This is why if you look at a map of the border between Tanzania and Kenya, Tanzania juts into Kenya to include Kilimanjaro on the otherwise dead straight border drawn up by the colonialists. The national park was established in 1973 and covers an area of 756 sq km.

Routes up the mountain

About 22,000 climbers attempt to get to the top of Kilimanjaro each year. The altitude at Marangu Gate is 1829 m and at Kibo/Uhuru Peak 5895 m – that's a long way up. Officially anyone aged over 12 may attempt the climb. The youngest person to climb the mountain was a 10-year-old, while the oldest was 79. However, it is not that easy, and estimates of the number of people who attempt the climb and do not make it to the top vary from 20 to 50%. The important things to remember are to come prepared and to take it slowly – if you have the chance, spend an extra day halfway up to give you the chance to acclimatize.

There are a number of different trails. The most popular is the Marangu trail, which is the recommended route for older persons or younger people who are not in peak physical condition. Even on this trail, the climbing tends to be much more strenuous than anticipated, which when combined with lower oxygen levels, accounts for the 20 to 50% failure rate to reach the summit.

The Marangu trail is the only one that uses hutted dorm accommodation. On the other routes, even though the campsites are called huts this actually refers to the green shacks. Some of these have fallen into disuse or are usually inhabited by the park rangers on the lower slopes, they are also sometimes used by the guides and porters. Trekkers are accommodated in tents carried and set up by the porters.

Marangu trail

This is probably the least scenic of the routes but it is the gentlest climb and has a crop of hotels at the beginning in Marangu and hutted accommodation on the way up. It is therefore the most popular.

Day 1 The national park gate (1830 m) is about 5 km north of the village of **Marungu**, along a road where most of the hotels are located. This is as far as vehicles are allowed. From here to the first night's stop at **Mandara Hut** (2700 m) is a walk of three to four hours. It is through *shambas* – small farms growing coffee – as well as some lush rainforest, and is an enjoyable walk, although it can be quite muddy. On the walk you can admire the moss and lichens and the vines and flowers, including orchids. There is an alternative forest trail, which branches left from the main track a few minutes after the gate and follows the side of a stream. It is a little slower than the main track, which it rejoins after about three hours. The Mandara Hut, near the Maundi Crater, is actually a group of A-frame huts that can sleep about 60 people. Mattresses, solar lighting and stoves are provided but nothing else. The complex was built by the Norwegians as part of an aid programme. There is piped water, flushing toilets and firewood available, and a dining area in the main cabin.

Day 2 The second day will start off as a steep walk through the last of the rainforest and out into tussock grassland, giant heather and then on to the moorlands, crossing several ravines on the way. There are occasional clearings through which you will get wonderful views of Mawenzi and Moshi far below. You can also enjoy the views by making a short detour up to the rim of Maundi Crater. You will probably see some of the exceptional vegetation that is found on Kilimanjaro, including the giant lobelia, Kilimanjaro's 'everlasting flowers', and other uncommon alpine plants. The walk to **Horombo Hut** (3720 m) is about 14 km, with an altitude gain of about 1000 m, and will take you five to seven hours. This hut is, again, a collection of huts that can accommodate up to 120 people. There are flushing toilets and plenty of water but firewood is scarce. Some people spend an extra day here to help get acclimatized and, if you are doing this, there are a number of short walks in the area but remember to move slowly, drink plenty of water and get lots of sleep. It is a very good idea to spend the extra day here – but there is the extra cost to be considered.

Day 3/4 On the next day of walking you will climb to the **Kibo Hut** (4703 m) or Mawenzi Hut, which is 13 km from Horombo. As you climb, the vegetation thins to grass and heather and eventually to bare scree. You will feel the air thinning, and it is at this altitude that altitude sickness may kick in. The most direct route is the right fork from Horombo Hut. It is stony and eroded, a climb of six to seven hours up the valley behind the huts, past **Last Water** and on to the **saddle**. This is the wide, fairly flat U-shaped desert between the two peaks of Mawenzi and Kibo; from here you will get some awe-inspiring views of the mountain. After **Zebra Rocks** and at the beginning of the saddle, the track forks. To the right, about three hours from Horombo Hut, is **Mawenzi Hut** and to the left across the saddle is Kibo Hut. The left fork from Horombo Hut is gentler and comes out on to the saddle 1 km from Kibo Hut. Kibo Hut is where the porters stay, so from here on you should just take the absolute bare essentials with you. It is a good idea to bring some biscuits or chocolate for the final ascent to the peak, as a lunch pack is not always provided. Mawenzi Hut sleeps about 60 people. There is a stone-built main block with a small dining room and several dormitory rooms with bunks and mattresses. There is no vegetation in the area and no water, unless there has been snow recently, so it has to be carried up from Last Water. However, the camp does sell bottled water and soft drinks but they are understandably expensive. Some people decide to try and get as much sleep as possible before the early start, while others decide not to sleep at all. You are unlikely to sleep very well because of the altitude and the temperatures anyway.

Day 4/5 On the final day of the climb, in order to be at the summit at sunrise, and before the cloud comes down, you will have to get up at about midnight. One advantage of beginning at this time is that if you saw what you were about to attempt, you would probably give up before you had even begun. You can expect to feel pretty awful during this final five-hour ascent, and many climbers are physically sick. You may find that this climb is extremely slippery and hard going. The first part of the climb is over an uneven trail to **Hans Meyer Cave**. As the sun rises, you will reach **Gillman's Point** (5680 m) – it is a wonderful sight. From here you have to decide whether you want to keep going another couple of hours to get to **Kibo/Uhuru Peak** (5895 m). The walk around the crater rim to Kibo Peak is only an extra 200 m but at this altitude it is a strenuous 200 m. At the peak there is a fair amount of litter left by previous climbers. You will return to **Horombo Hut** the same day, and the next day (**Day 5/6**) return to Marangu, where you will be presented with a certificate.

Mweka trail
This trail is the most direct route up the mountain. It is the steepest and the fastest. It begins at Mweka Village, 13 km north of Moshi.

Day 1 The first day's walk takes six to eight hours. The trail follows an old logging road, which you can drive up in good weather, through the *shambas* and the forest, for about 5 km. It is a slippery track that deteriorates into a rough path after a couple of hours. From here it is about 6 km up a ridge to the **Mweka Huts** (3100 m) where you camp; they are some 500 m beyond the tree line in the giant heather zone. Water is available nearby from a stream in a small valley below the huts, five minutes to the southeast, and there is plenty of firewood. There are no toilets.

Day 2 From the Mweka Huts follow the ridge east of the Msoo River through heathland, open tussock grassland and then on through alpine desert to the **Barafu Huts** (4400 m), a walk of six to eight hours. There are no toilets and no water or firewood available – you will need to bring it up from Mweka Huts.

Day 3/4 From the Barafu Huts the final ascent, on a ridge between **Rebmann** and **Ratzel** glaciers takes about six hours up to the rim of the crater between **Stella** and **Hans Meyer Points**. From here it is a further hour to **Kibo/Uhuru Peak**. At the lower levels the path is clearly marked, but it becomes obscured further up. It is steep, being the most direct non-technical route. Although specialized climbing equipment is not needed, be prepared for a scramble. To catch the sunrise you will have to set off no later than 0200 from Barafu Huts. You return to the huts the same day, and make the final descent the next day (**Day 4**).

Umbwe trail
The climb is hard, short and steep but is a wonderfully scenic route to take to reach **Kibo/Uhuru Peak**. However, it is not recommended for inexperienced climbers. Many climbers descend this way after climbing up by a different route. To get to the start of the trail, take

the turning off the Arusha road about 2 km down on the right. From there it's 14 km down the Lyamungu Road, right at the T-junction towards Mango and, soon after crossing the Sere River, you get to **Umbwe** village (1400 m).

Day 1 ⓘ *Umbwe to Bivouac I, 4-6 hrs' walk.* From Umbwe village, the track continues through smallholding farms for about 6 km before you get to the start of the trail proper. There is a sign here, and the trail branches to the left and climbs quite steeply through the rainforest along the ridge between the Lonzo River to the west and Umbwe River to the east. In several places it is necessary to use branches to pull yourself up. You will reach the first shelter, a cave, about six to eight hours' walk from Umbwe. This is **Bivouac I** (2940 m), an all-weather rock shelter formed from the rock overhangs. It will shelter about six or seven people. There is firewood nearby and a spring about 15 m below under a rock face.

If you made an early start and are fit and keen, you can continue on to **Bivouac II** on the same day. However, most climbers take an overnight break here, camping in the forest caves.

Day 2 ⓘ *Bivouac I to Barranco Hut, 5 km, 4-5 hrs' walk.* From the caves, continue up, past the moorland and along the ridge. It is a steep but magnificent walk, with deep valleys on each side of the ridge and the strange 'old man's beard' – a type of moss – covering most of the vegetation. The second set of caves is **Bivouac II** (3800 m), three to four hours from Bivouac I. There are two caves – one about five minutes further down the track (you can camp here). There is a spring down the ravine about 15 minutes to the west.

From the second set of caves, the path continues less steeply up the ridge beyond the tree line before reaching **Barranco** or **Umbwe Hut** (3900 m). Barranco Hut is about five hours away from the first caves or two hours from Bivouac II. The path is well marked. About 200 m beyond the hut is a rock overhang, which can be used for camping. There is one pit latrine, water is available about 250 m to the east and firewood is available in the area. Some people may choose to spend an extra day at Barranco Hut to acclimatize to the altitude.

Day 3/4 ⓘ *Barranco Hut to Lava Tower Hut, 3-4 hrs' walk.* Just before reaching Barranco Hut, the path splits in two. To the left, the path goes west towards **Shira Hut** (five to six hours) and the northern circuit, or you can climb the west lateral ridge to the **Arrow Glacier Hut** (now defunct after it was buried in an avalanche) towards the **Lava Tower Hut** (4600 m), about three to four hours away. Up this path the vegetation thins before disappearing completely on reaching the scree slopes. The campsite at Lava Tower Hut is very barren and there is no shelter, so you need to be prepared for the extreme cold. There are no toilets, but water is available in a nearby stream.

Day 4/5 ⓘ *Lava Tower Hut to Kibo/Uhuru Peak, 4-6 hrs' walk.* Having spent the night at Lava Tower Hut, you will want to leave very early for the final ascent. Head torches are imperative and, if there is no moonlight, the walk can be quite difficult. Climb up between **Arrow Glacier** (which may have disappeared completely if you are there towards the end of the dry season) and **Little Breach Glacier** until you get to a few small cliffs. At this stage the course follows the Western Breach summit route and turns to the right heading for the lowest part of the crater rim that you can see. This part of the walk is really steep on scree and snow, and parts of it are quite a scramble. From December to February, crampons and ice axes are recommended. Having reached the crater floor, cross the **Furtwangler Glacier**

snout to a steep gully that reaches the summit plateau about another 500 m west of **Kibo/ Uhuru Peak** (5895 m), returning to **Mweka Hut**, among the giant heathers on the Mweka trail, for an overnight stop.

Day 5/6 ① *Descent from Mweka Hut to Mweka Gate, 14 km, 5-7 hrs' walk*. The return journey can be achieved in approximately half the ascending time.

Umbwe trail – alternative route
Day 3/4 ① *Barranco Hut to Bafaru Hut, 5 km, 4-5 hrs' walk*. The route is well marked at lower levels but not at higher altitudes. If you take the path to the right from **Barranco Hut** (eastwards on the southern circuit) you will cross one small stream and then another larger one as you contour the mountain to join the **Mweka trail**. The path then climbs steeply through a gap in the **West Breach**. From here you can turn left to join the routes over the south glaciers. Alternatively, continue along the marked path across screes, ridges and a valley until you reach the **Karangu Campsite**, which is a further two to three hours on from the top of the Breach. A further couple of hours up the **Karangu valley** (4000 m) will come out at the **Mweka-Barafu Hut** path. If you go left down along this, you will get to the **Barafu Hut** after one to 1½ hours. If you go straight on for about three hours, you will join the Marangu trail just above the **Horombo Hut**.

Day 4/5 ① *Barafu Hut to Kibo/Uhuru Peak to Mweka Hut, 5-6 hrs' walk to crater rim plus another hour to Uhuru Peak*. Parties heading for the summit set off around midnight to 0100, reaching the crater at Stella Point. If the weather conditions are favourable, **Kibo/ Uhuru Peak** (5895 m) is normally reached by first light. From here it is often possible to see the summit of Mount Meru to the west. Descend to **Mweka Hut** for an overnight stop.

Day 5/6 ① *Descent from Mweka Hut to Mweka Gate, 14 km, 5-7 hrs' walk*.

Machame trail
This trail is considered by some to be the most attractive of the routes up Kilimanjaro. It is between Umbwe trail and Shira trail and joins the latter route at Shira Hut. The turn-off to the trail and the village of Machame is to the west of Umbwe, off the main Arusha–Moshi road.

Day 1 From the village to the first huts takes about nine hours, so be sure to start early. Take the track through the *shambas* and the forest to the park entrance (about 4 km), from where you will see a clear track that climbs gently through the forest and along a ridge that is between the Weru Weru and Makoa streams. It is about 7 km to the edge of the forest, and then four to five hours up to the **Machame Huts** (3000 m), where you camp. There are pit latrines and plenty of water down in the valley below the huts, and firewood is available close by.

Day 2 From the Machame Huts go across the valley, over a stream, then up a steep ridge for three to four hours. The path then goes west and drops into the river gorge before climbing more gradually up the other side and on to the moorland of the Shira Plateau to join the Shira Plateau trail near the **Shira Hut** (3800 m). This takes about five hours. From the Shira Plateau you will get some magnificent views of Kibo/Uhuru Peak and the Western Breach. The area is home to a variety of game including buffalo. The campsite at the Shira Hut is used by people on the Shira Plateau trail, as well as those on the Machame trail. There is plenty of water available 50 m to the north and firewood nearby, but no toilets.

Day 3 onwards From here there are a number of choices. You can go on to the **Barranco Hut** (five to six hours, 3900 m) or the **Lava Tower Hut** (four hours, 4600 m). The path is well marked. The ascent includes scrambling over scree, rocks and snow fields – tough at times and probably only suited to experienced hikers. It goes east from Shira Hut until it reaches a junction where the North Circuit route leads off to the left. The path continues east, crossing a wide valley before turning southeast towards the Lava Tower. Shortly before the tower a route goes off to the right to Barranco Hut and the South Circuit route. To the left the path goes to **Arrow Glacier Hut** (not in use) and the Western Breach.

Shira Plateau trail
This route needs a 4WD vehicle and so, for this reason, is little used. The road can be impassible during wet periods. However, if you do have access to such a vehicle and are acclimatized, you can get to the **Arrow Glacier Hut** in one day.

The drive is a complex one and you may need to stop and ask the way frequently. Pass through West Kilimanjaro, drive for 5 km and turn right. At 13 km you will pass a small trading centre on the left. At 16 km you will cross a stream followed by a hard left. At 21 km you will enter a coniferous forest which soon becomes a natural forest. The plateau rim is reached at 39 km. Here the track continues upwards gently and crosses the plateau to the roadhead at 55 km. Just before the roadhead, about 19 km from **Londorossi Gate**, is a rock shelter. This site is suitable for camping and there is a stream nearby. From the roadhead you will have to walk. It is about 1½ hours to **Shira Hut** (3800 m). From here you continue east to join the Umbwe trail to the **Lava Tower Hut**. The walk is fairly gentle and has magnificent views.

Loitokitok trail
This, and the Shira Plateau trail, both come in from the north, unlike the other trails. It used to start on the Kenya border and was known as the Rongai trail (and is still today confusingly referred to as that) but the start has been shifted eastward to start in Tanzania from the village of Loitokitok and it has been renamed. You register at the Marangu Gate and then operators transfer you to the village and the trail head, which takes about 2½ hours.

The first part of the trail crosses maize fields and then a pine plantation and is not very steep. Beyond is heather and moorlands until you reach **First Cave** (2600 m), where you camp. It is a total of approximately five to six hours or 8 km to the caves from the trail head.

From these caves follow the path that heads towards a point just to the right of the lowest point on the saddle. You will pass **Bread Rock** after about 1½ hours. The track then divides. To the right is the **Outward Bound Hut** that you will almost certainly find locked. The path continues upwards to the saddle towards the **Kibo Huts** – a climb of three to four hours. To the left another path crosses towards the **Mawenzi Hut**.

The Summit Circuit
A route around the base of Kibo, the Summit Circuit links Horombo, Barranco, Shira and Moir Huts. The southern section of the circuit is most spectacular, as it cuts across moorland, in and out of valleys and under the southern glaciers.

Contents

Footprint features

Border crossings

At a glance

⊖ **Getting around** The centre's easily walkable (but not at night), and *dala-dalas*, buses and taxis are all over the town. Tour operators can help you trek Mt Meru or explore Arusha National Park.

● **Time required** 1-2 days to sort out safari arrangements and see the town, another day for a trip around the National Park, 3 days to climb Mt Meru and 1 day to recover.

☼ **Weather** Mostly warm and sunny, but Mt Meru can be tough in the rainy season from end of Mar-May and the summit, at over 4000 m, can be cold at any time of year.

✕ **When not to go** The city is accessible all year. You may want to avoid Mt Meru in rainy season, when the climb can be hard-going, slippery and sometimes dangerous.

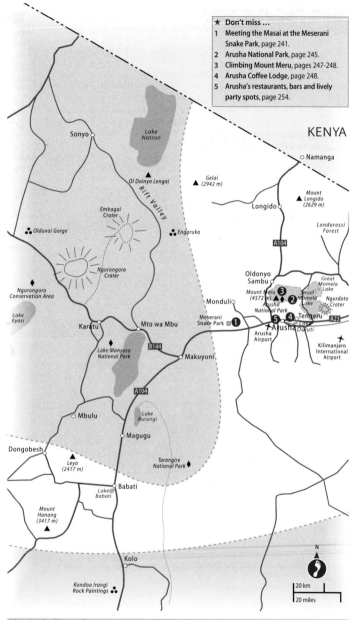

★ Don't miss ...
1 Meeting the Masai at the Meserani
   Snake Park, page 241.
2 Arusha National Park, page 245.
3 Climbing Mount Meru, pages 247-248.
4 Arusha Coffee Lodge, page 248.
5 Arusha's restaurants, bars and lively
   party spots, page 254.

KENYA

Sonyo

Lake
Natron

Ol Doinyo Lengai

Gelai
(2942 m)

Namanga

Mount
Longido
(2629 m)

Longido

Rift Valley

Londorossi
Forest

Embagai
Crater

Engaruka

Olduvai Gorge

Ngorongoro
Crater

Oldonyo
Sambu

Great
Momela
Lake

Ngorongoro
Conservation Area

Monduli

Lake
Eyasi

Karatu

Mto wa Mbu

Meserani
Snake Park 1

Mount Meru
(4572 m)

3

Arusha
National Park

Small
Momela
Lake

2

4

Tengeru

Ngurdoto
Crater

A23

Lake
Duluti

Kilimanjaro
International
Airport

5

Arusha

Arusha
Airport

B144

Lake Manyara
National Park

Makuyuni

A104

Mbulu

Lake
Burungi

Magugu

Dongobesh

Leya
(2417 m)

Tarangire
National Park

Babati

Lake
Babati

Mount
Hanang
(3417 m)

Kolo

Kondoa Irangi
Rock Paintings

N

20 km

20 miles

In the northern highlands of Tanzania, beneath the twin peaks of Mount Meru and Mount Kilimanjaro, Arusha is the safari capital of the country. It is a pleasant town, set at an altitude of 1380 m above sea level, and is the halfway point between Cairo and Cape Town (the actual point is in a field 20 km or so to the south of town). The drive up from Dar es Salaam to Arusha passes through the semi-arid grass plains, gradually becoming greener, more cultivated and more heavily populated; Mount Meru, in the Arusha National Park, appears on the right with its fertile, cultivated slopes. Built by the Germans as a centre of colonial administration in the early 20th century, Arusha was a sleepy town with a garrison stationed at the old boma and a few shops around a grassy roundabout. But from its backwater status amidst the farmlands and plantations of northern Tanzania, Arusha has today been transformed into one of the busiest Tanzanian towns after Dar es Salaam. Its prominence has particularly increased in recent years, since becoming the headquarters of the East African Community and being the host town for the Rwandan War Crimes Tribunals. The International Conference Centre has witnessed the signing of some of the most important peace treaties and international agreements in modern African history. Arusha is also the starting point for safaris in the north of Tanzania to the Serengeti, Ngorongoro, Lake Manyara, Tarangire, Olduvai Gorge and Arusha national parks. It can be very busy with tourists, mostly either in transit to, or returning from, these attractions. The dusty streets are filled with 4WD game-viewing vehicles negotiating potholed roads and Masai warriors in full regalia mingling with tourists clad in crisp khaki. There are lots of good hotels and restaurants, and tourism has made Arusha a very prosperous town.

Arriving in Arusha → *Colour map 1, A4. 3°20'S 36°40'E. Phone code: 027. Population: 1,300,000. Altitude: 1380 m.*

Getting there

Arusha is 80 km from Moshi and 650 km from Dar es Salaam. **Kilimanjaro International Airport** ① *off the A23/Moshi road, T027-255 4252, www.kilimanjaroairport.co.tz*, is 40 km east of Arusha and 55 km west of Moshi, and is well served by domestic flights and some international flights. If you fly into Kilimanjaro International Airport with **Precision Air**, their shuttle buses will meet the incoming flights and charge around US$10 to Arusha. Passengers travelling with other airlines will have to get a taxi for about US$50, or can arrange to be picked up or dropped off by one of the hotels, lodges or safari companies. The Nairobi–Arusha–Moshi shuttle buses also call in at the airport (see Kenya–Tanzania shuttle services box, page 15). Closer to town is the smaller **Arusha Airport**, 10 km west along the road to Dodoma. This is mostly used for charter flights and scheduled services operated by **Air Excel**, **Coastal Air**, **Regional Air** and **ZanAir**.

The road between Dar es Salaam and Arusha has recently been upgraded and is now smooth tar all the way. The journey by bus takes eight to nine hours. It is also only 273 km south of Nairobi, with the Namanga border with Kenya being roughly halfway. The two cities are linked by regular shuttle buses (see box, opposite) and the journey normally takes around 5½ hours. ▸▸ *For further details, see Transport, page 263.*

Getting around

The town is in two parts, separated by a small valley through which the Naura River runs. The upper part, to the east, contains the government buildings, post office, most of the top-range hotels, safari companies, airline offices, curio and craft shops, and the huge Arusha International Conference Centre (AICC), which is on East Africa Community Road (Barabara ya Afrika Mashariki). This road used to be called Simeon Road; the name Simeon Road has now been given to the road further east that links Old Moshi Road and the Nairobi–Moshi Road, near the Impala Hotel (formerly Nyerere Road). This can be quite confusing when reading local maps. Further down the hill and across the valley to the east are the commercial and industrial areas, the market, small shops, many of the budget hotels and the bus stations. In the middle of the centre is the clock tower and roundabout. From here, Sokoine Road neatly bisects the town to the west and continues further out of town to become the main road that goes to both Dodoma and the parks of the northern circuit. To the southeast of the clock tower is Old Moshi Road, along which some of the better hotels are located. *Dala-dala* run frequently up and down the main throroughfares, costing US$0.30, taxis are everywhere and should cost little more than US$3-4 for a short journey around town.

Safety

Alas safety is becoming an increasing concern in Arusha and muggings have become more common. Taxis are advised at night, and extra caution should be taken around the market and bus station, where pickpockets (especially street children) are common. If you are in a vehicle, ensure that it is securely locked.

Tourist information

Information for tourists on Arusha and the surrounding attractions can be obtained from the following places. The **Tanzanian Tourist Board** ① *Information Centre, 47E Boma Rd,*

Border crossing: Tanzania–Kenya

Namanga

Namanga is the busiest border between Tanzania and Kenya and is open 24 hours. It is 108 km north of Arusha and 162 km south of Nairobi on a newly tarred road. Immigration and customs are quick and efficient. Visas for both Kenya and Tanzania can be bought in US dollars, UK pounds or euro cash. Remember you don't need to get another visa to return to Kenya if you've only been to Tanzania (and vice versa). If you are on a safari, or using one of the daily shuttle bus services between Nairobi and Arusha and Moshi (see page 15), then the drivers/guides will assist with all border procedures.

If you are in your own vehicle, you need to show your Carnet de Passage, or for a car registered in Kenya or Tanzania, the registration document, and you'll be issued with a temporary import permit. You will also be required to take out third party insurance for either Kenya or Tanzania; the insurance companies have kiosks on both sides of the border.

You are advised to take great care if changing money on the black market (which is illegal in both Kenya and Tanzania), as there are many scams practised at this border. If going to Kenya, there's a branch of **Kenya Commercial Bank**, with an ATM, about 500 m from the border on the Kenyan side or wait until you get to a bank in either Nairobi or Arusha.

T027-250 3402/3, www.tanzaniatouristboard.com, Mon-Fri 0800-1600, Sat 0830-1330, is a useful source of local information and holds a list of registered tour companies as well as a 'blacklist' of rogue travel agencies (see page 259). They also provide copies of 'The official Arusha City Map', which has the latest street names (see above).

The **Tanzania Cultural Tourism Programme** office ① *T027-205 0025, www.tanzania culturaltourism.com, Mon-Fri 0800-1600, Sat 0830-1330*, is at the National Natural History Museum on Boma Road (see page 240). These projects were set up in conjunction with SNV, the Netherlands Development Agency, and the office has leaflets outlining the different initiatives, which directly involve and benefit the local people. It is best to make reservations and arrangements here before going out to the individual locations (which you can also do at the Tanzanian Tourist Board office, above). To date, this initiative has involved 28 villages around Arusha, Kilimanjaro, Iringa, Pangani, Mbeya and other regions. These programmes are an excellent way to experience traditional customs, music and dance and modern ways of life in rural areas. They tend to be off the beaten track, giving a very different tourist experience. An example is the **Usambara Mountains Cultural Tourism Programme** (see page 204). The tours offered by each programme have been described by one traveller as relatively expensive but worth the cost. See page 242, for the ones in the immediate region.

Ngorongoro Conservation Authority Information Office ① *Boma Rd, T027-254 4625, www.ngorongorocrater.org, Mon-Fri 0900-1700, Sat 0900-1300*, is a couple of doors along from the tourist information office. There's not much to pick up here in the way of leaflets, but it does sell some books and maps of the national parks, and there is an interesting painting on the wall that shows all the parks in the northern circuit, which gives a good idea where they all are in relation to each other. There is also a model showing the topography of the Ngorongoro Crater. The head office of **Tanzania National Parks Authority (TANAPA)** ① *Dodoma Rd, T027-250 3471, www.tanzaniaparks.com, Mon-Fri 0800-1600*, stocks booklets on the national parks at much more competitive prices than

Arusha

Where to stay 🛏
Africa Tulip **13** *D5*
Arusha **19** *C4*
Arusha Backpackers **27** *C1*
Arusha Coffee
  Lodge **2** *C1*
Arusha Crown **25** *B2*
Arusha Naaz **18** *C4*
Arusha Travel Lodge **8** *D6*
Arusha View
  Campsite **28** *B5*

Bay Leaf **6** *C6*
East African **4** *D5*
Everest Inn & Chinese
  Restaurant **1** *D5*
Flamingo **29** *C2*
Ilboru Safari Lodge **7** *A6*
Impala **11** *D6*
Karama Lodge **5** *D6*
Klub Afriko **16** *A6*
Le Jacaranda **12** *D6*
L'Oasis Lodge **14** *A6*

Masai Camp **3** *D6*
Naura Springs **31** *A4*
New Safari **21** *C4*
Onsea Country Inn
  & Guesthouse **9** *A6*
Outpost Lodge **23** *D5*
Pamoje Expeditions **30**
Palm Court **26** *C1*
Pepe One & Pepe's
  Restaurant **32** *B5*
Sinka Court **20** *C3*

Spices & Herbs & Ethiopian
Restaurant **10** *D6*

Restaurants 🍴
Blue Heron **2** *C6*
Cio Gelati **4** *D1*
Dolly's Patisserie **7** *C2*
Dragon Pearl **20** *D6*
Jambo Coffee House
& Makuti Garden **9** *C4*
McMoody's **13** *C2*

Patisserie **11** *C4*
Picasso Café **1** *D6*
Shanghai Chinese **18** *D1*
Steers **12** *C4*

Bars & clubs 🍸
Chrystal Club & Disco **24** *C3*
Colobus **26** *D6*
Empire Sports Bar **5** *D1*
Greek Club **25** *D6*
Matongee **16** *C4*

Triple A **22** *A1*
Via Via **27** *B5*

elsewhere, and is a useful resource if you require specialist information. It also provides information about the accommodation options in the more remote national parks.

There are also a couple of noticeboards with feedback bulletins from travellers at **Dolly's Patisserie** on Sokoine Road (see page 256) and the **Jambo Makuti Garden** on Boma Road (see page 255). There is a superb colour map of Arusha and the road to Moshi by Giovanni Tombazzi, which can be obtained from bookshops (see page 257) or **Hoopoe Safaris** on India Street (see page 260).

Places in Arusha

Centre

The centre of town is the **clock tower**, which was donated in 1945 by a Greek resident, Christos Galanos, to commemorate the Allied victory in the Second World War. The German Boma now houses the **National Natural History Museum** ① *north end of Boma Rd, T027-250 7540, 0900-1700, US$2.70*, opened in 1987. The building was built by the Germans in 1886 and it has an outer wall, with block towers at each corner. Inside the fortifications are a central administrative building, a captain's mess, a soldiers' mess, a guard house and a large armoury. A laboratory has been established for paleoanthropological research (study of man's evolution through the record of fossils).

The museum contains the celebrated **Laetoli Footprints**, dating back 3,500,000 years. Three hominids walking on two legs have left their tracks in solidified volcanic grey ash. The discovery was made at Laetoli, about 30 km southwest of Olduvai Gorge, by Andrew Hill, who was visiting Mary Leakey's fossil camp in 1978. Another display of interest is the tracing of the evolution of man based on the findings at Olduvai Gorge (see page 285).

The **Tanzanite Museum** ① *on the 3rd floor of the Blue Plaza Building, India St, T027-250 5101, www.tanzaniteexperience.com, Mon-Fri 0900-1600, Sat 0900-1300, free*, is nearby and explains about the history, mining and processing of tanzanite, found only in Tanzania, on the foothills of Kilimanjaro. There's a shop here where you can buy certified gems.

North of the museum, the huge **Arusha International Conference Centre (AICC)** ① *T027-250 3161, www.aicc.co.tz*, is made up of three main blocks – the Kilimanjaro, Ngorongoro and Serengeti wings. It has been an important centre for international deliberations, with recent events such as the Rwandan War Crimes Tribunal and the Burundi peace negotiations taking place here. The centre also has a bank, post office, foreign exchange bureau and cafeteria, as well as various tour operators and travel agents.

On the east side of East Africa Road, just north of the AICC complex, is the former **State House**, a small but handsome building with double gables and a green tin roof. This was the residence of the provincial commissioner in the colonial period. Nowadays it houses the Nyere Centre for Peace Research.

Old Moshi Road

In the colonial period Europeans settled in the area adjacent to the River Themi, along Old Moshi Road, and to the north and south of it. The Asian community lived near their commercial premises, often over them, in the area between Boma Road and Goliondoi Road. Africans lived further to the west on the far side of the Naura River. On the north side of the Old Moshi Road is **Christ Church Anglican Cathedral**, built in the 1930s in traditional English style of grey stone with a tiled roof and a pleasant interior. The cathedral is surrounded by a vicarage and church offices. Further along the road there are several bungalows with red tile roofs and substantial gardens. These housed government servants. One building in particular, the **Greek Club** (Hellenic Club), stands out with its classical porticos, on the corner of Old Moshi Road and Njiro Road.

Makongoro Road

The **Arusha Declaration Monument** is set on a roundabout past the police station on the Makongoro Road. Also commonly referred to as the Uhuru (Freedom) Monument, it has four concrete legs that support a brass torch at the top of a 10-m column. Around the base are seven uplifting scenes in plaster. The Declaration of 1967 outlined a socialist economic and political strategy for Tanzania. The nearby **Arusha Declaration National Museum** ① *T027-250 7800, www.arushamuseum.ac.tz, 0900-1700, US$1,* is dedicated to this landmark in Tanzania's history, outlining the evolution of Tanzania's political and economic development. It also has historic photographs of the German period and a display of traditional weapons including clubs, spears and swords. South of the museum is a small park containing the **Askari Monument**, dedicated to African soldiers who died in the Second World War. On the east side of Azimio Street is an interesting **temple**, with a portico, fretworked masonry and a moulded coping.

Arusha School

Arusha School dominates the area on the left bank of the Themi River. It is sited on sloping ground, has huge eucalyptus trees and is surrounded by a large swathe of playing fields. Nyerere's two sons were taught there. It also hosted the meeting of the Organization of African Unity (OAU) Heads of State in 1966, which included Nyerere, Obote, Kaunda, Moi (as vice president), Haile Selassie and Nasser. On the opposite side of School Road near Arusha School is the **Masai and Crafts Market**, which has a good selection of crafts and souvenirs.

Around Arusha → *For listings, see pages 248-264.*

Meserani Snake Park

① *25 km from Arusha on road to the Ngorongoro Crater and Serengeti, T027-253 8282, www.meseranisnakepark.com, 0800-1800, US$2. See also Camping, page 253.*
Meserani houses mostly local snake species, with the non-venomous snakes housed in open pits, and the spitting cobras, green and black mambas and boomslangs kept behind glass. There are other reptiles, including monitor lizards, chameleons, tortoises and crocodiles, and also a few species of birds that are orphaned or injured for whom a temporary home is provided at the park. There are gardens, a campsite, a restaurant and a bar. Run by Barry and Lynn Bale from South Africa, this project works very well with the local community and the local Masai village. Some of the snakes in the park were brought in by the local Masai, who instead of killing snakes that may harm livestock, captured and took them to the park. The Bales also provide antidote treatment for snake-bites and other basic health services for the Masai and other local communities free of charge, as well as providing antivenom for most of Tanzania. There is an excellent museum of the local Masai culture, which has mock-ups of Masai huts and models wearing various clothing and jewellery, and a Masai guide will explain the day-to-day life of the Masai. Local craftspeople sell their goods, and camel rides and treks can be arranged to meet the people in the Masai village.

Lake Duluti

Just south of the **Serena Mountain Village Hotel**, about 15 km from Arusha along the Moshi road, this small crater lake, fringed by forest, provides a sanctuary for approximately 130 species of birds, including pied and pygmy kingfishers, anhinga, osprey and several species of buzzards, eagles, sandpipers, doves, herons, cormorants, storks, kingfishers and barbets. Reptiles, including snakes and lizards, are plentiful too. The pathway around the lake starts off broad and level, but later on it narrows and becomes more difficult to negotiate. There are wonderful views of Mount Meru and, occasionally, the cloud breaks to reveal Mount Kilimanjaro. 'Ethno-botanical' walks are available, starting from the hotel through the coffee plantation and circumnavigating the lake. The walks are accompanied by guides who are knowledgeable about the flora and birds.

Cultural tourism programmes

Several villages on the lower slopes of Mount Meru, north of Arusha, have initiatives that are part of the **Tanzania Cultural Tourism Programme**. Profits from each are used to improve the local primary schools, kindergartens, clinics and the like, and provide jobs at a community level. Further details and bookings of the programmes described below can be obtained from the office at the Museum/Old Boma or the Tanzanian Tourist Board tourist information centre in Arusha (see page 236), www.tanzaniaculturaltourism.com. The other option is to discuss with your tour operator what you would like to do and they may be able to incorporate one or more of these visits into a longer safari.

Ng'iresi Village

ⓘ *7 km from Arusha north of the Moshi Rd, transportation by pickup truck can be arranged at the Arusha offices.*

Half-day guided tours of farms and local development projects, such as irrigation, soil terracing, cross breeding, bio gas and fish nurseries. Longer tours can involve camping at a farm and a climb of **Kivesi**, a small volcano with forests where baboons and gazelle live. The Wa-arusha women will prepare traditional meals or a limited choice of Western food.

Ilkiding'a Village

ⓘ *7 km north of Arusha along the road signposted to Ilboru Safari Lodge from Moshi Rd.*

You will be welcomed in a traditional boma, be able to visit craftsmen and a traditional healer, and walk through farms to one of several viewpoints or into **Njeche Canyon**. A three-day hike is also available, stopping at various villages and culminating in a visit to a Masai market. The guides of both this and the Ng'iresi programme are knowledgeable and have a reasonable standard of English.

Mulala Village

ⓘ *1450 m above sea level on the slopes of Mt Meru, about 30 km from Arusha. The turn-off is just before Usa River; follow signs for the Dik Dik Hotel; after the hotel, the road climbs for about 10 km.*

This programme is organized by the Agape women's group. There are walks through the coffee and banana farms to Marisha River, or to the top of Lemeka hill for views of mounts Meru and Kilimanjaro, and on to the home of the village's traditional healer. You can visit farms where cheese- and bread-making and flower-growing activities have been initiated. The women speak only a little English but interpreters can be arranged.

Mkuru camel safari

ⓘ *North side of Mt Meru, the camp is 5 km from Ngarenanyuki Village, which is 5 km beyond the Momela gate of Arusha National Park.*

The Masai of this area began keeping camels in the early 1990s and there are now over 100 animals. Camel safaris of half a day or up to one week, towards Kilimanjaro, to Mount Longido, or even further to Lake Natron can be arranged. Alternatively, there are walks through the acacia woodland looking for birds, or up the pyramid-shaped peak of Ol Doinyo Landaree. In the camel camp itself, it is possible to see the Masai carry the new-born camels to their overnight shelters and to watch them milk the camels. The guides are local Masai who have limited knowledge of English, communicating largely by hand signals – another guide to act as translator can be arranged with advance notice. There are several simple tents at the camel camp, or you can bring your own, and meals can be prepared if notice is given.

Mount Longido

ⓘ *The town of Longido lies 80 km north of Arusha on the main road to Namanga and Kenya Take a* dala-dala *from Arusha towards Namanga; the journey to Longido should take about 1½ hrs.*
Mount Longido (2629 m) rises up steeply from the plains 100 km north of Arusha on the border with Kenya and forms an important point of orientation over a wide area. To climb Mount Longido is useful preparation for Mount Meru or Mount Kilimanjaro. The **Longido Cultural Tourism Programme** is an excellent way of supporting the local Masai people and learning about their lifestyle and culture. There are several walking tours of the environs, including a half-day 'bird walk' from the town of Longido across the Masai plains to the bomas of Ol Tepesi, the Masai word for acacia tree. On your return to Longido you can enjoy a meal cooked by the local women. The one-day walking tour extends from Ol Tepesi to Kimokonwa along a narrow Masai cattle trail that winds over the slopes of Mount Longido. On clear days there are views of Kilimanjaro and Mount Meru and, from the north side, there are extensive views of the plains into Kenya. The tour includes a visit to a historic German grave. There is also a more strenuous two-day tour climbing to the top of the steep Longido peak, following buffalo trails guarded by Masai warriors armed with knives and spears to protect you. Accommodation is in local guesthouses, Masai bomas or at campsites. Part of the money generated by this cultural tourism project goes to the upkeep of the cattle dip in Longido. The Masai lose about 1500 head of cattle per annum, mainly because of tick-borne disease. Since Masai life is centred around their livestock this creates serious problems as reduced herd size means less work, income and food. Regular cattle dipping eradicates tick-borne diseases.

Babati and Mount Hanang → *Colour map 1, A4.*

Kahembe's Trekking and Cultural Safaris ⓘ *T0784-397 477, www.kahembeculturalsafaris. com, or make arrangements through the Tanzania Cultural Tourism Programme (above). There are regular bus services from Arusha to Babati (172 km) from 0730, 3 hrs; once there, ask for Kahembe's Guest House, a 5-min walk from the main bus stand.*
Babati is 172 km southwest of Arusha on the A104 road to Dodoma. It's a small market town straddling the main road, and the mainstay of the economy is maize farming. The plains around the town are home to cattle herders and, among these people, the Barbaig's traditional culture is still unchanged and unspoiled. The women wear traditional goatskin dresses and the men walk around with spears. A number of imaginative local tours can be arranged for around US$40 per person per day, and English-speaking guides who know the area will help you around, while a Barbaig-born guide will tell you about Barbaig culture. There is the chance to participate in local brick- and pottery-making and beer brewing, and to visit development projects like cattle and dairy farming, or piped water projects. The small **Lake Babati** is about a 10-minute walk from the town, and you can

organize canoe rides to see the few pods of hippos and the birdlife. Arrangements include full-board accommodation in local guesthouses and in selected family homes.

Lying to the southwest of Babati, **Mount Hanang** (3417 m) is the ninth-highest peak in East Africa and the fourth highest in Tanzania and is a challenge for more adventurous trekkers. **Kahembe's Trekking and Cultural Safaris** (see above) can arrange a trek up Mount Hanang along the Katesh route for around US$120 per person. The Katesh route can be completed in one day, with the ascent and descent taking a minimum 12 hours in total, but this is not recommended for inexperienced hikers, and an overnight on the mountain is usually arranged, sleeping in tents or caves. Independent exploration of the area is possible but not common.

Arusha National Park

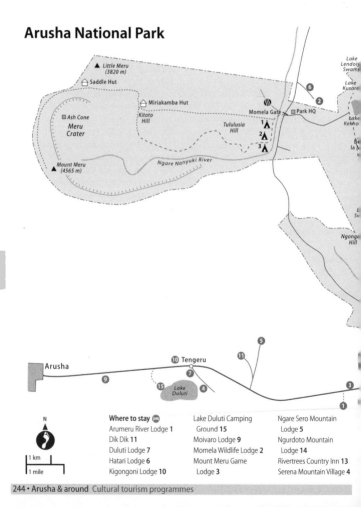

Little Meru (3820 m)
Saddle Hut
Miriakamba Hut
Kitoto Hill
Ash Cone
Meru Crater
Mount Meru (4565 m)
Ngare Nanyuki River
Tululusia Hill
Momela Gate
Park HQ
Lake Lendoi Swamp
Lake Kusare
Lake Kekho
Ngong Hill
Tengeru
Arusha
Lake Duluti

N
1 km
1 mile

Where to stay
Arumeru River Lodge 1
Dik Dik 11
Duluti Lodge 7
Hatari Lodge 6
Kigongoni Lodge 10

Lake Duluti Camping
Ground 15
Moivaro Lodge 9
Momela Wildlife Lodge 2
Mount Meru Game
Lodge 3

Ngare Sero Mountain
Lodge 5
Ngurdoto Mountain
Lodge 14
Rivertrees Country Inn 13
Serena Mountain Village 4

ⓘ *T027-255 3995, www.tanzaniaparks.com, 0630-1830, US$35, children (5-16) US$10, vehicle US$40, park fees for canoeing are US$20 per person for a half day and US$40 for a full day.*

The 542-sq-km Arusha National Park, which contains Mount Meru, is remarkable for its range of habitats. It encompasses three zones: the highland montane forest of **Mount Meru** to the west, where black-and-white colobus and blue monkeys can be spotted; **Ngurdoto Crater**, a small volcanic crater inhabited by a variety of mammals in the southeast of the park; and, to the northeast, **Momela Lakes**, a series of seven alkaline crater lakes, home to a large number of water birds. On a clear day it is possible to see the summits of both Mount Kilimanjaro and Mount Meru from Ngurdoto Crater rim. There are numerous hides and picnic sites throughout the park, giving travellers an opportunity to leave their vehicles, and this is one of the few of the country's parks where walking is permitted. Climbing Mount Meru or enjoying the smaller trails that criss-cross its lower slopes is a popular activity for visitors to the park. Although it only takes three days to reach the crater's summit, it's something of a short, sharp shock – a quieter, but some say more challenging, alternative to the famous peak of nearby Mount Kilimanjaro. Along the lower slopes, paths through ancient fig tree forests, beside crystal-clear cascading rivers and waterfalls make a relaxing day's hike for visitors who don't want to attempt the longer and more arduous climb. Canoeing on Small Momella Lake, where there are several hippos and interesting birdlife, is also an option for the active, and allows you the chance to see wildlife from a slower, quieter perspective. **Green Footprint Adventures** operate these canoeing safaris (see page 260).

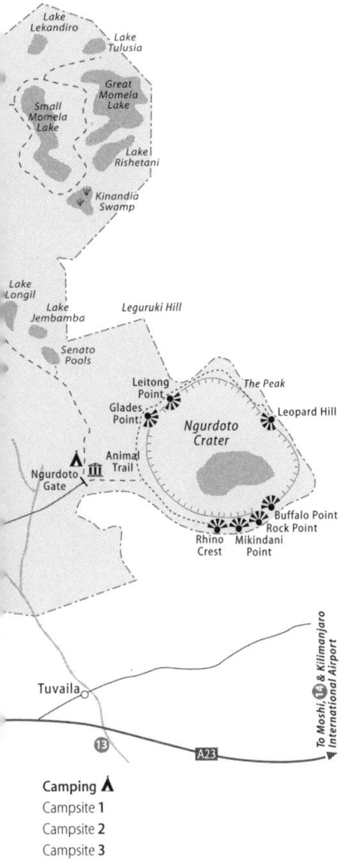

Arriving in Arusha National Park

Getting there Arusha National Park is about 25 km east of Arusha and 58 km from Moshi. The single road into the park is a good one, and the turning off the main road (A23) between Arusha and Moshi, about 35 km from **Kilimanjaro International Airport**, is at Usa River and is clearly signposted. From the airport the landscape changes from the flat dry and dusty Sanya Plain, gradually becoming greener, more fertile and more cultivated. Take the turning (on the right if

Map labels: Lake Lekandiro, Lake Tulusia, Great Momela Lake, Small Momela Lake, Lake Rishetani, Kinandia Swamp, Lake Longil, Lake Jembamba, Leguruki Hill, Senato Pools, Leitong Point, Glades Point, The Peak, Leopard Hill, Ngurdoto Crater, Animal Trail, Ngurdoto Gate, Buffalo Point, Rock Point, Rhino Crest, Mikindani Point, Tuvaila, A23, To Moshi & Kilimanjaro International Airport

Camping ▲
Campsite 1
Campsite 2
Campsite 3

you are heading towards Arusha) and follow the gravel road until it divides; the right-hand fork leads to the **Ngurdoto Gate**. This is coffee country and you will see the farms on each side of the road. On reaching the park entrance, the landscape changes to dense forest.

There's a second gate, **Momela Gate**, from which you access Mount Meru, to the north of the park. There are two routes leading to Momela Gate, both starting where the road divides north of Usa River. The road to the northwest is known as the Outer Road (25 km) and National Park fees are not payable if in transit on this route. The only available transport are pickup trucks, which take a few passengers and go to the village of Ngare Nanyuki, beyond the Momela Gate. It is permissible to walk this route too. The right fork takes you to the road that runs northeast via Ngurdoto Gate towards Ngurdoto Crater, before turning north (18 km) towards the Momela Crater Lakes; this route attracts the National Park fee. These roads through the park meet up again at the Momela Gate.

The best time to visit is October to February. If you don't have your own vehicle, many safari companies offer day trips from Arusha or Moshi. At the main entrance a small museum provides information on the bird, animal and plant life of the park. There are several excellent lodges around Usa River and on the lower slopes of Meru.

Background

Mount Meru (4565 m) is believed to have been formed at around the time of the great earth movements that created the Rift Valley, about 20 million years ago. The crater was formed about 250,000 years ago when a massive explosion blew away the eastern side of the volcano. A subsidiary vent produced the volcano of Ngurdoto, which built up over thousands of years. In a way similar to Ngorongoro, when the cone collapsed the caldera was left as it is today. Ngurdoto is now extinct, while Meru is only dormant, having last erupted about 100 years ago. The lava flow from this eruption can be seen on the northwest side of the mountain. It was at around this time in 1872 that the first European, Count Teleki, a Hungarian, saw the mountain. The Arusha National Park was established in 1960. The Howard Hawks film *Hatari* was made here in 1962, starring John Wayne, Elsa Martinelli, Red Buttons and Hardy Kruger.

Arusha National Park is home to giraffe, zebra, elephant, hippo, buffalo, spotted hyena, blue and black-and-white colobus monkey, bush buck, red forest duiker, reed buck, waterbuck and warthog. There are no lions; leopard are present though they are rarely seen. Birds include cormorants, pelicans, ibis, flamingos and grebes.

Ngurdoto Crater

There are over 50 km of tracks within the park but no roads have been built into the Ngurdoto Crater in order to protect and preserve it. From the Ngurdoto Gate a road leads east towards the Ngurdoto Crater. This area is known as the 'connoisseur's park' – rightly so. The road climbs up through the forest until it reaches the rim. At the top you can turn left or right to go around the crater clockwise or anti-clockwise. The track does not go all the way round the rim of the crater so you will have to turn round and retrace your tracks back to the main road. You will be able to look down on to the animals in the crater below but will not be able to drive down. The crater is about 3 km in diameter, and there are a number of viewing points around the rim from which you can view the crater floor, known as the 'park within the park'. These include Leitong Point (the highest at 1850 m), Glades Point, Rock Point, Leopard Hill, Rhino Crest and Mikindani Point. From this latter point you will be able to see Mount Kilimanjaro in the distance.

Climbing Mount Meru

The walk up Mount Meru involves a 3500-m altitude hike, frequently climbed up and down within three days. The last section of the walk to the summit is very steep. It is easy to underestimate the common problems associated with this walk – altitude sickness and frostbite. Snow is not unknown at the summit. On the ascent you will pass through the changing vegetation. The first change is to lower montane forest at about 2000 m, then to higher montane forest. The road climbs up the mountain to the heath zone at about 2439 m from where you can climb to the peak.

From the road and the park headquarters a track leads up to the **Miriakamba Hut**, which takes about three hours. The trail continues as a steady climb through montane forest, where there is an abundance of birds and black-and-white colobus monkeys. The first mountain hut sleeps about 48 people, while the second, **Saddle Hut**, sleeps about 24. Both huts provide firewood. It is a three-hour walk between the two huts but it is a steep climb. Having reached Saddle Hut you can spend the afternoon climbing **Little Meru** (3820 m), which takes about 1½ hours. From Saddle Hut the climb up to the rim of Mount Meru and around to the summit usually starts at 0200 in order to see the sunrise from the top. It's a steep climb to **Rhino Point** (3800 m), before continuing along an undulating ridge of ash and rock to reach **Cobra Point** (4350 m). The final ascent from Saddle Hut is difficult, cold and can be dangerous, but the views of the cliffs and crater rim are stunning: you can see the ash cone rising from the crater floor and Kilimanjaro floating on the morning clouds. Most of the tour operators in Arusha, and some in Moshi, can arrange climbs. Like the Kilimanjaro climb, there are a number of park fees to climb the mountain that are paid to the Tanzania National Parks. Though these are not quite as expensive as for Kili, nevertheless expect to pay in the region of US$400 for a package, including park fees, guide, porters, food and accommodation in mountain huts.

Momela Lakes route

From Ngurdoto Gate, if you take the left track you will reach the Momela Lakes. This track goes past the Ngongongare Springs, Lokie Swamp, the Senato Pools and the two lakes, Jembamba and Longil. At the peak of the dry season they may dry up but otherwise they are a good place to watch the animals and, in particular, the birdlife. At various spots there are observation hides. At **Lake Longil** there is a camping and picnic site in a lovely setting.

From here, the track continues through the forest, which gradually thins out, and, through the more open vegetation, you will be able to see Mount Meru. The Hyena Camp (Kambi ya Fisi) is reached at the point where you will probably see a pack of spotted hyenas. Beyond this there is a small track leading off the main track to **Bomo la Mengi** – a lovely place from which to view the lakes. Unless the cloud is down, you will also be able to see Kilimanjaro from here. The main track continues past two more lakes – **Lake El Kekhotoito** and **Lake Kusare** – before reaching the Momela Lakes.

The **Momela Lakes** are shallow alkaline lakes fed by underground streams. Because they have different mineral contents and different algae, their colours are also different. They contain few fish but the algae attract lots of birdlife. What you see will vary with the time of year. Flamingos tend to move in huge flocks around the lakes of East Africa and are a fairly common sight at Momela Lakes. Between October and April the lakes are also home to the migrating waterfowl, which spend the European winter in these warmer climes.

The track goes around the lakes reaching the **Small Momela Lake** first. This lake often has a group of hippos wallowing in it. Follow the road anti-clockwise and you will pass **Lake Rishetani**, which is a fantastic emerald green colour. Along this route you will be able to stop off at the various observation sites. The next lake that you will get to is the **Great Momela Lake**, which has a huge variety of birdlife and is a lovely spot. The last two lakes are **Tulusia** and **Lekandiro**, where you may see animals grazing.

Mount Meru → Colour map 1, A4.

The other major attraction of Arusha National Park is Mount Meru (4565 m), the second-highest mountain in Tanzania and also the fifth-highest in all Africa. The mountain lies to the west of the Ngare Nanyuki road in the western half of the park. There is a road that leads up the mountain to about 2439 m from the **Momela Gate**, passing through an open space called **Kitoto** from where there are good views of the mountain, but vehicles are no longer allowed to pass this way.

⊙ Arusha listings

For sleeping and eating price codes and other relevant information, see pages 22-26.

● Where to stay

The best hotels in the Arusha area are out of town in the foothills of Mt Meru. They have fine gardens, good standards and a charming atmosphere. They are recommended above similar priced hotels in Arusha or its outskirts. If you do not have your own transport, most will offer transfers from town and many are used as part of a safari package. At the budget end of the market there are a number of cheap hotels around the stadium and market that cost as little as US$10 and are good value, but be aware of safety issues and ensure your door is locked securely.

Arusha *p236, map p238*
$$$$ Arusha Coffee Lodge, 5 km west of town on the road to the crater near Arusha Airport, T027-250 0630, www.elewana collection.com. One of the most luxurious options in Arusha, set on a working coffee estate, with 30 stunning spacious chalets with balconies, fireplaces, facilities to make

coffee, enormous beds with mosquito nets, hardwood floors and wooden decks, Zanzibar-style furniture and Persian rugs. Very elegant lounge and a restaurant for fine dining (see Restaurants, page 254) with dressed up tables and leather sofas, plus a swimming pool.
$$$$ Onsea Country Inn and Guest Cottage, Baraa Rd, about 5 km outside Arusha off Moshi Rd, T0787-112 498, www.onseahouse.com. In a beautiful location overlooking the hills and Mt Meru, this stylish boutique hotel owned by Belgians Dirk and Inneke Janssens has 5 rooms, 3 in the main house and 2 in the guest cottage across the road, which can be used as one huge family suite. All rooms are elegantly furnished and there's a swimming pool in tranquil gardens. Excellent restaurant on the terrace of the main house with stunning views, see page 254.
$$$$-$$$ The Arusha Hotel, near the clock tower, T027-250 7777, www.thearusha hotel.com. Formerly the site of an old German hotel built in 1894, of which the splendid restaurant is the only surviving feature. The 86 elegantly decorated rooms, with a/c, satellite TV and Wi-Fi, have

balconies overlooking the swimming pool or the beautiful gardens running down to the Themi River. There's a gym, bar with garden terrace, restaurant serving Italian and Indian dishes, a good bookshop, gift/craft shop and a foreign exchange bureau.

$$$ African Tulip, 44/1 Serengeti Rd, T027-254 3004, www.theafricantulip.com. A fairly new hotel, owned by **Roy Safaris**, with 29 rooms decorated in smart contemporary style with an African safari theme, all with window seats overlooking the grounds or the roof garden that, appropriately, is full of African tulips. Rooms have a/c, flat-screen TV, Wi-Fi and minibar. There's a chic Zanzibar bar, a Baobab-themed restaurant and a pool in lawned gardens.

$$$ Arusha Travel Lodge, off Njiro Rd, 9 km to the southeast of town and 6 km after the Njiro Shopping Complex, T0786-288 740, www.arushatravellodge.com. Newly opened by **Victoria Expeditions Safaris & Travels** (page 263) and set in a quiet suburb on the edge of town, this has neat en suite rooms (some triple) in low whitewashed buildings with a/c, satellite TV and Wi-Fi, restaurant and secure parking. Pickups can be arranged from Kilimanjaro International Airport and Arusha centre.

$$$ The Bay Leaf, 102 Vijana Rd, T027-254 3055, www.thebayleafhotel.com. Arusha's newest boutique hotel set in a charming house in a quiet leafy street just a few mins' walk from the centre. It has just 6 individually decorated suites, some with colonial antiques and luxurious drapes, modern bathrooms with power showers, Wi-Fi, no pool but a mini-garden and terrace, and they plan to open spa facilities. Best known for its superb gourmet restaurant (see page 254) and the high standard of food carries through to the fantastic breakfasts for overnight guests.

$$$ East African Hotel, Nelson Mandela (Old Moshi) Rd, T0786-066 060, www.east africanhotel.com. Aimed predominantly at the conference market, but will appeal to those looking for a large, modern, purpose-built (some would say anonymous) hotel with good facilities, the 144 rooms are spacious with satellite TV and Wi-Fi and some have mini-kitchens. There's a bar and coffee shop, restaurant, and rates include a generous buffet breakfast, swimming pool and gym.

$$$ Impala Hotel, 500 m down Nelson Mandela (Old Moshi) Rd from the clock tower, T027-254 3082/7, www.impalahotel. com. 177 rooms in a modern block with satellite TV and Wi-Fi, pleasant garden and patio, swimming pool, 4 good restaurants, including an excellent Indian one, 3 bars/coffee shops, 24-hr room service, gift shop and bureau de change. Arranges tours and safaris through **Classic Tours** (see page 260). They run their own Nairobi–Arusha–Moshi shuttle bus (see box, page 15). A useful hotel with several amenities but somewhat impersonal service.

INFO@ARUSHATRAVELLODGE.COM
www.arushatravellodge.com

$$$ Karama Lodge & Spa, 3 km from town off the Nelson Mandela (Old Moshi) Rd, turn off just past Masai Camp, T0754-475 0188, www.karama-lodge.com. 22 thatched, stilted log cabins built on the hillside in a pretty tract of forest. It's close enough to town but is very peaceful and has good views of Meru and Kilimanjaro. Colourful rooms have hanging chairs on the balcony. There's a rustic bar, and the restaurant uses ingredients from the garden. A popular choice for a rest after climbing Kilimanjaro or Meru and, although it doesn't have a full spa as such, it does have a swimming pool and offers massages, body scrubs and yoga.

$$$ Naura Springs Hotel, East Africa Community Rd, about 500 m from AICC on the opposite side of the road, T027-205 0001/8, www.nauraspringshotel.com. You can't miss this 14-storey, blue-glass building housing Arusha's newest hotel. Beautifully crafted wooden carvings decorate the communal areas but, beyond that, the place has little character. The bar and main restaurant are by the cavernous reception lobby and there are lawns and a pool, with another bar and restaurant. The beauty salon and gym are still being built. The 125 rooms are spacious but soulless, with flat-screen TVs and fridges; some are more attractive than others but the views are great.

$$$ New Safari, Boma Rd, T027-250 3261, www.thenewsafarihotel.com. Friendly hotel, conveniently located in the New Safari Complex, which also houses businesses such as internet cafés and bureaux de change. Very smart modern building, nice terrace restaurant on the 1st floor with good views of Meru, 48 rooms with TV, internet connection for laptops, and minibar with soft drinks. Doubles from a good-value US$115.

$$$-$$ Ilboru Safari Lodge, 2 km east of town off the Moshi Rd, T0754-270 357, www.ilborusafarilodge.com. Well managed by a Dutchman, this popular and good-value lodge has 30 simple but comfortable en suite rooms in thatched rondavaals with a Masai theme, some triple and family rooms,

plus a pretty, grassy campsite with good ablutions (US$10 per person). There's an excellent restaurant (see page 255) that also serves Dutch-style pancakes, and a German beer garden. The large swimming pool is open to non-guests (0900-1800) for a small fee. Interesting activities offered include traditional tingatinga painting and Swahili cookery classes.

$$ Arusha Crown Hotel, Makongoro Rd, T027-250 8523, www.arushacrownhotel. com. A modern hotel and very centrally located (though at first glance it seems a pretty rough and ready back street), with 38 rooms on 6 floors. The decor is stylish (though it's very much a business travellers' hotel with 24 single rooms), internet access, good restaurant open to non-guests. A single is US$60, a twin or a double US$74, excellent value in this price range. The rooms facing north overlook Meru and directly into the stadium – if there's a match on you can watch the football from bed.

$$ Arusha Naaz Hotel, near clock tower on Sokoine Rd, T027-250 2087, www.arusha naaz.net. Once you get through the bizarre shopping centre entrance and head up the small staircase, the 21 a/c rooms are centred around a little internal courtyard and are clean, with en suite bathrooms, 24-hr hot water, fans and mosquito nets, restaurant with good food (closed in evening), internet access. You can also hire cars from here.

$$ Pamoja Expeditions, Serengeti Rd, T027-250 6136, www.pamojaexpeditionslodge. com. Rooms are in thatched bungalows in the garden, simply furnished with whitewashed walls, nets and satellite TV, small pool in the gardens with plastic chairs and sunbeds, internet café, bar and basic restaurant. Lacking in character compared to its neighbour, Outpost Lodge (see below).

$$-$ Le Jacaranda, Vijana Rd, T027-254 4624, www.chez.com/jacaranda. 23 African-themed rooms, small but clean with private bathrooms and decorated with Masai artwork, some are in the main building, which was a colonial farmhouse, while others are dotted around the gardens. Facilities include internet access, comfortable bar area with sofas on a terrace overlooking the gardens, a rather bizarre 'home-made' but fun crazy golf course, and the restaurant serves everything from Chinese to Swahili with plenty of vegetarian options (see page 255). Doubles from US$55.

$$-$ Outpost Lodge, 41 Serengeti Rd, off the Nelson Mandela (Old Moshi) Rd, near **Impala Hotel**, T027-254 8405, www.outpost tanzania.net. Good and long-established budget option with 25 en suite rooms in spacious garden cottages, plus dorms/family rooms in the main house sleeping up to 6, nothing fancy and with old-fashioned furnishings but clean with reliable hot water, mosquito nets and fans, full English breakfast included. A new swimming pool has recently been added together with **Café Mambo**, a cheerful café and bar, with chilled music, around the pool area.

$ Arusha Backpackers, Sokoine Rd, T027-250 4474, www.arushabackpackers.co.tz. This is a popular low-budget option with good facilities, including a lively bar and restaurant on the top floor with Wi-Fi, the 34 rooms are sparsely furnished and some are like windowless cells with nothing but bunk-beds and a chair, but good value at US$15 for a double including breakfast. There are also some dormitories with 2 sets of bunk beds for US$7 per person. Communal toilets and showers.

$ Everest Inn, Nelson Mandela (Old Moshi) Rd, near the **Impala**, T0767-255 277, www. everest-inn.com. 7 clean and comfortable rooms at the back of this popular Chinese restaurant (see page 255), with modern bathrooms, satellite TV and Wi-Fi and friendly and helpful hosts. There are pleasant tropical gardens at the front of the restaurant, which serves excellent Sechuan food.

$ Hotel Flamingo, Kikuyu St, near the market, T027-254 8812, flamingoarusha@ yahoo.com. A good low-budget option, with 9 spotlessly clean, light and airy rooms with mosquito nets and own bathrooms. Friendly

staff and a pleasant bar area that serves soft drinks only, and can serve very early breakfasts if need be (if you're catching an early bus, for example).

$ Hotel Pepe One, just off Church Rd, T0784-365 515, www.hotelpepeone.co.tz. This popular restaurant now has 5 rooms, all off the main reception area, which are simple but newly decorated with good, modern, tiled bathrooms, nets and TV. Tidy and clean but a bit cramped. Lively restaurant serving a varied menu (see page 255) and it's in a quiet location in pretty grounds. Good value at US$45 for a double; breakfast is an extra US$5.

$ Klub Afriko Hotel and Safaris, Kimandolu, 3 km from town on the Moshi Rd, T027-254 8878, www.klubafriko.com. Set in tropical gardens in a quiet neighbourhood just outside town, with 7 airy en suite bungalows, decorated with local artwork, good (pre-arranged) meals, friendly bar with satellite TV. All in all a reasonable set up if you're on one of their safaris but a little bit far from town otherwise.

$ L'Oasis Lodge, 2 km out of town, in the quiet residential area of Sekei, off the Moshi Rd, T027-250 7089, www.loasislodge.com. 22 en suite rooms, some on stilts and some in the main building, and 13 smaller twin budget rooms with shared bathrooms, although some are a little dark and dreary. However, good food, with continental and healthy dishes (some vegetarian and the Greek-inspired salads are good) and there's a casual laid-back lounge and bar by the swimming pool which serves burgers and pizzas. Pool with fish and wading birds, a dining area, bar, internet café and curio shop.

$ Palm Court Hotel, 500 m from the bus station off Wachagga St, T0754-975 468. A friendly low-budget option with rooms around the restaurant. Rates include breakfast and are more expensive if you want your own bathroom. Basic but clean, nets, shared hot showers, laundry service, small restaurant, bar, tea and coffee, lounge with satellite TV, exceptionally good value.

$ Sinka Court, Swahili St, near the market, T027-250 4961, sinkacourthotel@hotmail.com. In a very modern block, 29 rooms with built-for-hotel furniture and excellent bathrooms, a/c, TV, mosquito nets, the larger rooms have fridges and floor to ceiling windows, though the view is not up to much as the hotel overlooks an ugly block of flats. Underground parking, restaurant and bar.

$ Spices & Herbs, a few metres north of the **Impala Hotel** off Nelson Mandela (Old Moshi) Rd, T027-254 2279. Well appointed, with a garden and veranda leading to the restaurant which specializes in Ethiopian cuisine (see Restaurants, page 255). The 20 rooms are set around a courtyard to the rear, small but comfortable with hot showers, some are adjoining for families. In the middle of the courtyard are some chairs and a satellite TV.

Camping

Arusha View Campsite, near the Natural History Museum, Boma Rd, T0754-040 810, www.africa-royal-trekking.com. Very central and home to the **Africa Royal Trekking** office (see Tour operators, page 260), very basic camping on a grassy site next to the Themi River, which mosquitoes love, only US$1.50 per person and you can hire tents for US$3 but you will need a sleeping bag.

Masai Camp, 3 km along Nelson Mandela (Old Moshi) Rd, T0754-507 131, www.masaicamptz.com. Shady camping spots on grassy terraces, US$5 per person, plus some budget rooms in huts with mosquito nets for US$10 per person The ablutions are spotless, with steaming hot water, there's an internet café, fantastic restaurant, and lively bar (see Restaurants, page 255). Highly recommended for backpackers. The excellent safari company, **Tropical Trails** (see page 262) is based here.

Around Arusha p241, map p244

$$$$ Duluti Lodge, 14 km from town toward Moshi, turn right at the sign and follow the road through a coffee plantation,

T0759-356 505, www.dulutilodge.com. One of the most luxurious places to stay on this side of Arusha, with 18 stunning chalets set among indigenous trees on a coffee farm, each has satellite TV, Wi-Fi, walk-through showers, contemporary African decor, dining room, wooden deck and bar (sundowners can be taken at an outdoor lounge area on the lakeshore), swimming pool and lovely gardens. Can organize guided nature walks, canoeing on the lake and day trips to Arusha National Park. The whole lodge is wheelchair accessible.

$$$$-$$$ Serena Mountain Village, 14 km out of town along the Moshi Rd, turn right at the sign, T027-255 3049, www.serenahotels.com. Quality lodge in an old colonial homestead nestled in a coffee plantation and overlooking Lake Duluti (see page 241). 42 thatched stone cottages with hand-carved African animals on the doors, excellent gardens, very good restaurant, relaxed open bar and impeccable service.

$$$ Arumeru River Lodge, 20 km from Arusha, off the Moshi Rd, near Usa River, T0732-979, www.arumerulodge.com. One of the newest options in the Usa River region, with 21 chalets set in pleasant gardens full of birds, 6 are more upmarket, with large terraces and Wi-Fi, and there's a 2-bed family cottage with kitchen. Bar and restaurant with good wholesome farm-style food, large solar-heated swimming pool, activities include forest and village walks with Masai guides.

$$$ Dik Dik, 20 km from Arusha off the Moshi Rd near Usa River, T027-255 3499, www.dikdik.ch. Set in 8 ha of tropical gardens on the slopes of Meru, 9 comfortable chalets with verandas and fireplace, swimming pool, good restaurant. Very proficiently run by Swiss owners, though it lacks African atmosphere and concentrates on running upmarket Kilimanjaro climbs. More reasonable rates are available if you are buying accommodation as part of a climb package.

$$$ Kigongoni Lodge, 10 km east of Arusha, 1 km before Tengeru, 1 km off the

Moshi Rd, T027-255 3087, www.kigongoni. net. On a 28-ha coffee farm with good views of Kilimanjaro and Meru, the lodge has 18 cottages, built with local materials, with fireplaces, verandas and 4-poster beds, some have Wi-Fi. The restaurant serves a set 3-course meal each night and there's a cocktail lounge and a swimming pool on top of a hill with fantastic views. Revenues from the lodge support a local foundation for mentally disabled children and their families. Guided walks available.

$$$ Moivaro Lodge, 7 km from Arusha off the Moshi Rd, T027-255 3243, www. moivaro.com. 42 lovely double- or triple-bed cottages with verandas, set in gardens in a coffee plantation. There's internet access, a swimming pool, good restaurant and bar, children's playground, massages, and a jogging or walking trail through the plantation.

$$$ Mount Meru Game Lodge, 20 km from Arusha off Moshi Rd near Usa River, T027-255 3643, www.mountmerugame lodge.com. Well run, high-standard establishment with 17 thatched bandas in a garden setting with 4-poster beds and verandas, charming atmosphere and very good restaurant. Impressive animal sanctuary for orphaned or injured animals, which includes baboons and vervet monkeys, and a large paddock is home to zebra, waterbuck and eland, as well as saddle-billed and yellow-billed storks, sacred ibis and ostrich.

$$$ Ngare Sero Mountain Lodge, 20 km east of Arusha on the Moshi Rd, T027-255 3638, www.ngare-sero-lodge.com. Just 1.5 km from the main road is a jacaranda avenue leading to a footbridge. You reach the lodge by crossing the lake on the footbridge and climbing steps up through the gardens, or by driving around the forest reserve to reach the car park. 10 garden rooms and 2 suites, pool and sauna in the garden, horse riding, yoga classes, trout fishing and trekking on Mt Meru can all be arranged, and you can play croquet on the

lawn. Formerly the farm of Hauptmann Leue, a colonial administrator from the German period; the name means 'sweet waters' and there are magnificent gardens with an estimated 200 bird species.

$$$ Ngurdoto Mountain Lodge, 27 km from Arusha, 3 km off Moshi Rd, T027-254 2217/26, www.thengurdotomountainlodge. com. Very smart lodge in beautiful grounds with a range of facilities on a 57-ha coffee estate. 60 rooms in double-storey thatched rondavaals, 72 rooms in the main building, and 7 suites, some rooms have disabled access, satellite TV, most with bathtubs with jacuzzis. Good views of Kilimanjaro and Meru, 3 restaurants, 2 bars, a coffee shop, 18-hole golf course, health club and fully equipped gym, 2 tennis courts, badminton court, swimming pool, toddlers' pool, children's play area and tour desk that can arrange all safaris. An excellent base in the region especially for families.

$$$ Rivertrees Country Inn, 20 km from Arusha, off the Moshi Rd, near Usa River, T0732-971 667, www.rivertrees.com. Set in natural gardens along the picturesque Usa River, this is a very elegant country lodge with excellent farm cuisine and personal service. There are 8 individually decorated rooms with bathrooms in the farmhouse and 2 garden cottages with additional decks and fireplaces. Swimming pool, and horse riding, village visits and walking trips can be arranged.

Camping

$ Lake Duluti camping ground, 11 km from town toward Moshi, turn right at the sign and follow the road through a coffee plantation. Secure camping and parking is in a grassy yard around the jetty and bar, though ablutions are basic. There is a basic restaurant with a limited choice of food and you may have to wait. Cold beers and sodas available and you can pay to get your laundry done.

$ Meserani Snake Park, 25 km out of town on the road towards the Ngorongoro

Crater and Serengeti, T027-253 8282, www.meseranisnakepark.com. A hugely popular spot with backpackers, independent overlanders and overland trucks; just about any safari company on the way to the parks will stop here. Lively atmosphere and friendly, the bar serves very cold beers. The campsite has hot showers and vehicles are guarded by Masai warriors. Meals from simple hamburgers to spit roast impala are on offer (see also page 241).

Arusha National Park *p245, map p244*
$$$ Hatari Lodge, about 50 km from Arusha, just outside Arusha National Park, 4 km to the northeast of the Momela Gate, T027-255 3456, www.hatarilodge.com. Named after the famous 1961 movie *Hatari* starring John Wayne, which was filmed in the area, this 'themed' lodge has fun retro 1960s decor – think bucket chairs, lime green walls and padded headboards. The 9 spacious chalets are set in a grove of yellowwood acacia trees and have fireplaces and verandas with views of Mt Meru. Very good food served in the dining room in an old colonial farm building, swimming pool, canoeing, game drives and walks with the Masai can be arranged. Rates are full board.
$$$ Momela Wildlife Lodge, close to Hatari Lodge above, 3 km to the northeast of the Momela Gate, T027-250 8104, www.lions-safari-intl.com/momella.html. John Wayne stayed here and the hotel was the production base for *Hatari*. The lodge will screen the film on request for guests. Beautiful gardens, with a swimming pool, but the 55 rondavaals are quite run-down now and could do with a refurbishment; it's overpriced at about US$120 for a double. Nevertheless, the views of Meru and Kilimanjaro are excellent, there are many plains animals and a huge variety of birds nearby, and it's well placed for visits to the Momela Lakes.

Camping
Arusha National Park Campsites, there are 3 campsites in the park at the base of Tululusia Hill, which are rather unimaginatively named 1, 2 and 3, and have water, long-drop toilets and firewood; US$20 per person. Book through Tanzania National Parks Authority head office, see page 237.

🍴 Restaurants

Arusha *p236, map p238*
$$$ Arusha Coffee Lodge, see Where to stay, page 248. Open 0800-2200. Fabulous setting in a luxurious lodge, lovely wooden building surrounded by decks and overlooking the swimming pool, fine china and crystal, very elegant, big fireplace in the bar area, superb service. At lunch there are set menus with at least 4 main courses to choose from, plus a snack menu. At dinner choose steak, pork, chicken or fish, and then pick a marinade and accompanying sauce, with a wide choice of veg and salad. Wines are from South Africa and Chile.
$$$ The Bay Leaf, see Where to stay, page 249. Open 0800-1400, 1800-2200. Excellent-quality food in this stylish new boutique hotel, including the quartet starter – a sample of 4 of the starter dishes – and gourmet mains using lamb, duck and rabbit, plus fresh ravioli and gnocchi, liqueur coffees and good choice of wines. Expensive, and portions are sometimes small, but a very inventive menu for Arusha and nice for a treat in the smart dining room.
$$$ Onsea House Country Inn, see Where to stay, page 248. Open for brunch, lunch and dinner, bookings essential. Stunning views overlooking the Monduli Mountains and Mt Meru. The Belgian chef here prepares brasserie dishes that are Belgian/French with an African influence, accompanied by fine wines. This is fast gaining a reputation as the best place to eat in Arusha.
$$ Blue Heron, Haile Selassie Rd, T027-254 8087, www.blue-heron-tanzania.com. Mon-Thu 0900-1700, Fri-Sat 0900-2300.

A colourful house set in beautiful gardens, the outside bar is built around a frangipani tree and tables are set on the lawns or under a giant sail-cloth on the terrace. Cakes, coffee and light lunches, wood-fired pizza oven, good range of pastas, steaks and sauces. Children are well catered for with a kids' menu, jungle gym and activity area.

$$ Dragon Pearl, Nelson Mandela (Old Moshi) Rd, near the **Impala**, T027-254 4107. Mon-Fri 1100-1500, 1800-2230, Sat-Sun 1230-2245. Pleasant outdoor setting in lovely gardens. A full range of Chinese and some Thai is served, specialities include fried wonton and sizzling dishes; try the crispy chilli prawns. It's a good choice for vegetarians and serves wines from South Africa. A Korean chef will grill meat at your table and serve it with sauces.

$$ Ilboru Safari Lodge, see Where to stay, page 250. Open 1000-2200. Popular spot serving a mix of international and Swahili cuisine, along with some Dutch dishes; try the Swahili stews, which include a delicious veggie option, or the excellent sweet and savoury pancakes. There's a relaxed atmosphere in the Masai-inspired restaurant and, if you're lucky, the staff choir will demonstrate their singing talents.

$$ Le Jacaranda, see Where to stay, page 250. Open 0900-2200. Restaurant and bar on an attractive upstairs wooden deck, lounge area downstairs, surrounded by pretty gardens. Continental, Indian, Chinese and Swahili meals, grills and steaks, and a wide selection of vegetarian options. BBQs at weekends.

$$ Masai Camp, see Where to stay, page 252. Open 1000-late. Good food and bar, excellent place to meet other travellers, serves Tex Mex, burgers, pizzas and the best nachos in East Africa on tables in a boma around a roaring fire. There are pool tables and a separate cocktail bar that opens in the evening; on Wed, Fri and Sat nights there's a DJ and dancing.

$$ Pepe's, at Hotel Pepe One, see Where to stay, page 251. Open 1200-1500, 1800-

2230. A lively Italian and Indian restaurant, well known for its pizzas and lasagne but the tandoori and tikka dishes are worth a try too and are served with buttery naan bread. Tables are set in pretty gardens or in the restaurant with Masai artwork.

$$ Shanghai Chinese Restaurant, Sokoine Rd near the bridge, beside **Meru Post Office**, T027-250 3224. Open 1100-1500, 1800-2230. This long-established Chinese has an extensive and fairly authentic menu; the hot and sour soup is highly recommended, service is quick and portions large. There are pleasant outdoor tables under thatch on a terrace with potted palms.

$$ Spices & Herbs Ethiopian Restaurant, see Where to stay, page 252. Open 1100-2300. Simple, informal Ethiopian place with good vegetarian options made from lentils, peas and beans, very good lamb and continental food (steaks, chops and ribs). Set in a beautifully landscaped garden full of birds. Good service, full bar and live music Thu-Sat.

$$-$ Everest Inn & Chinese Restaurant, Nelson Mandela (Old Moshi) Rd, near the **Impala Hotel**. Open 1200-1500, 1800-2200. Popular Chinese restaurant set in an atmospheric old house or tables in the pleasant tropical gardens. Excellent Sechuan food; try the garlic prawns or duck with pancakes. Well-stocked bar and friendly hosts, also has some simple rooms round the back (see Where to stay, page 251).

$$-$ Picasso Café, by Kijenge Supermarket, Simeon Rd, T0756-448 585. Open 0900-2300. A modern a/c café and a great place for an upmarket breakfast or brunch, with a full English for US$7. It's also a popular lunch spot, serving sandwiches, crêpes, burgers and delicious cakes and more substantial meals in the evening. Wine and beer served too and has Wi-Fi.

$ Jambo Coffee House & Makuti Garden, Boma Rd just south of the **New Safari Hotel**, T027-250 3261. Open 0800-2200. Superb breakfasts, baguettes and stuffed chapatis, burgers, juices and shakes during the day and afternoon tea 1400-1700 with cakes and muffins. Dinner from 1930, fish, steaks, ribs and vegetarian dishes and a good wine list. The art on the walls is for sale.

$ McMoody's, on the corner of Sokoine and Market St, T027-254 4013. Tue-Sun 1000-2200. McDonald's-inspired fast food for those hankering after fries and milkshakes. It has a peculiar circular staircase and mirrored walkway that goes absolutely nowhere. There is an internet café next door and you can take your drinks in. There's another branch at the Njiro Shopping Complex, see page 258.

Cafés

Cio Gelati, TFA Shopping Centre, Sokoine Rd. Open 0800-1900. Snacks, samosas, cold orange juice, 14 flavours of ice cream, sundaes, milkshakes, cappuccino, espresso. Uses fresh ingredients and no eggs.

Dolly's Patisserie, Sokoine Rd, south of the market. Mon-Sat 0900-1800. Very smart, with modern counters and spotless tiles, fantastic freshly baked French bread, cakes and sweets, excellent biryanis, kormas and masalas, hot and cold drinks.

The Patisserie, Sokoine Rd, just down the hill from the clock tower. Mon-Sat 0730-1800, Sun 0830-1400. Most visitors to Arusha gravitate here as it's so central and it sells freshly baked breads, pies, cakes, cookies, croissants, Indian snacks, fresh juices, cappuccino, espresso and hot chocolate, as well as a couple of lunches, such as omelette and chips or chicken curry. There are counters and a few tables to sit at; it also doubles up as an internet café.

Steers, near the clock tower. Open 0900-2100. South African fast-food chain selling ribs and burgers, sodas and shakes in a/c and spotless environment.

☻ Bars and clubs

Arusha p236, map p238

There are a number of popular places in town and almost all the hotels and many of the restaurants have bars. There are also several in the new **Njiro Shopping Complex** (see page 258), 3 km out of town on Njiro Rd.

Crystal Club & Disco, Seth Benjamin Rd. Open most nights from 2200. Large dance floors with 2 rooms (techno and African/trance) and pool tables. Very lively at weekends, has a wide selection of drinks.

Colobus Club, Nelson Mandela (Old Moshi) Rd just past the **Impala Hotel**. Fri-Sat 2100-0600. Popular disco in town, and open for most of the night at the weekend, 2 large dance floors, several bars and pool tables.

Empire Sports Bar, in the TFA Shopping Centre behind **Shoprite**, off Sokoine Rd, T0754-695 670. Open 1000-late. A large modern bar, with high ceiling and mezzanine floor, pool tables, dart board, long bar, large TVs for watching sport and some tables outside in the courtyard. Popular with expats.

Greek Club, Nelson Mandela (Old Moshi) Rd, T0713-510 813. Tue, Wed and Fri-Sun 1200-1400, 1730-late. Set back from the road in a large white house with Grecian pillars out front. Sports bar with large TVs for football, darts board and pool table. Outdoor tables on a terrace or in the garden where there's a children's playground. The menu features Greek food, plus burgers, salads and baked potatoes with fillings.

Matongee, Nelson Mandela (Old Moshi) Rd. 1200-late. Outside tables in a spacious garden with *nyama choma* barbecues and plenty of cold beer. Relaxed and good value. Popular with local people.

Triple A, Nairobi Rd, Wed, Fri and Sat, 2100-0500. Also open on Sun afternoons to allow the kids to get down and boogie. This is easily the largest and most popular nightclub in Arusha with a big range of music including R&B and hip hop. Enormous dance floor, pool tables, 2 bars, gets completely packed, also runs its own FM radio station.

Via Via, Boma Rd, T0754-384 922.
Mon-Thu 1000-2200, Fri-Sat 1000-late.
A popular bar in the gardens of the Natural
History Museum, set in a series of thatched
bomas with garden seating, the sandwiches
and snacks are passable but the hot meals
are poor. Occasional live bands and on
Thu night there's sometimes traditional
dancing/acrobatics.

Around Arusha *p241, map p244*
If you are looking for a party with other
travellers the best places to go are the
Meserani Snake Park and the Masai Camp.

⊕ Entertainment

Casino
Safari Casino, at the Arusha Hotel (see Where
to stay, page 248), open from 1200 for the
slot-machines and from 1700 for the gaming
tables and stays open until 0400 or 0500.

Cinema
Century Cinemax, in the Njiro Shopping
Complex, 3 km out of town on Njiro Rd
(see page 258), T0755-102 221. A 2-screen
cinema showing movies at 1400 and 1900,
either Hollywood or Bollywood. Tickets are
around US$6, though oddly you pay a little
more to sit on the balcony. Closed Mon.

⊙ Shopping

Arusha *p236, map p238*
Bookshops
Arusha Hotel bookshop sells international
newspapers and magazines as well as books.
A Novel Idea, TFA Shopping Centre, see
below, T0754-271 374, www.anovelidea
tanzania.com. The best bookshop in Arusha.
Stocks a wide range of up-to-date novels,
coffee table books on Africa, guide books,
maps, intelligent Africana titles, as well as
wrapping paper and greeting cards. Prices
are steep as everything is imported, but
nevertheless one of the best ranges of
books in Tanzania.

Kase Stores, Boma Rd, T027-250 2640.
A very large shop with a good selection
of books, stationery and postcards.

Crafts
There are some craft shops on Goliondoi
Rd and near the clock tower with some
very good examples of carvings. The curio
markets crammed between the clock tower
and India Rd are brimming with carvings,
masks, beads and some unusual antique
Masai crafts, including masks, drums,
headrests and beaded jewellery, similar
items are available at the **Masai Craft Market**
on School Rd. Tingatinga paintings (see box,
page 56) are for sale at various outlets,
including the **Il Boru Safari Lodge** and at a
gallery opposite the **Meserani Snake Park**.
Cultural Heritage Centre, 3 km out of town
on the road towards Dodoma and the crater.
A massive structure showcasing some of
the finest of African art, though, of course,
it is very expensive. The items are of very
high quality: carvings, musical instruments,
cloth, beads and leatherwork from all over
the continent. They can arrange shipping
back to your home country and there is a
DHL branch office on site. Many of the safari
companies stop here en route to the parks.

Markets and shopping centres
The main **market** is behind the bus station
along Market St and Somali Rd. It is very good
for fruit, locally made basketware, wooden
kitchenware and spices, and is very colourful.
The range of fresh produce is very varied and
you can buy just about every imaginable fruit
and vegetable. If you are shopping, then be
prepared to haggle hard and visit a variety
of stalls before deciding on the price. Market
boys will help carry goods for a fee. In the
rainy season watch where you are stepping –
it becomes a bit of a quagmire.
   Small supermarkets are found along
Sokoine Rd, Moshi Rd and Swahili St.
These sell imported food and booze as
well as household goods.

Njiro Shopping Complex, 3 km out of town on Njiro Rd. A fairly new centre with a few shops, ATMs, restaurants and a cinema. The **Village Supermarket** has a good range of imported items and an excellent butchery. **TFA Shopping Centre**, also known as the **Shoprite Centre**, at the end of Sokoine Rd, beyond Meru Post Office and opposite the long-distance bus station, Mon-Fri 0900-1900, Sat 0800-1700, Sun 0900-1300. This is an enormous supermarket (South African chain) selling just about anything you might be looking for. The centre also has banks with ATMs, an internet café, an ice cream parlour, restaurants and several other shops, including a branch of **Woolworths**, another South African chain for quality clothes. TFA stands for the Tanganyika Farmers' Association, which owns the centre.

⚙ What to do

Arusha *p236, map p238*
Golf
Gymkhana Club, Haile Selassie Rd out towards the High Court, T0754-400 350, www.arushagolf.com. 9-hole golf course. Temporary membership available and clubs and caddies can be hired. Also has facilities for tennis and squash.

Horse and camel riding
Horse safaris are increasingly popular and can be arranged through the tour operators in Arusha. Most of these begin from Usa River, which is 22 km from Arusha on the Moshi road. For camel rides guided by a local Masai, see **Mkuru Camel Safari**, page 242.
Equestrian Safaris, based on a farm on the slopes of Mt Meru, T0754-595 517, www.safaririding.com. Offer day rides, and 3- to 14-day horse safaris around Kilimanjaro, Meru and Lake Natron. These are for experienced riders, as several hours a day are spent in the saddle. A real opportunity to explore terrain where vehicles cannot go. Full-board rates, inclusive of meals and fly

camping, are around US$300 per day.
Meserani Snake Park (see page 241). Ride a camel to a nearby Masai village.

Swimming
Some of the hotels allow non-guests to use their pools for a small fee. Try the **Il Boru Safari Lodge** or **Impala Hotel**.

Tour operators
Note The cost of taking foreign-registered cars into the national parks in Tanzania means that it is usually cheaper to go on a safari in a Tanzania-registered vehicle.

There are over 100 tour operators and safari companies based in Arusha who organize safaris to the different national parks in the northern circuit (see next chapter). Most also offer Mt Kilimanjaro and Meru treks, holidays in Zanzibar, hotel and lodge reservations, vehicle hire, charter flights, cultural tours and safaris to the other parks. The list below is far from comprehensive. It is just a matter of finding one you like and discussing what you would like to do. See box opposite, for further information. Many have also adopted cultural or environmental policies – supporting local communities, schools or empowerment projects – which are worth thinking about when choosing a safari operator. On the downside, travellers have reported that rival tour companies sometimes double up, with 2 or 3 groups sharing the same cars and other facilities – all paying different amounts. As a result, itineraries are changed without agreement. It is a good idea to draw up a written contract of exactly what is included in the price agreed before handing over any money. Sometimes touts (known in Arusha as 'fly-catchers') for rival tour companies are very persistent and this can be very frustrating. To get them off your back, tell them you have already booked a safari, even if you haven't. Once in Arusha, give yourself at least a day or 2 to shop around and organize everything. Likewise, allow for

How to organize a safari

→ Figure out how much money you are willing to spend, how many days you would like to go for, which parks you want to visit and when you want to go.

→ If you have the time before arriving in Arusha, check out the websites and contact the safari operators with questions and ideas. Decide which ones you prefer from the quality of the feedback you get.

→ Go to the Tanzania Tourist Board at the clock tower and ask to see the list of licensed tour operators. Also ask to have a copy of the companies that are blacklisted and that are not licensed to operate tours.

→ Pick 3-4 tour operators in your price range.

→ Shop around. Talk to the companies. Notice if they are asking you questions in order to gain an understanding of what you are looking for, or if they are just trying to book you on their next safari (regardless of what would be the best for you). Also, are they open about answering your questions and interested in helping you get the information you need. Avoid the ones that are pressuring you.

→ Make sure you understand what is included in the price, and what is not.

Normally, breakfast on the first day and dinner/accommodation on the last day is not included.

→ Listen to the salesperson and guide. They have current news about which parks are best at the moment. If they recommend you a different itinerary than you originally planned, it is probably the best itinerary for game viewing. They know the best areas to visit depending on the time of year and where the animals are in their yearly migrations.

→ Get a contract with all details regarding itinerary, conditions and payment.

→ Ask what kind of meals you can expect. If you are on a special diet, confirm that they can accommodate your needs.

→ Ask how many people will be on the safari. Make sure there is enough room in the vehicle for people and equipment.

→ Talk to the guide. Make sure that he is able to communicate with you, and that he is knowledgeable.

→ If possible, inspect the vehicle you will be using beforehand. If you are going on a camping safari or trek, ask to see the equipment (tents, sleeping bags, etc).

---

at least 1 night in Arusha on the final day of your safari as you will usually return late.

Blacklist At the tourist office there is a blacklist of rogue travel agencies, unlicensed agents and the names of people who have convictions for cheating tourists. It is recommended that you cross-check before paying for a safari. In addition, when going on safari, check at the park gate that all the fees have been paid, especially if you plan to stay for more than a day in the park. Also check that the name of the tour company is written on the permit. Sadly, there is a lot of cheating at present, and many tourists have fallen victim to well-organized scams. The tourist office also has a list of accredited tour companies, and you can find more on the Tanzania Association of Tour Operators website: www.tatotz.org. For details of other safari companies, both within Tanzania and overseas, see page 39.

Aardvark Expeditions, Nelson Mandela (Old Moshi) Rd, Kijenge, T0754-759 120, www.aardvark-expeditions.com. Good reports about this company, which operates mostly mid-upper range safaris and treks. As well as Meru and Kilimanjaro, they also offer treks to Ol Donyo Lengai and to Olmeti and Empakai Craters, and safaris across the country.

Adventureland Safaris, Sokoine Rd, T027-250 8360, www.adventurelandsafari.com. All safaris, Kili and Meru climbs, cultural tours to the Lake Natron and Lake Eyasi regions, trips to Zanzibar. Budget operator.

Africa Royal Trekking, based at **Arusha View Campsite**, see Where to stay, page 252, T0754-040 810, www.africa-royal-trekking.com. Safaris, Meru and Kilimanjaro climbs.

African Trails Ltd, Njiro Rd, T027-254 9183, www.africantrails.com. Mid-range and budget tours to the major parks.

Angoni Safaris, AICC, www.angoni.com. Safaris throughout Tanzania, cultural tours including trekking and donkey rides.

Bobby Tours, Goliondoi Rd, T027-250 3490, www.bobbytours.com. Good-value camping safaris, expect to pay around US$900 for a 5 day/4 night safari to the crater and Serengeti.

Bush Buck Safaris, Simeon Rd, T027-250 7779, www.bushbuckltd.com. An established operator with more than 20 years' experience, all safaris, hotel reservations, special arrangements for honeymooners, all the vehicles are 4WD landrovers, not minibuses.

Classic Tours & Safaris, Impala Hotel, see Where to stay, page 249, T027-254 3082, www.theclassictours.com. Safaris to the northern circuit plus mountain climbs and 1-day tours to Arusha and Tarangire national parks, all budgets.

Duma Explorer, Njiro Rd, T0787-079 127, www.dumaexplorer.com. Consistently good feedback from readers for this company, good-value northern circuit safaris and Kili climbs, some of their profits support a local school, excellent guides and food.

Easy Travel & Tours Ltd, New Safari Hotel, see Where to stay, page 250, T027-250 3929. In Dar, see page 72, www.easytravel.co.tz. Budget tours to all the Tanzanian parks, mountain trekking for Kili and Meru, also a general travel agent and can book flights.

Fortes Safaris, Nairobi Rd, T027-254 4887, www.fortes-safaris.com. Mid-range operator using the Serena and Sopa lodges in the parks, and can also arrange car hire, www.fortescarhire.com.

Good Earth Tours and Safaris, Arusha Municipality Rd, T0732-902 655, www.goodearthtours.com. Kili climbs, safaris, beach holidays, standard and luxury lodges.

Green Footprint Adventures, Sekei Village Rd, T0784-203 000, www.greenfootprintactive.com. Offer more adventurous activities, such as canoeing in Manyara and Arusha national parks, night game drives in Manyara, and mid- to high-budget safaris specializing in small camps and lodges.

Hima Tours & Safaris, Shule Rd, T027-250 7681, www.himatoursnsafaris.com. A variety of tours to all the parks and can also arrange mountain-bike and camel safaris.

Hoopoe Safaris, India St, T027-250 7011, www.hoopoe.com. Consistently recommended by travellers and a frequent award-winning company for its excellent commitment to local communities and conservation. Range of safaris and climbs and unusual trekking itineraries with the Masai. Run exclusive safaris using their **Kirurumu Under Canvas** tented camps, www.kirurumu. net. Some of the permanent camps are listed in the relevant chapters, some move seasonally. Highly recommended.

JMT African Heart, just outside town, not far from **Ilboru Safari Lodge**, T0732-975 428, www.africanheart.com. Luxury and budget safaris. Horseback, motorbike and mountain bike safaris, cultural treks, Kili climbs, Zanzibar.

JM Tours Ltd, Plot 15, Olorien, T027-254 3310, www.jmtours.co.tz. Specializing in travel planning for disabled travellers, school exchange programs and cultural tourism.

Kearsley Travel & Tours, Col Middleton Rd, T027-250 8043, www.kearsley.com. Established safari operator with over 60 years' experience.

Klub Afriko Safaris, at the Klub Afriko **Hotel**, see page 251, T027-254 8878, www. klubafriko.com. Various safaris, specializing in Serengeti, Tarangire, Zanzibar and Kilimanjaro.

Laitolya Tours & Safaris, Meru Plaza, Esso Rd, T027-254 7536, www.laitolya.com. Northern circuit, Mikumi, Udzungwa and Bagamoyo. Scheduled and custom-made.

Leopard Tours, Nelson Mandela (Old Moshi) Rd, Kijenge, T027-250 3603, www.leopard-tours.com. One of the bigger tour operators offering safaris in the northern circuit, Kilimanjaro climbs, cultural and historical tours, and beach trips.

Lions Safari International, Sakina/Nairobi Rd, T027-250 6423, www.lions-safari-intl. com. Good, professional company operating camping and lodge 3-11 day safaris.

Moon Adventure Tours & Safaris, Seth Benjamin Rd, opposite Meru School, T027-250 4462, www.moon-adventure-safaris. com. Low-cost camping safaris, Ngorongoro Highlands trekking, birdwatching safaris.

Nature Beauties, Nelson Mandela (Old Moshi) Rd, T027-254 8224, www.nature beauties.com. Alternative routes and trekking safaris with a strong focus on sustainability of environment.

Nature Discovery, PO Box 10574, T0732-971 859, www.naturediscovery.com. Tailor their trips, including Kilimanjaro and Oldonyo Lengai climbs, to the traveller and their budget.

Predators Safari Club, Namanga Rd, Sakina, T027-250 6471, www.predators-safaris.com. Wide range of safaris, from luxury lodges to camping all over Kenya and Tanzania, good national park combination packages, professionally run.

Ranger Safaris, Wachagga St, T027-250 3023, www.rangersafaris.com. Easily one of the biggest safari operators in Tanzania with a wide choice of lodge and camping safaris from 3 to 10 days and regular departure dates.

Roy Safaris Ltd, 44 Serengeti Rd, T027-250 2115, www.roysafaris.com. Good value and experienced operator offering both luxury lodge and camping safaris to the Northern

Circuit game parks and Kili and Meru treks, as well as treks in the Ngorongoro highlands, trips to Zanzibar and cultural tours.

Shidolya Safaris, AICC, T027-254 8506, www.shidolya-safaris.com. Lodge or camping safaris, Kili climbs and 1-day birdwatching safaris in Arusha National Park.

Simba Safaris, between Goliondoi Rd and India St, T027-254 9115, www.simba safaris.com. Kili climbs, reservations for Pemba and Mafia, safari packages, lots of departure dates.

Skylink Travel & Tours, Goliondoi Rd, T027-250 9108, www.skylinktanzania.com. Quality travel agent for flights, also has offices in Dar and Mwanza, agent for Avis Rent-a-Car.

Sunny Safaris Ltd, Col Middleton Rd, T027-250 8184, www.sunnysafaris.com. A very good fleet of game-viewing vehicles, lodge and camping safaris, mountain trekking, mountain bike and walking safaris.

Takims Holidays Tours and Safaris, Uhuru Rd, T027-250 8026, www.takimsholidays. com. An established operator with over 20 years' experience. Photographic safaris to all the national parks, including Serengeti, Kilimanjaro, Selous and Ruaha.

Tanzania Serengeti Adventure, Nelson Mandela (Old Moshi) Rd, T027-250 4069 www.abouttanzania.com. Range of lodge or budget camping safaris and Zanzibar bookings.

Tanzania Travel Company, AICC, T027-250 3349, www.tanzaniatravelcompany.com. Experienced and reliable, offering a range of classic and budget safaris, Kili and Meru climbs, cultural tours, trekking with Masai and trips to Zanzibar.

Tropical Trails, Masai Camp on Nelson Mandela (Old Moshi) Rd, T027-250 0358, www.tropicaltrails.com. Experienced operator offering northern circuit safaris

aimed at the budget and mid-range traveller, Lengani, Meru and Kilimanjaro climbs, cultural tours and crater highland trekking. **Victoria Expeditions Safaris & Travels**, Meru House Inn, Sokoine Rd, T027-250 0444, www.victoriatz.com. Professionally run safaris and trekking, Northern Circuit with 2-7 days camping, Zanzibar beach holidays, Kili climbs. **Wild Frontiers**, reservations Johannesburg, T+27-(0)72 927 7529, www.wildfrontiers. com. Excellent tour operator offering safaris across Tanzania, particularly northern circuit parks and Kilimanjaro treks. They also run lovely mobile camps in the Serengeti and Ngorongoro. Highly recommended. **Wildersun Safaris and Tours**, Joel Maeda Rd, T027-254 8847, www.wildersun.com. Standard safaris and can also organize half-day canoeing trips to Arusha National Park and Lake Duluti. **WS Safaris Ltd**, Moshono Village, near Baraa Primary School, T027-250 4004, www.wssafari.com. Offering a range of safaris including Kili climbs and trekking in the Ngorongoro Highlands.

⊖ Transport

Arusha *p236, map p238*
Air
Kilimanjaro International Airport, T027-255 4252, www.kilimanjaroairport.co.tz, is 40 km east of Arusha and 55 km west of Moshi off the A23. For details of getting to and from the airport, see Getting there, page 236. For details of international airlines serving Kilimanjaro, see Essentials, page 11.

Fly 540 has daily flights to **Dar**, some of which are on a circuit with **Zanzibar**, and flights to/from **Nairobi**, which connect with flights to **Mombasa**. Precision Air has daily flights to **Dar**, some of which are also on a circuit with **Zanzibar**, and **Mwanza**. They also have daily flights to/from **Nairobi** in Kenya, and **Entebbe** in Uganda.

Closer to town is **Arusha Airport**, 10 km west along the road to Dodoma.

Air Excel has daily scheduled circuits between Arusha, **Zanzibar** and **Dar**, and another circuit from Arusha to the lodges in the **Serengeti**. They also touch down at **Kilimanjaro** to meet Air Kenya flights from Wilson Airport in Nairobi.

Coastal Air has daily flights to/from **Dar**, which connect to **Zanzibar**, to **Tanga**, which continues on to **Zanzibar**, to **Grumeti** and the other airstrips in the **Serengeti**, and to **Ruaha** via **Manyara**, **Tarangire** and **Dodoma**.

Regional Air operates similar circuits to Air Excel between Arusha, **Zanzibar** and **Dar**, and the lodges in the **Serengeti**.

ZanAir has daily flights between Arusha and **Dar** and Arusha and **Zanzibar**, one of which continues to **Pemba**.

Airline offices Air Excel, Goliondoi Rd, T027-254 8429, www.airexcelonline.com. Coastal Air, Boma Rd, T027-508 038, www. coastal.cc. Ethiopian Airlines, New Safari Hotel Complex, Boma Rd, T027-250 6167, www.flyethiopia. com. **Fly 540**, Blue Plaza Building, India St, T0756-540 540, www.fly 540.com. KLM, New Safari Hotel Complex, Boma Rd, T027-250 8062/3, www.klm.com. Precision Air, New Safari Hotel Complex, Boma Rd, T027-250 6903, www.precision airtz.com. **Regional Air**, Nairobi Rd, T027-250 541, www.regionaltanzania.com.

Bus, dala-dala and shared taxi
There are now 2 bus stations in Arusha. The first is on Zaramo St just to the north of the market and buses from here mostly go to places not too far away. Buy your ticket from the driver on the day of travel. There are regular buses and *dala-dala* to **Moshi**, 1½ hrs, US$1.50. You can also get a shared taxi, which will be more expensive.

Long-distance buses go from the new bus station opposite the TFA/Shoprite Shopping Centre at the western end of Sokoine Rd. There are reported to be thieves operating around the Arusha bus stations and there are certainly many persistent touts. Go directly to the bus companies' offices and make sure the company's stamp is on the ticket. There are daily departures to **Tanga** via **Moshi**, 7 hrs, US$7, and to **Mwanza**, via either the **Serengeti**, **Singida** or **Nairobi** (see below). There are countless departures each day to **Dar**, 9 hrs, around US$15 'Deluxe', and US$10 'semi-luxury'. Both **Dar Express**, Colonel Middleton St, T0744-946 155, and **Royal Coaches**, Colonel Middleton St, T027-250 7959, offer a fast, reliable service. **Scandinavia Express Services Ltd**, Kituoni St near the police mess, south of the local bus station, T027-250 0153, www.scandinaviagroup.com, are recommended for reliability and safety and, as well as daily services to **Dar**, they offer a daily service to/from **Mwanza**, 20 hrs, US$22, via **Nairobi** (you will have to buy a transit visa for Kenya; US$20).

To Kenya *Dala-dala* take 4 or 5 hrs from here, depart regularly through the day; the border crossing is efficient (see page 237), but of course you will have to swap vehicles at the border. The better option are the through shuttle services to **Nairobi**, see box, page 15, which depart at 0800 and 1400 daily, US$30, and can be booked through hotels or tour operators. These include **Impala Shuttle**, at the Impala Hotel (see Where to stay page 249), T0754-678 678, www.impalashuttle.com, and **Riverside Shuttle**, ACU Building, Sokoine Rd, T027-250 2639, www.riverside-shuttle.com.

Car hire

Most of the tour operators (see page 258) can organize car hire. Also try **Easy Travel & Tours Ltd**, New Safari Hotel, see Where to stay, page 250, T027-250 3929, www.easy travel.co.tz, or **Fortes Safaris**, Nairobi Rd, T027-254 4887, www.fortes-safaris.com, www.fortescarhire.com. **Skylink Travel & Tours**, Goliondoi Rd, T027-250 9108, www.skylinktanzania.com, is the agent for **Avis**, www.avis.com.

Cars can also be hired at the **Arusha Naaz Hotel** and **Impala Hotel**.

❶ Directory

Arusha *p236, map p238*
Immigration Immigration office, East Africa Community Rd, T027-250 3569, Mon-Fri 0730-1530 for visa extensions. **Medical services** In the event of a serious medical emergency, you will be transferred to Nairobi. **Arusha International Conference Centre (AICC) Hospital**, Nelson Mandela (Old Moshi) Rd, T027-250 2329, www.aicc. co.tz; **Mount Meru Regional Hospital**, opposite AICC, East Africa Community Rd, T027-250 3351-3. **Police** Makongoro Rd, T027-250 3541. Always inform the police of any incidents – you will need a police statement for any insurance claims.

East African wildlife

Introduction

A large proportion of people who visit East Africa do so to see its spectacular wildlife. This colour section is a quick photographic guide to some of the more fascinating mammals you may encounter. We give you pictures and information about habitat, habits and characteristic appearance to help you when you are on safari. It is by no means a comprehensive survey and some of the animals listed may not be found throughout the whole region. For further information about East Africa's mammals, birds, reptiles and other wildlife, see the Land and environment section of the Background chapter, page 429.

The Big Nine

It is fortunate that many of the large and spectacular animals of Africa are also, on the whole, fairly common. They are often known as the 'Big Five'. This term was originally coined by hunters who wanted to take home trophies of their safari. Thus it was, that, in hunting parlance, the Big Five were elephant, black rhino, buffalo, lion and leopard. Nowadays the hippopotamus is usually considered one of the Big Five for those who shoot with their cameras, whereas the buffalo is far less of a 'trophy'. Equally photogenic and worthy of being included are the zebra, giraffe and cheetah. But whether they are the Big Five or the Big Nine, these are the animals that most people come to Africa to see and, with the possible exception of the leopard and the black rhino, you have an excellent chance of seeing them all.

■ **Hippopotamus** *Hippopotamus amphibius*. Prefers shallow water, grazes on land over a wide area at night, so can be found quite a distance from water, and has a strong sense of territory, which it protects aggressively. Lives in large family groups known as 'schools'.

■ **Black rhinoceros** *Diceros bicornis*. Long, hooked upper lip distinguishes it from white rhino rather than colour. Prefers dry bush and thorn scrub habitat and in the past was found in mountain uplands. Males usually solitary. Females seen in small groups with their calves (very rarely more than four), sometimes with two generations. Mother always walks in front of offspring, unlike the white rhino, where the mother walks behind, guiding calf with her horn. Their distribution was massively reduced by poaching in the late 20th century, and now there are conservation efforts in place to protect black and white rhino and numbers are increasing. You might be lucky and see the black rhino in Ngorongoro Crater and in the Selous.

■ **White rhinoceros** *Diceros simus*. Square muzzle and bulkier than the black rhino, it is a grazer rather than a browser, hence the different lip. Found in open grassland, it is more sociable and can be seen in groups of five or more. Probably extinct in much of its former range in East Africa, it still flourishes in some places.

Opposite page:
Leopard with a kill.
Above left:
Black rhinoceros.
Above right:
White rhinoceros.
Right:
Hippopotamus.

■ **Common/Masai giraffe** *Giraffa camel-opardis*. Yellowish-buff with patchwork of brownish marks and jagged edges, usually two different horns, sometimes three. Found throughout Africa, several differing subspecies.

■ **Common/Burchell's zebra** *Equus burchelli*. Generally has broad stripes (some with lighter shadow stripes next to the dark ones) that cross the top of the hind leg in unbroken lines. The true species is probably extinct but there are many varying subspecies found in different locations across Africa.

■ **Leopard** *Panthera pardus*. Found in varied habitats ranging from forest to open savannah. It is generally nocturnal, hunting at night or before the sun comes up to avoid the heat. Sometimes seen resting during the day in the lower branches of trees.

■ **Cheetah** *Acinonyx jubatus*. Often seen in family groups walking across plains or resting in the shade. The black 'tear' mark is usually obvious through binoculars. Can reach speeds

of 90 kph over short distances. Found in open, semi-arid savannah, never in forested country. Endangered in some parts of Africa. More commonly seen than the leopard.

■ **Elephant** *Loxodonta africana*. Commonly seen, even on short safaris, elephants have suffered from the activities of ivory poachers in East Africa. Tarangire is famous for its elephant population, with as many as 4000 at certain times of the year. Elephants are also prevalent in all other parks in Tanzania.

■ **Buffalo** *Syncerus caffer*. Were considered by hunters to be the most dangerous of the big game and the most difficult to track and, therefore, the biggest trophy. Generally found on open plains but also at home in dense forest, they are fairly common in most African national parks. They need a large area to roam in, so are not usually found in the smaller parks.

■ **Lion** *Panthera leo* (see page i). The largest of the big cats in Africa and also the most common, they are found on open savannah. They are often not disturbed at all by the presence of humans and so it possible to get quite close to them. They are sociable animals living in prides or permanent family groups of up to around 30 animals and are the only felid to do so. The females do most of the hunting.

Left: Common giraffe.
Above: Common zebra.
Opposite page top: Elephant.
Opposite page middle: Cheetah.
Opposite page bottom: Buffalo.

Top: Chimpanzee. **Left**: Chacma baboon. **Right**: Vervet monkey.

■ **Vervet monkey** *Chlorocebus pygerythrus*, 39-43 cm. A smallish primate and one of the most recognized monkeys in Africa. Brown bodies with a white underbelly and black face ringed by white fur, and males have blue abdominal regions. Spends the day foraging on the ground and sleeps at night in trees.

■ **Chimpanzee** *Pan troglodytes*, 0.6-1.2 m tall. A primate that is the closest living relative to a human being, with black/brown fur, and human-like fingers and toes. Uses tools, has a complex structure of communicating and displays emotions, including laughing out loud.

■ **Chacma baboon** *Papio ursinus*. An adult male baboon is slender and weighs about 40 kg. Their general colour is a brownish grey, with lighter undersides. Usually seen in trees, but rocks can also provide sufficient protection, they occur in large family troops and have a reputation for being aggressive where they have become used to the presence of humans.

Larger antelopes

■ **Beisa oryx** *Oryx beisa*, 122 cm. Also known as the East African oryx, there are two sub-species; the **common Beisa oryx** is found in semi-desert areas north of the Tana River, while the **fringe-eared oryx** is found south of the Tana River and in Tanzania. Both look similar with grey coats, white underbellies, short chestnut-coloured mane, and both sexes have long straight ringed horns. They gather in herds of up to 40.

■ **Common waterbuck** *Kobus ellipsiprymnus* and **Defassa waterbuck** *Kobus defassa*, 122-137 cm. Very similar with shaggy coats and white markings on buttocks: on the common variety, this is a clear half ring on the rump and around the tail; on the Defassa, the ring is a filled-in solid area. Both species occur in small herds in grassy areas, often near water.

Top: Beisa oryx. **Bottom left:** Defassa waterbuck. **Bottom right:** Common waterbuck.

■ **Sable antelope** *Hippotragus niger*, 140-145 cm, and **Roan antelope** *Hippotragus equinus* 127-137 cm. Both are similar in shape, with ringed horns curving backwards (both sexes), longer in the sable. Female sables are reddish brown and can be mistaken for the roan. Males are very dark with a white underbelly. The roan has distinct tufts of hair at the tips of its long ears. The sable prefers wooded areas and the roan is generally only seen near water. Both species live in herds.

■ **Greater kudu** *Tragelaphus strepsiceros*, 140-153 cm. Colour varies from greyish to fawn with several vertical white stripes down the sides of the body. Horns long and spreading, with two or three twists (male only). Distinctive thick fringe of hair running from the chin down the neck. Found in fairly thick bush, sometimes in quite dry areas. Usually lives in family groups of up to six, but occasionally in larger herds of up to about 30.

■ **Topi** *Damaliscus korrigum*, 122-127 cm. Very rich dark rufous, with dark patches on the tops of the legs and more ordinary looking, lyre-shaped horns.

■ **Hartebeest** The horns arise from a bony protuberance on the top of the head and curve outwards and backwards. There are two sub-species: **Coke's hartebeest** *Alcephalus buselaphus*, 122 cm, is a drab pale brown with a paler rump; **Lichtenstein's hartebeest** *Alcephalus lichtensteinii*, 127-132 cm, is also fawn in colour, with a rufous wash over the back and dark marks on the front of the legs and often a dark patch near the shoulder. All are found in herds, sometimes they mix with other plains dwellers such as zebra.

■ **White-bearded wildebeest** *Connochaetes taurinus*, 132 cm. Distinguished by its white beard and smooth cow-like horns, often seen grazing with zebra. Gathers in large herds, following the rains.
■ **Eland** *Taurotragus oryx*, 175-183 cm. The largest of the antelope, it has a noticeable dewlap and shortish spiral horns (both sexes). Greyish to fawn, sometimes with rufous tinge and narrow white stripes down side of body. Occurs in groups of up to 30 in grassy habitats.

Top: White-bearded wildebeest. **Middle:** Coke's hartebeest. **Bottom:** Eland.

Smaller antelope

■ **Bushbuck** *Tragelaphus scriptus*, 76-92 cm. Shaggy coat with white spots and stripes on the side and back and two white, crescent-shaped marks on neck. Short horns (male only), slightly spiral. High rump gives characteristic crouch. White underside of tail is noticeable when running. Occurs in thick bush, often near water, in pairs or singly.

■ **Kirk's dikdik** *Rhynchotragus kirkii*, 36-41 cm. So small it cannot be mistaken, it is greyish brown, often washed with rufous. Legs are thin and stick-like. Slightly elongated snout and a conspicuous tuft of hair on the top of the head. Straight, small horns (male only). Found in bush country, singly or in pairs.

■ **Steenbok** *Raphicerus campestris*, 58 cm. An even, rufous brown with clean white underside and white ring around eye. Small dark patch at the tip of the nose and long broad ears. The horns (male only) are slightly longer than the ears: they are sharp, smooth and curve slightly forward. Generally seen alone, prefers open plains and more arid regions. A slight creature that usually runs off very quickly on being spotted.

■ **Bohor reedbuck** *Redunca redunca*, 71-76 cm. Horns (males only) sharply hooked forwards at the tip, distinguishing them from the oribi (see page xiii). It is reddish fawn with white underparts and has a short bushy tail. It usually lives in pairs or in small family groups. Often seen with oribi, in bushed grassland and always near water.

■ **Grant's gazelle** *Gazella granti*, 81-99 cm, and **Thomson's gazelle** *Gazella thomsonii*, 64-69 cm (see page xii). Colour varies from a bright rufous to a sandy rufous. Grant's is the larger of the two and has longer horns. In both species the curved horns are carried by both sexes.

■ **Common (Grimm's) duiker** *Sylvicapra grimmia*, 58 cm (see page xii). Grey-fawn colour with darker rump and pale colour on the underside. Its dark muzzle and prominent ears are divided by straight, upright, narrow pointed horns. This particular species is the only duiker found in open grasslands. Usually the duiker is associated with a forested environment. It is difficult to see because it is shy and will quickly disappear into the bush.

■ **Oribi** *Ourebia ourebi*, 61 cm (see page xiii). Slender and delicate looking with a longish neck and a sandy to brownish-fawn coat. It has oval-shaped ears and short, straight horns with a few rings at their base (male only). Like the reedbuck, it has a patch of bare skin just below each ear. Lives in small groups or as a pair and is never far from water.

Above: Bushbuck.

■ **Suni** *Nesotragus moschatus*, 37 cm (see page xiii). Dark chestnut to grey-fawn in colour with slight speckles along the back, its head and neck are slightly paler and the throat is white. It has a distinctive bushy tail with a white tip. Its longish horns (male only) are thick, ribbed and slope backwards. They live alone and prefer dense bush cover and reed beds.

Top: Kirk's dikdik. **Bottom left:** Bohor reedbuck. **Bottom right:** Steenbok.

■ **Impala** *Aepyceros melampus*, 92-107 cm. One of the largest of the smaller antelope, the impala is a bright rufous colour on its back and has a white abdomen, a white 'eyebrow' and chin and white hair inside its ears. From behind, the white rump with black stripes on each side is characteristic and makes it easy to identify. It has long lyre-shaped horns (male only). Above the heels of the hind legs is a tuft of thick black bristles (unique to impala), which are easy to see when the animal runs. There is also a black mark on the side of abdomen, just in front of the back leg. Found in herds of 15 to 20, it likes open grassland or sometimes the cover of partially wooded areas and is usually close to water.

Top: Thomson's gazelle. **Bottom:** Common duiker.

Top left: Oribi. Top right: Suni. Bottom: Impala.

Other mammals

There are many other fascinating mammals worth keeping an eye out for. This is a selection of some of the more interesting or particularly common ones.

■ **African wild dog** or **hunting dog** *Lycacon pictus*. Easy to identify since they have all the features of a large mongrel dog: a large head and slender body. Their coat is a mixed pattern of dark shapes and white and yellow patches and no two dogs are quite alike. They are very rarely seen and are seriously threatened with extinction (there may be as few as 6000 left). Found on the open plains around dead animals, they are not in fact scavengers but effective pack hunters.

■ **Spotted hyena** *Crocuta crocuta*. High shoulders and low back give the hyena its characteristic appearance and reputedly it has the strongest jaws in the animal kingdom. The spotted variety, larger and brownish with dark spots, has a large head and rounded ears. The **striped hyena**, slightly smaller, has pointed ears and several distinctive black vertical stripes around its torso and is more solitary. Although sometimes shy animals, they have been known to wander around campsites stealing food from humans.

Top: African wild dog.
Middle: Spotted hyena.
Bottom: Black-backed jackal.

■ **Black-backed jackal** *Canis mesomelas*, 30-40 cm tall. Also known as the silver-back jackal, a carnivore with dog-like features, a long muzzle, bushy tail and pointed ears. So-called for the strip of black hair that runs from the back of the neck to the tail.

■ **Warthog** *Phacochoerus aethiopicus*. The warthog is almost hairless and grey with a very large head, tusks and wart-like growths on its face. It frequently occurs in family parties and when startled will run away at speed with its tail held straight up in the air. They are often seen near water caking themselves in thick mud, which helps to keep them both cool and free of ticks and flies.

■ **Rock hyrax** *Procavia capensis*. The nocturnal rock hyrax lives in colonies amongst boulders and on rocky hillsides, protecting themselves from predators like eagles, caracals and leopards by darting into rock crevices.

■ **Caracal** *Felis caracal*. Also known as the African lynx, it is twice the weight of a domestic cat, with reddish sandy-coloured fur and paler underparts. Distinctive black stripe from eye to nose and tufts on ears. Generally nocturnal and with similar habits to the leopard. They are not commonly seen, but are found in hilly country.

Top: Warthog. **Middle:** Rock hyrax.
Bottom: Caracal.

Contents

At a glance

⊖ **Getting around** The best option is local tour operators, who cater for every budget. There is some public transport to towns near park borders, then you'll need to book day trips into parks.

❂ **Time required** At least 3 days for the Serengeti and a day for Ngorongoro Crater. If you want to go off the beaten track, spend a couple of days in Manyara or Tarangire – both are worth exploring.

☽ **Weather** Warm and sunny for most of the year, although evenings can be cool, especially Jun-Oct. Light rains Nov-Dec and heavy rains end of Mar-May. Hot and sticky before the rains.

✖ **When not to go** Roads in the parks can be challeging and often impassable during the rainy season (Apr-May), with access to the crater floor sometimes restricted.

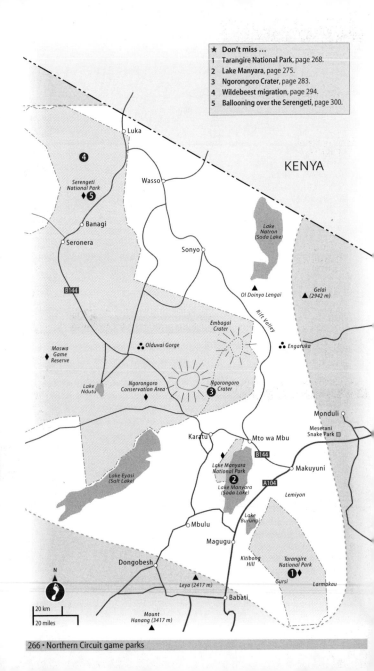

★ **Don't miss ...**
1 Tarangire National Park, page 268.
2 Lake Manyara, page 275.
3 Ngorongoro Crater, page 283.
4 Wildebeest migration, page 294.
5 Ballooning over the Serengeti, page 300.

KENYA

Luka

Wasso

❹

Serengeti
National Park
♦ ❺

Banagi

Seronera

Sonyo

Lake
Natron
(Soda Lake)

B144

Ol Doinyo Lengai ▲

▲ Gelai
(2942 m)

Rift Valley

Embagai
Crater

Olduvai Gorge

Engaruka

Maswa
Game
Reserve

Ngorongoro
Conservation Area

Ngorongoro
Crater
❸

Lake
Ndutu

Monduli

Karatu

Mto wa Mbu

Meserani
Snake Park

B144

Lake Manyara
National Park
❷

Makuyuni

A104

Lake Eyasi
(Salt Lake)

Lake Manyara
(Soda Lake)

Lemiyon

Lake
Burungi

Mbulu

Magugu

Kitibong
Hill

Tarangire
National Park
❶ ♦

Dongobesh

Gursi

Larmakau

▲ Leya (2417 m)

N

Babati

20 km
20 miles

Mount
Hanang (3417 m)

Everything you imagine Africa to be is here in the Northern Circuit Game Parks, from the soaring masses of wildebeest galloping across the plains of the Serengeti, to the iconic image of a lone acacia tree at sunset, to exclusive *Out of Africa*-style lodges deep in the bush. By now, the area is extremely experienced in catering for tourists – it's the most visited region of Tanzania – and it's able to provide for most budgets from the über-luxurious to the camping backpackers.

Despite its popularity, it's still easy to escape the crowds. Tarangire National Park, famous for its elephants and quirky baobab trees, is overlooked by many travellers wanting to head for the big names in game parks, and yet it has a gentle beauty and varied landscapes with tremendous birdlife as well as game. Then there's Lake Manyara National Park, where the lake becomes a blanket of pink, as flamingos come here to feed on their migratory route. Also in this region are the little-visited Lake Natron and Ol Doinyo Lengai volcano – a challenging climb for robust walkers – which offer a glimpse into the rural lives of the local Masai.

Ngorongoro Crater never disappoints and, because of its steep sides, it has almost captive wildlife. Even if you see nothing, the stunning landscapes within this 265-sq-km caldera 600 m below its rim are reward enough. And last, but far from least, there's the vast Serengeti. From December to April it's the scene of the world's most famous mass migration, when hundreds of thousands of wildebeest pound the path trodden for centuries to the Masai Mara – definitely a sight not to be missed.

Arriving at the Northern Circuit game parks

About 80 km west of Arusha on the road towards Dodoma, there is a T-junction at Makuyuni. The entrance to the Tarangire National Park is 20 km to the south of this junction, off the Arusha–Dodoma road, whilst the road that heads due west goes towards Lake Manyara, the Ngorongoro Crater and the Serengeti. This road used to be notoriously bad, with deep ruts and potholes, but it was upgraded a few years ago to smooth tar all the way to the gate of the crater. The drive to the gate of the Ngorongoro Conservation Area takes about four hours and is a splendid journey. On clear days, you'll have a view of Mount Kilimanjaro all the way, arching over the right shoulder of Mount Meru. You will go across the bottom of the Rift Valley and, at the small settlement of Mto wa Mbu, pass the entrance to the Lake Manyara National Park at the foot of the Great Rift Escarpment. Just beyond the entrance to the park, the road climbs very steeply up the escarpment and there are wonderful views back down onto Lake Manyara. From here, the country is hilly and fertile, and you will climb up to the Mbulu Plateau which is farmed with wheat, maize and coffee. The extinct volcano of Ol Deani has gentle slopes and is a prominent feature of the landscape.

All the safari operators offer, at the very least, a three-day and two-night safari of the crater and Serengeti, most offer extended tours to include Tarangire or Manyara, and some include the less visited Ol Doinyo Lengai and Lake Natron. There is the option of self-drive, but as non-Tanzanian vehicles attract much higher entrance fees into the parks, this is not normally cost effective. ▸▸ *For more information on national park fees and safaris, see page 10. For safari tour operators in Arusha, see page 258.*

Tarangire National Park

Tarangire National Park, established in 1970, covers an area of 2600 sq km and is named after the river that flows through it throughout the year. Unjustifiably considered the poor relation to its neighbouring parks, Tarangire may have a less spectacular landscape and does make you work harder for your game, but it also retains a real sense of wilderness reminiscent of more remote parks like Ruaha and Katavi. It's famous for its enormous herds of elephant that congregate along the river; it is not unusual to see groups of 100 or more, including some impressive old bulls. The best time to visit is in the dry season from July to September, when the animals gather in large numbers along the river. There are fewer people here than in Ngorongoro and that is very much part of the attraction. One of the most noticeable things on entering the park are the baobab trees, instantly recognizable by their massive trunks. As the park includes within its boundaries a number of hills, as well as rivers and swamps, there is a variety of vegetation zones and habitats. The river rises in the Kondoa Highlands to the south and flows north through the length of the park. It continues to flow during the dry season and so is a vital watering point for the animals of the park, as well as those from surrounding areas.
▸▸ *For listings, see pages 272-273.*

Park information

Tanzania National Parks Authority (TANAPA), off the Dodoma road (A104), 100 km south of Arusha and about 20 km south of Makuyuni, the park entrance is 7 km off the main road, www.tanzaniaparks.com, 0630-1830, US$35, children (5-16) US$10, vehicle US$40.

Wildlife

The Tarangire National Park forms a 'dry season retreat' for much of the wildlife of the southern Masailand. The ecosystem in this area incorporates more than just Tarangire National Park. Also included are the Lake Manyara National Park to the north and a number of 'Game Controlled Areas'. The largest of these are the Lake Natron Game Controlled Area

Tarangire National Park

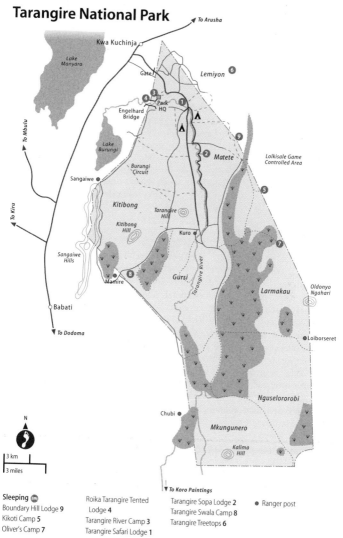

To Arusha

Kwa Kuchinja

Lake Manyara

Gate

Lemiyon **6**

To Mbulu

3
4 Park
HQ
Engelhard
Bridge **1**

9

2 Matete

To Kiru

Lolkisale Game Controlled Area

Lake
Burungi

Burungi
Circuit

Sangaiwe ●

Kitibong

Tarangire
Hill

5

Kitibong
Hill

Kuro ●

Sangaiwe
Hills

7

Mamire ● **8**

Gürsi

Larmakau

● Oldonyo
Ngahari

Babati ○

To Dodoma

● Loiborseret

N

Chubi ●

Nguselororobi

3 km
3 miles

Mkungunero

Kalima
Hill

To Koro Paintings

Sleeping 😴
Boundary Hill Lodge **9**
Kikoti Camp **5**
Oliver's Camp **7**

Roika Tarangire Tented
Lodge **4**
Tarangire River Camp **3**
Tarangire Safari Lodge **1**

Tarangire Sopa Lodge **2**
Tarangire Swala Camp **8**
Tarangire Treetops **6**

● Ranger post

Tsetse fly

The tsetse fly is a little larger than the house fly and is found over much of East Africa, including Tanzania. It is a carrier of the disease known as 'sleeping sickness' or African trypanosomiasis, known as *nagana* among the people of Tanzania. This disease can be deadly to cattle and is therefore of great economic concern to large rural areas of Africa. The presence of the tsetse fly has meant that large areas of Tanzania are uninhabitable by cattle and, consequently, human beings, as farmers need to live where their livestock grazes. Instead, these regions are left to the wild animals, as interestingly, the tsetse fly does not affect them. Since the colonial era, the areas have been gradually designated as national parks and game reserves. Tanzania is probably the worst affected

by tsetse fly of all the countries in East Africa, which goes some way to explain why 23% of the country is in designated parks and reserves. Tsetse flies can also infect humans with sleeping sickness – the disease affects the central nervous system and does indeed make you sleepy during the day – but cases in humans are very rare. Occasionally there have been endemics of sleeping sickness in East Africa, but these usually occur when large groups of people are dispersed, refugees for example, into an infected area. Tsetse flies, however, do administer a wicked bite, so try and steer clear of them. They are attracted to large objects and certain smells and dark colours – like cows. If you are riding a horse, a tsetse fly is more likely to bite the horse than you.

further north and the Simanjiro Plains Game Controlled Area towards Arusha. The Mto wa Mbu Game Controlled Area, the Lolkisale Game Controlled Area and Mkungunero Game Controlled Area are also included. The key to the ecosystem is the river, and the main animal movements begin from the river at the beginning of the short rains around October and November. The animals moving north during the wet season include wildebeest, zebra, Thompson's gazelles, buffalo, eland and hartebeest. The elephant population in this park was estimated at around 6000 in 1987 but numbers are believed to have fallen since then because of poaching. At the height of the rainy season the animals are spread out over an area of over 20,000 sq km. When the wet season ends, the animals begin their migration back south and spend the dry season (July-October) concentrated around the River Tarangire until the rains begin again.

The number of species of birds recorded in Tarangire National Park has been estimated at approximately 300. These include migrants that fly south to spend October-April away from the winter of the northern hemisphere. Here you may spot various species of herons, storks and ducks, vultures, buzzards, sparrowhawks, eagles, kites and falcons, as well as ostrich.

**Routes → ** *Colour map 1, A4. 3°50'S, 35°55'E. Altitude: 1110 m.*

The park is large enough for it not to feel crowded even when there are quite a few visitors. There are a number of routes or circuits that you can follow that take you to the major attractions.

Lake Burungi circuit

Covering about 80 km, this circuit starts at the Engelhard Bridge and goes clockwise, along the river bank. Continue through the acacia trees until about 3 km before the Kuro Range Post where you will see a turning off to the right. Down this track you will pass through a section of Combretum-Dalergia woodland as you head towards the western boundary of the park. The route continues around and the vegetation turns back to parkland with acacia trees and then back to Combretum as the road turns right and reaches a full circle at the Engelhard Bridge. Water levels have fallen and Lake Burungi is almost dry. If you are very lucky you may see leopard and rhino in this area, although the numbers of rhino have reportedly decreased.

Lemiyon area

This route covers the northern area of the park bound on each side by the eastern and western boundaries park and to the south by the river. This is where you will see the fascinating baobab trees, with their large silvery trunks and gourd-like fruits. Their huge trunks enable the trees to survive through a number of rain failures and they are characteristic of this type of landscape. Also found here are acacia trees, which provide food for giraffe. Other animals that you expect to see are wildebeest, zebra, gazelles and elephant.

Kitibong Hill circuit

This track covers the west section of the park and is centred on Kitibong Hill. It includes acacia parkland in the east and Combretum-Dalergia woodland in the west, the Gursi floodplains to the south, and the foothills of Sangaiwe Hills, along the western boundary of the park. This area is home to a variety of plains animals, including buffalo and elephant.

The Gursi and Lamarkau circuit

The grasslands found in the south of the park are home to many plain-grazing species. You are also likely to see ostrich here. During the wet season a large swamp forms in what is known as Larmakau – a corruption of the Masai word *'o'llakau'*, meaning hippo, which can be seen here.

Without a 4WD you will not be able to see much of the southernmost section of the park and, during the wet season, it is often impassable to all vehicles. There are two areas in the south – Nguselororobi to the east and Mkungunero in the southwest corner. The former is mainly swamp, with some plains and woodland, and, if you are lucky, you might see cheetah here. Mkungunero has a number of freshwater pools that serve to attract many different species.

Tarangire Conservation Area

The Tarangire Conservation Area is a 585 sq km area on the eastern boundaries of the park set aside by the local villages. The region comprises four distinct areas, the Lolkisale Conservation Area, the Naitolia Concession Area, the Makuyuni Elephant Dispersal Area, and the Lolkisale Livestock and Wildlife Zone. The Conservation Area was established to protect the main wet-season migration route from the park and to provide the animals with a natural sanctuary from the demands of modern farming methods, such as extensive deforestation by illegal charcoal collectors and years of indiscriminate poaching. What makes this whole project unique is that revenue goes directly into the local community and members of these same communities are being employed by tourism-based services within the area (see **Boundary Hill Lodge**, below). The local craftsmen have been involved in building the new lodges in the area using local renewable materials from the surrounding regions; the village councils sit on the board of directors; and women empowerment projects and local schools have received funding from the project. For more information visit www.tarangireconservation.com.

❹ Tarangire National Park listings

For sleeping and eating price codes and other relevant information, see pages 22-26.

❷ Where to stay

Tarangire National Park *p268, map p269*

$$$$ Boundary Hill Lodge, located just outside the park within the Lolkisale Conservation Area, T0787-293 727, www.tarangireconservation.com. This lodge – part-owned by the local Masai community and benefiting community projects – has 8 rooms built on the hillside, all affording total privacy with unobstructed views over the savannah and swamps. The rooms are individually designed, some with outdoor baths and toilets with a view. The restaurant and bar are set on attractive stone terraces. Walking safaris, night drives and fly camping available. Rates from US$260 per person, including activities and transfers to and from Arusha.

$$$$ Kikoti Camp, in the conservation area adjoining the park, reservations **African Conservancy Company**, Arusha, T027-250 8790, www.africanconservancycompany. com. A small luxury tented lodge built amongst a landscape of ancient boulders, baobab, mopane and fig trees, with 18 spacious tents with grass roofs and wooden decks. Large eating boma with outside campfire and comfortable deck chairs. Bush breakfast and lunches are served in secluded areas, sundowners on Kikoti Rock. Bush walks as well as game drives on offer and visits to the local Masai village. Rates from US$425 per person.

$$$$ Oliver's Camp, in the eastern part of Tarangire National Park, email for a list of agents, reservations@asiliaafrica.com, www.asilialodges.com. Intimate small luxury camp of 10 tents under thatch, with outdoor showers, well spaced out with views of a waterhole. Also a library and drinks tent, open-air dining with the manager and guides who offer walking safaris and game drives during the day. One tent is in a secluded location in the bush for honeymooners, carefully designed to blend into the landscape. From US$475 per person full board.

$$$$ Sanctuary Swala, on the edge of the Gursi swamp, reservations **Sanctuary Retreats**, UK, T+44 (0)20-7190 7728, www.sanctuaryretreats.com. Comprises 12 extremely comfortable tents raised on a wooden deck above the ground under acacia trees, each has its own butler and there's silver service dining in the restaurant that has been constructed around a baobab tree; a stunning infinity pool overlooks a waterhole and it's a first-class site for birdwatching. The staff and management team at Swala have initiated a conservation project that has recently led to the building of a school in a village that borders Tarangire. Rates US$520-765 per person full board.

$$$$ Tarangire River Camp, within a concession area set aside for conservation by the local Masai community of Minjingu, which borders Tarangire in the northwest, 3.5 km from the main gate, reservations Arusha, T0732-978 879, www.mbalimbali. com. In a beautiful setting overlooking the river and the Masai Steppes, and shaded by a giant baobab tree, are 21 well-equipped tents with wooden decks. The main building is an elegant elevated thatch-and-timber structure comprising a main lounge, wildlife reference library, dining room and cocktail bar. Rates US$175-225 per person full board.

$$$$ Tarangire Treetops, in the conservation area, reservations Arusha, T027-250 0630, www.elewanacollection. com. The 20 enormous rooms at this lodge take the form of stilt houses, constructed 3-5 m up in huge baobab and marula trees on a wooded hillside overlooking the Tarangire Sand River. It really is a beautiful and luxurious lodge, but its weakness lies in its location, being a considerable distance on rough roads from the main game-viewing areas in Tarangire. Nevertheless, excellent food and service, a swimming pool, walking safaris and night drives on offer. Rates US$630-845 per person full board.

$$$$-$$$ Tarangire Sopa Lodge, in the northeast of the park, about 30 km from the main gate, signposted, reservations Arusha, T027-250 0630-9, www.sopalodges.com. If you like intimate lodges, then this might disappoint. A large luxury lodge with 75 suites, opulent lounges, bars and restaurant. Excellent food and barbecues, large landscaped swimming pool on the edge of a rocky gorge and a shop. There are more personal choices of accommodation in the park, but this is a good option for families and offers good out-of-season reductions. Rates from US$200-550 for a double full board.

$$$ Roika Tarangire Tented Lodge, just outside the park boundary on the banks of the river about 5 km from the park gate, reservations Arusha, T027-250 9994, www. tarangireroikatentedlodge.com. Tented camp set in 20 ha, with 20 rooms themed to individual animals, with stunning wood carvings on everything from lamp stands to bedposts. Rather obscure concrete 'animal' baths extend the theme – check out the elephant bath if you can. It's not as scenically striking as its neighbour the **Tarangire River Camp**, and they seem to have gone overboard on the concrete stones in the bar, but it does have a quirky charm. Rates from US$160 for a double full board.

$$$ Tarangire Safari Lodge, 10 km into the park from the gate, lodge T027-253 1447, reservations, Arusha, T027-2544752, www.tarangiresafarilodge.com. This is a lovely lodge with 35 tents and 5 rondavaals set on an escarpment overlooking the Tarangire River and the acacia-studded plains, with beautiful sunrises. Not luxurious but comfortable, good restaurant and bar with a large swimming pool, children's pool with slide, and considerable discounts for children. This area is relatively free of tsetse flies, which are a problem in other areas of the park. Excellent value considering its location within the park. Rates from US$130 per person full board.

Camping

The National Park's public campsite is 5 km into the park from the gate and set amongst a grove of impressive baobab trees. Toilet and shower facilities are simple but above average, US$30.

There are also 12 special campsites; water and firewood are provided but there are no other facilities. Nor have they been sympathetically located in decent positions with nice views. They are, however, generally pleasant and pretty remote, US$50. These are used by the safari operators on camping tours. Further information is available from Tanzania National Parks Authority (TANAPA), head office, see page 237.

Mto wa Mbu to Lake Natron

From the turn-off on the Arusha–Dodoma road, the route northwest heads through the small town of Mto wa Mbu, home to many distinctive red-clad Masai. This used to be a popular stop for safari-goers who wanted to rest and have a break from the bumpy road, but these days the smooth tarmac carries vehicles straight through town. It is, however, the closest town to Lake Manyara National Park gate and, from here, another road goes north to Lake Natron. There are fabulous views over Manyara from the road that climbs from Mto wa Mbu towards the crater.
▶▶ *For listings, see pages 278-281.*

Getting there

There are community initiatives that can arrange a visit to this region, using the local Masai people as guides, for example the **Mkuru Camel Safari Cultural Tourism Programme** (see page 242) or the **Engaruka Cultural Tourism Programme** (see below). Several tour operators also offer cultural tours in this region using the local people as guides. These include **Hoopoe, Roy Safaris, Takim's Holidays** and **Klub Africo Safaris** (see Tour operators in Arusha, page 258).

Mto wa Mbu → *For listings, see pages 278-281. Colour map 1, A4.*

Mto wa Mbu (meaning Mosquito Creek) is a small, busy market town selling fruit and vegetables grown by the surrounding farms. It is on the route from Arusha to the northern safari circuit of Ngorongoro and Serengeti and only 3 km away from the gate of Lake Manyara National Park. You are likely to be welcomed to the town by people trying to sell the arts and crafts on display in the Masai central market, a cooperative of about 20 curio sellers, behind which is a fresh food market. However, all curios offered here seem to be more expensive than those in Arusha. Mto wa Mbu is a colourful town that's developed over recent years to accommodate its visitors. There's a new supermarket, bureau de change (though most of the curio sellers accept US dollars cash), and bikes are available for hire along the main street. It's worth exploring beyond this main street if you get chance, as you'll find plenty of local bars, a fruit and vegetable market and several local guesthouses for around US$10 a night if you're on a very limited budget.

The area around Mto wa Mbu was dry and sparsely populated until irrigation programmes began in the 1950s, which transformed the area into an important fruit and vegetable-growing region. (Look out for the distinctive red bananas for sale.) The accompanying population growth turned Mto wa Mbu into a melting pot of cultures. There is greater cultural diversity in this area than elsewhere in Tanzania, so in one day you can sample Chagga banana beer, or see a farmer from the Kigoma region make palm oil. The Rangi use papyrus from the lakes to make beautiful baskets and mats, and the Sandawe continue to make bows and arrows, which are used to hunt small game. On the surrounding plains, the Masai tend their cattle and, on Thursdays, there are Masai cattle markets. Seeing so many red-robed Masai men all together is quite a striking sight.

The **Mto wa Mbu Cultural Tourism Programme** ⓘ *further information available from the Tanzania Cultural Tourism Programme office, or the Tanzanian Tourist Information Centre, both on Boma Rd in Arusha, see page 236, www.tanzaniaculturaltourism.com,* offers an opportunity to support the local inhabitants and learn about their lifestyle. Walking safaris with Masai guides through the farms in the verdant oasis at the foot of the Rift Valley can be arranged. There are walks to Miwaleni Lake and waterfall, where papyrus plants grow in abundance, or an opportunity to climb **Balaa Hill**, which overlooks the whole town. Alternatively, you can rent a bicycle and cycle through the banana plantations to see the **papyrus lake**. The landscape is awe-inspiring, with the escarpment rising vertically up into the sky on one side and the semi-desert stretching away to the horizon on the other. The guides are all former students of Manyara secondary school and have a reasonable standard of English. Profits from the tours are invested in development projects and for the promotion of energy-saving stoves.

Lake Manyara National Park → For listings, see pages 278-281. Colour map 1, A4.
3° 40'S, 35° 50'E.

On the way to Ngorongoro Crater and the Serengeti, Lake Manyara is well worth a stop in its own right. Set in the Great Rift Valley, Lake Manyara National Park lies beneath the cliffs of the Manyara Escarpment and was established in 1960. It covers an area of 325 sq km, of which 229 sq km is the lake. The remaining third is a slice of marshes, grassland and acacia woodland tucked between the lake and the escarpment, whose reddish brown wall looms 600 m on the western horizon. ▸▸ For more information on national parks, see page 10.

Lake Manyara National Park

Where to stay
Kiruruma Tented Lodge 2
Lake Manyara 1
Lake Manyara Serena Lodge 3
Lake Manyara Tree Lodge 6

Park information
The only entrance gate is just to the west of Mto wa Mbu, 120 km from Arusha on the road to the crater and Serengeti; there's an airstrip near the park gate. www. tanzaniaparks.com, 0630-1830, US$35, children (5-16) US$10, vehicle US$40.

Background
The lake is believed to have been formed two to three million years ago when, after the formation of the Rift Valley, streams poured over the valley wall accumulating in the depression below. It has shrunk significantly and was probably at its largest about 250,000 years ago. In recent years it has been noted that water levels are falling in several of the lakes in the region, among them Lake Manyara. This trend often coincides with the development of salt brines, the rise of which is anticipated.

Wildlife
The park's ground water forests, bush plains, baobob-strewn cliffs and algae-streaked

hot springs offer incredible ecological variety in a small area. Lake Manyara's famous tree-climbing lions make the ancient mahogany and elegant acacias their home during the rainy season and are a well-known but rather rare feature of the northern park. In addition to the lions, the national park is also home to the largest concentration of baboons anywhere in the world. Other animals include elephants, hippo and plains animals, as well as a huge variety of birdlife, both resident and migratory. At certain times of the year, Lake Manyara feeds thousands of flamingos, which form a shimmering pink zone around the lakeshore. The 400 or so species of bird found here also include ostrich, egrets, herons, pelicans and storks. Also seen are African spoonbills, various species of ibis, ducks and the rare pygmy goose. As with all the other parks, poaching has been a problem in the past and has affected the elephant population in particular. It was a shock when the census of 1987 found that their population had halved to under 200 in just a decade. At the gate of the national park is a small **museum** displaying some of the park's bird and rodent life.

Routes

The only track through the park from the gate is good enough for most vehicles but, as it goes through the ground water forest before crossing the Marere River Bridge, it may be closed during the wet season. The best time to visit, therefore, is during the dry months, July to October, although the wetter months of December to February and May to July are the best times for birdwatching and for seeing the waterfalls on the cliff faces. The forest, as its name suggests, is watered not by rainfall, but by the high water table produced by seepage from the volcanic rock of the rift wall. The first animals you will see on entering the park will undoubtedly be baboons.

About 500 m after the Marere River bridge, the road forks. To the left the track leads to a plain known as **Mahali pa Nyati** (Place of the Buffalo), which has a herd of mainly old bulls cast out from their former herds. There are also zebra and impala in this area. This is also the track to the **Hippo Pool**, formed by the Simba River on its way to the lake and home to hippos, flamingos and many other water birds.

Back on the main track the forest thins out to bush and the road crosses the Mchanga River (Sand River) and Msasa River. Shortly after this latter bridge, there is a turning off to the left that leads down to the lakeshore, where there is a peaceful picnic spot. Soon after this bridge, the surroundings change to acacia woodland. This is where the famous tree-climbing lions are found, so drive through very slowly and look for a tail dangling down through the branches.

Continue down the main road crossing the Chemchem River and on to the Ndala River. During the dry season you may see elephants digging in the dry riverbed for water. At the peak of the wet season the river may flood and the road is sometimes impassable as a result. Beyond the Ndala River the track runs closer to the Rift Valley Escarpment wall that rises steeply to the right of the road. On this slope are many different trees to those on the plain and, as a result, they provide a different habitat for various animals. The most noticeable are the very impressive baobab trees with their huge trunks.

The first of the two sets of hot springs in the park are located where the track runs along the wall of the escarpment. These are the smaller of the two and so are called simply **Maji Moto Ndogo** (Small Hot Water). The temperature is about 40°C, heated to this temperature as it circulates to great depths in fractures that run through the rocks created during the formation of the Rift Valley. The second set of hot springs is further down the track over the Endabash River. These, known as **Maji Moto**, are both larger and hotter, reaching a temperature of 60°C. You are supposed to be able to cook an egg here in about 30 minutes. The main track ends at Maji Moto and you have to turn round and go back the same way. In total the track is between 35 and 40 km long.

North of Mto wa Mbu

Engaruka → *Colour map 1, A4.*

Engaruka, one of Tanzania's most important historical sites, lies at the foot of the Rift Valley escarpment, 63 km north of Mto wa Mbu on the road to Ol Doinyo Lengai and Lake Natron. The access road along here as far Lake Natron (about 120 km north of Mto wa Mbu) is very rough and is really only feasible in a 4WD. Masai cattle graze on the surrounding plains and dust cyclones often arise on the horizon. They are feared as the 'devil fingers' that can bring bad luck when they touch people.

In the 15th and 16th centuries the farming community here developed an ingenious irrigation system made of stone-block canals with terraced retaining walls enclosing parcels of land. The site included seven large villages. Water from the rift escarpment was channelled into the canals that led to the terraces. For some unknown reason, the farmers left Engaruka around 1700. Several prominent archaeologists, including Louis Leakey, have investigated these ruins but, to date, there are many questions left unanswered about the people who built these irrigation channels, and why they abandoned the area. The ruins are deteriorating because, with the eradication of the tsetse fly, Masai cattle now come to graze in this area during the dry season, causing extensive damage.

The **Engaruka Cultural Tourism Programme** ⓘ *further details available from the Tanzania Cultural Tourism Programme office, or the Tanzanian Tourist Information Centre, both on Boma Rd in Arusha, see page 236, www.tanzaniaculturaltourism.com,* offers half-day tours of the ruins or visits to local farms to see current farming and irrigation methods. A Masai warrior can also guide you up the escarpment – from where there are views over the ruins and surrounding plains – pointing out trees and plants the Masai use as food and medicine along the way. In one day you can climb the peak of **Kerimasi** to the north of the village and there is a two-day hike up Kerimasi and then **Ol Doinyo Lengai** volcano (see below). The sodium-rich ashes from the volcano turn the water caustic, sometimes causing burns to the skin of the local Masai's livestock. Moneys generated are used to exclude cattle from the ruins and to start conservation work, and also to improve the village primary school. There is no formal accommodation but it is possible to camp.

Ol Doinyo Lengai → *Altitude: 2886 m.*

ⓘ *As the mountain lies outside the conservation area, no national park fees are payable.*

Ol Doinyo Lengai, the 'mountain of God', is Tanzania's only active volcano. It is north of and outside the Ngorongoro Conservation area in the heart of Masailand, to the west of the road to Lake Natron. This active volcano is continuously erupting, sometimes explosively but more commonly just subsurface bubbling of lava. It is the only volcano in the world that erupts natrocarbonatite lava, a highly fluid lava that contains almost no silicon, and is also much cooler and less viscous than basaltic lavas.

The white deposits near the summit are weathered natrocarbonatite ash and lava, and are interpreted by the Masai as symbolizing the white beard of God. The last violent eruption was in 1993, but lava has occasionally flowed out of the crater since then, indeed, there were minor eruptions as recently as 2007 and 2008. Only physically fit people should attempt the climb; note that the summit is frequently wreathed in clouds.

Although it is possible to climb the mountain, the trek up to the crater is an exceptionally demanding one. In parts of the crater that have been inactive for several months, the ground is so soft that one sinks into it when walking. In rainy weather the light brown powdery surface turns white again because of chemical reactions that occur when the lava absorbs water. Climbs are frequently done at night, as there is no shelter on the mountain and it gets extremely hot. The gradient is very steep towards the crater rim. A guide is required and you are strongly advised to wear sturdy leather hiking boots to protect against burns should you inadvertently step into liquid lava. Boots made of other fibres have been known to melt. Another safety precaution is to wear glasses to avoid lava splatter burns to the eyes. Both **Lake Natron Tented Camp** and **Engare Sero Lake Natron Camp**, see Where to stay, page 280, can organize guided climbs with the Masai – the ascent usually begins at midnight to reach the peak around dawn; expect to pay in the region of US$250 for two people; the cost goes down for larger groups.

Lake Natron → *Colour map 1, A4.*

This pink, alkaline lake is at the bottom of the Gregory Rift (part of the Great Rift Valley), touching the Kenyan border about 250 km from Arusha. It is surrounded by escarpments and volcanic mountains, with a small volcano at the north end of the lake in Kenya, and the much larger volcano, Ol Doinyo Lengai, to the southeast of the lake (see above). The lake is infrequently visited by tourists because of its remoteness, but numerous Masai herd cattle around here. The route from Arusha is through an area rich with wildlife, depending on the season, particularly ostriches, zebra and giraffe.

The lake has an exceptionally high concentration of salts and gets its pink colour from the billions of cyano-bacteria that form the flamingo's staple diet. There are hundreds of thousands of lesser flamingos here, as this lake is their only regular breeding ground in East Africa. Often more of the birds are found here than at either Lake Magadi in Kenya or Lake Manyara. Lake Natron is also an important site for many other waterbird species, including palearctic migrants. A few kilometres upstream on the Ngare Sero River are two **waterfalls**. Follow the river from the campsite: with the occasional bit of wading, it is a hike of about an hour.

◉ Mto wa Mbu to Lake Natron listings

For sleeping and eating price codes and other relevant information, see pages 22-26.

◉ Where to stay

Mto wa Mbu *p274*

$$$$ E Unoto Retreat, 14 km from Mto wa Mbu on the road to Lake Natron, T0787-622 724, www.maasaivillage.com. A Masai-inspired lodge nestling into the Rift Valley escarpment that resembles an authentic Masai village and blends into the surroundings. The 25 luxurious rooms are in separate bandas with nice views over Lake Miwaleni, which is home to many hippo. 4 of the bandas are designed for wheelchair users, and the honeymoon suite has a personal butler and luxurious heavy wood furniture. A small infinity pool overlooks the lake, bikes can be hired and guests are encouraged to interact with the local Masai on guided walks to the top of the Rift escarpment and to local villages, where the hotel owners recently built a school.

$$$ Migunga Tented Camp, outside Lake Manyara National Park, just a couple of kilometres before the gate, reservations Arusha, T027-250 6135, www.moivaro.com. This lovely tented camp is set in 14 ha of acacia forest in a secluded part of Migungani

Village. Bushbuck and other antelope are sometimes seen on the property. 19 spotless, self-contained tents, dining room and bar under thatch, which are atmospherically lit at night with hurricane lamps. Less luxurious than the normal tented camps, but much more affordable, and rates include meals. Mountain biking, bird walks and village tours can be arranged.

$$$-$ Kiboko Tented Lodge, 2 km before town on the Arusha Rd, 2 km from the main road, reservations Arusha, T027-250 2617, www.kibokobushcamp.com. 12 self-contained permanent tents in a lovely tract of acacia forest, set well apart under thatched roofs, though sparsely furnished with small beds and with unattractive concrete showers and toilets, but reasonably good value for US$60 per person. Also has a large campsite (US$5 per person) with plenty of space for vehicles, a kitchen area under thatch with cutlery and crockery, but only 2 toilets and showers. Restaurant and bar in a large thatched building which looks rather tired, can organize Masai dancing.

$$-$ Jambo Lodge & Campsite, in Mto wa Mbu, just a few doors away from **Twiga Campsite**, T027-2503 5553, www.njake. com. A well-maintained budget option in pleasant gardens, with 16 spotless en suite rooms in 2-storey houses with satellite TV, fridge, reliable hot water and terrace or balcony. Swimming pool, restaurant and baobab tree bar. Spacious camping ground with good ablutions facilities, US$7 per person or US$20 if hiring a tent. If you get to Mto wa Mbu under your own steam, they can organize day trips to Manyara or the crater for about US$130 per person if there are 4 people, as well as longer lodge safaris.

$$-$ Twiga Campsite & Lodge, left of the main road in Mto wa Mbu going towards the gate of Lake Manyara National Park, T027-253 9101, www.twigacampsitelodge. com. There are some decent grassy tent pitches (US$10 per person) at the back with plenty of shade, hot showers, a curio shop and a reasonable bar and restaurant

area near the swimming pool. Restaurant serves chicken, beef and rice, etc, and plenty of cold beer. The 24 new rooms are an improvement on the old ones and well worth the extra dollars, with satellite TV, fridge and fans. They're at the far end of the camp and so don't get as much noise from the street as the 10 older rooms, which have hot water but no fans and are fairly basic. Again, they can organize affordable short safaris and have tents and camping equipment for hire.

Camping

Sunbright Campsite, near Mto wa Mbu, signposted on the right off the main road towards Ngorongoro Crater, you can book through the Arusha office but you shouldn't need to, T027-250 6708, www. sunbrighthotels.com. This pretty campsite is set in lovely gardens dotted with palms and is a good option for independent travellers. Tents and bedding are available to rent, and there are good hot showers and a spacious bar and restaurant under thatch for basic meals with a satellite TV. US$7 per person.

Lake Manyara National Park *p275, map p275*

$$$$ Kirurumu Tented Lodge, reservations, **Hoopoe Safaris**, Arusha T027-250 7011, www.kirurumu.net. Built on the escarpment in a stunning location overlooking the lake, 27 well-appointed tents on solid platforms under thatched roofs, plus 2 honeymoon suites and 2 family cottages, all with splendid views, excellent service and meals. Relaxing bar with views over Lake Manyara, activities include walks with the Masai, and mountain biking and fly-camping can be arranged. Rates from US$345 per person full board. There are plans to open a similar camp in Tarangire – contact them for details.

$$$$ Lake Manyara Tree Lodge, www.lakemanyara.com, reservations, Johannesburg, South Africa, T+27-(0)11- 809 4313, www.andbeyond.com. Set in the heart of a mahogany forest in the remote southwestern region, this is the only lodge within the park and is nicely designed to exert minimal impact on the environment. The 10 luxurious treehouse suites are crafted from local timber and makuti palms, and have outside shower, deck, fans, mosquito nets and butler service. There's a dining boma where guests can watch what is going on in the kitchen, breakfast and picnics can be organized on the lakeshore, and there's a swimming pool. Rates US$755-1095 per person full board, but for this you get an impeccable safari experience.

$$$$-$$$ Lake Manyara Hotel, 300 m above the park, reservations, Arusha, T027-254 4595, www.hotelsandlodges-tanzania. com. On the escarpment overlooking the lake and park with wonderful views. This old-fashioned safari lodge is built in low concrete blocks, but the 100+ rooms have recently been renovated. There's a beautiful swimming pool in established gardens, a TV room, babysitting service, restaurant and bar (although there have been some negative reports about the food). Village walks and guided mountain-bike trails arranged. Rates US$175-370.

$$$$-$$$ Lake Manyara Serena Safari Lodge, on the edge of the eastern Rift Valley's Mto wa Mbu escarpment, reservations Arusha T027-254 5555, www. serenahotels.com. The main attraction here is the lovely infinity pool with views over to the lake. 67 rooms in round bungalows all with lake views, 2 rooms available for wheelchair users, Wi-Fi available. Offers 'soft adventures' – mountain biking, forest hikes, nature and village walks, night game drives, canoe safaris when the lake isn't too shallow and children's programmes – available to everyone, not just staying guests. Manyara is, perhaps, the weaker of the 3 Serena lodges in the area, but remains a good and reliable option with fantastic views. Rates US$205-460 for a double full board.

Camping
There are 2 public campsites at the entrance to the park, with water, toilets and showers, US$30. There are 3 special campsites inside the park itself, all of which must be pre-booked as part of a safari and can only be used by one group at a time, US$50. Bookings through **Tanzania National Parks Authority (TANAPA)** head office, Arusha, see page 237.

Lake Natron *p278*
$$$$ Engare Sero Lake Natron Camp, at Engare Sero village, southwest of the lake, T0732-978 931, www.ngare-sero-lodge.com. This camp was set up in conjunction with the Engare Sero village on the lakeshore to assist the local Masai in benefiting from tourism income; it employs the Masai as guides, and you can organize short rides on their camels. The 8 simple tents under low-level thatched roofs, a dining tent and bar area are located next to a freshwater stream where you can cool off. Follows eco-principles, with, for example, compost toilets and a generator that is run on vegetable oil. A good range of activities, including walks with the Masai and the climb of Ol Doinyo Lengai, can be arranged.

$$$ Lake Natron Tented Camp, southwest of the lake, operated by **Moivaro**, T027-250 6315, www.moivaro.com. 9 self-contained spacious permanent tents with showers and flush toilets, thatched dining room and bar, swimming pool, solar power in all tents and dining room. You can also camp here (US$15 per person), and they have tents and bedding for hire if necessary. The camp is an excellent base from which to explore the surrounding area on hikes and visit Masai villages; they can also organize the climb of Ol Doinyo Lengai. Transfers from and to Arusha can be arranged if you have no transport.

Camping
Independent overlanders report that it is possible to bush camp reasonably close to

the lake, or near the waterfalls on the Ngare Sero River, if fully self-sufficient. Remember that lions may visit the area to drink.

⊖ Transport

Mto wa Mbu *p274*
Bus and dala-dala
There are regular buses and *dala-dala* between **Arusha** and Mto wa Mbu, which take about 2 hrs and cost around US$2. Some of these go on to **Karatu** (below).

Lake Manyara National Park *p275, map p275*
Air
Air Excel and Regional Air have daily scheduled round-trip circuits between **Arusha** and the lodges in the **Serengeti** and will touch down at the airstrip near Manyara's park gate on request. **Coastal Air** will again touch down at Lake Manyara on their daily circuit between **Arusha**, the lodges in the **Serengeti** and **Mwanza**. Schedules are on the websites; see Arusha Transport, page 263, for contact details.

Ngorongoro Conservation Area

The Ngorongoro Conservation Area encompasses the Ngorongoro Crater, Embagai Crater, Olduvai Gorge – famous for its palaeontological relics – and Lake Masek. Lake Eyasi marks part of the southern boundary and the Serengeti National Park lies to the west. The Ngorongoro Crater is often called 'Africa's Eden', and a visit to the crater is a main draw for tourists coming to Tanzania and a definite world-class attraction. A World Heritage Site, it's the largest intact caldera in the world, containing everything necessary for the 30,000 animals that inhabit the crater floor to exist and thrive. ▸▸ *For listings, see pages 288-291.*

Arriving in Ngorongoro Conservation Area → *Colour map 1, A4. 3°11'S 35°32'E.*

Getting there and around The entrance gate to the Ngorongoro Conservation Area is 190 km west of Arusha, 25 km from Karatu and 145 km from the Serengeti and is reached via the Arusha–Serengeti road (B144). At Karatu, is the turning off to **Gibb's Farm**, 5 km off the main road. From this junction you turn right, climbing towards the park entrance at **Lodware Gate**; as the altitude increases the temperature starts to fall. Your first view of the crater comes at **Heroes' Point** (2286 m). The road continues to climb through the forest to the crater rim. It is sometimes possible along this road to spot leopard that inhabit the dense forests at the top of the crater. During the long rains season (April-May) the roads in the park can be almost impassable, so access to the crater floor may be restricted. The best times to visit are December to February and June and July. There's an airstrip near **Crater Village**, which is the service point for the lodges at the top of the crater,

Tourist information The entrance to the Ngorongoro Conservation Area is on the Arusha–Serengeti road (B144), www.tanzaniaparks.com, www.ngorongorocrater.org, 0630-1830, US$50, children (5-16) US$10, vehicle US$40, note: only Tanzanian-registered vehicles are allowed down into the crater itself, for which there is an additional Crater Service Fee of US$200 per vehicle. ▸▸ *See also Arriving at Ngorongoro Crater, page 284.*

Background

The Ngorongoro Conservation Area was established in 1959 and covers an area of 8288 sq km. In 1951 it was included as part of the Serengeti National Park and contained the headquarters of the park. However, in order to accommodate the grazing needs of the

Masai people's livestock, it was decided to reclassify it as a conservation area. In 1978 it was declared a World Heritage Site in recognition of its beauty and importance. Where the road reaches the rim of the crater you will see memorials to Professor Bernhard Grzimek and his son Michael. They were the makers of the film *Serengeti Shall Not Die* and published a book of the same name (1959, Collins). They conducted surveys and censuses of the animals in the Serengeti and Ngorongoro parks and were heavily involved in the fight against poachers. Tragically, Michael was killed in an aeroplane accident over the Ngorongoro Crater in 1959, his father returned to Germany, where he set up the Frankfurt Zoological Society. He died in 1987 requesting in his will that he should be buried beside his son in Tanzania. Their memorials serve as a reminder of all the work they did to protect this part of Africa.

Karatu → *Phone code 027.*

The small but burgeoning town of Karatu lies on the Arusha–Serengeti road (B144) and is 28 km after Mto wa Mbu, 140 km from Arusha and 25 km before the gate of

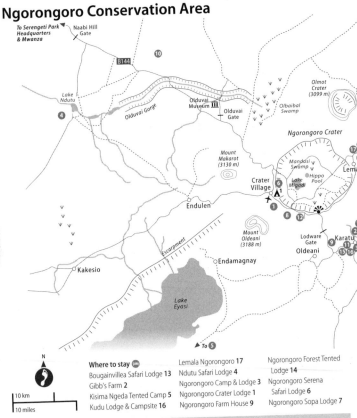

Ngorongoro Conservation Area

Where to stay
Bougainvillea Safari Lodge 13
Gibb's Farm 2
Kisima Ngeda Tented Camp 5
Kudu Lodge & Campsite 16
Lemala Ngorongoro 17
Ndutu Safari Lodge 4
Ngorongoro Camp & Lodge 3
Ngorongoro Crater Lodge 1
Ngorongoro Farm House 9
Ngorongoro Forest Tented Lodge 14
Ngorongoro Serena Safari Lodge 6
Ngorongoro Sopa Lodge 7

the Ngorongoro Conservation Area. In the past, the area around Karatu was of great importance to the German colonial administration. The region's cool climate, verdant hills, and pleasing views made it popular with settlers and farmers, and coffee was a main crop grown for export. Today, a few large farms that remain in private hands still cultivate the cash crop on the hills and small valleys outside of town. With completion of the tarred road from Arusha to the gates of Ngorongoro, Karatu has more recently come into its own and now spreads for several kilometres along the highway. It is locally dubbed 'safari junction' and for good reason. All safari vehicles en route to the parks in the Northern Circuit pass through here. Because of its proximity to the crater, more and more lodges and campsites are springing up. Some offer very good and, in some cases, much cheaper alternatives to staying within the confines of the Ngorongoro Conservation Area. However, the disadvantage is not having the views that the lodges on the rim of the crater afford. As well as the accommodation options listed below, those on an organized camping safari may find themselves staying at one of the many other campsites around Karatu, as the

Ngorongoro Wildlife Lodge 8
Octagon Safari Lodge 15
Olduvai Camp 10
Plantation Lodge 11

Rhino Lodge 12

Campsites ▲
Simba Campsite 1

cheaper companies use these instead of the more expensive **Simba Campsite** at the top of the crater (which, incidentally, gets overcrowded, has poor facilities and can be extremely cold). These cheaper campsites cater exclusively to groups who have their own cooks, though there are often also bars to buy beers and soft drinks.

There are three banks in town and all have ATMs. For those on self-drive safaris, this is the last place to buy provisions and fuel before entering the Ngorongoro Conservation Area (see Shopping, page 291). Petrol stations spread from one end of town to the other.

There are plenty of buses throughout the day between Arusha and Karatu. One option for budget travellers wanting to visit the Ngorongoro Crater is to catch public transport as far as Karatu, stay overnight and then take a half-day safari to the crater the next morning, returning to Arusha the following afternoon. This is considerably cheaper than booking a safari from Arusha.

Ngorongoro Crater → For listings, see pages 288-291. Colour map 1, A4.

The crater has an area of 265 sq km and measures between 16 and 19 km across. The rim reaches 2286 m above sea level and the crater floor is 610 m below it. The crater floor is mainly grassy plain, interspersed with a few tracts of sturdy woodland. Scrub heath and remnants of montane forests cloak the steep slopes. There are both freshwater and brackish lakes, and the main water source is Lake Migadi in the centre of the crater, a soda lake that attracts flocks of pink-winged flamingos and plenty of contented hippos who remain partially submerged during the day and graze on grass at night. The views from the rim overlooking Ngorongoro Crater are sensational, and you can pick out the wildlife as dots on the crater floor.

Arriving at Ngorongoro Crater

All the lodges and the public campsite are around the rim of the crater. The descent into it is by way of two steep roads, which are both one-way. You enter by the **Windy Gap** road and leave by the **Lerai** road. The Windy Gap branches off the Serengeti road to the right and descends the northeast to the floor of the crater 610 m below. The road is narrow, steep and twists and turns as it enters the crater, which is rather like a huge amphitheatre.

Most people go down into the crater on an organized safari from Arusha (see page 258), or join one in Karatu. Access onto the crater floor is limited to half a day per visitor, and safaris enter either early in the morning or early in the afternoon. Access is restricted to registered tour operators in Tanzanian-registered vehicles and, for most of the year, only 4WDs are allowed. If you have your own vehicle, you are allowed to take it through the Ngorongoro Conservation Area (and beyond into the Serengeti) but you are not allowed to take it down into the crater. However, there is the option to leave your own vehicle at the top and to hire Land Rovers and drivers in Crater Village where you pick up the ranger; this is cheaper than hiring through the lodges.

Background

The name 'Ngorongoro' comes from a Masai word *Ilkorongoro*, which was the name given to the group of Masai warriors who defeated the previous occupants of the area, the Datong, around 1800. The sounds of the bells – 'koh-rohng-roh'– that the Masai wore during the battle were said to have terrified their enemies into submission. The Masai refer to the Ngorongoro Southern Highlands as 'O'lhoirobi', which means the cold highlands; the Germans also referred to the climate, calling these the 'winter highlands'. Ngorongoro is believed to date from about 2,500,000 years ago – relatively recent for this area. It was once a huge active volcano and was probably as large as Kilimanjaro. After its large major eruption, as the lava subsided, its cone collapsed inwards leaving the caldera. Minor volcanic activity continued, and the small cones that resulted can be seen in the crater floor. To the northeast of Ngorongoro crater are two smaller craters, Olmot and Embagai. From the crater, on a clear day you should be able to see six mountains over 3000 m.

Wildlife

The crater is home to an estimated 30,000 animals, and visitors are almost guaranteed to get a good look at some or all of the Big Five. About half of this number are zebra and wildebeest. Unlike those in the neighbouring Serengeti, these populations do not need to migrate, thanks to the permanent supply of water and grass through both the wet and the dry seasons. Thanks to the army of pop-up minibuses that go down each day, the animals are not afraid of vehicles and it's not unusual for a pride of lions to amble over and flop down in the shade of a minibus. However, recently introduced regulations limit the number of vehicles around an animal or kill to five, in an effort to reduce the impact of hordes of over-eager safari vehicles surrounding the wildlife. The crater's elephants are mostly old bulls with giant tusks. The females and calves prefer the forested highlands on the crater rim and only rarely venture down into the grasslands. There are no giraffe; because of the crater's steep sides, they can't climb down, and there is a lack of food at tree level.

Embagai Crater → *For listings, see pages 288-291. 2°55'S 35°50'E.*

Embagai Crater (also spelt Empakaai) can be visited in a day from any lodge at the Ngorongoro rim. The caldera is approximately 35 sq km. You can walk down to the 80-m deep, alkaline **Lake Emakat**, which partly occupies the caldera floor. The vegetation is predominantly highland shrubs and grassland, but there are small patches of verdant, evergreen forest in the southern part of the caldera. Buffalo, hyenas, leopards and various species of bats may be seen. Birdlife is prolific and includes the lammergeyer, Egyptian vulture, Verreaux's eagle, pelicans, storks, flamingos, duck, sandpiper, doves, kingfishers and ostrich. This is an isolated, beautiful place, accessible by 4WD only. You need to be accompanied by a ranger because of the buffaloes.

Olduvai Gorge → *For listings, see pages 288-291. Colour map 1, A4.*

Olduvai Gorge, a water-cut canyon up to 90 m deep, has become famous for being the site of a number of archaeological finds and has been called the 'cradle of mankind'. Lying within the Ngorongoro Conservation Area to the northwest of the crater, the site is about 10-15 minutes off the main road between Serengeti and Ngorongoro. Olduvai comes from the Masai word *oldupai*, which is the name for the type of wild sisal that grows in the gorge.

Archaeological finds

Olduvai Gorge first aroused interest in the archaeological world as early as 1911, when a German, Professor Katurinkle, found some fossil bones while looking for butterflies in the gorge. These caused great interest in Europe and, in 1913, an expedition led by Professor Hans Reck was arranged. They stayed at Olduvai for three months and made a number of fossil finds. At a later expedition in 1933, Professor Reck was accompanied by two archaeologists, Dr Louis Leakey and his future wife, Mary.

The Leakeys continued their work and, in July 1959, 26 years later, discovered 400 fragments of the skull *Australopithecus-Zinjanthropus boisei* – the 'nutcracker man' – who lived in the lower Pleistocene Age, around 1,750,000 BC. A year later the skull and bones of a young *Homo habilis* were found. The Leakeys assert that around 1.8 to two million years ago there existed in Tanzania two types of man: *Australopithecus-Zinjanthropus boisei* and *Homo habilis*. The other two, *Australopithecus africanus* and *arobustus*, had died out. *Homo habilis*, with the larger brain, gave rise to modern man. *Habilis* was a small, ape-like creature and, although thought to be the first of modern man's ancestors, is quite distinct from modern man. Tools, such as those used by *Homo erectus* (dating from one to 1½ million years ago), have also been found at Olduvai, as well as at Isimila near Iringa. Other exciting finds in the area are the footprints of man, woman and child found in 1979 at Laetoli (a site near Olduvai), made by 'creatures' that walked upright. These possibly date from the same period as *Australopithecus afarensis*, popularly known as 'Lucy', whose remains were discovered near Hadar in Ethiopia in 1974. Dating back 3.6 to 3.8 million years, they pushed back the timing of the beginnings of the human race even further. In 1986, a discovery at Olduvai by a team of American and Tanzanian archaeologists unearthed the remains of an adult female dating back 1,800,000 years. In total the fossil remains of about 35 humans have been found in the area at different levels.

Prehistoric animal remains were also found in the area, and about 150 species of mammals have been identified. These include the enormous Polorovis, with a horn span of 2 m, the Dinotherium, a huge, elephant-like creature with tusks that curved downwards, and the Hipparion, a three-toed, horse-like creature.

At the site there is a small **museum** ① *open until 1500, may be closed during the wet season (Apr-end Jun), entrance US$3*. The building was built in the 1970s by the Leakeys to house their findings. It holds displays of copies of some of the finds, a cast of the footprints and pictures of what life was like for Olduvai's earliest inhabitants. You can go down into the gorge to see the sites, and there will usually be an archaeologist to show you around. All safari operators pull in here on the way past.

Around Olduvai Gorge

Nearby places of interest include **Nasera Rock**, a 100-m monolith on the edge of the Gol Mountain range – it offers stunning views of the southern Serengeti and is a great vantage point from which to watch the annual wildebeest migration. This is sometimes called the Striped Mountain, so named for the streaks of blue-green algae that have formed on the granite. **Olkarien Gorge**, a deep fissure in the Gol Mountains, is a major breeding ground for the enormous Ruppell's griffon vulture.

A geological feature of this area are shifting sand-dunes, or *barchan*, crescent-shaped dunes lying at right angles to the prevailing wind. They usually develop from the accumulation of sand around a minor obstruction, for example a piece of vegetation. The windward face has a gentle slope but the leeward side is steep and slightly concave. The *barchans* move slowly as more sand is deposited; they range in size from a few metres to a great size, as seen in the Sahara or Saudi Arabia.

Lake Nduto

Lake Ndutu is a soda lake in the Ndutu woodlands in the western part of the Ngorongoro Conservation Area. Rarely visited, it is home to many flamingo, plains game mammals and their attendant predators. You can explore this area on game drives from **Ndutu Safari Lodge**, and there's a special campsite on the lakeshore used by some of the safari companies.

Lake Eyasi → *For listings, see pages 288-291. Colour map 1, A4.*

Arriving at Lake Eyasi

Access to Lake Eyasi is from the Kidatu–Ngorongoro road. The journey takes about 1½-2 hours, driving southwest of Karatu and the Ngorongoro Crater. There are few tourist facilities here but in recent years it has been included in walking safaris by several companies. There are no set itineraries for the five-day and four-night hiking and camping tours but they generally start at Chem Chem Village from where the guides start their search for a Hadzabe camp. Once there, hikers can freely participate in the Hadzabe daily activities, including mending bows, collecting herbal poisons for the arrows, actual hunts, gathering of firewood, plants, water, etc.

Landscape and wildlife

This soda lake, one of several lakes on the floor of the Rift Valley, is sometimes referred to as the 'forgotten lake'. It is larger than Lakes Manyara or Natron and is situated on the remote southern border of the Ngorongoro Conservation Area, at the foot of Mount Oldeani and the base of the western wall of the Rift Valley's Eyasi Escarpment. The Mbula highlands tower to the east. Seasonal water levels vary greatly but, following the trend in the region, the lake levels are falling and salt brines have developed. It is relatively shallow even during the rainy season. Lake Eyasi mostly fills a *graben*, an elongated depression of the earth's crust that is commonly the site of volcanic and/or earthquake activity. The Mbari River runs through the swampy area to the northeast of the lake known locally as **Mangola Chini**, which attracts much game. The northeastern region of the lake is a swampy area fringed by acacia and doum palm forests. Nearby are some freshwater springs and a small reservoir with tilapia fish. These springs are believed to run underground from Oldeani to emerge by the lakeshore. There are several kopjes (see page 294) close to the lake. Wildlife includes a profusion of birdlife, including flamingos, pelicans and storks, as well as leopards, various antelope, hippos and many small primates.

People

Two ancient tribes inhabit this area. The **Hadzabe** people (also called the Watindiga), who live near the shore, are hunter-gatherers, still live in nomadic groups, hunt with bows and arrows and gather tubers, roots and fruits. These people are believed to have their origins in Botswana; their lifestyle is similar to the San (of the Kalahari) and the Dorobo (of Kenya). It is estimated that they have lived in this region for 10,000 years. Their language resembles the click language associated with the San. Their hunting skills provide all their requirements – mostly eating small antelopes and primates. Their hunting bows are made with giraffe tendon 'strings', and they coat their spears and arrows with the poisonous sap of the desert rose. They live in communal camps that are temporary structures constructed in different locations depending on the season.

Nearby is a village of **Datoga** pastoral herdsmen, also known as the Barabaig or Il-Man'ati (meaning the 'strong enemy' in the Masai language). The Datoga are a tall, handsome people who tend their cattle in the region between Lake Eyasi and Mount Hanang. The Masai drove them south from Ngorongoro to Lake Eyasi about 150 years ago and remain their foes. They live in homes constructed of sticks and mud, and their compounds are surrounded by thornbush to deter nocturnal predators. Like the Hadzabe, the Datoga speak a click language and they scarify themselves to form figure of eight patterns around their eyes in a series of raised nodules.

Archaeological excavations of the nearby **Mumba cave shelter** were undertaken in 1934 by Ludwig and Margit Kohl-Larsen, and their discoveries included many fossilized hominoid remains: a complete prehistoric skull, molars and prehistoric tools, such as knives and thumbnail scrapers. Animal remains included rhino, antelope, zebra, hippo and catfish. The Mumba cave also contained ochre paintings. It is believed that the Mumba cave shelter was occupied over the years by various people.

⦿ Ngorongoro Conservation Area listings

For sleeping and eating price codes and other relevant information, see pages 22-26.

⦿ Where to stay

Karatu *p282, map p282*
All the lodges in and around Karatu can organize day trips to the crater among other safaris and activities.

$$$$ Gibb's Farm, 4 km from Karatu, T027-253 4397, www.gibbsfarm.net. At the edge of a forest facing the Mbulu Hills to the southeast, this charming 80-year-old farmhouse set in lush gardens is still a working farm and coffee plantation, originally built by German settlers in 1929. Accommodation is in 22 luxurious farm cottages, recently upgraded and all with private verandas, garden bathrooms and open fireplaces. The restaurant produces excellent meals using organic vegetables grown on the farm. And there's a spa with a difference – a traditional Masai healer provides treatments made from local plants and materials, either in your cottage or in his thatched house, the Engishon Supat.

$$$$ Ngorongoro Forest Tented Lodge, 3 km from Karatu on the road to **Gibb's Farm**, T027-250 8089, www.ngorongoro forestlodge.com. Also overlooking the Ngorongoro Forest Reserve, this stylish lodge has 7 spacious and attractive tented rooms elegantly furnished and with both indoor and outdoor showers. The lounge bar overlooks the forest reserve and the wildlife corridor to Lake Manyara, with vast windows and a telescope for stargazing.

$$$$ Plantation Lodge, 4 km towards the crater, 2 km from the main road, badly signposted so look hard, T027-253 4405 www.plantation-lodge.com. Accommodation in exquisitely stylish rooms on a coffee estate. A huge amount of work has gone into the safari-style decor. The 16 individual and spacious rooms are in renovated farm buildings throughout the

grounds. There are several places to sit and drink coffee or enjoy a sundowner, and you can choose to eat at grand dining tables on your veranda, in huge stone halls, in the garden, or in the main house with the other guests. The honeymoon suite has a vast bed, fireplace, jacuzzi and sunken bath, some units are whole houses which are ideal for families, and there's a swimming pool.

$$$$-$$$ Ngorongoro Farm House, on a 200-ha coffee farm 5 km from the gate to the crater, T0767-333 223, www.tanganyikawildernesscamps.com. There are 50 rooms spread between 3 separate camps, attractively built in the style of an old colonial farm. In the main thatched building is the restaurant, with a wooden terrace overlooking the farmland and flower beds, and excellent food using fresh vegetables from the farm. There's a large swimming pool, and they can arrange farm tours or nature walks with the Masai. One of the less expensive options outside Karatu from US$200 for a double.

$$$ Bougainvillea Safari Lodge, signposted to the left if going out of town towards the crater, 300 m off the main road, T027-253 4083, www.bougainvillealodge.net. Fairly newly built with 32 comfortable rooms in brick chalets with verandas, 2 have adjoining rooms for families, arranged around a large swimming pool, although the gardens have yet to mature. Good meals in the dining room as the chef used to work at **Gibb's Farm**, breakfast and lunch are generous buffets while dinner is a set menu, bar with wicker couches, curio shop and internet café, and can organize massages.

$$$ Octagon Safari Lodge, 1 km outside Karatu signposted on the left off the main road towards the Ngorongoro gate, T027-253 4525, www.octagonlodge.com. Owned by Rory and Pamela, an Irish-man and his Tanzanian wife, this lodge is set in beautiful African gardens. The 12 wood and bamboo chalets and 2 stone cottages that sleep 4 all have a Masai theme, are en suite and have balconies looking out onto the gardens. The Irish bar has plenty of whiskies to choose from, along with Guinness, and the food has received good reports. Can organize walking or mountain-bike tours in the surrounding countryside. Rates from US$55 per person B&B, dinner US$20, and picnic lunch boxes can be arranged.

$$$-$ Kudu Lodge and Campsite, signposted to the left if going out of town towards the crater, 600 m off the main road, T027-253 4055, www.kudulodge. com. Established and popular lodge with welcoming staff. Accommodation is in comfortable and well-maintained en suite rondavaals and cottages dotted around the mature tropical gardens, which sleep a total of about 50 people in doubles, triples or 2-bed family units with kitchens; rates start from US$140 for a double and a 50% discount is available in low season. The large shady campsite, often used by safari groups, has separate cooking shelters and good ablution blocks with hot water; camping US$15 per person. Enormous bar with satellite TV, pool table, fireplace and lots of couches, and acrobatic shows are put on in the evening, internet café, gift shop and good, affordable restaurant. The newest addition is a swimming pool with a delightful full-size statue of an elephant providing a fountain from its trunk. Safaris and other activities, such as mountain biking, can be organized.

$$$-$ Ngorongoro Camp & Lodge, on the main road in the middle of Karatu next to a petrol station and bank, T027-253 4287, www.ngorongorocampandlodge.net. This is a good mid-range option, with 32 neat and tidy double rooms, with space for extra beds, and good showers with plenty of hot water. Full breakfast included. Cosy bar with fireplace and satellite TV, restaurant serving reasonable continental and Indian dishes, a well-stocked supermarket and an internet café. Room rates are overpriced at US$140 for a double but nevertheless, a friendly

and comfortable place to stay. Camping is available for US$7 per person. The campsite is 100 m from the main lodge on one of the back roads and there is a bar and kitchen area for the safari cooks.

Ngorongoro Crater *p283, map p282*
For other accommodation options within 20 km of the Ngorongoro Crater, outside the conservation area's boundary, see Karatu, above.

$$$$ Lemala Ngorongoro, closed Apr-May, reservations Arusha, T027-254 8952, www.lemalacamp.com. A pricey option from US$640 per person, but the only tented camp experience on the crater rim and an alternative to the large lodges. It is near the quiet Lemala access route into the crater on the eastern rim, the same road used by guests at the nearby **Ngorongoro Sopa Lodge**. The 8 double tents and 1 family tent sleeping 4-5 are set up in an acacia forest, and have gas heaters (essential for the chill), wood floors with rugs, solar lights and en suite flush loos and safari bladder showers. The mess tent is surprisingly well furnished given its location, with giant sofas, lamps and bookshelves. There is Masai dancing and talks after dinner. They also operate a seasonal tented camp in the Ndutu region of the Ngorongoro Conservation Area Nov-Apr; check the website for information.

$$$$ Ngorongoro Crater Lodge, www.ngorongorocrater.com, reservations, Johannesburg, South Africa, T+27-11-809 4313, www.andbeyond.com. A lodge has been on this spot since 1934, but it was completely rebuilt in 1995, and the architecture and style is simply magnificent. It's the most luxurious lodge on the rim of the crater, very romantic and opulent. The individual cottages offer butler service, sumptuous decor, a fireplace and even an Ipod station. With unobstructed views down into the crater even from the bathrooms, this is a special place to stay. Very expensive at US$790-1500 per person, but fully inclusive of meals, drinks and game drives. The lodge supports local schools, clinics and health initiatives.

$$$$ Ngorongoro Wildlife Lodge, T027-254 4595, www.hotelsandlodges-tanzania.com. This ugly 1970s concrete block was originally built as a government hotel on the rim of the crater. It has wonderful views and the facilities are fine, with 80 comfortable and newly refurbished rooms with balconies overlooking the acacia forest on the floor of the crater. Bar with log fire, TV room with satellite TV, restaurant serving either buffets or à la carte, although there have been poor reports about the quality. Zebra can be seen on the lawns, and the surrounding trees are full of fairly tame birds.

$$$$-$$$ Ngorongoro Serena Safari Lodge, reservations Arusha, T027-254 5555, www.serenahotels.com. Luxury development built to the highest international standards out of wood and pebbles. Stunningly perched on the rim of the crater, and each of the rooms has its own rock-enclosed balcony. Telescope provided on main balcony to view the crater. The centre of the public area is warmed by a roaring fire and lit by lanterns. Friendly staff, good food and has its own nursery in the gardens to plant indigenous plant species. Offers hiking and shorter nature walks. Local Masai make up 25% of staff. Doubles from US$250 in low season.

$$$$-$$$ Ngorongoro Sopa Lodge, reservations, T027-250 0630-9, www.sopa lodges.com. Luxury lodge with 92 suites, all enjoying uninterrupted views into the crater. Spectacular African rondavaal design with magnificent lounges, restaurant and entertainment areas, swimming pool and satellite TV. Most of the lodges are on the southern or western crater rim, but the Sopa is on the unspoilt eastern rim, way off the beaten track. Unfortunately, this means an extra 45- to 50-km journey (one way) over poor-quality roads.

$$$ Rhino Lodge, T0785-500 005, www.ngorongoro.cc. Jointly owned by **Coastal Air**

and the **Pastoralists Council of Ngorongoro**, which represents local Masai communities, this former hunter of the first conservationist to the area was reopened in 2008 after extensive rebuilding and helps to support 6 local Masai villages. It's the only mid-budget option on the crater rim, though it's set back a bit and lacks the drop-dead views right into the crater. It offers good value, with 24 simply furnished, Masai-inspired rooms, all en suite with balconies overlooking the forests. Restaurant and bar area are simple with huge fireplaces, and dinners are communal buffets followed by Masai dancing. Rates are US$120 per person full board.

National Park campsites

Simba Campsite, about 2 km from Crater Village. A public campsite with showers, toilets and firewood, but facilities have deteriorated and water supplies are irregular – make sure that you have sufficient drinking water to keep you going for the night and the game drive the next day. Given that you are camping at some elevation at the top of the crater, this place gets bitterly cold at night, so ensure you have a warm sleeping bag. It gets very busy with tour groups, with up to 200 tents at any one time. The hot water runs out quickly – so don't expect to have a shower here. Many budget safari companies use this site, though **Karatu** is quite frankly a better option. If in your own vehicle, there is no need to book. Just pay for camping (US$30 per person) along with park entry when you enter at the gate. In your own vehicle there is also the option of dropping into the lodges for a meal or drink.

Elsewhere in the reserve there are 5 special campsites (US$50 per person), usually used by the safari companies going off the beaten track.

Olduvai Gorge *p285, map p282*
$$$$ Ndutu Safari Lodge, reservations Arusha, T027-253 7015, www.ndutu.com.

Established in 1967 by professional hunter George Dove, Ndutu is one of the earliest permanent lodges in the Crater/Serengeti area and has become something of an institution over the years. On the southern shore of Ndutu soda lake, amongst acacia woodland, it's in a good position for the migration in the calving season, midway between the Ngorongoro Crater and Seronera Lodge in the Serengeti (90 km to both) and it's near to the Olduvai Gorge. Sleeps 70 in 34 stone cottages. Bar and restaurant, fresh ingredients from Gibb's Farm, restricted use of water as it is trucked in. Ndutu was home for over 20 years to the famous wildlife photographer Baron Hugo van Lawick, one of the first filmmakers to bring the Serengeti to the attention of the world. He died in 2002 and was granted the honour of a full state funeral before being buried at Ndutu.

$$$$ Olduvai Camp, just south of the Serengeti border, closest lodge to the Olduvai Gorge, reservations Arusha, T0784-228 883, www.olduvai-camp.com. In a lovely setting around a giant kopje, the highlight here are the 3 head guides who are all Masai warriors from the villages immediately around the camp; you can go walking with them in the Ngorongoro Highlands. Facilities are simple, the 17 tents are of a modest size with thatched roofs and wooden floors, furnished with the basic essentials, en suite bathrooms have flush toilets and bladder showers. The public spaces are limited to 2 small thatched rondavaals and an open fire pit, and there's a platform right on top of the rocks with a telescope. Has a generator, and lanterns are provided at night. Rates from US$455 per person full board. Compared to the other giant impersonal concrete lodges,

this is an intimate, rustic camp that offers the opportunity to sleep on the plains amongst the local Masai.

Lake Eyasi *p286, map p282*
$$$$ Kisima Ngeda Tented Camp, on Lake Eyasi, a remote southern corner of Ngorongoro Conservation Area and about 2 hrs' drive from the crater rim, at the foot of Mount Ol Deani, reservations@ kisimangeda.com, www.kisimangeda.com. There are 7 tents here right on the lakeshore, with thatched roofs, en suite stone baths, wooden furniture, electric lights and plenty of space. Activities include canoeing on the lake, walks, mountain biking and meeting the Hadzabe people, and a new addition is a swimming pool. Wholesome food includes vegetables grown in the local villages, dairy products from the Hadzabe people's cattle and tilapia fish from the lake. Far from luxurious and it's a rough road to get here, but the cultural experience is unique.

O Shopping

Karatu *p282, map p282*
For those on self-drive safaris this is the last place to buy food before entering the Ngorongoro Conservation Area and, beyond, the Serengeti. There's a market on the left-hand side of the road if coming from Arusha which has a good variety of fresh food; meat can be bought from the small butcher at the back and bread from the kiosks. There's also a small supermarket at the **Ngorongoro Camp & Lodge**, see Where to stay, page 289. However, given that Arusha is less than 2 hrs' drive away, there's a far better choice of shopping there, especially at **Shoprite** on your way out of town.

Serengeti National Park

The Serengeti supports the greatest concentration of plains game in Africa. Frequently dubbed the eighth wonder of the world, it was granted the status of a World Heritage Site in 1978 and became an International Biosphere Reserve in 1981. Its far-reaching plains of endless grass, tinged with the twisted shadows of acacia trees, have made it the quintessential image of a wild and untarnished Africa. Large prides of lions laze easily in the long grasses, numerous families of elephants feed on acacia bark, and giraffes, antelope, monkeys, eland and a whole range of other African wildlife is here in awe-inspiring numbers. The park is the centre of the Serengeti Ecosystem – the combination of the Serengeti, the Ngorongoro Conservation Area, Kenya's Masai Mara and four smaller game reserves. Within this region live an estimated three million large animals. The system protects the largest single movement of wildlife on earth – the annual wildebeest migration. This is a phenomenal sight: thousands upon thousands of animals, particularly wildebeest and zebra, as far as the eye can see. ➽ *For more information on national parks and safaris, see page 10. For listings, see pages 296-300.*

Arriving at Serengeti National Park ➔ *Colour map 1, A4. 2°40'S, 35°0'E.*

Getting there There are several airstrips inside the park used by charter planes arranged by the park lodges or on scheduled circuits to/from Arusha by **Air Excel**, **Coastal Air** and **Regional Air**.

By road, the Serengeti is usually approached from the Ngorongoro Conservation Area. From the top of the crater the spectacularly scenic road, with a splendid view of the Serengeti plains winds down the crater walls on to the grasslands below. Along here the Masai tribesmen can be seen herding their cattle in the fresher pastures towards the top of the crater. Shortly before the Serengeti's boundary, there is the turning off to Olduvai Gorge where most safari companies stop. Then, entry is through the **Naabi Hill Gate** to the southeast of the park, where there is a small shop and information centre. From here it is 75 km to **Seronera**, the village in the heart of the Serengeti, which is 335 km from Arusha.

Approaching from Mwanza or Musoma on the shore of Lake Victoria, take the road east and you will enter the Serengeti through the **Ndabaka Gate** in the west, through what is termed as the Western Corridor to the Grumeti region. This road requires 4WD and may be impassable in the rainy season. There is a third, less frequently used gate in the north, **Ikoma Gate**, which lies a few kilometres from Seronera. This also goes to Musoma but, again, is not a very good road.

Getting around Most tourists are usually on a safari from Arusha, or there are a few that can be arranged from Mwanza, but it is possible to explore in your own vehicle. However, the roads are quite rough and you can expect hard corrugations (especially the road from Naabi Hill to Seronera, where there are deep ruts). In many regions of the park there is a fine top soil known locally as 'black cotton', which can get impossibly sticky and slippery in the wet. This is especially true of the Western Corridor. The dry season should not present too many problems. The Park Headquarters are at Seronera and there are airstrips at Seronera, Lobo and Grumeti, and at many of the small exclusive camps.

Park information Tanzania National Parks Authority (TANAPA), on the Arusha–Serengeti road (B144), www.tanzaniaparks.com, www.serengeti.org, 0630-1830, US$50, children (5-16) US$10, vehicle US$40.

Climate The dry season runs from June to October, the wet between March and May and, in between, is a period of short rains, during which time things turn green. At this time of year there are localized rain showers but it's more or less dry. With altitudes ranging from 920 to 1850 m, average temperatures vary from 15 to 25 °C. It is coldest from June to October, particularly in the evenings.

Serengeti National Park

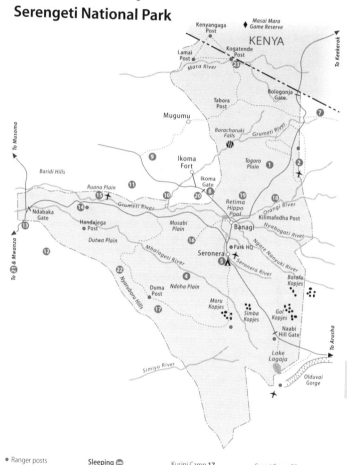

- • Ranger posts

Sleeping

Bilila Lodge Kempinski **19**
Faru Faru Lodge **10**
Grumeti Serengeti Tented
   Camp **15**
Ikoma Bush Camp **8**
Kijereshi Lodge **12**
Klein's Camp **7**

Kusini Camp **17**
Lobo Wildlife Lodge **2**
Mapito Tented Camp **20**
Mbalageti **22**
Mbuzi Mawe **18**
Migration Camp **1**
Sabora Lodge **11**
Sasakwa Lodge **9**

Sayari Camp **23**
Serena Kirawira Camp **14**
Serengeti Serena Lodge **16**
Serengeti Sopa Lodge **4**
Serengeti Stopover **13**
Seronera Wildlife Lodge **5**
Speke Bay Lodge **21**

Background

The name is derived from the Masai word 'siringet' meaning 'extended area' or 'endless plains'. A thick layer of ash blown from volcanoes in the Ngorongoro highlands covered the landscape between three and four million years ago, preserved traces of early man, and enriched the soil that supports the southern grass plains. Avoided by the pastoralist Masai because the woodlands had tsetse flies carrying trypanosomiasis (sleeping sickness), the early European explorers found this area uninhabited and teeming with game. Serengeti National Park was established in 1951 and, at 14,763 sq km, is Tanzania's second largest national park (after Selous). It rises from 920 to 1850 m above sea level and its landscape varies from the long and short grass plains in the south, the central savannah, the more hilly wooded areas in the north and the extensive woodland in the western corridor. The **Maswa Game Reserve** adjoins its western border.

Wildebeest

During the rainy season the wildebeest, whose population has been estimated at around 1,500,000, are found in the eastern section of the Serengeti and also in the Masai Mara in Kenya to the north. When the dry season begins at the end of June, the annual migration starts as the animals move in search of pasture. Just before this, they concentrate on the remaining green patches, forming huge herds, the rutting season begins and territories are established by the males, who then attempt to attract females into their areas. Once mating has occurred, the herds merge together again and the migration to the northwest begins. The migrating animals do not all follow the same route. About half go west, often going outside the park boundaries, and then swing northeast. The other half go directly north. The two groups meet up in the Masai Mara in Kenya. To get to the west section of the Serengeti and the Masai Mara, where they will find pasture in the dry season, the wildebeest must cross a number of large rivers and this proves too much for many of them. Many of the weaker and older animals die during the migration. Needless to say, predators follow the wildebeest on their great trek and easy pickings are to be had. The animals have to cross the Mara River, where massive Nile crocodiles with thickset jaws lick their lips in anticipation of a substantial feed. For any visitor to Tanzania, the herds are a spectacular sight. They return to the southeast at the end of the dry season (October-November) and calving begins at the start of the wet season (March).

Other wildlife

The Serengeti is also famous for cheetah, leopards and lions, some of which migrate with the wildebeest while others remain in the central plain. Prides of lions are commonly seen; leopards are most frequently detected resting in trees during the daytime along the Seronera River, whereas cheetahs are usually spotted near the Simba Kopjes. The elephant population in Serengeti was estimated to have fallen five-fold during the mid 1970 to 1980s thanks to poaching, though, since then, the numbers have slowly increased. Birdlife is prolific and includes various species of kingfishers, sunbirds and rollers, ostrich, egrets, herons, storks, ibis, spoonbills and ducks. Birds of prey include Ruppell's vulture and the hooded vulture, several varieties of kestrels, eagles, goshawks and harriers.

Routes

If you are approaching the Serengeti from the southeast (from the Ngorongoro Conservation Area), **Lake Ndutu**, fringed by acacia woodland, lies southeast of the main road (see page 286). Next you will reach the **Short Grass Plains**. The flat landscape is broken by the **Gol Mountains**, to the right, and by kopjes. The grass here remains short during both the wet and dry seasons. There is no permanent water supply in this region as a result of the nature of the soil. However, during the rains, water collects in hollows and depressions until it dries up at the end of the wet season. It is then that the animals begin to move on. The **Southern Plains** provide nutritious grasses for the wildebeest and, when the short rains come in November, these mammals move south to feed. In February-March, 90% of female wildebeest give birth and the plains are filled with young calves.

Naabi Hill Gate marks the end of the Short Grass and beginning of the **Long Grass Plains**. Dotted across the plains are **kopjes**. These interesting geological formations are made up of ancient granite that has been left behind as the surrounding soil structures have been broken down by centuries of erosion and weathering. They play an important role in the ecology of the plains, providing habitats for many different animals from rock hyraxes (a small rabbit-like creature whose closest relation is actually the elephant) to cheetahs.

The kopjes that you might include the **Moru Kopjes** in the south of the park to the left of the main road heading north. You may be lucky enough to see the Verreaux eagle, which sometimes nests here. The Moru Kopjes have a cave with Masai paintings on the wall and a rock called **Gong Rock** after the sound it makes when struck with a stone. There are also the **Simba Kopjes** on the left of the road before reaching Seronera, which, as their name suggests, are often a hideout for lions.

Passing through the Long Grass Plains in the wet season from around December to May is an incredible experience. All around, stretching into the distance, are huge numbers of wildebeest, Thompson's gazelle, zebra, etc.

The village of **Seronera** is in the middle of the park, set in the **Seronera Valley**. It forms an important transition zone between the southern grasslands and the northern woodlands. The area is criss-crossed by rivers and, as a result, this is where you are most likely to spot game. It is reached by a gravel road, which is in fairly good condition. Seronara is the best area to visit if you can only manage a short safari. It has a visitor centre, and the research institute is based here. It also contains a small museum noted for its giant stick insects (near the lodge). In the approach to Seronera the number of trees increases, particularly the thorny acacia trees. You can expect to see buffalo, impala, lion, hippo and elephant. If you are lucky, you might see leopard.

About 5 km north of Seronera the track splits. To the left it goes to the Western Corridor, and to the right it goes to Banagi, where it splits again to go northeast to the Lobo area and beyond to the Mara River, and northwest to Ikoma Gate. **Banagi** was the site of the original Game Department Headquarters before it became a national park, and to the north of here the land is mainly rolling plains of both grassland and woodland with a few hilly areas and rocky outcrops. Just to the west of Bangagi, off the main track to Ikoma Gate, is the **Retima Hippo Pool**, which is about 20 km north of Seronera.

In the northeast section of the park is the **Lobo Northern Woodland**. Wildlife remains in this area throughout the year, including during the dry season. The area is characterized by rocky hills and outcrops, where pythons sunbathe, and woodlands frequented by elephants fringe the rivers. Lobo is the site of the **Lobo Lodge**, 75 km from Seronera. Further north is the **Mara River**, with riverine forest bordering its banks. This is one of the rivers that claims many wildebeest lives every year during the migration. You will see both hippo and crocodile along the river banks.

If you take the left-hand track where the road splits north of Seronera, you will follow the **Grumeti Western Corridor**. The best time to follow this track is in the dry season (June-October) when the road is at its best and the migrating animals have reached the area. Part of the road follows, on your right, the **Grumeti River**, fringed by lush riverine forest, home to the black-and-white colobus monkey. On the banks of the river you will also see huge crocodiles basking in the sun. The **Musabi** and **Ndoha Plains** to the northwest and west of Seronera respectively can be viewed if you have a 4WD. The latter plain is the breeding area of topi, and large herds of up to 2000 will often be found here. All but the main routes are poorly marked.

◉ Serengeti National Park listings

For sleeping and eating price codes and other relevant information, see pages 22-26.

◉ Where to stay

Serengeti National Park *p292, map p293*
Inside the park
Rates for the lodges and camps in the Serengeti vary widely over the course of the year – sometimes by a few hundred dollars – and are determined by the season (rates are reduced by as much as 50% during the long rains, especially in Apr-May when some camps close altogether) and when the migration is expected to pass through.

$$$$ Bilila Lodge, about 20 km north of the Retima Hippo Pool, T0778-888 888, www.bililalodgeserengeti.com. Opened in 2009, this has set the benchmark for luxury lodges in the park, with 62 a/c rooms with satellite TV, Wi-Fi and minibars. The 16 suites and villas have their own plunge pools, kitchenette and butlers, all have stunning views and a telescope on each balcony or terrace. There's an infinity pool with views over the plains, a gym, spa, library, business centre, wine cellar, boma, pub and restaurant, and the whole architecturally impressive stone-and-thatch complex is centred on 2 very active waterholes. Rates start at US$370 per person.

$$$$ Grumeti Serengeti Tented Camp, Western Corridor, 93 km west of Seronera and 50 km east of Lake Victoria, www.grumeti.com, reservations Johannesburg, South Africa, T+27-(0)11-809 4314, www.andbeyond.com. Overlooks a tributary of the Grumeti River that teems with hippo and crocodile. Central bar/dining area near the river, swimming pool, 10 charming, custom-made tents with stylishly colourful decor. Expensive at US$755-1095 per person, but fantastic service and a great location, especially during the migration. Balloon safaris are also available from the lodge.

$$$$ Mbalageti, in the Western Corridor of the park, reservations Mwanza T028-262 2387, www.mbalageti.com. In an attractive location on Mwamyeni Hill, with 360° views over the plains and Mbalageti River. The 24 luxury tented chalets are set out in 2 groups – those facing sunrise and those facing sunset, all beautifully furnished and the suites have outdoor baths on private terraces. There are also 14 slightly cheaper lodge rooms. The lounge is full of African tribal carvings and antiques, and the swimming pool, restaurant, bar and outdoor spa with tranquillity pool have fantastic views over the plains. Doubles US$360-400 full board.

$$$$ Migration Camp, built within the rocks of a kopje in the Ndassiata Hills near Lobo, overlooking the Grumeti River, reservations Arusha, T027-250 0630, www.elewanacollection.com. Award-winning luxury camp which provides excellent views of the migration. The 20 richly decorated tents include a secluded honeymoon tent and a family tent sleeping 6; each one is surrounded by a 360° veranda, and there are many secluded vantage points linked by timber walkways, bridges and viewing platforms. There's also a swimming pool, bar and restaurant. Rates US$630-740 per person full board.

$$$$ Sanctuary Kusini, at the Hambi ya Mwaki-Nyeb Kopjes in the southwest, near the border with the Maswa Game Reserve, reservations **Sanctuary Retreats**, UK, T+44 (0)20-7190 7728, www.sanctuaryretreats. com. Closed Apr-May. Well off the usual tourist track, the camp is situated in a conchoidal outcrop of kopjes, offering superb views, with 12 stylish tents, 1 of which is a honeymoon suite, hospitable camp managers arrange sundowners on cushions up on the kopjes and candlelit dinners each evening. There's also a library and lounge. Rates US$520-800 per person.

$$$$ Sayari Camp, in the far north of the Serengeti, near the Kenyan border, reservations through **Asilia Lodges**, email them and they'll send you a list of agents, reservations@asiliaafrica.com, www. asilialodges.com. Formerly a mobile camp that followed the migration, this is now a permanent tented camp and one of the few in this remote region near the Mara River, with 15 luxurious and comfortable tents, the mess tent has a bar, lounge, library and restaurant centred around a campfire, and there's an infinity swimming pool and spa, attentive service. Income from the camp supports education and employment in the nearby villages. Rates US$550-770 per person full board.

$$$$ Serena Kirawira Camp, western Serengeti, reservations Arusha, T027-254 5555, www.serenahotels.com. A luxuriously appointed all-inclusive tented camp 90 km from Seronera in the secluded Western Corridor area. A member of Small Luxury Hotels of the World group. All the 25 tents have Edwardian decor and great views across the plains. The central public tent is adorned with exquisite antiques, including an old gramophone, and the swimming pool overlooks the plains. Doubles US$340-840 full board.

$$$$ Serengeti Wilderness Camp, 25 km east of Seronera, overlooking the Ngare Nanyuki River, reservations Arusha, T027-254 3068, www.tanzaniawildernesscamps.com. You really feel you're in the heart of the bush at this camp, which is semi-permanent and

moved every 3 months or so depending on the season to follow the game, producing minimal impact on the environment. Unpretentious and friendly, guests here rave about the quality of the food. There's a large dining tent and bar, with a separate lounge area. The 10 comfortable tents have bucket showers and solar-powered lighting. A great option if you want more of a bush experience but one that comes with home comforts. Rates US$450-730 per person full board.

$$$$-$$$ Lobo Wildlife Lodge, northeast of Seronera in the Lobo area, 45 km from the border with Kenya, reservations, Arusha, T027-254 4595, www.hotelsandlodges-tanzania.com. One of the oldest lodges in this part of the park, built in the 1960s, this 4-storey stone-and-timber lodge with 75 rooms, some of them adjoining for families, is well-camouflaged among clusters of large boulders. The swimming pool and bar, both dug into the rock, afford good views over the savannah and there's an active waterhole, as well as a buffet restaurant, TV room, gym and curio shop. Doubles US$170-350 full board.

$$$$-$$$ Mbuzi Mawe Tented Camp, in the northeast of the park, about 45 km from Seronera, reservations Arusha, T027-254 5555, www.serenahotels.com. Built around rocky kopjes, Mbuzi Mawe means 'the place of the klipsringer' in Kiswahili and you'll see several of them skipping up the rocks here, no longer shy of people. It's a charming, understated camp with 16 tents stylishly decorated with private verandas, a relaxing bar and restaurant, a fire-pit and stone terrace, and friendly staff. Doubles US$230-660 full board.

$$$$-$$$ Serengeti Serena Safari Lodge, 20 km north of Seronera Village, reservations Arusha, T027-254 5555, www. serenahotels.com. Another super-luxurious establishment in an idyllic central location with superb views towards the Western Corridor. Set high overlooking the plains, the lodge is constructed to reflect the design of an African village. Each of the 66 rooms is a stone-walled and thatched rondavaal, with wooden balcony, natural stone bathrooms, a/c, central heating, carved furniture and Makonde carvings. Also has a spa and infinity pool with views over the Serengeti. Doubles US$225-655 full board.

$$$$-$$$ Serengeti Sopa Lodge, in the previously protected area of Nyarboro Hills north of Moru Kopjes, reservations T027-250 0630, www.sopalodges.com. A good-value offering from the Sopa group decorated in an African-village theme with murals, giant pots and thatch. There are 69 rooms and 4 suites, excellent views of the Serengeti plains through double-storey window walls in all public areas, multi-level buffet restaurant and lounges, swimming pool, gift shop and TV room. Doubles US$180-550 full board.

$$$$-$$$ Seronera Wildlife Lodge, in the centre of the Serengeti, near the village of Seronera, T027-254 4595, www.hotelsand lodges-tanzania.com. This large lodge really is at the heart of the Serengeti. Good game viewing year round, but also significant visitor traffic. The public areas are very cleverly built into a rocky kopje, as is the swimming pool (making it look like an attractive natural pool). The bar is especially nice, but the 75 rooms are in unattractive and old-fashioned accommodation blocks built in the 1970s. Restaurant, shop, bar and viewing platform at the top of the kopje (beware of the monkeys). Campers at the nearby public campsites are allowed into the bar in the evenings (suitably dressed), as driving around the immediate vicinity of Seronera is permitted until 2200. Doubles US$160-420 full board.

National Park campsites There are several public campsites around Seronera. Be prepared to be totally self-sufficient and, if you are self-driving, bring food with you as there is little available in Seronera Village. It is not necessary to pre-book the public campsites; you simply pay for camping when you enter the park: US$30 per person. Facilities vary but most have nothing

more than a long drop and are completely unfenced. The animals do wander through at night so ensure that you stay in your tent. Camps are regularly visited by hyenas each night scavenging for scraps, and lions have also been known to wander through in the middle of the night.

Outside the park
The lodges and camps outside the national park boundaries are able to offer additional night drives and game walks.

$$$$ Buffalo Luxury Camp, on a private concession area on the northeastern boundary of the park, just south of the Kenyan border, T0753-888 5555, www. buffaloluxurycamp.com. One the Serengeti's newest permanent tented camps, with 20 tents, well furnished in a contemporary style; 15 are referred to as 'suite tents' with raised sleeping areas and surprisingly spacious tiled bathrooms, and there are 5 smaller and cheaper 'chalet tents'. Lounge with fireplace, bar/library and terrace restaurant with views over the Loliondo Hills. Rates from US$570 per person full board.

$$$$ Klein's Camp, on a private ranch on the northeastern boundary of the park, just south of the Kenyan border, reservations, Johannesburg, South Africa, T+27-(0)11-809 4313, www.kleinscamp.com, www.and beyond.com. Named after the American big game hunter Al Klein, who in 1926 built his base camp in this valley. The ranch is located on the Kuka Hills between the Serengeti and farmland, which forms a natural buffer zone for the animals and overlooks the wildlife corridor linking the Serengeti and the Masai Mara. 10 super-luxury stone-and-thatch cottages, the dining room and bar are in separate rondavaals with commanding views of the Grumeti River Valley, and there's a swimming pool. Rates US$650-1090 per person full board.

$$$$ Sasakwa Lodge, Sabora Tented Camp and **Faru Faru Lodge**, these 3 lodges are located in a 350,000 ha private concession area near the Grumeti River and Ikoma Gate, owned by **Singita**, one of Africa's top safari brands with many lodges in southern Africa, www.grumetireserves. com, www.singita.com. **Sasakwa** has been built in the style of an Edwardian manor house and has 9 luxury cottages and 1 4-bedroomed house (with separate staff quarters), each with fireplace, private infinity pool and deck with telescope. It is set on a hill with stunning views over the main migration route in the Western Corridor. Facilities include a gym and yoga room, spa, an equestrian centre, tennis courts and they have their own balloon. This flagship property costs a hefty US$1200-1700 per person, but for this you'll get unsurpassed luxury in an amazing location. **Sabora** is a classic tented camp reminiscent of the 1920s safari style and has 9 tents, and **Faru Faru** is a beautifully designed stone-and-thatch lodge constructed around 2 rim-flow swimming pools with 9 suites and 1 villa. Both are located further down the hill on the plains and rates are US$850-1200 per person.

$$$$-$$$ Mapito Tented Camp, 5 km outside the park, signposted left off the main road, 1 km from Ikoma Gate, then about 4 km drive on a dirt-track, T0732-975 210, www.mapito-camp-serengeti.com. More affordable than lodges within the park, from US$280 for a double full board, this relaxing camp has 13 large en suite tents with hot water bucket showers and solar-powered electricity. The lounge, bar and restaurant is in an impressive and unusual double-storey timber-and-canvas structure with a giant thatched roof.

$$$ Ikoma Tented Camp, 2 km from Ikoma Gate, reservations Arusha, T027-250 6135, www.moivaro.com. This camp has the concession for the area to operate game drives and walks, and works in close collaboration with the local Masai villages. It is comfortable, secluded and sheltered in a grove of acacia trees, with 31 spacious tents and a bar and dining area under thatch around a central fire-pit. Simpler and slightly cheaper than some of the more luxurious

tented camps above; rates are from US$180 per person full board. There's also a campsite here (**$**) with hot showers and a thatched kitchen area or you can eat at the restaurant; very useful for self-drivers coming from the Musoma direction.

$$$ Speke Bay Lodge, on the shores of Lake Victoria, off the main road (B6), 15 km from Ndabaka Gate and 125 km from Mwanza, T028-262 1237, www.spekebay. com. A lovely, cheaper alternative to staying in the Serengeti if you fancy a break from the bush. Run by a Dutch couple, this lodge on the shores of Lake Victoria has 8 round en suite bungalows, spacious and spotless, with a mezzanine floor for triple beds, plus 12 cheaper permanent tents under thatched roofs with shared toilets and hot showers. The bar and restaurant are on a terrace overlooking the beach. With well-established gardens, over 250 bird species and a pod of 10 hippos within its 85 ha, it's a mini nature reserve in its own right. The lodge offers bird walks, canoe trips with local fishermen and boat hire.

$$-$ Serengeti Stopover, along the Mwanza–Musoma road (B6) on the western edge of Serengeti, 141 km east of Mwanza and 1 km west of Ndabaka Gate, T028-262 2273, www.serengetistopover.com. 10 simple self-contained chalets with TVs, fans and nets, some with verandas and lounge areas, doubles from US$60, and a campsite for US$10 per person. There's a good basic restaurant that does the best fish and chips in the area, caught fresh that day from Lake Victoria, which is within walking distance. Its proximity to the park means that game can be present and you could avoid park entrance fees. Unlike safaris from Arusha, the lodge can arrange day trips into the park that can be very good value. It is run as a community initiative with the local Sukuma people, and tours can be arranged to the local villages. Recommended for budget travellers; you can jump off any of the buses that go between Mwanza and Musoma.

☉ What to do

Serengeti National Park *p292, map p293*

Balloon safaris

Serengeti Balloon Safaris, desks at Serengeti Serena Safari Lodge, Serengeti Sopa Lodge, and Seronera Wildlife Lodge see Where to stay, above, reservations Arusha, T027-254 8967, UK office T+44 (0) 122 587 3756, www.balloonsafaris.com. Balloon safaris are available for US$500 per person from the central (Seronera), southern Serengeti and Western Corridor lodges and camps. The normal drill is a 0500 pickup to the balloon site to watch them being inflated, a 60- to 90-min balloon flight at sunrise, followed by a champagne breakfast and transport back to your lodge. Especially during the months of the migration, this is often the highlight of visitors' trips to Tanzania. Although expensive, the experience is well worth the treat. Given that there are only 3 balloons, it is essential to pre-book, but any of the lodges can check if there's last-minute space available. No children under 7.

⊖ Transport

Serengeti National Park *p292, map p293*

Air

Air Excel and **Regional Air** have daily scheduled round-trip circuits between **Arusha** and the lodges in the Serengeti. **Coastal Air** have a daily circuit between **Arusha**, the lodges in the Serengeti and **Mwanza**, which returns the same way. Schedules are on the websites; see Arusha Transport, page 263 for contact details.

Contents

Footprint features

Border crossings

Around Lake Victoria

At a glance

⊖ **Getting around** Mwanza and
the regional towns are connected
by bus and *dala-dala*, and journey
times are becoming increasingly
shorter and more comfortable
thanks to major road-building in
this part of Tanzania. However, there
are some vast distances covering
hundreds of kilometres, so local
ferries or flights are often a more
pleasant option.
◐ **Time required** 5-7 days; 1-2 days
in each of the towns to enjoy their
lakeside setting, and a visit to
Rubondo Island National Park to
see wildlife away from the hordes.
☼ **Weather** Mostly warm during
the day, with cool evenings. Apr-
May has the most rainfall, although
showers aren't uncommon at any
time. Coolest in Jun-Sep.
✕ **When not to go** If using
Mwanza as a base for the Serengeti's
Western Corridor, avoid the heavy
rains Apr-May.

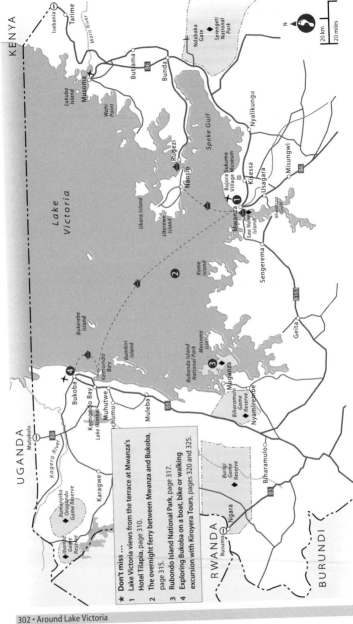

KENYA

Isebania

Tarime

Mara River

Serengeti National Park

Ndabaka Gate

B6

Butiama

Bunda

Musoma

Lukuba Island

Wahi Point

Speke Gulf

Nyalikungu

Kisessa

Misungwi

B6

Usagara

Bujora Sukuma Village Museum

Rugezi

Nansio

Mwanza

Mwanza Gulf

Ukara Island

Ukerewe Island

Saa Nane Island

Sengerema

Lake Victoria

Kome Island

2

Bukerebe Island

Kemondo Bay

Bumbiri Island

Maisome Island

Geita

B163

4

Bukoba

Kemondo Bay

Lake Ikimba

Muhutwe

Chumu

Muleba

B8

Rubondo Island National Park

Muganza

Biharamulo Game Reserve

Nyamirembe

3

Kagera River

Mutukulu

B3

Karagwe

Rumanyika Orugundu Game Reserve

Ibanda Game Reserve

Biharamulo

Burigi Game Reserve

B3

UGANDA

RWANDA

Rusumo

Ngara

BURUNDI

Don't miss ...
★ Lake Victoria views from the terrace at Mwanza's
  Hotel Tilapia, page 310.
1 The overnight ferry between Mwanza and Bukoba,
  page 315.
2 Rubondo Island National Park, page 317.
3 Exploring Bukoba on a boat, bike or walking
4 excursion with Kiroyera Tours, pages 320 and 325.

N

20 km
20 miles

Lake Victoria, bordered by Kenya, Tanzania and Uganda, is the largest freshwater lake in Africa and the second largest in the world after Lake Superior in North America. Occupying a shallow depression at an altitude of 1135 m, it covers 69,490 sq km, is the source of the White Nile and provides a livelihood for millions of people living around its shores, not only in Tanzania but in Kenya and Uganda, too. This area is a long way from the coast of Tanzania and, for many years, transport links left much to be desired. However, while many of the roads to Mwanza through central Tanzania are still generally in a poor state, this is changing slowly as mining activity to the south of the lake is encouraging road-building and the opening up of access routes. There is also access by train or by air (though both these services can be erratic) or by road through Kenya, Uganda and Rwanda. In fact, thanks to the vast distances across the dull, dry, flat and largely empty interior of Tanzania, Mwanza, the principal city in the region, is closer to Kampala and Kigali than it is to Dar es Salaam.

Mwanza itself is a busy city and, surprisingly, given its location, the second largest in Tanzania; the export of fish from Lake Victoria is big business here, and it has trade links with nearby Kenya. Bukoba, on the western side of the lake, is in a very attractive setting. Neither of these towns feature high on the usual tourist itinerary, though the western section of the Serengeti National Park can be accessed from this region, and the most notable attraction on the lake is the Rubondo Island National Park.

Getting there and around

Mwanza has an airport, and there are regular flights from both Dar es Salaam and Arusha with **Precision Air**, **Fly 540**, and **Coastal Air**. There are also some flights from Mwanza to the smaller airstrip at Bukoba and charter flights to Rubondo Island National Park. The major tarred road that accesses the region from Kenya, the B6 to Mwanza, has turn-offs to Musoma and the Serengeti National Park. The roads from the coast and Dodoma to Lake Victoria cover vast distances, and many in the region are very poor, especially after rain. However, road conditions are improving rapidly, thanks to the gold-mining operations in the Geita region, and there has been substantial road-building in the lake region in the last few years. For example, the road from Mwanza around the south of the lake to Bukoba and on to the Mutukulu border with Uganda has been tarred, so journey times and public transport are improving on this route all the time. There are frequent buses from Mwanza to the border with Kenya and beyond, and some of the long-distance buses to Arusha and Dar es Salaam take the route via Kenya. But there are also cross-country buses across the interior – a route that used to take days rather than hours. The other option to get to Mwanza is by train on the Central Line railway from Dar es Salaam (see box, page 18). There are also a number of ferry services operating on Lake Victoria, notably the Mwanza–Bukoba car and passenger ferry.➤➤ *For further details, see Transport, page 315.*

Eastern Lake Victoria

The Tanzania towns of Musoma and Mwanza and the nearby islands offer the opportunity to witness the majesty of Lake Victoria. Mwanza, the second-largest town in Tanzania, is the springboard for the ferry across the lake to Bukoba on the western shore, easily the best method of getting to the other side, and the terminus for the Central Line railway. ➤➤ *For listings, see pages 309-316.*

Musoma → *Colour map 1, A3. 1° 50'S, 34° 30'E. Phone code: 028. Population: 150,000.*
This small port is set on the east shores of Lake Victoria, 102 km southwest of the border with Kenya at Isebania (see box, opposite). It's near the Ndabaka Gate (0600-1600) to the Western Corridor of Serengeti National Park (see page 292) and so should be one of the centres for safaris to the park, but, because of its general inaccessibility, it has not developed as such. There is little reason to come here, although the views over the lake are very good, and it is a bustling and friendly town and capital of Mara Region. It is possible to pop in on your way to or from Kenya, but it can be by-passed completely, as the B6 between the border and Mwanza runs 18 km inland. It's another 222 km southwest to Mwanza, and a steady stream of buses and *dala-dalas* run between the two towns; some *dala-dalas* also go to Isebania. The weekday market, when women bring their crops of mangoes and green leafy vegetables, ripe avocados and bunches of bright yellow bananas to sell is worth seeing; as are the many varieties of boats on the lake, from large ferries and transport barges to *ngalawa* fishing boats and dugout canoes. Small boats can be taken across the bay and to the little islands nearby for around US$1 per person. They leave from the fish market and harbour on the north shore, not far from the **Afrilux Hotel**.

Border crossing: Tanzania–Kenya

Isebania

Isebania is a small settlement that straddles the B6, which, over the border in Kenya, becomes the A1. The border is open 24 hours and the crossing is efficient and quick. Visas for both Tanzania and Kenya are available, but remember that if you've only gone into Tanzania and are going back to Kenya, you don't need to buy another visa to re-enter, as long as your original one is still valid.

There are money changers on both sides of the border and you can change a small amount of currency to last until you get to the next bank. If coming from Tanzania, the first banks (with ATMs) you'll reach in Kenya are in Migori, 20 km north of the border. If coming from Kenya, the first banks in Tanzania are in Musoma and Mwanza, which are both some considerable distance away.

It is 325 km from Mwanza to Isebania, on a good tarred road; and there are plentiful petrol stations en route. The road passes the Serengeti National Park's Ndabaka Gate (0600-1600) to the Western Corridor of the park, which is 195 km before Isebania. There is little accommodation between Mwanza/Musoma and the border, but some places to stay near Ndabaka Gate (see page 299). Once in Kenya, the road first goes to Kisii, which is 90 km north of Isebania, where the road splits; the B3 goes northeast to Nakuru (295 km), where it joins the A104 to Nairobi, 393 km from Isebania. The A1 continues north from Kisii to Kisumu, 195 km north of Isebania.

Some Tanzanian long-distance buses between Mwanza and Arusha and Dar es Salaam take the route via Kisii, Nakuru and Nairobi in Kenya, as the roads are far better than in the interior of Tanzania. (You will have to buy a transit visa for Kenya; US$20.) Note that the buses from Nairobi on this route leave Nairobi late in the evening and cross the border at first light – travel by bus at night in Tanzania is not permitted, which is why the buses do the Kenyan section during the night. Also note that it can get very cold at night in Kenya's Western Highlands, so dress appropriately. There are also *dala-dalas*, which go to Isebania from Mwanza and Musoma on the Tanzanian side, and *matatus* from the border to Kisii and Kisumu on the Kenyan side.

There is a very poor choice of accommodation in and around Kisii – not much more than a clutch of simple board and lodgings. The better option is to overnight in either Kisumu or Nakuru (or one of the other Rift Valley towns), depending on which direction you're going in; see the *Footprint Kenya Handbook*.

Electricity and water supplies can be erratic in Musoma, and the small hotels will not have generators. None of the hotels currently take credit cards, although there are branches of **Barclay's Bank** and **National Bank of Commerce**, which have ATMs.

Around Musoma

Butiama The home village of Julius Nyerere (see box, page 405) is 48 km southeast of Musoma, off the B6. To get here, there are infrequent *dala-dalas* from Musoma. If you are driving, head along the B6 south towards Mwanza. Ignore the first signposted junction to Butiama, which leads you along 17 km of very bad dirt track; instead take the second junction, which is 11 km of tarmac road to Butiama. The village has the **Julius K Nyerere Museum** ① *T028-262 1338, 0930-1800, US$5*, which commemorates Nyerere's life and work. Exhibits document the rise of Nationalism, the Independence movement and the

Lake Victoria

Lake Victoria is one of the most important natural water resources in the sub-Saharan region of Africa. It is has a surface area of approximately 69,500 sq km, with an adjoining catchment area measuring 184,000 sq km. The Tanzania share of the lake is 49%, Kenya's share is 6% and Uganda has 45%. The surrounding lake communities in all three countries equal approximately 30 million people, a large proportion being totally dependent on the lake for water, food and economic empowerment. Despite its vast size, Lake Victoria remained one of the last physical features in Africa to be discovered by the 19th-century explorers from Europe. Early charts depict a vague patch of water lying to the north and east of the 'Mountains of the Moon' (today's Rwenzori Mountains in Uganda), but it was not until 1858 that explorers Speke and Burton stumbled on to its southern shore near Mwanza in Tanzania. Speke later wrote that he felt no doubt that the lake gave birth to the River Nile, the source of which had been the subject of so much speculation and the object of many explorers' expeditions. He said "the lake at my feet is the most elusive of all explorers' dreams, the source of the legendary Nile".

Lake Victoria is relatively shallow and has a gentle slope to the shores, so any slight change in water level affects a large land area. Its mean depth is 40 m, the deepest part is 82 m. The water balance is dominated by evaporation and rainfall in the lake, with contributions from river inflow and outflow. The outflow of water, into the River Nile through the Owen Falls Dam in Uganda, accounts for only 20% of water loss from the lake. The remaining 80% is taken by evaporation. Similarly, the inflow through the many rivers from the catchment area only contributes 15-20%, while rainfall on the lake accounts for 80-85%. Of the inlets, the River Kagera, which flows from Rwanda, contributes about 46%, Kenya's Nzoia and Sondu/ Miriu rivers about 15% and 8% respectively, and Tanzania's Mara River about 10-15%.

There is a wide variety of fish in the lake. Scientifically, it is puzzling that so many diverse species unique to these waters could evolve in so uniform an environment. Biologists speculate that hundreds of thousands of years ago, the lake may have dried into a series of smaller lakes causing these brilliantly coloured cichlids to evolve differently. These fish are greatly sought after for aquariums. One unique characteristic for which cichlids (tilapia being the best known) are noted is the female's habit of nursing its fertilized eggs and young in its mouth. To many of the people of Lake Victoria, the cichlids are their livelihood – the catch, preparation (sun-drying) and sale of these fish are an important resource for them. Lake Victoria is also a home to a predator fish, the Nile perch, introduced into the lake some 20 years ago as a sport fish.

Warning Lake Victoria is infected with bilharzia (Schistosomiasis) so swimming close to the shore is not recommended.

early history of Tanzania, as well as displaying various items of interest that belonged to Tanzania's first president, including a copy of Plato's *Republic*, translated into Kiswahili by hand. Nyerere was buried in Butiama after his death in 1999, and his grave lies not far from the humble dwelling where he was born 77 years before. If there's no one around at the museum, ask at the army base just before and someone will find the curator to let you in.

Mwanza → *For listings, see pages 309-316. Colour map 1, A3. 2° 30'S, 32° 58'E. Phone code: 028. Population: 3,200,000.*

Mwanza lies on a peninsula that juts into the lake and is the largest Tanzanian port on Lake Victoria. With a population of roughly 3.2 million, it is also Tanzania's second largest city. It is surrounded by rocky hills, and the land is dominated by granite outcrops, some of which are very impressive and look as if they are about to topple. The road approach (B6) from the north is spectacular, tunnelling through some vast boulders. As the railway terminus and major lake port, Mwanza is a bustling and lively city. It has close trade links with Kenya, and there is a steady stream of trucks on the B6 to and from the border. It was founded in 1892 as a regional administrative post for the Germans and a commercial centre to control mainly export production of the cotton-growing areas in the Lake Victoria region. It was captured by the British in 1916. The railway line, built by the British, reached Lake Victoria in 1928 and was considered vital for the development of the northwest area. Today, fishing is a major commercial activity in this area, though maize, cotton and sweet potato plantations around here produce large volumes of cash crops that pass though Mwanza on their way to market. The produce from the lake region is gathered here and is then transported to the coast by rail or to Kenya by road. Recently, the town has received a major economic boost with the South African takeover of the **Mwanza Brewery**, and the substantial gold-mining developments in Shinyanga and around Geita, where several massive and ambitious mines have been operating since the late 1990s. More are expected to open to exploit Tanzania's large gold deposits in the southern lake region. Although the city has few attractions for the visitor, it makes a good base from which to explore nearby Rubondo Island National Park and the western parts of the Serengeti.

Arriving in Mwanza

Getting around Taxis can be found near the bus and train stations or outside the **New Mwanza Hotel**. *Dala-dalas*, locally known as 'express', are well distributed throughout the town and are the most popular and cheapest means of transport. ▶▶ *For further details, see Transport, page 314.*

Places in Mwanza

Although there are few formal sights in Mwanza, it's an interesting city in which to walk and drink in Tanzanian street life. The colonial centre of Mwanza was around the port on the west side of the town. Among the historic buildings in this area are the **Primary Court**, dating from the German period, and the **Mahatma Gandhi Memorial Hall** from the British period. The **clock tower** has a plaque recording that on 3 August 1858, on Isamilo Hill, a mile away, John Hanning Speke first saw the main water of Lake Victoria, which he later proved to be the source of the Nile.

The former colonial residences are spread over **Capri Point** to the south of town, which today is the wealthiest area of the city; social life is centred on the **Mwanza Club** and its golf course, and the **Yacht Club**. One of the celebrated sights is **Bismarck Rock**, which appears, precariously balanced, just south of the ferry terminal on Nasser Road. It is named after the German Chancellor (1815-1898) under whom the town of Mwanza was established as an administration centre in German East Africa in the 1890s.

Around Mwanza

Saa Nane Island ⓘ *Motorized boats from Mwanza depart on demand from the jetty, 1 km south of the centre, off Station Rd just before the Hotel Tilapia, 1100-1600 and return 1200-1700 and take about 20 mins. Combined boat and entry fee is about US$5, but this is expected to increase if the island receives national park status.* This 0.7-sq-km island is not far from Mwanza and is little more than a grassy outcrop of rock. Originally it was opened as a wildlife sanctuary in the 1960s and, for many years, was not much more than a glorified zoo, with cramped enclosures for animals, such as leopard, lion, hyena and monkeys. However, today these animals have been removed, the cages are empty, and the island

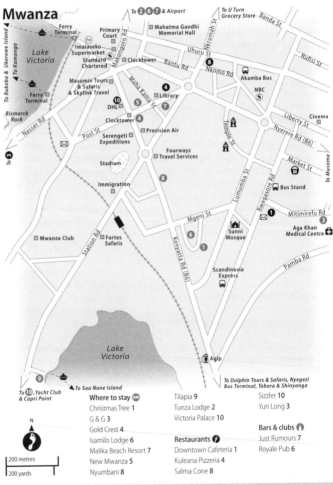

Mwanza

Where to stay 🛏
Christmas Tree **1**
G & G **3**
Gold Crest **4**
Isamilo Lodge **6**
Malika Beach Resort **7**
New Mwanza **5**
Nyumbani **8**
Tilapia **9**
Tunza Lodge **2**
Victoria Palace **10**

Restaurants 🍴
Downtown Cafeteria **1**
Kuleana Pizzeria **4**
Salma Cone **8**
Sizzler **10**
Yun Long **3**

Bars & clubs 🍸
Just Rumours **7**
Royale Pub **6**

is currently being considered for national park status by the Tanzania National Parks Authority (TANAPA; www.tanzaniaparks.com). For now, it has free-ranging impala and vervet monkeys; rock hyrax are commonly seen sunning themselves on the rocks; hippo and monitor lizard can be seen around the shores, and there is plentiful birdlife, including fish eagle, pied kingfisher and cormorants. You can walk all over the island and maybe have a picnic, and there are some bandas with tables near the jetty; be wary, however. as you may encounter pythons and crocodiles in the undergrowth, and the monkeys (given the island's history as a zoo) are used to people and may attempt to steal food. Ensure you pre-arrange for the boatman to come and pick you up again from the jetty.

Bujora Sukuma Village Museum ⓘ *16 km from Mwanza on the Musoma road, reached by taking a* dala-dala *from the bus station near the market in Mwanza to Kisessa, then walking the remaining 2 km, 0800-1800, US$5, children (under 16) US$2.50, which includes a 1-hr guided tour and the snake dance.* Originally set up by missionaries from Quebec in 1952, the museum celebrates the traditions and culture of the Sukuma, who make up one of the largest tribal groups in Tanzania. Exhibits include an unusual two-storey royal pavilion in the shape of the royal stool (which symbolizes the Sukuma royal throne), shrines and traditional instruments, including a drum collection. Traditional dances are held when the museum is busy, usually on a Saturday, and include the impressive Sukuma snake dance or *Bugobogobo*, which is performed with a live python. You can camp here for US$3 per person.

Ukerewe Island The 530-sq-km Ukerewe Island is the largest island in Lake Victoria. It lies about 45 km north of Mwanza and can be reached by ferry, which takes about three hours (see Transport, page 315). It is also possible to go by road – east round the lake to **Bunda** and then west along a dirt road along the north shore of Speke Gulf, crossing the **Rugezi Channel** by a shorter car and passenger ferry service (3.8 km) to Ukerewe Island. There are only irregular *dala-dalas* on the last leg of this route, so it may be necessary to hitch. The shoreline of Ukerewe Island is carved into numerous bays, and it is surrounded by at least a dozen smaller islands. Inland, it features low rocky hills interspersed with a scattering of small villages and subsistence smallholdings which mostly grow cassava and rice. The island is very pretty and provides a perfect example of how rural people in these parts rely on the lake, but there is little else to attract the tourist. The largest settlement is **Nansio**, where there are a number of small board and lodgings and cheap restaurants and, if you ask around, bikes can be hired to explore the island.

ⓔ Eastern Lake Victoria listings

For sleeping and eating price codes and other relevant information, see pages 22-26.

ⓦ Where to stay

Musoma *p304*
There are 2 excellent options south of Musoma near the Ndabaka Gate of the Serengeti National Park, **Serengeti Stopover**, and **Speke Bay Lodge**, see page 299.

$$$$ Lukuba Island, reservations, Arusha, T027-254 8840, www.lukuba.com. This is primarily a fishing lodge on Lukuba Island, and guests are transferred from Musoma by boat, which takes around 45 mins. Accommodation is in 5 stone thatched cottages and 3 permanent tents nestled in the island's forest, with lake views, good cuisine (mostly fish) and friendly management. Activities include fishing excursions by dhow, kayaking, and there's a little sand beach and a swimming pool. It is possible to catch Nile perch in these waters, and otters and monitor lizards are frequently seen around the island.

$$-$ Peninsula Beach Resort, 2 km south of town towards the pleasant suburb of Makoko, south of the airstrip, T028-264 2546. Whitewashed building in what was once a formal colonial home on the beach. Rooms are either in unattractive metal huts or better wooden cabins dotted around the large boulders in the grounds and have a/c, TV, hot water and fridge. It is a little overpriced for the standard, but the location next to the lake is pleasant. Large restaurant serving Western and Indian dishes, separate beach area with a swimming pool (not always open) and boats.

$ Afrilux Hotel, Karume St, 500 m from the bus stand, T028-262 0031. Very good-value, self-contained rooms, with hot water, fans and satellite TV in a modern 4-storey block. The management is friendly, there's a restaurant serving filling local and Indian meals and a large garden bar area; this is not a bad place to eat in the evening, though service is notoriously slow.

$ Hotel Matvilla, Mkendo St, opposite Barclay's Bank, T028-262 2445, www.matvilla hotel.com. Musoma's newest hotel has been built above the **Musoma Emporium**, and has 25 modern though rather small rooms with spotless tiled bathrooms and reliable hot water, a/c and satellite TV. The attached open-air bar and restaurant is set in a well-tended garden with palm trees and has a varied menu of local and continental dishes, and, if there's a conference on, buffet meals. They are planning to open a campsite to the west of the town on a spot among the rocks at the tip of the peninsula; ask at the hotel for details.

$ Tembo Beach Hotel, at Old Musoma Pier, 2 km west of town, T028-262 2887. Hotel with lovely private beach bordered with planted shrubs on the peninsula, with 7 self-contained rooms in a long wooden block with porches and hot water, some

have extra beds in the loft (they are in the process of building 5 more). There's also a sandy, shady campsite, with separate ablution block and plenty of space for vehicles, and a good bar and restaurant, which serves excellent grilled fish. It's a little dilapidated, but very peaceful, with wonderful views of the lake, especially at sunset, and they rent out bikes. Doubles US$30, camping US$8 per person.

Mwanza *p307, map p308*

In the last few years there has been a mushrooming of new purpose-built hotels in Mwanza; mostly aimed at local business travellers and almost all have conference facilities. As such, some may seem characterless but, for the visitor, there is now an excellent choice of mid-range places to stay with modern facilities.

$$$ Gold Crest Hotel, Kenyatta Rd, T028-250 6058, www.goldcresthotel.com. Opened in 2011 in a smart white tower block, with lake views from the top floors and good facilities. The rooms and suites have a/c, satellite TV, Wi-Fi, modern dark-wood made-for-hotel furnishings, some have balconies (and quite bizarrely) double circular beds. Facilities include 2nd-floor bar with balcony and good city views, TVs for sports and a good choice of cocktails and whiskies. There's a coffee shop with Wi-Fi selling freshly made cakes, a buffet restaurant and swimming pool. Doubles from US$140.

$$$ Hotel Tilapia, Station Rd, near the jetty for ferries to Saa Nane Island, 1 km southwest of town, T028-250 0517, www.hoteltilapia.com. On the lakeshore, with 40 chalet-style rooms with a/c or fans, satellite TV and fridge. There are also 7 small cabin rooms on a boat moored on the lake by the hotel. Lovely swimming pool where non-guests can swim for a small fee, and a gym. Indian, Thai and Japanese restaurants and a decking bar overlooking the lake (see Restaurants, page 312). Fax and internet services, and they can arrange car hire. Doubles from US$110.

$$$ Malika Beach Resort, 8 km from town and 5 km before the airport, signposted off Makongoro Rd, T028-256 1111, www. malaikabeachresort.com. A newly built resort set among the boulders on the lakeshore not far from the airport, with 32 rooms in very impressive double-storey villas with conical roofs, each with large balcony and lake views, Wi-Fi, power showers and a/c. There's a great swimming pool built right on the lake's edge, a children's playground, grassy lawns, restaurant serving continental and Indian dishes, a coffee shop and bar. This is a fairly ambitious development but reports are good so far. Doubles from US$150.

$$$-$$ Isamilo Lodge, 3 km from town towards the airport, signposted to the right of the Makongoro Rd, T028-254 1627, www.isamilolodge.com. A bit out of the way in the Isamilo Hills, but reputedly this is built on the spot where John Hanning Speke first saw Lake Victoria in 1858. It has 20 comfortable rooms with a/c, satellite TV, Wi-Fi, minibar and veranda, most with harbour, city and distant lake views. The rooms are in neat red-tiled buildings that climb up the hillside with a series of staircases and bridges. There's a restaurant and bar with pleasant outdoor terrace that maximizes the view; the menu is small but includes fresh fish, pizza and Indian food, and there's a swimming pool. Doubles from US$80.

$$$-$$ Victoria Palace Hotel, at Capri Point, 1 km south of town beyond the **Hotel Tilapia**, T028-250 3068, www.victoriapalace hoteltz.com. In a rather garish pale cream and blue-glass tower, this is another business/conference hotel but well positioned in a peaceful part of town near the lakeshore, with 39 a/c rooms and neat furnishings. The attractive public areas are built around rocks, and there's a nice swimming pool, restaurant, bar, gym, sauna and steam room, and massages can be arranged. Doubles from US$95.

$$ New Mwanza Hotel, central on Post St, T028-250 2528, www.newmwanzahotel. com. Mwanza's principal central hotel is in

an ugly concrete block, but is well run with attentive and helpful staff and management. The 54 rooms have a/c, satellite TV and Wi-Fi. Extensive facilities include **King's Casino**, with a number of tables and slots, 24-hr coffee shop and room service, **Blue Moon** disco, bar and restaurant (see Restaurants, page 312), swimming pool, gym, sauna and steam room. Doubles from US$65.

$$-$ Nyumbani Hotel, Kenyatta Rd, T028-250 2021-3, www.nyumbanihotels.com. A massive new steel and blue-glass block that dominates Mwanza's skyline with 100+ rooms, with Wi-Fi, flat-screen satellite TV, tea- and coffee-makers, a/c, lovely furnishings in creams and browns. Rooms either look out across the lake or, on the other side, over the giant boulders above town, and are superb value from just US$55 for a double and US$35 for a single. Facilities include smart restaurant, rooftop swimming pool and bar with sweeping views, and underground car park.

$$-$ Tunza Lodge, Ilemela Beach, near the village of Hemla, 10 km north of town and 3 km from the airport, signposted off Makongoro Rd, T028-256 2215, www. renair.com. A simple and friendly South African-run beach resort with 13 rooms, all with en suite bathrooms, plus camping on the beach with simple (cool) showers in reed huts. Nice gardens leading down to the beach but remember Lake Victoria has bilharzia and swimming close to the shore is not recommended. Fishing trips, waterskiing and windsurfing can be arranged. Good bar and restaurant in pleasant thatched building right on the sand, and Nile perch is a speciality. Doubles from US$70, camping US$10 per person.

$ Christmas Tree, Karuta St, just off Mgeni St, T028-250 2001. Inexplicably named, but one of the more friendly and popular of the many board and lodgings in the back streets, in a modern 3-storey block, with 30 simple rooms with fans, nets, hot water in bathrooms and some have TV. There's a good-value restaurant for local meals and it's a 5-min walk into town for the better restaurants and bars.

$ G & G Hotel, Mitimrefu Rd, opposite the Aga Khan School and not far from the bus station, T028-254 2351, www.gnghotel.com. A 7-storey block with 43 rooms, with a/c, Wi-Fi and satellite TV, rather small and stuffy with old-fashioned furniture but with neat tiled bathrooms and good value at US$40 for a double and US$30 for a single. The **Serengeti Restaurant** serves a reasonable selection of cheap and filling African and international dishes, such as chicken and chips, and the **Ngorongoro Bar** has plenty of cold beer.

❼ Restaurants

Musoma *p304*

There are a few basic food canteens around town, but the best restaurants are at Musoma's hotels (see Where to stay, above).
$ Rehema Café, at the Anglican Diocese Compound, just off the main road between Musoma Primary School and the second-hand clothes market, T022-278 3941. Mon-Fri 0800-1600, Sat 0800-1300. Run by a church missionary group, this small, delightful and unexpected café with garden seating offers real espresso coffee, cakes, light lunches and Sat-morning breakfast. All profits are used for the Rehema Project, which helps disadvantaged women and children in Musoma. Highlights are the banana cake, peanut cookies, smoothies and fresh juices, and the ladies are exceptionally friendly.

Mwanza *p307, map p308*

Again, the best places to eat are at the hotels (see Where to stay, above), whether you're staying or not. If these are hosting local conferences, a buffet lunch or dinner may be served and, if you're a guest, you will be able to join in. During the day, there are a number of cheap restaurants serving up barbecued meat, fried chicken and stews. These include the **Downtown Cafeteria ($)**, opposite the bus stand, which is clean and smart, with good juices and coffees, and is

a very useful place to wait for a bus if you have luggage.
$$$-$ Hotel Tilapia, Station Rd, 1 km southwest of town, see Where to stay, page 310. The best of the hotels for eating, with 4 restaurants inside in the basement and outside on the roof, serving Chinese, Japanese and Indian food. The thatched bar has a grassy terrace and is a fine place for a sundowner with sweeping views of the lake; it gets lively at the weekends and is very popular with expat miners who come into town for R&R. Taxis wait outside and should cost in the region of US$2 back to town if it's a late night.
$$ New Mwanza Hotel, central on Post St, see Where to stay, page 311. The main restaurant opens 1200-2300. The Indian food here is superb and very authentic, cooked by Indian chefs, but there's also a good choice of continental dishes and grilled tilapia fish from the lake, and good buffet breakfasts (from 0700), which is just the job if you've come off the ferry from Bukoba early in the morning. The coffee shop is open 24 hrs.
$$ Yun Long, 5-min walk from the ferry terminal along Nasser Rd, T0744-609 790. Open 1200-2300. Fantastic setting in lovely gardens, with all the tables right on the edge of the lake with views of Bismarck Rock. There's a large bar under thatch, with a full range of imported drinks, 2 pool tables, and satellite TV; this is not a bad place to come for a sundowner. Try the Chinese-style tilapia fillet with chilli or sweet and sour sauce.
$ Kuleana Pizzeria, Post St, near the **New Mwanza Hotel**, T028-256 0566. Open 0900-2100. Set in a gravel courtyard with tables under thatch and serving pizzas, sandwiches made with home-baked bread, salads, cakes and desserts; the fresh juices are very good, and you can have a beer, but only if you're ordering food. It's run by a charity that supports street kids.
$ Sizzler, Kenyatta Rd, T0741-341 118. Open 1000-1530, 1800-2200. Good-quality international, Chinese and Indian food, especially the Indian dishes which are a

good choice for vegetarians with excellent naan and roti breads. It's also well known for its whole BBQ chicken, which is cooked on a charcoal grill outside and served with chips or rice. No alcohol.

Cafés
Salma Cone, corner of Barti St and Nkrumah St. 0900-1800. Coffee, snacks and excellent ice cream – try the chocolate sundae with nuts or the thick milkshakes – and the best fresh passion fruit juice in town. Always busy, especially with Indian families.

🍷 Bars and clubs

Mwanza *p307, map p308*
Just Rumours, Station Rd, close to the New Mwanza Hotel. Bar with a modern interior and mirrored glass on the exterior, satellite TV and big screen, pool tables, dance floor very popular at the weekends from about 2300.
Royale Pub, just off Mgeni St. A big outdoor bar under a large canopy, most of the awnings are made from UN tarps, barbecued meals, busy all day, friendly service.

🎭 Entertainment

Mwanza *p307, map p308*
King's Casino, 1st floor of the New Mwanza Hotel. Opens at 1200 for the slots, 1700 for the gaming tables, until 2400. Roulette and black jack, slot machines and bar, free drinks to players, no entry fee. The **Blue Moon** disco is also in the hotel.

O Shopping

Mwanza *p307, map p308*
The massive **Central Market** is to the east of town, near the bus station and hemmed in by Market St, Pamba Rd and Rwagasore Rd. It sells just about everything imaginable in its tightly packed lanes, but be very wary of pickpockets and clamouring street kids selling the likes of plastic bags or offering services, such as carrying your shopping.

Stalls sell fish, spices, fresh fruit and vegetables, and souvenirs, including drums. Masai jewellery, Sukumu fertility masks, *kikois* and *kangas* (sarongs) can all be picked up at much cheaper prices than in the more touristy areas of Tanzania. The raggedy *dukas* (small shops) around the market and in the back streets sell anything from cheap jeans and shoes made in China, to radios and mousetraps.
U Turn Grocery Store, corner of Nkrumah and Hospital St, T028-250 0865. Mon-Fri 0800-2000, Sat 0800-1400, Sun 1000-1300. This is Mwanza's best supermarket for imported goods, including chocolate and booze, and it also sells frozen meat and toiletries. It's fairly expensive but has an impressive range of products. A similar range of imported items can be found at the **Imalaseko Supermarket**, Mon-Sat 0800-1900, Sun 1000-1400, at the clock tower roundabout next to Standard Chartered Bank.

⚓ What to do

Mwanza *p307, map p308*
Tour operators
Dolphin Tours & Safaris, in the Mkuyuni Industrial area, 6 km from town off the Shinyanga road, T028-255 1141, www.carhire.co.tz. Car hire, including 4WDs to take into the parks. They can also organize tailor-made safaris from Mwanza, including 2- or 3-day trips to the Serengeti and Ngorongoro Crater.
Fourways Travel Services, corner of Station and Kenyatta Rds, T028-250 2620, www.fourwaystravel.net. Very helpful travel agent for fishing and wildlife safaris, airport pickups and flight tickets.
Fortes Safaris, Station Rd, T028-250 1804, www.fortessafaris.com. Has more than 40 vehicles for car hire and safaris, including a 6-day/5-night safari to the Northern Circuit parks starting in Mwanza and finishing in Arusha (or vice versa).
Masumin Tours & Safaris and **Skylink Travel**, Kenyatta Rd, T028-250 0192,

www.masuminsafaris.com. Safaris to the parks in the Northern Circuit from Mwanza, also offers short- or long-term car hire. Shares an office with **Skylink** who also have offices in Dar and Arusha, T028-250 0233, www.skylinktanzania.com. Quality travel agent for flights, also agents for **Avis** car hire, www.avis.com.

Serengeti Expeditions, Kenyatta Rd, opposite the **New Mwanza Hotel**, T028-254 2222, www.serengetiexpedition.com. Safaris to the Northern Circuit and car hire.

⊖ Transport

Musoma *p304*
Air
The airstrip in Musoma is practically in the middle of town and runs adjacent to the main road. Some of the **Precision Air** (see below) flights between **Mwanza** and **Dar**, also touch down in Musoma 4 times a week, but only if there are enough passengers.

Bus
Musoma lies 18 km from the main road (B6) that goes from Mwanza to the Kenya border at Isebania (see page 305), but the international through buses between Mwanza and Kenya do not stop here. However, there are regular direct buses and *dala-dalas* to/from **Mwanza** from the bus stand, which is behind Kusaga St in the centre. The 222-km trip takes 3 hrs and costs around US$4. There are also *dala-dalas* to/from the border (95 km), after which you'll have to get another minibus (*matatu*) in Kenya.

Mwanza *p307, map p308*
Air
Mwanza Airport is 12 km north of the city on the lakeshore; follow Makongoro Rd out of town. Taxis meet the flights, and almost all the hotels can arrange pickups/drop-offs for about US$10. Given that some flights come from Kenya, the airport has immigration facilities and visas are available on arrival.

Auricair, at the airport, T028-250 0096, www.auricair.com, runs a daily flight between **Bukoba** and Mwanza (45 mins), which leaves Bukoba at 0700 and leaves Mwanza at 1745, US$120 1 way. Also operates air transfers between Mwanza and **Rubondo Island National Park** (see page 318 for details).

Coastal Air, at the airport, T028-256 0441, www.coastal.cc, has daily flights to/from **Arusha** (2 hrs 15 mins) via the airstrips in the **Serengeti**. They can also organize charter flights between Mwanza and **Kigali** in Rwanda (1 hr).

Precision Air, Kenyatta Rd, T028-250 0819, and at the airport, www.precisionairtz.com, has direct daily flights between Mwanza and **Dar** (1 hr 30 mins), although some also touch down in **Musoma** and **Shinyanga**, while others are on a circuit with **Zanzibar** and **Kilimanjaro**. They also have a daily direct flight to/from Mwanza and **Nairobi** (1 hr 40 mins); and to/from **Bukoba**, Mon, Wed and Fri (45 mins).

Bus
The main bus stand is off Mitimirefu Rd and is fairly organized, with kiosks around the edge selling tickets. However, many of the long-distance services now go from the new **Nyegezi Bus Terminal**, which is 10 km south of town on the Shinyanga road. The two are linked by *dala-dalas*, or you can take a taxi for around US$6.

Locally, there are plenty of buses and *dala-dalas* to **Musoma** costing little more than US$4 and taking 3 hrs. Now that the short **Kamanga Ferry** across the Mwanza Gulf (see below) is operational, and the B163 via Geita, and the B8 to Bukoba are almost entirely tarred, there are through buses that cover the 385 km between Mwanza and **Bukoba** and take 7-8 hrs: US$9. However, the more enjoyable way of getting between the two is by ferry (see below).

Further afield, buses go to **Dar** and **Arusha** via **Nairobi**, 20 hrs, US$22 (you will have to buy a transit visa for Kenya;

US$20). The buses go north across the Kenya border, then to Nairobi via **Kisii**, **Kericho** and **Nakuru**, then south to cross the **Namanga** border into Tanzania again, and onward to Arusha and Dar. If you're only going to **Nairobi**, it takes about 12 hrs and costs US$15. Both **Scandinavia Express**, Rwagasore St, T028-250 3315, www.scandinaviagroup.com, and the equally good Kenyan company, **Akamba Bus**, Uhuru St, T0728-250 0727, www.akambabus.com, offer services on this route; for more information, see box, page 305.

There are other services to **Dar** across the interior of Tanzania via **Shinyanga**, **Singida**, **Dodoma** and **Morogoro**, which, in theory, should take about 14 hrs, but in reality may take nearer 20 hrs, US$25. Though the roads are not in great condition and the ride is bumpy, the roads in the central region are steadily improving. The stretch between Singida and Dodoma has recently been tarred, so now this route is fully tarred between Singida and Dar, which has reduced journey times considerably. Additionally, the B6 road between Mwanza and **Tabora** is almost all tarred now, and there are a couple of buses a day via **Shinyanga**, taking about 7 hrs, US$9.

Buses also go to **Arusha** through the **Serengeti National Park** and **Ngorongoro Conservation Area**, 12-15 hrs, US$25. This service leaves very early in the morning and goes via **Bunda** on the road to the Kenyan border, which is tarred, then branches off on either a horrendously bad dirt road to the Serengeti's Ikoma Gate, or via the Serengeti's Ndabaka Gate, 10-15 km south of Bunda on the B6a. It then goes through the park via **Seronera** and out again into the Ngorongoro Conservation Area at Naabi Hill Gate. It does not stop to look at any animals and takes a little under 2 hrs to cross the Serengeti. The bus continues past the crater (though of course does not go down into it) to **Karatu** and then on to Arusha, arriving there late at night. Although this service is the quickest method of getting between Mwanza and Arusha, foreigners will have to pay the US$50 entrance fee for both the Serengeti and the crater, which means another US$100 is added to the US$25 bus ticket. This makes it an expensive option, with the added disadvantage of speeding past the animals in a crowded bus without being able to stop. An alternative is to arrange a safari of the Serengeti and the crater with one of the tour operators in Mwanza and asked to be dropped off at the end in either Karatu or Arusha.

Car hire
The tour operators can organize car hire (see page 313).

Ferry
The ferry terminal is off Nasser Rd to the west of the city centre. This is easily the most reliable, enjoyable and comfortable way to travel on to **Bukoba**. The boats, the *MV Serengeti* and the *MV Victoria*, though old, have recently been refitted. There is a ferry on Sun, Tue and Thu from Mwanza to **Bukoba**, and on Mon, Wed and Fri from Bukoba to Mwanza, both leaving at 2100 and taking 11-12 hrs. Fares are US$18/1st class; US$13/2nd class, and US$9/3rd class. In addition, there's US$5 port tax. 1st class provides a berth in a 2-person cabin, 2nd class in a 4-person cabin, and 3rd class is seating or deck space. Earplugs can be a help. Both boats have a restaurant/bar serving passable fish (tilapia or Nile perch) or chicken and chips/rice and warm beers/sodas.

To get to **Ukerewe Island** (page 309), there are daily passenger and car ferries (3½ hrs) that leave both Mwanza and Ukerewe at 0900 and 1400, but check times locally, US$4 per person, US$6 per vehicle. The alternative route is to drive east round the lake to Bunda and then west along a dirt road along the north shore of Speke Gulf, crossing the Rugezi Channel by a shorter car and passenger ferry service (20 mins) to the island. These depart at 3-hr intervals 0700-1800, US$0.50 per person and US$2 per vehicle.

The other short passenger and car ferry service is west across the Mwanza Gulf to **Kamanga**, which leads to the B163 road to Geita, 85 km from Kamanga (see Geita, below). This is the shortest and most direct route to **Bukoba** and the **Rwanda border** and saves more than a 400-km drive around via Shinyanga. The ferry leaves from Mwanza at a separate jetty just south of the main ferry terminal, it takes 30 mins and departs every hour from both sides 0730-1830, US$1 per person and US$3 per vehicle.

Train
Mwanza is the terminus for the Lake Victoria branch of the Central Line from **Dar es Salaam** (1227 km). The trip may involve changing trains at **Tabora** (10 hrs from Mwanza).

You can also get to **Kigoma** by train from Mwanza (via Tabora). See box, page 18, for full details of timetables and fares.

ⓘ Directory

Musoma p304
Medical services Musoma Hospital is next to the market, T028-262 2111.

Mwanza p307, map p308
Immigration Immigration office, opposite the railway station, T028-250 0585, Mon-Fri 0730-1530. **Medical services** Aga Khan Medical Centre, Mitimirefu Rd, T028-250 2474, www.agakhanhospitals. org, is the best private hospital in this part of Tanzania and is affiliated to the Aga Khan Hospital in Dar. **Police station**, Kenyatta Rd near the ferry terminal.

Western Lake Victoria

The western shores of Lake Victoria were formerly known as the West Lake Region, until Uganda's Idi Amin attempted to annex the area in 1978, during the short-lived Uganda-Tanzania War. It was subsequently renamed the Kagera Region, after the Kagera River that flows from Rwanda through northern Tanzania and into Lake Victoria. More recently, the areas along the borders were the locations of massive refugee camps to house people fleeing conflicts in Rwanda and Burundi in the 1990s. As such, the region was largely denied some of the infrastructure afforded to the rest of the country. But, things are changing, thanks largely to the mining enterprises around Geita to the south of the lake, between Mwanza and Bukoba. Many roads are being tarred to serve the mines, and there has been a rapid influx of people attracted to the area, which in turn has seen former small settlements, such as Geita, flourish into small towns. This growth is expected to continue as the exploitation of the rich gold reefs continues. Nevertheless, further north, the principal town of Bukoba remains little more than a sleepy backwater. With a scenic position on the lakeshore in this far northwestern corner of Tanzania, Bukoba has a relaxed atmosphere and provides a useful access route to Uganda. Further south, the highlight of the region is the Rubondo Island National Park, where the forests harbour a number of species of game and bird. ►► *For listings, see pages 322-326.*

Geita
Geita lies 90 km west of Mwanza on the recently tarred B163 from the Kamanga Ferry over the Mwanza Gulf (see page 315). Once no more than a sprawling village just south of the lakeshore, it has grown in leaps and bounds since the first gold mine opened in this region in 2000. It's now a fully fledged town of perhaps 150,000 people and serves the miners (expats and Tanzanians). The first reef was discovered here in the early 1900s and, for a short time, the Germans mined the 'Bismarck Reef'; but this fell out of production following defeat in the

Border crossing: Tanzania–Rwanda

Rusumo

Rusumo border is on the B3, 103 km northwest of the junction with the B8 at **Lusahunga**. From here, the B8 goes south to Kigoma (346 km) and north to Bukoba (210 km); 50 km north of the junction towards Bukoba, the B163 branches off to Mwanza (442 km from Lusahunga). The B3 itself heads across country from Lusahunga to eventually reach Singida (506 km). Those in private vehicles must be aware that there have been incidents of banditry on the roads to the southwest of Lake Victoria. From the border it is roughly 160 km on a fairly good road to/from Rwanda's capital, Kigali, which is served by regular minibuses, which take about four hours. In the other direction, there are buses leaving very early each day from Ngara, 10 km from the border post on the Tanzania side, and arriving at Mwanza in the evening. Minibuses link the border with Ngara, where there is a clutch of basic board and lodgings if you need to stay overnight, which you may need to do if you are coming from the Kigali direction and have to wait for the buses the following morning.

Visas for Tanzania and Rwanda (for those who need them) are available at the border. For drivers, third-party insurance is available from kiosks on both sides of the border. In Rwanda, you are required by law to carry a pair of red warning triangles to set up on the road in the event of a breakdown. There are money changers to swap Tanzania shillings to Rwanda francs (or vice versa). The border is open 0600-1800 but note, Rwanda is one hour behind Tanzanian time. The border itself is a high bridge over the Kagera River and Rusumo Falls. It gained international notoriety during the 1994 Rwandan genocide, when thousands of bodies were washed under the bridge and hundreds of thousands of refugees fled over the bridge into Tanzania to escape the fighting.

First World War. Things changed rapidly when Tanzania opened up to foreign investment in the mid-1990s, and the modern-day gold prospectors (Ashanti and Anglo-American, among others) began exploration. Today, the Geita Gold Mine is the largest gold producer in Tanzania, and there are eight other mines in the region. Since the outset, the foreign companies are required to pay royalties to the Tanzanian government for the gold; Tanzania is now the world's third-largest gold producer, after South Africa and Ghana, and gold is the principal export-earner for the country. As a hastily and rather haphazardly developed mining town, Geita is still a pretty rough-and-ready place, with no formal facilities for travellers yet. There is a clutch of very basic board and lodgings on the main road (B163) aimed at hopeful miners migrating to town (the expats live in the mine company compounds). But it does have general stores and petrol stations, if you're passing through, and there are new hotels in the pipeline. From Geita, it's another 122 km to Biharamulo (see page 319).

Rubondo Island National Park → *For listings, see pages 322-326. Colour map 1, A2.*
2° 30'S, 31° 45'E.

Rubondo Island National Park is an island northwest of Mwanza and directly south of Bukoba. The park encompasses Rubondo Island as well as several smaller islands nearby. It was gazetted in 1977 with a total area of 460 sq km, about 240 sq km of which is land. It is rarely visited and, unless you're opting for the expensive option of flying there, access is only by small boat from the mainland (although the boat trip itself is fantastic); you are dropped right on the beach and can either stay in the one luxury lodge or the park's simple bandas and campsite. Other than these and the airstrip, there is nothing on the island except verdant dense jungly forests, papyrus swamps with beautiful flowering orchids, and empty sandy beaches. The added bonus is you're likely to have the place almost to yourself.

Arriving in Rubondo Island National Park

Getting there Air transfers from Mwanza are arranged by the charter airline, **Auric Air** (T028-250 0096, www.auricair.com). In Mwanza, flights connect with **Precision Air** flights that come from Dar and Kilimanjaro, and with **Coastal Air** services from Arusha and the camps in Serengeti. So, a visit to Rubondo can be combined with a safari of the parks in the Northern Circuit. ►► See Transport, page 325.

You can also drive the 265 km from Mwanza to **Muganza** along the lakeshore where there is a **Tanzania National Parks Authority (TANAPA)** office. This route goes west from Mwanza around the southern lakeshore via the newly tarred B163 and **Kamanga Ferry** (see page 315) to Geita, and Nyamirembe. The turn-off from the B163 is at Bwanga, 85 km west of Geita. You can also drive to Muganza from Bukoba, which is roughly 190 km; there's a turn-off from the B8 to Nyamirembe and Muganza at Biharamulo. Once there, the TANAPA speedboat journey to Rubondo takes about 30 minutes and costs US$100 for a maximum of six people. No vehicles are allowed on the island, although you can arrange with the park rangers to leave your vehicle at Muganza. If you are not in your own vehicle, contact the tour operators in Mwanza (page 313), or **Kiroyera Tours** in Bukoba (page 325) who can organize transport to Muganza and the boat. Once on the island, there is a truck that is used to transport visitors from the boat, which lands on the beach on the west side of the island, to the **Rubondo Island Camp** and the **National Park Bandas & Campsite** (see Where to stay, page 323) on the east side of the island near the Park HQ. You can walk all over the island but must be accompanied by a TANAPA guide/park ranger; this can be organized at the camps or the Park HQ.

Park information Tanzania National Parks Authority (TANAPA), www.tanzaniaparks. com, US$20, children (5-16) US$5. If you intend to fish, a three-day fishing licence costs US$50.

Wildlife

There are a number of different vegetation types on the island providing differing habitats for a variety of animals. With a high water table, the island is able to support dense forest. Other vegetation includes more open woodland, savannah grassland and swamps. There is little 'big game' on the island, although some has been introduced, including giraffe, elephant, chimpanzee and the black-and-white colobus monkey. Many of these animals were relocated here

Rubondo Island National Park

Chitebe Island
Chitende Island
Rubiso Island
Kageye & Park HQ
National Park Bandas & Campsite
Kalela Island
Ibozya Bay
Miso Island
Mlaga
Iloba Island
Chambuzi Island
Manylla Island
Mamba Island
Lake Victoria
Chitoma Bay
Lukaga
Lukukuru
Izilamouda Island
N
2 km
2 miles

Where to stay
Rubondo Island Camp 1
Ranger post ●

in the 1970s, when the island was identified as a safe haven in the fight against poaching and land encroachment. They live alongside other animals indigenous to the island, which include crocodile, hippo, bushbuck, sitatunga (a swamp-dwelling antelope only found here and in Selous), vervet monkeys, genet, mongoose, monitor lizard and spotted-necked otter (the latter is rare, but can be seen swimming in the bays around Rubondo). The park is good for hiking (you must always be accompanied by a park ranger) and has wonderful birdlife, with more than 420 recorded species. You are likely to spot fish eagle, martial eagle, sacred ibis, saddle-billed stork, kingfishers, water fowl, cuckoos, bee eaters and sunbirds. There are also flocks of African grey parrots, which were released here after being confiscated from illegal exporters. While the waters around the island are probably safe from the risk of bilharzia, swimming is ill-advised as the Nile crocodiles around the island are known to reach lengths of 5 m.

Biharamulo and around → *Colour map 1, A2. 2° 25' S, 31° 25' E.*

Continuing west for another 122 km from Geita on the B163 is Biharamulo, a well-laid-out town that served as an administrative centre during the German period. There are some fine colonial buildings, and the entrance to the town is along a tree-lined avenue. The **Old Boma** has been restored and, at present, houses government offices.

This is the nearest town to the **Biharamulo Game Reserve** (below). From here, it is roughly 175 km to Bukoba on the newly tarred B8, via the villages of **Muleba** (where there's a petrol station) and **Kemondo Bay** (where the Mwanza–Bukoba bus stops an hour before/after Bukoba to offload bananas and charcoal). The road runs close to the lakeshore and, in some stretches (particularly between Kemendo Bay and Muleba), offers great views looking down on to the vivid blue waters of the lake. Avoid driving at night along this road (and indeed the road from Mwanza), as there have been incidents of banditry on vehicles as recently as 2009; plenty of *dala-dalas* ply the route between Biharamulo and Bukoba during the day.

South of Biharamulo, and after about 40 km, the B8 reaches **Lusahunga**, which is the turn-off on to the B3 to the Rwanda border (see box, page 317).

Biharamulo, Burigi and other northwest game reserves

Adjacent to Rubondo Island National Park on the mainland and straddling the B8 road are the **Biharamulo Game Reserve** (1300 sq km) and, adjoining to the west, the **Burigi Game Reserve** (2200 sq km), but these have no facilities and receive no visitors. Because of the proximity of the large numbers of displaced Rwandan refugees, who were put in camps on the edge of the reserves during the 1990s Rwandan crisis, the flora and fauna of the game reserves have been greatly depleted. Many of the animals were poached; trees were cut down for fuel, and large tracts of land were cleared for the cultivation of crops. However, the reserves are still believed to be home to some klipspringer, dik-dik, oribi and impala, and the birds have been less adversely affected by human encroachment. They include saddle-billed storks, the rufous-bellied heron, several varieties of starling, sunbird and weaver, the grey kestrel and the fish eagle. Look out for these as you drive along the B8 through the reserves.

Other game reserves in northwest Tanzania were also adversely affected, including **Moyowosi Game Reserve**, **Ibanda Game Reserve** and **Rumanyika Game Reserve**, which cover a total area of 14,500 sq km. It is estimated that the mammal population decreased by 90% in this combined area after the arrival of the refugees in the 1990s.

Bukoba → *For listings, see pages 322-326. Colour map 1, A2. 1° 20'S, 31° 59'E. Phone code: 028. Population: 100,000.*

The compact town of Bukoba is set in a bay between lush hills and has a population of around 100,000. Although it receives few visitors, it has a university, an airstrip, and is Tanzania's second-largest lake port. For several centuries, until Bukoba was established by the Germans at the end of the 19th century, Karagwe, some 100 km inland, was the principal centre in the region. The Bahinda, a cattle-herding people from the interior, operated a feudal system where chiefs took tributes from their subjects; the wealth of the area was based on cattle that were raised successfully, despite problems with tsetse flies (see box, page 270).

This is a lovely part of Tanzania – green and fertile and with a very relaxed way of life. The major food crop here (as in much of the area around the lake) is *matoke*. This is the green banana you will see grown everywhere. It is peeled, wrapped in banana leaves and cooked very slowly by steaming. Vanilla is another recently introduced cash crop. The major commercial crop is coffee, which has contributed significantly to the wealth of the

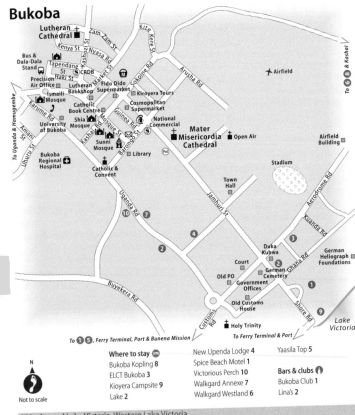

Bukoba

Where to stay
Bukoba Kopling **8**
ELCT Bukoba **3**
Kioyera Campsite **9**
Lake **2**

New Upenda Lodge **4**
Spice Beach Motel **1**
Victorious Perch **10**
Walkgard Annexe **7**
Walkgard Westland **6**

Yaasila Top **5**

Bars & clubs
Bukoba Club **1**
Lina's **2**

N
Not to scale

The Hen and the Hawk: a Bukoba fable

Once upon a time a hen and a hawk who were friends lived together in the same hut. One day, during a great famine, the hen went off in search of food. She was successful for she met a man who had some bananas. As she was carrying her load home, she met the hawk who asked her how she had got the bananas. The hen, standing on one leg and hiding the other in her feathers, replied that she had paid for them with her foot. The hen told the hawk that he must also buy some food with his foot.

The hawk agreed that this was indeed fair and went off in search of some food. He met a man and offered his leg in return for some food. The man agreed, cut off the hawk's leg and then gave him some food. The hawk had great difficulty walking home with only one leg, trying to balance the load.

When the hawk eventually reached home he saw the hen standing on two legs. He was extremely angry with the hen, saying that although the hen was supposed to be his friend, she had cheated him. The hawk told the hen that he could not forgive her and would kill her. The hen replied that he would never succeed in killing her for she would run away. Sure enough the hen ran away and lived with man, while the hawk and all his descendants remain determined to kill the hen and its offspring. This is why the hawk will always try to kill any hen that it sees.

---

area. There is a coffee factory near the jetty. Unfortunately, the world price has fallen in recent years, with notable effects on the people of this district. There are quite a few aid projects in this area, so a number of expat aid workers live here. Huge deposits of nickel and cobalt have been discovered in the area, and there are plans to exploit these.

Arriving in Bukoba

Getting there Bukoba is a long way from anywhere else by road but, thanks to the recent tarring of the B8 road south, journey times are becoming shorter, buses are more frequent, and there are now direct buses from Mwanza around the south of the lake. The most pleasant way to get to Bukoba is by ferry from Mwanza, and there are also a few flights from Mwanza too. Bukoba is not far from the border with Uganda at Mutukulu, and is a five- or six-hour journey from Kampala, Uganda's capital, so this is another option for reaching the northwest lakeshore in Tanzania. ▶▶ *See Transport, page 325, for further information.*

Getting around Taxis can be found at the port and market, and *dala-dalas* run from the bus stand to outlying villages. Bicycle taxis, known in these parts as *piki-pikis*, are widely used for short journeys.

Places in Bukoba

Near the lakeshore is a group of buildings from the German period. **Duka Kubwa**, the first general store in the town and the first stone building in Bukoba, is on the corner of Jamhuri Road and Aerodrome Road. Originally the market was in this area but, during the British period, it was moved about a kilometre inland. When the British took the town in 1914, in their excitement they blew up the German Boma (which was on the site of Holy Trinity Church) and the German Post Office, which was on the lakeshore under the heliograph (a device for sending messages by mirrors); today only the concrete foundations remain.

Mutukulu

The Mutukulu border (0600-1800) is 82 km northwest of Bukoba on the recently tarred B8. From the border it is another 218 km to Uganda's capital, **Kampala**, via Masaka (89 km), again on a good tarred road. With the border crossing, it should take five or six hours between Bukoba and Kampala, and there are through buses between the two. However, **Masaka** is the junction with the main road that goes across Uganda to the east, towards the game parks and gorillas, so you may choose not to go to Kampala at all. The border is fairly efficient and visas for both countries are available, as is third-party insurance for drivers. Remember, because of the East Africa customs agreement, you are permitted to travel between Tanzania, Kenya and Uganda on single-entry visas without getting re-entry visas for each of these countries, as long as the visas you have are valid. There are banks with ATMs in Bukoba, Masaka and Kampala.

Later the British regretted their impetuosity – they had no administrative centre and had to make use of the German Hospital (now called the **Old Boma** and currently housing part of the University of Bukoba). Across the road from the **Lake Hotel** is a **German cemetery**. Further west is an area of European housing up in the hills. Beyond the aerodrome runway to the east is **Nyamukazi** fishing village. Between **Lake Hotel** and the lakeshore is the former Gymkhana Club, where there was a cricket pitch, a golf course and tennis courts; it's now called the **Bukoba Club** (see page 325). The centre of town has many Asian-style buildings, now very shabby.

The **Mater Misericordia Cathedral** (Roman Catholic) is an extraordinary building on a huge scale in spectacular style. When it was originally constructed in 1968 the dome began to subside. All the cladding was removed, new foundations inserted under the building, and the whole shebang raised 3 m on hydraulic jacks. The levitation was done a millimetre at a time and took 10 weeks.

The **Lutheran Cathedral** is an altogether more modest and practical construction in modern style. The Evangelical Lutheran Church of Tanzania (ELCT) has a large presence in Bukoba, and runs the Huyawa Orphans Project and **ELCT Bukoba Hotel**, see Where to stay, page 323 (both near the **Lake Hotel**), the Nyumba ya Vijana Youth Centre (near the Bukoba Regional Hospital) and a bookshop and internet café on Market Street.

◉ Western Lake Victoria listings

For sleeping and eating price codes and other relevant information, see pages 22-26.

◉ Where to stay

Rubondo Island National Park *p317, map p318*
Both of these are near the Park HQ on the east side of the island, while the **Tanzania National Parks Authority (TANAPA)** boat lands on the beach on the west side. The airstrip is about midway. A TANAPA truck is used to ferry visitors between these and the camps and the drive from the boat takes about 20 mins.

$$$$ Rubondo Island Camp, in a shady tract of forest along the lake shore, reservations **African Conservancy Company**, Arusha, T027-250 8790, www.african conservancycompany.com. The only formal camp on Rubondo Island, with 10 tents on concrete bases under thatch, set apart from each other with verandas and lovely views overlooking the lake and beach, each has hot water and electricity. Rustic central area, with dining room, fresh fish obviously features, while the rest of the food is flown in (nothing can be grown on the island because of its national park status), bar, lots of lounging space, and small swimming pool set in an outcrop of rock. Walking and fishing safaris can be arranged. Most people visit here as part of a package that includes flights.

$ National Park Bandas & Campsite, 1 km from the park HQ and about the same distance from the **Rubondo Island Camp**. There are camping facilities and banda accommodation but they are very basic, so you are advised to take all your own equipment and food. However, the bandas have beds with mosquito nets, and there are long-drop loos, bucket showers and a cooking shelter. Costs for bandas and camping US$30 per person, children (5-16) US$5. This option is mostly used by the tour operators from Mwanza or Bukoba on organized trips. You are permitted to walk from the camp to enjoy a meal or a drink at the tented camp, though you need to give some notice for them to prepare food, and you may be able to get warm beers and sodas from the Park HQ. For further information, contact the **Tanzania National Parks Authority (TANAPA)** head office in Arusha, see page 237.

Bukoba *p320, map p320*

$$ Victorious Perch Hotel, Uganda Rd, T028-222 0115, www.victoriousperchhotel. com. Bukoba's newest hotel in a neat red-tiled 3-storey block. Guests are welcomed at the entrance by a 'victorious perch' – a large concrete fish/ornamental fountain. The rooms are neat, with modern bathrooms and walk-in showers. Indoor and outdoor bars with satellite TV, restaurant with nice covered terrace and reasonable Western meals. Buffets can be organized for groups. There's an internet café and secure gated car park.

$$ Walkgard Westland Hotel, 3 km southwest of Bukoba on the slopes of Kashuru Hill, overlooking the lake, T028-222 0935, www.walkgard.com. Has 42 comfortable rooms with en suite bathrooms, satellite TV, balconies with great views, but old-fashioned furnishings. Very nice swimming pool with sun loungers. Rates include full English breakfast. Friendly staff can organize boat trips and tours to the local sites. Good restaurant with a varied menu, including some Chinese and Indian dishes, so there's always something for vegetarians, also pool café and bar. Easily the best place to stay in the area. It also runs the **Walkgard Annexe Hotel**, along Uganda Rd, which has another 13 spacious and comfortable rooms, with a/c, TV, and fridge, and offers reasonable food with barbecues, buffets, and a bar.

$$-$ ELCT Bukoba Hotel, off Aerodrome Rd, near the lakeshore and the **Lake Hotel** (below), T028-222 3121, www.elctbukoba hotel.com. This is the guesthouse of the Evangelical Lutheran Church of Tanzania and has 22 neat self-contained rooms in simple brick buildings in well-tended gardens, spotlessly clean with tiled floors, TV and a/c. Also curio shop, internet café, restaurant (no bar) and large secure car park. There's often a local conference on, and it feels a little institutionalized, but it's well run, and they can organize a car with driver for local excursions. Doubles from US$40. You can actually walk to the airport from here.

$$-$ Bukoba Kopling Hotel, on Kashuru Hill, 3 km southwest of Bukoba, near the **Walkgard Westland Hotel**, T028-222 1236, www.kolpingguesthouses-africa.com. Set in lawned grounds with excellent elevated views of the lake, this is in a dated concrete 3-storey block, but the carpeted rooms are modern and comfortable, with a/c, satellite TV and, rather surprisingly, well-stocked minibars, and some have balconies. Good restaurant and bar which, among other dishes, does pizza and varied buffet meals if there's a conference on, and they bake their own bread. You can relax in the gardens or pay a small fee at the **Walkgard**, down the road to use their swimming pool.

$ Kamachumu Inn, around 50 km south of Bukoba, the turning for Kamachumu is at Muhutwe on the B8, T028-222 2466, www.kamachumuinn.com. A fairly remote, but cosy country inn on the 1800-m plateau of Kamachumu, about 40-50 mins' drive south from Bukoba. All rooms are in rondaavals and have satellite TV (the more expensive have their own bathroom), and are linked by paved pathways in the pleasant, well-tended gardens. They have their own bakery for bread and pastries, grow their own vegetables and produce dairy products from their own cows, so the food in the restaurant is fresh and organic; you can also get tilapia fish from the lake, and beer is available. Village tours can be organized, and they provide packed lunches for hikes to nearby waterfalls.

$ Kioyera Campsite, on the lakeshore, at the end of Jamhuri St, T028-222 0203, www.kiroyeratours.com. Run by the excellent **Kiroyera Tours**, see page 325, this the best place for budget travellers to head, with a shady campsite right on the beach (US$4 per person or you can rent a tent) and a clutch of thatched domed bandas (US$10 per person), clean shared ablutions, reliable hot showers, volleyball court in the sand, pool table, sun loungers and an excellent bar and restaurant, serving the likes of tilapia fish from the lake, beef stew, chicken and chips, and the charismatic cook here will have a go at pizzas. They have their own boat and can organize fishing trips using traditional bamboo rods, and the excursions run by **Kiroyera Tours** are highly recommended.

$ Lake Hotel, on the lakeshore at the end of Jamhuri St, T028-222 0232. This, the oldest hotel in Bukoba, is in a rambling and imposing timbered colonial building, offering simple accommodation in 14 rooms with fans, TV and hot water, but everything's old and musty. It's a better place to come for the restaurant, which has a good variety of food, including many Western dishes

and excellent barbecued kebabs. Nice atmosphere in the outside terrace beer garden with a view of the lake; it gets busy especially at the weekends. Camping is possible in the car park, but you need to negotiate for a room for bathroom facilities.

$ New Upenda Lodge, Rwaijumba St, off Jamhuri St, T028-222 0620. Courtyard with bar, offers 16 rooms, 3 are larger with extra sitting room, all have hot water, satellite TV and large beds; the modern kitchen serves Tanzanian and European dishes. Rooms from about US$15.

$ Spice Beach Motel, on the lakeshore, on the lower road to and just north of the port, T028-222 0142. The lovely lakeside location makes up for the several fairly tatty rooms in this modern bungalow, but they do have TV, hot water and a/c; you can get a bed here for less than US$15. Very good bar and restaurant serving chicken and chips, grills and kebabs; if you order the day before they will lay on an Indian meal, and there's a pool table and TV. This is a particularly charming spot at night, when ferry boats are docked at the port, and it's a good place for waiting for the evening ferry to Mwanza, even if you're not staying here.

$ Yaasila Top Hotel, next to **Spice Beach** on the lakeshore, 2 km from town and a short walk from the port, T028-222 1251, reservations@yaasila.com. In a nice location with lake views, the 13 en suite rooms (US$25) have a balcony, TV and fridge, and there are 3 budget rooms with shared bathroom (US$12). There's a restaurant and 3 bars: 1 in the leafy garden, 1 on the 2nd floor with balcony overlooking the beach, and 1 with a *nyama choma* grill next to the conference centre, which also has satellite TV, a dart board and pool table for guests.

❼ Restaurants

Bukoba *p320, map p320*
There are numerous daytime canteen-style places around town that serve inexpensive fish, meat, rice, beans, *matoke*, samosas, fried

chicken and sausages and chips. Most also sell delicious fresh fruit juices. In the evening the best places to eat are at the hotels.

🎵 Bars and clubs

Bukoba *p320, map p320*
Bukoba Club, opposite the Lake Hotel. This old colonial club is run-down now, but is a delightful venue to have a beer in the evening before sunset, with tables set over a grassy area with pleasant views over the lake. Many local people come for an evening together here, and basic food includes very good 'fish in foil' cooked on a brazier in a tin shed in the car park. Indians sometimes play cricket on the open grassy area near the club. **Lina's**, Uganda Rd. A 24-hr bar serving plenty of cold beer, thatched outside seating, blaring TVs showing football and music channels, there's often dancing on weekend nights.

🛒 Shopping

Bukoba *p320, map p320*
Bukoba's market is fairly large and is in the centre of town. There are sections for fruit and veg, *matoke*, grains, meat, fish, clothing and assorted items both in and around the covered market area.
Cosmopolitan Provision Store, also known as **Mama Cosmo**, Jamhuri St, south of the market. 0830-1800. Sells many imported Western items, including cheese, wine, biscuits and chocolate, and is a good place to stock up on snacks for the ferry.
Fido Dido Supermarket, corner of Jamhuri St and Sokoine Rd, also close to the market. Mon-Sat 0830-2000, Sun 1000-1300. A similar set-up for Western imported goods, fresh bread and refrigerated meat.

⏰ What to do

Bukoba *p320, map p320*
Kiroyera Tours, Sokoine Rd, near the market T028-222 0203, www.kiroyeratours.com. Mon-Sat 0800-1800. A very friendly and

helpful set-up in Bukoba, which also serves as the de facto tourist office and is actively encouraging tourism in the Kagera region. Can assist with booking flights, ferry and train tickets (for a booking fee), and can organize car hire with a driver. Tours include overnight trips to **Rubondo Island National Park** and several inexpensive walking and cycling cultural tours in and around Bukoba that may visit the market, a drum-making workshop, a school or orphanage. They can also arrange fishing and sightseeing boat excursions to the nearby islands. Discuss with them what you want to do and perhaps allow a full day with one of their excellent guides.

🚌 Transport

Rubondo Island National Park *p317, map p318*
Air
The **Auric Air** transfer to Rubondo leaves **Mwanza** on Mon, Wed and Fri at 1700 and takes 30 mins, US$160 one way/US$320 return. In Mwanza, this flight connects with the **Precision Air** flights that have come from **Dar** and **Kilimanjaro**, and with **Coastal Air** services from **Arusha** and the camps in the **Serengeti**. On the return leg, the **Auric Air** flight goes back to **Mwanza** on Mon, Wed, Fri and Sun at 1550. Once in Mwanza, it connects with the **Precision Air** flight to **Dar**, but not the one to Kilimanjaro or the Coastal Air flight back to Serengeti/Arusha; in order to take these flights the next day, you'll need to spend a night in Mwanza. (It is essential to confirm all these schedules.)

Bukoba *p320, map p320*
Transport to and from Bukoba is fitful. Buses, ferries and flights are all rescheduled on a regular basis, depending on demand, and you must check before you travel. See box, page 322 for details about crossing the border with Uganda, and page 317 for the border with Rwanda, both of which are within striking distance of Bukoba.

Air

Bukoba's airstrip is on Aerodrome Rd, which runs to the south of town along the lakeshore. There are flights between Bukoba and **Mwanza**; see page 314, for details of onward flights from Mwanza. In the event that your first arrival to Tanzania is via the Kagera region, it is actually feasible to fly to **Entebbe International Airport** near **Kampala** in Uganda, which is served by numerous international airlines. You can then get a bus from Kampala to Bukoba (about 5-6 hrs). **Kiroyera Tours** (see above) can also arrange private transport between Entebbe International Airport and Bukoba. **Auricair**, at Mwanza Airport, T028-250 0096, www.auricair.com, has a daily flight between Bukoba and **Mwanza** (45 mins), which leaves Bukoba at 0700 and leaves Mwanza at 1745, from US$120 1 way.

Precision Air, Mosque St, near the bus stand, T028-222 0545, www.precisionairtz.com, flies between Bukoba and **Mwanza**, Mon, Wed and Fri (45 mins), leaving Mwanza at 1035 and leaving Bukoba at 1135, from US$120 1 way.

Bus

The bus stand is in the centre of town near the clock tower, where the bus companies have their kiosks, but you can also get information on buses from **Kiroyera Tours**, see above.

Through buses cover the 385 km between **Mwanza** and Bukoba in 8-10 hrs, US$9, although the more enjoyable way of getting between the two is the ferry (see below).

Tashrif, T028-222 0427, and **Tawfiq Executive Falcon**, T028-222 0427, have buses to **Dar**, via **Nzega**, **Singida**, **Dodoma**, and **Morogoro** (up to 24 hrs), US$25. This route still covers some considerable distance on bumpy dirt roads on parts of the B3 in the interior, but the route is now paved from Bukoba as far south as **Biharamulo**, and from Singida to Dar.

Services also go to **Kigoma**, though these are rough rides on poor roads, and each journey can take days rather than hours. These depart very early in the morning at about 0500, generally only go twice a week and in wet season less frequently.

There are a few companies that run daily buses from Bukoba to **Kampala** in Uganda, which take 5-6 hrs, US$10. They usually depart from Bukoba about 0600-0700 and return from Kampala in the early afternoon (also see box, page 322).

Ferry

This is easily the most reliable and comfortable way to travel to **Mwanza**. For details, see page 315. The ferry makes a stop in **Kemondo Bay** 1 hr before/after Bukoba.

⊙ Directory

Bukoba *p320, map p320*
Medical services Bukoba Regional Hospital, in the centre of town off Uganda Rd, T028-222 0927.

Contents

At a glance

🚌 **Getting around** There are plenty of buses between the main towns but, while the roads are improving, these cover some vast distances. The best option for getting to Kigoma and Lake Tanganyika is the Central Line train. You can only access Gombe and Mahale by boat.

⏱ **Time required** At least 2 days to see each of the Gombe Stream and Mahale Mountains national parks, and at least 36 hrs for the train journey from Dar. Allow yourself plenty of time and flexibility to get to your destination.

🌤 **Weather** Dry and dusty, but relatively cool in the towns during Jun-Oct. Light rains Nov-Mar and then heavy rains until Jun.

✖ **When not to go** Gombe, Mahale and Katavi can theoretically be visited all year but can be hard-going and slippery during the rainy season (Apr-May).

Central Region

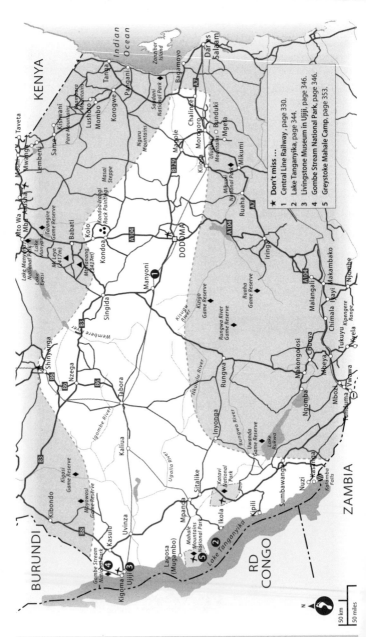

Don't miss ...

★ Central Line Railway, page 330.

1 Lake Tanganyika, page 344.

2 Livingstone Museum in Ujiji, page 346.

3 Gombe Stream National Park, page 346.

4 Greystoke Mahale Camp, page 353.

KENYA

Indian Ocean

Zanzibar Island

Dar es Salaam

BURUNDI

RD CONGO

ZAMBIA

DODOMA

Lake Tanganyika

The central route from Dar es Salaam to Kigoma in the far west passes through a number of different landscapes and vegetational zones. The distance between the towns is large and much of this route is sparsely populated. The major towns that you pass through are Morogoro, Dodoma and, finally, Tabora, before reaching Kigoma. The Central Railway line is the focus of this route, and it follows the old slave and caravan trail from the coast to Lake Tanganyika. Until a few years ago, the appalling roads hampered travel (and in some cases development) in what is a largely rural area, but major road-building projects are currently opening up the central region. On the shores of Lake Tanganyika are Mahale Mountains and Gombe Stream national parks, both famous for their substantial chimpanzee populations. Also in the west of the region is the Katavi National Park, which is so remote that it only receives a handful of visitors each year. These parks are not easy to get to but nevertheless offer safari experiences away from the hordes of pop-up minibuses on the Northern Circuit, in landscapes that are more wild and untouched.

Getting there and around

Air There are some flights between Dar es Salaam and Kigoma and Shinyanga with **Precision Air**. The easiest option for getting to Katavi National Park is by flying, and safaris here are usually arranged with an additional trip by air to the Mahale Mountains National Park.

Rail For access to the destinations in the central area and for budget travellers not wanting to take the expensive flights to Kigoma, the best option is the train. The **Central Line** goes from Dar to Morogoro, then heads northwest through Dodoma to Tabora, where it splits, and the two lines go either to Mwanza on Lake Victoria (see page 307) or Kigoma on Lake Tanganyika. To either destination this is a lengthy journey, but the train is an interesting experience and relatively comfortable, especially if you travel first class. It stops at dozens of stations en route through the central area (hence the 40- to 48-hour journey time between Dar and Kigoma), and at each, the villagers meet the train to sell their wares – anything from live chickens to wooden spoons.

Road Although there are some buses that link the towns, they are infrequent, uncomfortable and slow, and some of the roads are very poor, especially after the rains. However, things are changing and there have been some major road-building operations in the Central Region and around Lake Victoria in the north in recent years. The Tabora–Nzega–Shinyanga–Mwanza road (B6), and the Singida–Dodoma road (B141/B129) are now tarred and, by the time you read this, the Nzega–Singida road (B3) may well be tarred too. This has reduced journey times considerably but there are still some long distances to cover by bus.

Dar es Salaam to Dodoma

From Dar, the A7 road heads inland for 195 km, via Chalinze, to Morogoro, where another road, the B129, and the railway veer off to cross the largely empty expanses of rural central Tanzania. The towns in the region have little to offer the visitor, but Morogoro is a lively centre surrounded by attractive mountains, and Dodoma holds the inauspicious title of being the capital of the country. ▶▶ *For listings, see pages 334-338.*

Chalinze → *Colour map 1, B5.*

Chalinze is a small town 110 km to the west of Dar es Salaam. It's essentially a truckstop and the main fuelling centre for travellers to north and south Tanzania. It is at the junction of the A7 from Dar, which continues west to Morogoro and beyond, and the A14 north to Tanga, Moshi and Arusha (see the North to Kilimanjaro and Moshi chapter, page 202). Chalinze has six petrol stations and dozens of little kiosks and bars, which makes it a buzzing place and a good spot to break a journey for 30 minutes. Look out for the young men who sell little home-made toy trucks and buses on the roadside – replicas of the passing vehicles, painted in the same colour and complete with company logos. About 200 m along the Dar road from the junction is a petrol station with a good restaurant, just look for the thatched roof. Most of the buses stop here for a quick break.

Morogoro → *For listings, see pages 334-338. Colour map 1, B5. 6° 50'S, 37° 40'E. Phone code: 023. Population: 206,000. Altitude: 500 m.*

Morogoro lies in the agricultural heartland of Tanzania and is a centre of farming in the southern highlands. Tobacco is grown in the region and accumulated here before going on to **market**, and fruit and vegetables from here are transported the 195 km to Dar es Salaam. The countryside is green and fertile, large sisal plantations predominate, and the market is probably the largest in the country and worth visiting to soak up the atmosphere. Just about anything that grows and can be eaten can be bought here. It's a good place to stock up on fresh produce if heading south to Malawi and Zambia. In addition to its agricultural importance, Morogoro is also the centre for missionary work that goes on in the country, and the various missions and their schools and hospitals are a central feature of the town. Morogoro is based at the foot of the **Uluguru Mountains**, which reach a height of 2630 m and provide a spectacular backdrop to the town; the peaks are often obscured by dramatic, swirling mists. It was here that Smuts was confident he would confront and destroy the forces of von Lettow in the First World War – only to be bitterly disappointed (see page 400). It was en route to Morogoro that Edward Sokoine, the Prime Minister, widely expected to be Nyerere's successor, was killed in a road accident in October 1984. The Agricultural University in Morogoro has been named after him.

Morogoro

Where to stay 🛏
Arc **2**
Hilux **4**
Mama Pierina **6**

Morogoro **3**
New Acropol **1**
New Savoy **15**
Oasis **13**

Restaurants 🍴
Dragonaire's **1**
Ricky's Café **2**

Not to scale

From Morogoro, the A7 road continues southwest through the **Mikumi National Park** (100 km) to **Iringa** and **Mbeya** and, ultimately, the Zambia and Malawi borders. Meanwhile, the B129 goes northwest to Dodoma and beyond, into central Tanzania. Morogoro is also the largest town near the **Selous Game Reserve** (see page 360).

Places in Morogoro

The old German **Boma** is to the south of the town in the foothills of the **Uluguru Mountains**, along Boma Road.

At the top of Kingalu Road there is a pretty **rock garden**, laid out around a mountain stream with a café.

The **War Cemetery** ① *south on Boma Rd and then turn west*, is interesting in that it records the deaths of men in both the German and the British and Empire Forces. There are two graves of Germans from before 1914: a postal officer and a train driver. Also here is the grave of Kannanpara John, born in Kerala, India, and the first Asian priest of the Diocese of Central Tanganyika. The involvement of the British Empire in the First World War is apparent from the 49 graves for troops and support service personnel of regiments from South Africa, Gold Coast, West Africa and the British West Indies, as well as East Africa. There is a special plinth to the 'Hindus, Mohammedans and Sikhs' who died in Imperial Service. These troops were accompanied by 'followers', including their families, traders and craftsmen, and three of these – 'Jim', 'Aaron' and 'Harr' – are recorded as having died in the fighting around Morogoro. The plinth for the Germans records about 180 dead, a mixture of German officers and African soldiers of the Schuztruppe (see box, page 401).

Uluguru Mountains

The Uluguru Mountains dominate Morogoro, with a range of impressive summits. The lower slopes are densely cultivated and terraced; higher up they are forested with some splintered rock bastions, and further back they rise to over 2630 m. There are some good hikes to seasonal waterfalls, through the cool forest full of colourful butterflies and flowers, such as African violets and busy lizzys. The forest is also home to vervet and black-and-white colobus monkeys, and numerous birds including three endemic to the Ulugurus: the Loveridge sunbird, the black cap shrike and Mrs Moreau's warbler. The best way to explore is on guided half- or full-day walks organized by the **Chilunga Cultural Tourism Programme** ① *office is on Kingalu Rd, just south of the the post office, T023-261 3323*, which is one of the excellent **Tanzania Cultural Tourism Programmes**. They can also organize cycling tours to local villages for perhaps a pottery-making demonstration or a visit to a traditional healer. Further details and bookings can be obtained from the **Tanzania Cultural Tourism Programme** office at the Museum/Old Boma or the Tanzanian Tourist Board tourist information centre in Arusha (see page 236), www.tanzaniaculturaltourism.com.

Dodoma → *For listings, see pages 334-338. Colour map 1, B4. 6° 8'S, 35° 45'E. Phone code: 026. Population: 325,000. Altitude: 1113 m.*

In the very heart of Tanzania, 455 km west of Dar es Salaam via the A7 and B129, Dodoma is the nation's official political capital and the seat of government in the country. The government legislature divide their time between here and Dar es Salaam. Much smaller and less developed than the country's commercial centre, Dodoma is on the eastern edge of the southern highlands; it's a dry, windy and some say desolate place to choose for a capital, lying at an altitude of 1330 m, giving it warm days and cool nights.

Dodoma was formerly a small settlement of the semi-pastoral Gogo people. Caravan traders passed through the plateau, and it developed into a small trading centre. It owes its growth to the Central Railway and the Germans' plan to take advantage of Dodoma as a trading and commercial centre. During the First World War the town was important as a supply base and transit point. In the years after the war, however, two famines struck the area and an outbreak of rinderpest followed. The British administration was less keen than the Germans to develop Dodoma as the administrative centre, its only real advantages being its central position and location on the railway line. But from 1932, Cape to London flights touched down here, and Dodoma received all Dar es Salaam's mail, which was then transferred by rail.

As it is in the very centre of the country, Dodoma was designated the new capital by the former president Nyerere. However the process of transfer has never fully taken off, and today only one government ministry has its permanent base in Dodoma. The area's water shortage and poor road network are important contributing factors, and thus the city functions as a capital only when parliamentary sessions are held. On the approach road from Dar is a sprawling housing estate of unfinished and empty houses – a one-time, unsuccessful effort to move civil servants here.

This is an important beef-producing area and delicious roasted meat can be found in the many open bars scattered around town. A cattle **market** (*mnada*) takes place each

Dodoma

Where to stay 🛏
Cana Lodge **8**
DM **1**
Kilondoma Inn **7**
Nam **4**
New Dodoma **3**
Peter Palm **5**
St Gaspar Hotel & Conference Centre **2**

Restaurants 🍴
Aladdin's Cave **1**
Leone L'Africano **2**

200 metres
200 yards

Saturday on Kondoa Road, 5 km from the centre. It is an important event for many locals and is an interesting spectacle. All in all, Dodoma is a peaceful town surrounded by a large number of missions, but there is little reason for tourists to stay here.

North of Dodoma → *Colour map 1, B4.*

About 180 km north of Dodoma on the A104, and 275 km southwest of Arusha in the Great Rift Valley, the **Kondoa Rock Art Sites** are the nearest attraction to Dodoma and are among the finest rock paintings in the world. They are a good example of ancient art and a further reminder of the existence of ancient humanity in this part of Africa (the rock shelters were used in the later Stone Age by the Bushmanoid tribes who were mainly hunters). The paintings vary in quality, size, style and colour. The most important are from the pre-agriculturalist period: red pigment outlines in streaky and silhouette styles more than 3000 years old. There are patterned designs, human and animal figures, mainly giraffe, eland and elephant, and hunting scenes. 'Late whites' from a later period are mostly abstract finger paintings. More than 100 sites were described by Mary Leakey in the 1950s but only recently have efforts been made to preserve and promote them, though they were designated as a UNESCO World Heritage Site in 2006. At **Kolo**, where interesting paintings are most accessible, guides must be hired from the visitors' centre office run by the Department of Antiquities. Alternatively, for the best tours of Kondoa, contact enterprising local guide Moshi Changai (T0784-948 858, www.tanzaniaculturaltours.com). Other sites include **Kinyasi**, **Pahl**, **Swera** and **Tumbelo**. Many of the shelters have fantastic views over the plains for miles around.

This region is not easy to get to, and the A104, also known as the Great North Road, between Dodoma and Arusha is not tarred and is still in a very poor state, especially after rain; buses from Dodoma can take four to 10 hours to cover the 160 km to Kondoa and Kolo, another 20 km further on. The better option is to organize a tailor-made excursion with one of the tour operators in Arusha (see page 258), which can add on an excursion to a safari to Tarangire National Park.

Mount Hanang, sometimes called the forgotten mountain and East Africa's ninth highest, rises some 1828 m above the Mangati Plain and, while it is accessed off the A104 road between Dodoma and Arusha, southwest of Babati, where there is a **Tanzania Cultural Tourism Programme**, it's a little closer to Arusha and is listed in that chapter, see page 242.

◉ Dar es Salaam to Dodoma listings

For sleeping and eating price codes and other relevant information, see pages 22-26.

◉ Where to stay

Morogoro *p331, map p331*
There is a dense crop of cheap board and lodgings on the streets around the market where you will get a bed and a mosquito net, and not much else, for around US$5.
$$ Morogoro Hotel, Rwegasore Rd, 2 km from town, follow Kingalu Rd south, T023-261 3270, www.morogorohotel.com.

69 rather odd domed-shaped a/c chalets, with satellite TV and fridge, old-fashioned furnishings but comfortable and in lovely gardens with good facilities, including restaurant offering local, Indian and Chinese dishes, cosy bar with large TV, swimming pool and its own 9-hole golf course. There's also a campsite (**$**) and plenty of secure parking. Doubles from US$60.
$$-$ Arc Hotel, 2 km from town off the Tanzam Highway towards Iringa, T0769-600 240, www.archotel-tz.com. Opened in 2009, this modern purpose-built hotel is probably

the best option in Morogoro, and most of the rooms have balconies or patios with views of the Uluguru Mountains, plus a/c and satellite TV. It's a little plain but neat, with tiled floors and modern bathrooms, good restaurant serving continental and Indian food, bar, secure walled car park and small garden. Can organize 1-day safaris to Mikumu National Park, 70 km away, so this is a good option if you don't have your own transport. Doubles from US$45.

$$-$ New Acropol, Old Dar es Salaam Rd, T0754-309 410, www.newacropolhotel. com. Run by a Canadian lady, this is more of a guesthouse than a hotel. It's set in very pretty gardens with 5 rooms, 1 suite has 2 bedrooms and sleeps up to 5, each with veranda, lovely furnishings, satellite TV, a/c and fridge. Varied menu with bar snacks, burgers and pizzas, and a selection of puddings, cakes and ice cream. Can organize walking tours in the Uluguru Mountains, bike hire and massages.

$ Hilux Hotel, Old Dar es Salaam Rd, T023-260 3946, hiluxhotel@yahoo.com. Functional, if a little faded, town hotel with good facilities aimed at businessmen and conference-goers. Rooms have a/c, satellite TV and en suite bathrooms with hot water, and include a full breakfast. A busy lively covered outdoor bar and restaurant offers a promising menu, including pasta, fish and grills, but food is mediocre and service is slow.

$ Hotel Oasis, Station Rd, T023-260 4178, www.hoteloasistz.com. Efficient and well run, a neat red-brick building with 37 clean rooms with a/c and TV (but check they're working). The nicest aspect is the refreshing outdoor swimming pool with mountain views. The large restaurant offers a wide range of Indian, Chinese and European dishes, as well as a buffet at the weekends, and this is probably the best food in Morogoro; there's also a well-stocked bar.

$ Mama Pierina, Station Rd next to Hotel Oasis, T0741-786 913, dshatzis@ hotmail.com. Family-run guesthouse with comfortably furnished veranda run by

Dimitri, a friendly Italian/Greek. Worn but comfortable rooms with fan, mosquito net and hot water, although they are in the process of being refurbished with a/c and TV, breakfast included. Probably best known for its good Greek, Indian and Italian dishes, including pizzas, and the restaurant and bar is popular with local expats and volunteers. Doubles from US$25.

$ New Savoy Hotel, just opposite the railway station, T023-260 3041. This was the former **Bahnhof Hotel**, built in the German period by the Greeks and the scene of an elaborate prank by von Lettow in the First World War (see page 400). It is now rather run down and shabby, but the buildings are impressive and set in attractive gardens. Rooms are spacious and provide functional accommodation for those on a budget who enjoy 'character' (such as the original Armitage Shanks sinks and plastic flowers). Food is available, and there's a lively bar offering a disco at the weekends.

Dodoma *p332, map p333*

The town can be very busy when parliament is in session or there is a CCM meeting, so try to book ahead. Many hotels are modern, featureless and mostly aimed at visiting civil servants, and usually offer single or very small double rooms. You will find all of them empty at the weekends when the town is exceptionally quiet.

$$$-$$ New Dodoma Hotel, close to the railway station, T026-232 1641, dodomahotel@kicheko.com. This was the old German Railway Hotel, with 91 rooms, on the small side with worn furniture, but some have balconies, a/c and satellite TV. There's an internet café, small swimming pool, gym, secure car park, restaurant serving continental, Chinese and Indian food and a bar. Everything is centred around an attractive courtyard. It's a good place to come to eat, even if you are not staying; food includes steak, chicken, Indian and Chinese. It's popular, and the best place to stay, but don't expect international standards.

$$-$ St Gaspar Hotel & Conference Centre, 7 km east of Dodoma on the Morogoro road (B129), T026 235 3038, www.stgasparhotel.co.tz. Built in 2007 as a large conference venue with a rather impressive pillared entrance, this has 73 good-standard rooms with a/c, satellite TV and minibar, 2 restaurants that serve buffets, if there's a conference on, and a bar where the outside area is under a huge baobab tree in nice gardens. Some distance from town so you'll have to take a taxi or a *dala-dala* towards Morogoro and asked to be dropped off outside.
$ Cana Lodge, 9th St, T026-232 1199. A modern block with chunky old-fashioned furniture, but a good option with 17 spotlessly clean rooms of various sizes (reflected in the price), with fans, satellite TV, hot water and mosquito nets. Small restaurant serving soups, snacks, a stab at Western pasta dishes and substantial breakfasts, which are included in the rates, and there's an internet café next door.
$ Hotel DM, Nduvo Rd, T026-232 1001. Friendly staff and good rooms with satellite TV, phone, massive double beds, nice tiled bathrooms and ceiling fans; some rooms have nets, others are sprayed. There's also a bar/restaurant on the top floor with tables on a breezy terrace overlooking town. Doubles from US$20 including breakfast.
$ Kilondoma Inn, Hospital St, south of Independence Sq, T0756-144 325. Tiny, tiny rooms really only suitable for 1 person though they do have double beds, with fans, mosquito nets, satellite TVs in cupboards above the beds, spotless bathrooms with reliable hot water, and you may be able to pick up Wi-Fi (while you're sitting on your bed). Breakfast included and is served on a tiny enclosed veranda.
$ Nam Hotel, Arusha Rd (A104), 2 km north of town, T0741-670 081, www.namtz.com. Well looked-after, quiet 3-storey block with 30 en suite rooms, all with phones, nets, carpet, some with satellite TV (same price), simple restaurant and bar on the roof which

sometimes holds a disco at the weekend. Doubles from US$20 with basic breakfast.
$ Peter Palm, Mjimpya St, T026-232 0154. A 3-storey block with miniscule rooms and only just enough space for the bed and bathroom, but clean and modern with TV, fans, hot water and cool white tiles throughout. Basic breakfast included, internet available and there's a shady communal balcony with seats.

North of Dodoma *p334*
Kondoa Rock Art Sites
You can camp near the visitors' centre but there is no other accommodation near the paintings.
$ New Planet Hotel, near the bus stand, Kondoa, 20 km south of Kola and 4 km west of the Dodoma–Arusha road (A104). A simple guesthouse in Kondoa that is used to international visitors and has small but clean single and double rooms with nets, and basic private bathrooms with hot water, and a reasonable restaurant. They can advise on how to visit the rock art sites.

⭐ Restaurants

Morogoro *p331, map p331*
There are few restaurants in Morogoro and the best are at the hotels, most of which are very good. Local canteens offer fried chicken, stews, chips and omelettes; the market has an excellent variety of fresh fruit, and some of the shops offer soft drinks and tinned food.
$ Dragonaire's, 3 km to the east of town along the Old Dar es Salaam Rd. 1500-2300. This is a favourite haunt amongst expats in town, in pleasant thatched buildings surrounded by green lawns and mountain views. The varied menu includes pizza, continental and Chinese dishes but expect a long wait, the bar has a pool table and satellite TV. It's a bit far from town to walk after dark but you can get a taxi. They also have 4 B&B rooms (**$**).
$ New Green Restaurant, near the clock tower on Station Rd. 1100-1600, 1900-2230.

Simple restaurant and bar, with excellent Indian food, good choice for vegetarians, plus local dishes and good grilled chicken, which is roasted over charcoal outside.

Cafés

Ricky's Café, Old Dar es Salaam Rd near the post office. 0900-1500. Almost worth coming into town for, if you're driving past Morogoro, this thatched area at the Oryx petrol station serves excellent coffees, milkshakes, burgers, toasted sandwiches and ice cream, and more substantial meals like grilled tilapia fish and stir-fry veg and noodles, and has a children's playground.

Dodoma *p332, map p333*

It might have been expected that the transfer of the seat of government would have seen the emergence of some reasonable restaurants but this doesn't appear to be the case at all. However, all the hotels have restaurants, the best of which is the New Dodoma Hotel, which also has a separate and good Chinese restaurant. There are several places in the back streets north of Mwangaza Av where you can get a whole chicken, chips and salad on a large plate to share. Unusually for Tanzania, among the many street stalls around town serving *mishkaki* (barbecued beef kebabs), you may find grilled pork, *kiti moto*.

\$\$ Leone L'Africano, Arusha Rd (A104), 2 km north of town, T0754-073 573. Tue-Fri 1700-2200, Sat-Sun 1200-1500, 1700-2200. The only decent stand-alone restaurant in Dodoma, in a semi-open circular thatched building in green grounds with a children's playground and a mini-golf course. Excellent Italian food, including grills, pizzas and home-made pasta, including gnocchi with lots of sauces to choose from. Friendly Italian owners and good choice of wine. Taxis wait outside.

Cafés

Aladdin's Cave, on Market St near the corner with Lindi Av. 0930-1300, 1500-1800.

An Indian-run shop selling lots of sweets and chocolate, home-made ice cream, milkshakes and juice, and some snacks like samosas and burgers. Doubles up as an internet café.

⊘ Shopping

Morogoro *p331, map p331*

GAPCO petrol station, near the market, also has an upstairs supermarket that sells a wide range of packet and tinned items but no alcohol.

Pira's Supermarket, Lumumba St, T023-260 4594. A wide range of items, including wines, cheeses and meat, including pork.

Dodoma *p332, map p333*

Yashna's Supermarket, Hatibu Av, behind the Gapco petrol station, T026-232 2694. Sells toiletries, booze including South African wine, frozen meat and ice cream (proudly proclaims it sells McCain's oven chips!) and a good range of other imported items including chocolate and snacks such as Pringles, so a good place to stock up for bus or train journeys.

⊖ Transport

Morogoro *p331, map p331*
Road

The enormous **Msamvu Bus Terminal** is a couple of kilometres out of town at the main junction of the A7 and the B129 to Dodoma. There are *dala-dalas* and taxis from here into town. There are numerous buses making the trip to **Dar** (2 hrs), US$3. Buses from Dar to **Mbeya** pass through Morogoro until midday, arriving in Mbeya at about 2000-2100 (US$13) and to **Iringa** (US$6). Buses also go to **Dodoma** (3 hrs), US$4.

Dodoma *p332, map p333*
Air

The airport is about 2 km north of town to the east of the A104/Arusha road. Despite it being the capital, there are very few flights to/from Dodoma. **Coastal Air**, Dar es Salaam T022-284 2700, www.coastal.cc, flies daily from **Dar** (1 hr 20 mins) at 0830, and returns from Dodoma at 1510, but the flight only runs if there are enough takers.

Bus

The main bus stand is opposite the town hall, 2 blocks up from Dar es Salaam Av. There are numerous buses to/from **Dar** (5-7 hrs), which go via Morogoro: deluxe, US$6.50, and semi-luxury US$5. There are a dozen or more companies including Scandinavia Express, which has a separate terminal on Dar es Salaam Av, T026-232 2170, www.scandinaviagroup.com.

There are other services that head northwest from Dodoma across the interior of Tanzania to **Singida** and then **Nzega**. From here, buses either go north via **Shinyanga** to **Mwanza**, or northwest to **Bukoba**. The roads in the central region are steadily improving thanks to on-going road building. However, there are still vast distances to cover – the Dodoma–**Mwanza** journey may take up to 20 hrs, for example. Most of these buses leave Dodoma in the early morning, so try and book a seat the day before. There are a few buses that cover the 440-km journey north from Dodoma to **Arusha** via Konoa on the A104, but this road is largely unsurfaced and the journey may take up to 2 days.

Train

The **Central Line** train passes through Dodoma and the railway station is in the centre of town. The train towards **Kigoma** and **Mwanza** via **Tabora** (where the train 'splits') arrives in Dodoma at 0810 Wed and Sat. The train towards **Dar** arrives in Dodoma at 1840 Fri and Mon. For more information see box, page 18.

ⓘ Directory

Morogoro *p331, map p331*
Medical services Aga Khan Medical Centre, Boma Rd, just south of the main roundabout, T023-260 4595, www.agakhan hospitals.org, is a private hospital which is affiliated to the Aga Khan Hospital in Dar. Morogoro Regional Hospital is on Old Dar es Salaam Rd in the centre of town.

Dodoma *p332, map p333*
Medical services Aga Khan Medical Centre, Sixth/Market St, in the centre of town near the Gapco petrol station, T026-232 1789, www.agakhanhospitals.org, again is a private hospital which is affiliated to the Aga Khan Hospital in Dar.

Tabora and around

The region around Tabora was once frequently crossed by Livingstone on his quest to explore central Africa but few people visit today and there is little of interest for the traveller to Tanzania. However, the Central Railway splits at Tabora and anyone riding the train will spend either a few hours or a whole day here depending on their direction of travel: to Mwanza via Shinyanga, to Kigoma or to Dar. ⟫ For listings, see pages 341-343.

Tabora → *For listings, see pages 341-343. Colour map 1, B3. 5° 25'S, 32° 50'E. Phone code: 026. Population: 127,000.*

The railway continues along the old caravan trading route to Tabora, founded in 1820 by Arab slave traders and of enormous historical interest. During the German occupation, Tabora was one of the most populated and prosperous towns in the whole of East Africa. From 1852 Tabora was the Arab's slaving capital (*Kazeh*) in Unyanyembe, the kingdom of Nyamwezi (Tanzania's second-largest tribe), with famous chieftains Mirambo and Isike. Ivory and humans were bartered in exchange for guns, beads and cloth. Its heyday was in the 1860s, when 500,000 caravans annually passed through the town and many trade routes converged here. The Germans realized this and constructed a fort. (Isike later fought the Germans here in 1892, and the Germans captured the town in 1893.)

The building of the Mittelland Bahn (the Central Railway) in 1912 increased the town's importance. It fell to Belgian forces from the Congo after 10 days' fighting on 11 September 1916. Tabora was a railway town by the time the British took over. The explorers Burton, Speke, Livingstone and Stanley all used the town as an important base for their journeys into more remote areas. Tabora School (1925) was important for nurturing future leaders, including Nyerere. However, these days not much happens here and it's little more than a collection of dusty streets. But it is here that the railway divides, one line going on to Kigoma, the other north to Mwanza, and for this reason people often stay a night here in order to change trains.

Places in Tabora

Tabora is dominated by the **Fort** (or boma) on a hill overlooking the town, built by the Germans at the turn of the 20th century. This is southeast of the town centre along Boma Road, at the junction of Boma Road and School Street. Do not take pictures as it is a military building. The **central market** is worth a wander around and has an excellent second-hand clothing section, which is cheaper than in some of the other cities.

Livingstone's Tembe ① *about 6 km outside the town at the settlement of Kwihara, 0800-1700, US$2*, is the major attraction in Tabora and is dedicated to Dr David Livingstone. Tembe means 'Arab house'. Henry Stanley stayed here for three months in 1871 on his way to find Livingstone (see box, page 340). Afterwards (in 1872) they returned to the house in Tabora; Stanley stayed for a month or so before returning to the coast, while Livingstone, who was in poor health, occupied the house for about 10 months to recuperate, before setting off on the final leg of his journey. He died less than a year later at Chitambo, Zambia. The museum, although run-down, is interesting and contains various letters, maps, pictures, etc, associated with the man, as well as with other early missionaries and explorers. To get there follow Boma Road south out of town past the fort; after the roundabout take the right-hand fork, a taxi there and back will cost around US$9.

Livingstone

David Livingstone was born on 19 March 1813 in Blantyre in Scotland. He had a strict Scottish upbringing, and his first job was in a factory. He studied during the evenings and, at the age of 27, finally qualified as a doctor. In 1840 he joined the London Missionary Society, was ordained in the same year and set off for Africa. On the voyage out he learnt to use quadrants and other navigational and mapping instruments, which were to prove vital skills during his exploration of uncharted parts of Africa. In 1841 he arrived in South Africa and journeyed north in search of converts.

In his first few years as a missionary, Livingstone gained a reputation as a surveyor and scientist. His first major expedition into the African interior came in 1853, lasted three years and included in 1855 the discovery of the Victoria Falls. When he returned to England in 1856 he was greeted as a national hero, was awarded a gold medal by the Royal Geographical Society, and was made a Freeman of the City of London.

He returned to Africa in 1858 and began his quest for the source of the Nile in 1866. This trip was funded by a grant from the British government, which enabled Livingstone to be better equipped than during his previous expedition. During this journey little was heard of him and rumours reached Britain of his apparent death. Henry Morton Stanley, a newspaper reporter for the *New York Herald*, was sent by James Gordon Bennett, his publisher, to find Livingstone. In 1871 Stanley found Livingstone's camp at Ujiji, a small town on the shores of Lake Tanganyika, greeting him with the now legendary, "Dr Livingstone, I presume?" At the time of the meeting Livingstone had run short of supplies, in particular quinine, which was vital in protecting him and his companions from malaria.

Livingstone set out on his last trip from near Tabora and continued his explorations until his death at Chitambo in what is now Zambia. His heart was buried at the spot where he died, his body embalmed and taken by Susi and Chumah, his two servants, to Bagamoyo (see page 80) from where it was shipped back to England. He was buried at Westminster Abbey and a memorial was erected at Chitambo.

Shinyanga → *For listings, see pages 341-343. Colour map 1, A3. Phone code: 028. Population: 107,000.*

Shinyanga, the principal town of Shinyanga province, is a major transport hub in this part of the central region with an airport and buses that go in every direction. It is 196 km north of Tabora on the B6 via Nzega, and can also be reached from Dodoma (530 km) via Singida and Nzega. It's 162 km south of Mwanza. It is a large, sprawling town with buildings and roads in poor condition, mostly built in the 1940s and 1950s when the area was thriving on gold, diamonds and cotton. During that time a large number of Europeans lived here and many vets from the UK were employed at a research station involved in eradicating rinderpest.

The area has been deforested – the timber being used for firewood – and now the region is hot, dry and dusty, featururing vast plains dotted with baobab trees. It is known for its cattle production, and African dew-lapped cows can be seen everywhere. There's still a lot of cotton here too, which is brought to the area's ginneries for processing. Rice is also grown, and just outside town are several large, circular, covered stores where the surplus is kept to be distributed in the event of crop failure. Additionally, gold is still found in the area, and

Williamson Diamond Mine

About 15 km along the B6 road to the northeast of Shinyanga you come to a turning on the right for the Williamson Diamond Mine (also referred to as the Mwadui Mine after the kimberlite pipe), where there is a tree-lined road leading up to the compound. It became well known as the first significant diamond mine outside South Africa, following the discovery of diamonds here in 1940 by a Canadian geologist Dr John Williamson. By the 1950s he had developed the Williamson Diamond Mine, the first in Tanzania, with state-of-the-art equipment and a labour force of several thousand, and he managed the mine until his death in 1958. In the 1960s the compound had its own hospital, churches, supermarket and schools, and a Dakota flew for weekly shopping trips to Nairobi from the on-site airstrip.

The Mwadui diamondiferous kimberlite pipe is one of the largest in the world but, in 1971, a decade after Tanzania's Independence, the government nationalized the mine, output was reduced significantly, and facilities fell into semi-disrepair. In 1994, De Beers revitalized the mine, and today it is part-owned by the Tanzanian Government (25%) and Petra Diamonds (75%). Only industrial diamonds are now mined, but the Williamson Mine holds the record for the world's longest-running uninterrupted diamond mining operation. The most famous stone ever mined here was the 'Williamson pink' diamond, found in October 1947, which was given to Princess Elizabeth as a wedding gift. It weighed 23.6 carats after cutting and polishing, and was a beautiful rose colour.

there are substantial gold mining developments in Shinyanga and around Geita, closer to Lake Victoria (page 316), where several massive and ambitious mines have been operating since the late 1990s and more are expected to open. These have, in part, contributed to the massive road-building that has been going on in the region in recent years.

The inhabitants are very friendly and there is no problem walking around, especially in the day time. Education has always been very important in Shinyanga and now there is a big college on the road to Kamborage Stadium. There is a sizeable Indian community and also many Africans of Arab descent, hence the large number of Muslims.

There are no large shops, but a great number of stores selling only a few items – many with a dressmaker and sewing machine outside. Every day there is a busy market selling just about everything. There's a branch of **National Bank of Commerce**, with an ATM, on the Mwanza road south of the railway station and **Shinyanga Motel**.

◉ Tabora and around listings

For sleeping and eating price codes and other relevant information, see pages 22-26.

◉ Where to stay

Tabora p339
$$-$ Orion Tabora Hotel, opposite the railway station, T026-260 4369. This is a historic German railway hotel (there used

to be a sign here warning that the hotel did not permit black people or dogs), with sweeping steps up to the outside terrace. Of the 35 rooms, the more modern ones around the back of the main building have mosquito nets and TV. There's good food, including curries and grilled fish and chicken, and you can eat in the formal dining room, the comfy bar in front of

the enormous satellite TV or on the lovely veranda. An extensive buffet breakfast is included in the price and, if you arrive off the train, you can eat breakfast here too. Nothing fancy, but easily the best option.
$ Fuma Hotel, off Lumumba Rd. 12 spotless rooms with nets around a small courtyard, each one is named after a month of the year, some with bathrooms for not much more. Good value, and secure parking behind a locked gate. Small restaurant and bar near the entrance.
$ Golden Eagle, Songeya Rd, T026-260 4623. A good location for early morning buses. Upstairs around a bright, freshly painted courtyard are 13 reasonable-value rooms with or without bathrooms, fans and mosquito nets, and with spotless white sheets. Simple food in the restaurant, including a couple of Indian (and vegetarian) dishes, and there's a small rooftop bar.
$ Hotel Wilca, Boma Rd, T026-2604105. Comfortable and well run, friendly staff, nice outdoor bar with pool table, *nyama choma* grill and good restaurant serving stews and curries. The rooms have en suite bathrooms with hot water, but there are only 10, so you may need to arrive early to get one. This is by far the best of a whole bunch of guesthouses in this area, most of which are very basic.

Shinyanga *p340*
$ Mwoleka, 1 block north of the bus stand, T028-276 2249. Simple and tatty, rooms are en suite and have hot water (though some only have bathtubs), mosquito nets and fans, but it is clean, has quite good food, and there's a bar and a locked compound for cars. This is the best of the basic places around the bus stand.
$ Shinyanga Motel, opposite the railway station, T028-276 2458. The best option in town and fairly recently refurbished in a 3-storey orange-painted block. The en suite rooms have fans, nets and hot water, pay a little more for a/c, some have small balconies. Bar and restaurant serving African and some Indian dishes.

🍴 Restaurants

Tabora *p339*
As in all small towns, there are a number of canteen places around Tabora open during the day for breakfast, snacks and grills, fresh juice and tea and coffee. These include the lively restaurant at the railway station, also known as the **Duka Bar**, which has outdoor tables under thatch, plenty of cold beer, and large-screen TVs to keep waiting passengers entertained with European football matches. Watch the mosquitoes around your feet in the evening here, though. All the hotels have reasonable restaurants – the best is at the **Orion Tabora Hotel** (see Where to stay, page 341).

Shinyanga *p340*
$ Green View Bar, on the main road between the bus stand and Catholic church. An attractive place under thatched rondavaals, and one of the few cheap places around town that is open in the evening. Serves good chicken and beef kebabs roasted over charcoal with chips or rice and cold beer. To one side of the road leading to the bar is a football pitch used by the locals, and most evenings the teams of shirts versus no-shirts can be seen playing.

🚌 Transport

Tabora *p339*
Bus
The Tabora bus stand is off Market St with a huge football stadium behind. It is fairly well organized, with the bus company kiosks around the perimeter. Buses go daily to **Mwanza** (8 hrs), via **Shinyanga** (4 hrs), and to **Dar** (16 hrs), via **Ngeza** (2 hrs), **Singida** (5 hrs), and **Dodoma** (11 hrs). There are also buses to **Mbeya** (20 hrs), but not every day and the B6 road south of Tabora is very rough and is impassable in places during the rainy seasons. Most services leave very early in the morning.

Train

Tabora is the place where the Central Line 'splits' to go to either **Kigoma** or **Mwanza**. If the train from **Dar es Salaam** is on time, it should get to Tabora at 1825 Wed and Sat and, once it is separated and attached to different locomotives, both services should depart again for Kigoma/Mwanza at 2130. In the other direction, both services should arrive in Tabora at 0400, and the Dar-bound train should depart at 0725. While the carriages are shunted around in Tabora (and you may have to swap carriages depending on which direction you are going in), you can get off the train, wander around the station, have a drink and snack in the bar, and generally enjoy watching the organized chaos of the trains being separated. However, during this very busy time, when there are hundreds of people at Tabora Station, ensure someone is watching your luggage at all times, even if it's in a locked train compartment, as petty theft can occur, including through train windows. For more details of the Central Line, see box, page 18.

Additionally to the main Central Line train, there's a side-line railway track that goes from Tabora to the tiny town of **Mpanda**, approximately 300 km across country (it doesn't even follow a road), which lies roughly midway on the (extremely rough) B8 road between Kigoma in the north and Tunduma on the Zambian border in the south. Just a few carriages are tacked on this locomotive that serves local villages along its route, and journey time is 10-15 hrs. It is scheduled to depart Tabora at 2100 on Mon and Fri and returns from Mpanda at 1300 on Tue and Sat. The only likely reason for travellers to use this train is to visit **Katavi National Park**, which can be reached independently without your own vehicle from Mpanda (see page 351 for details).

Shinyanga *p340*
Air

There is a grass airstrip a few kilometres out of town toward Mwanza. When the cows are shooed off, **Precision Air**, Dar es Salaam, T022-286 0701, www.precisionairtz.com, has a flight to/from **Dar**, which leaves Dar at 0940, arrives in Shinyanga at 1140, departs again at 1210 and arrives back in Dar at 1410.

Bus

Shinyanga is 162 km from **Mwanza**. The road between the 2 has recently been tarred and the journey takes a little over 2 hrs. There are a great number of buses in every other direction.

Train

Shinyanga is on the Central Line railway on the branch line between **Mwanza** and **Tabora**. See Tabora Transport, above.

❶ Directory

Shinyanga *p340*
Medical services Shinyanga General Hospital is in the centre of town, T028-22235/6.

Lake Tanganyika

Despite its remote location in the extreme northwest of Tanzania, Lake Tanganyika has a number of attractions. Here are the attractive lakeside national parks of Mahale and Gombe, famous for their chimpanzee populations, and further south is the wild and scenic Katavi National Park. A safari here gives you the feeling of having the park to yourself. The region is an adventurous destination to get to and explore for the budget traveller by train or ferry, though reasonably accessible for those who can afford to visit by plane. ▶▶ *For listings, see pages 352-356.*

Kigoma → *Colour map 1, B1. 4° 55'S, 29° 36'E. Phone code: 028. Population: 80,000. Altitude: 800 m.*

Capital of the Western Region of Tanzania, Kigoma is a small, sleepy town 1254 km west of Dar es Salaam, with one tree-lined main road. It overlooks Lake Tanganyika on its western side and has scenic rolling hills to the east. It is the main railway terminus in the west of the country for the Central Line Railway that was built in the early 20th century to transport agricultural goods from the African hinterland to the coast. Just a few kilometres to the south is the old Arab slave trading settlement of Ujiji (see below), the famous meeting place of Stanley and Livingstone. Most people come here on their way to Burundi or Zambia across the lake on the steamer *MV Liemba* (see box, page 345) or else on their

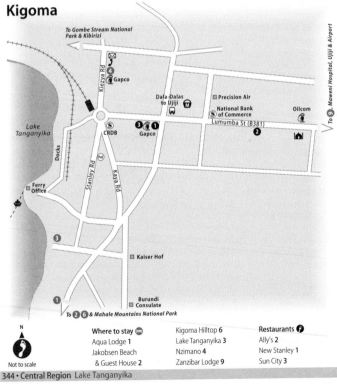

Kigoma

Where to stay
Aqua Lodge **1**
Jakobsen Beach
& Guest House **2**
Kigoma Hilltop **6**
Lake Tanganyika **3**
Nzimano **4**
Zanzibar Lodge **9**

Restaurants
Ally's **2**
New Stanley **1**
Sun City **3**

N
Not to scale

MV Liemba

The steamer *Liemba*, originally named *Gotzen*, was built in Germany in 1913 and transported at great expense to Kigoma where it was reconstructed. Its first trial runs took place in June 1915 and average speeds of around 8 knots were reached. It was the flagship of the German flotilla on Lake Tanganyika and was used during the First World War as armed transport, particularly to carry troops down the lake from Kigoma to Kasanga. The *Gotzen* was the largest ship on the lake at this time and could carry about 900 men in a quarter of the time that it took the dhows to do the same journey.

In June 1916 the Gotzen was attacked by Belgian planes but was not too seriously damaged. In July of the same year, when the railway to Kigoma was captured, the Germans scuttled her.

After the war, the Gotzen was raised from the deeps and refitted. On 16 May 1927 the ship was rechristened *Liemba*, the name by which Lake Tanganyika had originally been known by local people, and in trials that month managed an average speed of 8.5 knots – not bad for a ship that had spent from 26 July 1916 to 16 March 1924 at the bottom of the lake. It is still in operation today.

Since then the *Liemba* has steamed the lake from end to end almost continuously, for a period of over 80 years (see page 355). She has probably completed the nearly 1000-km, week-long round trip between Kigoma and Mpulungu in Zambia over 4000 times, perhaps steaming over 4 million kilometres. She is generally believed to be the oldest operational passenger vessel in the world.

---

way to **Gombe Stream National Park** (see page 346). The **Mahale Mountains National Park**, also famous for chimpanzees, lies to the south of Kigoma but is very remote and is accessed most easily by plane from Kigoma (see page 349).

The **railway station** is a very imposing building built before the First World War by the Germans. The nearby **Kaiser Hof**, another German building, was built for the Kaiser and today is used as the State House (do not take photographs). Intriguingly, there is a tunnel between this house and the railway station which was a secret escape route for the Kaiser. The major industry in Kigoma is fishing and this is mostly done in the afternoon, when hundreds of dhows set sail across the lake from **Kibirizi Village**, 3 km north of Kigoma. In this village you can see the fishermen building dhows or stringing fishing nets together. There is also a large depot here for the petrol companies that transport fuel across the lake.

Ujiji → *Colour map 1, B1.*
ⓘ *There are regular dala-dalas to and from Kigoma, ask to be dropped off at Livingstone St, and the museum is a few mins' walk towards the lake.*

This small market village 6 km south of Kigoma has a thriving boat-building industry. It used to be the terminus for the old caravan route from the coast, and the resulting Arab influence is clear to see. The houses are typical of the coastal Swahili architecture and the population is mainly Muslim. The **post office** on Kigoma Road is a substantial structure, dating from the German period. It is, however, most famous for being the place where the words 'Dr Livingstone, I presume' were spoken by Henry Morton Stanley (see page 340). The two men met on the 10th November 1871. The site where this is thought to have occurred is marked by a plaque and a museum, between the town and what used to be the shore, on Livingstone Street. The original mango tree, under which the two gentlemen met, died in the 1920s, but there are two very large mango trees that are supposed to have been grafted from the original one. After the meeting, Livingstone left Uijiji and went to Tabora with Stanley. In the **Livingstone Museum** ① *0800-1800, free entry, but a tip of US$2-3 is expected*, the curator will show you around for a small tip and tell you the story. He will also proudly tell you about the day he met Michael Palin when he visited here during the making of *Pole to Pole*. In the main building of the museum are some faded drawings and books and rather comical brightly painted, full-size papier mâché figures of the two men shaking hands. There is also a small plaque in the grounds to Speke and Burton, the first Europeans to set eyes on Lake Tanganikya on 14 February 1858.

Gombe Stream National Park → *For listings, see pages 352-356. Colour map 1, B1.*
4° 38'S, 31° 40'E.

In the extreme northwestern corner of Tanzania on the shore of Lake Tanganyika and sharing a border with Burundi, Gombe Stream National Park is one of Tanzania's most remote. The park is most famous for the work of Jane Goodall, the resident primatologist who spent many years in its forests studying the behaviour of the endangered chimpanzees. Guided walks deep into the forest to observe and sit with the extraordinary primates for an entire morning are possible and are an incredible experience. Aside from chimpanzee-viewing, many other species of primates and mammals live in Gombe Stream's tropical forests, as well as a wide variety of birdlife.

Arriving in Gombe Stream National Park
Getting there The park headquarters are on the lakeshore at **Kasekela**, which is 23 km north of Kigoma. The main purpose of the park is for research rather than tourism and facilities are minimal: there are just two places to stay, the **Gombe Forest Lodge**, and the **National Park Bandas and Campsite**, see Where to stay, page 353. The park can be visited all year round. You can get a basic boat fairly easily from **Kibirizi**, a village 3 km north of Kigoma. They normally leave around 1400-1500 and the trip takes about three hours. These boats are actually lake taxis that serve the villages on the lakeshore immediately north of Kigoma, but they will go to Kasekela and charge around US$4 each way. Arrange with the boatman what time they will pick you up the next day; they usually pass Kasekela first thing in the morning. Because of these timings, it is essential to spend at least two nights in the park in order to go chimp-tracking (allow up to five hours for this; walks usually go at sunrise). The better option is to charter one of the boats from Kibirizi, which, with a bit of negotiation, you can do for US$50-60. You can also organize a transfer by motorboat from the **Kigoma Hilltop Hotel** in Kigoma (see Where to stay, page 352). These cost around US$500 for the return trip, can carry up to 12 people and take about 1½ to two hours each way. Of course, the easiest option, if you can afford it, is to book a package and stay at the **Gombe Forest Lodge**, which organizes its own boat transfers for guests, as well as charter flights to Kigoma.

Park information Tanzania National Parks Authority (TANAPA), www.tanzaniaparks. com, park open 0630-1830, US$100, children (5-16) US$20, a guide for chimp-tracking is US$20 for a group of up to six people. Note: children under 15 cannot go chimp-tracking.

Background
In 1960 Jane Goodall set up the area as a chimpanzee research station (see box, page 348). She wrote a book on the findings of her initial research called *In the Shadow of Man*, and

her early years of work were filmed by Hugo van Lawick, the wildlife photographer. This attracted much publicity to the reserve and, in 1968, the Gombe Stream National Park was established. It covers an area of 52 sq km, making it the smallest park in Tanzania. It is made up of a narrow, mountainous strip of land about 16 km long and 2.5 km wide that borders Lake Tanganyika. The mountains, which rise steeply from the lake to 681-1500 m, are intersected by steep valleys, which have streams running in them and are covered in thick gallery forest (that is, the river banks are wooded, but beyond is open country).

Wildlife

There are approximately 100 chimpanzees in the park divided into three family troops. They each guard their territory fiercely. One of the groups often goes down to the valley, so you can see them from there. Alternatively, there are a number of observation points around the park, and the rangers usually know where to go to see them. However, there is no guarantee that you will see the chimpanzees during your visit. They are less visible here than at Kibale Forest in western Uganda. Other primates include red-tailed and blue colobus monkeys. Birdlife is also prolific and includes various barbets, starlings, sunbirds, kingfishers, the palm-nut vulture, crowned eagle and the rufous-bellied heron.

Gombe Stream National Park

Chimpanzee-tracking

It is compulsory to take a guide with you to the forest. If you're not staying at the lodge, a guide for chimp-tracking can be organized at the Kasekela park headquarters, and walks take anywhere between 30 minutes and five hours, depending on where the chimps are. Most depart early in the morning, when the rangers have a better idea where the chimps may be, as they can trace evidence of their overnight nests. As chimpanzees can catch many of our diseases, you will not be allowed to go chimp-tracking if you have a cold or any other infectious illness. From the National Parks camp and park headquarters, there is a trail leading to a lovely waterfall just over 2 km away in a valley. If there are no chimps in this valley, one of the guides will take you further into the forest to try and track them down. It can be hard, slippery walking up and down the valleys through the forest. You are permitted to walk along the beach without a guide; there you may see a troop of partially habituated olive baboons, but do not get too close as they are still dangerous wild animals.

Jane Goodall

Jane Goodall was born in 1934 in England. She had an early interest in animals and a longing to go to Africa. Her chance came in 1957, when she visited a friend's farm in Kenya, and met Louis Leakey, archaeologist and curator of the Natural History Museum in Nairobi. She became his assistant and accompanied the Leakeys on archaeological digs to Olduvia Gorge. Louis then revealed his plans to send her to Gombe in Tanganyika (now Tanzania) to study chimpanzees. Previously, few studies of chimpanzees had been successful, usually because the size of the party of researchers frightened the chimps off. Leakey believed that Goodall had the patience and temperament to endure long-term isolation in the wild, while she observed chimps alone.

In 1960, 26-year-old Jane went to Gombe with her mother Vanne Morris-Goodall. The presence of Vanne was necessary to satisfy the concerns of government officials in Kigoma that a young European woman shouldn't live in the bush without a companion. (In later years, Vanne became great friends with Louis and co-authored the book *Unveiling Man's Origins* with him in 1969, and it was in her apartment in London where Leakey died in 1972.) Jane and Vanne set up camp on the shore of Lake Tanganyika in the Gombe Stream Reserve (now the Gombe Stream National Park). Over time, Jane established a non-threatening pattern of observation of the chimps, appearing at the same time every morning on the high ground near a feeding area. Within a year, the chimps had got used to her presence and allowed her to get within 50 m.

One of Jane's major breakthroughs was the discovery of tool-making among the chimps, who made twigs into implements to catch insects. Though many animals had been observed using tools, it was previously thought that only humans made tools. Leakey arranged for Jane to return to the UK, where she earned a doctorate in ethology at Cambridge in 1964, before returning to Tanzania in 1965 to set up the Gombe Stream Research Centre. Her subsequent findings revealed that chimps engage in long-term warfare and have definite characters, as well as emotions, courtship rituals and family ties.

Her 52-year fascination with the closest living species to humans has been invaluable for our understanding of chimps, and she is today regarded as the world's authority on the species.

In 1977 she founded the Jane Goodall Institute, which today continues field research on chimpanzees and supports community-based conservation and development programs. Jane has written many books, has more than 20 honorary doctorates from universities worldwide and has earned many awards for her environmental work. In 2003, she became a Dame of the British Empire. She now travels the world speaking about chimpanzees and the resolution of environmental threats to the planet.

Mahale Mountains National Park → *For listings, see pages 352-356. Colour map 1, B1.*

This is another chimpanzee sanctuary, established in 1985 as a national park covering an area of 1613 sq km, and lying at an altitude of over 1800 m. The park is about half way down the eastern shore of Lake Tanganyika, 120 km south of Kigoma. Although Gombe is more famous, the primate population in Mahale Mountains is more numerous, and sightings, more regular and prolonged (reputedly, the only person who stayed in Mahale and didn't see chimps, was Bill Gates). Hikes to their habitation areas are accessible and not strenuous. As well as being the premium location in all Africa for viewing chimpanzees in the wild, Mahale Mountains is also in a stunningly beautiful lakeshore setting, with superb white sand beaches and clear water for swimming (though check with the lodge staff before swimming, as some parts of Lake Tanganyika are affected by bilharzia).

Arriving in Mahale Mountains National Park

Getting there There are no roads running into the park and the only access is by boat or plane. The park office is at **Bilenge**, where all fees are paid. From here there is a boat transfer to **Kasiha** village, 10 km south of Bilenge, the departure point for chimp walks; this is also the location of the national park rest camp. The best time to visit is May to September, during the drier months. The most practical, though most expensive, way of getting there is by charter flight direct to the park's landing strip. These can be organized as part of a package through the luxury lodges or tour operators in Arusha (page 258) or Dar es Salaam (page 72); many of the packages also include stays in Katavi National Park (see page 351) and flights go via Katavi en route between Mahale and Arusha. A cheaper alternative is to organize a boat transfer from the **Kigoma Hilltop Hotel** in Kigoma (see Where to stay, page 352). Motorboats cost in the region of US$800 per return trip, can carry up to 12 people and take four to six to eight hours each way.

In theory, it is also possible to take the lake ferry *(MV Liemba)* to the park from Kigoma, though this is an adventurous option, see page 355. The ferry is scheduled to leave Kigoma on Wed at 1600 and you get to **Lagosa** (also known as Mugambo), which is 15 km north of the park boundary, after about 10 hours. The return ferry passes Lagosa on Sat but, again, in the middle of the night at any time between 2100 and 0700. If you arrive by ferry, you will then have to get a small boat to take you from the ferry to the shore; a national park boat meets the *MV Liemba* and transfers passengers to the park headquarters at Bilenge, which takes about three hours, and then it's another 10 km to Kasiha and the rest camp. This must be pre-

Mahale Mountains National Park

Where to stay 🛏
Kungwe Beach Lodge **3**
Greystoke Mahale **1**
National Park Rest
    Camp **2**   Ranger Post ●

N
Not to scale

arranged, which is difficult (visit the **Tanzania National Parks Authority (TANAPA)** head office in Arusha, T027-250 3471, www.tanzaniaparks.com, page 237, or ask at the **Kigoma Hilltop Hotel** in Kigoma). You'll also need to organize the return boat transfer back to the ferry at Bilenge. If you do opt for the ferry, then, of course, you will have to stay at Mahale for a week (and the ferry is far from reliable).

The final option is to take a lake taxi from **Kibirizi** village, 3 km north of Kigoma, which stops at the villages on the lakeshore south of Kigoma. But this is ill-advised as they are no more than simple timber boats, there is no shelter, they are overcrowded, and the journey could take anything from 15 to 25 hours.

Park information Tanzania National Parks Authority (TANAPA), www.tanzaniaparks.com, www.mahalepark.org, park open 0700-1800, park fees US$80, children (5-16) US$30; a guide for chimp-tracking is US$20 for a group of up to six people. Note that children under 12 cannot go chimp-tracking.

Wildlife

The park is largely made up of montane forests and grasslands and some alpine bamboo. The eastern side of the mountains is drier, being in the rain shadow, and the vegetation there is the drier miombo woodland, which is found over much of west Tanzania and east DR Congo. The highest peak reaches 2460 m, and the prevailing winds from over the lake, when forced up to this level, condense and ensure a high rainfall. The wildlife found here is more similar to that found in western Africa than eastern. Other than the chimpanzees, it includes porcupine, giant forest squirrel, colobus monkeys (both red and the Angolan black and white), blue duiker and Sharpe's grysbok, although there are also more common savannah animals, such as giraffe, zebra, warthog and roan and sable antelope. Indeed, animals such as the leopard and lion have reappeared in the area in recent years, although these are rarely (if at all) seen. Birdlife includes the fish eagle, kestrel, kingfisher, barbet and starling, similar to those found at Gombe Stream. The chimpanzee population has been the focus of much research by scientists from around the world. According to a recent census there are now more than 700 individuals in about 15 communities. Some of these groups are accessible to visitors, others are the subject of research studies, but most live undisturbed deep inside the forest.

Chimpanzee-tracking

Guides can be organized through the lodges, or at the rest camp at Kasiha and at the park headquarters at Bilenge. Rules are a little more stringent than at Gombe. Again you are not permitted to visit the chimps if you are sick or have an infectious disease. No more than six people are allowed in each group and, once found, no more than an hour is permitted in the presence of the troop, after which the guide will move you away. If the chimps are moving and the viewing is interrupted, that allotted hour is paused and resumed again when the chimps are relocated. Like Gombe, treks can last from anything from 30 minutes to five hours depending on where you may find the chimps, and most depart early in the morning, when the rangers have a better idea where the chimps may be, as they can trace evidence of their overnight nests.

Katavi National Park is 40 km southeast of Mpanda town, 205 km north of Sumbawanga and sits astride the main Mpanda–Sumbawanga road. It was upgraded to a national park in 1974 and now covers an area of 4471 sq km. Travelling south from Mpanda or north from Tunduma (the border town of Tanzania and Zambia), the road passes through the park. However, its isolation and lack of facilities mean that it receives few tourists (about 200 a year). As such, it offers unspoilt wildlife viewing in a remote location far off the beaten track.

Arriving in Katavi National Park

Getting there The main entrance gate and the **Tanzania National Parks Authority (TANAPA)** park headquarters is close to **Sitalike** village, 40 km south of Mpanda. The easiest way to reach Katavi is by charter flight and there are airstrips at Sitalike near the gate outside the park, and at Ikuu and Mlele inside the park. The lodges or tour operators organize this. If driving, it's a tough but scenic drive from either Mbeya in the south via Sumbawanga (550 km), Kigoma in the north via Mpanda (390 km), or Tabora in the northeast via Mpanda (415 km), but all these routes are rough and become impassable in the wet; a 4WD (and possibly a GPS) is essential. If travelling overland, allow plenty of time to get there and back. It is possible to reach Mpanda by rail from Tabora (there's a branch line from the Central Line, see Tabora Transport page 342), then to catch a *dala-dala* (or charter your own – all *dala-dalas* in this region are 4WDs) the 40 km to Sitalike. There is basic accommodation in Mpanda and a basic resthouse at the park headquarters at Sitalike (see Where to stay, page 354). Hiring a 4WD vehicle with a driver is possible at the park headquarters and costs around US$100 per day or per 100 km (whichever comes first), which you can also use to get to the upmarket lodges, in the unlikely event you are staying in one and are not arriving by charter plane.

Park information TANAPA, www.tanzaniaparks.com, www.katavipark.org. 0630-1830, park fees US$20, children (5-16) US$5, vehicle US$40.

Wildlife

The scenery is as varied as it is pristine. Flood plains of thick reeds and dense waterways are home to a huge population of hippo and, in the woodlands to the west, forest canopies shelter herds of buffalo and elephant. Seasonal lakes fill with dirt-coloured water after the rains, and animals from all corners of the park descend on them to drink. The park is characterized by miombo woodland and acacia parkland, as well as some water-logged grassland plains. There is a large swampy area around the Katuma River, which joins the two lakes in the park – Lake Katavi and Lake Chada. The park is famous for its sable and roan antelope, rarely found in other Tanzanian parks, and also for its large populations of elephant (an estimated 4000) and buffalo, which can be seen in herds 1000 strong. It also has a high density of crocodiles, Defassa water buck, topi, eland, hartebeest and greater kudu. Other large mammals seen here include hippo, crocodile, zebra, spotted hyena, various antelope, as well as lion and, if you are lucky, leopard. Over 400 species of birds have been identified. The park has many waterbirds and birds of prey, including the black heron, Dickinson's kestrel, bee-eaters, strikes, weavers, nightjars and the go-away bird. The best time to visit is in the dry season from July to October, when the flood plains retreat and the Katuma River becomes no more than a narrow muddy trickle forming the only source of water and attracting huge herds of game. This is when hippo-viewing is at its most spectacular – up to 200 at a time can be seen crowded together in the shallow water, and territorial fights between the males is common.

Further south

Sumbawanga → *Colour map 1, B2. Phone code: 025.*
This is a fairly large but unremarkable town on the rough B8, which runs parallel to but some way inland from the lakeshore. It is 205 km south of Kitavi National Park and 312 km north of Tunduma, which is on the A104, the main road through southwest Tanzania. Sumbawnga has some impressive buildings, in particular the Roman Catholic church, a large market selling second-hand clothes and a separate one selling a wide range of fruit, vegetables and fish. The town is very clean, with a newly laid tarmac main road. Although its name is said to mean 'witch people', there's nothing here to see or do, and it only has very basic facilities. But you are likely to pass through on the southern route to Kitavi National Park from Mbeya, or from **Kasanga**, which lies 110 km to the southwest on the lakeshore and is the last port of call in Tanzania for the *MV Liemba* ferry from Kigoma (see Kigoma Transport, page 355). If you've come off the ferry at Kasanga, you'll need to swap buses in Sumbawanga and get another to Tunduma and beyond to Mbeya.

⊕ Lake Tanganyika listings

For sleeping and eating price codes and other relevant information, see pages 22-26.

⊕ Where to stay

Kigoma *p344, map p344*
$$$ Kigoma Hilltop Hotel, 2 km south of town on a headland overlooking the lake, T028-280 4437, reservations **Mbali Mbali Lodges & Camps**, Dar es Salaam, T022-213 0553, www.mbalimbali.com. Upmarket and recently refurbished resort, without doubt the best place to stay in Kigoma, with endless lake views and 30 a/c cottages with satellite TV, Wi-Fi, fridge and balcony. There are 2 restaurants serving good Indian food and local fish, including Nile perch, and a very attractive poolside terraced bar, swimming pool, gym, tennis courts. Tours to their luxury camps at Gombe and Mahale (see page 353) by motorboat and private plane can be arranged and, closer to the hotel, they can arrange short fishing and boat trips, or tours to the Livingstone Museum in Ujiji. Doubles from US$110.
$$$-$$ Lake Tanganyika Hotel, overlooking the lake, T028-280 3052, www.laketanganyikahotel.com. This is an old building, formerly the **Tanganyika Beach Hotel**, which was completely refurbished

and reopened in 2009, with beautiful views from the terraced lawns where you can walk down to the water. The smart a/c rooms have satellite TV and Wi-Fi, and there's a bar and restaurant serving good food, and a lovely additional tented bar area on the lakeshore where there is a disco on Sat. Doubles from US$85.
$$-$ Jakobsen Beach & Guest House, 6 km south of Kigoma, T0713-331 215, www.kigomabeach.com. To get here follow the lakeshore road south of the **Kigoma Hilltop Hotel**, or get a *dala-dala* from Kigoma towards the village of Katonga. About 800 m before Katonga, there is a signposted turn-off to the right, which goes to the lodge and beach (a 15- to 20-min walk). This is a lovely forested spot run by a Norwegian couple with self-catering accommodation (there's no restaurant so bring everything you need from Kigoma). The guesthouse is up the hill from the beach, with 4 rooms and shared fully equipped kitchen and bathroom (a housekeeper can help with cooking and cleaning). You can take just 1 room or the whole house, which sleeps 10 in total. The grassy campsite also has a number of pre-erected walk-in tents under thatched roofs, shared toilets and (cold) showers, kerosene

lamps are provided and, if you want to BBQ, firewood and cutlery and crockery are available. Very friendly and very peaceful and has a beautiful sandy beach with thatched sunshades; the water here is perfect for swimming and reputedly bilharzia-free (check first), and they rent out snorkelling gear and kayaks.

$ Hotel Nzimano, Kiezya Rd near the post office, 500 m from the railway station, T028-280 2276, www.tourism.kigomadiocese. org. This is a church-run guesthouse in an old-fashioned but neat red-brick block set in flowering gardens with lake views. The rooms, with or without bathrooms, are plain but functional and cheap, from US$12. There's no bar or restaurant but with notice they can organize local meals, and rates include a basic cold breakfast. Profits from the hotel go directly to the Diocese of Kigoma, which runs many institutions in the region, such as schools, health centres, children's homes and a hospital.

$ Zanzibar Lodge, Mwanga, on the Ujijiji road about 2 km from Kigoma, T028-280 3306. Nowhere near the lake, but handy if catching buses (which depart from Mwanga) and one of the better board and lodgings in town. The smart double-storey block has clean rooms with nets and fans, some with TV, that surround a central courtyard, and a restaurant and bar for local food. Those with en suite are around US$10, while those with shared bathrooms, US$5.

Gombe Stream National Park p346, map p347

$$$$ Gombe Forest Lodge, reservations Mbali Mbali Lodges & Camps, Dar es Salaam, T022-213 0553, www.mbalimbali. com. Near the Mitumba Stream at the northern end of the park on the lakeshore on a spacious beach, the 7 en suite tents are on raised wooden decks facing the lake and are under big shady mango trees. There is a small reception area made out of local wood, with a thatched roof and wooden deck, where there is a library, a curio shop, a

bar and lounge. Meals are taken either in the main mess tent or on the beach. Electricity comes from a generator. Rates are US$375-470 per person per night and include boat transfers and chimp-tracking but not entrance fees. Most people stay 2 nights with 2 opportunities to go chimp-tracking and, perhaps, an afternoon on the beach, and spend a night either before or after at the Kigoma Hilltop Hotel, which is also run by Mbali Mbali Lodges & Camps.

$ National Park Bandas & Campsite, bookings can be made through the Tanzania National Parks Authority (TANAPA) head office in Arusha, see page 237. The basic buildings here are rather grim blocks and the verandas are caged in to protect you from baboons and chimpanzees. There is a hostel that sleeps 12 people but this can only be used for organized groups, and there are 5 simple bandas with 4 beds in each; mosquito nets are provided but you need to bring sleeping gear and all cooking equipment and food, and there's a campsite, with very basic shared latrine toilets and cold showers, taps and a fireplace and grill. You may be able to get one of the ladies that live in the staff accommodation near the park HQ to cook you a local meal. The price for bandas and camping is US$20 per person.

Mahale Mountains National Park
p349, map p349

$$$$ Greystoke Mahale, operated by Nomad Safaris, info@nomad-tanzania. com, www.nomad-tanzania.com. They do not take direct bookings, email them and they'll send a list of their agents. In a stunning spot on a white-sand beach, where the forest-clad Mahale Mountains plunge into Lake Tanganyika. Established in 1992, Greystoke was the first accommodation in Mahale and remains the best place to stay by some considerable margin. The 6 suites are open-fronted, with adjoining bathrooms and upstairs decks. Apart from trekking to see the chimps, kayaking and snorkelling is on offer and they have their own dhow for fishing trips. The staff will arrange intimate dinners on the beach for couples and there's a fantastic bar on a rocky headland with very good food and service. One of the finest safari camps in Tanzania with a price tag to match.

$$$$ Kungwe Beach Lodge, on a sandy beach near the park HQ, reservations **Mbali Mbali Lodges & Camps**, Dar es Salaam, T022-213 0553, www.mbalimbali.com. The 8 luxury tents are raised on wooden platforms overlooking the lake, each very private with 4-poster beds, outdoor shower and a wooden veranda; there's a communal lounge, dining area, curio shop, library and beach hut complete with chunky cushioned lounge beds. Electricity comes from a generator. Rates are US$445-560 per person per night and include boat transfers and chimp-tracking but not entrance fees. Can also organize fishing for Nile perch, snorkelling and kayaking. Again, run by **Mbali Mbali Lodges & Camps** and people usually visit with a combined stay at **Kigoma Hilltop Hotel**.

$ National Park Rest Camp, Kasiha Village, 10 km south of the park office at Bilenge. Bookings can be made through the park's website, www.mahalepark.org, or the **Tanzania National Parks Authority (TANAPA)** head office in Arusha, see page 237. Facilities are minimal, bring all bedding, food, drinking water and cooking equipment from Kigoma, though there is a fireplace with grill and firewood, and a local cook can be hired to help you make meals. There are 4 rooms with shared bathrooms and 5 newer rooms with en suite bathroom, though there is no running water or electricity, so bucket showers and paraffin lamps are provided.

Katavi National Park *p351*

$$$$ Chada Katavi, operated by **Nomad Safaris**, www.nomad-tanzania.com. They do not take direct bookings, email them and they will send a list of their agents. Accessed by private plane, this is a superb bush camp

in the heart of the park, offering unsterilized safaris for people who really want to get out in the wilds. 6 luxury tents, excellent food, game drives, guided walks, fly camping safaris, elegantly hosted but still refreshingly simple and earthy.

$$$$ Katavi Wildlife Tented Camp, reservations **Foxes of Africa**, Dar es Salaam, T022-286 2357, www.katavi.org. Tented camp camouflaged from the animals in a clump of trees on the banks of the Katuma River. 8 modestly furnished tents spread well apart with viewing decks with hammocks overlooking the plains. The double-storey thatched central building is semi-open and has lounge, bar and dining area. Usually visited on a flying safari with their camp in Ruaha National Park.

$$$$ Katuma Bush Lodge, reservations **Mbali Mbali Lodges & Camps**, Dar es Salaam, T022-213 0553, www.mbalimbali.com. Fully refurbished in 2011, this lies in the centre of the park on the Katisunga Plains, with 10 spacious tents elevated on wooden decks. The central mess area has a lounge, bar, dining area, outdoor fire-pit, swimming pool and viewing deck. Game drives, game walks and BBQ dinners in the bush can be arranged. Often combined with a flying safari to their camps in Gombe Stream and Mahale.

$$$$ Palahala Camp Katavi, reservations **Firelight Expeditions**, Arusha T027-250 8773, www.firelightexpeditions.com. Set in a grove of very tall doum palms near the Kapapa River, with 8 unusual octagonal-shaped tents on elevated platforms, each 90 sq m in size and well furnished with a large veranda, lit by hurricane lamps and connected to the main tent by sandy walkways. Good food, game drives and walks and picnic breakfasts in the bush can be arranged.

$ Park Headquarters Resthouse, at the Sitalike Gate. This is primarily used by TANAPA staff, but they'll rent out the 4 basic rooms to visitors. Rooms have mosquito nets and a shared bathroom with warm water, and you can get a plate of hot food and warm beers/sodas at the staff recreation room, which has satellite TV. This is where you can arrange to hire a vehicle and driver (see page 351) but you may also be able to negotiate for one of the armed rangers to take you on a game walk in the area.

$ Super City Hotel, in Mpanda, 40 km north of the park entrance at Sitalike, T028-282 0459. You are likely to stay in Mpanda if accessing the park by public transport and via the train from Tabora (see Tabora Transport, page 342). This is a fenced compound about a 500-m walk up the hill from the railway station (not a station as such, but where the railway track ends) and 1.5 km south of town on the Sumbawanga road, with basic rooms with mosquito nets and running water. There's a restaurant and bar, which sells reasonable grilled fish and chicken chips/rice. You can get a *dala-dala* to Sitalike (for Katavi) outside.

Sumbawanga *p352*
$ Mbizi Forest Hotel, Meku Bar St, T025-280 2746. Despite its odd name (it's in a dusty back street with not a tree in sight), this is a good basic option, with 10 very clean rooms from US$15 with TV and modern tiled en suite bathrooms, and there's a pleasant restaurant and bar with tables outside in the garden.
$ Moravian Conference Centre, Nyerere Rd, central, T025-280 2853. A church-run guesthouse in a fairly new 3-storey block. Rooms with or without bathrooms from US$10, breakfast included, nothing remarkable but spotlessly clean, and there's a canteen with satellite TV serving basic local dishes, but of course no alcohol. You can use their internet and there's a secure car park.

❶ Restaurants

Kigoma *p344, map p344*
There are a number of places around town to get a cheap hot meal during the day, such as grilled chicken or fish, beef stew and the like with rice or *ugali*. Try **Sun City** and the **New Stanley Restaurant**, on the main road near

the market, or **Ally's**, along Ujiji Rd going east. There are also a number of food stalls around the station. The best restaurants are at the hotels. If you want to eat and drink with a lake view, head for the **Kigoma Hilltop Hotel**, or the **Lake Tanganyika Hotel**.

❷ Transport

Kigoma *p344, map p344*
Air
The airport is 5 km east of the town centre and just north of Ujiji. Taxis meet the flights and the hotels can arrange transfers. **Precision Air**, just off the main street opposite the market, T028-280 4720, www.precisionairtz.com (closed in the middle of the day when the man in the office goes to the airport to meet the flight) has flights between Kigoma and **Dar** on most days (depending on demand), which go via **Mwanza**, where it departs at 1040, arrives in Kigoma at 1140, leaves again in 1205 and arrives back in Mwanza at 1315.

Bus
Long-distance bus services go from **Mwanga**, 2 km from Kigoma on the Ujiji road, where there are several bus company kiosks. Services go to **Mwanza** and **Bukoba**, though these are rough rides on poor roads and each journey can take days rather than hours. These depart very early in the morning about 0500, so enquire the night before. To get to **Dar** by bus, most local people go to Mwanza first. The better option is the train (see below).

Ferry
The famous ferry on Lake Tanganyika is the *MV Liemba*, see box, page 345. For information phone the booking office in Kigoma, T028-280 2811, or alternatively contact the head office of the **Marine Services Company Ltd**, in Mwanza, T028-250 0491, www.mscltz.com.

The ferry leaves Kigoma at 1600 on Wed for **Mpulungu** (Zambia), arriving there at

1000 on Fri morning, then departs from Mpulungu again at 1600 on Fri afternoon and arrives back in Kigoma at 1000 on Sun; a 42-hr journey. However it stops at lots of small ports on the way, and is more than often delayed (sometimes by up to 12 hrs) as it unloads and loads cargo and passengers. The most interesting of these small ports to visitors are **Lagosa**, the jump-off point for the **Mahale Mountains National Park** (see page 349 for details of this option) and **Kasanga**, the last port in Tanzania before Mpulungu, and an option for getting to **Mbeya** and southwest Tanzania. At Kasanga, buses meet the ferry and go to **Sumbawanga** (see page 352), where you can swap buses and get another one to **Tunduma** and **Mbeya**.

Fares: Kigoma–Mpulungu (Zambia) 1st class US$45, 2nd class US$34, 3rd class US$18; Kigoma–**Lagosa**; US$17/US$12/US$7; and Kigoma–**Kasanga** US$42/US$31/US$17, plus US$5 port tax. The journey can be very crowded and rowdy at times. 3rd class is benches or deck space; 2nd-class cabins are small, hot and stuffy with 4 or 6 bunks; 1st-class cabins have 2 bunks, a window, fan, and meals and drinks are available. If at all possible, book and pay for your ferry ticket in advance and most certainly as soon as you arrive in Kigoma or Mpulungu.

The port in Kigoma is fairly organized and there is a large seating area under a tin roof for waiting passengers. There is an **immigration** and **customs** post but, given that many passengers arriving from Zambia may get off the ferry before Kigoma, Tanzania immigration and customs officials come on board the boat at Kasanga, the first port of call in Tanzania. Visas for Tanzania are available and are paid for in US$ cash. Zambian immigration and customs are found on arrival at Mpulungu and, again visas for Zambia are available.

At **Kibirizi**, a village 3 km north of Kigoma, down at the boat yard, local motorboat taxis depart on routes to the other villages along the lakeshore, and it's possible to catch these to both Gombe Stream and Mahale Mountains national parks (see pages 346 and 349 for details). You can get to Kibirizi by walking north along the railway track from Kigoma.

Train
Kigoma is the Lake Tanganyika terminus of the Central Line, and the fine old German-built railway station is in the middle of town. The journey to/from **Dar** is 1254 km and takes about 40 hrs. There is also the option of changing at Tabora for the Mwanza-bound branch of the train. See box, page 18, for details.

Sumbawanga *p352*
There are regular buses to/from **Mbeya** via **Tunduma**, which leave from both at 0600-0700 and take around 8 hrs, US$7. Heading to or from **Kasanga** on Lake Tanganyika, 110 km from Sumbawanga, there are a couple of buses a week (usually to tie in with the arrival of the ferry) and a few pick-up trucks daily, generally leaving before noon – ask around at the market.

Directory

Kigoma *p344, map p344*
Embassies and consulates Burundi Consulate, in a house just out of town on the road to the Hilltop Hotel, T028-280 2865. **Medical services** Maweni Hospital, T028-280 2671, 1 km or so down the road towards Ujiji.

Contents

Footprint features

Border crossings

Southern Tanzania

At a glance

⊕ Getting around For the Selous and Ruaha, unless you have your own vehicle, it's best to use a tour operator because public transport is very limited. Local buses and *dala-dalas* travel between the main towns in the region, where there are plenty of taxis.

⊕ Time required 5-7 days for a safari, another 5 days to take in the towns and hike in the highlands.

⊕ Weather The highlands can be quite cool and have higher rainfall. The best time to visit the parks is during the dry season Jun-Nov, when the temperatures are warm but not too overpowering.

⊗ When not to go Avoid the rainy season, end Mar-May, on the more remote roads away from the Tanzam Highway.

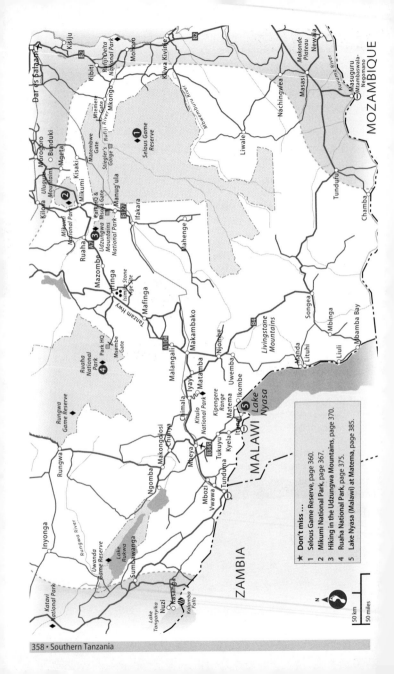

MOZAMBIQUE

ZAMBIA

MALAWI

★ Don't miss ...
1 Selous Game Reserve, page 360.
2 Mikumi National Park, page 367.
3 Hiking in the Udzungwa Mountains, page 370.
4 Ruaha National Park, page 375.
5 Lake Nyasa (Malawi) at Matema, page 385.

N

50 km
50 miles

The little-visited south of Tanzania has lots to offer, from the country's largest wilderness area in the Selous, to the pretty Kitulo National Park, tiny in comparison to its vast neighbour yet bursting with rare flowers. Wildlife-lovers who want to escape the safari convoys should come to this region – although you may work harder to see your game, you'll rarely see the crowds of the Northern Circuit. Frequently dubbed the 'Southern Circuit', the parks here, particularly Ruaha National Park and the Selous, a UNESCO World Heritage Site, have some fabulous lodges and are teeming with birdlife as well as animals, while the Udzungwa Mountains National Park protects ancient forests that are home to forest antelope and monkeys and is ideal terrain for hiking.

The major towns in the southwest are Iringa and Mbeya. Mbeya is on the TAZARA Railway that links Tanzania with Zambia. Road communications are good; the main road that cuts through southwest Tanzania, referred to as the Tanzam Highway, is the extension of Zambia's Great North Road and the continuation of the road that runs down the length of Lake Malawi in Malawi to the south. Take time to chill at Matema, on Lake Nyasa's northernmost shore (the Tanzanian name for the lake), and stroll along its beach, or explore the lush highlands, with high peaks and crater lakes, around Tukuyu and Mbeya.

Getting there and around

From Dar es Salaam, the Tanzam Highway heads out to Chalinze and Morogoro (see page 330). To the south of it are the limited road access points to the Selous Game Reserve, whilst 70 km to the southwest of Morogoro, the A7 road runs through a 50-km stretch of the Mikumi National Park. Beyond the Mikumi National Park, the road climbs into the Kitonga Hills, which are part of the Udzungwa Mountains. It is quite a journey, with sharp bends and dense forest all around. Part of the road runs alongside the Ruaha River gorge, often dubbed 'Baobab Valley' by veteran overlanders. Eventually the road levels out to the plateau and Iringa. To the northwest of Iringa is the Ruaha National Park. Mbeya lies 390 km to the southwest, along the A104 road, which passes though vast pine plantations and rural farms. About midway between the two towns is the junction with the B4 road that heads due south to the little-visited extreme south of Tanzania, around Songea and the eastern shore of Lake Nyasa (Malawi). Except for the steep climb up to Iringa through Baobab Valley, where the tar has melted, the Tanzam Highway is in fairly good condition. From Dar es Salaam there are regular buses linking the towns on this route.

The TAZARA railway (see boxes, page 18 and page 385) runs from Dar to Mbeya and on to Zambia. The train stops at intermediate stations on the way and, in theory, you would think some of these would be convenient for the sights. It stops in Kisaki in the north of the Selous Game Reserve, and at Manug'ula, which is just 1 km from the gate of the Udzungwa National Park, for example. But, in reality, as the train departs from Dar es Salaam at 1450 on Tuesday and Friday, it arrives in these places at inconvenient times, and the service is notoriously unreliable. The Selous Game Reserve and Ruaha National Park are served on daily scheduled circuits by **Coastal Air**, designed to transfer safari-goers from the coast to the Southern Circuit parks.

Selous Game Reserve

This enormous reserve in south Tanzania, first established in 1922, is the largest park in Africa and the second largest in the world, covering an area of 55,000 sq km or 5% of Tanzania's total area, making it roughly the size of Switzerland and four times larger than the Serengeti. The Selous' ecosystem as a whole is made up of a few conservation areas, namely Mikumi in the north and the Kilombero game-controlled area in the west, covering in total over 90,000 sq km of pristine wilderness virtually devoid of human influence. It is home to over one million large animals, including over half of Tanzania's elephant population. From the visitor's point of view, all these facts and figures can be a bit misleading, given that the majority of visitors are restricted to the area north of the Rufiji River. South of here has hitherto been the sole domain of trophy hunters, who, for a hefty fee, are allowed to shoot a restricted quota of wildlife in private concession areas only, the proceeds ostensibly going towards further conservation. The landscape in the north is largely open grassland and acacia woodland, cut across by slivers of riverine forest and patches of miombo woodland. Its rivers, hills and plains are home to roaming elephant populations, the area's famous wild dogs and some of the last black rhino left in the region, though the density of animals in the park is lower than that of other parks. During a game drive here you are unlikely to see any other vehicles, and the Selous offers you a chance to see a wild and expansive Africa, far from paved roads and curio shops

▶▶ *For listings, see pages 364-366.*

Frederick C Selous: Greatest of the White Hunters

Born in 1852 in London, the young Selous went to Rugby school. An early expedition saw him trek to a lake 25 km from Rugby, strip off, swim through the icy water to a small island and shin up a tree to collect eight blue heron's eggs. On returning to school he was rewarded by being made to copy out 63 lines of Virgil for each egg. Undeterred, and inspired by the writings of Livingstone, Selous wanted to visit Africa. After toying with the idea of becoming a doctor, he travelled to South Africa in 1871, and rapidly established himself as a supreme tracker and hunter.

Hunting was tough. The rifles were heavy muzzle-loaders, and powder was carried loose in one pocket, ignition caps in another and a supply of four ounces of lead bullets in a pouch. It was not uncommon for a hunter to be knocked out of the saddle by the gun's recoil and accidents were common.

Selous killed much game in his early years, partly for trophies in the case of lion and rhinoceros, for ivory in the case of elephants, and anything else as meat for his party. His techniques were based on absorbing the skills of African hunters and trackers, and in 1881 he published the first of a series of highly successful books on his methods and exploits, *A Hunter's Wanderings in Africa*. In 1887 he began a career of paid work leading safaris for wealthy clients, which culminated in a huge expedition organized for President Roosevelt in 1909. (A young British diplomat in South Africa, H Rider Haggard, based Allan Quatermain on Selous and his adventures in his novel *King Solomon's Mines*, published in 1895.)

During one visit to England, Selous took delivery of a new .450 rifle at his hotel an hour before he was due to catch the boat train from Waterloo to return to Africa. There was no time to test the sights and alignment on a rifle range, so Selous ordered a cab to stand by, flung open his bedroom window, squeezed off five shots at a chimney stack, checked that the grouping was satisfactory with his binoculars, swiftly packed the rifle and skipped down to the cab, pausing only to remark that he had heard shots on his floor and that the manager had better look into it.

By 1914, Selous, now married, had retired to Surrey and busied himself with running his own natural history museum. At the outbreak of war, despite being 63, he was determined to serve in East Africa, where he felt his skills would be useful. He joined the Legion of Frontiersmen, a colourful outfit that included French Legionnaires, a Honduran general, Texan cowboys, Russian émigrés, some music hall acrobats and a lighthouse keeper.

In January 1917, scouting in the campaign against General von Lettow Vorbeck (see page 400), he was killed by a German sniper at Beho Beho on the Rufiji River (now part of Selous Game Reserve).

Arriving in Selous Game Reserve → *Colour map 1, B5. 9° S, 38° E.*

Getting there The most convenient way of getting to the reserve is certainly by air and there are airstrips at most of the camps; the flight takes about 35 minutes from Dar es Salaam. ➤➤ *For details, see Transport, page 366.*

The northern part of the reserve, which is where the camps are, is accessed by the **Matambwe** and **Mtemere** gates. If driving, take the Dar es Salaam–Kibiti–Mkongo road. The B2 road is tarmac as far as **Kibiti** (145 km south of Dar and the last place you will be able to get petrol), and then it is fairly rough dirt and a 4WD is necessary. It is then 30 km from Kibiti to Mkongo, where a west turning will take you on the final 75 km to Mtemere

Gate. In total this route is about 270 km from Dar and will take about six to seven hours. The other road you can take is the Tanzam Highway/A7 as far as Morogogo, from where the turn-off leads 140 km, via Matombo and Kisaki, to Matambwe Gate; again a 4WD is needed. This route is a total of 330 km from Dar and will take four to five hours.

Getting around You will have to bring plenty of fuel from Dar es Salaam, Morogoro or Kibiti for your whole stay in the reserve; there are no car repair facilities here, and drivers are advised to carry essential items, such as tools, spare tyre, tyre repair kit, shovel and drinking water. Because of its inaccessibility, most people go to the Selous on organized safaris from Dar, see page 72. However, it's also possible to arrange a road transfer directly with the camps.

Apart from seeing the Selous by road, other popular ways are on foot or by boat. Because the Selous is a game reserve, rather than a national park, its visitors are subject to

Selous Game Reserve north

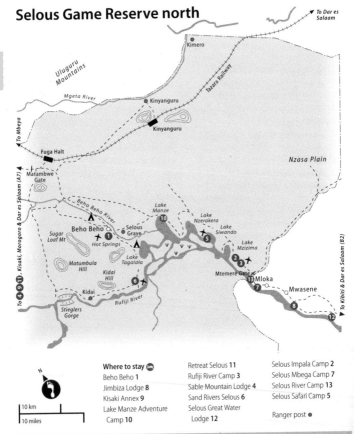

Where to stay 🏠
Beho Beho 1
Jimbiza Lodge 8
Kisaki Annex 9
Lake Manze Adventure
Camp 10

Retreat Selous 11
Rufiji River Camp 3
Sable Mountain Lodge 4
Sand Rivers Selous 6
Selous Great Water
Lodge 12

Selous Impala Camp 2
Selous Mbega Camp 7
Selous River Camp 13
Selous Safari Camp 5

Ranger post ●

10 km
10 miles

fewer restrictions and it is one of the few protected wildlife areas where you are allowed to walk; all camps can arrange walking safaris. You will normally set off early in order to avoid the worst of the midday sun and you must be accompanied by an armed ranger. Animal sightings tend to be rarer on walking safaris, as the animals frequently shy away from humans. However, it is very pleasant to be able to stretch your legs and get a different perspective of the country. Trekking safaris of several days are also a possibility, as is fly camping away from the main lodges. Some lodges arrange boat trips up the Rufiji River.

Park information Open 0630-1830, US$50, children (5-16) US$30, vehicle US$40. If you stay at a camp outside the reserve's boundaries, you don't have to pay the entry fee; however, at these camps there is normally a conservation fee of US$15-25 per person. You will also have to pay entry fees on game drives that enter the reserve.

Climate The best time to visit is July to October. The camps and lodges are closed at the peak of the wet season from Easter to June, when the rains render many of the roads impassable, but check as they have been known to stay open in drier years.

Background

The park is named after Captain Frederick Selous, a British explorer and hunter who wrote a book about the region and his travels, and was killed in action in January 1917 while scouting in the area (see box, page 361). His grave is at the foot of the Beho Beho Hills.

The game reserve has an interesting history. In the days of the slave trade the caravan routes passed through the park. It is said that the occasional mango groves that can be seen, grew from the mango stones discarded from the caravans on their way from the coast. In the early 20th century, during German colonial rule, some of this area was designated as game reserves but in those days big game hunting was the most significant activity. In 1910 Kaiser Wilhelm gave part of the reserve to his Kaiserin as an anniversary gift. Hence the nickname 'Shamba la Bibi', meaning 'The Woman's Field', for the section of Selous north of the Rufiji River. In 1922, the land area was increased and named after Frederick Selous. From then until 1975, when the current boundaries were delineated, the reserve's size increased steadily, so as to include major animal movement corridors (particularly those of elephants, who wander over vast distances during the course of their lives), and today it covers 55,000 sq km.

Wildlife

This vast, wonderfully diverse and well-watered habitat has the right ingredients to to sustain an unusually high number of animals of all shapes and sizes, as well as support an extraordinary array of different vegetation types. The statistics speak for themselves: the Selous has over 2100 species of plant, 350 species of bird (including heron, fish eagle, kingfisher, various waterfowl and birds of prey), 60,000 elephant, 108,000 buffalo and an estimated 1300 of the world's approximate 4000 remaining African wild dogs. Other animals you may see include lion, hippo, crocodile, black rhino, and just about every African antelope there is.

Visiting Selous Game Reserve

Rufiji River

Central to the park and, perhaps, its greatest attraction is the mighty Rufiji River (where most of the camps are located), home to one of the largest crocodile and hippo populations in Africa, and swarming with fish which, in turn, attract numerous birds. The river has formed several large lakes on its northern bank, navigable by boat and sheltered by beautiful palm forests. This river and its associated water system has the largest catchment area of any river in East Africa; it rises from the south and becomes the Rufiji where the Luwegu and Mbarangandu join. Other rivers join it and, further north, it swings east before it is forced through Stiegler's Gorge. At its delta, opposite Mafia Island, millions of tonnes of silt are deposited every year during the wet season, and the river swells to such an extent that it renders much of the park inaccessible. During the dry season it subsides and sand banks are revealed.

Stiegler's Gorge

Named after a German explorer who was killed here by an elephant in 1907, Stiegler's Gorge is in the north of the reserve at the junction of the Rufiji and Ruaha rivers. It is a 40-km, two-hour drive from Matambwe Gate. It is a bottleneck, as the water from this huge catchment area is forced through the narrow gorge. The gorge is about 7 km long, 100 m wide and deep. If you have a head for heights there is a cable car that spans it.

Beyond the gorge, the river widens again and splits to form a number of lakes – Tagalala, Manze, Nzerakera, Siwando and Mzizima. The swampy area is home to many animals that congregate here especially when water is scarce during the dry season, in particular elephant, buffalo and, of course, hippo, sometimes in large numbers.

Maji Moto

Other attractions in the park include the hot springs known simply as Maji Moto (hot water in Kiswahili). These are on the eastern slopes of Kipalala Hill and the water flows down into Lake Tagalala. You get to them by walking (with a ranger at all times) up the ravine. The water emits a strong smell of sulphur. The highest springs are the hottest, while further down they are sufficiently cool for you to be able to swim in them.

◉ Selous Game Reserve listings

For sleeping and eating price codes and other relevant information, see pages 22-26.

◉ Where to stay

Selous Game Reserve *p360, map p362*
$$$$ Beho Beho, in the reserve, perched on the lower slopes of Namikwera Hill overlooking Kipalala Hill; no direct bookings, email them for a list of their agents, www.behobeho. com. Panoramic views over the Rufiji River flood plain, with 8 a/c stone cottages, open-air showers and spacious verandas that have Zanzibari day beds. Lounge and dining area, billiards room and swimming pool. One of the first camps to open in the northern sector and still one of the most luxurious. Rates include full board and all activities – game drives and boat and walking safaris.

$$$$ The Retreat Selous, outside the reserve to the west, on the Great Ruaha River, a 30-min drive from the airstrip at Matambwe, reservations Dar, T0783-213 951, www.retreat-africa.com. The newest luxury camp in the Selous region (it opened in 2007), with 12 tented suites, either on a hilltop or on the riverbank, Arabian-style billowing fabrics, copper free-standing baths with a view, antique furniture and Persian rugs. Some have their own plunge pools. The main building has cool arches and roof decks, and is modelled on and built on the site of a First World War observation post. Dining tables are set up on sandbanks next to the river, swimming pool with thatched pool bar, walks, drives, canoeing and spa treatments on offer. However, it's located in a former hunting concession and game is scarcer than in other areas, although this will change in time.

$$$$ Rufiji River Camp, in the reserve, overlooking the Rufiji River, reservations Dar, T0784-237 422, www.rufijirivercamp.com. This, the oldest camp in the reserve, has 20 tents with bathrooms, electricity and mosquito nets, spaced out along the river in an attractive tract of woodland. Restaurant, bar, swimming pool and a choice of fishing, boat safaris, game drives or walking safaris. Run by **Foxes Safari Camps** and often visited with their camps in Ruaha and Katavi national parks.

$$$$ Sand Rivers Selous, in the reserve, overlooking the Rufiji River, operated by **Nomad Safaris**, www.nomad-tanzania.com; no direct bookings; email them for a list of their agents. The most luxurious and isolated of the lodges, with only 4 super-exclusive tented and thatched suites with their own vast patios, plunge pools, semi-open bathrooms, Rufiji River views, superb food and service, and the main building has its own swimming pool set in the rocks next to the river and comfortable lounge. Walking safaris, boat rides and fly camping can be arranged. Often included in a flying safari with their other camps in Ruhaha and Mahale Mountains national parks.

$$$$ Selous Impala Camp, in the reserve, on the banks of the Rufiji River, not far from Mtemere Gate, reservations Dar, T022-245 2005, www.adventurecamps.co.tz. A popular rustic camp with 8 fairly small but comfortable and nicely furnished en suite tents raised on wooden platforms, 2 of which are 'double' tents (next to each other) for families, less lavish than most and as such, considerably less expensive. Offers all the usual activities, as well as fishing and fly camping, and there's a relaxing pool that overlooks the river.

$$$$ Selous Safari Camp, in the reserve, in the lake area, reservations **Selous Safari Co**, Dar, T022-211 1728, www.selous.com. A luxury tented lodge overlooking Lake Nzerakera, which adjoins the Rufiji River, it

may remain closed longer than other camps because it's on the floodplain. 13 individual tents, divided between the north and south camps. Each has its own swimming pool, lounge and dining areas. The tents in the north camp can be booked in their entirety (either 4 or 6 tents sleeping 8-12 people) as an exclusive option. Impeccable and attentive service. Animals wander freely around the camp at night, including elephant and hippo. Boats and fishing equipment are available, and morning and evening game drives are included.

$$$$-$$$ Sable Mountain Lodge, just outside the reserve, 10 km along the road from Kisaki, a 20-min drive from the airstrip at Matambwe, reservations **A Tent With a View Safaris**, Dar, T022-211 0507, www.selouslodge.com. 8 comfortable stone cottages, the honeymoon cottage overlooks a small waterhole, plus 4 luxury tents and 1 double-storey villa suitable for families. Swimming pool over a natural spring and treehouse overlooking a waterhole. Useful for people who don't want inclusive game drives, as they will also take bookings on a simple full-board basis from US$145 per person. As well as game drives, walks and boat rides, village visits can be organized.

$$$ Jimbiza Lodge, outside of the reserve, 4 km from Mtemere Gate, reservations Dar, T022-261 8057, www.jimbizaselous.com. On the Rufiji River, a neat thatched and timber bush lodge with 15 rooms either in bandas or permanent tents, a couple are on elevated platforms in the trees and most have uninterrupted views of the river. Bathrooms have warm water, no-frills but comfortable and personable, good wholesome food, bar and small swimming pool. All game activities on offer.

$$$ Lake Manze Adventure Camp, in the reserve, in the lake area, reservations Dar, T022-260 1747, www.lakemanze.com. Set in a grove of tall doum trees on the banks of Lake Manze, this is owned by **Coastal Air** and is a simple camp with a natural feel. 12 spacious tents with verandas are set well apart from each other. The main section, with lounge, bar and dining area, is open under a huge thatch roof with sand floor. Nothing fancy but a good location next to an ancient elephant trail, and all game activities are on offer, including fishing from the lakeshore, which is a pleasant activity while watching out for animals.

$$$ Selous Great Water Lodge, outside the reserve, 9 km from Mtemere Gate to the east, T0784-361 951, www.selouslodge. co.tz. A small, friendly and rustic lodge on the Rufiji River, with 3 thatched family bandas sleeping up to 5, 1 double rondaval and a double treehouse on a 2-m elevated platform, outside dining area and bar, with a fire-pit and chill-out area on the sandy riverbank and hammocks strung out in the trees. Usual game drives, plus riverbank walks, village visits, boat rides and fishing can be arranged. Good value from US$95 per person full board.

$$$ Selous Mbega Camp, reservations, **Baobab Village Co Ltd**, Dar, T022-265 0250, www.selous-mbega-camp.com. This is 2 camps, and the option is to spend a night or 2 in each. The **Main Camp**, outside the reserve, just 500 m from the Mtemere Gate in the east, is set in a pretty tract of forest on the Rufiji River with 12 tents and a 2-bedroomed stone house. The restaurant and bar are built around a mahogany tree. **Kisaki Annex** is outside the reserve to the northwest, 4 km from Kisaki village, and is set on a hilltop with views of the Uluguru Mountains. It has 5 tents, restaurant and bar and a campsite (**$**). It's very basic, just simple beds and not much else, but both are in nice locations, with a good varied menu and excellent service. They are good value from US$100 per person, full board. Village visits and walks are also available.

$$$-$ Selous River Camp, outside the reserve but less than 500 m from Mtemere Gate, close to the **Selous Mbega Camp**, T0784-237 525, www.selousrivercamp.com.

Budget option but still in a great location in a lovely forested spot close to the Rufiji River, with a collection of either en suite thatched bandas with home-made (from tree branches) 4-poster beds that can sleep up to 4 or permanent tents under thatch, but these are A-frames as opposed to walk-in tents, with camp beds, palm mats and chairs and good shared stone bathrooms with hot water. There's also a grassy campsite with tap, firewood and ablution block, and meals can be provided for campers. Boat trips, village walks and game drives are arranged. Rates vary but start from US$65 per person full board, and camping is US$10 per person.

Camping

You can camp beside the bridge over the Beho Beho River a few kilometres northwest of **Beho Beho** itself, and at a site beside **Lake Tagalala**. There are no facilities apart from a pit latrine, so bring everything with you. Small fires made with dead wood are permissible and rainwater can be collected nearby. Camping fees must be paid in advance at one of the gates, US$30, children (5-16) US$5.

✪ Transport

Selous Game Reserve p360, map p362
Air

Most of the camps have their own airstrips, and those that don't can arrange transfers; you must specify which airstrip you want to go to, and you'll even be asked again once on the flight. **Coastal Air**, Dar, T022-284 2700, www.coastal.cc, has 3 flights a day on a circuit to/from **Dar** (35 mins), some of which also go to **Ruaha** and will touch down at **Udzungwa Mountains National Park** on request. Some continue on to/from Dar to **Zanzibar** without having to change planes. **Zan Air**, Zanzibar, T024-223 3670, www.zanair.com, has a daily flight from **Zanzibar** via **Dar** that arrives in the Selous at 1015 and departs again at 1100.

Mikumi National Park

Between the Uluguru Mountains and the Lumango range, Mikumi is the fourth largest park in Tanzania and has a wide variety of wildlife that is easy to spot and well used to game viewing; the park is popular with weekend visitors as it only takes about four hours on a good road to drive the 300 km from Dar es Salaam. It borders the Selous Game Reserve and Udzungwa Mountains National Park, and the three locations make a varied and pleasant safari circuit. Mikumi has a pretty, undulating landscape with good resident game, but it is not as spectacular as the other parks. ⤷ *For listings, see page 369.*

Arriving in Mikumi National Park → *Colour map 1, B5. 7° 26'S, 37° 0'E. Altitude: 549 m.*
Getting there From Morogoro the main Tanzam Highway/A7 road travels through cultivated land for about 100 km before reaching the boundary of the park; in the other direction, it's 200 km northeast of Iringa. The national park is on both sides of the road, so drive with care. The speed limit along this stretch is 50 kph and the road now has speed bumps – animals had been killed before by speeding vehicles. This is one of the easiest parks to visit without your own transport, as all the buses stop in the town of Mikumi, on the A7 road 6 km east of the park gate. Safaris can be arranged at the hotels in and around Mikumi (see Where to stay, page 369). There is also an airstrip near the park headquarters; flights from Dar es Salaam take 45 minutes.

Mikumi National Park

Where to stay 🛏
Mikumi Bush Camp **4**
Mikumi Wildlife Camp **1**
Genesis Motel **3**

Stanley's Kopje **2**
Tan Swiss Lodge **5**
Vuma Hills **6**

Waterholes ⊛

Park information Tanzania National Parks Authority (TANAPA), www.tanzaniaparks.com, 0630-1830, US$20, children (5-16) US$5, vehicle US$40.

Background
The park was gazetted in 1964 during the construction of the Morogoro–Iringa highway and is set in a horseshoe of the towering Uluguru mountain range, which rises to 2750 m and covers an area of 3230 sq km. It lies between the villages of Doma and Mikumi from which it takes its name. Mikumi is the Kiswahili name for the borassus palm found in the area.

Wildlife
The landscape is typically woodland and grassy plains, which are fed by the Mkata River flood plain, an area of lush vegetation that attracts a number of animals throughout the year. These include lion, eland, hartebeest, buffalo, wildebeest, giraffe, zebra, hippo and elephant. Up to 300 species of birds stop over on migratory routes over Tanzania, so birdlife is particularly abundant here, with many species present that are seen infrequently in the game parks of northern Tanzania. They include the violet turaco and the pale-billed hornbill, along with various species of storks, pelicans, herons, ibis, kestrels, kites and eagles. The Mikumi forest elephants are much smaller than their big game park counterparts and are mainly grazers, so they do not cause as much damage to the trees. It's not unusual to see them, and sometimes lion, from the main road, especially in the evening or at night. They seem quite accustomed to the traffic that rumbles past.

Visiting Mikumi National Park
From the park gate the road leads to the floodplain of the **Mkata River**, which is particularly important for the wildlife. To the north the floodplain remains swampy throughout the year, while in the south, water channels drain to the Mkata River. Here you will see, among other animals, elephant, buffalo and hippo. About 15 km northwest of the park gate there are **hippo pools** where there are almost always a number of hippos wallowing in the mud.

Other areas worth visiting are the **Choga Wale** area and **Mwanambogo** area – the latter can only be reached in the dry season. The track is to the east of the flood plain and heads north towards the Mwanambogo Dam. The **Kisingura circuit** is another popular drive, as is the **Kikoboga** area, where you are likely to see elephant, particularly in December and January.

The road that goes along the river is a good one to take for game viewing. It passes through a patch of woodland and some swampy areas before coming on to the grasslands of the Chamgore. **Chamgore** means 'place of the python' and has two waterholes that are always ideal for spotting game. **Hill Drive** leads up the foothills of the Uluguru Mountains from where you will get wonderful views all around. The vegetation is miombo woodland and the ebony tree grows here.

To get to the south part of the park take the track that branches off opposite the park entrance, which heads towards an area called Ikoya. Here you will see sausage trees, *Kigelia africana*, with their distinctive pods hanging down. This is also where you may see leopard.

◉ Mikumi National Park listings

For sleeping and eating price codes and other relevant information, see pages 22-26.

◉ Where to stay

Mikumi National Park *p367, map p367*
The small town of Mikumi has a number of cheap hotels and guesthouses.
$$$$ Stanley's Kopje, in the north of the park near the Mkata River, reservations **Foxes Safari Camps**, Dar, T0784-237 422, www.tanzaniasafaris.info. Luxury tented camp raised on wooden decks overlooking the Mkata River floodplain in a peaceful location in the north of the park. 8 large thatched tents with bathrooms and 2 double beds, scattered around a granite kopje with views in every direction. There's a central boma area for eating and a small swimming pool.
$$$$ Vuma Hills, in the Vuma Hills in the south of the park, **Foxes Safari Camps**, Dar, T0784-237 422, www.tanzaniasafaris.info. A classic safari camp with 16 luxury tents, bathrooms, private verandas and colonial decor. The dining area and bar overlook the swimming pool, and serve good wholesome food (produce comes from their nearby highland farm). Both these **Foxes Safari Camps**, are often visited on flying safaris with their other camps in Selous and Katavi.
$$$ Mikumi Wildlife Camp, about 300 m off the main road to the right, near the park headquarters, reservations Dar, T022-260 0352, www.mikumiwildlifecamp.com. 12 very comfortable stone bandas, some with 3 or 4 beds in 1 or 2 rooms – good value for families or groups. Bar and lounge under a huge fig tree, dining room in a rondavaal, small stone swimming pool, and there is an observation tower for game viewing. Rates are more at the weekend.
$$-$ Mikumi Bush Camp, off the A7, 3 km to the west of the park gate towards Mikumi and 2 km to the south of the road, reservations Dar, T022-550 0200, www.mikumibushcamp.com. Good budget option,

especially if you don't have a vehicle, set in a glade of acacia trees with 7 large pre-erected dome tents with camp beds and chairs, and a grassy campsite, flush loos and cold showers. US$50 per person, camping US$15per person. Cooked breakfast is included in rates, and sandwiches for lunch and a set meal for supper are available. You can organize a safari vehicle and driver here for US$400 per day for up to 5 people, which includes the car and driver's entry fees but not your own, or they can organize overnight safaris from Dar or longer safaris which include the Udzungwa Mountains National Park.
$$-$ Genesis Motel, Mikumi Village on the Iringa side, T023-262 0466. A simple, friendly roadside motel with 30 rooms in bandas, each with a double and single bed and hot water; breakfast is included. There's a campsite (US$5 per person), with basic toilets and cold showers. Restaurant with reasonable menu of local and Western dishes, nice bar with satellite TV, secure parking. Snake park attached.
$$-$ Tan-Swiss Lodge, Mikumi Village on the Dar side, T0755-191 827, www.tan-swiss.com. Well-run brightly painted lodge with double, triple and family rooms in chalets, with a/c and mosquito nets, plus 2-bedroom bungalows with extra satellite TV, and a campsite, all set back from the main road. Doubles from US$55, camping US$5 per person. Good restaurant and bar serving continental, Indian and Chinese dishes with garden tables and kids' playground, worth stopping at, even if you're just passing. Can organize very well-priced safaris into the park for up to 5 people from US$140 per vehicle for half a day, plus park entry fees, and can provide packed lunches to take with you. Also available are trips to Udzungwa Mountains National Park.

Camping
National Park Campsite, about 4 km into the park from the main gate. Water and firewood usually available, very basic and expensive at US$30, children (5-16) US$5.

Udzungwa Mountains National Park

The Udzungwa Mountains rise up from the western edge of the Selous Game Reserve. Botanical diversity is exceptional, and the park is host to a large number of endangered bird species as well as forest antelope and monkeys. This is a forest area and covers approximately 1990 sq km lying between 250 and 2576 m (on the highest peak, Luhomero). Views from the peaks of the mountains, towards the Selous Game Reserve and the distant Indian Ocean coast, are incredible and well worth the effort. To the south lies the green Kilombero Valley, with the jagged slopes of the Mbarika Mountains clearly visible rising out of the lowlands 100 km away. There are no roads or tracks through the park but guided walks are available; it's a lovely place to walk, and hikers will have the park to themselves. Paths lead through sunshine-dappled glades surrounded by trees rising to 30 m, their buttresses covered with mosses, lichens and ferns. ▶▶ *For listings, see pages 371-372.*

Arriving in Udzungwa Mountains National Park → *Colour map 1, B5. 7° 50'S, 37°E.*

Getting there The park is about six hours' drive from Dar es Salaam and 65 km from the Mikumi National Park. To reach the park headquarters, turn south off the main Tanzam Highway (A7) at Mikumi on to the B127, and follow the signs to Ifakara. The tarmac road continues 34 km to Kilombero and crosses the Ruaha River to Kidatu. From here the road is good gravel and descends 700 m through a gorge to the Kilombero River floodplain and the **Ilovo Kilombero Sugar Estate** (where the airstrip is). After another 24 km you will reach **Mang'ula**; the signposted turning for the park headquarters and **Msosa Gate** (1 km) is on the right. Buses to Ifakara can drop off here, and you can also arrange tours from the hotels and lodges at Mikumi (see Where to stay, page 369). By air, **Coastal Air** will fly to the airstrip at Kilombero near Mang'ula (but only on request) on its circuit of the Southern Circuit parks. ▶▶ *For further details, see Transport, page 372.*

Park information Tanzania National Parks Authority (TANAPA), T023-262 0224, www. tanzaniaparks.com, www.udzungwa.org, 0630-1830, US$20, children (5-16) US$5, a guide/ranger costs US$10 per group of up to eight.

Wildlife

The Udzungwa Mountains are part of the Eastern Arc Range of mountains, which stretch from southern Kenya to southern Tanzania. The Eastern Arc are small and fragmented mountains, each block having a patchwork of dense tropical forests with high rainfall. River catchments protected within the park boundary are important for hydroelectricity production, local communities' water supply and agriculture. The national park protects more than 2500 plant species, of which 160 are used locally as medicinal plants. Over 300 animal species have been recorded, including 18 vertebrate species found only in the Eastern Arc Mountains. The recently discovered Sanje mangabey and the Iringa red colobus are thought to be endemic to the region; other primates include the black and white colobus, blue and vervet monkey and yellow baboon. There are also numerous forest antelope, such as blue duiker and bushbuck, and, although less frequently seen, elephant, buffalo, lion and leopard are present. More than 250 species of bird are found here, and endemics are the rufous-winged sunbird and Udzungwa partridge.

Hiking

A variety of trails are available to suit different abilities, including short half-day trails, such as the popular walk to **Sanje Waterfall**, which plunges 170 m through a misty spray into the forested valley below. There are also mountain climbing trails, with overnight camping, and long-range wilderness trails taking several days. The park can be visited at any time of year, though the paths can be slippery in the wet. The dry season is June to October before the short rains, but be prepared for rain at any time.

⊙ Udzungwa Mountains National Park listings

For sleeping and eating price codes and other relevant information, see pages 22-26.

⊙ Where to stay

Udzungwa Mountains National Park
p370
$$$-$ Udzungwa Forest Tented Camp (Hondo Hondo), bordering the park in the Kilombero Valley, just before the turning for the park HQ and Msosa Gate, operated by **Wild Things Safaris**, reservations Dar, T0784-479 427, www.udzungwaforestcamp.com. An excellent new set-up and the perfect place to explore the park. Accommodation is in 6 secluded tents under thatch, with furnishings made from natural local materials, outdoor bathrooms and verandas (U$120 per person full board). Separately on another part of the site are 5 simple thatched huts (US$60 per person full board or US$18 bed only), and a beautiful grassy campsite with hot showers (US$6 per person or you can hire a tent with bedding for US$12). Great forest views, with monkeys easily spotted in the trees, over 80 species of bird have been seen from the camp and they have their own nature trail through the forest and surrounding farmland. There's also a bar and restaurant, good wholesome food and excellent cooked breakfasts, including pancakes, hash browns and bacon. Can organize transfers to the start of the hiking trails and rents out mountain bikes, plus 1- to 3-day fully catered camping trips into the park for the longer hiking trails with porters and all equipment (from US$130 for an overnight trip including park fees), and canoeing on the Kilombero River near Ifakara, which is home to hippo. Can pick up from the airstrip, train or from Mikumi.
$ Udzungwa Mountains Views Hotel, 500 m south of the turning to the park HQ and Msosa Gate and just before Mang'ula, T023-262 0260. Owned by the **Genesis Motel** in Mikumi and a similar set-up, with budget rooms in bandas in a pleasant garden surrounded by the forest, and there's a campsite (US$5 per person) with basic toilets and cold showers. Restaurant and

Hondo Hondo
udzungwa forest tented camp
Beautiful tented rooms with open air bathrooms and views up to the mountains
One of the most Responsible and Sustainble projects in Tanzania
Hiking in the stunning pristine forests
Swimming in crystal clear plunge pools
Primate and bird watching from the bar
Cycling and village tours
www.udzungwaforestcamp.com

bar for basic meals, and can organize local guides for hiking.

Camping
There are 3 designated campsites just inside the park and within 1-3 km of the park HQ. They are very pretty, and spaces have been cleared next to streams, but other than long-drop toilets, there are no facilities and they are expensive at US$30, children (5-16) US$5. Bring everything with you.

☉ Transport

Udzungwa Mountains National Park
p370
The tiny settlement of **Mang'ula** on the Mikumi–Ifakara road (B127) is the unexpected transport hub for the park, and is only just over 1 km from the park HQ and Msosa Gate.

Air
The airstrip is at the **Ilovo Kilombero Sugar Estate** near Kidatu, which is 24 km or about a 20-min drive north of Mang'ula on the main road towards Mikumi. **Coastal Air**, Dar, T022-284 2700, www.coastal.cc, has a daily flight (but only on request and with a minimum of 2 people) on its circuit from **Dar** and the Southern Circuit parks, including **Selous** and **Ruaha**. You'll be able to hire a local car for a lift from the airstrip or, if you're staying at **Udzungwa Forest Tented Camp (Hondo Hondo)**, they'll pick you up.

Bus
Fairly regular buses and *dala-dalas* run between **Mikumi** and **Ifakara** and will drop off in **Mang'ula**. There is the odd direct bus between **Dar** and Ifakara, but there's a much better choice of buses between Dar and Mikumi on the main A7 road.

Iringa and around

From Mikumi the road steadily climbs upwards to the chilly highlands of Iringa, which is set on a plateau 502 km southwest of Dar es Salaam and 390 km northeast of Mbeya on the Tanzam Highway (A7). It commands a panoramic view over the surrounding boulder-strewn countryside and, on arrival, you will notice a distinct drop in temperature and vendors on the roadside arranging rows of welly-boots and jackets to sell. Be sure to take warm clothes. Maize, vegetables, fruits and tobacco are grown in the fertile soil around here and, consequently, the welcoming town has an excellent market, where you can barter for almost every vegetable under the sun. About 120 km west of Iringa, Ruaha National Park is a huge undeveloped wilderness, whose ecology is more like that of southern Africa. ➤ *For listings, see pages 377-380.*

Arriving in Iringa ➔ *Colour map 1, B4. 7° 48'S, 35° 43'E. Phone code: 026. Population: 112,000. Altitude: 1635 m.*

Getting there The main bus stand is in town on Uhuru Avenue, but, if travelling on a bus which is not terminating in Iringa, you may find yourself getting off at the bus stand on the main road at the bottom of the hill, 2 km outside Iringa town. There are taxis and regular *dala-dalas* into town.

Places in Iringa

During German occupation, the German military constructed the town as a fortified defence against marauding Hehe tribal warriors intent on driving them out of the region. **Gangilonga Rock**, a site just outside the town, is a legendary spot where the Hehe chief at that time, Chief Mkwawa, met with his people and decided how to fight the Germans in an uprising of 1894. He was finally defeated in 1898 but, refusing to be captured by the Germans, he committed suicide.

The pleasant albeit slightly chilly climate attracted settlers, and there is an impressive legacy of German colonial architecture, including the old **Boma**, the **Town Hall**, the

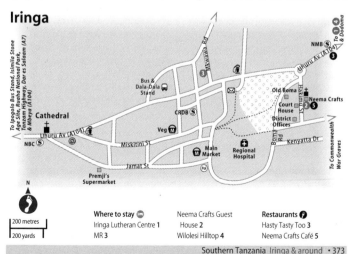

Iringa

Where to stay
Iringa Lutheran Centre 1
MR 3
Neema Crafts Guest House 2
Wilolesi Hilltop 4

Restaurants
Hasty Tasty Too 3
Neema Crafts Café 5

Neema Crafts

Neema is the Kiswahili word for 'grace', and Neema Crafts (Hakimu St, opposite the District Commissioner's Office and just to the right of the clocktower roundabout, T0786-431 274, www.neemacrafts.com) is a unique set-up in Iringa and a flagship enterprise in Tanzania that is well worth visiting and supporting. It started life in 2003 as a project of the Anglican Diocese of Ruaha in Iringa with three young deaf men being taught in one room, a £400 grant from a UK charity and a bag of elephant dung (which they were being taught how to make into handmade paper). At the time of the centre's establishment, the 2002 national census had recorded that some 10% of Tanzania's population were classified as having severe disabilities. The Iringa region had one of the highest rates in the country, reaching 15% in some districts and was also one of only a few regions with no projects in existence to cater for the needs of disabled people. Since then the project has grown in leaps and bounds, and now employs more than 125 disabled people from Iringa and the surrounding area, who have been trained in a wide variety of crafts and skills. All participants have been lifted out of extreme poverty and reliance on street begging to achieve a degree of self-sufficiency and a greatly improved level of self-esteem. Today the centre has several workshops, a gift shop, café, internet café and a newly opened guesthouse (see Where to stay, page 378). The running costs have been covered almost entirely by revenue from sales of the goods sold, plus donations from visitors and supporters.

You can browse in the shop (Mon-Sat 0900-1830), where the staff (all disabled) will happily show you around the workshops and tell you about the centre and the other numerous projects it runs in the region. The excellent selection of crafts include items created from paper (handmade from elephant-dung, dried maize leaves or recycled paper), plus beaded jewellery made from recycled glass; home-made candles; woven items, such as *kikoys* and scarves, using locally grown cotton; some lovely ceramics using clay from the hills around Iringa and a kiln that is powered by recycled engine oil; and on-site tailors who make clothes and bags. The centre now supplies many upmarket safari lodges in Tanzania with decor items. The excellent café (see Restaurants, page 380) is entirely run by deaf people, except for the member of staff manning the till, who is physically disabled. The café purposely challenges visitors to communicate in a different way with their waiter or waitress when placing their order, and the unique menus have printed diagrams on how to sign in Kiswahili. The café has Wi-Fi, a second-hand book exchange, a balcony with views across town, and the internet café is next door.

Hospital and **Post Office**. Iringa was also the site of several battles during the First and Second World Wars, and **Commonwealth War Graves** are just outside town.

Isimila Stone Age Site
ⓘ *About 20 km from town towards Mbeya, and then 2 km to the south of the main road. Buses going towards Mbeya can drop you on the main road or you can take a taxi from Iringa. Entry US$3.*

This is considered to be one of the finest stone age sites in East Africa. Once a shallow lake, now dried up, the site was discovered in 1951 by a South African, D Maclennan, and excavated in 1957-1958 by Dr Clark Howell and G Cole, sponsored by the University of Chicago. Soil erosion in a *korongo* (a watercourse, which is dry for most of the year) exposed a great number of Acheulian stone tools, including pear-shaped axes, cleavers and spherical stones, which had been artificially shaped. They are believed to date from 60,000 years ago. Also among the finds were fossilized animal bones, including a now extinct form of hippopotamus (*H Gorgops*), whose eyes protruded like periscopes, and a short-necked giraffe (*Sivatherium*). It is believed that early hominoids used this area as both a watering place and a place to hunt the animals that came to drink there. A small museum was built on the site in 1969 and displays some of the tools, fossils and bones found during excavations.

Iringa to Makambako

South of Iringa, the Tanzam Highway continues on its way the 390 km to Mbeya. Note that, from Iringa, the A7 becomes the A104 (though it's one continuous road); the latter has crossed the interior of Tanzania from Arusha via Dodoma and Iringa to join the A7. From Iringa the road cuts through mixed woodland and savannah as well as cultivated land. Towards the end of the rainy season the scenery looks almost Mediterranean, with its cultivated rolling hillsides flecked with the yellow of sunflower crops and wild flowers. Gradually it opens up to savannah, and various side roads will lead you off the main road into the Usangu Plains. Roughly midway between Iringa and Mbeya is the junction town of Makambako, which developed because of its station on the TAZARA Railway and because it is a stop for road traffic passing through from Zambia. Heading south from here on the B4 through fertile, rolling hills leads down to the eastern side of Lake Nyasa (Malawi) and Mbamba Bay, via the towns of Njombe and Songea (see box, page 386).

Ruaha National Park → *For listings, see pages 377-380.*

Ruaha National Park is one of the most remote parks in Tanzania, and visitor numbers reflect that: 2500 per annum to Ruaha, compared to 250,000 to the Serengeti. Yet it is Tanzania's second largest national park, with vast concentrations of buffalo, elephant, gazelle, and over 400 bird species. Elephants are found here in some of the highest concentrations in the country, travelling in matriarch-led herds through ancient grazing lands to seasonal sources of water. The **Ruaha River** is the main feature of the park and meanders through its borders. Most of the national park is on the top of a 900-m plateau, whose ripples of hills, valleys and plains make the game-viewing topography uniquely beautiful. Small mountains run along the southwest borders of the park, and their tree-covered slopes are visible in the distance. During the rainy seasons, dry river beds swell with the biannual deluge and, within days, a thin coating of green covers all the land in sight.

Arriving in Ruaha National Park

Getting there Ruaha is 470 km from Dar es Salaam and 120 km from Iringa. From Iringa and the Tanzam Highway the road passes through densely populated countryside until the development gradually thins out and the vegetation becomes miombo woodland. The road is well maintained dirt and the journey should take around two hours, but a 4WD is recommended in the wet and for the tracks within the park. After about 60 km from Iringa, the turning off to the right to the park is indicated. It is another 50 km down this road to the park boundary and from there about 10 km to Ibuguziwa Gate, where you pay the park entrance fees and cross the Ruaha River. About 1 km beyond the river there is a junction. To the right the track goes to **Msembe** and the park headquarters, and to the left to **Ruaha**

River Lodge. Night driving is not permitted, so arrive at the gate in plenty of time to reach your camp. There is an airstrip at the park headquarters for light aircraft, and there are flights with **Coastal Air** on their circuit of the Southern Circuit parks from Dar. ▸▸ *For details, see Transport, page 380.*

Park information Tanzania National Parks Authority (TANAPA), www.tanzaniaparks. com, 0630-1830, US$20, children (5-16) US$5, vehicle US$40.

Climate Visiting is possible during both the dry 'yellow' season and the wet 'green' season, even in January when the rain is heaviest, because the rains are short and most of the roads are all-weather. However, in the wet season the grass is long and game viewing is almost impossible, so it's best to visit from July to December.

Background
Ruaha National Park was classified a national park in 1964. The area was part of Sabia River Game Reserve, established by the German colonial government in 1911 and later renamed the Rungwa Game Reserve. It covers an area of 12,950 sq km, which is the size of Belgium, and ranges from 750 m to 1900 m above sea level. The park gets its name from the river that forms part of its boundary. The name *Ruaha* is from the word *Luvaha*, which means

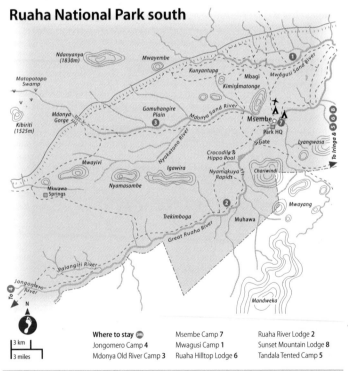

Ruaha National Park south

Where to stay 🛏
Jongomero Camp **4**
Mdonya Old River Camp **3**
Msembe Camp **7**
Mwagusi Camp **1**
Ruaha Hilltop Lodge **6**
Ruaha River Lodge **2**
Sunset Mountain Lodge **8**
Tandala Tented Camp **5**

3 km
3 miles

'great' in the Hehe language. The river is vital to the economy of the country, for it supplies much of Tanzania with electricity through hydroelectric power from the dam at Kidatu. Further downstream, the Ruaha joins the Ulanga to form the Rufiji River.

Wildlife

There is a wide variety of wildlife in this park, largely due to the different vegetation types found here. There are four major vegetation zones: the river valleys, the open grassland, the miombo woodland, and undulating countryside where baobabs dominate. Animals include elephant, lion, zebra, giraffe, African wild dogs, ostrich, greater and lesser kudu, impala and many other antelope and, in the river, hippo and crocodile. There are over 480 recorded species of bird in the park. The rare Eleonora's falcon may be sighted here, as well as the pale-billed hornbill and violet-crested turaco. Pel's fishing owls are also seen, as well as several species of bat. Unfortunately, poaching here was a serious problem in the 1970s and 1980s, and the animal population suffered enormously, in particular rhinos, which were once found here, but are now extinct in the park. The elephant population also plummeted during the 1980s, but has recovered well, and there are now thought to be about 12,000 elephant migrating though the greater Ruaha River ecosystem.

Visiting Ruaha National Park

Around Msembe is bush country, with acacia and baobab trees, and elephants are often found here. Along the river, particularly during the dry season, many animals congregate, and you may see confrontations between lion and buffalo. You can expect to see elephant, giraffe, baboon, warthog, buffalo, zebra, all sorts of antelope and, if you are lucky, leopard and cheetah. In the river itself are both hippo and crocodile.

The **Mwagusi Sand River** joins the Ruaha about 10 km from Msembe. If you cross this river and follow the track you will get to **Mwayembe Hill** and the escarpment where there is a salt lick often frequented by elephant and buffalo.

The **Mdonya Sand River** joins the Ruaha between the ferry and the park headquarters. From the ferry a drive southwest will take you past the **Nyamakuyu Rapids** and Trekimboga to where the Jongomero joins the Ruaha, about 40 km upriver. This is a good place to see hippo and crocodile. Roan and sable antelopes, which are difficult to see elsewhere, can also been seen here.

◉ Iringa and around listings

For sleeping and eating price codes and other relevant information, see pages 22-26.

◉ Where to stay

Iringa and around *p373, map p373*
$$-$ Wilolesi Hilltop Hotel, 1 km northeast of the roundabout along the Dodoma (A104) Rd, take a signposted left turn up into the Wilolesi Hills, T026-270 0007, www.wilolesihilltophotel.com. A modern hotel in a suburb, set in a variety of buildings that climb up a granite hillside with good views across town. 26 rooms with nets, fans, hot water and balconies, the smallest doubles start from US$35, suites with extra lounge from US$70. Restaurant and bar are arranged in neat thatched huts in the pleasant gardens.
$ Iringa Lutheran Centre, Kuwawa Rd, T026-270 0722, www.iringalutherancentre.com. A simple church-run place with single, double and triple rooms from US$20 per person, freshly painted, spotlessly clean, and newish bathrooms with hot water, an adequate cold breakfast is included and supper is available but must be pre-ordered.

A little bit out of town to the east, about a 10-min walk from the bus stand.

$ MR Hotel, Mkwawa Rd, near bus station, T026-270 2006, www.mrhotel.co.tz. A 4-storey block, the rooms are big and have hot showers and satellite TV, but are old fashioned and a little worn around the edges. Reasonable restaurant, which, unusually, offers some vegetarian dishes and, usefully for drivers with an early start, they can organize breakfast from 0530. Transport to Ruaha National Park can be arranged.

$ Neema Crafts Guest House, at Neema Crafts (see box, page 374), Hakimu St, T0786-431 274, www.neemacrafts.com. Newly opened in 2011, there are 10 large, cheery guest rooms, some for families, on the top floor of the centre above the workshops, with bathrooms and hot water, home-made furniture, mosquito nets, Wi-Fi (or there's an internet café next door) and good views over town; US$30 for a double with breakfast. You can eat at the restaurant, but, as it's church-affiliated, there's no booze; there are bars nearby.

$ Riverside Campsite, at an attractive site on the Little Ruaha River, 12 km northeast of Iringa, 1.5 km off the road to Dar (the Tanzam Highway), T0787-111 663, www. riversidecampsite-tanzania.com. A friendly and rustic place, with 12 simple chalets and tented bandas (from US$12) in a lovely forested spot near the river, some are en suite and 1 is a family banda with self-catering facilities. There's also a grassy campsite (US$5 per person), as well as hot showers, a bar, a barbecue area under a large tree, and all meals are available but they need a bit of notice. Horse riding can be arranged at the nearby farm, mountain bikes for hire, village tours and refreshing swimming in the river. Also has a 4WD and can arrange safaris to Ruaha National Park. Buses and *dala-dalas* will drop off on the main road.

Iringa to Makambako *p375*
$$$ Highland Fishing Lodge, Mufindi, go past **Kisolanza Farm** and turn off at

Mafinga, just past a Total petrol station 80 km southwest of Iringa; head towards Sawala along this unsurfaced road for 30 km until a signposted turning to the left; follow signs for a further 11 km, reservations **Foxes Safari Camps**, Dar, T0784-237 422, www. tanzaniasafaris.info. Above the Great Rift Valley, south of Iringa, in the scenic southern highlands and set among the tea plantations are 9 well-appointed log cabins that command fine views across the valley and have bathrooms and private verandas. There is a TV room with pool table, living room with large log fires and dining room serving meals cooked using fresh produce from the farm. Full board, and activities include mountain biking, horse riding, birdwatching, walking, canoeing and swimming in dammed pools. Trout fishing available at extra cost (this is thought to be the only place where naturally bred rainbow trout are found in Tanzania). They can pick you up from the main road at Mafinga or Iringa.

$$$-$ The Old Farm House, Kisolanza Farm, 50 km southwest of Iringa and 20 km before Mafinga, adjacent to the Dar–Mbeya Rd; buses will drop off at the gate, T0754-306 144, www.kisolanza.com. Charming old house and the home of the Ghaui family for over 70 years, with 2 thatched farm guest cottages with fireplaces set in their own flowering gardens (rates for these are full board and they can accommodate families). About 1 km away there's a campsite with another 4 smaller en suite cottages and 4 chalets that share showers and WC with campers, and there's also a stone-built BBQ and plenty of shade. At another location on the farm is a separate campsite for overlanders (many overland trucks stop here on their way through southern Tanzania), which also has a bar. The restaurant and main bar for all is at the main house. Pleasant climate at an altitude of over 1600 m, large freshwater dam offers excellent swimming and fishing, and fresh food, including bread, meat and eggs, is available to buy.

Ruaha National Park *p375, map p376*

$$$$ Jongomero Camp, in the remote southwestern sector of Ruaha, reservations Selous Safari Co, Dar T022-211 1728, www. selous.com/jongomero-camp. A luxury tented lodge set under shady acacia trees on the banks of the Jongomero Sand River, with 8 large and well-appointed en suite tents under enormous thatched roofs, with spacious private verandas, comfortable dining and living areas, natural rock pool for swimming, excellent food and good service, airstrip for direct access, full board rates and game drives included, and walking safaris can also be organized.

$$$$ Mdonya Old River Camp, near Mdonya Falls, a 2-hr drive from the airstrip, reservations Dar, T022-260 1747, www.mdonya.com. A rustic tented camp with 12 tents, with verandas, open-air showers and toilets in reed walls, 1 is a 'double' family tent, centred around a large lounge/dining/bar tent overlooking a sand river that is a natural wildlife corridor. All game drives and meals included. Additional walking safaris to the Mdonya Falls with a bush breakfast can be organized.

$$$$ Mwagusi Camp, a 30-min drive from the airstrip, reservations **Wings Over the Wild Ltd**, in the UK, T+44-(0)1822-615 721, www.mwagusicamp.com. Stylish, luxurious, and without doubt the best safari camp in the park, overlooking the Mwagusi Sands River, which does not dry up and so attracts all kinds of wildlife throughout the year. It has 10 luxury thatched tented rooms, each with verandas overlooking the river, with hammocks and sunken seating area, superb food and fine wines, and expert safari guides for drives and walks.

$$$$ Ruaha River Lodge, 18 km south of Msembe, reservations through **Foxes Safari Camps**, Dar, T0784-237 422, www. tanzaniasafaris.info. This, the oldest lodge in the park, is in a wonderful setting and has 20 comfortable stone bandas with verandas, some have river frontage, and the main thatched lodge is an unusual structure built on and around a kopje overlooking the Ruaha River. Several decks with sweeping views lead off from the comfortable lounges, dining room and bar.

$$$$ Tandala Tented Camp, outside the park, 13 km before the park gate, T026-270 3425, www.tandalatentedcamp.com. Not as luxurious or as expensive as the other places but in a nice setting among baobab trees, with 10 comfortable tents built on elevated platforms, bathrooms in thatch and stone, solar power, leather sofas in the lounge area, nice bar with pool table crafted out of old railway sleepers. The food is good and there's a lovely swimming pool surrounded by a wooden deck. They offer game drives into the park and, as it's outside the boundary, they can also do night drives around the camp. Can pick up from Iringa.

$$$ Ruaha Hilltop Lodge, outside park, 20 km before the park gate, T026-270 1806, www.ruahahilltoplodge.com. A rustic, well-run safari lodge and, as the name suggests, built on a hill overlooking miombo woodland and with views into Ruaha: a lovely spot for sunsets. Accommodation is in 12 simply furnished but comfortable en suite cottages, each with its own balcony and linked by stone paths to the main thatched building, which has the restaurant, bar and a curio shop. This is one of the cheapest options around Ruaha, from US$160 a double full board, and they can organize game drives into the park, as well as walks, village tours and transport from Iringa.

$$$ Sunset Mountain Lodge, outside park, 16 km before the park gate, reservations Dar, T022-245 1024, www.ruahaventure.com. A friendly option on the slope of the Idelemle Mountain, with broad views across the surrounding bush and, again, a fine vantage point for watching the sunset. There are 11 en suite thatched cottages, with mosquito nets, basic furnishings and hot water, some have 3 beds, as well as a bar and restaurant with pool table and satellite TV. Good meals and packed lunches are provided, and game drives to the park and walks to a local Masai village can be arranged. Low season rates start from US$60 per person full board, which is excellent value.

Camping

Msembe Camp, at the park HQ. In a good area for game and not far from the river, but basically part of the staff village (and next to the staff school), with 11 rather ugly and hot corrugated-tin rondavaals with bedding and mosquito nets and a campsite with cold showers and pit latrines. At US$40 for the huts and US$30, children (5-16) US$5, for camping, there are much better options.

🍴 Restaurants

Iringa and around *p373, map p373*
The hotels are the best bet for an evening meal, but there are a couple of good cafés that are worth coming into town for, even if you're just driving past Iringa. There are plenty of cheap places around the market for local food.
$ Hasty Tasty Too, Uhuru Av, near the clock tower roundabout. Mon-Sat 0700-2000, Sun 0800-1400. Indian-run café with outdoor tables serving a good variety of meals and snacks, including burgers, cakes, coffees, milkshakes and toasted sandwiches. Good place to come for breakfast – try the cheese omelette. Popular with expats.
$ Neema Crafts Café, Hakimu St, T0786-431 274, www.neemacrafts.com. Mon-Sat 0900-1830. Part of the Neema Crafts community initiative employing deaf and disabled people (see box, page 374), this is a great place to eat. It serves Italian paninis, salads, home-made cakes and ice cream, and good cappuccinos and lattes made with Tanzanian coffee, and there's a book exchange and Wi-Fi. By the time you read this it may also be open in the evening to serve the new guesthouse (see above).

🛍 Shopping

Iringa and around *p373, map p373*
The **market** offers a variety of fresh foods and a number of grocery shops around the

side of the market sell packaged European foods. Try **Premji's Supermarket**, on Jamat St. The **Iringa Service Station**, on the Tanzam Highway/A7 at the turn-off to town, sells dairy items, such as fresh milk, yoghurt and cheese, as well as fresh bread from **Kisolanza Farm** (see Where to stay, page 378).

🚌 Transport

Iringa and around *p373, map p373*
Air
There's an airstrip off the A104 to the north of town. **Auricair**, Dar, T022-212 6043, www.auricair.com, is a charter airline that runs a daily flight, if there is the demand, between **Dar** and Iringa and **Mbeya**. It leaves Dar at 0750, arrives at Iringa at 0915, Mbeya 0925, departs again at 1215, Iringa 1225 and gets back to Dar at 1400.

Bus
Buses leave from the main bus stand in the centre of town, where the bus kiosks are. The through buses between Dar and Mbeya don't come into town but stop at the Ipogolo bus stand on the Tanzam Highway, from where you can get taxis and *dala-dalas* 2 km into town. There are numerous buses to/from **Dar** (7 hrs, US$7) and **Mbeya** (5 hrs, US$9), as well as the other towns on the Tanzam Highway and **Dodoma** (10 hrs, US$12).

Ruaha National Park *p375, map p376*
Air
Coastal Air, Dar, T022-284 2700, www.coastal.cc, has 3 daily flight to/from **Dar** and **Zanzibar** on its circuit with the **Selous**.

ℹ Directory

Iringa and around *p373, map p373*
Medical services Iringa Regional Hospital, in the centre of town to the east of the market, T026-702 264.

Mbeya and around

From Makambako, the Tanzam Highway climbs up and down 175 km to Mbeya, the major agricultural capital in the country's southwest region. The Mbeya mountain range lies to the north and the Poroto mountain range lies to the southeast. Large coffee and tea plantations, banana farms and fields of cocoa are all grown around the region and come to Mbeya for packaging and transport. Mbeya's location also makes it an ideal transit point for travel by road and rail between Tanzania and neighbouring Zambia and Malawi. Other towns in the Mbeya region worth heading for are Tukuyu, on the road to the border with Malawi, which offers good trekking in the surrounding hills, and Matema, on the shores of Lake Nyasa (Malawi), a remote and traditional settlement with spectacular lakeside scenery. ▸▸ *For listings, see pages 388-393.*

Mbeya ➔ *Colour map 1, C3. 8° 54'S, 33° 29'E. Phone code: 025. Population: 280,000. Altitude: 1737 m.*
The town of Mbeya, 830 km from Dar es Salaam, was founded in the late 1920s when the gold mines at Lupa became active (they continued to be productive until they closed in

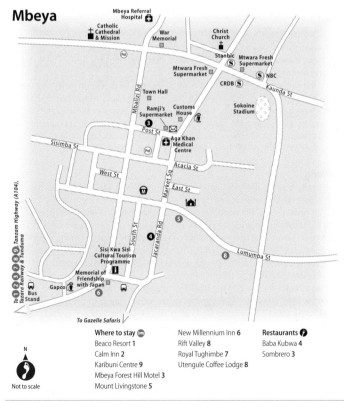

Where to stay
Beaco Resort **1**
Calm Inn **2**
Karibuni Centre **9**
Mbeya Forest Hill Motel **3**
Mount Livingstone **5**

New Millennium Inn **6**
Rift Valley **8**
Royal Tughimbe **7**
Utengule Coffee Lodge **8**

Restaurants
Baba Kubwa **4**
Sombrero **3**

1956). It also grew as a strategic stop-off for both the Tanzam Highway and the TAZARA railway, and attracted many farmers and entrepreneurs during both the German and British occupations. Today, being only 132 km from the Zambian border at Tunduma (see box, page 383) and the last main station on the TAZARA railway line, it is a popular overnight stop and important trading centre and has developed into a bustling, if a little run-down, town. Its setting in the southern highlands, surrounded by small-scale farms that make the most of the good climate, is very attractive. It's a major producer of bananas, potatoes and rice, and much of the maize grown in the region is transported from here to other parts of Tanzania.

Excursions
Although there is little of interest in Mbeya itself, it is an excellent point from which to make excursions into the outstandingly beautiful surrounding countryside of the southern highlands. There are endless options, particularly for hikers and cyclists. Tourism is still a micro industry in this region which may explain the laid-back and unobtrusive approach of the available tour guides. ▶▶ *To organize a guide, see What to do, page 391.*

Between Mbeya and Lake Rukwa is the small town of **Galula**, at the northern end of the Songwe River Valley. Galula has an imposing Catholic church built by the French White Fathers. Nearby are lake deposits indicative of a previously much larger lake, and evidence of Iron Age and Late Stone Age sites have been found on the river terraces.

At **Mapogoro**, northeast of the Lupa Goldfields, close to the village of Njelenje, volcanic rock shelters were identified in 1990 by researchers from the University of Alberta. Many artefacts of the Late Stone Age were found.

The **Mbozi Meteorite** is a 12-tonne mass, believed to be the eighth largest in the world and to have landed over 1000 years ago. The meteor is roughly rectangular in shape and approximately 5 m in diameter. There is evidence that many small samples have been removed for analysis, judging from what appear to be saw indentations in several places. It is 40 km southwest of Mbeya, along the road to Zambia; take the turning off just after Mbowa, it's a good 10-15 km from the highway. For the Poroto Mountains, see page 384.

Trekking
The mountain to the north of the town, part of the Mbeya Range, is **Kaluwe** (known as Loleza Peak), which rises to 2656 m. It can be reached in about two hours and is well worth it, if you have a spare afternoon. The view from the summit is breathtaking and, if you enjoy a good romp, the pathway is quite rugged and steep. The hillsides are dotted with wild flowers, and the peace is only disturbed by cattle bells and birdsong. From Mbeya, turn right just after the Catholic cathedral and mission and head straight – find the path that leads up a slope and follow it (it passes a number of Christian monuments and crosses along the way). This leads to the summit.

Mbeya Peak, rising to 2826 m, is the highest peak in the range and looms to the north above the town. There are two possible routes, one harder than the other. The first is down a track about 13 km along the Chunya Road. From the end of this track, the climb will take about one hour, including a walk through eucalyptus forest and high grass. The second, more difficult route is only recommended for those prepared for a steep climb and, in parts, a real scramble. This begins from the coffee farm at Luiji. There is very good accommodation here at the **Utengele Coffee Lodge** (see Where to stay, page 388). At the top you can catch your breath and admire the view for miles around.

Border crossing: Tanzania–Zambia

Tunduma–Nakonde

The Tunduma–Nakonde border is on the A104, 113 km southeast of Mbeya, and just over 1000 km northeast of the capital of Zambia, Lusaka. The border is open 0600-1800 but note, Zambia is one hour behind Tanzanian time. There are frequent *dala-dalas* from Mbeya to the border, which take two hours, but very little in the way of public transport on the Zambian side except for minibuses that link the villages. The road is reasonable – tarred with a few stretches of potholes – but there are no facilities for a very long way. However, there are through buses (try **Scandinavia Express**) between Dar es Salaam and Lusaka (29 hours, US$38), via Morogoro, Iringa and Mbeya, although these can get stuck at the border for a considerable time and there are often delays. Visas and third-party insurance are available for both countries, and there are money changers.

Note The other possible ways to cross into Zambia from Tanzania is by the TAZARA train between Dar es Salaam and Kapiri Mposhi in Zambia, via Morogoro, Iringa and Mbeya, see box, page 385, or by the *MV Liemba* ferry on Lake Tanganyika from Kigoma to Mpulungu in Zambia, see box, page 345 and Kigoma Transport, page 355.

Another worthwhile, but also energetic trek is to **Pungulume** (2230 m) at the west end of the range. It is approached from the road at its base near Njerenji. Alternatively, follow the ridge from Mbeya Peak. (Avoid this trek in the wet season.)

Probably one of the best viewpoints in the Mbeya Range is known as **World's End**. From here you will see the Usangu Flats and the Rift Valley Escarpment; the view is really quite breathtaking. To get to it, go about 20 km down the Chunya Road, due north of Mbeya beyond World's End to a forest camp, and take the track off to the right.

The **Poroto Mountains**, southeast of Mbeya, are home to a wide variety of birdlife, including Livingstone's turaco and the green barbet. There are also several species of kingfisher, woodpecker and eagle.

Kitulo National Park

ⓘ *www.tanzaniaparks.com, 0630-1830, US$20, children (5-16) US$5, vehicle US$40.*

This 416 sq km park is quite beautiful and was, unusually, primarily established to protect its flora rather than its wildlife. It is known locally as Bustani ya Mungu – God's Garden – because of the sheer number of endemic plants here, including 45 species of orchids, yellow-orange red-hot pokers and a medley of aloes, proteas, geraniums, giant lobelias, lilies and aster daisies. With over 350 species of plants, the landscape during December to March is awash with colour, but the paths are also sadly awash with mud. It's by far the best time to come if you're a botanist; otherwise you may prefer to visit between September and November when the hiking will be more comfortable. Its location on Kitulo Plateau at an altitude of 2600 m between the Kipengere, Poroto and Livingstone mountain ranges ensure that distant views are just as attractive, and there are some excellent hiking trails here. There are no large mammals but mountain reedbuck and eland are present, and it's good for bird-watchers, being home to the endangered blue swallow and the rare Denham's bustard.

Getting there The park headquarters is at **Matamba Village**, and is reached via a twisting dirt road from **Chimala** (4WD only), which is 78 km east of Mbeya off the main Mbeya–Dar es Salaam (A104) road. The last 26 km to Matamba is a difficult but spectacular stretch of road and is dubbed Hamsini na Saba, meaning '57' in Kiswahili, after the number of hairpin bends. From Matamba, it's about another hour's drive or roughly a three-hour walk to the top of the plateau in the park. It is possible to hike from here across the Livingstone Mountains to **Matema** on Lake Nyasa (Malawi), see page 385, but this will take all day, and it's preferable to be with a guide (see What to do, page 391). **TANAPA** are planning to set up campsites in the park, but at present the only accommodation is a couple of very basic board and lodgings in Matamba. Otherwise, it's a long journey back to Mbeya or Matema.

Tukuyu and around → For listings, see pages 388-393. Colour map 1, C3. Altitude: 1615 m. 9° 17'S, 33° 35'E.

This is a small town about 70 km south of Mbeya, on the road (B345) to Lake Nyasa (Malawi). It was an administrative centre for the Germans, and there is a group of colonial buildings to the southeast of the town, but, all in all, it's a pretty dreary place and appears quite bleak when hidden under swirling mists. On the other hand, it has a glorious location in the scenic **Poroto Mountains**. There's nothing to keep you in the town itself but a great deal to see in the surrounding countryside. The dark volcanic soils sustain a fertile productive region swathed in banana trees and fresh mountain air. Tukuyu is an important tea-growing area, and the road to Kyela is lined with picturesque tea plantations.

Trekking

Tukuyu is a good centre for trekking but it is necessary to engage a guide (see What to do, page 391). Among the local attractions are **Mount Rungwe**, the most important mountain in this area and, at 2961 m, the highest mountain in southern Tanzania. Its slopes are vast and wild, with over 100 sq km of uninhabited forest, upland scrub and rock terrain. It is accessed from Isangole, 10 km north of Tukuyu, and will take at least a full day to climb. Other attractions are the **Masoko Crater Lake**, 15 km to the southwest, and the **Kaporogwe Falls**, south of Tukuyu, which are around 40 m high and in an attractive lush setting. Halfway down there is a cave behind the falls, which it is possible to enter. There's good swimming in the pool at the bottom. To reach them go about 6 km down the main road towards Kyela to the Ushirika Village bus stop. From there, it's about 2½ hours to walk, or you can hire a bicycle at the main road (with or without rider).

Ngozi Crater Lake, about 20 km north of Tukuyu in the Poroto Mountains, is a beautiful lake lying in the collapsed crater of an extinct volcano, the sides of which plunge down steeply from a rainforest-covered rim. The forest is home to colonies of colobus monkeys. Witch-doctors are said to call upon ancestral powers here, and local legend claims that there is an underwater snake-like monster hidden deep in the waters of the lake, causing the surface waters to change colour from time to time. To get there catch a *dala-dala* going to Mbeya up to Mchangani Village (this takes 1-1½ hours). It's advisable to arrange for a guide at Mchangani to take you up to the lake, as the route is by no means obvious, and it's a two-hour walk from the main road to Ngozi. The second half of the walk entails a steep climb through rainforest before you emerge at the crater rim. From here the views across the lake are spectacular. You could camp at the top, in which case you would be there for sunset and dawn.

Daraja la Mungu (Bridge of God), also known as Kiwira Natural Bridge, is an unusual rock formation spanning a small river close to Tukuyu. To get there take a *dala-dala* going to Mbeya and get off at Kibwe (12 km north of Tukuyu). Here, change to another *dala-dala* waiting at the beginning of the road branching off to the left. It's a further 12 km down

TAZARA railway

The TAZARA (Tanzania and Zambia Railway Authority) railway runs from Dar es Salaam to Kapiri Moshi in Zambia. It was built by the Chinese between 1970 and 1975 and is an impressive feat of engineering. The track covers 1870 km, passes over 300 bridges, through 23 tunnels and past 147 stations. At a cost of US$230 million, this was the largest railway project at the time since the Second World War. The railway was Zambia's answer to the closure of its routes to Southern African ports, as a result of Rhodesia's Unilateral Declaration of Independence in 1965. Initially, it was meant to handle all of landlocked Zambia's freight, and it did. But since the reopening of the southern routes,

following Independence in Mozambique in 1975 and the coming of majority rule in Zimbabwe in 1980, Zambia's dependency on the Dar es Salaam port has lessened. As a result, the volume of cargo along the railway has been considerably reduced. However, its passenger trains, built to carry 600-plus people, are almost always full to capacity and, for people living along the route, the train is the cheapest and most convenient link to the rest of Zambia or Tanzania. The railway is also a lifeline to villagers living along its route. When they hear the train coming, people bearing baskets full of red onions, potatoes, rice, bananas, tomatoes, plantains and oranges rush to meet it.

this rough road. There are apparently also hot springs (*maji ya moto*) a little further on and nearby is Kijunga waterfall.

Kyela → *Colour map 1, C3.*

The 61-km road from Tukuyu to Kyela is incredibly scenic, lined with glistening tea plantations and with a drop in altitude of more than 1000 m. Kyela is a small commercial centre northwest of Lake Nyasa (Malawi) and the nearest town to the Malawi border at Songwe (see box, page 388). The surrounding countryside is fertile, abounding with banana plants, mango trees, maize, bamboo and also rice, particularly prized throughout Tanzania; much of it is transported to Dar es Salaam after harvest. Unfortunately, the town itself doesn't match its attractive surroundings and lies some 10 km inland from the lake; it is dusty and characterless and, on arrival, you'll probably be keen to get out as soon as possible. Matema, which is on the lake itself, is a far nicer place to stay.

Matema → *For listings, see pages 388-393. Colour map 1, C3.*

Matema is the secret paradise of the southwest of Tanzania, and a walk along the lakeshore here will simply take your breath away. The slopes of the Livingstone Mountains – vertiginous rock, meadows and plunging waterfalls – provide a backdrop for the blue waters and sandy beaches of the lake. Although it's not the easiest place to reach, especially by public transport – vehicles to Matema are painfully slow, uncomfortable and extraordinarily overcrowded – don't be put off by travellers' tales of woe; it is well worth the trip. To get there, turn off to the left (south) just before the Malawi border, where a gravel road takes you the 43 km to Matema. This is Tanzania's closest answer to a rustic lakeside resort, like those found further south in Malawi; there are a couple of simple places to stay or camp, and it is still far from being overrun with tourists. The village itself is very friendly, with banana trees, flowers and pigs, dogs and chickens milling around. In the market, bamboo wine is drunk literally by the bucket load, and grilled meat (especially pork) is offered by the vendors.

A walk along the mountainside to the village of **Ikombe**, the site of a former mission, is a highly recommended excursion. The mountainside comprises steep slopes and deep valleys, which are home to fresh mountain streams, butterflies and wild flowers Alternatively, it is possible to hire a dug-out canoe, which takes 30 minutes each way between Matema and Ikombe, depending on the wind. Enquire locally about excursions and you will be sure to find a willing and helpful guide who will ensure that the relevant permission is sought. The beach at Ikombe is safe for swimming and reportedly clear of bilharzia, but check locally. There are supposed to be hippos and crocodiles in the river that flows into the lake about 3 km or so west of the village, it is a pleasant walk along the beach.

The **Wakisi**, one of the peoples who make up the population of the surrounding area, are well known throughout Tanzania for their pottery skills. The role of the Wakisi women is not only to raise and rear children, farm and look after the home but also to make the pots – a woman's skill affects her ability to marry. In the market in Matema large piles of Wakisi pots can be seen bound up awaiting transportation to Mbeya, Iringa and even as far away as Dar es Salaam.

Tanzam Highway to Lake Nyasa (Malawi)

Approximately 550 km long, 75 km at its widest point, and with a surface area of about 29,600 sq km, Lake Nyasa (Malawi) is the third largest lake in Africa (after lakes Victoria and Tanganyika), and the eighth largest lake in the world. In Tanzania it's known as Lake Nyasa (meaning 'body of water', the name Livingstone gave it when he first set eyes on it in 1859); in Malawi, it's Lake Malawi, and in Mozambique, it's Lago Niassa. However, today it's universally referred to as Lake Malawi.

In Tanzania, the most likely place to approach the lake is on the western side at Matema (page 385), to the south of Mbeya; but it's also possible to reach the eastern shore at Mbamba Bay, which, as the crow flies, is less than 40 km north of the Mozambique border (though you can't cross anywhere in this part of Tanzania). Mbamba Bay is a modest village on a glorious bay, surrounded by hills on the eastern shore of the lake and, if it was in Malawi, it would be heaving with tourists. But it's not and it isn't and, apart from the beautiful undeveloped beach, there's little reason to come here as it's not on the way to anywhere else. Nevertheless, the route south to the lake, along the Tanzam Highway and via the sizeable towns of Njombe and Songea, will appeal to overlanders with their own vehicles and anyone with time on the hands for the bus journey. But be prepared to stay only in basic board and lodgings in the towns and villages.

The turn-off to the B4 is at **Makambako**, which is roughly midway between Iringa and Mbeya. The B4 is in good condition as far as Songea but then it deteriorates considerably for the 170 km from Songea to Mbamba Bay. It is very rough in parts, the bridges are occasionally severely damaged, and it becomes treacherous in the wet. Once at Mbamba Bay, there is the option of getting the once-weekly ferry across to Itungi on the northwest side of the lake (see box, page 393).

Set among attractive green rolling highlands, **Njombe** is 60 km south of Makambako and is an undistinguished Tanzanian town at an altitude of 1859 m and with a cool climate all year round. There are several wattle and tea plantations in the district, some of which can be seen on the road between Iringa and Mbeya. The town was established as a centre for the rich farming country of the southern highlands, possibly because of the aerodrome,

The Maji Maji Rebellion

Songea and the surrounding area is home to the Ngoni, a group descended from an offshoot of the Zulus who came from South Africa, fleeing the rule of King Chaka, in the mid-19th century. They were hunters and farmers and, later on, strongly resisted the German colonial settlement. From 1905 to 1907, there was an extensive two-year insurgence against the Germans, triggered by the harsh working conditions in the cotton plantations. It was known as the Maji Maji Rebellion and was led by a witch-doctor named Kinjekitile, who told his followers that, with the help of his magic potion which could transform bullets into water, they would be invincible. Warriors shouted '*maji maji*' (meaning 'water water'), while going into battle armed only with swords, pangas and clubs, convinced that in doing so they would disable the German arms. The rebellion was finally suppressed locally, when the Ngoni chiefs were all hanged in Songea by the Germans in 1907. The tree used to execute the local chieftains survives.

an early refuelling point en route to South Africa. Njombe is very much the centre of missionary activity. There is a single high street with a few shops and a number of basic guesthouses can be found around the bus stand.

The provincial headquarters of Southern Province and with a population of around 130,000, **Songea**, 270 km south of Makambako, was comparatively isolated until the construction of the sealed road. Now there are several daily buses between Makambako and Songea, via Njombe, which take around five or six hours. Tobacco is the main cash crop in the area, although Mbinga, to the south, is an important centre for coffee-growing and, to the east, towards Tunduru, are a couple of sapphire mines that have been operating since the late 1990s. These are presently small scale, but they have been producing some high gem-quality stones, so mining activity in this region is expected to increase. Songea, named after a Ngoni chief, is a pleasant enough place and, although there is little to keep you in the town itself, it is surrounded by attractive rolling countryside and hills, which are good for walking in. There are petrol stations, a market, general stores, a couple of banks with ATMs, and a clutch of basic board and lodgings near the bus stand, which is just west of the market on the road to Mbamba Bay.

The route from Songea to Mbamba Bay is very scenic, passing up, down and around the green hills before descending to Lake Nyasa (Malawi). As the road descends, the vegetation changes from that of pine and eucalyptus trees, to miombo bush and mango trees. The road is bad, however, and the journey is pretty difficult in the rainy season. In the dry season there are sometimes buses from Songea that leave very early in the morning, but mostly local landrovers make the journey, and then only sporadically so. Without your own transport, the only option is to get as far as Songea and wait. The scenic surroundings and pretty coconut palm-lined beaches of **Mbamba Bay** may well be enough to entice you into waiting. Many of the houses here are made in the traditional style, with sun-baked bricks, topped with thatch made from a long grass called *nyasi*. The magnificent **Mohalo Beach**, reportedly over 20 km in length, lies 4-5 km south of the village, and can be reached by walking along the road to Mbinga or, alternatively, by hiring a dug-out canoe to take you around the headland. There is another long beach to the north of the village. Both have pure white sand, and you can admire the fish darting about in the clear water. There are dug-out canoes parked on the beaches, their fishing nets spread

Border crossing: Tanzania–Malawi

Songwe

Warning Touts are a real problem around the bus station in **Mbeya**, don't fall for the scam of buying a ticket all the way to Malawi. At the time of writing, no buses from Mbeya actually cross the border, and you will end up paying for the whole trip but only going as far as Kyela; the touts promise that a bus will meet you at the Malawian side of the border but, of course, it never materializes.

The Songwe border is 140 km southeast of Mbeya and 50 km north of Karonga in Malawi. The border is open 0600-1800 but note: Malawi is one hour behind Tanzanian time. There are frequent buses to **Kyela** (see page 385) from Mbeya, which take three hours. There are some buses (including **Scandinavia Express**) that have direct services between Dar es Salaam and Kyela (13 hours); ask to be dropped off at the turn-off to the border, before you reach the town of Kyela, from where it is about 5 km to the border and you can hitch or get a bicycle taxi.

Visas are available for Tanzania, and most nationalities do not require a visa for Malawi. There are kiosks for third-party insurance for drivers. Money changers will start plaguing you from the turn-off to the border. As there are no banks on either side, exchange rates aren't great but you'll need Malawi kwacha or Tanzania shillings for bus rides until you get to the next banks (in Mbeya or Karonga). After Tanzanian immigration formalities, you cross the bridge over the Songwe River to Malawi immigration on the other side and, after a few minutes' walk, there is a bus stand where you can pick up a bus to **Karonga** (two hours), where public transport continues on to Mzuzu, Lilongwe and Blantyre.

out on the sand, fish drying on stalls, women washing clothes and utensils, and children swimming and splashing in the water. The village has a post office, police station, a few little *dukas* (small shops), and only a couple of very basic places to stay; however, you will find a bed, meal and a beer or you can camp on the beach.

◉ Mbeya and around listings

For sleeping and eating price codes and other relevant information, see pages 22-26.

⬤ Where to stay

The better and more secure places to stay are along the Tanzam Highway (A104), which lies about 800 m to the south of town.

Mbeya *p381, map p381*
$$$ Utengule Coffee Lodge, 20 km northwest of Mbeya on a coffee estate beneath Mbeya Peak and 90 km from the Zambian border, T0753-020 901, www.

riftvalley-zanzibar.com. The signposted turning is roughly 12 km from Mbeya on the main road, it is then about another 8 km to the hotel. A charming country lodge set on a 200-ha coffee estate, with restaurant, bar, 16 comfortable rooms, verandas and good mountain views. They serve very good home-grown food and, naturally, good coffee (they also run the **Zanzibar Coffee House**, page 155). There's a swimming pool, squash and tennis court, and a lovely grassy campsite (US$10 per person). Mountain bikes can be hired, and it is a good base for excursions into the mountains, for which guides can be arranged. Doubles from US$125.

$$ Beaco Resort, Tunduma Rd, near St Mary's School, off the main Tanzam Highway, 5 mins' drive to the west of town, T025-250 4441, www.beacoresort.com. A friendly small hotel opened in 2010, so everything is very fresh, with small but neat rooms, a/c, satellite TV and made-for-hotel furnishings in a collection of newly built red-brick blocks. A restaurant and bar, with a pleasant palm-filled courtyard, serve local and Western dishes and there's a large secure car park.

$$ Mbeya Forest Hill Motel, Tanzam Highway, 5 mins' drive to the west of town, T025-250 3173, www.mbeyaforesthillmotel. com. A fairly new roadside motel behind a petrol station with views of Mbeya Peak, nothing fancy and predominantly a local conference venue, but with comfortable rooms in low-storey buildings with a/c and satellite TV, swimming pool, gym, bar and restaurant, and secure parking behind a gated wall.

$$ Mount Livingstone Hotel, opposite mosque on Lumumba St, T025-250 3334, www.twiga.ch/TZ/mtlivingstone.htm. Possibly Mbeya's most established hotel, centrally located, with a private drive and pleasant gardens. All 40 rooms have bathrooms with hot water and satellite TV. Clean, comfortable, professionally run and recently renovated. The bar has an extensive wine and cocktail list, and there's good food in the restaurant. Doubles from US$65.

$$-$ Calm Inn Hotel, Tanzam Highway, 5 km east of town, T025-250 2402, www.calminnhotel.com. Set in a walled compound and a rather odd structure – basically 2 large, 3-storey buildings connected by an elevated bridge, but it's another new option in Mbeya and has decent rooms with kettle, fan and satellite TV, but dated furniture. There's a restaurant, bar and rooftop terrace. The plastic flowers laid out on the bed are a welcome touch. Doubles from US$40.

$ Karibuni Centre, 500 m off the Tanzam Highway at the Mbalizi Evangelical Church, T025-250 3035, www.twiga.ch/TZ/ karibunicenter.htm. A church guesthouse run by a Swiss missionary in a peaceful forest area with spotlessly clean but spartan en suite rooms, but cheap from US$5 per person. Good simple meals are served in the restaurant (Mon-Sat) and you can camp in the compound (US$3 per tent). Safe parking for vehicles.

$ New Millennium Inn, opposite the main bus stand, T025-250 0599. One of the better cheap board and lodgings around the bus stand and very convenient for early starts or late arrivals. Rooms vary from singles with shared bathroom to en suite doubles with satellite TV, hot water and mosquito nets. Staff are friendly, and the simple restaurant has passable local food and the odd curry, and may attempt something like spaghetti bolognaise. Doubles from US$10.

$ Rift Valley, town centre, T025-250 4351, www.twiga.ch/TZ/riftvalley.htm. Multi-storey hotel with 75 en suite rooms, basic and a little tatty with simple furniture, but passable with mosquito nets and hot water. There's a restaurant for local dishes, 2 bars and a disco (which may get noisy) at the weekends. Doubles from US$20.

$ Royal Tughimbe Hotel, Mbilizi Township, off the Tanzeem Highway, 2 km east of Mbeya, T0754-384 975, www.royaltughimbe hotel.com. A popular if old-fashioned roadside stop and rather unmissable thanks to the life-size concrete elephants and giraffes at the entrance. 22 simple rooms with satellite TV and fridge, reasonable restaurant serving continental, Chinese and Indian dishes, bar, internet café and walled car park. Doubles from US$25.

Tukuyu *p384*

$$-$ Landmark Hotel, in the centre of town at the main crossroads, T025-255 2450. This impressively smart and professionally run hotel is an unexpected find, with a large manicured garden, mirrored windows and shining granite-topped reception desk. The 27 neat rooms have a/c, satellite TV, and some have balconies with great views over town and the mountains. Camping available in the grounds for US$4. There's a bar, large restaurant with a reasonable menu, and car park.

$ DM Motel, on the main Mbeya–Kyela road just south of the market, T025-255 2332. Clean and simple accommodation in low buildings with corrugated-tin roofs in a compound with a pleasant small garden, trimmed hedges and a kids' playground. There are 10 rooms, with or without bathrooms, and a bar; food can be arranged with notice.

Camping
Bongo Camping, at Kibisi village, 4 km north of Tukuyu and 700 m off the Mbeya–Kyela road, T0784-823 610. A lovely spot in the foothills of Mt Rungwe, surrounded by tea and banana plantations and popular with overlanders coming from Malawi (the border is a 1-hr drive). Great springy grass, clean toilets and showers, cooking shelter, meals such as chicken/vegetables with rice/chips are available, US$6 per tent, or you can rent a tent and bedding for US$8. It's a community-run enterprise that supports a local pre-school/kindergarten which you can visit, and they can also organize local guides to take you on tours of the tea estates.

Kyela p385
There is little reason to stay in Kyela when Matema on the lakeshore is so tantalizingly close. There are several basic guesthouses in the centre offering a bed in a bare room and shared bathroom for around US$5.

$ Kyela Resort, on the main road 1.5 km from town towards Tukuyu, T025-254 0452. This is a fairly modern roadside place in a neat group of whitewashed buildings with red tiled roofs. The comfortable rooms are set in a long building with their own entrances, and have fans, mosquito nets, tiled bathrooms and reliable hot water.

There's a large restaurant and bar with outdoor tables in the garden and secure parking. Doubles from US$30.

$ Matema Beach Hotel, on the main road 500 m from town towards Tukuyu, T0754-404 860. Rather a silly name given that it's not in Matema nor on the beach, but a reasonably comfortable local conference hotel, which has 30 small rooms with a/c, TV, some with kettle and fridge, internet access, restaurant, bar and large terrace. It's cheap from US$20 for a double.

Matema p385
Note Bilharzia is present in the lake off Matema. However, there are some deep places along the shoreline where it may not be (remember bilharzia is a parasite that is spread by human activity in the water). Ask locally for advice on where to swim. All these places can organize dug-out canoes for boat trips, bicycle hire and may be able to rustle up gear for snorkelling. The nearest bank with an ATM is in Tukuyu – make sure you have cash.

$ Matema Lake Shore Resort, T025-250 4178, www.twiga.ch/TZ/matemaresort.htm. Popular with expats, spotlessly clean and well run, the resort has 8 en suite rooms in double-storey wooden beachfront chalets, the largest sleeps up to 5, with mosquito nets and little verandas or balconies, from US$10 per person, and you can negotiate to camp here. The beach is raked and cleaned daily and planted with palms to create some privacy for sunbathing. There's a small restaurant but a little notice is needed for meals, or you are permitted to self-cater in the kitchen. It's church-run so no alcohol available, but you can get beers in the village.

$ Matema Lutheran Guest House, T0787-275 164, www.matemabeachview.com. A similar set-up to above and also church-run, with 14 mud-brick and thatched self-contained bandas on the beach with mosquito nets (from US$10 per person), plus a 2-bedroomed house with kitchen and gas cooker that is ideal for families/groups (from

US$35), and it's possible to camp (US$4). There's a beach kiosk that serves snacks and (warm) drinks (no alcohol), and meals can be pre-ordered in the dining room.

Camping
Blue Canoe Safari Camp, formerly known as **Crazy Crocodile Camp**, T0783-575 451, www.bluecanoelodge.com. A rustic campsite set on a beautiful wide sandy beach, also has a clutch of simple bamboo and grass thatch huts backed by coconut and papaya trees (by the time you read this there may be some bandas). Toilets and showers are basic but clean, there's a rustic bar with reed walls built in the sand, and a campfire is lit in the evening; meals can be organized.

🍴 Restaurants

Mbeya *p381, map p381*
Like all small towns, there are a number of canteen places around Mbeya that offer fried chicken, stews, chips and omelettes. These include **Baba Kubwa**, Jacaranda Rd, and **Sombrero**, just off Post St, which both have a wide variety of African and Indian dishes and snacks. For evening meals, all the hotels have restaurants; the best of these is at the **Mount Livingstone Hotel**, see Where to stay, above, which has a good choice of meat grills and some Chinese and Mediterranean dishes.

🛍 Shopping

Mbeya *p381, map p381*
The market has an excellent variety of fresh fruit, and some of the shops around the market offer soft drinks and tinned food. **Mtwara Fresh** is a locally run supermarket with outlets in the centre of town, which has some imported items, plus fresh bread and cheese. Also try **Ramji's Supermarket**, Post St, next to the post office.

⚑ What to do

Mbeya *p381, map p381*
Gazelle Safaris, Jacaranda St, south from the market, T025-250 2482, www.gazellesafaris. com. A British/Tanzanian operation that organizes everything from local day trips and hikes to safaris across Tanzania. They also arrange flights and car hire.
Sisi Kwa Sisi Cultural Tourism Program, Mbalizi Rd, near the Memorial of Friendship with Japan, T0754-463 471, www.sisi-kwa-sisi. com. Mon-Sat 0800-1600. Theoretically open daily 0800-1800, although during the 'low season' the hours may be revised. Literally meaning 'Us for Us', this is one of the excellent **Tanzania Cultural Tourism Programmes**. Sisi Kwa Sisi offers tours of the area and uses profits to help the local community, in this case through agricultural projects. Tours offered include visits to all attractions in the Mbeya, Tukuyu and Matema areas, with the chance to experience the traditional local cultures. There are also a variety of guided hikes including 2- to 3-hr climbs of Loleza and Mbeya peaks, visits to Ngozi Crater Lake and Kijungu Waterfall. The guides and the staff in the office are a mine of local information and speak excellent English. Depending on transport, an average day trip costs US$15-20 per person. Further details and bookings of the programmes can be obtained from the **Tanzania Cultural Tourism Programme** office at the Museum/Old Boma or the Tanzanian Tourist Board tourist information centre in Arusha (see page 236), www.tanzaniaculturaltourism.com.

Tukuyu *p384*
Rungwe Tea & Tours, near the post office, T0784-293 042, www.rungweteatours.com. A community-based tour operation with profits benefiting local villages. Tours include visits to local tea farms and attractions, including Mt Rungwe, Ngozi Crater Lake, Daraja la Mungu (the Bridge of God) and Kaporogwe Falls. Good reports, friendly staff and knowledgeable guides.

⊖ Transport

Mbeya *p381, map p381*
Air
The airstrip in Mbeya is to the south of the Tanzam Highway (A104) about 5 km south of town. A new airport to serve the southern highlands near Songwe and the Malawi border is presently being planned. Auricair, Dar, T022-212 6043, www.auricair. com, is a charter airline that runs a daily flight, if there is the demand, between **Dar** and **Iringa** and Mbeya. It leaves Dar at 0750, arrives at Iringa at 0915, Mbeya at 0925, departs again at 1215, Iringa at 1225 and gets back to Dar at 1400.

Bus
Touts are a real problem around the bus station here and will do their utmost to sell you tickets. Only buy tickets from the bus company offices and, in particular, don't fall for the scam of buying a ticket all the way to **Malawi**, see border box, page 388.

Scandinavia Express, at the main bus stand, T025-250 4305, www.scandinavia group.com, buses are very regular to Dar via **Morogoro** (10-12 hrs, US$11). There are many other bus companies that cover the Dar route, but choose carefully as some stop frequently on the Tanzam Highway, which makes the journey much longer. Scandinavia Express through buses between **Dar** and **Lusaka** in Zambia also stop in Mbeya (see border box, page 383. There are also frequent buses to **Kyela** (3 hrs, US$3), for the Malawi border (see border box, page 388), via **Tukuyu**. There are a couple of weekly buses to **Tabora** on a poor road (20 hrs, US$10).

Train
The TAZARA trains between Dar and **New Kapiri Moshi** in Zambia stop in Mbeya and at the border at Tundumu: the express service in both directions on Sat, and the slower service on Wed (see box, page 18). With its glass exterior and sweeping steps,

the impressive **TAZARA** railway station is 4 km outside town on the Tanzam Highway (A104) towards Zambia. Trains are often full, and booking in advance is advised. In Mbeya, try and purchase tickets the day before travel, as although it is possible on the day, the queues are long and chaotic. The route between Mbeya and Dar passes through lovely countryside. However, the frequent stops and jerky motions involved in braking and acceleration, mean that the journey is quite a tiring experience.

Tukuyu *p384*
Bus
Frequent buses and *dala-dalas* stop in Tukuyu between **Mbeya** and **Kyela** and it's roughly 70 km to each. The bus stand is just off the main Mbeya–border road.

Kyela *p385*
Bus
You have to be an early riser to catch a bus going to **Dar** (US$12, 13 hrs); most leave between 0400 and 0500 and pick up passengers at **Tukuyu** and sometimes **Mbeya** too. Scandinavia Express, T025-254 0514, www.scandinaviagroup.com, has a direct bus that departs at 0600. There are frequent buses and *dala-dalas* to **Mbeya** (3 hrs, US$3), via Tukuyu. All buses drop off and pick up at the turn-off to the Malawi border at Songwe, which is 5 km before Kyela (see border box, page 388). The route to **Matema** goes via the village of **Ipinda**, 14 km north of Kyela, and the two are linked by *dala-dalas*, which are usually pickup trucks, but the later you leave it the less chance you have of arriving at Matema on the same day due to scant transport for the last leg of the 27-km journey between **Ipinda** and Matema. There are buses from Ipinda to Matema but they are irregular and tend not to run after midday; set off early from Kyela to ensure a link to Matema. There are also *dala-dalas* to **Itungi**, on the lakeshore 10 km east of Kyela, for the Nyasa ferry (see box, page 393).

Ferries on Lake Nyasa (Malawi)

There is an erratic ferry service between **Itungi**, which is 10 km to the east of Kyela on the western side of Lake Nyasa (Malawi), and Manda and Mbamba Bay (page 386) on the eastern side. The boats are run by **Marine Services Company**, based in Mwanza, Customer Information Centre T028-250 3079, www.mscltz.com; ticket office in Kyela, T0737-134 971.

The *MV Songea* departs from Itungi on Thursday at 1300 and travels around the lake, stopping frequently at villages (including Matema, page 385), as far as **Mbamba Bay**, where it arrives on Friday at around 0900. The return journey leaves Mbamba Bay on Sunday at 0800 and gets back to Itungi on Monday at around 0600. While this boat occasionally crosses to **Nkhata Bay** in Malawi, it only does so if there's enough freight on board, so don't rely on it to get to Malawi. If you do get across the lake, then there is an immigration office in Mbamba Bay where you can get an exit stamp from Tanzania or buy an entry visa. Most nationalities do not need visas for Malawi.

The *MV Iringa*, follows the same route but only goes as far as Manda, a small village north of Mbamba Bay. It leaves Itungi on Tuesday at 1100 and arrives in Manda at around 2200, departing again on Wednesday at 1600 and arriving back in Itungi on Tuesday at around 1600.

However, these timetables can be a work of fiction; there are frequent delays and, on occasions, given that both vessels are old and often need repairing, the boats simply won't run at all. Tickets can be bought at the port and arriving several hours before the estimated time of departure will ensure that you have time to buy tickets and read several novels before there's even a hint of movement. A first class ticket to Mbamba Bay will cost about US$20. First class cabins are for two people and are small but comfortable. Try to get a cabin facing the lakeshore. In third class you get a wooden bench, if you're lucky, and plenty of company. Many passengers end up sleeping on the floor, so be prepared (second class seems to have disappeared). Food and drink is theoretically available on board, but don't count on it. If you can cope with these uncertainties, however, travelling on the lake is a great way to get a slice of local life and at the same time take in some of the beautiful shoreline scenery.

Matema *p385*
Bus
From Matema to **Kyela**, again transport is scarce and buses to **Ipinda** leave early in the morning. Once in Ipinda there are plenty of *dala-dalas* to Kyela.

❶ Directory

Mbeya *p381, map p381*
Medical services Aga Khan Medical Centre, Post St opposite the post office, T025-250 2265, www.agakhanhospitals.org, for malaria testing and other minor ailments, provides an efficient service; **Mbeya Referral Hospital**, Hospital Hill Rd, to the north of town, is the main state hospital in the region, T025-250 3577, www.mbeyareferralhospital.org.

Contents

Background

History of Tanzania

Earliest times

From oral history, archaeology, linguistic analysis and anthropology (although no written records), a certain amount can be deduced about the early history of Tanzania. The Olduvai Gorge (see page 285) has become known as the cradle of mankind, and the era of Australopithecine man probably lasted several million years. The bones of two types of hominids from the Australopithecine era found there have provided evidence of human evolution. These are *Zinjanthropus*, the 'Nutcracker Man' and *Homo habilis*, the 'Handy Man'. They lived together about two million years ago and, until recently, it was thought that *Homo habilis*, capable of using tools, evolved into *Homo erectus*, and then into modern man – *Homo sapiens*. But this is now under some debate, as in 2001, in the Lake Turkana region of Kenya, a *Homo erectus* complete skull (1.4 million years old) was found within walking distance of an upper jaw of a *Homo habilis* (1.5 million years old). This proved that they must have lived in the region at the same time, and one theory now is that they evolved from another, older common ancestor: a missing link that has not yet been found.

By about 500,000 years ago *Homo erectus* was on the scene (sometime between the Australopithecine and *Homo sapiens* eras). The brain was larger and the hands more nimble and, therefore, better at making tools. The development of tool-making is clearly seen at Olduvai Gorge. The different layers of rock contain tools of different ages, which show the development from crude tools to more efficient and sharper implements. Another collection of such tools can be found at Isimila near Iringa (see page 374).

The Middle Stone Age saw the further development of hunter-gatherers, who used tools and were advanced in human ingenuity and craftsmanship and the use of fire. Progress accelerated in the Late Stone Age, which began about 100,000 years ago, and there are a number of sites from this era in Tanzania, particularly well known because they are the locations of rock painting.

The virtual disappearance of these people was a result of the migration and expansion of other people who were more numerous and more advanced. The most significant factor about these migrating people was that instead of being hunter-gatherers they were food producers – either by agriculture or by keeping livestock. They spoke the language of the Cushitic group (legendary biblical descendants of the Cush in Ethiopia, Somalia and north Sudan) and came from the north from around 1000 BC onwards. They did not have iron-working skills and this meant that the efficiency of their agriculture was limited.

Bantu migration

Later still, during the past 1000-2000 years, two other groups migrated into the area. These were both Negroid but were of different linguistic groups: the Bantu from the west and the Nilo-Hamite pastoralists from the north. A process of ethnic assimilation followed; the Cushitic intermarried with the newcomers and adopted their languages. The Bantu possessed important iron-processing skills, which greatly improved agricultural efficiency and this enabled population growth. There was not one single migration but a series of waves of various groups, expanding and contracting, assimilating and adapting. The present ethnic mix is a result of this process over many centuries.

The most recent of the Nilotic migrations was by the Masai. By about the year 1800 they had reached the area around Dodoma, where their advance was stopped by the Gogo and the Hehe (see page 332). Their reputation as a warrior tribe meant that the north part of Tanzania was largely avoided by slave traders and caravan routes.

As a result of these migrations, north and central Tanzania has great ethnic diversity. In this part of the country there are Khoisan, Cushitic, Nilotic and Bantu-speaking peoples. The rest of the country is entirely Bantu-speaking; indeed about 95% of Tanzanians born today are born into a family speaking one of the Bantu dialects. Swahili itself is a Bantu tongue and this has developed into the national language and, as such, is a significant unifying force.

Arab traders
Initially Swahili was a coastal language and developed as the language of trade. The earliest visitors to Tanzania were Arab traders who arrived on the coast, and their influence can be seen in the coastal settlements, such as Kilwa (see page 112). By the 13th century there was a bustling trade on the coast. Initially the trade was dominated by the Persians, Arabs, Egyptians, Indians and Chinese but the Arab influence began to dominate and, with it, the spread of Islam. The major trading objects were gold, ivory and rhino horns, exchanged for guns, textiles and beads. These coastal towns were very much orientated towards the sea and away from the interior until the beginning of the 16th century, when the development of long-distance trade led to more integration. Caravan routes began to extend from the coast to the Congo and Buganda.

Portuguese seafarers
By the mid-15th century the Portuguese had arrived on the scene – Vasco da Gama noted the beauty of Kilwa – and attempted to take control of the gold trade. The Portuguese were later expelled by the Arabs and the influence of the Arabs increased again. A period of reduced trading activity followed, until the latter half of the 18th century when it flourished again, although this time the commodity was slaves. Around 1776 the only trading route inland went southwest from Kilwa to the area around Lake Nyasa, and this became increasingly important through the slave trade. During the 18th century Kilwa became East Africa's major slave-trading port, drawing first on the peoples of southeast Tanganyika and then on the Lake Nyasa area.

During the 19th century the trade pattern shifted, as a result of the changes in the supply of ivory. During the first half of the century, most of the ivory had come from within what was to become Tanganyika. However, as Tanganyika's elephants were destroyed, so the price of ivory rose. Prices at Tabora are reported to have increased tenfold between 1846 and 1858, and the hunters began to look further afield, eventually leaving Tanganyika altogether. As the hunters moved away, the chiefs in these areas lost their major source of revenue, and it was this that led some of them to look to the new trade in slaves.

The slave trade
Caravan routes into the interior developed in the 19th century, and trade centres developed at places such as Ujiji and Tabora. Humans and ivory were exchanged for guns, beads and cloth. The slaves were largely obtained by bartering with the local chiefs rather than by force. Some of the more militarized tribes raided their neighbours and 'prisoners of war' were then sold on to the Arabs as slaves. Convicted criminals were often sold as slaves and this penalty was sometimes extended to include their families.

The size of the slave trade remains a matter of speculation. However, it has been estimated that approximately 1,500,000 slaves from the interior reached the coast and that 10 times that number died en route. Bagamoyo was a terminus of the caravan route and, from there, the slaves were taken to Zanzibar, which developed into an important trading centre. The slaves were either put to work in the plantations of Pemba and Zanzibar or were shipped to the Middle East.

By the 1830s, Zanzibar had become sufficiently prosperous from the sale of slaves and spices for the Omani Sultan Seyyid Said to move his capital from Muscat to Zanzibar. For some time Britain tried to suppress the slave trade by signing various agreements with the Omani Sultans but it was not until 1873 that the trade was officially abolished when an agreement was signed with Sultan Barghash (Seyyid Said's successor). However, this prohibition was implemented only slowly and the practice continued on the mainland for some years. By the 1880s the internal market for slaves had become more important than the external.

The first Europeans

The first Europeans in this part of Africa (since Vasco da Gama) were missionaries and explorers. In 1844, John Krapf, a German working for the Church Missionary Society of London, arrived in Zanzibar. He was joined by John Rebmann, who was to become the first European to set eyes on Mount Kilimanjaro in 1848. The two British explorers Burton and Speke, sent by the Royal Geographical Society, arrived in Zanzibar in 1856 and journeyed along the caravan routes into the interior. In 1858 Speke came across the huge expanse of water, which he named Lake Victoria. Dr Livingstone was perhaps the most celebrated of all the missionaries, being found, after no news of him for several years, by HM Stanley, a newspaper reporter (see box, page 340).

By the 1880s considerable numbers of Europeans were arriving in East Africa as missionaries, big game hunters, traders and adventurers. Some had political ambitions, including two Germans, Carl Peters and HH Johnson, who wanted to see this part of Africa under the control of Germany. They formed the Society for German Colonization, from which emerged the German East Africa Society. Emissaries of the Society signed 'protective treaties' with unsuspecting and often illiterate chiefs from the interior. These so-called treaties of friendship were then used by the German East Africa Company to exploit the areas that they covered with the apparent agreement of local authorities.

Both Germany and Britain made claims over East Africa, which were resolved by a series of agreements. The Berlin Conference of November 1884 to February 1885 was convened by Bismarck and was important in demarcating European spheres of influence in Africa. This saw the recognition of the German 'protective treaties' and, by early 1885, several chiefdoms were formally placed under the control of the German East Africa Company. Three years later, the Germans were shaken by an uprising of both Arabs and Africans, and the German government took control in 1891. The Anglo-German Agreement of November 1886 defined the north boundary from the coast inland to Lake Victoria. A month later another agreement saw the defining of the boundary with Mozambique. These and various other treaties saw Zanzibar, Pemba and a 16-km coastal strip go to the Sultan under British Protectorate rule in 1890, while what is now mainland Tanzania, Rwanda and Burundi became German East Africa. But it was not until 1898 that German rule was secured and consolidated with the death of Mkwawa, chief of the Hehe, who had resisted German domination.

Mount Kilimanjaro

While Germany and Britain were deciding the north boundary, Kaiser Wilhelm I insisted that Mount Kilimanjaro should be German because it had been discovered by a German, John Rebmann. Queen Victoria generously 'gave' the mountain to her grandson, the future Kaiser Wilhelm II, on his birthday in 1886, reportedly explaining, by way of justification,

Central and northern railways

The first railway to be constructed in Tanganyika was the Tanga (Northern) line, which began when the German authorities decided in 1891 that a metre-gauge line should be built from Tanga to Muheza, and then on to Korogwe. Eventually this line would be continued on to Moshi and Arusha. A small port was built at Tanga to land equipment and material, and the construction of the line began in 1893. Labour was scarce and, at times, had to be imported from Mozambique making progress slow. It took two years for the laying of just 40 km as far as Muheza. Financial difficulties caused construction to be halted periodically but the line finally reached Korogwe in 1902 and Moshi in 1911. Unfortunately much of this line, built at great expense over a long period of time, was destroyed by the Germans as they retreated in 1914.

Meanwhile, the central route of the old slave trail to Lake Tanganyika was receiving attention. Dar es Salaam had been made the capital of the German protectorate in 1891, and talk of the construction of a railway began soon after. However, delays again ensued and it was not until 1905 that construction began on a line from Dar es Salaam to Morogoro. This was to be built by a private company with a grant from the Imperial German Government. The Maji Maji rebellion created problems with the supply of labour, but the line reached Morogoro in December 1907. By 1914 the line had been extended as far as Kigoma, although it was clear that it had

little commercial value and traffic was extremely light.

Planning continued for other lines, but the First World War intervened, and much of the work already carried out was destroyed. Most of the bridges between Dar es Salaam and Kigoma were blown up, and the rolling stock destroyed. A line was built during the war, linking the Tanga line to the Kenya railway system, which facilitated the advance and occupation of Tanga by the British.

Following the war, many repairs were carried out so that the goods traffic on the railways increased. However, the problems returned with the depression of the 1930s, which severely affected revenues. The non-metre gauge lines were closed, and about 40% of the staff were laid off. The Second World War saw an increase in the activities of the railways and, following the war, the 'Groundnut Scheme', involved the hasty construction of a branch line from Lindi on the coast to Nachingwea, one of the areas where groundnuts were to be grown. The scheme was a monumental failure, the expected traffic never materialized, and the line was abandoned.

In 1948 the railway and port services in Tanganyika were amalgamated with the Kenya and Uganda railways under the East Africa High Commission. A regional authority, East African Railways & Harbours (EAR&H), ran the railways until 1977 when the East African Community collapsed, severing the rail link through Taveta to Kenya, with Tanzania assuming responsibility for its own network.

that "William likes everything that is high and big". The boundary was thus moved so that Kilimanjaro is now found within Tanzania. Instead of marking the boundary by pencilling it in with a ruler from the coast to Lake Victoria in one go, a freehand detour was made when the ruler hit the mountain, before carrying on again with the ruler and pencil on the far side.

The German colonial period

There were a number of phases of German colonial rule. The first, around the turn of the 20th century, saw attempts at establishing a settler economy. This was to be based in the north highlands, with agriculture as the mainstay of the economy. It was initially not a great success. Revolts occurred in Bagamoyo, Pangani and Tanga, which were all crushed. The best-known uprising was the Maji Maji rebellion, which occurred in the south of the country from 1905 to 1906 (see box, page 387). Discontent was initially aroused over a cotton scheme that benefited the Africans little, although they were obliged to provide all the manual labour. The uprising was unique in eastern Africa for it was cross-tribal and included a large area – almost the whole of the country south of Dar es Salaam.

The uprising led to a major reappraisal of German colonial policy. The administrators realized that development would be almost impossible without a contented local population. This period saw the building of the railway to Tabora to open up the area to commerce, and crops such as coffee and groundnuts were encouraged. Economic activity increased and a world boom led to the re-emergence of a settler cash crop economy as the most significant part of colonial policy. In particular, the boom saw prices of sisal and rubber soar. Most farming took place along the coast and on the slopes of Mount Kilimanjaro and Mount Meru. Inland, the threat of the tsetse fly hindered development, as domestic animals could not be raised in affected areas. Missionary activity led to the growth of clinics and schools.

First World War

With the outbreak of hostilities in Europe, the German commander General Paul von Lettow Vorbeck realized that his meagre forces could not defeat the British but he resolved to aid Germany's efforts in the European theatre of war by tying up as many British military resources as possible. Von Lettow, his German officers and African troops conducted an astonishing rearguard campaign, retreating from Kenya through what is now Tanzania and Mozambique, and was undefeated when Germany surrendered in Europe.

Von Lettow arrived in Dar es Salaam at the start of 1914 to take command of the German forces. He was 44 years old, son of a general, a professional soldier and experienced in bush warfare from service in German South West Africa (now Namibia). His forces consisted of around 2500 *Schutztruppe askaris* in 14 field companies (see box, opposite), and he promptly signalled his intentions by capturing Taveta across the border in Kenya. The British assembled a force of 5000 mainly British, South African and Indian troops, and von Lettow withdrew to begin his epic, 4000-km, four-year campaign. When faced by overwhelming odds, von Lettow fell back, but at defendable positions, although always hopelessly outnumbered, he inflicted fearful losses on his adversaries, most notably at Tanga and Kibata.

The British fared better when commanded by the South African, Jan Christian Smuts, for 11 months in 1916. A rare combination of intellectual, politician and soldier, he later became Prime Minister of South Africa. During the war, however, he found himself pursuing an infuriatingly elusive and surprisingly humorous foe. He was convinced that he would trap and destroy von Lettow's troops in Morogoro, where retreat to the south was blocked by the Ulunguru Mountains. But as his forces marched into the town, they heard a mechanical piano playing *Deutschland Ueber Alles* in the Bahnhof Hotel and, in the empty *Schutztruppe* barracks, on every item of furniture, was a piece of human excrement.

Never defeated, at the end of the campaign von Lettow and his force numbered 155 Germans, 1156 *Schutztruppe askaris* and about 3000 camp-followers made up of porters and *askari* wives and children, many of the latter born during the campaign. Over 250,000

Schutztruppe – an African fighting elite

It was recognized by the Germans from the start that white troops in East Africa would be nothing more than a 'walking hospital'. So, under German officers, an African fighting force of *askaris* was recruited, thoroughly drilled, trained, disciplined and well paid – 30 rupees a month for privates (about US$80 in present-day values) and 150 rupees for non-commissioned officers.

The *Shutztruppe* became an elite. The uniform was a khaki jacket, trousers and puttees and a black leather belt with ammunition pouches. Head gear was a kepi – rather like a khaki fez with a chin-strap and a gold Imperial eagle on the front. The non-commissioned officers decorated their *kepis* with feathers. Each soldier had his own servant (an *askari*-boy). When travelling, a *Schutztruppe*

private would send his *askari*-boy ahead to a village with a cartridge. This was an order to the local headman to have ready four beds (one for the *askari*, one for his rifle, one for his ammunition pouch and one for his uniform) – and some 'blankets' – a selection of the village girls.

Tough, resilient and brave, around 150 *askaris* made up a field company that included two machine-gun teams. With several hundred porters carrying food and ammunition, each company was highly mobile. During the First World War, the British were contemptuous of these African troops, thinking they would collapse when faced with European and Indian forces. In the event, the *Schutztruppe* was never defeated, and inflicted fearful losses on the British and their allies.

Allied troops had been thrown against them at one time or another during the four years. But with their ultimate defeat in the First World War, the Germans lost control of German East Africa. The northwest, now Rwanda and Burundi, went to the Belgians. The rest was renamed Tanganyika, and the British were allocated a League of Nations mandate.

Von Lettow returned to Germany, entered politics in 1920 and for 10 years was a Deputy in the Reichstag. In 1930 he resigned and, in 1935, Hitler suggested he become Ambassador to Britain. Von Lettow declined. It is said he told Hitler to 'go fuck himself', but von Lettow subsequently denied he had ever been that polite. In 1958, at the age of 88, von Lettow returned to Dar es Salaam. He was met at the dockside by a crowd of elderly *Schutztruppe askaris* who carried him shoulder-high to an official reception at Government House. In 1964 the German Bundestag finally voted the funds to settle the back-pay owing to the *Schutztruppe* at the surrender in 1918. Over 300 veterans, some in faded and patched uniforms presented themselves at Mwanza. Only a handful had their discharge papers. Those who didn't were handed a broom and taken through arms drill, with the orders given in German. Not one man failed the test. The same year, at the age of 94, von Lettow died.

The British period

From 1921, Britain introduced the policy of Indirect Rule, which had proved effective in other parts of colonial Africa. This involved giving a degree of political responsibility to local chiefs and ruling through them. Economic development between the wars was negligible. Tanganyika had few exportable products; unlike Uganda, there was no major cash crop, such as cotton, suited to production by small African farmers. The most significant export was sisal, a spiky plant that yields fibres that can be made into ropes and twine, but this required long-term, large-scale, capital-intensive investment and was not suitable for small-scale African production. It was produced almost entirely by British and Asian companies with a local workforce. The most successful African cash crop was coffee, grown by the Chagga on the slopes of Mount Kilimanjaro, and by the Haya west of Lake Victoria. Coffee-growing was extended to Africans by the British in 1922. Previously only settlers were allowed to grow coffee on estates established by the Germans from 1910.

Most British settlers went to Kenya, where there was already a sizeable settler community and where the highlands provided an attractive climate. Moreover, the British presence seemed more secure in Kenya, which was a colony. The League of Nations mandate required Britain to prepare Tanganyika for eventual self-government, and the British kept expenditure on administration, infrastructure and education to a minimum.

The 1920s saw the emergence of the first African political groups. In 1922 the African Civil Servants Association of Tanganyika Territory was formed in Tanga and, in 1929, the Tanganyika African Association (TAA). Throughout the 1930s and 1940s, unions and agricultural cooperatives developed. These were not primarily political associations, although their formation obviously led to increased political awareness. The major issues were land-use policies, aimed in particular at soil conservation, and the eviction of Africans to make way for white settlers. The African population in 1950 was about eight million, compared to an Asian population of 55,000 and European population of 17,000. However, Europeans and Asians dominated local government councils even in areas that were almost exclusively African. These were issues upon which the TAA focused. In 1953 Julius Nyerere became the leader of the TAA and the movement towards Independence developed momentum. In July 1954, at a meeting of all political elements, the Tanganyika African National Union (TANU) was created with the slogan *Uhuru na Umoja* (Freedom and Unity).

There were two major strengths to this movement in comparison to similar movements in other parts of Africa. Firstly, there was no dominating tribal group and, secondly, Swahili had developed into the major language, encouraged by German colonial policy, and this served as an important unifying force. A further point of relevance in the run-up to Independence was that, after the Second World War, Tanganyika was given UN Trustee status in place of the mandate. Both the mandatory system and the trusteeship system were very important because they meant that controversial issues could be referred to the UN Council, unlike in other colonial territories. In December 1956 Nyerere addressed the UN General Assembly's Fourth (Trusteeship) Committee, which gave him a platform to present the views of Tanganyikans to the outside world.

The first elections were held in two phases, in September 1958 and February 1959, and TANU won a sweeping majority. These were multiracial elections, but even the European and Asian candidates owed their success to TANU. Tanganyika attained Independence on 9 December 1961, with Nyerere as the first Prime Minister. The constitution was subsequently changed and Tanzania became a republic, with Nyerere as President.

Post-Independence Tanzania

In 1964 Zanzibar and Tanganyika merged to form Tanzania (see page 140). An awkward union has resulted, in which Zanzibar has retained its own President, Parliament, a full range of Ministries and handles most of its own finances. The President of Zanzibar was, *ex officio*, one of the two Vice-Presidents of Tanzania, until the multi-party elections in 1995. Despite having a population that is less than 5% of the total, Zanzibar has almost a third of the seats in the Tanzanian Assembly.

After Independence, there was pressure to replace Europeans with Africans in the administration and the business sector. There was also considerable demand for basic education and health services. Although economic progress was significant in these early years, there was an impatience at the slow pace of development, and Nyerere made plans for a bold, radical change.

This culminated in the 1967 **Arusha Declaration**, a programme of socialist development accepted by TANU and which was then amplified in a number of pamphlets by Nyerere. Its two main themes were egalitarianism and self-reliance, and it was broadly based on the Chinese communist model. (It has been said that Tanzania took the Chinese model, mistakes and all, and then added a few mistakes of its own.) Politicians were subject to a leadership code, which required that they had no private sources of income and no more than one house or car. Banks, plantations and all major industries were nationalized. The cornerstone of the programme was the villagization and agricultural collectivization programme known as *Ujamaa*. This, and efforts in the rest of the economy, would, it was hoped, lead to the development of a just and prosperous society. Education was considered to be one of the most important aims of the programme and, as a result, Tanzania achieved some of the highest literacy rates in Africa. In the initial years there was success, too, in extending basic health care in the rural areas.

Ujamaa

Ujamaa, a programme for advancement in the rural areas, was an important element in post-Independence Tanzanian philosophy. Intended to involve the voluntary movement of people into villages, its major objective was to raise output through collectivization and large-scale agricultural production. Emphasis was also put on the social benefits: the provision of services, such as piped water, electricity, schools and clinics. Self-reliance was the key, and the villages were meant to be set up and run by the villagers themselves.

There were three phases of villagization in the decade from 1967. The first was voluntary movement on a locally selective basis, combined with compulsory movement in Rufiji and Handeni, which were areas worst affected by drought and flood. From 1970 to 1973 this was replaced by a 'frontal approach', whereby incentives were given for people to move to villages, which included financial and technical assistance. The reluctance of people to move of their own accord meant the targets were not reached and, after 1973, these methods were replaced by the use of force in support of rapid villagization. The results were dramatic. In 1970 the villagized population stood at about 500,000, or less than 5% of the population. After the first year of compulsory movement, Nyerere claimed that there were over nine million people – or about 60% of the mainland population, living in villages. Force was justified on the grounds that people could not always see what was best for them and had to be shown the way. As it is easier to provide amenities such as piped water and electricity to people grouped in villages, the *Ujamaa* did provide some benefits.

However, attempts to farm collectively were disastrous, and agricultural output fell. The programme was vigorously resisted in the major coffee-growing areas of Kagera (west of Lake Victoria) and in the Kilimanjaro region. By 1977, the *Ujamaa* programme was effectively abandoned, although considerable villagization remains.

Late 20th century to the present

In 1973, it was decided to move the capital city from Dar es Salaam on the coast to Dodoma in the centre. The position of this city is suitable in so far as it is on communication networks and is in the centre of the country, about 320 km inland. However, it is also a dry and desolate area, and the major problem with the plan has been the cost of moving. A Presidential official residence, the Prime Minister's office and a National Assembly building have all been established there, but the cost of relocation and the unwillingness of government employees have forced the rest of central government to remain in Dar.

In 1975, a law was passed that gave legal supremacy to TANU as the national political party and, in 1977, TANU and the Afro-Shirazi party (which had taken control in Zanzibar after the revolution) merged to form *Chama Cha Mapinduzi* (CCM), the 'party of the Nation'. The 1970s saw the gradual disintegration of the East Africa Community (EAC), which involved Kenya, Tanzania and Uganda in a customs union and provision of common services. Tanzania and Kenya had different ideological perspectives, and the three countries could not agree on the distribution of the costs and services of the EAC. Things came to a head over East African Airways. The failure of Tanzania and Uganda to remit funds to Kenya caused Kenya to 'ground' the airline (conveniently when all the planes were sitting on the tarmac in Kenya), and Tanzania reacted by closing the border with Kenya in February 1977. The border was only reopened in 1983 after the ownership of the EAC's assets was finally agreed.

In 1978, Tanzania's relations with neighbouring Uganda worsened, and skirmishes on the border were followed by an announcement by Idi Amin that Uganda had annexed the Kagera salient. This is an area of about 1800 sq km of Tanzanian territory west of Lake Victoria. The Organization of African Unity (OAU) applied pressure, which caused Uganda to withdraw, but fighting continued. In January 1979, a Tanzanian force of over 20,000 invaded Uganda; Amin's army capitulated, and the Tanzanians rapidly took control of the southern part of the country. The invading force had withdrawn by 1981, having spent the interim period in Uganda overseeing the election of Milton Obote for the second time. A remarkable feature of this episode is that, despite being the only African country ever to win a war in the 20th century, this event is not celebrated in Tanzania. The only monument is a small pyramid on columns, located on the road from Bukoba to Masaka, just south of the border. It is dedicated to the 16 Tanzanian soldiers who died in the war.

In 1985, Nyerere decided to step down as President of Tanzania (the first President in post-Independence Africa to retire voluntarily). He remained as Chairman of the party (CCM) before formally retiring from politics in 1990. Vice-President Sokoine, who had been widely thought of as Nyerere's successor, had been killed in a car crash in October 1984. Ali Hassan Mwinyi, who was then President of Zanzibar, was nominated to be the sole candidate for President and was elected in October 1985.

Throughout the early 1980s, Tanzania had been put under pressure to accept economic reforms suggested by the World Bank and International Monetary Fund. These financial institutions, as well as Western governments, aid donors and foreign investors argued that the socialist development strategy had led to a crisis, involving falling incomes, decaying infrastructure, deteriorating health and educational provision and a climate of petty corruption. For many years Tanzania resisted changes but, eventually, the climate of opinion changed in 1986, under Mwinyi, a market economy strategy was adopted, and Tanzania began an economic recovery.

In 1993, Tanzania allowed political parties other than CCM to form. In October 1995 there were elections in which CCM won a substantial majority of seats in the Union Assembly. The Presidency was won by the CCM candidate, Benjamin Mkapa, Mwinyi having retired after two terms in office. Mkapa won comfortably with 62% of the vote, and the practice of having two Vice-Presidents (with one being the President of Zanzibar) was discontinued.

In 1995, the main opposition in Zanzibar, the Civic United Front (CUF) ran CCM very close in both the Zanzibar Assembly and in the race for the Zanzibar Presidency. There were allegations of election fraud, supported by evidence from international observers.

Julius Nyerere

Julius Kambarage Nyerere was born in 1922 in Butiama, east of Lake Victoria. He was the Roman Catholic son of a Zanaki chief. His father died having had 26 children by 18 wives. The name Nyerere means 'caterpillar' in the Zanaki language and was supposed to have been given to Nyerere's father because, at the time of his birth (around 1860), the countryside was infested with them. Nyerere attended a boarding school in Musoma and, from 1937, the Tabora Government Secondary School. He was baptized in 1943 and the same year he entered Makerere College, Uganda. After Makerere he returned to Tabora, where he taught history and biology at St Mary's Catholic Boys' School, operated by the White Fathers. In 1949, he went to Edinburgh University and, in 1952, obtained his Master of Arts in Economics and History (he was the first Tanzanian to be educated in Britain). In 1953 he married Maria Gabriel Magigo, who was also a Catholic of the Msinditi tribe and was to become its first woman teacher. He paid the traditional bride-price of six head of cattle for her and they had seven children.

Nyerere subsequently took a teaching post at the Catholic Secondary School of St Francis at Pugu, a few kilometres west of Dar es Salaam, and it was from here that he became involved in politics. In 1954 he became president of the Tanzania African Association and was instrumental in converting this into the political organization TANU. He was appointed a temporary member of the Tanganyika Legislative Council in 1954, and a full member of the Legislative Assembly in 1958, where he remained until his assumption of the Presidency in 1962. In his acceptance speech, he said "We will light a candle on the top of Kilimanjaro which will shine beyond our borders, giving hope where there is despair, love where there is hate, and dignity where before there was only humiliation."

While some of his policies were criticized, throughout his term he placed great faith in rural African people and their traditional ways of life. He resigned as President in 1985 and became known as 'Mwalimu', which means teacher. He moved back to his childhood home of Butima and continued to be an advocate for poor African countries around the world. He was undoubtedly one of Africa's greatest statesmen, admired for his integrity, modest lifestyle and devotion to equality and human rights. On his death in October 1999, the ANC released a statement: "The organization weeps in memory of this giant amongst men ... an outstanding leader, a brilliant philosopher and a people's hero – a champion for the entire African continent."

Nonetheless, CCM formed the administration in Zanzibar, and Salim Amour was installed as Zanzibar's President. It was around this time that various Zanzibari separatist groups formed in exile, some wishing merely for Independence, others pressing for an independent Islamic state, but splits within the separatist movement have enabled the government to contain the problem so far.

The 2000 election was fought by fewer parties, but the opposition was still divided, and CCM and Mkapa had comfortable victories. In Zanzibar the incumbent President, Salim Amour, having completed two terms, was prevented from running again. His successor as CCM candidate for the Presidency was Amani Karume, son of the former President. On election day there was chaos at the polls, and elections in 16 constituencies had to be re-run. Despite opposition claims of electoral fraud, the outcome was a victory for CCM and Karume. Seif Shariff Hamad, the CUF leader, got the remaining 33%. His party won 16 assembly seats on the island of Pemba. Both parties signed a reconciliation agreement in 2001, and Zanzibar is set to remain part of Tanzania. But the CUF, which enjoys strong support on Pemba, has called for greater autonomy, and some CUF members have called for Independence. In 2005, Zanzibar presented its new flag, the first time for over 40 years that the archipelago has flown its own flag since uniting with Tanganyika to form Tanzania in 1964, though Zanzibar's government has stressed the adoption of a flag does not mean that this is a move towards Independence.

In April 2004, Tanzania celebrated its 40th birthday as an independent country and, in 2005, went to the polls again. Mpaka had already served for two terms and the constitution didn't allow him to stand for a third. There were 10 party candidates for presidency but Jakaya Mrisho Kikwete from the CCM, the former Minister of Foreign Affairs under Mpaka, won a land-sliding 80% of the vote and became the fourth president of Tanzania. Karume kept his position on Zanzibar with 53% of the vote, though this time round it was much closer, with Shariff Hamad getting 46%. Nevertheless the election was largely without incident. Again, in 2010, Kikwete and the CCM won the national elections with a majority of 61%.

Meanwhile, on Zanzibar, after a referendum in 2010, a power-sharing agreement between the CCM and CUF was negotiated and, since then, Zanzibar has been administered by a unity government; as on the mainland, the national 2010 election passed peacefully on the islands. The former vice-president, Ali Mohamed Shein, replaced Karume as president. As Shein comes from Pemba but is a member of the CMM, this has been hailed as a diplomatic success that strikes a happy medium on the islands and should save Zanzibar from future political turmoil between the CMM and CUF.

Overall, since 1995, Tanzania's political stability has remained excellent. The government has stayed secure in a period that has seen the advent of multi-party democracy and economic policies that have changed from socialism to capitalism. There is still significant room for improvement on poverty reduction, public services and infrastructure but, on the whole, Tanzania is fairly stable and has good prospects for the future. Fairly young (he was only 55 when he became president), Kikwete is well respected and, during his 10-year term as Minister of Foreign Affairs, was involved in conflict resolution for troubled neighbours Burundi and the Democratic Republic of Congo (DRC) and was the Chairperson of the African Union from 2008 to 2009. During this term, his most notable success was his involvement in brokering the power-sharing deal between Mwai Kibaki and Raila Odinga after neighbouring Kenya's 2007 election crisis. He was close to Nyerere and, to some degree, his governing philosophies of investing in people have been influenced by Nyerere. Education is one of his priorities and, since 2005, 1500 new secondary schools have been built across Tanzania and a new university opened in Dodoma in 2007. Other successes include progressive anti-corruption initiatives and the launch of a nationwide voluntary HIV/AIDS-testing programme; Kikwete and his wife were the first to take the test.

People of Tanzania

The population is largely made up of mixed Bantu groups but there are 129 recognized ethnic groups, of which the Sukuma, Haya, Nyakyusa, Nyamwezi and Chagga have more than one million members.

The largest ethnic groups are the Sukuma and the Nyamwezi, and, although no group makes up more than 15% of the population, about a dozen of the largest groups make up about 50% of the population. Most of these are of Bantu origin (see page 396), although there are some Nilotic groups as well, and about 95% of the population is Bantu-speaking. The most important Bantu language is Swahili (Kiswahili in the language), a language which is the mother tongue of the people of Zanzibar and Pemba as well as some coastal people. Swahili became a *lingua franca* before the colonial period in some areas and this was encouraged by both the Germans and the British. In 1963 it became the national language.

Sukuma

This is Tanzania's largest ethnic group and makes up about 16% of the population. The name means 'people of the north', and the group lives just to the south of Lake Victoria around Mwanza. In the pre-colonial period they were organized into a large number of small chiefdoms. They practise mixed agriculture, with both cattle-herding and cultivation. This is also an important cotton-growing area.

Nyamwezi

The Nyamwezi people are found to the south of the Sukuma people in north Tanzania and in many ways are similar to them. Like the Sukuma, they were formerly made up of a large number of very small chiefdoms. Some of these chiefs tried later to dominate wider areas. Their identity is fairly recent and rather fragile. They are primarily a cultivating people and have established a reputation as traders. The name means 'people of the moon'.

Makonde

These people are located in the southeast part of the country and are fairly isolated on the Makonde Plateau. Although they are one of the five largest groups, the Makonde have been little affected by colonial and post-colonial developments. They are renowned for being a conservative people who are determined to defend their way of life. This is facilitated by the difficulty in reaching this part of Tanzania. Even today, communications with the southeast are poor, particularly during the wet season. The Makonde are perhaps most famous for their beautifully crafted woodcarvings. They are also found in Mozambique.

Chagga

The Chagga (or Chaga) are found around the south slopes of Mount Kilimanjaro and around Moshi, and constitute the third-largest group in Tanzania. They are greatly advantaged by living in a fertile and well-watered region, which is ideally suited to the production of coffee. They were also one of the first groups to be affected by the Christian missionaries, in particular the Roman Catholics and Lutherans, and this meant that the initial provision of education in the area was ahead of many other areas. The high level of education and the opportunity of cash-cropping have resulted in a comparatively high level of income and also a relatively high level of involvement in community activity. One example is the cooperative production and marketing of coffee.

Haya

The Haya people are different from most other ethnic groups in Tanzania. They live in the far northwest of Tanzania, to the west of the shores of Lake Victoria. Although they have common traditions, social system, culture and language as well as territorial identity, they are divided into several chiefdoms, which suggests that, in this case, political unity is not an essential part of tribal identity. The Haya are cultivators, growing coffee and plantains, and live in densely populated villages. Exactly similar to the situation in Kilimanjaro region, the high altitude of the west of Lake Victoria provided a pleasant climate for missionaries, and the Catholics and Protestants competed for converts by providing education here; this history, combined with the production of coffee, had a beneficial effect on the economy.

Hehe

The Hehe people live in the central south region of Tanzania around Iringa. They have a strong sense of identity, and have their own more or less distinctive social system and culture, with a unifying political system. However, within this group there are differences in the way of life and social systems between those who live in the drier eastern parts of the region and those in the wetter uplands to the west. These are caused by environmental factors as well as the effects of distance. Despite this, one observer has suggested that there is a greater unity and identity among the Hehe than there is within any other group of people.

Masai

The Masai (also spelt Maasai) inhabit the north border area with Kenya, but are found as far south as Morogoro and Tabora. To people outside Tanzania, they are probably the best-known traditional 'tribe', with their striking costume and reputation as fierce and proud warriors, and they are resident near many of the game parks and reserves in Tanzania and Kenya. They are a spectacular group of tall, slender cattle-herders, living off milk, blood and meat. All life is centred on cattle, and the number of cows and children a man has is a measure of his wealth. Young men leave to become *moran* before returning to begin family life. As *moran*, they carry spears, wear distinctive red garments and have elaborately decorated faces, bodies and hair. The women have shaven heads and often wear many coils of beads on their necks and shoulders. Clans are governed by elders who discuss matters and make decisions. Houses are built within *manyattas* – a sort of kraal that protects the cattle from wild animals at night.

Shirazi

The Shirazi is the name given to people who are a mixture of Africans and people who are said to have come at a very early time from the Shiraz area of Iran. They are divided into three 'tribes' called the Hadimu, Tumbatu and Pemba. The Africans are descendants of mainlanders, who came to the islands of Zanzibar and Pemba, often as slaves, although later of their own accord. Descendants of the Shirazis have intermixed with other Swahili people and have become more African in race, speech and culture.

Swahili

This is the general term given to the coastal people, who have a Muslim-orientated culture. They are the descendants of generations of mixing of slaves, migrant labourers and Afro-Arabs. Archaeological evidence suggests the Swahili have inhabited the East African coast since the first century AD. Arabic and Chinese medieval documents record the presence of a people involved in the long-distance trade of ivory, slaves, gold and grain in exchange for textiles, beads, weapons and porcelain. The Swahili were, and are, an urban people, living in 'stone towns' up and down the coast and on Zanzibar island. The language is Kiswahili, which is spoken by about 90 million people in East Africa.

Other African groups

The **Hi** people are a small group of click-speakers. They are hunter-gatherers and live on the southwest shores of Lake Eyasi, in the central north part of Tanzania. Other click speakers found in Tanzania include the **Hadzabe** and the **Sandawe**. The Hadzabe live in the same area as the Hi and the groups are believed to be closely related. The Sandawe live in the interior central region of Tanzania to the north of Dodoma. The **Dorobo** are a small group of hunter-gatherers who are found throughout Masailand and in Kenya.

Non-Africans

This group makes up under 1% of the population of Tanzania and comprises Europeans, Asians and Arabs.

Tanzania land and environment

Geography

Tanzania is a large coastal country (approximately 945,000 sq km), which lies just below the equator and includes the islands of Pemba and Zanzibar between 1° S and 11° S latitude and 30° to 40° E longitude. It is bounded by Kenya and Uganda to the north, Rwanda, Burundi and the Democratic Republic of Congo (DRC) to the west, Zambia, Malawi and Mozambique to the south. Temperatures range from tropical to temperate, moderated by altitude. Most of the country consists of high plateaux but there is a wide variety of terrain, including mangrove swamps, coral reefs, plains, low hill ranges, uplands, volcanic peaks and high mountains, as well as depressions such as the Rift Valley and lakes. Dar es Salaam is the main port and there are hydro-electric schemes on the Rufiji and Pangani rivers. Mineral deposits include diamonds, gold, gemstones (tanzanite, ruby, emerald, green garnet, sapphire), graphite, gypsum, kaolin and tin.

Climate

Because Tanzania lies below the equator, the coolest months occur during the northern hemisphere's summer, and all year-round the weather remains pleasant and comfortable. There is a long dry season between June and October, when temperatures range from around 10°C in the northern highlands to about 23°C on the coast. On the plains and the lower-altitude game reserves, the temperatures from June to October are warm and mild. On the coast, these months are some of the most pleasant to visit, with balmy, sunny weather much of the day and cooling ocean breezes at night. This is followed by short rains in November and December. January to March can be very hot, with temperatures of 25-35°C across the country (with the exception of Kilimanjaro and Meru), and are followed by heavy rains in April and May. The timing of the rains has been less regular in recent years and the volume also varies from year to year, and from region to region. Short rains have tended to spread from November to May, with a drier spell in January and February. In northeast Tanzania, the long rains are in March to June. A quarter of the country receives an annual average of 750 mm of rain, but in some areas it can be as high as 1250 mm. The central area of the country is dry, with less than 500 mm per annum. In many areas two harvests can be grown each year. ▸▸ *For more information on when to visit, see page 4.*

Vegetation

Tanzania is justifiably famous for its flora and fauna. In areas of abundant rainfall, the country is lush, supporting a huge range of plants, and the wide variety of geographical zones support a corresponding diversity of flora. The majority of the country is covered in savannah-type vegetation, characterized by the acacia. The slopes of Kilimanjaro are covered in thick evergreen temperate forest from about 1000 m to 2000 m; then to 3000 m the mountains are bamboo forest; above this level the mountains are covered with groundsel trees and giant lobelias. Mangroves are prolific in the coastal regions.

Wildlife

Mammals

Practically everyone travelling around East Africa will come into contact with animals during their stay. Of course there is much more than the big game to see and you will undoubtedly travel through different habitats from the coast to the tropical rainforests but the mammals are on the top of most people's 'to see' lists. ▸▸ *See East African wildlife colour section in the middle of the guide.*

Big Nine The 'Big Five' (**elephant**, **lion**, **black rhino**, **buffalo** and **leopard**) was the term originally coined by hunters who wanted trophies from their safaris. Nowadays the **hippopotamus** is usually considered one of the Big Five, whereas the buffalo is far less of a 'trophy'. Equally photogenic and worthy of inclusion are **zebra**, **giraffe** and **cheetah**. Whether they are the Big Five or the Big Nine, these are the animals that most people come to Africa to see and, with the possible exception of the leopard, you have an excellent chance of seeing all of them.

The **lion** (*Panthera leo*), which weighs in at around 250 kg for a male, is the second largest cat in the world after the tiger. Lions are unlike other cats in that they live in large prides consisting of related females and offspring and a small number of adult males. Groups of female lions typically hunt together for their pride, being smaller, swifter and more agile than the males, and unencumbered by the heavy and conspicuous mane, which causes overheating during exertion. They act as a coordinated group in order to stalk and bring down the prey successfully. Totally carnivorous, they prey mostly on large antelope or buffalo. Visually, coloration varies from light buff to yellowish, reddish or dark brown; the underparts are generally lighter and the tail tuft is black. They communicate with one another with a range of sounds that vary from roaring, grunting and growling to meowing. Roars, more common at night, can reach sound levels of over 110 decibels and be heard from distances of up to 8 km.

The **leopard** (*Panthera pardus*) is an equally impressive cat but less likely to be seen as it is more nocturnal and secretive in its habits. It hunts at night and frequently rests during the heat of the day on the lower branches of trees. Well camouflaged, its spots – typically dark rosettes with a tawny-yellow middle – merge into foliage or blend well into less sparse grassland. Its habitat is extremely diverse, and it can survive in high mountainous and coastal plains regions as well as rainforests and deserts.

The **cheetah** (*Acinonyx jubatus*) is well known for its running speed; in short bursts it has been recorded at over 90 kph. But it is not as successful at hunting as you might expect with such a speed advantage. The cheetah has a very specialized build: long and thin with a deep chest, long legs and a small head. But the forelimbs are restricted to a forward and backward motion, which makes it very difficult for the cheetah to turn suddenly when in hot pursuit of a small antelope. Cheetahs are often seen in family groups walking across the plains or resting in the shade.

The **elephant** (*Loxodonta africana*) is the largest land mammal and, weighing in at up to six tonnes, with an average shoulder height of 3-4 m, it is awe-inspiring by its very size. Sociable by nature, elephants form groups 10-20 strong led by a female matriarch, and it is wonderful to watch a herd at a waterhole. Elephants are herbivores and are voracious and destructive feeders, sometimes pushing over a whole tree to get to the tender shoots at the top. Although they have suffered terribly from the activities of poachers in recent decades, they are still readily seen in many of the game areas.

The **white rhino** (*Ceratotherium simum*) and the **black rhino** (*Diceros bicornis*) occur naturally in Tanzania. Unfortunately, they too have suffered severely from poaching for their horns and, sadly, this is still an issue even today. Their names have no bearing on the colour of the animals as they are both a rather non-descript dark grey. The name of the white rhino is derived from the Dutch word '*wijd*' which means wide and refers to the shape of the animal's mouth. It has a large square muzzle, and this reflects the fact that it is a grazer and feeds by cropping grass; its preferred habitat is grasslands and open savannah with mixed scrub vegetation. The black rhino, on the other hand, is a browser, usually feeding on shrubs and bushes, using its long, prehensile upper lip which is well adapted to the purpose; it lives in drier bush country and usually alone. The horn of the rhino is not a true horn, but is made of a material called keratin, which is essentially the same as hair.

The **buffalo** (*Syncerus caffer*) was once revered by the hunter as the greatest challenge for a trophy, and more hunters have lost their lives to this animal than to any other. This is an immensely strong animal with particularly acute senses. Left alone as a herd, buffalo pose no more of a threat than a herd of domestic cattle. The danger lies in the unpredictable behaviour of a lone bull which, when cut off from the herd, becomes bad-tempered and easily provoked. While you are more likely to see buffalo on open plains, they are equally at home in dense forest. To see a large herd peacefully grazing is a great privilege and one to remember.

The most conspicuous animal in water is the **hippopotamus** (*Hippopotamus amphibius*), a large beast with short stubby legs that can weigh up to four tonnes. However, the hippo is quite agile on land. During the day it rests in the water, rising every few minutes to snort and blow at the surface and, at night, it leaves the water to graze. A single adult animal needs up to 60 kg of grass every day and, to achieve this, obviously has to forage far. The banks near a river or waterhole with a resident hippo population will be very bare and denuded of grass. Should you meet a hippo on land, keep well away; if you get between it and its escape route to the water, it may well attack. Hippos need water not only to prevent their skin from drying out, but also to regulate their body temperature.

The **giraffe** (*Giraffa camelopardalis*) may not be as magnificent as a full-grown lion, or as awe-inspiring as an elephant, but its elegance as a small party strolls across the plains is unsurpassed. Both male and female animals have horns, though in the female they may be smaller. A mature male can be over 5 m high to the top of its head. They are browsers and can eat the leaves and twigs of a large variety of tall trees, thorns presenting no problem. The lolloping gait of the giraffe is very distinctive and is caused by the way it moves its legs at the gallop. A horse will move its diagonally opposite legs together when galloping, whereas the giraffe moves both hind legs together and both forelegs together. It achieves this by swinging both hind legs forward and outside the forelegs. The giraffe has a yellowish-buff coat with the characteristic patchwork of brownish markings with very jagged edges. In most animals there are only two horns, though occasionally animals are seen with three horns.

The **zebra** is another easily recognized animal. It forms herds, often large ones, sometimes with antelope. The **common** or **Burchell's zebra** (*Equus burchelli*) has broad stripes which cross the top of the hind leg in unbroken oblique lines. Although they all look identical, each individual has a different pattern of stripes. These stripes are a form of camouflage which breaks up the outline of the body. At dawn or in the evening, when their predators are most active, zebras look indistinct and may confuse predators by distorting distance. A zebra defends itself by kicking its hind legs, which is far more effective then it sounds and even large predators like lion find it difficult to bring down an adult.

Larger antelope The first animals that you will see on safari will almost certainly be antelope; these are by far the most numerous group to be seen on the plains. Like giraffe and the zebra, all antelopes are herbivores but they have keratin-covered horns which makes them members of the *Bovidae* family. They vary greatly in appearance, from the tiny dikdik to the large eland and, once you have learnt to recognize the different sets of horns, identification of species should not be too difficult. For identification purposes they can be divided into the larger ones, which stand at about 120 cm or more at the shoulder, and the smaller ones under that height.

The largest of all the antelopes is the **eland** (*Taurotragus oryx*), which stands 175-183 cm at the shoulder. It is cow-like in appearance, with a noticeable dewlap and shortish spiral horns present in both sexes. The general colour varies from greyish to fawn, sometimes with a rufous tinge, with narrow white stripes on the sides of the body. It occurs in herds of up to 30, in a wide variety of grassy and mountainous habitats. The eland will travel large distances in search of food and will eat all sorts of tough woody bushes and thorny plants.

Not quite as big, but still reaching 140-153 cm at the shoulder, is the **greater kudu** (*Tragelaphus strepsiceros*). Although nearly as tall as the eland, it is a much more slender and elegant animal altogether. Its general colour also varies from greyish to fawn and it has several white stripes running down the sides of its body. The male carries very long and spreading horns, which have two or three twists along their length. A noticeable and distinctive feature is a thick fringe of hair which runs from the chin down the neck. The greater kudu prefers fairly thick bush, sometimes in quite dry areas, and usually lives in family groups.

Its smaller relative, the **lesser kudu** (*Strepsiceros imberis*), looks quite similar, with similar horns, but stands only 99-102 cm high. It lacks the throat fringe of the bigger animal, but has two conspicuous white patches on the underside of the neck. It inhabits dense scrub and acacia thickets in semi-arid country, usually in pairs, sometimes with their young.

The **roan antelope** (*Hippotragus equinus*) and **sable antelope** (*Hippotragus niger*) are similar in general shape, though the roan is somewhat bigger, being 140-145 cm at the shoulder, compared to the 127-137 cm of the sable. In both species, both sexes carry ringed horns which curve backwards, and these are particularly long in the sable. There is a horse-like mane present in both animals. The sable is usually glossy black with white markings on the face and a white belly. The female is often a reddish brown in colour. The roan can vary from dark rufous to a reddish fawn and also has white markings on the face. The black males of the sable are easily identified, but the brownish females can be mistaken for the roan. Look for the tufts of hair at the tips of the rather long ears of the roan (absent in the sable).

Another large antelope with a black and white face is the **oryx** (*Oryx beisa*), which stands 122 cm at the shoulder. It is a striking creature with a black line down the spine and a black stripe between the coloured body and the white underparts. This is not an animal you would confuse with another. Its horns are long and straight and sweep back behind their ears – face-on they look V-shaped. It is found in herds in arid and semi-desert country.

The two **waterbuck** are very similar, both being about 122-137 cm at the shoulder, with distinctive shaggy grey-brown coats. The males have long, gently curving horns which are heavily ringed. The two species can be distinguished by the white mark on the buttocks. In the **common waterbuck** (*Kobus ellipsiprymnus*) this forms a clear half ring on the rump and round the tail, whereas in the **Defassa waterbuck** (*Kobus defassa*) this ring is filled in, forming a white patch. Both animals occur in small herds, in grassy areas, often near water. Solitary animals are also often seen. They are fairly common.

The **wildebeest** (*Connochaetes taurinus*) is well known to many people because of the spectacular annual migration through the Serengeti National Park. It is a big animal about 132 cm high at the shoulder, looking rather like an American bison from a distance, especially when you see the huge herds straggling across the plains. The impression is strengthened by its buffalo-like horns (in both sexes) and humped appearance. The general colour is greyish with a few darker stripes down the side. It has a noticeable beard and long mane. Wildebeest are well known for their distinctive snorts and grunts when alarmed, when they also toss their massive heads about nervously – being the favourite prey of lions they have to be ever on the alert. They occur in herds of 20 to 30 individuals and are often found grazing with zebra.

The four remaining large antelope are fairly similar. Three of these four are **hartebeest** of various sorts and the fourth is called the **topi**. All four antelope have long, narrow horse-like faces and rather comical expressions. The shoulders are much higher than the rump giving them a very sloped back appearance, especially in the three hartebeest. They have short, curved horns, carried by both sexes. In the three hartebeest the horns grow out of a bony protuberance on the top of the head and curve outwards as well as backwards. One of the hartebeests, **Jackson's hartebeest** (*Alcelaphus buselaphus*; about 132 cm) is similar in colour to the **topi** (*Damaliscus korrigum*; about 122-127 cm), being a very rich dark rufous in colour. But the topi has dark patches on the tops of the legs, a coat with a rich satiny sheen to it and more ordinary-looking lyre-shaped horns. Of the other two hartebeest, **Coke's hartebeest** (*Alcephalus buselaphus*; about 122 cm), is usually considered to be a subspecies of Jackson's hartebeest, but is a very different colour, being a more drab pale brown with a paler rump. Finally, **Lichtenstein's hartebeest** (*Alcephalus lichtensteinii*; about 127-132 cm) is also fawn in general colouration, but usually has a rufous wash over the back. Also look out for dark marks on the front of the legs and, often, a dark patch on the side near the shoulder. All four of these antelope are found in herds, and sometimes they mix with other plain dwellers such as zebra. The hartebeest has the habit of posting sentinels: solitary animals who stand on the top of anthills keeping a watch out for predators.

Smaller antelope The remaining common antelopes are a good deal smaller than those described above. The largest is the **impala** (*Aepyceros melampus*), which is 92-107 cm at the shoulder and is bright rufous in colour with a white abdomen. From behind, the white rump with black lines on each side is characteristic. Only the male carries the long, lyre-shaped horns. Just above the heels of the hind legs is a tuft of thick black bristles which are surprisingly easy to see as the animal runs. Also easy to see is the black mark on the side of abdomen, just in front of the back leg.

Two slightly smaller antelope are **Grant's gazelle** (*Gazella granti*), about 81-99 cm at the shoulder, and **Thomson's gazelle** (*Gazella thomsonii*), about 64-69 cm at the shoulder. They are superficially similar. Grant's, the larger of the two, has longer horns, but this is only a good means of identification when the two animals are seen together. The general colour of both varies from a bright rufous to a sandy rufous. In both species the curved horns are carried by both sexes. Thomson's gazelle can usually be distinguished from Grant's by the broad black band along the side between the rufous upper parts and white abdomen, but not invariably, as some forms of Grant's also have this dark lateral stripe. If in doubt, look for the white area on the buttocks, which extends above the tail on to the rump in Grant's, but does not extend above the tail in Thomson's. The underparts are white. Thomson's gazelle, or "Tommies", are among the most numerous animals that inhabit the plains of Kenya and Tanzania. You will see large herds of them, often in association with other game. Grant's gazelle occurs on rather dry grass plains.

The **Bohor reedbuck** (*Redunca redunca*) and the **oribi** (*Ourebia ourebi*) are not really very similar, but they do both have a curious and conspicuous patch of bare skin just below each ear. The horns (carried only by males) are quite different, being sharply hooked forwards at the tip in the Bohor reedbuck, but straight in the oribi, and this is enough to distinguish them. There is a slight difference in size, the Bohor reedbuck being about 71-76 cm at the shoulder and the oribi only about 61 cm. The oribi is more slender and delicate looking than the Bohor reedbuck, and has a proportionally longer neck. Both animals are a reddish fawn, but the oribi tends to be duller or more sandy in appearance. Both oribi and Bohor reedbuck are usually seen in pairs in bushed grassland, never far from water.

The last two of the common smaller antelopes are the **bushbuck** (*Tragelaphus scriptus*) which is about 76-92 cm at the shoulder, and the tiny **Kirk's dikdik** (*Rhynchotragus kirkii*), only 36-41 cm. Both are easily identified. The bushbuck's coat has a shaggy appearance and a variable pattern of white spots and stripes on the side and back, and two white crescent-shaped marks on the front of the neck. The horns, present in the male only, are short, almost straight and slightly spiralled. The animal has a curious high rump which gives it a characteristic crouching appearance. The white underside of the tail is noticeable when it runs. The bushbuck tends to occur in areas of thick bush, especially near water. They lie up during the day in thickets, but are often seen bounding away when disturbed. They are usually seen either in pairs or singly. Kirk's dikdik is so small it can hardly be mistaken for any other antelope. In colour it is a greyish brown, often washed with rufous. The legs are noticeably thin and stick-like, giving the animal a very fragile appearance. The snout is slightly elongated, and there is a conspicuous tuft of hair on the top of the head. Only the male carries the very small straight horns.

Other mammals Although the antelope is undoubtedly the most numerous species to be seen on the plains, there are others worth keeping an eye open for. Some of these are scavengers, which thrive on the kills of other animals. They include the dog-like jackals, of which there are two species that you are likely to come across. Both species are similar in size (about 86-96 cm in length and 41-46 cm at the shoulder). The **black-backed jackal** (*Canis mesomelas*), which is the most common and ranges throughout the region, is a rather foxy reddish-fawn in colour, with a noticeable black area on its back. This black part is sprinkled with a silvery white, which can make the back look silver in some lights. The **side-striped jackal** (*Canis adustus*) is generally greyish fawn in colour, with a variable and sometimes ill-defined stripe along the side. Jackal can be seen in most parks, often near lion kills, but are also common on farmland. The other well-known plains scavenger is the **spotted hyena** (*Crocuta crocuta*), which is a fairly large animal, 69-91 cm high. Its high shoulders and low back give it a characteristic appearance. Brownish in colour with dark spots and a large head, it usually occurs singly or in pairs, but occasionally in small packs. The slightly smaller **striped hyena** (*Hyaena hyaena*), 65-80 cm high, is seen less often as it's more nocturnal than the spotted hyena, and quickly returns to its lair at sunrise. Its coat colour varies from grey to light brown with vertical black stripes along the length of the body and dark legs. When hungry, hyenas are aggressive creatures; they have been known to attack live animals and will occasionally try to steal a kill from lions. They always look dirty because of their habit of lying in muddy pools which may be to keep cool or alleviate the irritation of parasites. If camping in unfenced campsites, be very wary of hyena – they have little inherent fear of humans, can get very close and will think nothing of sniffing out and stealing food. A favourite and common plains animal is the comical **warthog** (*Phacochoerus aethiopicus*). A member of the pig family, it is unmistakeable, being grey in colour and almost hairless, with a very large head, tusks and wart-like growths on the face. These are thought to protect the eyes as it makes sideways sweeps into the earth with its tusks, digging up roots and tubers. The warthog is often seen in family groups and, when startled, the adult will run at speed with its tail held straight up in the air, followed by its young.

In suitable rocky areas, such as *kopjes*, look out for an animal that looks a bit like a large grey-brown guinea pig. This is the **rock hyrax** (*Heterohyrax brucei*), an engaging and fairly common animal that lives in communities; during the morning and afternoon you will see them sunning themselves on the rocks. Perhaps their strangest characteristic is their place in the evolution of mammals. The structure of the ear is similar to that found in whales, their molar teeth look like those of a rhinoceros, two pouches in the stomach resemble a condition found in birds, and the arrangement of the bones of the forelimb are like those of the elephant.

The **caracal** (*Felis caracal*), also known as the African lynx, is roughly twice the size of a domestic cat, with reddish sandy fur and paler underparts. The graceful cat has very characteristic tufts of black hair at the end of its pointed ears. It is very good at bush camouflage, and is scarcely noticed when lying still against the earth, though it is an adept hunter and possesses great speed and lightning reflexes; it can easily snatch a flying bird out of the air. Like a leopard, it often takes prey into a tree to be eaten.

The most common and frequently seen of the monkey group are the baboons. The most widespread species is the **olive baboon** (*Papio anubis*), which occurs almost throughout the region. This is a large (127-142 cm), heavily built animal, olive brown or greyish in colour. Adult males have a well-developed mane. In the eastern part of Kenya and Tanzania, including the coast, the olive baboon is replaced by the **yellow baboon** (*Papio cynocephalus*; 116-137 cm), which is a smaller and lighter animal, with longer legs and almost no mane in the adult males. The tail in both species looks as if it is broken and hangs down in a loop. Baboons are basically terrestrial animals, although they can climb very well. In the wild they are often found in acacia grassland, often associated with rocks, and are sociable animals living in groups called troops. Females are frequently seen with young clinging to them. In parts of East Africa they have become very used to the presence of man and can be a nuisance to campers. They will readily climb all over your vehicle hoping for a handout. Be careful; they have a very nasty bite and can carry rabies.

The smaller monkey that also makes a nuisance of itself is the **vervet** or **green monkey** (*Cercopithicus mitis*), which is the one that abounds at campsites and often lodges. It has a black face framed with white across the forehead and cheeks. Its general colour is greyish tinged with a varying amount of yellow. The feet, hands and tip of the tail are black.

Chimpanzees (*Pan troglodytes*) are not animals you will see casually in passing; you have to go and look for them. They occur only in the forests in the west of Tanzania. They are large black apes that can weigh up to 60 kg and stand 90-160 cm at the shoulder. They have short fur, no tail and pink or black skin on the face and hands. They are a sociable animal and live in family groups of up to 20 individuals.

Birds

East Africa is one of the richest areas of birdlife in the world. The total number of species exceeds 1300, and it is possible and not too difficult to see 100 different species in a day. You will find that a pair of binoculars is essential. The birds described here are the common ones and, with a little careful observation, you will soon find that you can identify them. They have been grouped according to habitat.

Urban birds The first birds that you will notice on arrival in any big city will almost certainly be the large numbers soaring overhead. Early in the morning the numbers are few, but as the temperature warms up, more and more are seen circling high above the buildings. Many of these will be **hooded vultures** (*Neophron monachus*; 66 cm) and **black kites** (*Milvus migrans*; 55 cm). They are superficially similar, rather nondescript brownish birds. They are, however, distinguished by the shape and length of the tail. The tail of the hooded vulture is short and slightly rounded at the end, whereas the black kite (which incidentally is not black, but brown) has a long, narrow tail that looks either forked when the tail is closed or slightly concave at the end when spread. In flight the kite uses its tail a lot, twisting it from side to side. Also soaring overhead in some cities you will see the **marabou stork** (*Leptoptilos crumeniferus*; 152 cm). Although this bird is a stork, it behaves like a vulture, in that it lives by scavenging. Overhead, its large size, long and noticeable bill and trailing legs make it easily identified. The commonest crow in towns and cities is the **pied crow** (*Corvus albus*; 46 cm). This is a very handsome black bird with a white lower breast that joins up with a white collar round the back of the neck. In towns along the coast you will see another member of the crow family, the **Indian house crow** (*Corvus splendens*; 38 cm). This slender, shiny black bird with a grey neck is not indigenous to Africa, but was introduced and is spreading along the coast.

In gardens and parks there are a number of smaller birds to look out for. The **dark-capped** or **common bulbul** (*Pycnonotus barbatus*; 18 cm) can be heard all day with its cheerful call of "Come quick, doctor, quick". It is a brownish bird with a darker brown head and a slight crest. Below, the brown is paler fading to white on the belly, and under the tail it is bright yellow.

There are a large number of weaver birds to be seen, but identifying them is not always easy. Most of them are yellow and black in colour, and many of them live in large noisy colonies. Have a close look at their intricately woven nests if you get the chance. The commonest one is probably the **black-headed weaver** (*Ploceus cucullatus*; 18 cm), which often builds its colonies in bamboo clumps. The male has a mainly black head and throat, but the back of the head is chestnut. The underparts are bright yellow, and the back and wings mottled black and greenish yellow. When the bird is perched and seen from behind, the markings on the back form a V-shape.

Also in parks and gardens, and especially among flowers, you will see members of another large and confusing bird family: the sunbirds. The thick-set and sturdy looking

scarlet-chested sunbird (*Nectarinia senegalensis*; 15 cm) often perches on overhead wires, allowing you to get a good look at it. The male is a dark velvety brown colour with a scarlet chest. The top of the head and the throat are an iridescent green. The tail is short. There are two common thrushes often seen in parks and gardens. They look rather similar, but do not occur in the same areas. The **olive thrush** (*Turdus olivaceous*; 23 cm) is the common thrush of the highlands, where it is often seen in gardens. The very similar garden thrush of lower areas is the **African thrush** (*Turdus pelios*; 23 cm). Both birds are brown, but the olive thrush is a much richer-looking bird, with a rufous belly and a bright orange bill. The African thrush has a wash of rufous on the side and is duller looking.

Birds of open plains Along with the spectacular game, it is here that you will see many of the magnificent African birds. In particular, there are two large birds which you will see stalking across the grasslands. These are the **ostrich** (*Struthio camelus*; 2 m) and the **secretary bird** (*Sagittarius serpentarius*; 101 cm). The secretary bird is so called because the long plumes of its crest are supposed to resemble the old-time secretaries who carried their quill pens tucked behind their ears. The bird is often seen in pairs as it hunts for snakes, its main food source. The ostrich is sometimes seen singly, but also in family groups. There are other large terrestrial birds to look out for, and one of them, the **kori bustard** (*Otis kori*; 80cm), like the secretary bird, quarters the plains looking for snakes. It is quite a different shape, however, and can be distinguished by its thick-looking grey neck (caused by loose feathers). It is particularly common in the Serengeti National Park and in the Masai Mara in Kenya. The other large bird that you are likely to see on the open plains is the **ground hornbill** (*Bucorvus cafer*; 107 cm). When seen from afar, this looks like a turkey but, close up, it is very distinctive and cannot really be mistaken for anything else. They are very often seen in pairs, and the male has bare red skin around the eye and on the throat. In the female this skin is red and blue.

Soaring overhead on the plains you will see vultures and birds of prey. The commonest vulture in game areas is the **African white-backed vulture** (*Gyps africanus*; 81 cm). This is a largish, brown bird with a white lower back, and the characteristic bare head of its family. Because they are commonly seen circling overhead, the white rump is sometimes difficult to distinguish. So look out for the other diagnostic characteristic – the broad white band on the leading edge of the undersurface of the wing. The **bateleur** (*Terathopius ecaudatus*; 61 cm) is a magnificent and strange-looking eagle. It is rarely seen perched, but is quite commonly spotted soaring very high overhead. Its tail is so short that it sometimes appears tailless. This, its buoyant flight and the black and white pattern of its underparts make it easy to identify.

Where there is game, look out for the oxpeckers. The commonest one is the **red-billed oxpecker** (*Buphagus erythrorhynchus*; 18 cm). These birds are actually members of the starling family, although their behaviour is not like that of other starlings. They associate with game animals and cattle and spend their time clinging to and climbing all over the animals while they hunt for ticks, which form their main food. There are other birds which associate with animals in a different way. For example the **cattle egret** (*Bubulcus ibis*; 51 cm), which follows herds and feeds on the grasshoppers and other insects disturbed by the passing of the animals. Occasionally, too, the cattle egret will perch on the back of a large animal, but this is quite different from the behaviour of oxpeckers. Cattle egrets are long-legged and long-billed white birds, most often seen in small flocks. In the breeding season they develop long buff feathers on the head, chest and back.

Birds of dry, open woodland The two habitats of open plain and dry open woodland form a vast area of Africa and most of the game parks come into these categories. As well as being quintessentially African, this dry open woodland with acacia thorn trees is an extremely rewarding area for birdwatching. It supports an enormous variety of species and it is relatively easy to see them.

The guinea fowl lives in flocks and if you surprise a group on the road they will disappear into the bush in a panic, running at great speed. There is more than one sort of guinea fowl, but they are rather similar, being a slate grey with white spots. The **vulturine guinea fowl** (*Acryllium vulturinum*; 59 cm) is a most handsome bird, with long blue, white and black feathers covering its neck and upper body. The rather small head itself is bare, hence the bird's name. The **helmeted guinea fowl** (*Numida meleagris*; 55 cm) is rather less handsome, but, with its dark slate and white-spotted plumage and the boney 'helmet' on its head, it is nonetheless a striking bird.

The tops of the thorn trees are used as observation perches by a number of different species. Especially noticeable is the **red-billed hornbill** (*Tockus erythrorhynchus*; 45 cm), which has blackish-brown back, with a white stripe down between the wings. The wings themselves are spotted with white. The underparts are white and the bill is long, curved and mainly red. As the bird flies into a tree the impression is of a black-and-white bird with a long red bill and a long tail. Another striking bird which perches on tree tops is the **white-bellied go-away bird** (*Corythaixoides leucogaster*; 51 cm). This gets its strange name from its call, "Go-away, go-away". It is a basically grey bird with a very upright stance. The top of the head carries a long and conspicuous crest. The belly is white and the long tail has a black tip. It is usually seen in small family parties.

The strange-looking, brightly coloured **D'Arnaud's barbet** (*Trachyphonus darnaudii*; 15 cm) is quite common in the dry bush country. The impression you get is of a spotted bird, dark with pale spots above, and pale with dark spots below. It has a long, dark, heavily spotted tail. Its call and behaviour is very distinctive. A pair will sit facing each other with their tails raised over their backs wagging them from side to side, and bob at each other in a duet. All the while they utter a four-note call over and over: "Do-do dee-dok". They look just like a pair of clockwork toys. Another brightly coloured bird is the **lilac-breasted roller** (*Coracias caudata*; 41 cm), which is very easy to see as it perches on telegraph poles or wires, or on bare branches. The brilliant blue on its wings, head and underparts is very eye-catching. Its throat and breast are a deep lilac and its tail has two elongated streamers. It is quite common in open bush country. Also often seen sitting on bare branches is the **drongo** (*Dicrurus adsimilis*; 24 cm), but this is an all-black bird. It is easily identified by its forked tail, which is fish-tailed at the end. It is usually solitary.

There are two common birds, which in the field look rather similar, although they are not related at all. These are the **white-crowned shrike** (*Eurocephalus rueppelli*; 23 cm) and the **white-headed buffalo weaver** (*Dinemellia dinemelli*; 23 cm). They both occur in small flocks in dry acacia country and are both thick-set, rather chunky birds, which appear basically dark brown and white. To distinguish between them look at the rump, which is red in the white-headed buffalo weaver, but white in the white-crowned shrike. This is usually easy to see as they fly away from you.

There are many different species of starling to be seen in eastern Africa, and most of them are beautifully coloured. Two of the most spectacular are the **Ashy starling** (*Cosmopsarus unicolor*; 32cm) and the **superb starling** (*Spreo superbus*; 18 cm). The superb starling is the more widespread of the two and is seen near habitation as well as in thorn bush country. The car park between the Serengeti National Park and the Ngorongoro Conservation Area is probably the best place to see the superb starling, so called because of its vibrant glossy colours. The Ashy starling is endemic to Tanzania and can only be found in the baobab trees in Tarangire National Park and around the Tarangire Safari Lodge. Both are fairly tame and are usually seen hopping about on the ground. Another long-tailed bird quite commonly seen in bush country is the **long-tailed fiscal** (*Lanius cabanisi*; 30 cm). It is black and white, and usually seen perched on wires or bare branches. It can be identified by its very long all-black tail and mainly black upperparts, which are grey on the lower back and rump.

Finally look out for three birds which, though small, are very noticeable. The **red-cheeked cordon-bleu** (*Uraeginthus benegalus*; 13 cm) is a lovely little blue bird, with a brown back and bright red cheek patches. They are seen in pairs or family parties, and the females and young are somewhat duller in colour than the males. They are quite tame and you often see them round the game lodges. In the less dry grasslands you can see the beautiful red and black bishop birds. There are two species, both of which are quite brilliant in their colouring. The brightest is the **red bishop** (*Euplectes orix*; 13 cm), which has brown wings and tail, and noticeable scarlet feathers on its rump. The almost equally brilliant **black-winged bishop** (*Euplectes hordeaceus*; 14 cm), may be distinguished from the red bishop by its black wings and tail and rather less obvious red rump. Both species occur in long grass and cultivation, often, but not invariably, near water.

Birds of more moist areas Although so much of eastern Africa consists of grass plains, to the west of the area there are moist wooded grasslands that support a very different variety of bird species. The tall and elegant **crowned crane** (*Balearica pavonina*; 1 m) is quite common near Lake Victoria, though it also occurs in much of the rest of the area as well. It cannot really be mistaken for anything else when seen on the ground. In flight, the legs trail behind and the neck is extended, but the head droops down from the vertical. Overhead flocks fly in loose V-shaped formation. The curious **hamerkop** (*Scopus umbretta*; 58 cm) is another unmistakable bird. It is a rather dull brown in colour and has a stout, moderately long bill. Its most distinctive feature is the large crest which projects straight backwards and is, rather fancifully, said to look like a hammer. It is a solitary bird, usually seen on the ground near water, sometimes even roadside puddles. It nests in trees and builds an enormous nest, which is so large and strong that it can easily support the weight of a man. Another common, rather dull-looking ground bird is the **hadada ibis** (*Hagedashia hagedash*; 76 cm). This is a greyish olive bird with a long down-curved bill and a green wash on the wings. It is almost invariably seen in pairs and flies off with its characteristic loud call "Ha-da-da, Ha-da-da". It is one of Africa's most familiar birds, and walks about on lawns and open spaces. The **black-and-white casqued hornbill** (*Bycanistes subcylindricus*; 70 cm), is yet another loud and conspicuous bird, but it is always seen in trees, and is particularly common in moist woodland in the west. The similar **silvery-cheeked hornbill** (*Bycanistes brevis*; 70 cm) replaces it to the east, though its habitat requirements are broadly similar. Both are basically black and white birds, but the wings of the silvery-cheeked hornbill are wholly black, whereas the black-and-white casqued hornbill has a large white patch on the black wings. Look also at the casque on top of the bill, which is carried by both species. This casque is all pale in the silvery-cheeked hornbill, but, as its name would suggest, black and white in the other bird. The moist forests and woodlands around Lake Victoria, which are the home of the black-and-white casqued hornbill, are also home to the **grey parrot** (*Psitticus erithacus*; 30 cm). This bird is usually seen in flocks and is best distinguished both in flight and at rest, by its bright red tail. The **paradise flycatcher** (*Terpsiphone viridis*; male 33 cm, female 20 cm) is very easily identified by its very long tail and bright chestnut plumage. The head is black and bears a crest. The tail of the female is much shorter, but otherwise the sexes are similar. It is seen in wooded areas, including gardens, and is usually in pairs. Another long-tailed bird is the **speckled mousebird** (*Colius striatus*; 36 cm).

They are usually seen in small flocks and follow each other from bush to bush. The mainly brown plumage has a speckled appearance and the tail is long and graduated. It has a red rather parrot-shaped bill and a crest.

Water and waterside birds The inland waters of Africa form a very important habitat for both resident and migratory species. A lot can be seen from the shore, but it is especially fruitful to go out in a boat, when you will get quite close to, among others, the large and magnificent herons that occur here. The king of them all is the aptly named **goliath heron** (*Ardea goliath*; 144 cm), which is usually seen singly on mud banks and shores, both inland and on the coast. Its very large size is enough to distinguish it, but the smaller **purple heron** (*Ardea purpurea*; 80 cm), which frequents similar habitat and is also widespread, may be mistaken for it at a distance. If in doubt, the colour on the top of the head (rufous in the goliath and black in the purple) will clinch it; also the purple is much more slender with a slender bill.

The flamingos are known to most people and will be readily identified. However, there are two different species which very often occur together. The **greater flamingo** (*Phoenicopterus ruber*; 142 cm) is the larger and paler bird and has a pink bill with a black tip. The **lesser flamingo** (*Phoenicopterus minor*; 101 cm) is deeper pink all over and has a deep carmine bill with a black tip. They both occur in large numbers in several lakes in Tanzania, the best known being Lake Manyara. The magnificent **fish eagle** (*Haliaeetus vocifer*; 76 cm) has a distinctive colour pattern. It often perches on the tops of trees, where its dazzling white head and chest are easily seen. In flight, its white head, chest and tail contrast with the black wings. It has a wild yelping call, which is usually uttered in flight. Try and watch the bird as it calls; it throws back its head over its back in a most unusual way.

There are several different kingfishers to be seen, but the most numerous is the black and white **pied kingfisher** (*Ceryle rudis*; 25 cm). This is easily recognized as it is the only black and white kingfisher. It is common all round the large lakes and also turns up at quite small bodies of water. It hovers over the water before plunging in to capture its prey.

In quiet backwaters with lily pads and other floating vegetation, you will see the **African jacana** (*Actophilornis africana*; 25 cm). This is a mainly chestnut bird almost invariably seen walking on floating leaves. Its toes are greatly elongated to allow it to do this. When flying away from you, the legs dangle right down distinctively. Do not confuse this with the **black crake** (*Limnocorax flavirostra*; 20 cm), which also frequents the quieter backwaters. This is an all slatey black bird with bright pink legs. It is rather shy and disappears into the vegetation at your approach; if you wait quietly it will reappear.

Books on Tanzania

Fiction and autobiography

Boyd, W *An Ice-cream War*, a neatly observed, humorous and sensitive tale set against the First World War campaign in East Africa.

Boyd, W *Brazzaville Beach*. Although written as a West African story, it's clearly based on Jane Goodall and the chimps of Gombe.

Dahl, R *Going Solo*, impressions of a young man sent out to work in the colonies before the First World War.

Hemmingway, E *Green Hills of Africa*, masterly short stories based on the author's East African visits in 1933-1934.

History

Hibbert, C *Africa Explored: Europeans in the Dark Continent; 1769-1889*, provides fascinating detail on the early explorers and their motivations, including the search for the source of the Nile.

Millar, C *Battle for the Bundu*, is an account of the First World War in German East Africa.

Packenham, T *The Scramble for Africa*, first published in 1974, this classic book documents the European colonization of Africa.

Natural history, wildlife and photography

Briggs P, *East African Wildlife*, is Bradt's comprehensive field guide on the animals you are likely to see on safari and is illustrated by photographs or watercolour drawings.

Goodall, J *In the Shadow of Man*, gives a flavour of what is involved in making a life's work of studying a particular species, in this case chimps.

Grzimek, B *Serengeti Shall Not Die*, is a classic account of this world-famous park

and one of the earliest publications to highlight the need for conservation of African animals.

Hosking D, Withers M *Collins Traveller's Guide – Wildlife of Kenya, Tanzania and Uganda*, is a good companion to any wildlife-watching trip to the region and covers numerous mammal, bird, reptile and tree species, with a good selection of photographs.

Jafferji, J and Rees, B *Images of Zanzibar*, superb photographs and a good introduction to, and souvenir of, Zanzibar. Javed Jafferi (www.javedjafferji.com) owns **Gallery Publications** (www.gallery-publications.net) in Stone Town, and over the last couple of decades has been a prolific book and magazine publisher; among his many other titles are: *A Taste of Zanzibar*, a Zanzibar recipe book; *Historical Zanzibar – Romance of the Ages*, an illustrated account of Zanzibar's turbulent past with archive photographs of the slave and ivory trade; and *Swahili Style*, which examines the unique blend of architectural styles that make up Zanzibar's historic quarter, illustrated with sketches and colour photographs. In total Javed has published 45 souvenir books on Tanzania, including some of the parks and reserves, and they can be bought in his own **Zanzibar Gallery** (page 162), and other shops in Stone Town, **A Novel Idea** bookshop in Dar es Salaam (page 70) and the duty-free shops at the airport.

Peterson, D *Jane Goodall: The Woman who Redefined Man*, is a biography of Goodall, from her early encounters with chimps as a research assistant, to her more recent worldwide conservation work.

Poliza M, *Eyes Over Africa*, is a stunning collection of photographs of Africa's landscapes, wildlife and people, many of them aerial, taken by renowned photographer Michael Poliza.

From page to screen

Adapted from a short story by Ernest Hemingway, *The Snows of Kilimanjaro* (1952) is a classic film starring Gregory Peck, Susan Hayward and Ava Gardner. Harry Street is an American writer who is on safari in Africa when he is accidentally scratched by a thorn, which leads to infection and ultimately death. As he lies delirious, with Kilimanjaro looming in the background, he recalls the lost loves of his life. *Hatari* (1962), starring John Wayne, is an adventurous comic romp about Americans capturing animals for zoos, and was filmed near Arusha with good scenic shots of Mount Meru. Much of *King Soloman's Mines* (1950), starring Deborah Kerr and Stewart Granger, was filmed in Tanzania. Adapted from Rider Haggard's book, it's a story of finding treasures in the unexplored interior of Africa. *Stanley and Livingstone* (1939) is about Stanley (Spencer Tracey) tracking down Livingstone (Cedric Hardwicke) on the banks of Lake Tanganyika. The German film, *Serengeti Shall Not Die* (1959), was the first wildlife documentary to be aired on television and put the Serengeti on the map as a tourist destination.

Contents

Footnotes

Useful words and phrases

Here are some useful words and phrases in Kiswahili. Attempting a few words will be much appreciated by Tanzanians.

Good morning	*Habari ya asubuhi*
Good afternoon	*Habari ya mchana*
Good evening	*Habari ya jioni*
Good night	*Habari ya usiku*
Hello!	*Jambo!*
A respectful greeting to elders, actually meaning: "I hold your feet"	*Shikamoo*
Their reply: "I am delighted"	*Marahaba*
How are you?	*Habari yako?*
I am fine	*Nzuri / Sijambo*
I am not feeling good today	*Sijiziki vizuri leo*
How are things?	*Mambo?*
Good/cool/cool and crazy	*Safi / poa / poa kichizi*
See you later	*Tutaonana baadaye*
Welcome!	*Karibu! (Karibu tena!)*
Goodbye	*Kwaheri*
Please	*Tafadhali*
Thank you	*Asante*
Sorry	*Pole*
Where can I get a taxi?	*Teksi iko wapi?*
Where is the bus station?	*Stendi ya basi iko wapi?*
When will we arrive?	*Tutafika lini?*
Can you show me the bus?	*Unaweza ukanioyesha basi?*
How much is the ticket?	*Tiketi ni bei gani?*
Is it safe walking here at night?	*Ni salama kutembea hapa usiku?*
I don't want to buy anything	*Sitaki kununua chochote*
I have already booked a safari	*Tayari nimeisha lipia safari*
I don't have money	*Sina hela*
I'm not single	*Nina mchumba / siko peke yangu*
Could you please leave me alone?	*Tafadhali, achana na mimi*
It is none of your business!	*Hayakuhusu!*
One	*moja*
Two	*mbili*
Three	*tatu*
Four	*nne*
Five	*tano*
Six	*sita*
Seven	*saba*
Eight	*nane*
Nine	*tisa*
Ten	*kumi*

Index → *Entries in bold refer to maps*

Advertisers' index

Credits

Footprint credits
Project Editor: Felicity Laughton
Layout and production: Emma Bryers
Proofreader: Sophie Jones
Cover and colour section: Pepi Bluck
Maps: Kevin Feeney

Managing Director: Andy Riddle
Content Director: Patrick Dawson
Publisher: Alan Murphy
Publishing Managers: Felicity Laughton,
Jo Williams, Nicola Gibbs
Marketing and Partnerships Director:
Liz Harper
Marketing Executive: Liz Eyles
Trade Product Manager: Diane McEntee
Account Managers: Paul Bew, Tania Ross
Advertising: Renu Sibal, Elizabeth Taylor
Finance: Phil Walsh

Photography credits
Front cover: Zebra. Harald Lange /
mauritius images
Back cover: A traditional dhow sailing
off Zanzibar. Bertrand Rieger / hemis.fr

Colour section
Page i: Nigel Pavitt / awl-images.com
Page ii: FB-Fischer / age fotostock
Page v: Louie Schoeman / Shutterstock.com
Page vi: BlueOrange Studio /
Shutterstock.com
Page vii: Dimitry Sukhov / Shutterstock.com
Page viii (top): Nigel Pavitt / awl-images.com
Page vii (bottom): Nigel Pavitt /
awl-images.com

Printed in India by Replika Press Pvt Ltd

Publishing information
Footprint Tanzania
3rd edition
© Footprint Handbooks Ltd
June 2012

ISBN: 978 1 907263 59 0
CIP DATA: A catalogue record for this book
is available from the British Library

® Footprint Handbooks and the Footprint
mark are a registered trademark of
Footprint Handbooks Ltd

Published by Footprint
6 Riverside Court
Lower Bristol Road
Bath BA2 3DZ, UK
T +44 (0)1225 469141
F +44 (0)1225 469461
footprinttravelguides.com

Distributed in the USA by Globe Pequot
Press, Guilford, Connecticut

Footprint Mini Atlas
Tanzania

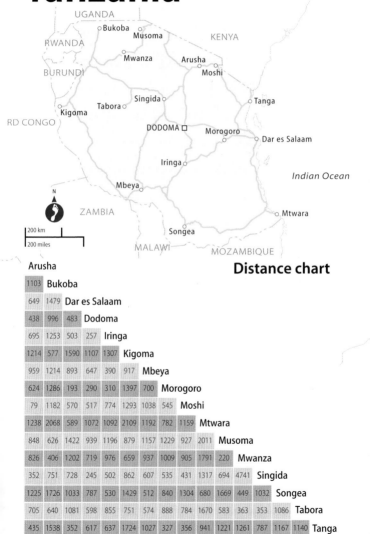

Distance chart

Arusha															
1103	Bukoba														
649	1479	Dar es Salaam													
438	996	483	Dodoma												
695	1253	503	257	Iringa											
1214	577	1590	1107	1307	Kigoma										
959	1214	893	647	390	917	Mbeya									
624	1286	193	290	310	1397	700	Morogoro								
79	1182	570	517	774	1293	1038	545	Moshi							
1238	2068	589	1072	1092	2109	1192	782	1159	Mtwara						
848	626	1422	939	1196	879	1157	1229	927	2011	Musoma					
826	406	1202	719	976	659	937	1009	905	1791	220	Mwanza				
352	751	728	245	502	862	607	535	431	1317	694	4741	Singida			
1225	1726	1033	787	530	1429	512	840	1304	680	1669	449	1032	Songea		
705	640	1081	598	855	751	574	888	784	1670	583	363	353	1086	Tabora	
435	1538	352	617	637	1724	1027	327	356	941	1221	1261	787	1167	1140	Tanga

Distances in kilometres 1 kilometre = 0.62 miles

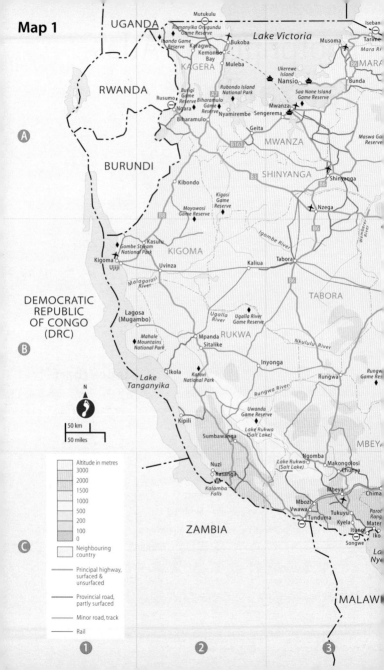

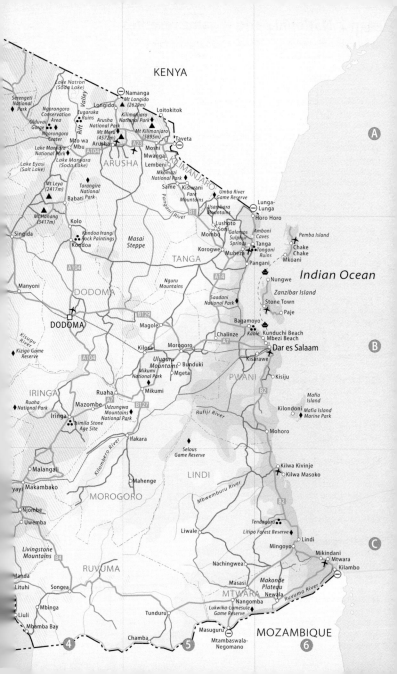

Map 2 National parks & game reserves

❶ Serengeti National Park
Far-reaching plains of endless grass, tinged with the twisted shadows of acacia trees, make this the quintessential image of wild, untarnished Africa. It supports the highest concentration of game in Africa.

❷ Ngorongoro Conservation Area
Often called 'Africa's Eden', Ngorongoro encompasses the volcanic Ngorongoro and Embagai craters, Olduvai Gorge – famous for its palaeontological relics – and Lake Masek. The crater is a world-class visitor attraction.

❸ Arusha National Park
In the shadow of mounts Kilimanjaro and Meru, this is a compact park with three varied habitats: the highland montane forest; a small volcanic crater inhabited by a variety of mammals; and a series of seven alkaline crater lakes.

❹ Kilimanjaro National Park
One of the most impressive sights in Africa, the highest mountain on the continent is visible from as far away as Tsavo National Park in Kenya. Kibo Peak rises to 5895 m.

❺ Gombe Stream National Park
One of Tanzania's most remote parks and famous for its chimpanzee populations.

❻ Mahale Mountains National Park
Another chimpanzee sanctuary with a larger population so there's more chance of sightings here than at Gombe.

❼ Katavi National Park
A very isolated park less frequented by tourists, Katavi is famous for its Roan and Sable antelope and large herds of buffalo.

❽ Lake Manyara National Park
Best known for its beautiful lake tinged by thousands of flamingos, while the acacia-studded shore is the habitat for elephants and tree-climbing lions.

❾ Ruaha National Park
Although little visited, this is Tanzania's second-largest national park, with vast concentrations of buffalo, elephant, gazelle and over 400 bird species.

❿ Udzungwa Mountains National Park
This forested area plays host to a large number of endangered bird species as well as forest antelope and vervet monkeys.

⓫ Selous Game Reserve
The largest park in Africa and the second largest in the world, Selous covers 5% of Tanzania's total area (although much is off limits to visitors). The area is famous for African wild dogs and some of the last black rhino left in the region.

⓬ Mafia Island Marine Park
The best deep-sea diving in Tanzania in protected coral gardens. The island is the meeting place of large oceanic fish and the vast variety of fish common to the Indian Ocean coral reefs.

Lake Victoria

Rumanyika Orugundu Game Reserve
Ibanda Game Reserve
Bukoba
Karagwe
Muleba
Ukerewe Island
Nansio
Saa Nane Island Wildlife Sanctuary
Rubondo Island National Park
Mwanza
Burigi Game Reserve
Ngara
Biharamulo Game Reserve
Biharamulo
Sengerema
Geita
Shinyanga
Kibondo
Nzega
Mayowosi Game Reserve
Kigosi Game Reserve
Igombe River
❺ Kasulu
Gombe Stream National Park
Kigoma
Ujiji
Uvinza
Kaliua
Tabora
Malagarasi River
Ugalla River
Lagosa (Mugambo)
Mpanda
Sitalike
Inyonga
❻ Mahale Mountains National Park
Ikola
❼ Katavi National Park
Lake Tanganyika
Rungwa River
Kipili
Uwanda Game Reserve
Lake Rukwa (Salt Lake)
Sumbawanga
Nuzi
Kasanga
Lake Rukwa (Salt Lake)
Ngomba
Makongolosi
Mbozi
Vwawa
Tunduma

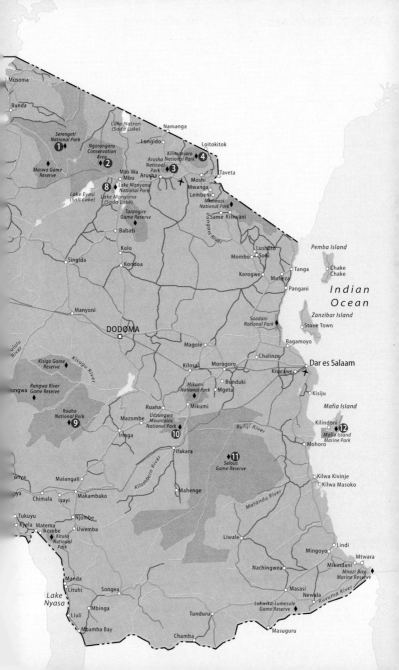

Map 3 Dive sites

Pemba Island

Africa's 'Emerald Isle' is the jewel in Tanzania's dive-site portfolio and is considered a world-class diving destination. On the west coast the deep waters of the Pemba Channel create dramatic walls and drop-offs. You may see sharks, eagle rays, manta rays, Napoleon wrasse, great barracuda, tuna and kingfish.

Zanzibar

Near Stone Town there are pristine coral gardens and a proliferation of marine life. Murogo Reef has some beautiful coral. Leven Banks on the north coast is near the deep water of the Pemba Channel and you may see big shoals of jacks and trevally. The east coast has the most talked about diving on Zanzibar and is also great for snorkelling.

Mafia Island

"Shallow Pemba with more fish", according to one diver. Mafia has beautiful reefs and spectacular fish life. Jino Pass and Dindini Wall are two good reefs to the northeast of Chole Bay. Here you can see huge malabar, potato and honeycomb groupers, giant reef rays, green turtles, great barracuda, kingfish, bonito, shoals of bluefin trevalley and snappers in their thousands.

Mainland sites

If you are not visiting Pemba or Zanzibar, try a dive around Dar. Ferns Wall, on the seaward side of Fungu Yasin Reef has barrel sponges, gorgonian fans, 2-m long whip corals and reef sharks. Big T Reef is a must for the experienced diver but only on a calm day. Off Latham Island you can see big game fish and hammerheads. Mnazi Bay Marine Reserve also has superb snorkelling and diving. Fabulous coral reef and turtles are common.

Map symbols

□	Capital city
○	Other city, town
⟷	International border
⟷	Regional border
⊖	Customs
⬭	Contours (approx)
▲	Mountain, volcano
⤙	Mountain pass
⏜	Escarpment
⟷	Glacier
⬚	Salt flat
⬚	Rocks
⸙	Seasonal marshland
⬚	Beach, sandbank
⁂	Waterfall
⌒	Reef
═══	Motorway
───	Main road
──	Minor road
╍╍╍	Track
⋯⋯	Footpath
──	Railway
⊶▬	Railway with station
✈	Airport
🚌	Bus station
Ⓜ	Metro station
╴╴╴╴	Cable car
┼┼┼┼	Funicular
⛴	Ferry
═══	Pedestrianized street
) (	Tunnel
⟶	One way-street
⫿⫿⫿	Steps
⟷	Bridge
▄▄▄	Fortified wall
⬚	Park, garden, stadium
●	Sleeping
❶	Eating
◑	Bars & clubs

▦	Building
▫	Sight
✝✝	Cathedral, church
⛩	Chinese temple
卌	Hindu temple
⚲	Meru
◖▲◗	Mosque
⏶	Stupa
✡	Synagogue
ⓘ	Tourist office
🏛	Museum
✉	Post office
Ⓟ	Police
Ⓢ	Bank
@	Internet
♪	Telephone
☎	Market
✚	Medical services
Ⓟ	Parking
⛽	Petrol
⛳	Golf
⁖	Archaeological site
◆	National park, wildlife reserve
❋	Viewing point
⋀	Campsite
⌂	Refuge, lodge
🏰	Castle, fort
↘	Diving
⫟⫮⫯	Deciduous, coniferous, palm trees
⸙	Mangrove
⌂	Hide
🍇	Vineyard, winery
⚗	Distillery
⟿	Shipwreck
⚔	Historic battlefield
⬄	Related map

Index

THE BEST OF TANZANIA chosen by millions of travellers

Emerson Spice

Mount Kilimanjaro

House of Spices

Top-rated places to stay

Emerson Spice
Stone Town
ⓞⓞⓞⓞⓞ
"Full marks for everything!"

Chumbe Island Coral Park
Zanzibar
ⓞⓞⓞⓞⓞ
"Eco paradise"

Next Paradise Boutique Resort, Pwani Mchangani
ⓞⓞⓞⓞⓞ
"Ideal for romantic
beach holidays"

Amazing attractions

Mount Kilimanjaro
Kilimanjaro National Park
ⓞⓞⓞⓞⓞ
"Once-in-a-life-time adventure"

Tarangire National Park
ⓞⓞⓞⓞⓞ
"Elephant families abound"

Ngorongoro Crater
Tanzania
ⓞⓞⓞⓞⓞ
"Hard to beat the concentration
of wildlife"

Popular restaurants

Cafe at Emerson Spice
Stone Town
ⓞⓞⓞⓞⓞ
"Lovely lunch amid the
wonderful chaos"

Lazuli
Stone Town
ⓞⓞⓞⓞⓞ
"You will find yourself ordering
two of every drink"

House of Spices
Stone Town
ⓞⓞⓞⓞⓞ
"Difficult to find but worth it"

ⓞⓞ **trip**advisor®

Plan your perfect trip with millions of candid traveller reviews.

– and much more

- ◆ Over 50 years experience arranging
  Kilimanjaro climbs - all routes
- ◆ Country hotel and safe camp-site
  with full amenities
- ◆ Relax by the pool set in extensive
  tropical gardens
- ◆ Daytrips to waterfalls, cultural
  sites and game parks

Marangu Hotel
PO Box 40, Moshi, Tanzania
Tel: 255 27 2756594/2756361 • Fax: 255 27 2756591
e-mail: info@maranguhotel.com • www.maranguhotel.com

Ask your African travel specialist to book Marangu Hotel